The Resur
A Critical Inquiry

The Resurrection:
A Critical Inquiry

MICHAEL J. ALTER

Library of Congress Control Number:		2014915069
ISBN:	Hardcover	978-1-4990-5404-0
	Softcover	978-1-4990-5405-7
	eBook	978-1-4990-5403-3

Print information available on the last page.

Scripture taken from the King James Version of the Bible.

Bibliographical reference:
1. Jesus Christ – Resurrection
2. Christianity – Controversial Literature
3. Bible N.T. – Criticism, Interpretation, etc.
4. Jesus Christ – Historicity

Rev. date: 02/25/2015

To order additional copies of this book, contact:
Xlibris
1-888-795-4274
www.Xlibris.com
Orders@Xlibris.com
541992

CONTENTS

Chapter 3: From Crucifixion to Death

Chapter 5: Friday Afternoon until Saturday Morning 207

Chapter 10: The Judas Episodes

Conclusion   **745**

Illustrations

Tables

PART III: Bibliography

DEDICATION

To my father, Moses Alter ז"ל

and

my mother, Frieda Alter

O LORD, my strength, and my fortress, and my refuge in the day of affliction, the Gentiles shall come unto thee from the ends of the earth, and shall say, Surely our fathers have inherited lies, vanity, and things wherein there is no profit (Jer 16:19).

Thus saith the LORD of hosts; In those days it shall come to pass, that ten men shall take hold out of all languages of the nations, even shall take hold of the skirt of him that is a Jew, saying, We will go with you: for we have heard that God is with you (Zech 8:23).

The lip of truth shall be established for ever: but a lying tongue is but for a moment (Prov 12:19).

These are the things that ye shall do; Speak ye every man the truth to his neighbor; execute the judgment of truth and peace in your gates (Zech 8:16).

The seal of God is truth (*b. Shabbat* 55a).

Truth hurts like a thorn, at first; but in the end it blossoms like a rose (Samuel ha-Nagid, *Ben Mishle*).

And ye shall know the truth, and the truth shall make you free (Jn 8:32).

Am I therefore become your enemy, because I tell you the truth? (Gal 4:16)

FOREWORD

I T IS NOT really surprising that there have been many books written about the resurrection of Jesus from both those who believe it is an historical fact and those who deny its historicity. It is hard to imagine another belief as important as this one is to Christianity. In the first letter of Paul to the Corinthians (15:14), he states its critical value for Christians: "**And if Christ be not raised, your faith is vain**." Put simply, Paul claims that if the Resurrection is not a fact, then Christianity is false.

Accordingly, if you are interested in the resurrection of Jesus, then this inquiry into the belief requires your attention. In addition, if you are a Christian or thinking about becoming one, this text may change the way you view the subject and provide a wholly new perspective on the issue.

This encyclopedic work by Mr. Alter is a complete analysis of everything in the New Testament that has any relationship to the death and resurrection of Jesus. He has basically divided the work in two parts. Before the first part, as an introduction, he discusses some of the methodological issues, like the nature of the Gospels themselves and the burden of proof. Then he progresses to the first part where there is a complete analysis of the events and issues in the Gospels related to the events from the Crucifixion until after the Resurrection. Every issue deals with a different problem or aspect of these events examined by comparing each of the gospel accounts of these events (when they exist in that gospel).

He starts with the dating issues. The first issue he discusses is one of significant importance; what year was the Crucifixion? He brings views using evidence from the New Testament for almost every year from 24 to 36 CE. Following this methodology, he analyses everything about the last days of Jesus as they are in the New Testament. For example, issue 3 deals with the well-known problem of which day in Nisan was the Crucifixion, the fourteenth or the fifteenth, this being a well-known contradiction between the Gospel of John and the synoptic Gospels of Mark, Matthew, and Luke. The problem is fully analyzed in contradiction 3.

This leads to the well-known contradiction, issue 4, which deals with whether or not the Last Supper was the Passover meal. He points out two contradictions, whether it is a Passover meal and a problem that occurs because of Mark's language describing the event. This second problem is one that is totally overlooked in the apologetic literature that I have seen. Following these two contradictions, he deals with a number of problems that have been posed by commentators and investigators into the gospel accounts. These are referred to as speculations as they are not strictly contradictions, but they do raise important questions/problems. Some are quite problematic to someone who is maintaining that the Resurrection accounts are factual. For example, in speculation #1 on issue #2, he points out some information that would indicate that the Crucifixion may not have been in the spring at all but rather in the fall. It is worth the time to carefully consider that.

Following discussions of the issues related to when the events occurred, he goes on to the Crucifixion and issues surrounding that. These include the differing accounts of the thieves (issue 8) and what Jesus said before he died (issue 9). Of course there are a number of issues around the different "miracles" that were to have occurred at that time (issues 10-13).

He then goes on to discussions of what happened after the Crucifixion including the burial. This includes the piercing of Jesus' side (issue 19) and Joseph of Arimathea (issues 20-22, 25). The mysterious Nicodemus is discussed in issue 28. He then goes on to discuss issues about the burial including (issue 34) the confusion in the Gospels as to who actually did the burying.

Following this he covers the events just after the burial. Issue 40 discusses the visit to Pilate after the burial, and in contradiction 48 and 49 he discusses the reliability of that and the many Christians who doubt that it is historical.

From issue 45, on he goes into the problems about the women going to the tomb. In issue 46 he shows how the accounts of the arrival times of the women are so confused that they are irreconcilable.

From there he goes on to the actual resurrection accounts and the many contradictions and problems with it based on the verses themselves. For example, issue 55 deals with the jumbled mess of who was at the tomb. Then the contradictory messages they were given is in issue 60. Following this all the actions of the apostles are covered in detail. In issue 77 he then turns to Judas and the contradiction over whether Judas actually repented or not. The first part ends with the appearances of Jesus to his followers and the problems with that: where he came, who he spoke to, and what actually happened.

It would not be possible here to go through every issue. I have just tried to point out some of the main ones. A quick look at the table of contents shows just how detailed and extensive the coverage is. To describe this first section as encyclopedic is to understate the depth of this study.

The second part, which will appear in the second volume of this series, deals with issues raised in Christian apologetic literature.

In view of the massive amount of material that is presented, it might be more appropriate to call this everything you wanted to know about the Resurrection (but were afraid to ask). There is something here for everyone with even the smallest interest in the subject. Scholars will find the format useful as will those who present challenges to Christians. Even Christians who wish to evaluate the claims that are made by Christianity will find here a presentation that is scholarly, objective, and sensitive. There is no bone to pick here by the author; it is "only the facts."

With that said, it cannot be denied that this work does present significant reasons to doubt the historicity of the Resurrection. The result is unquestionable. Much of what is here demonstrated is not found in any other work, and even when it does occur in other works, it is not in such an easily understood manner. There may be a point or two in favor of those who believe in the Resurrection that may have been overlooked by accident. But even if this is a given, the preponderance of evidence shows that the Resurrection is myth and not history. It is certainly not something one should base a life's decision on.

I am certain that anyone who reads this book will come away with the same evaluation as I have; it is in indispensable addition to one's library. It will become a constant reference and resource for all those interested in the truth.

Rabbi Moshe Shulman
Executive Director, Judaism's Answer
New York, January 12, 2014

PREFACE

I N 2003, I was challenged by an adamant believer in Jesus to prove that Jesus did *not* physically rise from the dead. The genesis of this text was, in fact, this direct challenge from an acquaintance during an interchange spanning several years. Two e-mail excerpts included:

> I did miss amongst all the good stuff your explanation in refutation of the *resurrection of Jesus*, which is of course the drawing card of many searchers. It is the glue holding the whole NT together (July 9, 2003).

> Of course for the Christian the real issue is the resurrection, which if true validates the whole exercise and if not the whole exercise is vitiated (November 15, 2003).

I naively accepted the challenge. What followed was totally unexpected and unforeseen. During the next eleven years, usually during summer vacation, I traveled to New York, Dallas/Ft. Worth, Chicago, and other cities to carry out my investigation of the Resurrection. These cities contain perhaps many of the most substantial theological collections in the United States. In particular, the theological seminaries in these cities have in their collections materials that cannot be found in most secular institutions of higher learning. The materials available were on a broad spectrum of theological studies: Christian apologetics, church doctrine, dogmatics, evidences of Christianity, and systematic theology. In addition, and importantly, these repositories harbored New Testament commentaries, introductions into the New Testament, numerous books dealing with the biography of Jesus, religious encyclopedias, and dissertations and theses.

To give laypeople an appreciation of the variety of material on Jesus alone, one only needs to examine the topics of study listed under the Library of Congress subject heading "Jesus Christ." The subject headings, all of which are related to this inquiry, seemed innumerable: historicity, descent into hell, apparitions and miracles, betrayal, three days in the tomb, denial by Peter, appearances, promises, burial, crucifixion, and date of death. Other topics studied included the Apostles' Creed, biblical exegesis, biblical typology, prophecy, the Ascension, the Exaltation, and, of course, the Resurrection. For most laypeople, many of these subjects have technical terms that are alien and probably meaningless. For priests, pastors, ministers, and theologians, these subjects comprise a substantial part of their theological curriculum and training.

The amount, depth, and scope of material related to Jesus's resurrection is not only voluminous—it is mindboggling. This researcher, for instance, can literally state that he examined and read over five thousand sources including journal articles, monographs, theses, dissertations, excerpts from books, entire books, and, finally, literature on the Internet. Therefore, this book will answer questions raised by the many resurrection accounts, and, more specifically, collect and critically examine the arguments advanced by proponents of Jesus's resurrection as well as his postmortem resurrection "appearances" and his ascension.

Further, for sake of discussion, this text adopts the "fundamentalist" Christian concept of a "resurrected" Jesus as the transformation of a corpse into a "spiritual body" or living supernatural body (*soma pneumatikon*). The well-known fundamentalist and Christian apologist William Lane Craig (1988, 127; cf. 2012, 375-76) described Jesus's resurrected body as follows: "Jesus rose to eternal life in a radically transformed body that can be described as immortal, glorious, powerful, and supernatural. In this new mode of existence he was not bound by physical limitations of the universe, but possessed superhuman powers."

Significantly, it must be understood that a resurrection is *not* the same as the "resuscitation" or "reanimation" of a body or the "reincarnation" or "immortality" of a soul. The following definitions may be helpful:

- **Resuscitation:** the restoration or revival of a person from a coma, unconsciousness, or apparent death back to the same earthly life. Therefore, the body has no changes in it and is subjected to death once again (House and Holden 2006, Chart 59).
- **Reanimation:** the rejoining of an earthly body with the same soul (or a new soul?) after a temporary separation.
- **Reincarnation:** the rebirth of a soul into a new and different but still physical and mortal body (common idea in some Eastern religions).
- **Immortality:** the inability to die, life continuing forever (especially a soul after its separation from a dead body).

Based upon Craig's interpretation of a "resurrection," it can be inferred that (1) Jesus was no longer able to die, (2) Jesus was no longer able to age, (3)

Jesus was no longer able to become sick, (4) Jesus was no longer able to become injured, and (5) Jesus was able to move at will instantaneously from place to place (Cavin 1995, 363; Martin 2011, 289). At the same time, since there is inadequate evidence to investigate these five inferences (except possibly #5), this text will only be concerned with the previously stated intention: a critical examination of the Resurrection story and those writings that support it.

Another term that must be defined is "ascension." In his master's thesis, Hook (1978, 4) advised that "when the doctrine of the ascension is discussed it is imperative in this day and age that one clarifies exactly what is meant when the term ascension is employed." Trotter (2005, 38-39; cf. Toon 1983, 198), writing for the *Dictionary for Theological Interpretation of the Bible*, wrote: "Ascension of Jesus Christ. Event, recorded most fully in Acts 1:1-11, by which Christ concluded his post resurrection appearances, left the earth, and was taken up into heaven, not to return physically until his second advent."

This book is divided into three major divisions:

PART I contains perfunctory material. In particular, it provides an overview of the issue of miracles and supernaturalism in terms of the topic: the burden of proof. Furthermore, this section discusses several relevant concepts that must be addressed before reading part II.

PART II, the main text, explores 113 issues that are examined in three formats. Each issue begins with a plain-and-simple description of the text. Here the concern is what the text means to the average person on the street two thousand years ago or today. This description is followed by a section of contradictions and speculations. Altogether 120 contradictions and 217 speculations are examined.

PART III consists of an extensive reference list, name index, and subject index.

In lieu of presenting the Christian scriptures in their traditional order—Matthew, Mark, Luke, and John—this book uses the historical and chronological sequence in which they were actually written. Therefore, the scriptural verses are presented in parallel columns from left to right: (1) the writings of Paul, when appropriate, (2) the Gospel of Mark, (3) the Gospel of Matthew, (4) the Gospel of Luke, including the Acts of the Apostles, and (5) the Gospel of John. The sequential analysis starts from approximately the time of Jesus's death and avoids most of his trial. It continues with the accounts detailing Jesus's (1) burial, (2) post-resurrection appearances, and (3) ascension.

Similarly to facilitate the readers' understanding, this text incorporates eighty-four tables and four illustrations. In addition, the text concludes with a healthy reference list. The references include opinions and sources from a wide range of perspectives. Furthermore, the text incorporates material that spans from dated, older sources to those current.

"Orthodox believers" in Jesus's resurrection will reject many of the statements and interpretations found in this text. The sources of the expressed materials cover large areas of both geography and history. The interpretations of Jesus's resurrection obviously changed over time and across cultures. It is also recognized that some Orthodox believers may charge this text as representative of liberal scholars and theologians or those characterized from the other end of the spectrum. In reality, this book presents scholars and theologians who cover the entire spectrum. Obviously, among religious believers, as well as among both skeptics and nonbelievers, there are diverse opinions. Groups whose input was sought include those termed by Christian fundamentalists as "nominal" Christians (e.g., biblical Unitarians), Jews, Muslims, and a broad group of generally areligious persons. The rationale behind employing the assistance of these views is multifaceted.

- "Orthodox Christian" scholars and theologians too often fail to raise critical and controversial points of inquiry because they are constrained by (1) the statements of faith and strictures of a theological college or seminary, (2) their previously held belief(s), and (3) their confessional stance.
- Many of the foremost authorities of Orthodox Christian theology may include former Christian theologians who turned apostate and those categorized as areligious thinkers.

In the Christian scriptures, 1 Thessalonians 5:21 challenges: "Prove all things; hold fast that which is good." Don Martin (2013), elaborating on this well-known verse from the Christian scriptures, wrote:

> The Greek word for "prove" is domimazo (the word in our verse has a different grammatical posture; hence, while the same word, the spelling differs) and it means, "To test, prove, etc." (Expository Dictionary of New Testament Words by W. E. Vines). Some insert ". . . with the expectation of approving," as this seems to be the fundamental idea in I Thessalonians 5: 21 (Ibid.) The word dokimazo is rendered "discern," "approvest," "examine," and "trieth" (Lk. 12: 56, Rom. 2: 18; I Cor. 11: 28; I Thes. 2: 4). Dokimazo in the expression "prove all things" (panta de dokimazete) is second person, plural, present tense, imperative mood, and active voice. Hence, "prove all things" is not an option

but an actual command, required of the Christian (imperative mood shows this). The fact that the tense is present indicates it is an ongoing command.

This text attempts to meet the challenge presented by the author of 1 Thessalonians with regard to Jesus's resurrection. It is hoped that the readers will respect that effort.

Several years ago, E. P. Sanders (2000, 39), a highly respected New Testament scholar, succinctly wrote:

> Research deals with probabilities, and it should not be able either to create or destroy faith; at its best, it can inform faith. Its actual task, however, is to illuminate the early period of the Christian movement for interested believers and unbelievers alike. Scholarship that *aims* at either supporting or damaging faith is, in my view, not true scholarship. Scholarship should be "disinterested," not the servant of a preferred set of conclusions.

This text faced several challenges in order to meet Sanders's ideal that "scholarship should be 'disinterested,' not the servant of a preferred set of conclusions." However:

- What is one to do if a believer in the Resurrection challenges your faith?
- What is one to do when evangelicals and missionaries openly witness and, in some cases, proselytize their religion to members of their family?

Stanton (1977, 64) suggested that rather than being a neutral observer, "empathy with the subject matter of the text is an essential presupposition."

An often-repeated theological claim or challenge of believers in Jesus runs accordingly: All you need to do is read the gospels' account of the Resurrection or any of the numerous popular texts, either evangelistic or apologetic in genre, and you will be convinced to accept "that Jesus died for our sins according to the scriptures; And that he was buried, and that he rose again the third day according to the scriptures" (1 Cor 15:3-4). One example of a challenge was issued by the late president and founder of Campus Crusade for Christ International William Bright. Bright (1999, xii) wrote:

> During my fifty-five years of sharing the good news of the Savior with the academic world, I have met very few individuals who have

honestly considered the evidence and yet deny that Jesus Christ is the Son of God and the Savior of men. To me, the evidence confirming the deity of the Lord Jesus Christ is overwhelmingly conclusive to any honest, objective seeker after truth. However, not all—not even the majority—of those to whom I have spoken have accepted Him as their Savior and Lord. This is not because they were *unable* to believe—they were simply *unwilling* to believe!

Bright's claim that the evidence is "overwhelmingly conclusive to any honest, objective seeker after truth" is not a matter of objectivity but a matter of subjective opinion. Although he and others claim to know and hold the absolute truth, this dogmatic view is rejected by many honest, objective seekers of the truth such as former ministers, pastors, and priests who came to a contradictory position after years of contemplation and study. Many, in fact, converted to other religions or became areligious.

Furthermore, one of the numerous advantages of the printed word is that it permits the reader time to turn pages back (or scroll down) to pause and reflect upon what has been read. However, this means of communication also creates a paradox for its author. That is, one of the shortfalls of the printed text is who delivers the last word, a topic literally raised in scripture:

> Proverbs 18:17. The first to present his case seems right, till another comes forward and questions him. (NIV)

In other words, critics of this text will ultimately have the last word. Therefore, opponents can cherry-pick a few contradictions (out of the 120!) and speculations (out of the 217!) and present to their readership a distorted view of the text as a whole. Furthermore, readers are reminded that the speculations presented in this text are nothing more than speculations.

Perhaps, at this point, several baseball analogies may be useful. For a pitcher, every pitch (or every contradiction or speculation offered in this text) does not need to be a strikeout or even a strike. Sometimes a ball, a walk to first base, or even a single can be advantageous and considered a win for the team. Similarly, a batter does not need to hit a home run with the bases loaded. Sometimes a deliberately fouled-off pitch or a single can be advantageous. So too, for the approximate 120 contradictions and 217 speculations a "home run" is not necessary to achieve an eventual win.

There is another issue this text deems important that must be clarified. Numerous times throughout this text the phrase "Christian apologists" will appear. This text includes *all* Christian apologists who are believers in Jesus. However, it is recognized that some "believers in Jesus" do not accept or acknowledge being called a Christian. Nonetheless, for the sake of convenience, this phrase is adopted. Second, this text does not mean to employ this phrase in a mean-spirited manner.

Gary R. Habermas (1984a, 171; cf. Sire 2006, 160), one of the leading Christian apologists, once lamented: "To date, too many evangelicals have been complacent, largely attempting to write to each other, repeating old presentations of evidence for Jesus' resurrection without really grappling with contemporary concerns. For this we deserve criticism." A similar lament could be stated but in reference to numerous opponents of Jesus's resurrection. This text, in part, attempts to correct that complacency. As Taussig (2004, 249) appropriately wrote in his conclusion to a critical book review of N. T. Wright's *The Resurrection of the Son of God*, "the complex ethical demands for honest and rigorous biblical interpretation in this postmodern world of seekers and multilaterality can be met."

In conclusion, this text critically surveys many of the voluminous evangelistic and Christian apologetic writings on the subject of Jesus's resurrection and responds to their claims, interpretations, and challenges. It is this author's belief that sufficient issues are refuted adequately for Christians and any others to rethink the truth of Jesus's claimed resurrection, post-resurrection appearances, and ascension.

ACKNOWLEDGMENTS

PRODUCING THIS TEXT was a cumulative team effort, and hence, I wish to express deep gratitude to the many people who made it possible. First, I must acknowledge Anthony Buzzard. Anthony is a prolific biblical Unitarian. During countless communiqués and dialogues, we discussed numerous beliefs that we shared in common such as Jesus is not God and God does not exist as a Trinity. However, Anthony definitely maintains that Jesus is the Messiah. This is a view unequivocally rejected by this writer. According to Anthony and others, there is overriding proof that Jesus is the Messiah: his physical, bodily resurrection. This physical, bodily resurrection is also the lynchpin for Christians who maintain that Jesus is God. In 2003, it was Anthony who challenged me to prove that Jesus was not physically resurrected. After eleven years of research, this book is the result of his challenge.

Second, I wish to acknowledge the assistance of Rabbi Moshe Shulman. He has been active in Kiruv Rechokim (Jewish Outreach), countering missionaries and teaching Torah and Chassidus for over twenty years. Rabbi Shulman has also been working with the major counter missionary organizations like Outreach Judaism and Jews for Judaism and with numerous counter missionaries over the world for over twenty years. Rabbi Shulman was coordinator of Messiah Truth Project's Outreach Services, providing information and counseling for Jews interested in leaving Messianic/Christian movements. Messiah Truth is nonprofit organization established to combat the deceptive missionary techniques of evangelical Christian denominations and the Messianic movements. He is the Executive Director of Judaism's Answer, an anti-missionary organization with an influential website: *http:// judaismsanswer.com*

Significantly, he assisted in editing this project and helped in reordering the flow of logic and clarity of the text. Furthermore, Rabbi Shulman continually offered poignant and relevant words based on his many years of experience of working in the field as a counter missionary. In fact, I highly recommend Rabbi Shulman for those seeking the services of a skilled lecturer, instructor, debater, or counter missionary facilitator.

I am also indebted to two copy editors who assisted in editing this book: Fran Ginsberg and Richard Signore. Copy editors are usually thought to merely check the mechanical details of the author's writing, such as spelling, punctuation, and grammar. However, they went beyond this narrow job description and in a literal sense raised insightful questions and enhanced the readability and clarity of the text.

Last, I wish to acknowledge the efforts of all the members of the Xlibris staff for their helpfulness throughout the production of this text.

ABBREVIATIONS

HEBREW BIBLE

Gen or Gn	Genesis
Exod or Ex	Exodus
Lev or Lv	Leviticus
Num. or Nm	Numbers
Deut or Dt	Deuteronomy
Josh	Joshua
Judg	Judges
1 Sam	1 Samuel
2 Sam	2 Samuel
1 Kgs	1 Kings
2 Kgs	2 Kings
Isa or Is	Isaiah
Jer	Jeremiah
Ezek or Ez	Ezekiel
Hos	Hosea
Joel	Joel
Amos or Am	Amos
Obad or Ob	Obadiah
Jon	Jonah
Mic or Mi	Micah
Nah or Na	Nahum
Hab or Hb	Habakkuk
Zeph or Zep	Zephaniah
Hag or Hg	Haggai
Zech or Zec	Zechariah
Mal	Malachi
Ps	Psalms
Prov or Prv	Proverbs
Job or Jb	Job

Song or (Cant)	Song of Songs (Song of Solomon, or Canticles)
Ruth	Ruth
Lam	Lamentations
Eccl	Ecclesiastes
Est	Esther
Dan or Dn	Daniel
Ezra	Ezra
Neh	Nehemiah
1 Chr or 1 Chron	1 Chronicles
2 Chr or 2 Chron	2 Chronicles

THE CHRISTIAN SCRIPTURES (NT)

Matt or Mt	Matthew
Mk	Mark
Lk	Luke
Jn	John
Acts	Acts of the Apostles
Rom	Romans
1 Cor	1 Corinthians
2 Cor	2 Corinthians
Gal	Galatians
Eph	Ephesians
Phil	Philippians
Col	Colossians
1 Thess or 1 Thes	1 Thessalonians
2 Thess or 2 Thes	2 Thessalonians
1 Tim or 1 Tm	1 Timothy
2 Tim or 2 Tm	2 Timothy
Ti	Titus
Philem or Phlm	Philemon
Heb	Hebrews
Jas	James
1 Pet or 1 Pt	1 Peter
2 Pet or 2 Pt	2 Peter
1 Jn	1 John
2 Jn	2 John

3 Jn	3 John
Jude	Jude
Rev or Rv	Revelation

THE APOCRYPHA and PSEUDEPIGRAPHA

Ass Mos or As Mos	Assumption of Moses (Testament of Moses)
2 Apoc Bar or 2 Bar	2 Apocalypse of Baruch
1 Enoch or 1 En	Book of Enoch (Ethiopian Apolcalypse)
2 Enoch or 2 En	Book of Enoch (Slavonic Apocalypse)
1 Macc or 1 Mc	1 Maccabees
2 Macc or 2 Mc	2 Maccabees
3 Macc or 3 Mc	3 Maccabees
Tob or Tb	Tobit
Ecclus or Sir	Ecclesiasticus
Wisd of Sol	Wisdom of Solomon

TRACTATES OF THE TALMUD

Git.	*Gittin*
Meg.	*Megillah*
Ned.	*Nedarim*
R.H. or *Rosh*	*Rosh HaShanah*
Sanh.	*Sanhedrin*
Sabb. or *Shab*	*Shabbat*
Sot.	*Sotah*
Yom.	*Yoma*

GENERAL

Ant.	*Antiquities of the Jews* by Flavius Josephus
AV	Authorized Version
b.	ben, bar, son of
BCE	Before the Christian Era
ca. or c.	*circa*, around, about
CE	Common Era
cf.	*Confer*, compare, refer to

ch.	Chapter
e.g.	*exempli gratia*, for example.
f. or ff.	Following verse or chapter (plural ff.).
Gk.	Greek
Heb.	Hebrew.
i.e.	id est, that is.
KJV	King James Version (Bible)
loc. cit.	*Loco citato*, in the place cited.
LXX.	Septuagint: the Greek version of the Hebrew Bible
MS.	Manuscript (Plural MSS.)
NB., n.b.	Note carefully
n.d.	No date, not determined
NIV	New International Version (Bible)
NRSV	New Revised Standard Version (Bible)
para. or par.	Paragraph
pl	Plural
R.	Rab, Rabban, Rabbenu, Rabbi.
RSV	Revised Standard Version (Bible)
RV	Revised Version of the Bible.
Sanh.	Sanhedrin.
Vulg.	The Vulgate: the Latin version of the Bible compiled by Jerome

( ) represent parenthesis that are found in the original text.

[ ] represent brackets that are original additions to the text.

[[ ]] represent double brackets employed in place of [ ] that are *not* found in the original text. These additions usually clarify or elaborate a point offered by the original source.

If there is a difference in the numbering of biblical verses between the Hebrew Bible and Christian scriptures, the Christian numbering is placed in brackets (e.g., Isa 9:5 [6 AV]).

In addition, unless otherwise indicated, the scriptural translation is based on the King James Version (Authorized). The rationale is (1) it is perhaps the most widely used English translation and (2) it is in the public domain.

Furthermore, contrary to *The Christian Writer's Manual of Style* (2004), as a matter of consistency, this text adopts the recommendation of the sixteenth edition of *The Chicago Manual of Style* by capitalizing religious events and concepts of major theological importance (e.g., the **C**rucifixion, the **R**esurrection, the **E**leven, and the **T**welve). However, when used generically, such terms are in lowercase. In addition, this text incorporates the rule (7.16, p. 354) for possessive proper nouns, including the singular form: Jesus's.

PART I

INTRODUCTORY REMARKS

CHAPTER 1

Perfunctory Material

TOPIC 1: Thirteen Assumed Facts in Reference to the Resurrection

FOR THE SAKE of discussion, this text will accept as a premise thirteen basic ideas or tenets. The first three assumed facts relate directly to God, whereas the last ten facts are in reference to Jesus. These last ten facts were adopted from E. P. Sanders's *In Jesus and Judaism* (1985, 11; cf. Ehrman 2012; Johnson 1996, 121-22; Lenowitz 1998, 34-49; Loke 2009, 570-84; Sanders 1993, 10):

1. God exists.
2. The Hebrew Bible is God's revealed word.
3. Miracles (i.e., supernatural events) can and definitely occur.
4. Jesus lived during the first century in Roman-occupied land that today is called Israel. (Bart Ehrman's *Did Jesus Exist?* is a tour de force argument in support of the historical Jesus by a self-proclaimed "agnostic with atheist leanings" p. 5).
5. Jesus spoke Aramaic and Hebrew.
6. Jesus was a Galilean who preached and healed.
7. Jesus selected disciples, and they are referred to as the Twelve.
8. Jesus confined his activity to Israel.
9. Jesus engaged in a controversy about the Temple.
10. Jesus was crucified outside Jerusalem by the Roman authorities.
11. Jesus was crucified during the rule of Pontius Pilate.
12. After his death Jesus's followers continued as an identifiable movement.
13. Some Jews openly resisted parts of the new movement (Gal. 1:13, 22; Phil. 3:6); and this persecution endured, at least, to a time near the end of Paul's career (2 Cor. 11:24; Gal. 5:11; 6:12; cf. Matt. 10:17; 23:34).

TOPIC 2: Reasons Why the Gospels and Others Portions of the Christian Scriptures Were Written

Commentators, scholars, and theologians (Aune 1988; Bailey 1995, 197-221; Blomberg 2007a, 298-303; Burridge 2004; Eddy and Boyd 2007, 309-61; Guelich 1991, 173-208; Gundry 1974, 97-114; Hurtado 1992, 276-82; Keener 2009a, 75-81; Klein, Blomberg, Hubbard, and Eckelberg 1993, 323-74; Talbert 1977; Tiede 1984, 1705-29) debate the issue regarding what genre the Gospels and other portions of the Christian scriptures were written. The text by Bailey and Vander Broek, *Literary Forms in the New Testament: A Handbook* (1992) provides definitions of over thirty literary forms, including examples of their use in the New Testament and comments regarding the value of genre recognition for interpretation. Various descriptions and labels include historical literature, historical biography, popular biography, Graeco-Roman biography, a folk book, tradition in a Middle Eastern peasant culture, cultic legend, document of faith, drama or mythography, letter writing (e.g., Paul's epistles), memoirs, Midrashic, narrative literature, novels, theological literature, and unique genre. In order to answer what genre these texts were written, it is necessary to determine the purpose of their respective authors. At the same time, it is the position of this text that the Gospels *are not* a biography, and they are not written to record history in a modern sense. In fact, these texts were primarily written for five and interwoven reasons.

First, the Gospels, and most of Paul's writings, are evangelistic in genre. That is, they call people to have faith in Jesus.

Second, they are exhortatory, written to encourage and assure believers in their faith.

Third, and directly tied to the former, these works have explicit theological purposes.

A. Mark wants to prove that Jesus is the Messiah and the Son of God (e.g., Mk 1:1).
B. Matthew's goal is to prove that Jesus is the Messiah *and* to make disciples of all nations, baptizing them in the name of the Father and of the Son and of the Holy Ghost. In addition, he wants his eleven disciples to teach new disciples to obey everything that Jesus commanded (e.g., Mt 1:1, 18; 28:19-20).
C. Luke writes his gospel to provide an orderly account that makes it possible to know the truth concerning the events that occurred (e.g., Lk 1:1-4).

D. John writes his gospel so one would come to believe that Jesus is the Messiah, the Son of God, and that through believing one could have life through his name (e.g., Jn 20:31).

Fourth, to achieve these ends, the primary means of these writers is to provide proofs in the forms of deeds, miracles, signs, and wonders assigned to Jesus. The foremost sign was Jesus's resurrection.

Fifth, these works were written approximately thirty to seventy years after Jesus's death, and many of the witnesses were dying off or dead. Therefore, the Gospels tell the story of Jesus for a generation who did not know any eyewitnesses or have access to firsthand accounts of the Jesus tradition.

In closing, reference must be made to Hans Küng's *On Being a Christian* (1976, 348). Unlike most authors, this liberal Catholic writer unabashedly stated what the Gospels really were.

> First difficulty. What is true of the Gospels as a whole is particularly true of the Easter stories: they are *not unbiased reports* by disinterested observers but depositions in favor of Jesus submitted in faith by supremely interested and committed persons. They are therefore not so much historical as theological documents: not records of proceedings or chronicles, but testimonies of faith. The Easter faith, which characterized the whole Jesus tradition from the very beginning, obviously determined also the Easter accounts themselves, thus creating extraordinary difficulties from the start for a historical scrutiny. It is in the Easter stories that we must ask about the Easter message.

TOPIC 3: Who Wrote the Gospels and Their Claimed Inerrancy

None of the Gospels identify their author. Instead, the names associated with each gospel were penned much later and became part of church tradition. Consequently, when this text employs the name Mark, it does not literally mean that Mark wrote the Gospel of Mark. Similarly, the use of the name Matthew does not mean that Matthew was the actual author of Matthew. The authors of these works are anonymous.

However, how do we know that the authors of the Gospels are anonymous? First, the *Criterion of Environmental Contradiction* and the *Criterion of Palestinian Environmental Phenomena* (cf. Stein 1980, 237-38) refute the claim that the Gospels were written by the names associated with them. That is, several of these texts betray the Palestinian social, domestic, agricultural, etc., customs and situations in the lifetime of Jesus. Second, numerous scholars maintain the position that the disciples were probably lower-class men, illiterate, and speaking Aramaic. Several were fisherman (Peter and John) and presumably never went to school or had very little schooling. For example, Acts 4:13 reported that Peter and John were "unlearned and ignorant men" (AV). However, Blomberg (2006) declares that "Acts 4:13 means that Peter and John were illiterate (the term *agrammatos* 'unlettered' in this context means not educated beyond the elementary education accessible to most first-century Jewish boys)." Therefore, based upon Blomberg's own words, it would have been impossible for the presumed authors to have written the Gospels because they were written by writers highly literate and skilled in Greek composition and rhetoric (cf. Ehrman 2012, 46-50).

Nonetheless, Ellis (1999, 36) rejects this assumption: "The second-century sources probably identify the four Evangelists correctly. The arguments against these identifications are not decisive and often rest on questionable assumptions, for example, that a Palestinian could not write Greek." Another argument that has been raised by Christian apologists is that Matthew is assumed to have been an educated tax collector. This apologetic is nothing more than speculation.

Because the topic of the Gospels' authorship is important, this text will cite numerous excerpts of relatively recent publications in the category of "Introduction to the New Testament" and the "Origin of New Testament Manuscripts" that challenges the position that the names penned to the four gospels are authentic.

In 2012, Hagner authored *The New Testament: A Historical and Theological Introduction*. His words about the Gospels' authors are significant:

> Mark (p. 164) *Probably* John Mark, son of Mary of Jerusalem (Acts 12:12), and cousin of Barnabas (Col 4:10). (Italics in the original)

> Matthew (p. 194): Although the disciple Levi-Matthew possibly was the collector and editor of the five Matthean discourses, the Gospel as it stands likely is the work of an unknown disciple or disciples of the Matthean circle—that is, associated with Matthew.

> Luke-Acts (p. 228): *Probably* Luke, "the beloved physician" (Col 4:14) and traveling companion of Paul (Italics in the original)

John (p. 256): Probability tips only very slightly in the direction of identifying the Beloved Disciple with the Apostle John as the author of an initial edition of this Gospel, which was then put into its present form by disciples of the Johannine school in Ephesus. It is possible, however that the author was John the Elder, to be distinguished from the Apostle.

In 2009, Russell Pregeant published his *Encounter with the New Testament: An Interdisciplinary Approach.* He wrote:

Mark (p. 111): Second-century tradition attributes the Gospel of Mark to someone named Mark, who supposedly received his information from Peter. It is often assumed that this is John Mark who appears as a companion of Paul in Acts and the Paul to whom Paul refers to in his letters. Mark was a common name, however, so that even if a Mark was the author, we cannot be certain about these connections.

Matthew (p. 128): Like its author, its place of composition is unknown.

Luke (p. 147): Second-century tradition identifies the author as Luke, a companion of Paul mentioned in his letter to Philemon.

There are good reasons to doubt this tradition, however.

John (p. 174): Second-century tradition assigned this Gospel to John, son of Zebedee, one of 'the Twelve' among Jesus' disciples. And it has often been assumed that the unnamed 'disciple whom Jesus loved,' who appears late in the story, was the same person. None of this is likely . . . . An alternative suggestion for the author is a 'Presbyter John' from Ephesus, although there is no solid evidence that there was such a person.

That same year, *The People's New Testament Commentary*, authored by Boring and Craddock (2009, 105) concisely stated: "As is the case with all of the New Testament Gospels, the Gospel of Mark is anonymous."

One year earlier, D. C. Parker's *An Introduction to the New Testament Manuscripts and Their Texts* (2008, 313) made several important comments about the titles (and the presumed authors) of the Gospels:

> The dates at which these titles are first found in manuscripts has to take into account the fact that they were sometimes added in a different hand from that of the scribe . . . No papyrus has any indication of having had running titles, which first appear in the fourth-century parchment Bibles. The fact that a title was added in a different hand (as in P4 and P66) does not itself mean that it was added very much later, or even that it was not written by the scribe, since a skilled writer will have commanded several styles.

> The oldest sure evidence of a contemporary name comes in the beginning of the third century in P75 of Luke and John, which contains the end of the first and beginning of the second book.

Two years earlier, Hurtado (2006, 27) contributed an article "The New Testament in the Second Century: Text, Collection and Canon" into a work *Transmission and Reception: New Testament Text-Critical and Exegetical Studies*. He opined:

> That is, I suggest that what changes in the post-150 CE period is a greater tendency to see texts as the *works of authors*, and so to cite them as such, rather than simply appropriating the contents of texts. And I further suggest that a major reason for a greater emphasis of texts as products of particular authors is the swirling controversies of the second century over heresies. This led Christians to place greater emphasis on authorship of writings as a way of certifying and/or promoting them. So, for example, whereas the canonical Gospels were composed without the authors identifying themselves, across the second century we see an increasing tendency to attribute and emphasize authorship of writings, including a greater tendency to attribute authorship to writings, for which authorship was not an explicit feature of the text (e.g., the canonical Gospels, Hebrews).

Similarly, deSilva (2004, 194), wrote in his *Introduction to the New Testament Contexts, Methods & Ministry Formation*:

> The Gospels' titles are not original to the authors—they were just "Gospels" and only became Gospels "according to Mark" and so forth as the churches began to use multiple Gospels side by side, requiring a clearer identification of each other one. The

identification was based on early church traditions about each Gospel's development rather than on internal evidence.

Burkett (2002, 121), in his *An Introduction to the New Testament and the Origins of Christianity*, also declared in no uncertain terms that the Gospels were authored by anonymous people:

> The New Testament canon contains four Gospels, bearing the titles "Matthew," "Mark," "Luke," and "John," respectively. We cannot be sure that these titles give the true names of the authors, since these headings were added to the Gospels years after they were written. The Gospels themselves tell us nothing about who wrote them or when they were composed.

Finally, in the most dated source that is cited, Perrin and Dulling (1982, 42) unabashedly stated in their *New Testament: An Introduction Proclamation and Parenesis, Myth and History*, second edition:

> The gospels were not written by eyewitnesses of the ministry of Jesus. They were written in the period between A.D. 70 and 100, forty years or more after the crucifixion, and originally they circulated anonymously. It has to be understood that in the ancient world it was quite common to attach important names to anonymous works, or to write in the name of the teacher or famous person from the past . . . Many modern scholars believe that the authoritative 'apostolic' names were attached to the gospels in the second century A.D. We simply do not know who wrote them, though as we shall see, the gospels themselves tell us a great deal about the gospel writers—the evangelist—and their concerns. But they do not tell us their names, and when we speak of "Matthew," "Mark," "Luke," or "John" we do so only for convenience; the actual names of the evangelists are forever lost to us.

Nonetheless, in direct opposition to the above, it must be acknowledged that there are advocates of tradition. For example, Ellis (1999, 36) unequivocally states in his *The Making of the New Testament Documents*: "The second-century traditions are of the highest probability for Luke and Mark, and apart from John they are undisputed, are without a satisfactory alternative and are inherently not improbable: one must resist the modern tendency to assume that in early Christianity only unknowns could be authors."

Further complicating matters, research demonstrates that the manuscripts in use were living documents. Consequently, variation is found in the approximate 5,600 surviving manuscripts. However, most of these manuscripts are not complete texts. Significantly, Metzger and Ehrman (2005, 51n80; cf. Swanson 1995)—writing in their *The Text of the New Testament Its Transmission, Corruption, and Restoration*, fourth edition—warn: "Lest, however, the wrong impression be conveyed from the statistics given above regarding the total number of Greek manuscripts of the New Testament, it should be pointed out that most of the papyri are relatively fragmentary and that only about 60 manuscripts (of which Codex Sinaiticus is the only majuscule manuscript) contain the entire New Testament."

Last, it is important to point out that the number of variants in the surviving manuscripts has been estimated to approximate over 250,000. Although most of these variants might be judged to be minor, in a number of situations they have important theological significance. In order to verify this claim, one only needs to type into an Internet search engine "List of major textual variants in the New Testament" or "List of Bible verses not included in modern translations." Several examples can be seen below:

Matthew 6:13 The Majority Text [MT] is in agreement with the Textus Receptus against the Critical Text [CT].

MT: And do not lead us into temptation, But deliver us from the evil one. For Yours is the kingdom and the power and the glory forever. Amen.

CT: And do not lead us into temptation, But deliver us from the evil one.

Matthew 24:36

MT: But of that day and hour no one knows, not even the angels of heaven, but My Father only.

CT: But of that day and hour no one knows, not even the angels of heaven, nor the Son, but My Father only.

Mark 11:26

MT: But if you do not forgive, neither will your Father in heaven forgive your trespasses.

CT: *Verse omitted*

Mark 16:15 is part of the Long Ending, and it is not considered authentic. This verse is significant because it contains Jesus's command for his disciples to evangelize the *Great Commission* to the entire world. "And he said unto them, Go ye into all the world, and preach the gospel to every creature."

Mark 16:16 is also part of the Long Ending, and it is not considered authentic. This verse is cited as evidence for the requirement of believer's baptism among churches of the Restoration Movement. Of greater import, this verse specifically discusses the requisite to obtain salvation or condemnation (judgment). "He that believeth and is baptized shall be saved; but he that believeth not shall be damned."

Mark 16:17a is also part of the Long Ending, and it is not considered authentic. This verse is specifically cited as biblical support for some denominations' teachings concerning exorcism and spiritual warfare. "And these signs shall follow them that believe; In my name shall they cast out devils; they shall speak with new tongues."

Mark 16:17b is also part of the Long Ending, and it is not considered authentic. This verse is specifically cited as biblical support for some denominations' teachings concerning the speaking in tongues. "And these signs shall follow them that believe; In my name shall they cast out devils; they shall speak with new tongues."

Mark 16:18a is another verse that is part of the Long Ending, and it is not considered authentic. This passage is important because the practice of snake handling and of drinking various types of poisons, found in a few offshoots of Pentecostalism, find their biblical support in this verse. "They shall take up serpents; and if they drink any deadly thing, it shall not hurt them; they shall lay hands on the sick, and they shall recover."

Luke 22:19b-20 is a disputed text which does not appear in some of the early manuscripts of Luke. The missing part of the verse deals with the institution of the Lord's Supper. "And he took bread, and gave thanks, and brake it, and gave unto them, saying, 'This is my body *which is given for you: this do in remembrance of me.*'"

1 Jn 5:7, the *Johannine Comma is* perhaps the most significant New Testament proof text for the Trinity. The last part of this verse is omitted from the NRSV, the NIV and the NASB. "For there are three that bear record in heaven, the Father, the Word, and the Holy Ghost: and these three are one."

Finally, the statistics mentioned above in reference to the number of variants in the surviving manuscripts demonstrate that in no way are the Christian scriptures inerrant.

TOPIC 4: Dating the Manuscripts

The dating of all manuscripts is subject to intense speculation. Conservative scholars [Hendricksen 1973, 97; J. A. T. Robertson 1976; Rieke 1972, 121-34] usually favor an older dating of the documents whereas liberals and skeptics place an earlier dating on these works. Carson (2007, 40) elaborated:

> The second edition of *The New Testament: An Introduction* by Norman Perrin and Dennis C. Duling (Harcourt Brace Jovanovich 1982, £25.25 pb) fits the NT documents into a doctrinaire history of NT Christianity reconstructed at the beginning of the book. The result is a pretty radical scheme. At the other end stands John A. T. Robinson, *Redating the New Testament* (/TPI nd, op), who argues that all the books in the NT canon were completed before AD 70 and that external ascriptions of authorship in early Christian tradition are remarkably accurate. *Both books deserve careful reading by the serious student, if only to discover how data can be made to fit such wildly different schemes.* [italics mine.]

Similarly, Timothy Luke Johnson (1996, 90) observed: "The dating of the four canonical Gospels is entirely a matter of scholarly deductions, based on arguments concerning literary dependence."

The Resurrection: A Critical Inquiry assumes that the works of Paul are the oldest of the Christian scriptures, and that they were penned approximately during the late forties to late fifties. Several of Paul's letters are *not* recognized as authentic. Timothy Luke Johnson (1999, 271), writing in his *The Writings of the New Testament: An Interpretation*, wrote: "Nearly all critical scholars accept seven letters as written by Paul: Romans, 1 and 2 Corinthians, Galatians, Philippians, 1 Thessalonians, and Philemon. There is almost equal unanimity in rejecting 1 and 2 Timothy and Titus. Serious debate can occasionally be found concerning 2 Thessalonians, Colossians, and Ephesians, but the clear and growing scholarly consensus considers them to be non-Pauline."

The scholarly consensus is that Mark 1-16:8 was authored between the late sixties and perhaps just after the destruction of the Second Temple by the Romans in 70 CE. In contrast, Mark 16:9-20 is generally acknowledged and recognized by scholars to have been written by another hand many years later. Notably, Farmer (1974) has rejected the scholarly consensus. In the literature these twelve verses are commonly referred to as the Markan Long Ending or the Markan Appendix.

(Interested readers should consult theses [Cox 1993; Eymann 1978; Lee 1958; Thompson 1980; Yang 2003]; entire books [Farmer 1974; Kelhoffer 2000]; portions of books [Aland and Aland 1989, 292; Fenton 1994, 1-7; Gundry 1993, 1009-21; Metzger 1994, 101-07; Watermann 2006, 26-83); and numerous articles (Hester 1995, 61-86; Holmes 2001, 12-23, 48-50; Petersen 1980, 151-66; Williams 1999, 21-35) written on this controversial topic.)

Matthew is assumed to have been written a few years later in the early eighties.

In contrast, Luke-Acts is speculated to have been written in the mideighties or later. Compounding matters, it is further disputed whether or not these texts were authored by the same person. As a side note, Tipler (1994, 306) cautions:

> The consensus of biblical scholars is that Luke was composed between A.D. 80 and 85, which would mean Luke was written some fifty years after Jesus' death. On this dating, it is very implausible that it would contain any eyewitness testimony, and even if it did, such testimony would be very unreliable at such a late date, for reasons I shall give below. [Note: Tipler supports the view that Luke was written before A.D. 70.]

Finally, John is assumed to have been written in the nineties, with its final redaction possibly between the years 100-110. Here, too, there is a controversy. Many scholars take the position that the last chapter (i.e., 21) was not written by the same author of the previous twenty chapters.

TOPIC 5: Burden of Proof

> 1 Cor 15:3, 4, 14-18 For I delivered unto you *first* of all that which I also received, how that Christ *died for our sins* according to the scriptures; And that he was buried, and that he rose again the third day according to the scriptures... And if Christ be not risen, then is *our preaching in vain, and your faith is also vain.* **Yea, and we are found false witnesses of God**; because we have testified of God that he raised up Christ: whom he raised not up, **if so be that the dead rise not**. For if the dead rise not, then is not Christ raised: And if Christ be not raised, *your faith is vain; ye are yet in your sins.* Then they also which are fallen asleep in Christ are perished. If in this life only we have hope in Christ, **we are of all men most miserable**.

The resurrection of Jesus has been variously referred to as the bedrock, core, cornerstone, foundation, keystone, and lynchpin upon which believers in Jesus stand. The implications of these words in 1 Corinthians 15 by the apostle Paul cannot be overemphasized. He unequivocally declares that if there were no resurrection then:

- Jesus is not raised (v. 13).
- There is no guarantee of resurrection of the dead (v. 13; 20-23).
- Our preaching is in vain (v. 14).
- Our faith is vain (v. 14, 17).
- Believers are false witnesses because they preached a false doctrine (v. 15).
- Believers are still in their sins (unforgiven) (v. 17).
- All the dead are perished (v. 18).
- There is no hope (v. 19).
- Believers are to be pitied above all men (v. 19).

Consequently, one can appreciate why Christian apologists are so adamant about the issue of Jesus's resurrection.

PROPONENTS OF THE RESURRECTION: THE BURDEN OF PROOF ARGUMENT

"The burden of proof in Jesus research refers to the question of historical veracity of the New Testament accounts of Jesus." (Winter, 2011, 843) A

THE RESURRECTION: A CRITICAL INQUIRY

fundamental issue is whether or not the accounts and details recorded in the Christian scriptures are considered reliable and trustworthy. Christian apologists and evangelical fundamentalists also referred by Craffert (2002, 95) as "supernaturalists" or "fundamentalist rationalists" take the position that the Christian scriptures, in particular references to Jesus's resurrection, are reliable and trustworthy until proven contradictory. They often claim that the "entire" burden of proof is on those who deny its historicity. Stein (1980, 227), a Christian apologist, even extends this point: "Of course, if through the investigation of an account one arrives at a 'general attitude' toward its historical veracity which is negative, then one cannot help but change the burden of proof, so that the historicity rather than the unhistorical nature of the accounts must be demonstrated. For this writer, however, this has in no way been demonstrated with regard to the gospel materials."

According to Christian apologists, the disciples and other eyewitnesses as recorded in the Christian scriptures believed themselves to have seen Jesus in actual physical presence, not as a "telegram," not as a ghost or phantom, and not as a spirit. These proponents and defenders of the Resurrection forcefully argue that opponents must show why the views of the recipients as recorded in the Christian scriptures of Jesus's appearances are "untenable" and why they are "not true." Christian apologists also extend this argument to the events and details leading up to the Resurrection, such as Jesus's trial, execution, body preparation, and burial. For example, Siniscalchi (2011, 370) passionately writes:

> Testimonies and other artifacts of history, whether oral or written, are often transmitted because the original compiler(s) firmly believed in their truth. Historians cannot escape such sources. If the resurrection occurred, then we would expect his followers to transmit zealously such a message about Jesus to subsequent generations. An absence of personal commitment on the part of the original witnesses would actually render their testimony less than credible.

In the opinion of many Christian apologists, the issue of miracles or supernatural events recorded in the Christian scriptures poses the most serious problem for skeptics. A common rebuttal, if not ad hominem, to skeptics or opponents of the Resurrection is that they do not believe in miracles and supernaturalism. As a case in point, Christian apologists argue:

1. Nonbelief in miracles is an unwarranted philosophical presumption, not a scientific conclusion.

2. Given that the existence of a transcendent Creator is granted as possible, miracles deserve serious consideration. (Geisler 2013, 317)

Williams (2000; cf. Siniscalchi 2011, 368) and other Christian apologists also regularly suggest that an antisupernatural presupposition skews the research of skeptics. That is, skeptics approach the text under the guise of doing dispassionate, unbiased historical research, when, from the beginning, the game has been fixed. For example:

1. Given miracles do not happen.
2. It can be concluded that Jesus did not perform any miracles.

Consequently, it is not surprising that different scholars come to negative findings at the conclusion of their study. As a result, Christian apologists argue that Jesus's resurrection is unbelievable if skeptics have already decided that events such as the Resurrection cannot occur. In other words, opponents and skeptics can be likened to people who look into a pool of water and observe a reflection of their own image. Needless to say, Christian apologists maintain that an a priori dismissal of miracles is not legitimate. For example, Blomberg (2004, 66; cf. Geisler 2013, 317) stated: "If God, by definition a supernatural being who created the universe, does exist, then we must allow for the possibility of his occasionally interrupting the normal scientific laws of cause and effect to create what we call a miracle." Taken one step further, Christian apologists maintain: given that God exists, there are good reasons to believe He "can" and "did" and "does" miraculously intervene in the affairs of mankind.

And, more recently, Keener (2011; cf. Griffith 1996, 307) defended Blomberg's position in his two-volume text *Miracles: The Credibility of the New Testament Accounts*. Two points from his detailed study bear consideration:

1. To exclude the possibility of some sort of suprahuman and possibly supernatural intelligent causation is to, a priori, rule out what may be a very plausible explanation of some evidence. Yet many Western intellectuals would exclude any miracle claim—even if it were the public raising of a person clinically dead for several days—merely on the presupposed grounds that miracles do not happen. How does the critic know that miracles do not happen? (p. 112)
2. The a priori modernist assumption that genuine miracles are impossible is a historically and culturally conditioned premise. This premise is not shared by all intelligent or critical thinkers and, notably, not by many people in non-Western cultures. (p. 764)

At the beginning of the last century, the Christian apologist James Orr (1908, 105; cf. Geisler 2013, 293-318; Gwynne 2001, 360) wrote: "Naturalism or supernaturalism—there is no escape from the alternative presented. There are consequently two, and only two, possible avenues of approach to these narratives, and according as the one or the other is adopted, the light in which they appear will be different." Rephrased almost ninety years later, Wildman (1998, 85) pointed out that it was important to note: "Between these two extremes [[exclusive supernaturalism and reductionist naturalism]] lies a hermeneutical war zone from which, supposedly, only one party may emerge victorious." Recently, Winter (2011, 846) rearticulated more tactfully, "In the New Quest the burden of proof became a hotly debated issue. Every writer and scholar on Jesus had to come down on one of two sides regarding the credibility of New Testament accounts, and the burden of proof was placed accordingly on the other side."

Consequently, Christian apologists argue that statements such as "extraordinary claims require extraordinary investigations" is a skeptical argument full of holes and difficulties. They point out:

1. Definitions of "extraordinary claims" vary based on prior beliefs and experiences.
2. Different people have different standards for what is "extraordinary evidence."
3. "Extraordinary evidence" is subject to perspective because those who have firsthand direct experience of the phenomena already have their "extraordinary evidence" while others who have not, do not.
4. The argument is based on an unproven premise that miraculous phenomena in the scriptures are either impossible or extremely improbable.
5. Just because something is improvable does not automatically put it in the same category as everything else that is improvable.

More recently Geisler and Turek (2004, 182) repeated the well-known phrase: "An absence of evidence is not evidence of absence." Obviously, the issue of extraordinary evidence as it relates to miracles and supernaturalism presents diverse views.

In closing, Christian apologists point out that *proving* a thing is a matter of degrees. Once you get outside of mathematics, it is nearly impossible to prove anything to certitude because each side can set up the hurdle for "proof" as high or as low as it likes. Therefore, too often in the real world people set the hurdle high for things they do not want to believe (e.g., Jesus's resurrection) and low for things they do want to believe (the denial of Jesus's resurrection).

SKEPTICS: THE BURDEN OF PROOF ARGUMENT

In direct contrast to the position articulated above, many opponents, detractors, and skeptics of Jesus's resurrection often take the position that the Christian scriptures must be reckoned unreliable and untrustworthy until proven otherwise innocent. With regard to accounts of the Resurrection, skeptics argue that placing the burden of proof on them is a logical fallacy and a form of *argumentum ad ignorantiam*, or shifting the burden of proof on the person who denies or questions the assertion in question. They claim that the source of the fallacy is the assumption that the assertion is true unless proven otherwise. The following questions can serve as an example:

> "OK, so if you do not think pink aliens have gained control of the U.S. government; can you prove it?"

> "OK, you do not think leprechauns exist; can you prove it?"

> "OK, you do not think yellow polka-dotted aliens exist; can you prove it?"

(cf. Licona 2010, 97-98). The point here should be obvious: the nonexistent is nothing. Thus, opponents and skeptics of the Resurrection maintain: "He who asserts must prove."

Further extending this argument, opponents and skeptics criticize the challenge of Christian apologists who change the rational concept of the burden of proof into the irrational concept of the burden of disproof. They dispute Christian apologists who say to opponents something akin to "reasonably prove that miracles did not occur" instead of attempting to reasonably prove that miracles did occur.

An obvious problem confronting opponents of Jesus's resurrection is that the primary existing account of the circumstances is found in accounts recorded by Jesus's disciples who, of course, were both believers and eventual missionaries for their cause. Even Siniscalchi (2011, 366), a Catholic apologist, writing in *The Heythrop Journal*, confirms this position. However, he adds:

> Sceptics are completely within their epistemological rights to insist that all the evidence for the resurrection comes from individuals who already believed in the risen Jesus. However, they are mistaken if they conclude that the biblical authors' beliefs about the resurrection of Jesus prevent us from having reliable information about the origins of Christianity.

Christian apologists claim that the disciples were believers because of what they had seen. However, it must be pointed out that this idea is merely a belief or statement of faith. There are numerous historians, scholars, and theologians who would beg to differ.

A cursory review of many standard reference texts, including those written by Christian apologists, state in no uncertain terms that Mark did not write Mark, Matthew did not write Matthew, Luke did not write Luke, and John did not write John. These names were merely appended to these respective works in order to gain prestige. At the absolute most it can merely be claimed that the authors of these texts spoke to witnesses. However, here too there is no incontrovertible evidence. Instead, many of the standard reference sources discuss and suggest that the texts evolved from an oral tradition. In fact, journal articles, chapters of texts, and entire texts have been devoted to this topic.

Skeptics can also reverse the earlier argument employed by Christian apologists: a pro-supernatural presupposition has skewed the believers' research from the beginning; therefore, it is not surprising that different scholars find a different Jesus at the conclusion of their study (cf. Hooker 1972, 581). Bultmann (1964, 343) stated this issue another way: "Every exegesis that is guided by dogmatic prejudices does not hear what the text says, but only lets the latter say what it wants to hear." The bottom line is that whenever a proof is presented, it is incumbent on the challenger to give the said proof an honest and truthful evaluation.

Skeptics could raise an extension to the pro-supernatural presupposition of Christian apologists. The pertinent question is whether or not Christian apologists have the same so-called anti-supernatural biases about everything "but" their Bible.

1. Do Christian apologists accept the miracle claims of ancient *non-*biblical documents? If not, why not?

2. Do Christian apologists have an "anti-supernatural bias" toward all miracle claims *except* biblical ones? If so, what is their rationale for this highly selective bias? (Note: They would probably argue the quality of the witnesses—again a subjective manner—or perhaps claim that the miracles came from Satan too. But again, opponents could also claim that it was Satan who deliberately misled the apostles and disciples.)

3. Do Christian apologists accept the miracle claims in the Book of Mormon, the Hindu Vedas, the Qur'an, Josephus's *Wars of the Jews,* Suetonius's *Twelve Caesars,* and other works of similar matter? If not, why not?

4. If it is reasonable to question such claims as these, why is it unreasonable to question comparable claims in the Bible on the same grounds that have led believers to reject nonbiblical miracles?
5. If believers believe one miracle, on what principle can they reject another?

Price (1993, 120) raised several additional points that bear consideration:

1. Do these conservatives/apologists, in fact, believe that if one grants the possibility of miracles one is thereby committed to believe every recorded miracle story ever told? In other words, if you believe miracles are possible, must they also believe too that the formation of legends is *im*possible?
2. What conservatives are really objecting to is that the standpoint of critical scholars does not require implicit belief in every Bible story. Whether critics hold "naturalistic presuppositions" is not really the issue, as previously noted. The sin of critics is that they do *not* approach the text *with* a presupposition, the presupposition that the Bible is inerrant.

Barker (2003, 313) raised a question related to another associated issue. If Christian apologists ask, "Why have you ruled out the supernatural?" I will say I have not ruled it out: I have simply given it the low probability it deserves along with the other possibilities. I might equally ask them, "Why have *you* ruled out the *natural*?" A further rebuttal to the accusation raised by Christian apologists is that it is not because of prejudices against supernatural phenomena that critical scholars and theologians come to the conclusions that they do. Continuing, (Locks 2003) added: "Rather a historian does not rule out in advance the possibility that certain stories in his sources are legendary, and non-fundamentalists are more at ease to face this possibility." Wildman (1998, 4) stated this position another way: "Secular historians regard traditional interpretations of the resurrection with suspicion because they are unconvincing, and not just because of a naturalistic bias."

Orr's statement (cited earlier) is an example of a false dilemma. First, it is possible to believe in the supernatural and that miracles are possible but that Jesus's resurrection was not one of them. For example, Orthodox Christians, traditional Jews, and Muslims believe in miracles. Therefore, as Baden Powell (1859, 285) wrote over a century ago: "At the present day it is not *a miracle*, but the *narrative of a miracle*, to which any argument can refer, or to which faith is accorded." Consequently, stating that the empty tomb and resurrection were either divine works or human works is simplistic at the least and deliberately misleading at the worst. Several issues and speculations in this text provide a controversial alternative view of the supernatural interpretation of Jesus's resurrection.

Given that miracles or supernaturalism exist, how much evidence is necessary for a miracle to be accepted? Ideally, in relation to the Jesus's resurrection, a miracle claim would be an event that requires "at the least very strong evidence." Opponents and skeptics of Jesus's resurrection contend that because of human fallibility, extraordinary claims require "extraordinary evidence." An obvious reason that extraordinary claims demand extraordinary evidence is for the obvious reason of balance.

Father Raymond E. Brown raised an additional point regarding the anti-supernatural argument of proponents of the Resurrection. Brown (1993, 608-09) was perhaps one of the foremost and renowned Catholic scholars. Below is his personal response to criticism by conservative Christian writers:

> Yamauchi ("Episode" 22) laments that Roman Catholic scholars (he mentions me as an example) are now accepting interpretations that were earlier proposed by antisupernatural critics of Christianity. I would ask two questions: First, for modern Catholic scholarship to gain Yamauchi's approval, would he reduce us accept as logical a *post hoc, propter hoc* attitude? That would reduce us to silence since almost every critical biblical position was earlier advanced by skeptics. Most of my coreligionists who use biblical criticism are perfectly aware of its origins but accept as wise the attitude of the church catholic since the time it first encountered Greek philosophy: Christians should put at the service of the gospel every truth or valid insight available, no matter the view points of those who first phrased it.

Brown raised two additional points:

- At the root of the problem I would find the erroneous supposition that scriptural narrative must be historical—a supposition that restricts divine freedom to use various types of literature to guide God's people (n103).
- It would be helpful if apologists for supernatural events answered the obstacles to the historicity of the said events. (p. 609)

In other words, the onus lies with the Christian apologist when challenges are made to claims of the Resurrection in the Gospels and elsewhere in the Christian scriptures.

In the opinion of Packham (1998):

> So does an extraordinary event require extraordinary evidence? If "extraordinary evidence" means "clear and convincing" evidence or evidence "beyond a reasonable doubt," then the answer is clearly "yes." But that requirement is a statement about the *sufficiency* of the evidence, not its nature. The evidence itself can be very ordinary, and, in fact, must be (since improbable explanations are inadmissible). But if a miracle really happens, there is no reason why there should not be evidence to prove it.

Elaborating this issue, Matson (1997, 7) wrote in *The Skeptical Review*: "To win his or her case, the skeptic need only show that the arguments in its favor are not compelling. The skeptic does not have to disprove the claims. The skeptic's claim is that supernatural miracles and miraculous prophecy should presently be rejected as extremely unlikely, not that they have been proven false beyond any possible doubt."

However, as previously discussed, the subject of Jesus's resurrection has a major obstacle in the eyes of many skeptics. The only supposed primary proof texts of Jesus's resurrection are the accounts recorded in the Christian scriptures. Since these texts are assumed by proponents to record eyewitness accounts they are nonetheless considered to lack reliability.

According to Lett (1990),

> in fact, testimony is always inadequate for any paranormal claim, whether it is offered by an authority or a layperson, for the simple reason that a human being can lie or make a mistake. No amount of expertise in any field is a guarantee against human fallibility, and expertise does not preclude the motivation to lie; therefore a person's credentials, knowledge and experience cannot, in themselves be taken as sufficient evidence to establish the truth of a claim. Moreover, a person's sincerity lends nothing to the credibility of his or her testimony. Even if people are telling what they sincerely believe to be the truth, it is always possible that they could be mistaken. Perception is a selective act, dependent upon belief context, expectation, emotional and biochemical states, and a host of other variables. Memory is notoriously problematic, prone to a range of distortions, deletions, substitutions and amplifications. Therefore the testimony that people offer of what they remember seeing or hearing should always be regarded as only provisionally and approximately accurate; when people are

speaking about the paranormal, their testimony should never be regarded as reliable evidence in and of itself. The possibility and even the likelihood of error are far too extensive (see Connor 1986).

In contrast, Michael Horner (1995) argued in a debate that extraordinary events require extraordinary evidence, which creates "a phantom standard that virtually nothing could meet." Similarly, Lenardos (n.d.) challenged the demand of opponents and skeptics of the Resurrection as "masquerading as a test." His rationale is that a detractor could be asking for any or all the following: (1) a higher quality of evidence, (2) a different kind of evidence, and (3) a greater amount of evidence. In the same way, Slick (2003; cf. Law 2011, 133-34, 49), writing for Christian Apologetic and Research Ministry, wrote:

> Nevertheless, when defending the Bible and dealing with the claim that "extraordinary claims require extraordinary evidence," address the following issues:
>
> 1. Will their presuppositions allow unbiased examination of the evidence?
> 2. What would qualify as extraordinary evidence?
> 3. What criteria are used to determine what extraordinary evidence is?
> 4. Are criteria for extraordinary evidence reasonable?

Thus, for Christian apologists, opponents and skeptics of Jesus's resurrection, whether or not a given miracle has occurred, becomes an historical matter that calls for investigation.

Once more, this brings us to the topic of burden of proof and specifically proving something that does not exist. Lowder (2000) wrote:

> Second, it is simply false that it is *impossible* to prove that something does not exist, for there are actually two ways to show the nonexistence of something. First, one can show that an object does not exist is to show that the object has incompatible properties. For example, square circles and married bachelors cannot exist *by definition*. Second, one can show that an object does not exist if the object's existence is incompatible with some actual fact about the world. For example, consider the claim that there is a rattle snake on my desk biting my fingers as I type this review. Yet I am unable to detect the snake or its bite with any of

my five senses. In this case, the lack of evidence of the snake is actually evidence for the nonexistence of that snake.

Perhaps one alternative to the miracle-supernaturalism controversy is to temporarily suspend all judgment and then evaluate all the relevant material with an objective and open mind. However, Winter (2011, 851) offers another option: "the burden of proof should rest with those presuming historical veracity as with those who deny it."

Hooker (1972, 580), over forty years ago, wrote: "It is the duty of every scholar, in considering every saying, to give a reasonable account of all the evidence; for he is not entitled to assume, simply in the absence of contrary evidence, either that a saying is genuine or that it is not."

Finally, the words of J. Warner Wallace (2013; cf. Crossley 2011, 49-75; Levine 2007, 78; Lüdemann 2005/6, 35), a Christian apologist, bear thought:

> The question is not whether or not we have ideas, opinions, or preexisting points of view; the question is whether or not we will allow these perspectives to prevent us from examining the evidence objectively. It's possible to have a prior opinion yet leave this presupposition at the door in order to examine the evidence fairly. We ask jurors to do this all the time. In the state of California, jurors are repeatedly instructed to 'keep an open mind throughout the trial' and not to "let bias, sympathy, prejudice, or public opinion influence your decision." The courts assume that people have biases, hold sympathies and prejudices, and are aware of public opinion. In spite of this, jurors are required to "keep an open mind." Jurors have to enter the courtroom with empty hands; they must leave all their *baggage* in the hall. Everyone begins with a collection of biases. We must (to the best of our ability) resist the temptation to allow our biases to eliminate certain forms of evidence (and therefore certain conclusions) before we even begin the investigation.

TOPIC 6: Exegesis versus Eisegesis

One of the most important considerations when evaluating an explanation or interpretation of a text is the writer's methodology. In general, there are two opposing methodologies: exegesis and eisegesis. Exegesis occurs when a person interprets a text based solely on what it says. That is, he extracts from the text what is there as opposed to reading into it what is not there. There are basic rules for proper exegesis: read the immediate context, related themes, word definitions, etc., that play a part in properly understanding what something says or does not say.

Exegesis is a theological term used to describe an approach to interpreting a passage in the Bible by critical analysis. Proper exegesis includes using the context around the passage, comparing it with other parts of the Bible, and applying an understanding of the language and customs of the time of the writing in an attempt to understand clearly what the original writer intended to impart. In other words, it is trying to "pull out" of the passage the meaning inherent in it.

In contrast, eisegesis evolves when a person interprets and reads information into the text that is not there. For example, CARM (Christian Apologetics and Research Ministry) cites 1 Corinthians 8:5, which says: "For though there be that are called gods, whether in heaven or in earth (as there be gods many, and lords many)." CARM points out that "with this verse, Mormons, for example, bring their preconceived idea of the existence of many gods to this text and assert that it says there are many gods. But that is not what it says. It says that there are many that are called gods. Being called a god doesn't make something an actual god. Therefore, the text does not teach what the Mormons say and they are guilty of eisegesis; that is, *reading* into the text what it does not say."

Stated another way, Claude F. Mariottini (2006) of the Northern Baptist Seminary wrote that:

> [E]isegesis is the approach to Bible interpretation where the interpreter tries to "force" the Bible to mean something that fits their existing belief or understanding of a particular issue or doctrine. People who interpret the Bible this way are usually not willing to let the Bible speak for itself and let the chips fall where they may. They start off with the up-front goal of trying to prove a point they already believe in, and everything they read and interpret is filtered through that paradigm. Stated another way, they engage in what the Bible refers to as "private interpretation."

In closing, a significant consideration when evaluating an interpretation from scripture is the writer's methodology. Christian apologists argue that skeptics employ eisegesis when interpreting the Bible. Similarly, skeptics contend that it is Christian apologists, more often fundamentalists, who employ eisegesis.

TOPIC 7: Omissions and Contradictions

Christian apologists often refute differences in the Gospel narratives as being omissions and *not* contradictions. The problems here are that (1) this Christian apologetic is a mere speculation since there is no way to know what the writers were thinking when they constructed their narratives, (2) it is, in fact, possible that the author of one of the gospels (or other portions of the Christian scriptures) was writing what he considered were actual facts and in so doing he was correcting and thus contradicting the earlier narratives, and (3) omissions can at times be considered contradictions when the missing material is highly relevant and significant. Thus skeptics argue that the absence of proof can be proof, but it is acknowledged not always.

Numerous times this text will present contradictions which fall under the Christian apologists' rubric of omission. When these contradictions are encountered, it must be remembered that the omissions here are extremely significant and something a normal person would not expect to see. For example, the author of Matthew stated that when Jesus died there was an earthquake, tombs were opened, and many bodies of the saints who had fallen asleep came out of their tombs and entered Jerusalem and appeared to many people. However, these events are not recorded elsewhere. It is this type of omission that is considered a valid contradiction.

TOPIC 8: Writing for a Specific Audience

Christian apologists often suggest that the writers of these texts were writing for a specific audience. The problems with this Christian apologetic are that (1) this is a speculation since there is no way to know what the writers were thinking when they constructed their narratives, (2) there is no way to know specifically when and where the narratives were authored, and (3) there is no means to determine who the narratives were being written for. Recently, several commentators (Bauckham et al. 1998) have challenged the long-held position that the gospel writers wrote for a specific audience.

Carson (2007, 49-50) commented that "a book edited by Richard Bauckham, *The Gospels for all Christians: Rethinking the Gospel Audiences* (Eerdmans 1998), nicely challenges a great deal of current critical thinking about the Gospels. The contributing authors present largely convincing evidence that all four Gospels were intended from the beginning to address all Christians, not hermetically sealed sectarian communities. The implications are substantial."

TOPIC 9: The Gospels Accounts Likened to Four Witnesses to a Car Accident

Christian apologists often suggest that the narratives could be likened to four people witnessing a car accident and providing differing accounts without them being contradictory. That is, the observers reported what each saw. Christian apologists actually go so far as to claim that the differences found in the Resurrection accounts actually substantiate their trustworthiness. Their argument runs something like this: people who conspire to testify to a falsehood rehearse carefully to avoid contradictions.

The shortfall with this Christian apologetic is that (1) not all the writers were eyewitnesses to the account, (2) the narratives were written approximately thirty to seventy years after the events, (3) at least Luke admitted in his preface that he was reporting hearsay, (4) the writings are believed to be a result of an evolving oral tradition, and (5) the writings are biased, written to evangelize and spread their theological propaganda (see topic 2 above).

TOPIC 10: Progressive Exaggeration

When read chronologically, the gospel narratives exemplify continual enhancement. For example, the author of Mark reported that there were several women whom were "looking on afar off" as Jesus was on the cross. Later, several of these women were described as having "beheld where he was laid." Therefore, the women only observed the location of the tomb in which Jesus was buried. However, there is no detail regarding their proximity to the tomb.

Matthew 27:55 initially described the women "there beholding afar off" during the Crucifixion. Later, Matthew 27:61 reported that the women were positioned "sitting over against the sepulchre." Gundry (1994, 582) interpreted this action of "sitting over against the grave" as vigil, exemplifying "care and concern for the persecuted that true discipleship requires."

Luke 23:49 also mentioned that the witnesses "stood afar off" during the Crucifixion: "And all his acquaintance, and the women that followed him from Galilee, stood afar off, beholding these things." Later, in Luke 23:55 the women not only "beheld the sepulchre," they also beheld "how the body was laid." Afterward, Luke had these women returning to their homes to prepare "spices and ointments" to anoint Jesus's body and then observe the Sabbath. These two actions demonstrate increasing discipleship and piousness.

Finally, John 19:26-27 specifically detailed that Jesus's mother and the disciple who he loved were also present at the cross. However, not only were they present but Jesus also had a conversation with them prior to his death. Furthermore, Jesus specifically "ordered" that the disciple whom he loved would be responsible for taking care of Mary, his mother.

> Jn 19:26 When Jesus therefore saw his mother, and the disciple standing by, whom he loved, he saith unto his mother, Woman, behold thy son!

> Jn 19:27 Then saith he to the disciple, Behold thy mother! And from that hour that disciple took her unto his own home.

The omission of these monumental and extremely noteworthy facts from the synoptic Gospels leads skeptics to doubt their historicity.

A second contrast in the synoptic narratives also bears thought. The three narratives grow in relation to their temporal distance from the event: approximately 70 CE to 85 CE the author of Mark 15:39 narrated that a singular person, the Roman centurion, watched Jesus die and then he declared: "Truly this man was the Son of God." Next, Matthew pluralized the "seeing" and "saying" by adding the soldiers as well who were guarding Jesus under the centurion's command. And later, Matthew 27:54 declared: "Now when the centurion, and *they*, that were with him, watching Jesus, saw the earthquake, and those things that they were done, *they* feared greatly, saying, Truly this was the Son of God." Gundry (1994, 578) likened this godly fear and confession to "the vanguard of the Gentiles who will flock into the church." Finally, Luke 23:47 turned Matthew's plural back into a singular and glorified God: "he *glorified God*, saying, Certainly this was a righteous man." However, in the next verse Luke 23:48 increases the number of witnesses and has the witnesses do more than just speak: "And *all the people* that came together to that sight, beholding the things which were done, *smote their breasts*, and returned." Obviously, here too the synoptic accounts demonstrate continual and progressive exaggeration.

PART II

CHRONOLOGICAL AND SEQUENTIAL ANALYSIS OF THE GOSPELS AND OTHER PORTIONS OF THE CHRISTIAN SCRIPTURES

THE TOPIC OF CHRONOLOGY

The initial issues below are concerned with the topic of chronology. This is an extremely complex, controversial, and diverse topic. In order to understand why there are so many conflicting theories regarding the dates associated with Jesus's claimed resurrection, it is necessary to be aware of the events before, during, and after his life.

CHAPTER 2

Chronology of the Crucifixion

ISSUE 1: The Year Jesus Was Crucified

1 Tim 6:13	Mk 15:1 And	Mt 27:2	Lk 23:1	Acts 3:13	Jn 18:29
I give thee charge in the sight of God, who quickeneth all things, and before Christ Jesus, *who* *before* *Pontius* *Pilate* witnessed a good confession;	straightway in the morning the chief priests held a consultation with the elders and scribes and the whole council, and bound Jesus, and carried him away, and delivered him *to Pilate.*	And when they had bound him, they led him away, and delivered him *to* *Pontius* *Pilate the* *governor.*	And the whole multitude of them arose, and led him *unto* *Pilate.*	The God of Abraham, and of Isaac, and of Jacob, the God of our fathers, hath glorified his Son Jesus; whom ye delivered up, and denied him *in the presence of* *Pilate*, when he was determined to let him go.	*Pilate* then went out unto them, and said, What accusation bring ye against this man?

THE ONLY CERTAINTY about the year of Jesus's death and claimed resurrection is that it must have occurred sometime during the ten years Pontius Pilate was procurator of Judea from 26 to 36 CE. This certainty is based primarily upon numerous citations in the Christian scriptures (see 1 Tim 6:13; Mk 15:1, 44; Mt 27:2, 13, 65; Lk 3:1; 23:1, 52; Acts 3:13; 13:28; Jn 18:29, 31; 19:38). Attempts to determine the exact year of Jesus's death can only be calculated by analyzing significant details and events before, during, and after his life (see table 1).

TABLE 1. A List of Significant Events Employed for Calculating the Date of the Crucifixion and Resurrection

Topic	Significance
1. Jesus was born when King Herod was still alive, and Herod died no later than 4 BCE.	It is possible to determine the earliest year that Jesus could have been born. Given that Herod the Great died in March or April of 4 BCE, Jesus was born no later than April of 4 BCE, and some scholars put it up to two years earlier. Adding thirty years (Lk 3:23) provides an approximation when Jesus started his ministry.
2. Luke 2:2 narrated that Emperor Augustus decreed a census.	Augustus ordered that a census to be taken on three different occasions: 28 BCE, 8 BCE, and 14 CE.
3. Luke 3:1-2 carefully states that John the Baptist commenced his ministry in the fifteenth year of Tiberius Caesar (Jesus was baptized by John subsequently).	The date of the fifteenth year makes it possible to determine the year that Jesus was baptized by John the Baptist and the year that Jesus was crucified within a year or two at the least. Tiberius Caesar began his reign on August 19, 14 CE, and John the Baptist's ministry began no earlier than the autumn of 29 CE.
4. King Herod executed John the Baptist for criticizing the marriage to his brother's wife (Mk 6:17-26; Mt 14:1-12).	Antipas went to war with Nabataean Aretas. The war was precipitated because Antipas divorced Aretas's daughter in order to marry Herodias.
5. Luke 3:23 records that Jesus was about thirty years old when he began his work.	Given that the date of Jesus's birth is known, it is possible to calculate the year that he began his ministry. Between 4 BCE when Herod died and 27 CE, there were about thirty years. Therefore, Jesus could not have started his ministry much later than that time.
6. John's narrative recorded three Passovers.	Assuming that the date Jesus started his ministry can be determined, so too can the year of its termination.
7. At the first Passover of Jesus's ministry, Jesus declared in John 2:20 that the Temple had been in continuous construction for forty-six years.	If the date of the Temple's commencement of construction is known, then the year of the commencement of Jesus's ministry can be calculated.

8.	King Herod began to build the Temple approximately 20/19 BCE.	This fact coincides with John 2:20 and provided information to calculate when Jesus started his ministry.
9.	Aretas (an Arab king of Petra) defeated Antipas in 36 CE.	Kokkinos (1989, 133-34) stated: "The Gospels place the death of John the Baptist during the time that Herodias was living with Antipas . . . Tiberius died in March A.D. 37 . . . Thus, as a logical consequence, the war of Aretas is dated to 36, the death of John the Baptist to 35, and the journey of Antipas to Rome and his subsequent marriage to Herodias to 33 or 34 . . . The Gospels are clear that the death of John preceded Jesus', and John's death in 35 places the Crucifixion in 36, the last possible year due to the ending of Pilate's prefecture."
10.	The date the last Passover was attended by Pontius Pilate was in 36 CE.	This year marked the termination date of Jesus's crucifixion since Pilate was the procurator during the trial.
11.	All four gospels agree that Jesus died a few hours before the commencement of the Jewish Sabbath (i.e., he died before nightfall on a Friday).	Given that Jesus was crucified on Friday, the fifteenth of Nisan, it is possible to eliminate various years that do not have the fifteenth coinciding with a Friday.
12.	Jesus was crucified when Pontius Pilate was procurator of Judea, which is well documented (Josephus, *Ant.* xviii) to span 26-36 CE.	Pilate held office for ten years. Therefore, it is possible to calculate the termination of his office and the time frame of the high priesthood of Caiaphas.
13.	Caiaphas was the high priest at the time of the arrest, trial, and crucifixion.	It is possible to calculate the year that Caiaphas assumed office and was terminated. The fact that the high priest Caiaphas (Mt 26:57; Jn 18:24) and the Roman procurator Pilate (Mk 15:1; Mt 27:2; Lk 23:1; Jn 18:29) presided at Jesus's trials limits the year of the Crucifixion to the period of their common jurisdiction, CE 26 to 36.
14.	Passover always falls on the fifteenth day of the month of Nisan (the name of the first Jewish lunar month of the spring).	Given that Jesus was crucified on Friday, the fifteenth of Nisan, it is possible to eliminate various years that do not have the fifteenth coinciding with a Friday.

15. The earth went dark during the Crucifixion (Lk 23:44).	Astronomers can calculate the viable dates of an eclipse.
16. The year that Paul became a convert.	Scholars assume that Paul converted approximately one to three years after the death of Jesus. This event helps to set the termination date of Jesus's crucifixion.

CONTRADICTION #1: The Year Jesus Was Crucified

Theologians, New Testament scholars, historians, standard reference sources, evangelicals, and even evangelical organizations are divided regarding the exact "year" Jesus was crucified and resurrected.

The reason for the vast differences in dates is simple to understand, for the calculations are based on different assumptions: primacy given to the synoptic Gospels (Nisan 15) or John (Nisan 14); noncanonical texts; the length of Jesus's ministry (approximately one year or three); and the Crucifixion on a Wednesday, Thursday, or Friday, to mention a few (see table 1). Theissen and Merz (1998, 160n29) comment that "one factor of uncertainty which present-day, absolutely accurate, astronomical calculations cannot remove is the weather. In antiquity the beginning of the month was fixed by the sighting of the new moon; if it was cloudy, this date could shift." Rationales for eleven selected years along with a listing of their proponents are found below. Out of convenience this text will most often adopt the commonly employed AD and BC terminology.

The Year AD 21

Eisler (1931, 16-20) and Vardaman (1998, 313-20; 1989, 55-82) postulate that Jesus was crucified in the year AD 21. This date is based on the following points:

FIRST METHOD:

Both writers base their calculations on the apocryphal work of the Acts of Pilate. This text reports that the death of Jesus took place during the consulship of Rubellius Geminus and Refius Geminus (Tertullian, *Adversus Judaeos* viii), which fell in the year AD 29. Eisler argues that one reason

Christians did not choose to avail themselves of this document is simply that these *Acta* contained "material highly offensive to them and hence of no use for missionary purposes." Eisler (p.17) also argues that Christian apologists fabricated a chronology that appeared in a work by Josephus, a first century Jewish historian:

> The Christian apologists could then do nothing else than fabricate a chronological argument by converting—a trifling change indeed!—the figure sixteen (Iς) for the number of years of Pilate's administration (*Ant.*, xviii. 4.1, § 89) into ten (I), and the corresponding number Δ (four years) for his predecessor Gratus (*Ant.*, xviii. 2. 2, §35) into IA (eleven years), thus making Pilate's administration begin in A.D. 26 instead of A.D. 19.

In addition, Eisler posits Valerius Gratus, who was Pilate's predecessor, assumed office in A.D. 15. Gratus was the first of the officials of Judea appointed by Tiberius in A.D. 15, just after the death of Emperor Augustus. During the next four years—A.D. 15, 16, 17, and 18—he appointed four high priests, each who held the office for one year. This view was maintained by the Talmud, *Yoma* 8b, where it is stated that procurators were in the habit of changing the high priest every year because on each occasion they received some reward or bribe money. The respective high priests were (1) Ismael, the son of Phabi; (2) Eleazar, the son of Ananus; (3) Simon, the son of Camithus; and (4) Joseph Caiaphas.

Then Josephus (*Ant.* 18, 2, 2) reported that "when Gratus had done those things, he went back to Rome, after he had tarried in Judea eleven years, when Pontius Pilate came as his successor." Therefore, Gratus's government lasted four years instead of the eleven years maintained by church tradition. Consequently, Pilate's assumed procuratorship must have started approximately in the fall of A.D. 18 (and not in A.D. 26). If Pilate was in power during three Passovers that Jesus ministered, the Crucifixion must have occurred in the year 21. And again, "The year A.D. 21 as the date of the passion, the date given for the trial of Jesus in the *Acta* published by Maximinus Daïa, would then fall entirely within the administration of Pilate" (p. 19).

Pilate permitted Caiaphas to remain in power for the next seventeen years instead of the traditional ten years reported in the corrupted Josephus. In A.D. 37, Caiaphas was finally removed from office when the reign of Pilate came to an end (*Ant.* 18, 4, 2).

SECOND METHOD:

Eisler postulates that:

1. Jesus was born in 12 BC,
2. he was twenty-six years old in AD 15,
3. Jesus began his ministry at about thirty, and
4. his ministry lasted six years.

THIRD METHOD:

Vardaman (1989, 55-82. esp. 77) bases his date on the following:

1. That Jesus was born in 12 BC agrees with Luke's statement (3:23) that "Jesus himself began to be about thirty years of age" at the time of his baptism by John (see tables #2 and 3).
2. The first year of the ministry of Jesus included late AD 15 and early-to-middle AD 16, at which time coins from Damascus were struck with microletters referring to the first year of Jesus's "reign."
3. The possibility of a copying error of Luke 3:1 reading year two instead of year fifteen.
4. The conversion of Paul should be dated earlier (AD 24-27).
5. The work of Josephus "accurately places Jesus's career (AD 15-19) in the same approximate historical context that the microletters point to—around AD 15-21" (see *Antiquities* 18, 48-83; cf. Eisler 1931, 19). See tables 2-3.

TABLE 2. Josephus's Chronology Assumed to be Chronologically Correct [Source: Modified from Jerry Vardaman, "Jesus' Life: A New Chronology," *Chronos, Kairos, Christos*, edited by Jerry Vardaman and Edwin M. Yamauchi. (Winona Lake: Eisenbrauns, 1989), 56-57.]

Numbered	Year	*Antiquities* Citations	Event
1.	AD 14-17	*Antiquities* 18:46ff.	Parthians requested then rejected Vonones.
2.	AD 17	*Antiquities* 18:52, 54	Silanus removed and Piso became governor of Syria.

3.	AD 15-18	*Antiquities* 18:52	Orodes ruled in Armenia.
4.	AD 17-19	*Antiquities* 18:54	Germanicus sent to East, poisoned by Piso (?).
5.		*Antiquities* 18:63-64	Josephus referred to Jesus.
6.	AD 19	*Antiquities* 18:65ff.	Mundus seduced Paulina; Tiberius overthrew Isis cult.
7.	AD 19	*Antiquities* 18:81-83	Fulvia cheated; Tiberius expelled Jews from Rome.

TABLE 3. When Jesus was about to Become Thirty (Lk 3:23) if Born by 5 BC [Source: Modified from Jerry Vardaman, "Jesus' Life: A New Chronology," *Chronos, Kairos, Christos*, edited by Jerry Vardaman and Edwin M. Yamauchi. (Winona Lake: Eisenbrauns, 1989), 58.]

Year	Age of Jesus	Year	Age of Jesus
5 BC	1	AD 16	21
4	2	17	22
3	3	18	23
2	4	19	24
1	5	20	25
AD 1	6	21	26
2	7	22	27
3	8	23	28
4	9	24	29
5	10	**25**	**30**
6	11	26	31
7	12	27	32
8	13	28	33
9	14	29	34
10	15	30	35

Nevertheless, there are numerous problems with Eisler's hypothesis. First, virtually the entire hypothesis is based on conjecture. Second, Jesus was known to be born before King Herod died, and that event occurred in 4 BC; Pilate did not assume office until AD 26. Consequently, Jesus could not have died before Pilate assumed office. In addition, (Jack 1933, 230) points out: "An important point is that both writers [[Luke and John]], acting on lines quite independent of each other, give the same date approximately within one year or so for the death of Jesus." Third, the Gospel of John reports that Jesus's ministry spanned only three Passovers—that is, three years.

Finally, several writers (Carrier 2002a, 39-41, 61; 2002b, 60-61; Hendin 1991, 28-30) have aggressively challenged Vardaman's claim of microletters: (1) there are no peer-review publications supporting this claim, (2) no other numismatist has ever visualized the same "microinscriptions" on the same coins or on other coins, (3) "it is not plausible that a celator who engraved a well-organized and beautifully executed coin design would scribble disorganized graffiti in entirely different inscription styles all over the die of that coin", (4) no photographs of the coins are presented, only line drawing, (5) the writings on the coins required technology that did not exist at the time (e.g., lenses or magnifying glasses and etching equipment) (given that nobody could read the inscriptions their incorporation seems meaningless), and (6) a later analysis of the coins at the British Museum employing a magnifying glass and digital microscope failed to confirm the conscriptions.

The Year AD 24

Steward (1932, 314) hypothesizes that Jesus was crucified in AD 24. His hypothesis is based on six converging lines:

1. The fact that AD 19 was the fifteenth year of the reign of Tiberius Caesar when John the Baptist came preaching in the wilderness, thus indicating AD 20 or 21 as the date of our Lord's baptism and AD 24 as the year of the crucifixion.
2. The fact that the crucifixion took place on Wednesday, the fourteenth of Nisan, in a year in which the fifteenth of Nisan fell on a Thursday: a coincidence that occurred in AD 24 but did not recur until AD 33.
3. Luke's statement that when our Lord began His mediatorial or high priestly work, He was about thirty years of age.
4. The dates of Paul's conversion and his first and second visits to Jerusalem in AD 27, AD 30, and AD 44, respectively.
5. The period of 483 years that, according to Daniel, was between the command to rebuild the city given in 460 BC, and the cutting off of the Anointed One, the Prince: a period that was exactly fulfilled in AD 24.
6. The report from China that the story of the crucifixion and the resurrection had reached their country sometime between AD 25 and 28, a maximum period of less than four years.

Again, the problem with this hypothesis is that Jesus was known to be born before King Herod died in 4 BC, and Pilate did not assume office until AD 26. Consequently, Jesus could not have died before Pilate assumed office.

The Year AD 27

King (1945, 145-47, 153) and Meyer (1923, 3:171) suggest that the Crucifixion took place in AD 27. They posit that the Crucifixion had to occur on a Friday, the fourteenth of Nisan. This only occurred on AD 27, 30, 33, and 36. Therefore, this date meets the minimum threshold requisite.

Hoehner (1974a, 337) rejects this date because "Luke 3:1-2 indicates that John the Baptist's ministry started in Tiberius' fifteenth year, which was AD 28/29. Jesus' ministry followed this and, therefore, the AD 27 date is not only questionable astronomically but is impossible biblically—if one takes Luke 3:1-2 seriously." In addition, Humphreys and Waddington (1989, 170; 1983, 744) point out, "Most scholars believe Pilate had been procurator for some time before the Crucifixion" (see Lk 13:1; 23:12).

The Year AD 28

Winter (1961, 175n5) speculates that Jesus died "perhaps in the year 28 CE." He cites Clements of Alexandria I (chapter xxi) 145, 5 (GCS Clemens II, p. 90; MPG 8, col. 885) that Jesus was crucified forty-two years and three months before the day on which the Romans destroyed Jerusalem. "This would correspond to the year 28 CE."

Jack (1933, 236) offers yet another possible explanation for the AD 28 crucifixion. Jesus declared in John 2:20: "Forty and six years has this temple been in building."

> As Josephus, in giving a single date, invariably computes it from the *de facto* kingship, it is clear that the Temple was begun between autumn B.C. 20 and autumn B.C. 19. It follows that the forty-sixth year *ended* in autumn A.D. 27, and the following Passover (at which the words referred to must have been uttered) would be that of A.D. 28. Thus, we have in the fourth Gospel a tradition which places the death of Jesus either at the Passover of A.D. 28, (if we reckon one cleansing of the Temple) or at that of A.D. 29 (if we reckon two).

An obvious argument against an AD 28 date is that Jesus could not have died before Pilate assumed office. Furthermore, Jesus's ministry coincides with John's record of three different Passovers.

The Year AD 29

Numerous writers (Depuydt 2002, 466, 478; Hölscher 1940, 26; Holtzmann 1904, 110; Lake 1912, 462-77; Loisy 1907, 386-89; M'Clintock and Strong 1873, 898; Norris 1877, 139-48; Nourse 1911, 484-88; Tertullian [*Adversus Judaeos* viii]; Turner 1898, 411-15; Wright 1893, 282) and others advocate the year AD 29 for the Crucifixion. Lasker (2004, 95-99) strengthens Depuydt's argumentation and concludes that "18 March, 29 C.E., remains plausible despite attempts to discredit it." Tertullian first presented this date because in that year March 23 was a Friday, and the pagans celebrated the death of one of their "resurrection" gods (*Adv. Jud.*, 8). He had heard they were emulating the Crucifixion of Jesus. Norris (1877, 140) also argues that this "year agrees with the constant tradition of the first five centuries (based doubtless on the *Acts of Pilate* before the document was corrupted)." Here he cites Tertullian's *Adversus Judaeos* viii; Augustine's *De civitate Dei Liber* (City of God) xviii, 54, etc.

On the other hand, Holtzmann (1904, 110) posits the following:

1. John the Baptist began his ministry in AD 28; this agrees with the ancient Christian tradition that the death of Jesus took place in the consulship of Rubellius Geminus and Rufius Geminus which fell in the year AD 29.
2. Clement of Alexandria also may be taken to mean (*Strom.* i. 21, 144 f.) that Jesus lived fifteen complete years under Augustus and fifteen complete years under Tiberius. This again points to the year AD 29 as being the year of Jesus's death.
3. Other synchronistic data of Luke also agrees.

The year 29 can absolutely be eliminated because in that year the Passover occurred at the beginning of the week. In addition, the date assumes a one-year ministry. Consequently, this cannot be reconciled with any of the other evidence. The Passover cannot occur that early.

The Year AD 30

Numerous writers advocate the year AD 30 for their choice as to when Jesus died. Research by Brown found 53 people supported this date; Blinzler (1959, 72-73) cites thirty-six proponents. Raymond Brown (1994a, 2:1375n50) cites Benoit, Brandon, Conzelmann, Dibelius, Flusser, Haenchen, Holtzmann, Jeremias, Leitzmann, Metzger, Olmstead, Schürer, Wikenhauser, and Zahn; Hoehner (1974a, 332) cites Blinzler (1959, 72-80), Madison (1963, 149-63), and Ruckstuhl (1965, 1-12). Other advocates for this date include Aldrich (1870, 429), *The Anchor Bible Dictionary*, volume 1 (1992, 1016), Cadoux (1937, 182), Fotheringham (1934, 142-62), Haggard (1912, 664-92), *The International Standard Bible Encyclopedia* (1939, 647 see Bible Chronology), Tabor (2006, 199), White (1980, 64), and *The Zondervan Pictorial Encyclopedia* volume 1 (1977, 331). Finally, A. T. Robertson and the *Dictionary of the Bible* (1963, 157) cite Lightfoot, Wieseler, Salmon, and Goguel.

According to church tradition, the Crucifixion had to occur on a Friday, the fourteenth of Nisan. This only occurred in the years 27, 30, 33, and 36. Therefore, the year 30 meets this requirement. Hoehner (1974a, 338) citing Blinzler, who by employing a Syrian chronology suggests that Tiberius's fifteenth year would be from Tishri 1, AD 27 to Tishri 1, 28. John the Baptist's ministry began then, and Jesus's ministry commenced at this point, which "is substantiated by John 2:20, where the temple had been in continuous construction for forty-six years since Herod began to build it in 20/19 BC" (p. 339). Finally, Blinzler states that Jesus's ministry lasted two years and some months.

Hoehner (1974a, 338-39) rejects this thesis for the following reasons:

1. It has some astronomical difficulty.
2. There is no proof that Luke employed a Syrian chronology.
3. Jesus was talking about the temple's edifice, which was completed in 18/17 BC as having stood for forty-six years, that is, the Passover of AD 30.
4. Jesus's ministry required more than "two years and does not explain the time note of John 4:35 or the unnamed feast of John 5:1."

Advocates of a later date argue that Jesus could not have died before the execution of John the Baptist which they calculate at approximately AD 35 or 36.

The Year AD 31

Ellen G. White (1917, 699; 1898, 233; 1888, 327-28, 410) along with other Adventist leaders helped form what is now known as the Seventh-day Adventist Church. She was an early advocate of an AD 31 crucifixion. This date is also supported in *The Seventh-day Adventist Bible Commentary* (Nichol 1980, 5:248-60). Hoeh (1959), a late evangelist of the World Church of God, posits that AD 31 was the *only* year in which a maximum eclipse of the full moon occurred around the time Pilate was in power. Furthermore, "only" in AD 31 do events fit the gospel account and both the astronomical and rabbinical evidence. For example, in that year, the fourteenth of Nisan, the Passover day on which Jesus would have been crucified, fell on Wednesday, April 25. The next day, Thursday, would have been the high feast day; and therefore, it would have been a Sabbath. If Jesus were crucified in the year 31, he would have been crucified on Wednesday and buried that evening before the high feast day Sabbath began. Consequently, his body would have remained in the tomb for three days (Thursday, Friday, and Saturday) and three nights (Wednesday, Thursday, and Friday), just as he predicted. Thus Jesus's resurrection would have taken place on Saturday evening, April 28. That would place his resurrection on Sunday, the first day of the week because the Jewish day begins at sundown. Thus, if one maintains a literal reading of Matthew 12:40—Jesus laid in the tomb for three complete days (seventy-two hours)—then the year 31 AD is possible.

Advocates are also of the opinion that the Jewish Talmud records in *Yoma* 39b events, which also occurred in 31 CE, supporting the date that Jesus was executed:

> Forty years before the Temple was destroyed [i.e., 40 years before AD 70, or in AD 31 by the Jewish method of inclusive counting] . . . the gates of the Hekel [Holy Place] opened by themselves, until Rabbi Yohanan B. Zakkai rebuked them [the gates] saying, Hekel, Hekel, why alarmist thou us? We know that thou art destined to be destroyed.

Further, forty years before the destruction of the Temple, the Sanhedrin was banished from the Chamber of Hewn Stone and sat in the trading station on the Temple Mount (*b. Shabbat* 15a). Therefore, forty years before the destruction of the Temple in AD 70 is AD 31—the very year that Jesus was crucified.

Proponents of year 31 also point to Daniel's sixty-nine-week prophecy to support their opinion. Daniel 9:25-26, from the going forth of the commandment to rebuild Jerusalem, issued and put into effect in the late summer or early fall of 457 BC, declared there would be sixty-nine prophetic weeks (7 + 62) until the Messiah would come. Proponents maintain that the sixty-nine prophetic weeks equaled four hundred and eighty-three years, and 483 years after 457 BC would bring us to the autumn of AD 27—the year in which Jesus began his ministry. Three and a half years later leads to an AD 31 crucifixion.

However, acceptance of the Wednesday crucifixion requires that the evidence from the other gospels be overlooked and rejects church tradition. Most significantly, numerous times the Gospels refer to the Sabbath. Again, advocates of a later crucifixion date previously mentioned would also refute this date.

The Year AD 32

Hoehner (1974a, 333-34) cites Anderson (1895, 97-105), Bammel (1952, 206-10), and Stauffer (1960, 22-43; 91-110) for advocating AD 32 for a crucifixion date. Anderson's theory posits that the year AD 32 is based on the sixty-nine weeks of Daniel 9, which he calculates to equal 483 years.

However, Monday, April 1, 32, can absolutely be eliminated because in that year the new moon and Passover occurred at the beginning of the week, and it is thus impossible to reconcile this with any of the other evidence. Anderson has also been criticized for employing faulty mathematics and assumptions.

The Year AD 33

Perhaps AD 33 is one of the most often cited years for Jesus's death. Advocates (Bacon 1909, 148; Hoehner 1992, 121-22; 1974a, 348; Maier 1989, 16; Mosse 2007, 176-77; Ogg 1940, 244-77; O'Herlihy 1946, 305; Reicke 1975, 183-84; Renan 1898, 41; 1864, 297; Turner 1965, 67-74) include historians, scholars, and theologians. Other supporters include Finegan (1998, 362, 67), Fotheringham (1934, 142-62; 1910, 122, 127), Keresztes (1989, 1:38, 43), and Humphreys and Waddington (1992, 331-51; 1989, 181; 1985, 2; 1983, 746). There are numerous arguments in support of this date.

1. According to tradition, the Crucifixion occurred on a Friday, the 14th of Nisan. Again; this only occurred in the years 27, 30, 33, and 36.
2. It is assumed that Jesus's ministry began in AD 29. This assumption coincides with John's record of three different Passovers.

3. Research by Humphreys and Waddington (1986, 746 cf. 1989, 178-79) confirms that 33 is sound astronomically since "the eclipse of 3 April AD 33 would probably have been seen by most of the population of Israel since the Jews on Passover Day would be looking for both sunset and moonrise in order to commence their Passover meal."

4. The dating is not limited to one dating system for reckoning the commencement of John the Baptist's ministry in Tiberius's fifteenth year (Lk 3:1-2).

5. The year 33 adequately explains in John 2:20 that the Temple edifice stood for forty-six years since its completion.

6. The characterization of Pilate's change of attitude, his attempt to save Jesus, and his yielding to the pressures of the Jews, is intelligible by the year 33. In addition, the Jewish threats to Pilate in John 19:12 were only viable in the year 33. Specifically, Brown (1994a, 2:1376) writes: "In some ways the political situation in 33 (after the fall of Sejanus in Rome in Oct. 31) would better explain Pilate's vulnerability to the pressures of the populace, however, that is too uncertain an argument to create a preference." Yet another rationale is that the friendship of Pilate and Herod Antipas is justifiable.

7. There was the earthquake and eclipse reported by Phylegon and Eusebius, dating the death of Jesus in the nineteenth year of Tiberius.

Brown points out two shortfalls with this date. First, the year 33 implies "too old a Jesus and too long a ministry, since he would have been almost 40 when he died and have had a public ministry of some 4 years" (p. 1376). Others argue that year 33, with a Friday crucifixion does not provide for a literal seventy-two hours in the tomb. Again, those advocating a year 35 or 36 would posit that the execution of John the Baptist precludes an execution in year 33. Finally, Aldrich (1882, 239) argues that Jesus's ministry then would have spanned six and a half years, yet only three Passovers are mentioned.

The Year AD 34

Sir Isaac Newton advocated a year AD 34 death based on his calculations. Martin Luther also supported AD 34 as part of a grand scheme explaining Daniel's Seventy Weeks. [See J. Barr, "Luther and Biblical Chronology," *BJRL* 72, 1 (1990), 61.]. Pratt (1991, 301-04) analyzed Newton's hypothesis:

Newton began by dating the baptism of Christ in AD 29 during the 15th year of Tiberius Caesar (Luke 3:1, 21). He then cited evidence for a total of five (rather than four) passovers during the ministry, implying an AD 34 crucifixion. Then Newton did the calendrical analysis almost exactly as has been done since: determining in which years the crucifixion day, 14 Nisan on the Judean calendar, could have been a Friday (John 19:14, 42). He stated that the Jews deemed the crescent 'visible about 18 h after the true conjunction,' which is optimistic even near the spring equinox. Using that rule to determine the first day of Nisan, he calculated the day of the week for 14 Nisan for the years AD 31-36. He thus excluded AD 31, 32 and 35 because 14 Nisan could not have been a Friday, which has been confirmed by all modern researchers. After next excluding AD 35 and 36 on historical grounds, he had narrowed the field to AD 33 April 3 and AD 34 April 23. He then found a final argument for AD 34 in the ripeness of the corn at passover, based on Luke 6:1 referring to the last day of passover two yrs prior to the crucifixion.

Nodet (2010, 351) and Humphreys and Waddington (1985, 5; 1983, 744) criticize this date on several grounds:

1. This year is too late because it would probably conflict with the probable date of Paul's conversion.
2. It falls more than a lunar month after the equinox.
3. Year 34 is only possible if the weather that spring had been exceptionally severe.
4. Newton's chief reason for advocating AD 34 was because April 23 was St. George's Day.

The Years AD 35/36

Keim (1883, 6:234-44) advocates the year 35 for the Crucifixion, whereas others (Baigent 2006, 52-53; Fox 1991, 33f, 423; Kokkinos 1989, 163; Lake 1912, 462-67; Schonfield 1974, 46-47; 51-53) specifically support the year 36.

Kokkinos (1989, 133-63), based on the following assumptions, calculates that Jesus died in AD 36:

1. According to Josephus, John the Baptist was not arrested before 34, he died in 35, and the death of John preceded Jesus. Therefore, this event placed the Crucifixion in 36.

2. The statement of Luke 3:1 referred to the commencement of John's preaching, *not* to the commencement of Jesus's ministry.
3. Jesus began his career at the closing of John the Baptist's career.
4. The statement of Paul in Galatians 2:1 should read "four" instead of "fourteen" years.
5. John recorded three Passovers in duration; and all are assumed to be in 34, 35, and 36.
6. Jesus was assumed to be born in 12 BC since this coincided with Halley's comet and the visit of the Magi.
7. John's gospel revealed that Jesus was forty-six at the time of the first Passover in 34 and that he was not yet fifty at the time of the Feast of Tabernacles.
8. Luke's phrase "about thirty years old" was meant to symbolize the age of King David; it need not be used for dating purposes.

The obvious problem with this hypothesis is that its foundation is based on a chain of assumptions and speculations. Hoehner (1974a, 337-38) also challenges this late date because "There is no indication in the gospels that Jesus' ministry lasted six years" and "the theory makes havoc of the gospels' chronology." Furthermore, Sanders (1993, 286-290) argues that a substantial rationale of a later date is based on Josephus's *Antiquities*. However, "many of the stories are not in chronological order." (p. 286)

Finally, the late controversial author and editor of *Freemasonry Today*, Michael Baigent (2006, 52-53), writes in *The Jesus Papers*:

> The Gospel of Luke (3:1, 23) states that Jesus was about thirty years old at the time of his baptism by John, and this was after the fifteenth year of the reign of Tiberius (as calculated in Syria)— AD 27. But he was baptized not long before John the Baptist was executed, and after John's death the Gospel of Matthew (14:13) describes Jesus as seeking refuge in the desert, perhaps fearing for his own life. What then was the date of the execution? It could not have been AD 27, for Matthew and Mark reported that John the Baptist was arrested by Herod Antipas for criticizing his marriage to Herodias—the wife of his brother, whom she had divorced—a marriage outlawed by Jewish law and also by one of the texts of the Dead Sea Scrolls, the Temple Scroll. Following this public criticism, John was executed. So far as can be ascertained, the marriage of Herod Antipas and Herodias took place in AD 35. Hence, John the Baptist was executed in AD 35. So Jesus must still have been alive at this date.

The last Passover attended by Pilate was AD 36. In other words, since Jesus is said in the Gospels to have been executed *after* John the Baptist's death and by the decision of Pilate, it must have been the Passover of AD 36 during which Jesus was crucified. This is later than most experts have placed the event, but if Jesus was born at the time of the census in AD 6, as stated by Luke (2:2), and if he was aged about thirty, AD 36 is just about the right time of the crucifixion—the crucifixion of the "Star of Bethlehem."

CONCLUSION

It must be remembered that Christian apologists (e. g., Clark 1957, 17; Köstenberger and Taylor 2014; O'Connell 2010, 144) maintain that the year Jesus died and was resurrected *is* the most important and significant event in the history of mankind. Yet historians, scholars, and theologians alike cannot pinpoint when these two momentous events occurred. In contrast, the years and in many instances the exact days listed below of various ancient dates are known with absolute and total clarity.

- Alexander the Great died on June 11, 323 BC.
- Augustus (Gaius Julius Caesar Octavianus) was born September 23, 63 BC.
- Tiberius Caesar Augustus was born on November 16, 42 BC.
- Julius Caesar was assassinated on March 15, 44 BC.
- Cassius and Brutus were defeated by Anthony and Octavian at the Battle of Philippi on October 23, 42 BC, followed by Brutus's suicide.
- King Herod I was elected king of the Jews by the Roman Senate in 37 BC.
- The Battle of Actium occurred in the seventh year of Herod's reign on September 2, 31 BC.
- Power was returned to the Roman Senate in 27 BC.
- Tiberius Claudius Germanicus was born on August 1, 10 BC.
- Herod the Great died in 4 BC.
- Augustus (Gaius Julius Caesar Octavianus) died on August 19, AD 14.
- Tiberius Caesar Augustus (born Tiberius Claudius Nero) died on March 16, AD 37.
- Gaius Caesar Augustus Germanicus (Caligula) was assassinated on January 24, AD 41.
- Agrippa I died in AD 44.

- Tiberius Claudius Germanicus died on October 13, AD 54.
- The Second Temple fell in AD 70.

In contradiction to the above, in issues 3 and 4, the exact day of the week or the exact date (fourteenth or fifteenth of Nisan) that Jesus was crucified is not known. In fact, the precise year that Jesus died as well as the date or day of his birth is not known. Obviously the date of these occurrences should be the most knowable events of the history of mankind, yet how is it possible that the dates of supposedly the "most stupendous miracles on record" (Clark 1957, 17; cf. Köstenberger and Taylor 2014; O'Connell 2010, 144) and the supreme events in the history of our world are totally unknown?

Marsh (1908, 37) offered three Christian apologetics why the chronology of this early date is unresolved:

1. Due partly to miscalculations.
2. Partly to loss of records.
3. "The followers of Christ were more occupied in preparing for the second coming of their Lord than in writing records and keeping dates, for they had misunderstood one of His sayings to imply that the end of all things was near."

Marsh's apologetics are excuses and speculations. First, in reverse order, there is no proof that the followers of Jesus were more occupied in preparing for the second coming than in writing records or keeping dates. Marsh is offering an argument based on silence, and there is no evidence to support it. Second, the "loss of records defense" is also speculation. How can one prove there was a loss of records if there never were any records that were lost? Third, although there is the possibility of miscalculations, here the error is in reference to presumably the most important event in the history of mankind. To argue that there were possible miscalculations is merely a convenient excuse, an argument based on silence, and pure speculation.

From this issue it is clear that nobody has the faintest idea when Jesus died! The year of Jesus's crucifixion is unknown, and the only certainty is that it must have occurred sometime during the ten years Pontius Pilate was procurator of Judea.

ISSUE 2: The Month and Season Jesus Was Crucified

Mk 11:1 And when they came nigh to Jerusalem, unto Bethphage and Bethany, at the mount of Olives, he sendeth forth two of his disciples, 2 And saith unto them, Go your way into the village over against you: and as soon as ye be entered into it, ye shall find a colt tied, whereon never man sat; loose him, and bring him. 3 And if any man say unto you, Why do ye this? say ye that the Lord hath need of him; and straightway he will send him hither. 4 And they went their way, and found the colt tied by the door without in a place where two ways met; and they loose him.	Mt 21:1 And when they drew nigh unto Jerusalem, and were come to Bethphage, unto the mount of Olives, then sent Jesus two disciples, 2 Saying unto them, Go into the village over against you, and straightway ye shall find an ass tied, and a colt with her: loose them, and bring them unto me. 3 And if any man say ought unto you, ye shall say, The Lord hath need of them; and straightway he will send them. 4 All this was done, that it might be fulfilled which was spoken by the prophet, saying,	Lk 19:29 And it came to pass, when he was come nigh to Bethphage and Bethany, at the mount called the mount of Olives, he sent two of his disciples, 30 Saying, Go ye into the village over against you; in the which at your entering ye shall find a colt tied, whereon yet never man sat: loose him, and bring him hither. 31 And if any man ask you, Why do ye loose him? thus shall ye say unto him, Because the Lord hath need of him. 32 And they that were sent went their way, and found even as he had said unto them. 33 And as they were loosing the colt, the owners thereof said unto them, Why loose ye the colt?	Jn 12:1 *Then Jesus six days before the passover* came to Bethany, where Lazarus was, which had been dead, whom he raised from the dead… Jn 12:12 On the next day much people that were come to the feast, when they heard that Jesus was coming to Jerusalem, 13 Took branches of palm trees, and went forth to meet him, and cried, Hosanna: Blessed is the King of Israel that cometh in the name of the Lord. 14 And Jesus, when he had found a young ass, sat thereon; as it is written,	Jn 18:28 Then led they Jesus from Caiaphas unto the hall of judgment: and it was early; and they themselves went not into the judgment hall, least they should be defiled; *but that they might eat the passover.* Jn 19:14 *And it was the preparation of the passover,* and about the sixth hour: and he saith unto the Jews, Behold your King!

5 And certain of them that stood there said unto them, What do ye, loosing the colt? 6 And they said unto them even as Jesus had commanded: and they let them go. 7 And they brought the colt to Jesus, *and cast their garments on him; and he sat upon him. 8 And many spread their garments in the way: and others cut down branches off the trees, and strawed them in the way. 9 And* they that went before, and they that followed, *cried, saying, Hosanna; Blessed is he that cometh in the name of the Lord: 10 Blessed be the kingdom of our father David, that cometh in the name of the Lord: Hosanna in the highest.*	5 Tell ye the daughter of Sion, Behold, thy King cometh unto thee, meek, and sitting upon an ass, and a colt the foal of an ass. 6 And the disciples went, and did as Jesus commanded them, *7 And brought the ass, and the colt, and put on them their clothes, and they set him thereon. 8 And a very great multitude spread their garments in the way;* others cut down *branches from the trees, and strawed them in the way. 9 And* the multitudes that went before, and that followed, *cried, saying,* Hosanna to the son of David: Blessed *is he that cometh in the name of the Lord;* Hosanna in the highest.	34 And they said, The Lord hath need of him. *35 And they brought him to Jesus: and they cast their garments upon the colt, and they set Jesus thereon. 36* And as he went, they spread their clothes in the way. 37 And when he was come nigh, even now at the descent of the mount of Olives, the whole multitude of the disciples began to rejoice and praise God with a loud voice for all the mighty works that they had seen; 38 *Saying, Blessed be the King that cometh in the name of the Lord: peace in heaven, and glory in the highest.*	15 Fear not, daughter of Sion: behold, thy King cometh, sitting on an ass's colt. 16 These things understood not his disciples at the first: but when Jesus was glorified, then remembered they that these things were written of him, and that they had done these things unto him.	

In the context of the last week of Jesus's life, *all* of the Gospels make a reference to a Passover. Traditionally "Palm Sunday" is the Sunday before Easter and commemorates Jesus's triumphal entry into Jerusalem prior to his execution. Therefore, according to the synoptic Gospels and the Gospel of John, the season of Jesus's crucifixion was the spring and was specifically at Passover. Consequently, Jesus's entry into Jerusalem occurred during the Hebrew month of Nisan, mid-March to early April. However, several scholars have advocated or discussed that the days prior to the passion of Jesus suggest that these events occurred during the autumn in the month of September, the fifteenth through the twenty-second day of the seventh Hebrew month of Tishri and specifically during the Feast of Tabernacles, Succoth.

CONTRADICTION #2 The Controversy Regarding the Garments

Prior to Jesus's entry into Jerusalem, presumably in March/April, Mark 11:7-8, Matthew 21:7-8, and Luke 19:35-36 reported that an unknown number of people laid down their *himatia* (in Greek, outer garments, or clothing) on both the colt and on the ground for Jesus's donkey to walk on as it carried Jesus. In contrast, John *omitted* any mention of people laying down their clothing on the ground for Jesus.

The description of people laying down their clothing is dubious. First, either the twelve disciples or these non-disciples were literally stripping down to their *epikarison* (in Hebrew, undergarments) and placing their clothing on the colt and on the road, or they were carrying an extra set of outerwear for this specific purpose. Second, it must be remembered that in those days people did not have numerous sets of clothes. (see *b. Shabbat* 113a) Often, many people had only the clothing they wore. Moxnes (1988, 91) writes:

> The description of clothing reveals the same picture of a simple life among most people. They wore a cloak (*himation*) as an outer garment ([[Lk]] 6:29) and under that a shirt, a tunic (*chitōn*, [[Lk]] 3:11; 6:29). Poor people might have to go without a shirt; to be the owner of two tunics apparently was a sign that one was relatively well-off ... Clothes were scare among the poor people, and thus objects for robbers ([[Lk]] 6:29), as with the man on a journey from Jerusalem to Jericho who was stripped of his clothes ([[Lk]] 10:30).

Similarly, in Middletown Bible Church (2014), it stated:

> Usually the Jews of Christ's day had at least one change of clothing.
> A man would be considered poor to have only one garment (see
> what John the Baptist said in Luke 3:11). In Matthew 10:10 Jesus
> told His disciples not to take an extra undergarment with them.

> Among the poorer people, the tunic was often the only clothing worn
> in warm weather. Wealthier people might wear the tunic alone inside
> the house, but they would not wear it without the outer garment
> outside the house. In the Bible the term "naked" is sometimes used
> of men who only have on their tunic (see John 21:7). To be dressed
> in such a scanty manner was thought of as "nakedness."

Assuming that it was the twelve disciples who were placing their garments
on the colt and on the ground, it does not seem realistic that this group of
wandering men without any means of revenue, other than support by several
women, would have "several" sets of clothing. And the problem remained,
even if non-disciples were the ones laying down garments, most people did
not have extra sets of clothing.

Fitzmyer (1985, 1250; cf. Carroll 2012, 385n2; Garland 2011, 771; Green
1997, 685n15; Kinman 2005, 245n56; Tannehill 1996, 283) posits that "the
cloaks on the road may be an illusion to the homage paid to the newly anointed
Jehu in 2 Kgs 9:13." However, several Christian commentators (Collins 2007,
519; Cranfield 1959, 350) point out a similar description of Cato Minor's soldiers
spreading their clothing at his feet when he was about to leave them. This
event appears in Plutarch's work *Vit. Cat. Minor* (Cato the Younger). "When
the time of Cato's military service came to an end, he was sent on his way, not
with blessings, as is common, nor yet with praises, but with tears and insatiable
embraces, the soldiers casting their mantles down for him to walk upon, and
kissing his hands, things which the Romans of that day rarely did, and only to a
few of their imperators" (see volume 8, 260-61 translation by Bernadotte Perrin,
Plutarch's Lives. New York: G. P. Putnam's Sons. 1919). Therefore, perhaps the
gospel narrators were adapting their account from an earlier literary tradition.

SPECULATION #1 Was the Crucifixion Really in the Fall and Not in the Spring?

Numerous commentators (Burkitt 1916, 139-49; Carrington 1952, 21-
23; Chilton 2008, 28; 2002, 22-23; Goguel 1933, 400; Kinman 1995, 116;

Hurtado 1989, 186; Keener 2003, 869; Kennard 1948, 172; Lane 1974, 390-91; Lenski 1943, 807; Manson 1951, 271-82; Mastin 1969, 76; Matson 1992, 503-05; C. W. F. Smith 1962-63, 130-46; 1960, 326; Myllykoski 2002, 71-72; Pope 1988, 24-25; Solowey 1987, 114-18; Tatum 1998, 134; Winter 1998, 152-55) discuss or imply in their commentaries that the immediate events detailed prior to Jesus's trial and crucifixion did not occur in the month of Nisan but rather in Tishrei. In other words, the original triumphal entry in Jerusalem was transferred to a different setting.

More overtly, Goguel (1933, 400) declares:

> As we have seen, Jesus did not enter Jerusalem a few days before the Passover but at the Feast of Tabernacles, in the month of September or October; he stayed there till the Feast of the Dedication, in December. Then he went away into retirement in Peraea; at the same time he remained in touch with his disciples in Jerusalem; he did not return to the capital until a short time before the Passover, 'six days before,' says John (xii. 1), that is to say, about the same time as his arrival is placed by the Synoptists.

Fitzmyer (1985, 1245) adds the following insightful comment: "If there is any validity to that argument [[i.e., the date]], it merely compounds the problem of the historical basis of the scene of Jesus' entry."

One reason for this speculation is the Hosanna controversy. All the gospel accounts, except Luke's, describe Jesus's entry into Jerusalem with the people declaring Hosanna. "Hosanna" is the Greek rendering of a Hebrew phrase meaning "Save now" (Ps 118:25); "Blessed be he that cometh in the name of the LORD" is the next verse of that Psalm (Ps 118:26). From a Christian perspective, the crowds naturally connected this royal procession to the common hope in the coming of the Son of David, and the reception that they gave Jesus supposedly identified him as the Davidic Messiah who would deliver them from oppression. However, the Christian rationale behind this reception is impossible because Jesus *never* taught publicly that he was the Messiah.

On the other hand, Hosanna was a customary form of acclamation at the Feast of Tabernacles. However, this feast is celebrated in September, just before the commencement of the civil year. During this celebration, the people carried in their hands bundles of boughs of palms, myrtles, etc. (Josephus, *Ant.* 12, 13, 6; 3, 10, 4). Furthermore, the words cited above virtually match, verbatim, what is said on Hoshanna Rabbah, the seventh day of Succoth. This celebration does not occur in mid-March but rather in September. In the opinion of Darrell Bock (2002, 314), professor of New Testament at the

Dallas Theological Seminary, "Luke's omission [[of celebratory actions]] may be motivated by the fact that this was a Jewish practice, often associated with the Feast of Tabernacles (*m. Sukkah* 3.1, 8-9, 12)."

In contrast, Chilton (2008, 86) writes:

> The Aramaic Targum [the targum is an early Aramaic translation, paraphrase, and interpretation of the Hebrew Bible] of the last chapter of the Book of Zechariah predicts that God's kingdom will be manifested over the entire earth when the offerings of *Sukkoth* are presented by both Israelites and non-Jews at the Temple. It further predicts that these worshipers will prepare and offer their sacrifices themselves, without the intervention of the middlemen. The last words of the book promise that "there shall never again be one doing trade in the sanctuary of the LORD of hosts at that time" (*Targum Zechariah* 14:21). The thrust of the targumic prophecy motivated Jesus in the dramatic confrontation he provoked in the Temple when he expelled both traders and their animals (Matthew 21:12-13; Mark 11:15-17; Luke 19:45-46; John 2:14-17). Zechariah's vision of a *Sukkoth* that restored the land to Israel and the Temple to the sacrifice God desired was a fundamental aspect of Jesus' purpose during his last months in Jerusalem.

The Controversy Regarding Jewish Traditions

Myllykoski (2002, 71-72) points out that there are at least two features that challenge the Christian tradition that Jesus was buried during the Passover festival. First, Mark (see 14:12; 15:1, 46) had Joseph of Arimathea purchasing Jesus's burial linen cloth during the Passover festival, that is the first day of Passover. However, work on a holy day (festival day) was a violation of God's command.

> Lev 23:6-7 And on the fifteenth day of the same month is the feast of unleavened bread unto the LORD: seven days ye must eat unleavened bread. In the first day ye shall have an holy convocation: ye shall do no servile work therein.
>
> Neh 10:31 And if the people of the land bring ware or any victuals on the sabbath day to sell, that we would not buy it of them on the

sabbath, or on the holy day: and that we would leave the seventh year, and the exaction of every debt.

Second, by contacting Jesus's body, Joseph remained impure for seven days after he had buried Jesus (cf. Num 19:16): "And whosoever toucheth one that is slain with a sword in the open fields, or a dead body, or a bone of a man, or a grave, shall be unclean seven days." The inability to participate in the Passover offering was also discussed in Numbers 9. Consequently, following John's chronology Joseph (and Nicodemus, see Jn 19:40) would not have been permitted to partake of the Passover meal.

The Controversy Regarding the Branches

Another reason that it may be speculated that Jesus's crucifixion did not take place in Nisan is because of the branches and palm trees detailed in several of the narratives. Mark 11:8 and Matthew 21:8 reported that "branches from the trees" were cut down and used as straw on the road but omitted details about what type of tree the branches came from. Nonetheless, Mark and Matthew clearly implied two significant facts: (1) these trees were standing *in* Jerusalem and (2) the branches were *leafy*.

The initial difficulty with these narratives relates to the branches described in Mark and Matthew. These oldest gospel narratives reported two specific actions: "others cut down branches off the trees" and "strawed them in the way."

> Mk 11:8 And many spread their garments in the way: and others cut down branches off the trees, and strawed them in the way.

> Mt 21:8 And a very great multitude spread their garments in the way; others cut down branches from the trees, and strawed them in the way.

The first problem relates to the Authorized Version's misleading translation. In Mark, the Greek text employed the word *stoibas* for "branches." This word, #4746 in the *Strong's Concordance*, appeared only once in the Christian scriptures. Strong (1890, 67) states: "a spread (as if tramped flat) of loose material for a couch, i.e. (by impl.) a bough of a tree so employed:-branch." Similarly, *Thayer's Lexicon* (1886, 588; cf. Vine 1939, 147) states: "(a) *a spread or layer of leaves, reeds, rushes, soft leaf twigs, straw,* etc., *serving for a bed.* b) that which is used in making a bed of this sort, *a branch full of leaves, soft foliage.*" Therefore, in Mark, the branches are *leafy* and such is the literal reading in the NSRV. Mark's account detailed *leafy* branches because it would not make sense to spread leafless sticks and dried twigs on a road in order to soften the road or to wave leafless sticks as a sign of celebration.

However, Matthew, writing after Mark, used the Greek term *klados* for "branches." This Greek term corresponds to #2798 in *Strong's Concordance*. Here, *Thayer's Lexicon* (1886, 347; cf. Vine 1939, 147) states that *klados* in Matthew 21:8 is "*a. prop. A young, tender shoot, broken off for grafting. b. univ. a branch.*" Therefore, Matthew has either omitted or deleted any allusion or suggestion of leafy branches. Perhaps the author or later redactors of Matthew recognized a potential error in Mark.

The problem with Mark's narrative is that there are *no* leafy branches in March (Nisan) during the time of Passover in Jerusalem because it is the wrong season. Therefore, either the narrative or the time sequence, the six days before the Passion and as a prelude to the Passover, is fallacious. Branches are waved during the fall harvest festival of Succoth.

> Lev 23:39-40 Also in the fifteenth day of the seventh month, when ye have gathered in the fruit of the land, ye shall keep a feast unto the LORD seven days: on the first day shall be a sabbath, and on the eighth day shall be a sabbath. And ye shall take you on the first day the boughs of goodly trees, branches of palm trees, and the boughs of thick trees, and willows of the brook; and ye shall rejoice before the LORD your God seven days.

Kinman too (1995, 116; cf. Hurtato 1989, 186) offers another relevant comment regarding the omission of the foliage in Luke specifically related to the timing of Jesus's entry into Jerusalem:

> A second possible explanation for the omission has to do with the timing of the entry. The impression given by Luke is that it takes place near Passover (Luke 22:1; cf. Mark 14:1). However, in Lev 23:40 and 1 Macc 13:51 the display of the foliage at a procession is connected with the Feast of Tabernacles and the celebration of Hanukkah, respectively. It is possible, therefore, that Luke would have seen the mention of the foliage as anachronistic and confusing to his readers. Indeed, the mention of it in Mark, Matthew and John has led some to debate the actual season of the entry in association with life-of-Jesus research.

In contrast to Mark and Matthew, Luke completely omits references to any branches at all. This omission is significant because Luke 1:1-4 claims to have carefully investigated "all things from the very first" and that he had written an orderly account so his reader would "know the certainty of those things." Luke possibly suspected a problem in these two earlier narratives: Mark using *leafy* branches out of season and Matthew having the people lay down *bare* branches on a road.

The Controversy Regarding the Palm Trees

John 12:13 alone specifically mentioned that these branches were from "palm" trees (*ta baia twn poinikwn*): "Took branches of palm trees, and went forth to meet him, and cried, Hosanna: Blessed is the King of Israel that cometh in the name of the Lord." Here the palm branches could be emblematic of triumph and victory. For example, their use in 1 Maccabees 13:51 (cf. 2 Macc 10:7) was on account of Simon's triumphal entry into Jerusalem. In the opinion of Farmer (1956), these branches were distinctive nationalist symbols and easily recognized as such (see especially 125-58). The fact that the people also waved branches is possible, although it is not explicitly stated.

Mastin (1969, 82), however, posits that "it would have been possible for the crowd, especially if it were small, to provide itself with such before it began what, on the Fourth Gospel's showing, was a planned demonstration." This action raises the issue of whether or not *palm* trees grew in Jerusalem and were readily available.

R. C. H. Lenski (1943, 807), a conservative Lutheran scholar, points out that palm branches had long before *disappeared* from Jerusalem: "In fact, the country has long ago been denuded of forests and of trees in general." Similarly, Lindars (1972, 422), commenting on John 12:13, writes:

> Palms do not grow commonly in the uplands, and they were usually brought up from the Jordan valley when required for ceremonial use . . . Matthew and Mark do not mention palms, but suggest that the disciples spontaneously cut branches of the trees growing in the locality. This suggests that the event has been reinterpreted in the course of the transmission of the tradition as a victory procession, or more likely as an equivalent of the Tabernacles procession for the water-pouring.

Research by Solowey (1987, 115-17), a Jewish detractor, substantiates the commentary of Lenski and Lindars: "<u>Palm trees do *not* grow in the Jerusalem area because of the high altitude and low temperature in winter.</u>" Elaborating on this point, Solowey writes:

> Date palms (botanical classification is Phoenix dactylifera) are the palms mentioned in the New Testament with reference to Palm Sunday...

> The date palm can survive a temperature as low as 20 degrees Fahrenheit but requires a mean temperature over 65 degrees Fahrenheit in order to flower and fruit. The mean temperature in Jerusalem in the winter is 41 degrees Fahrenheit for the low. Of course it sometimes gets much colder and it even snows in Jerusalem...

> Date palms grow in cities like Jericho which had always been famous for them. Jericho is about 40 km (24.84 miles) east of Jerusalem. But Jericho lies approximately 200 meters (656 feet) below sea-level in the Jordan Rift, while the altitude of Jerusalem is about 800 meters (2,624 feet) above sea level. The original palm still grows in hot regions only in the low places in Israel as Jericho, the Jordan Valley, the Beisan Valley, the Negev, and the southern Gaza Strip.

Finally, Malina and Rohrbaugh (1998, 210), writing in the *Social-Science Commentary on the Gospel of John*, provide a photograph of a date palm, the *Phoenix dactylifera*, in their text. Beneath the photograph they wrote: "It is the only native palm tree in the Holy Land. Actually, *it is native only to desert oases, e.g., Jericho, 'the city of palms'*" (Deut 34:3; 2 Chr 28:13), but was highly valued for its fruit and transplanted from very ancient times to other sites." [italics mine]

What can then explain John's specific inclusion of palm trees? Carson (1991, 432) maintains that that "From about two centuries earlier, palm branches had already become a national, (not to say nationalist) symbol" and were "no longer restrictively associated with Tabernacles." Keener (2003, 869) offers another Christian apologetic that branches from palm trees were brought to Jerusalem in preparation for Jesus's arrival. He then adds that "whether one judges the use of palm branches likely will depend on one's prior disposition toward the historicity of the Johannine tradition."

In conclusion, the Gospels stated that Jews shouted Hosanna and waved palm branches during the week-long festival of Passover. However, palm branches and Hosanna are associated specifically with Sukkot, not Passover. Bock (1996, 1557) concurs: "This action had eschatological significance at the Feast of Tabernacles, but is surprising here before this feast." Put more aptly, as an analogy, this would be like a story of people saying Happy New Year and setting off fireworks at Christmas or Easter (Carr 1999).

ISSUE 3: The Specific Date Jesus Was Crucified: Nisan 14 or Nisan 15

| Mk 14:12 *And the first day of unleavened bread, when they killed the passover*, his disciples said unto him, Where wilt thou that we go and prepare that thou mayest eat the passover? 13 And he sendeth forth two of his disciples, and saith unto them, Go ye into the city, and there shall meet you a man bearing a pitcher of water: follow him. 14 And wheresoever he shall go in, say ye to the goodman of the house, The Master saith, Where is the guestchamber, *where I shall eat the passover with my disciples?* 15 And he will shew you a large upper room furnished and prepared: there make ready for us. 16 And his disciples went forth, and came into the city, and found as he had said unto them: and *they made ready the passover.* 17 And in the evening he cometh with the twelve. 18 And as they sat and did eat, Jesus said, Verily I say unto you, One of you which eateth with me shall betray me. 19 And they began to be sorrowful, and to say unto him one by one, Is it I? and another said, Is it I? 20 And he answered and said unto them, It is one of the twelve, that dippeth with me in the dish. | Mt 26:20 Now when the even was come, he sat down with the twelve. 21 And as they did eat, he said, Verily I say unto you, that one of you shall betray me. 22 And they were exceeding sorrowful, and began every one of them to say unto him, Lord, is it I? 23 And he answered and said, He that dippeth his hand with me in the dish, the same shall betray me. 24 The Son of man goeth as it is written of him: but woe unto that man by whom the Son of man is betrayed! it had been good for that man if he had not been born. 25 Then Judas, which betrayed him, answered and said, Master, is it I? He said unto him, Thou hast said. 26 And as they were eating, Jesus took bread, and blessed it and brake it, and gave it to the disciples, and said, Take, eat; this is my body. 27 And he took the cup, and gave thanks, and gave it to them, saying, Drink ye all of it; | Lk 22:1 Now the feast of unleavened bread drew nigh, which is called the Passover.

Lk 22:7 Then came the day of unleavened bread, when the passover must be killed. 8 And he sent Peter and John, saying, Go and prepare us the passover, that we may eat. 9 And they said unto him, Where wilt thou that we prepare? 10 And he said unto them, Behold, when ye are entered into the city, there shall a man meet you, bearing a pitcher of water; follow him into the house where he entereth in. 11 And ye shall say unto the goodman of the house, The Master saith unto thee, Where is the guestchamber, *where I shall eat the passover with my disciples?* 12 And he shall shew you a large upper room furnished: there make ready. 13 And they went, and found as he had said unto them: *and they made ready the passover.* 14 And when the hour was come, he sat down, and the twelve apostles with him. | Jn 18:28 Then led they Jesus from Caiaphas unto the hall of judgment: and it was early; and they themselves went not into the judgment hall, least they should be defiled; *but that they might eat the passover.*

Jn 19:14 *And it was the preparation of the passover,* and about the sixth hour: and he saith unto the Jews, Behold your King! |

21 The Son of man indeed goeth, as it is written of him: but woe to that man by whom the Son of man is betrayed! good were it for that man if he had never been born. 22 And as they did eat, Jesus took bread, and blessed, and brake it, and gave to them, and said, Take, eat: this is my body. 23 And he took the cup, and when he had given thanks, he gave it to them: and they all drank of it. 24 And he said unto them, This is my blood of the new testament, which is shed for many. 25 Verily I say unto you, I will drink no more of the fruit of the vine, until that day that I drink it new in the kingdom of God. 26 And when they had sung an hymn, they went out into the mount of Olives.	28 For this is my blood of the new testament, which is shed for many for the remission of sins. 29 But I say unto you, I will not drink henceforth of this fruit of the vine, until that day when I drink it new with you in my Father's kingdom. 30 And when they had sung an hymn, they went out into the mount of Olives.	15 And he said unto them, With desire I have desired to eat this passover with you before I suffer: 16 For I say unto you, I will not any more eat thereof, until it be fulfilled in the kingdom of God. 17 And he took the cup, and gave thanks, and said, Take this, and divide it among yourselves: 18 For I say unto you, I will not drink of the fruit of the vine, until the kingdom of God shall come. 19 And he took bread, and gave thanks, and brake it, and gave unto them, saying, This is my body which is given for you: this do in remembrance of me. 20 Likewise also the cup after supper, saying, This cup is the new testament in my blood, which is shed for you.	

The scholarly consensus is that both the synoptic Gospels and the Gospel of John agree that Jesus was crucified on a Friday. Nonetheless, there are some who maintain that Jesus was crucified on either a Wednesday or Thursday. Consequently, one of the many controversial problems regarding Jesus's crucifixion is determining its exact date. The synoptic Gospels, on a simple reading, agree that Jesus was crucified on Passover day, the fifteenth of Nisan. In contrast, John had Jesus being executed on the eve of Passover, the fourteenth of Nisan.

CONTRADICTION #3 Nisan 14 or Nisan 15

The Gospels present conflicting dates for Jesus's crucifixion: the synoptic Gospels supported a Nisan 15 chronology while John indicates a Nisan 14 date. The Hebrew Bible states unequivocally that the paschal lambs were to be slaughtered on the fourteenth of Nisan and entirely consumed at the Passover meal that same evening, starting on the fifteenth of Nisan. This *command* is found in Leviticus:

> Lev 23:4 These are the feasts of the LORD, even holy convocations, which ye shall proclaim in their seasons.
>
> Lev 23:5 In the fourteenth day of the first month at even is the LORD'S passover.
>
> Lev 23:6 And on the fifteenth day of the same month is the feast of unleavened bread unto the LORD: seven days ye must eat unleavened bread.
>
> Lev 23:7 In the first day ye shall have an holy convocation: ye shall do no servile work therein.
>
> Lev 23:8 But ye shall offer an offering made by fire unto the LORD seven days: in the seventh day is an holy convocation: ye shall do no servile work therein.

Mark's narrative, essentially repeated by Matthew and Luke, plainly describes Jesus's death on the *first* day of Passover. Mark 14:14 narrates that Jesus sent two disciples to locate a place to eat the passover.

> Mk 14:14 And wheresoever he shall go in, say ye to the goodman of the house, The Master saith, Where is the guestchamber, *where I shall eat the passover with my disciples?*

In verse 16 the disciples carries out Jesus's command:

> Mk 14:16 And his disciples went forth, and came into the city, and found as he had said unto them: *and they made ready the passover.*

The statement "made ready the passover" means that they made sure the guestchamber was unleaven. This unleavening would have taken place on the fourteenth of Nisan. Then, in verse 17, they ate the passover:

> Mk 14:17 And in the evening he cometh with the twelve.

According to the Hebrew Bible's mode of counting, a new day starts at evening; therefore, it was now the fifteenth of Nisan. Then in verse 53

Jesus was arrested and taken to the high priest. Starting in chapter 15, Mark states that it was now the morning and Jesus was delivered to Pilate. Verses 3 through 15 narrates the examination of Jesus and the rendering of the verdict. From verses 16 through 41, Jesus is taken away, humiliated, and crucified. Collectively, these events occurred on the fifteenth of Nisan. Finally, in verse 42 Mark reports that the Sabbath is about to approach: "And now when the even was come, because *it was the preparation, that is, the day before the sabbath.*" Significantly, here "the preparation" was not for the Passover but for the Sabbath, which would not start until sunset. Therefore, this was still the fifteenth of Nisan.

John began the thirteenth chapter of his gospel by saying, "Now *before* the feast of the passover, when Jesus knew that his hour was come that he should depart out of this world unto the Father." This opening statement is highly noteworthy and significant, and must not be overlooked. John plainly states that the last meal with Jesus's disciples was on the day *before* the actual Passover lamb meal of Leviticus 23:5-6. Then the author of John adds a critical detail when the Jews were transferring Jesus over to Pontius Pilate to be crucified on the morning of the Crucifixion:

> Jn 18:28 Then led they Jesus from Caiaphas unto the hall of judgment: and it was early; and they themselves went not into the judgment hall, *lest they should be defiled; but that they might eat the passover.*

Why were these Jews so concerned about "that they might eat the passover" (AV) if they had *already* eaten the passover meal, as the synoptic accounts related? To reiterate, this concern does not make any sense given that they had already eaten the passover.

Third, John provided another important fact at the end of Jesus's trial and before Pilate rendered his verdict. Here John's words bear careful consideration:

> Jn 19:14 *And it was the preparation of the passover,* and about the sixth hour: and he saith unto the Jews, Behold your King!

What time is it? The author of John declares, "And it was the preparation of the passover" (AV). In other words, according to Leviticus 23, the time was approximately late afternoon of the fourteenth of Nisan, which directly coincides with when the lambs were to be slaughtered (Nolland 2005, 1045).

Another reason John could not have Jesus crucified on the fifteenth of Nisan is that, according to the Hebrew Bible, the paschal lamb was not slain until the evening of the fourteenth of Nisan. However, Deuteronomy 16:2, 5-6 demonstrated that the disciples would have also had a problem with *where* to slay a passover lamb had they desired to kill one.

> Deut 16:2 Thou shalt therefore sacrifice the passover unto the LORD thy God, of the flock and the herd, in the place which the LORD shall choose to place his name there.

> Deut 16:5 Thou mayest not sacrifice the passover within any of thy gates, which the LORD thy God giveth thee:

> Deut 16:6 But at the place which the LORD thy God shall choose to place his name in, there thou shalt sacrifice the passover at even, at the going down of the sun, at the that thou camest forth out of Egypt.

During Jesus's life, the Temple in Jerusalem was the place where God had commanded the Jewish people to slaughter the Passover lambs. However, Jesus's disciples positively could not have gone into the Temple at the beginning of the thirteenth of Nisan, the month of Abib as recorded in Deuteronomy 16:1. The disciples could not perform the sacrifice because the priests and Levites had to assist them in the slaughter of their Passover lambs. Moreover, the Jewish authorities who then controlled the Temple ritual would not have permitted anyone to slay their Passover lambs approximately twenty-one hours before ritual allowed. (France 1986, 47) Since the priests controlled and supervised the slaughter of the Passover lambs in the court of the Temple, this would have been an impossibility.

In conclusion, the synoptic accounts have the paschal lambs being slaughtered and the guestchamber being prepared on the fourteenth of Nisan. That evening, now the fifteenth of Nisan, Jesus ate his last meal; he was then arrested and examined by the religious leadership. During the morning, still on the fifteenth, Jesus was brought to Pilate, determined guilty, and crucified. In contrast, John had Jesus being arrested, tried, and executed on the day of preparation, the fourteenth of Nisan, the day of the passover.

Unequivocally, there is a clear contradiction of the texts. In a court of law, if two witnesses claimed that the same murder occurred on different days and there was no additional evidence, their testimonies would be excluded. The following three tables illustrate this indisputable contradiction.

TABLE 4. Thursday Through Sunday Timeline Based on the Synoptics

THURSDAY SYNOPTICS		FRIDAY SYNOPTICS		SATURDAY SYNOPTICS		SUNDAY SYNOPTICS	
Night	*Day*	*Night*	*Day*	*Night*	*Day*	*Night*	*Day*
	The lambs are slaughtered in the Temple.	The Passover Seder.	The First Day of Passover: a holy day.	The Sabbath and "the next day, that followed the day of preparation" (Mt 27:62).		The First Day of the Week.	
		The Jewish Community celebrates the Passover Seder.		1. The chief priests and Pharisees visit Pilate.		When the sabbath was past, three women bought spices (Mk 16:1).	1. The women left very early in the morning.
		1. Jesus and his disciples celebrate the Passover Seder.	1. Jesus is brought before Pilate and tried.	2. They went and made the sepulchre sure, sealing the stone, and setting a watch (Mt 27:62-66).			2. At sunrise the women came upon the sepulchre (Mk 16:1-2).
		2. Jesus is arrested.	2. Jesus is crucified, dies, and is buried.				
		3. Jesus is tried before Caiaphas.	3. The women returned home, and prepared spices and ointments prior to the Sabbath (Lk 23:56).				
PREPARATION DAY FOR PASSOVER							
14 NISAN		**15 NISAN**		**16 NISAN**		**17 NISAN**	

Two views of John affect the interpretation of table 5. First, John's chronology has a Friday crucifixion and a Friday Passover (NB: The majority view adapted to the synoptic Gospels' chronology). Therefore, this is the day after the Crucifixion. Here the Crucifixion would be occurring on the fourteenth of Nisan.

TABLE 5. Thursday Through Sunday Chronology Based on the Majority View

THURSDAY GOSPEL OF JOHN		FRIDAY GOSPEL OF JOHN		SATURDAY GOSPEL OF JOHN		SUNDAY GOSPEL OF JOHN	
Night	*Day*	*Night (Literally Thursday evening by our modern mode of reckoning)*	*Day* The lambs are slaughtered in the Temple.	*Night*	*Day* The Sabbath and Passover.	*Night*	*Day* The First Day of the Week.
		1. Jesus and his disciples celebrated a non-Passover Seder: "Now before the feast of passover" (Jn 13:1).	1. Jesus was brought before Pilate in the hall of judgment when "it was early" (Jn 18:28) and tried.				
		2. Jesus was arrested (Jn 18:1-12).	2. Jesus was crucified, died and buried.				
		3. Jesus was taken to Annas (Jn 18:13), then to Caiaphas (Jn 18:24).					
		PREPARATION DAY FOR PASSOVER.		SABBATH and PASSOVER [*an high day* (Jn 19:31)].			
13 NISAN		14 NISAN		15 NISAN		16 NISAN	

TABLE 6. Comparison of Mark and John: Timelines

THE GOSPEL OF MARK	THE GOSPEL OF JOHN (Assuming a Friday crucifixion.)
The preparation day for the Passover went from about *Wednesday at 6 p.m. until Thursday 6 p.m.* which was the 14th day of the first month.	The preparation day for the Passover went from about *Thursday at 6 p.m. until Friday 6 p.m.* which was the 14th day of the first month.
The Day of Preparation (The 14th of Nisan): The Passover lamb is sacrifice later in the afternoon.	The Day of Preparation (The 14th of Nisan): The Passover lamb is sacrifice later in the afternoon.
The Passover meal took place on *Thursday evening*, the 15th of Nisan.	The Passover meal would take place on *Friday evening*, the 15th of Nisan.
Jesus's Last Supper *was* supposedly a Passover Seder. It occurred on a Thursday [modern reckoning], the evening *after* the Passover lambs were brought to the Temple in the afternoon and slaughtered. This event is based on Ex 12:7-8 and Lev 23:5.	Jesus's Last Supper was *not* a Passover Seder. It occurred on a *Thursday* [modern reckoning], the evening *before* the Passover lambs were brought to the Temple and slaughtered.
After the *Passover Seder* on that Thursday evening and probably about midnight, Jesus was arrested.	After a *regular supper* on that Thursday evening and probably about midnight, Jesus was arrested.
On Friday, *the 15th of Nisan*, around dawn, Jesus was taken to Pilate.	On Friday, *the 14th of Nisan*, around dawn, Jesus was taken to Pilate.
Pilate, on Friday morning, *the 15th of Nisan*, heard the case against Jesus (the trial).	Pilate, on Friday morning, the *14th of Nisan* heard the case against Jesus (the trial).
Jesus was crucified on the *15th* of Nisan at 9:00 a.m., the morning *after the Passover Seder was eaten*.	Jesus was crucified on the *14th* of Nisan about noon, the day *before the Passover Seder* (i.e., on the day of preparation) was eaten. Therefore, Jesus died on the *same day* as the Passover *lamb was slaughtered*.

ISSUE 4: The Last Supper as a Passover Meal

Mk 14:12 *And the first day of unleavened bread, when they killed the passover,* his disciples said unto him, Where wilt thou that we go and prepare that thou mayest eat the passover? 13 And he sendeth forth two of his disciples, and saith unto them, Go ye into the city, and there shall meet you a man bearing a pitcher of water: follow him. 14 And wheresoever he shall go in, say ye to the goodman of the house, The Master saith, Where is the guestchamber, *where I shall eat the passover with my disciples?* 15 And he will shew you a large upper room furnished and prepared: there make ready for us. 16 And his disciples went forth, and came into the city, and found as he had said unto them: and they made ready the passover. 17 And in the evening he cometh with the twelve. 18 And as they sat and did eat, Jesus said, Verily I say unto you, One of you which eateth with me shall betray me.	Mt 26:19 And the disciples did as Jesus had appointed them; *and they made ready the passover.* 20 Now when the even was come, he sat down with the twelve. 21 And as they did eat, he said, Verily I say unto you, that one of you shall betray me. 22 And they were exceeding sorrowful, and began every one of them to say unto him, Lord, is it I? 23 And he answered and said, He that dippeth his hand with me in the dish, the same shall betray me. 24 The Son of man goeth as it is written of him: but woe unto that man by whom the Son of man is betrayed! it had been good for that man if he had not been born. 25 Then Judas, which betrayed him, answered and said, Master, is it I? He said unto him, Thou hast said. 26 And as they were eating, Jesus took bread, and blessed it and brake it, and gave it to the disciples, and said, Take, eat; this is my body.	Lk 22:1 *Now the feast of unleavened bread drew nigh, which is called the Passover.* Lk 22:7 Then came the day of unleavened bread, *when the passover must be killed.* 8 And he sent Peter and John, saying, Go and prepare us the passover, that we may eat. 9 And they said unto him, Where wilt thou that we prepare? 10 And he said unto them, Behold, when ye are entered into the city, there shall a man meet you, bearing a pitcher of water; follow him into the house where he entereth in. 11 And ye shall say unto the goodman of the house, The Master saith unto thee, Where is the guestchamber, where I shall eat the passover with my disciples? 12 And he shall shew you a large upper room furnished: there make ready.	Jn 18:28 Then led they Jesus from Caiaphas unto the hall of judgment: and it was early; and they themselves went not into the judgment hall, least they should be defiled; *but that they might eat the passover.* Jn 19:14 *And it was the preparation of the passover,* and about the sixth hour: and he saith unto the Jews, Behold your King!

19 And they began to be sorrowful, and to say unto him one by one, Is it I? and another said, Is it I? 20 And he answered and said unto them, It is one of the twelve, that dippeth with me in the dish. 21 The Son of man indeed goeth, as it is written of him: but woe to that man by whom the Son of man is betrayed! good were it for that man if he had never been born. 22 And as they did eat, Jesus took bread, and blessed, and brake it, and gave to them, and said, Take, eat: this is my body. 23 And he took the cup, and when he had given thanks, he gave it to them: and they all drank of it. 24 And he said unto them, This is my blood of the new testament, which is shed for many. 25 Verily I say unto you, I will drink no more of the fruit of the vine, until that day that I drink it new in the kingdom of God. 26 And when they had sung an hymn, they went out into the mount of Olives.	27 And he took the cup, and gave thanks, and gave it to them, saying, Drink ye all of it; 28 For this is my blood of the new testament, which is shed for many for the remission of sins. 29 But I say unto you, I will not drink henceforth of this fruit of the vine, until that day when I drink it new with you in my Father's kingdom. 30 And when they had sung an hymn, they went out into the mount of Olives.	13 And they went, and found as he had said unto them: and they made ready the passover. 14 And when the hour was come, he sat down, and the twelve apostles with him. 15 And he said unto them, With desire I have desired to eat this passover with you before I suffer: 16 For I say unto you, I will not any more eat thereof, until it be fulfilled in the kingdom of God. 17 And he took the cup, and gave thanks, and said, Take this, and divide it among yourselves: 18 For I say unto you, I will not drink of the fruit of the vine, until the kingdom of God shall come. 19 And he took bread, and gave thanks, and brake it, and gave unto them, saying, This is my body which is given for you: this do in remembrance of me. 20 Likewise also the cup after supper, saying, This cup is the new testament in my blood, which is shed for you.	

The "Last Supper" commonly refers to the final meal Jesus had with the twelve disciples and, perhaps, others immediately prior to his arrest and crucifixion. According to the tradition of mainline Christianity, this event was a celebration of the Passover meal. Fitzmyer (1985, 1378) points out that "The term "Last Supper" is never found in the NT itself. It has been developed from the reference to Jesus "dining" with his disciples "on the night on which he was betrayed" (1 Cor 11:23-25; cf. Jn 13:12). The requisites of the Passover are detailed in Leviticus 23:5-14 and Deuteronomy 16:1-8. Was the Last Supper actually a Passover meal or a memorial meal prior to Passover? Depending upon which commentators are read, there is absolute uncertainty. O'Toole (1992, 234), writing in *The Anchor Bible Dictionary*, succinctly states the problem associated with the academic research concerning the Last Supper: "Numerous analyses of the Last Supper have led to a remarkable variety of interpretations, many of which appear to have been influenced by the confessional stances of their proponents."

CONTRADICTION #4 The Last Supper as a Passover Meal

The the writings of Paul and the Gospels present contradictory details as to whether or not the Last Supper was a Passover meal. Mark, Matthew, and Luke seemingly reported that the Last Supper was a Passover meal (Bock 1996, 1951f; Jeremias 1966, 41-62 with 14 parallels; Stein 1996, 203f; and others). In contrast, others (Bockmuehl 1996, 92; Bruce 1971, 191-92; Catchpole 2000, 272-86; Frederick 1911, 503-09; Fuller 1954, 70-71; Geldenhuys 1951, 650; Jeremias 1967, 899; Mackinnon 1967, 203; Peake 1920, 215-16; Routledge 2002, 203-21; Schweizer 1967, 29-32; Taylor 1953, 664-65; Theissen and Merz 1998, 426-27) refute, raise questions about, or doubt that Jesus's Last Supper was a Passover meal. In general, Matthew and Luke agree with Mark. Consequently, *this* text will exclusively examine Mark as representative of the synoptic Gospels.

RELATIONSHIP TO THE SYNOPTICS

The entire case for identifying the Last Supper as a Passover meal rests almost entirely on a five-verse paragraph found in Mark 14:12-16:

TABLE 7. Analysis of Mark's Narrative of the Last Meal

VERSES FROM MARK	ANALYSIS
Mk 14:12 And the first day of unleavened bread, when *they killed the passover*, his disciples said unto him, Where wilt thou that we go and prepare that thou mayest eat the passover? (see Mt 26:17-19; Lk 22:1, 7)	1. The text declared that on *the first day of unleavened bread* Jesus's disciples made a request of him. 2. The text declared that on *the day when the Passover lamb was sacrificed*, Jesus's disciples made a request of him. 3. Therefore, *a lamb was clearly implied* by declaring "they killed the passover." 4. Jesus's disciples requested to know *where they were to go and make preparations for him to eat the passover.*
Mk 14:13 And he sendeth forth two of his disciples, and saith unto them, Go ye into the city, and there shall meet you a man bearing a pitcher of water: follow him (see Lk 22:8-10).	Jesus made an effort to hold the meal in Jerusalem, the required location for a Passover meal.
Mk 14:14 And wheresoever he shall go in, say ye to the goodman of the house, The Master saith, Where is the guestchamber, where I shall eat the passover with my disciples? (see Mt 26:18; Lk 22:10-13)	1. The text discussed the location *where they were to eat the passover.* 2. Here eating "the" passover must refer to the paschal lamb.
14:15 And he will shew you a large upper room furnished and prepared: there make ready for us (see Mt 26:18-19; Lk 22:11-12).	The word "prepared" referred to having been *made unleavened.*
Mk 14:16 And his disciples went forth, and came into the city, and found as he had said unto them: and they made ready the passover (see Mt 26:18-19; Lk 22:13).	1. The Passover meal had to be and was celebrated *in Jerusalem*, although Jesus had his lodgings in Bethany. 2. *The location was prepared by removing the leaven from it* [on the night of Nisan 14] *to make ready for the Passover Seder.*

Besides the details above, there are three extremely vague and ambiguous suggestions that the last meal was a Passover meal. These details include

(1) the drinking of wine, (2) the giving of thanks, and (3) the singing of a hymn.

Several writers (Bock 1996, 1951-53; Jeremias 1966, 41-62; Keener 2009a, 298; Stein 1996, 203-04; Theissen and Merz 1998, 423-26) discuss additional common features identified in the entire narrative:

1. The Passover meal was consumed at night, whereas, at other times, the main meal was usually eaten in the late afternoon.
2. Like the Passover meal, the bread was eaten in the middle of the meal and not at the start (Mk 14:20).
3. The interpretation of the meal's elements recalled the Passover. That is, it was customary during the Passover meal to describe the significance of certain items that were paralleled by Jesus's discussion of the bread and wine.
4. The Passover fellowship "had to consist of at least ten persons and this was the average number assumed that a one-year-old lamb could provide sufficient food for about ten people" (Jeremias 1966, 47).
5. The meal was eaten while those in attendance recline (Mk 14:18).
6. Jeremias (1966, 53) posits that Jesus and his disciples specifically drank *red wine* at the Last Supper as presumably opposed to the more common white or black wine. This argument is based on older traditions that red wine must be drunk at the Passover meal and was a binding prescription.

RELATIONSHIP TO JOHN

On the other hand, there are numerous objections to the Last Supper being a Passover meal. Significantly, John's Last Supper could *not* have been a Passover meal because it occurred on the fourteenth of Nisan. Substantiating this point, John mentions that Judas Iscariot mysteriously left the supposed Last Supper with a moneybag. The disciples immediately presumed that he was taking money to purchase food for the festive meal:

> Jn 13:29 For some of them thought, because Judas had the bag, that Jesus had said unto him, Buy those things that we have need of against the feast; or, that he should give something to the poor.

John's explanation for this action makes absolutely no sense! Why would Judas have purchased food for the Passover feast if, according to the first three gospels, they had just eaten it? Furthermore, the purchase of food on the fifteenth of Nisan would be a violation of Leviticus 23:7, working on a holy day.

Second, there was no mention of the Passover lamb in John's narrative. According to John, Jesus was the Passover lamb (see speculations 5 and 6). Consequently, he could not, by definition, eat the Passover since the Passover lamb was slaughtered before the Passover on the annual Preparation Day.

Later, Jesus was arrested and brought to Pilate for examination. John 18:28 states: "Then led they Jesus from Caiaphas unto the hall of judgment: and it was early; and they themselves went not into the judgment hall, lest they should be defiled; but that they might eat the passover." It makes no sense for the Jewish leadership to refuse entry into Pilate's hall of judgment—that is, a gentile's domain—and to fear becoming ritually defiled if the Passover had already occurred. That is, if the Jewish leadership had already participated in a Passover meal, the leaders did not need to fear becoming defiled, which would have excluded them from the Seder.

A few verses later, John 18:39 states that there was a tradition to release a prisoner *at* the Passover: "But ye have a custom, that I should release unto you one at the passover: will ye therefore that I release unto you the King of the Jews?" That is, John reports that the releasing of a prisoner was carried out in honor of the *upcoming* Passover. Obviously, the releasing of a prisoner *after* the Passover would in no way honor the Passover. Honoring could only occur by freeing the prisoner *before* the Passover.

Next, John 19:14-16 confirms that Jesus was sentenced prior to the Passover: "And it was the preparation of the passover, and about the sixth hour: and he saith unto the Jews, Behold your King! But they cried out, Away with him, away with him, crucify him. Pilate saith unto them, Shall I crucify your King? The chief priests answered, We have no king but Caesar. Then delivered he him therefore unto them to be crucified. And they took Jesus, and led him away."

Finally, John 19:30-31 corroborates that Jesus died prior to the Passover: "When Jesus therefore had received the vinegar, he said, It is finished: and he bowed his head, and gave up the ghost. The Jews therefore, because it was the preparation, that the bodies should not remain upon the cross on the sabbath day, (for that sabbath day was an high day,) besought Pilate that their legs might be broken, and that they might be taken away." Plainly, John has Jesus dying on the Preparation Day of the Passover.

RELATIONSHIP TO PAUL

It can also be argued that Paul's Last Supper was *not* a Passover meal. Consequently, Paul agrees with John's later narrative. This indicates that, like John, he associated Jesus with the paschal lamb. Paul, writing approximately 50-57 CE, predates the first gospel by about fifteen to twenty years and the Fourth Gospel by seemingly fifty years. His writings provide virtually no support that the Last Supper was a Passover meal. As a matter of fact, his comments seem to indicate the contrary.

1. Nowhere was the last supper meal called the actual Passover meal of Leviticus 23.
2. In 1 Corinthians 5:7 Paul refers to Jesus as "our passover." This indicates that, like John, he associated Jesus with the paschal lamb.
3. In 1 Corinthians 11:23, Paul conveys no awareness that the meal might have been a Passover observance. Specifically, there is no explicit mention of any details related to a Passover meal. That is, when Paul refers to the Last Supper, he significantly does not say "on the night of Passover" but instead refers to "the night in which the Lord was betrayed."
4. In 1 Corinthians 11:23, Paul uses the regular Greek word *artos* for "bread," not the proper designation for unleavened bread. The proper Greek term for "unleavened bread" is *azyma*, which Jerome renders as *azymorum* (see below.)

Furthermore, Tabor (2006, 200) posits that "if this meal had been the Passover, Paul would have surely wanted to say that, but he does not." In brief, there is no support for a Passover meal in the works of Paul.

In summary, the synoptic Gospels, in part, tended to indicate that the Last Supper was a Passover meal. Mark's narrative presented several anomalies or inconsistencies, perhaps suggesting that the Last Supper was *not* a Passover meal (see below). Smith (2003, 255) writes: "Thus, even if Jesus did celebrate a Passover meal with his disciples as his last meal, we do not have a clear reminiscence of such a meal in the description we now have." Or as the apologist N. T. Wright (1996, 555; cf. 1999, 84) suggests, "it seems to me virtually certain that the meal in question was *some kind of* Passover meal." In contrast, John unmistakably does not have a Passover meal. Paul's letters are doubtful and unclear as to whether or not Jesus's last meal was a Passover meal. What can be said is that Paul is seemingly tilted toward John. In conclusion, the lack of consensus regarding Jesus's last meal among historians, scholars, and theologians raises doubt as to its historicity.

CONTRADICTION #5 The Wrong Name in Mark 14:12

In error, Mark 14:12 identifies that "the first day of unleavened bread," the fifteenth of Nisan, is the time when the priests *sacrifice* ("killed" in the AV) the Passover lamb. In actuality, the slaughtering would have occurred on the fourteenth of Nisan. Here it must be understood that, according to the Hebrew Bible (Gen 1:8, 13, 19, 23, and 31), a new day starts at sunset. Therefore, the "first day of unleavened bread" started at sunset from our modern perspective. Second, the lamb was *eaten* on the fifteenth, not *slaughtered* on that day.

SPECULATION #2 Anomaly 1—Unexplained Rupture of the Storyline

In Mark 14:2, the chief priests and scribes express the desire to apprehend Jesus and dispose of him two days *before* the Passover meal. However, in verse 12, the Passover meal has *already* arrived. These two conflicting chronologies are seemingly left unreconciled. That is, declaring that on "the first day of unleavened bread" Jesus would be preparing for the Passover is clearly wrong since, according to Leviticus 23:6-7, on "the first day of unleavened bread" the Passover would have already taken place the night before on the evening of Passover. Unmistakably, the day before the Passover meal is not the day of Passover. Consequently, Cook (1999, 18-25; also see Black 2011, 287; Cook 2011, 254-57; 2010, 72) inquires:

1. Did something go wrong with the plan to arrest Jesus before the feast?
2. If yes, something did go amiss and the time for the Passover meal had already arrived before his arrest. How could Mark neglect to tell us what had gone awry?

If everything went as planned and Jesus was, in fact, arrested and disposed of *before* the Passover meal, then clearly the Last Supper was *not* a Passover meal. A possible resolution of this anomaly is that the chief priests and scribes did not put into action any plans they had perhaps designed. Instead they left the details to be determined and carried out by Judas (see verses 10 and 11).

Another solution offered by Jeremias (1966, 72-73) is that 14:2 was not necessarily understood as a temporal or chronological reference. Instead, Jeremias posits that *"it may well be local, 'in the presence of the festal crowd.'"*

SPECULATION #3 Anomaly 2—the Consequences of Following Judas

In Mark 14, it is told that

> Mk 14:1 After two days was the feast of the passover, and of unleavened bread: and the chief priests and the scribes sought how they might take him by craft, and put him to death.

> Mk 14:2 But they said, Not on the feast day, lest there be an uproar of the people.

Here there are two significant points that need to be noted. First, the religious leaders did *not* want Jesus arrested on the feast day. Second, their rationale was provided: Jesus's arrest would cause an uproar of the people. Later, in verse 43, Judas led a multiple of people from ("sent from" in the NIV) none other than the chief priests and the scribes and the elders on the first day of Passover to arrest Jesus: "And immediately, while he yet spake, cometh Judas, one of the twelve, and with him a great multitude with swords and staves, from the chief priests and the scribes and the elders." Consequently, the Jewish leadership did what actually they were afraid to do: have Jesus arrested and put to death on the feast day of Passover.

SPECULATION #4 Jesus as the Paschal Lamb

John having Jesus being crucified on the fourteenth of Nisan, the day before Passover, seemingly contradicts the synoptic Gospels. If the synoptic Gospels are correct, where did John get his idea that the Crucifixion occurred on the fourteenth of Nisan? One possible idea identified by Finegan (1998, 355 #608) and Hoehner (1974a, 335n33; cf. Peake 1920, 216) is that this idea came from the apostle Paul, writing in 1 Corinthians 5:7, when he declared: "For even Christ our Passover [[lamb]] is sacrificed for us." Hoehner (1974a, 335n33), the distinguished professor of New Testament Studies at the Dallas Theological Seminary, maintains that the idea that Jesus was crucified on the fourteenth of Nisan is also supported by the *Gospel of Peter 3*. However, it should be noted that Paul did *not* say that Jesus died on the same day as the Passover lamb.

Furthermore, it is speculated that John was familiar with Paul's agenda to remove the legal feast from Christianity (e.g., Heb 8:13: "In that he saith, A new covenant, he hath made the first old. Now that which decayeth and waxeth old is ready to vanish away") and to exhibit Jesus as the end of the law and of all sacrifice. Consequently, John must make it appear that Jesus did *not* eat a Passover lamb on the appointed day and, therefore, did *not* institute the Lord's Supper. Why is this so? The reason is very simple: Jesus himself was now to become the Passover lamb, which was slain on the fourteenth and *not* the fifteenth of Nisan.

SPECULATION #5 John's Theological Agenda of the Lamb of God

A rationale for the narrative accounts by the author of John is theological. The Gospel of John was attempting to reinforce a *theological* point that Jesus was "the Lamb of God who takes away the sins of the world":

1. John is the only gospel in which Jesus is identified as "the Lamb of God who takes away the sins of the world." From the very start of the Gospel of John, John the Baptist, Jesus's forerunner, declared that Jesus was "the Lamb of God."

   Jn 1:29 The next day John seeth Jesus coming unto him, and saith, Behold the Lamb of God, which taketh away the sin of the world.

   Jn 1:36 And looking upon Jesus as he walked, he saith, Behold the Lamb of God!

   In contrast, the most frequent allusion to Jesus as a lamb is found in the last book of the Christian scriptures, the book of Revelation, in which he is designated by that term twenty-eight times.

2. Jesus's death represents the salvation of God just as the sacrifice of the lamb represents salvation for the ancient Israelites during the Passover exodus. Furthermore, John is the only gospel in which Jesus dies on the same day as the Passover lamb, that is, the day of preparation. This concept is also mentioned in 1 Peter 1:19: "But with the precious blood of Christ, as of a lamb without blemish and without spot."

3. John is the only gospel in which Jesus dies at the same hour, just after noon, to unequivocally demonstrate that Jesus really was the Lamb of God.
4. Jesus died at the same place (Jerusalem) as the Passover lambs.
5. Jesus died at the hands of the same people, the Jewish leaders, especially the priests, as the Passover lambs.
6. John 19:31-37 is the only gospel in which Roman soldiers pierce Jesus's side with a spear rather than break his legs on the cross in order not to violate the prohibition found in Exodus 12:46 about breaking bones of the paschal lamb.
7. The month of Nisan has the sign of the lamb. Coincidentally, during the first century, the spring equinox, the time of Passover, is in the zodiacal sign of Aries the Lamb. It was the age of the lamb.
8. On March 21 the sun rose in the sign of the lamb. Coincidentally, the season of spring occurs when lambs are born, and this coincides with the Resurrection accounts.

In conclusion, John attempts to reinforce a *theological* point that Jesus is "the Lamb of God who taketh away the sin of the world." (Jn 1:29)

SPECULATION #6 Questions Raised about the Lamb of God

The Gospels do not record any historical words attributed to Jesus that demonstrated that he conceived of his death as a propitiatory sacrifice to save mankind from its sins! Why then did Jesus not once, during his ministry, either in private to his disciples, as recorded in the Gospels or as part of his public teaching, ever announce indisputably and unequivocally a divinely ordained scheme for the redemption of mankind? If the salvation of the world was at stake, as Christians proclaim, would it not have been reasonable, in plain and unequivocal terms, to have declared this plan to those whose benefit it was supposedly intended?

Yet another pertinent point must be asked: if the synoptic writers agree with the Fourth Gospel that the lamb was the antitype of Jesus, as John insisted, why is it that the synoptic Gospels describe the communion at the Last Supper with Jesus raising the matzo and declaring, "This is my body"? (Mk 14:2; Mt 26:26; Lk 22:19). Logically, it would be assumed that Jesus should have raised the paschal lamb.

SPECULATION #7 John Writing to Appeal to the Gentiles

Another possible reason John is written as it is, in order to appeal to a second-century church that had already become predominantly gentile and, therefore, had incorporated well-known pagan practices with elements of the Jewish faith. Moderate scholars are of the opinion that John was written in approximately 95 CE or even later outside of Judea. Extending this notion that the Gospel of John was written outside of Judea, perhaps the author or final redactor of John was more concerned about writing to a non-Jewish audience who knew little or nothing of the Jewish Passover Seder tradition.

SPECULATION #8 The Use of *Artos* (Bread)

Another argument against a Passover meal is that Mark 14:22, Matthew 26:26, and Luke 22:19 employ the Greek word *artos* (bread) instead of the word *azyma* (unleavened bread): a Passover meal requires unleavened bread. Gagne (2007, 419-20) elaborates:

> One other point of this feast is that only unleavened bread could be used as the Matzah. It was forbidden for any bread to be used that contained leaven. In all three passages in Matthew 26,26, Mark 14,22 and Luke 22,19 the word that is used is **ἄρτος** [[*artos*]] or according to Strong's, a raised loaf indicating that this had been prepared with leaven. This would have been a breaking of the law of Passover. The word for unleavened is **ἄζυμος** [[*azumos*]] and is found nine times in the New Testament for unleavened. In my studies, I have found only a few writers that even acknowledge the usage of 'raised loaf' in these passages, and this must call into question as to whether the Lord's Supper was really an observance of Passover. All of the other rituals connected to the Passover, mentioned in the previous paragraph, are also strangely absent from this meal.

Commentators (Jeremias 1966, 62-66; Stein 1996, 202) counter that the term *artos*; and its Hebrew equivalent terms employed in the Hebrew Bible, the LXX, the Mishna, and the Targums, describe showbread, which consisted of unleavened bread. Furthermore, Philo, a first-century Jewish scholar, explicitly refers to the unleavened bread of the Passover as *artos* (see *De specialibus legibus* 2.158). Similarly, Bock (1996, 1953) wrote that *artos* "is sometimes used of unleavened bread (Exod 29:23; Lev 7:12; 8:26; Num 6:15; Josephus, *Antiquities* 3.6,6 §143; 8.3.7 §90; *Jewish Wars* 5.5.5 §217)."

Nonetheless, Stein (1996, 202)—a senior professor of New Testament interpretation at the Southern Baptist Theological Seminary, Louisville, Kentucky—raises a substantial challenge to this notion: "The main difficulty with this alternative suggestion is that the writers of the Synoptic Gospels clearly wanted their statements to be understood as indicating that the Last Supper was part of a Passover celebration (see, for example, Mk 14:12, 14, 16; Lk 22:15)."

SPECULATION #9 Symbolism of the Bread and Wine and the Lack of a Lamb

JESUS'S SYMBOLISM OF THE WINE

The very thought of eating human flesh or drinking blood is totally repulsive in civilized sensibility and utterly unimaginable in Judaism (Bramer 2010, 140-71; Cahill 2002, 168-81; Carmichael, 1991, 103; *The Catholic Layman* 1853, 74-75; Fenton 2001, 97-111; Maccoby 1986, 118; Montefiore 1968, 332; Vermes 2008, 14). "The gravity of blood eating is so extreme, in fact, that it trumps even the uttermost instinct for survival" (Bramer, 2010, 157). Yet during the last meal, Mark 14:22, 24 narrates that Jesus referred to the consumption of the bread and wine, saying: "Take, eat: this is my body . . . This is my blood of the new Testament." However, eating the blood of an animal is explicitly forbidden in the Jewish scriptures:

> Lev 17:10 And whatsoever man there be of the house of Israel, or of the strangers that sojourn among you, that eateth any manner of blood; I will even set my face against that soul that eateth blood, and will cut him off from among his people.

> Lev 17:11 For the life of the flesh is in the blood: and I have given it to you upon the altar to make an atonement for your souls: for it is the blood that maketh an atonement for the soul.

> Lev 17:12 Therefore I said unto the children of Israel, No soul of you shall eat blood, neither shall any stranger that sojourneth among you eat blood.

Consequently, the Torah is explicit; in fact, there are two penalties for eating blood. Bramer (2010, 17) unequivocally and vividly explains the significance of this offense:

> The double penalty for eating blood, (a) having God's face set personally against the offender, and (b) being cut off (*karet*) from the religious life, constituted the most terrible and terrifying penalty imaginable in Jewish law, and amounted to a cultic death sentence, since it was, in effect, the antithesis of atonement (*kipper*). It cannot be underscored enough that the eating of blood amounted to one of the most potent taboos in the Hebrew cult, to the extent that the very thought or suggestion of consuming blood, even in a figurative sense, would have been met with absolute horror and revulsion by any Jew.

Oddly, in response to Jesus's command, these Jewish disciples, who presumably were familiar with this commandment, were totally silent.

JESUS'S SYMBOLISM OF THE BREAD

Eating human flesh, even symbolically, occurs nowhere in all Jewish tradition. However, Moses warned the people of Israel that if they did not obey God's commandments and statutes that there would come a day of reckoning: "And thou shalt eat the fruit of thine own body, the flesh of thy sons and of thy daughters, which the LORD thy God hath given thee" (Deut 28:53). Therefore, it must be asked, how were the disciples to understand that they were to eat the body of Jesus who was *about* to be put to death? Also, how were they to understand that they were to drink his blood, though not the blood present in his body, but rather his blood that was about to be shed in the near future? (See Jn 6:53-66)

Keener (2009a, 300) writes:

> When Jesus claims that the bread "is" his body he is not claiming any biochemical connection between the two. Presumably he means that the bread "represents" or stands for his body in some sense; the disciples presumably would have understood his words here no more literally than they would have taken the normal interpretation of Passover elements, some of which may have been

in widespread use this early: "This is the bread of affliction that our ancestors ate when they came from the land of Egypt." (By no stretch of the imagination did anyone suppose that they were re-eating the very bread the Israelites had eaten in the wilderness.) Those who ate of this bread participated by commemoration in Jesus' affliction in the same manner that those who ate the Passover commemorated in the deliverance of their ancestors. The language of Passover celebration assumed the participation of current generations in the exodus event.

On the other hand, assuming that Keener is wrong, why did not even one disciple speak up and ask Jesus to clarify this teaching? After all, earlier, in Matthew 16:22, even Peter challenged Jesus when he foretold his death: "Then Peter took him, and began to rebuke him, saying, Be it far from thee, Lord: this shall not be unto thee." Yet here there is not as much as one question being asked.

ABSENCE OF THE SYMBOLIC LAMB

Another reason for questioning the interpretation of the Last Supper is based on the recorded storyline: why did Jesus fail to mention that the lamb symbolized himself if it were really on the table? Furthermore, nowhere in the writings of Paul or the Gospels is the reader informed that Jesus had a lamb slaughtered in the Temple and cooked during the day for their evening meal. Although this may have been a deliberate omission on the part of Paul and the gospel writers, the absence of this highly significant detail should be collectively taken into consideration with regard to the other issues raised in this section.

SPECULATION #10 Jesus Left the Last Supper

Jesus's Last Supper could *not* have been a Passover meal. Christian apologists posit that Jesus fulfilled the Passover typology of the first Passover that is detailed in Exodus 12; it contains or details the events leading up to, including, and following the Last Supper. However, this Christian apologetic is false. According to Exodus 12:22, "and ye shall take a bunch of hyssop, and dip it in the blood that is in the bason, and strike the lintel and the two side posts with the blood that is in the bason; and none of you shall go out at the door of his house until the morning."

In direct contradiction, after eating the supposed Passover meal, Jesus left the house and went out into the garden/valley.

> Mk 14:26 And when they had sung an hymn, they went out into the mount of Olives.

> Mt 26:30 And when they had sung an hymn, they went out into the mount of Olives.

> Lk 22:39 And he came out, and went, as he was wont, to the mount of Olives; and his disciples also followed him.

> Jn 18:1 When Jesus had spoken these words, he went forth with his disciples over the brook Cedron, where was a garden, into the which he entered, and his disciples.

This action of Jesus and his disciples leaving the house is unequivocally against the command recorded in Exodus 12:22 that they must stay inside their dwelling until morning. Therefore, assuming that John and Mark agreed that Jesus was crucified on the fifteenth of Nisan and that the Last Supper was, in fact, the Passover meal, Jesus violated the instructions for the first Passover in Egypt. (Note: The instructions recorded in Exodus 12:22 did not refer to future Passover observances. It was a one-time occurrence. However, if Jesus's life was considered a *fulfillment* (or typology) of the Hebrew Bible, then he was deficient in this requisite.) On the other hand, if Jesus did not violate the command to stay in his dwelling, he must not have been participating in a Passover meal.

SPECULATION #11 Criticisms Identified by Theissen, Merz, and Others

In their text *The Historical Jesus: A Comprehensive Guide* (1998, 426-27; cf. O'Toole 1992, 234; Peake 1920, 215-16; Schweizer 1967, 29-32), Theissen and Merz identify several criticisms of the interpretation of the Last Supper as a Passover meal. In addition to those criticisms previously discussed, they also identify:

1. Leviticus 23—the Passover pilgrimage festival is required to be celebrated annually. "Had Jesus celebrated his farewell meal as a Passover meal, it would have led to the origin of an emphatically

annual meal. However, all Christians celebrate the Lord's supper, which they derived from that last supper, every week (and even more often, cf. e.g., Did. 14.I; Pliny, *Ep.* X, 96, 7; Justin, *Apol.*, I, 67, 3, 7)."

2. Mark 14:55—"Legal proceedings on the Passover would be an offence against the commandment relating to festivals—especially a trial with a death sentence."

3. Mark 15:6—"A Passover amnesty would make sense only if the person freed had an opportunity to take part in the Passover. Nowadays no one would proclaim an amnesty on Christmas Eve and not release those pardoned until 25 December" (cf. Watson [1995, 123] concisely states why the release reported in Mark 15:6 is inherently improbable: "The festival was over.")

4. Mark 15:21—"Simon the Cyrene is coming from the field. Certainly it is not explicitly said that he is returning from work (which was forbidden at festivals), but that would be a natural way to understand the note—especially as he is then conscripted into abhorrent work: he has to bear Jesus' cross."

5. Mark 15:46—"Joseph of Arimathea buys a linen cloth for burying Jesus. It is hard to imagine his finding a merchant to sell him such a thing on a high feast day."

Almost one hundred years earlier, Frederick (1911, 503) offered another rationale as to why Jesus's last meal was not a Passover meal. He pointed out that the law forbade any change in the time and ceremonies of the Passover: "Ye shall keep it in his appointed season: according to all the rites of it, and according to all the ceremonies thereof, shall ye keep it" (Num 9:3). Then, Frederick specifically cited Ex 12:11: the people were required to eat it with "shoes on your feet, and your staff in your hand."

Yet the night that it is claimed Jesus ate the Passover, "the disciples were shoeless when Jesus washed their feet." Frederick wrote: "It is evident that either Jesus and his disciples had no respect for the law, or they did not eat the Passover the night in which he was betrayed."

In addition, Theissen and Merz (1998, 425) identify three differences between Jesus's last meal and the Passover detailed in later rabbinic texts:

1. At the last supper Jesus interpreted for his disciples the symbolism of the bread and wine while they were being distributed. In contrast: "[T]he Passover liturgy interprets the event before the main meal."

2. Jesus provided a general interpretation of both "elements," that is, he interpreted the bread and wine as a whole. In contrast: "[T]he

Passover liturgy interprets only the special nature of the elements: not the bread but the *unleavened* bread."

3. "Jesus makes his disciples drink from one cup." In contrast: "At the Passover meal each has his own cup."

Jocz (1967, 4:609), writing in *The Zondervan Pictorial Encyclopedia of the Bible*, makes an interesting point that is often ignored, one regarding Jeremias's often-cited apologetic. He writes that "Jeremias provides some fourteen features suggestive of a paschal meal (op. cit. pp. 136ff.), yet he admits that from the NT evidence no uniform answer is possible" (TWNT, V, 895ff.). Specifically, in the *Theological Dictionary of the New Testament* (1967, 5:899) he tersely states: "As to the important question whether the Last Supper was a Passover meal the Gospels do not give consistent information. The Synoptics say that it was (Mk 14:12-16 and par.; Lk 22:15), but John seems to place the Last Supper on the night of 13th-14th Nisan, 18:28, cf. 19:14."

Similarly, Eduardo Schweizer (1967, 30-31) devotes an entire text to this topic, *The Lord's Supper According to the New Testament*. In chapter 6, he writes "Was Jesus' Last Meal A Celebration of the Passover?" In rebuttal he offers:

> All this corresponds to the prescribed observance of a Passover night. On the other hand, women also take part in the Passover, and usually a guest blesses the cup. The words of interpretation do not correspond to those spoken at Passover, where for instance the particular meaning of the unleavened bread is expounded. The execution of Jesus on Passover day is not impossible, although it is hard to imagine. Moreover, the Lord's Supper, unlike the Passover, was hardly celebrated only once a year in the earliest church. In fact, according to Acts 20:6 ("but we sailed away from Philippi after the days of Unleavened Bread") and the *Epistle of the Apostles* 15 (26), and among the Quartodecimans, the Passover probably had nothing to do with the Lord's Supper. Red wine was drunk at every festive or otherwise special meal. The reclining position at the table is frequently mentioned in all four Gospels. That the disciples lingered within the confines of the city is not presented as anything unusual in John 18:2, Luke 21:37, 22:39, while John 13:29 is used as a literary device by the evangelist, and does not, therefore, point to a special night on which the poor are to be found on the streets. By and large, the arguments against a Passover meal seem more persuasive, especially the lack of any

reference to the Passover in what are probably the oldest passages in Mark (and in Paul).

Klawans (2001, 29-30) criticizes Jeremias's long list of parallels as they were too general to be decisive. For example, he writes:

1. That Jesus ate a meal in Jerusalem, at night, with his disciples is not so surprising. It is also no great coincidence that during this meal the disciples reclined, ate both bread and wine, and sang a hymn. While such behavior may have been characteristic of the Passover meal, it is equally characteristic of practically any Jewish meal.
2. An ancient Christian church manual called the Didache also suggests that the Last Supper may have been an ordinary Jewish meal. In Chapters 9 and 10 of the Didache, the eucharistic prayers are remarkably close to the Jewish Grace After Meals (*Birkat ha-Mazon*). While these prayers are recited after the Passover meal, they would, in fact be recited at *any* meal at which bread was eaten, holiday or not. Thus, this too underscores the likelihood that the Last Supper was an everyday Jewish meal.

Bornkamm (1960, 161) adds:

1. The Passover lacked "given by the master of the house during the meal with his family."
2. The Passover meal lacked "in remembrance of the past liberation of the people from Egypt."

Falkson (April 25, 2006; cf. Barry Smith 1993, 40-41) elaborates on this latter point and identifies missing elements one would expect to see at a Passover meal:

1. Missing is the quintessential element, namely, that God had ordained an annual commemoration of that momentous time when He freed the Jews from Egyptian slavery.
2. Missing is the pivotal Passover commandment in Exodus 13:8-10 "And thou shalt tell thy son," the story of how we were slaves in Egypt for four hundred years and how we were freed by the mighty hand of God and brought to the land of Israel.

Klawans (2001, 27, 30-31; Barry Smith 1993, 5-6) points out that several Judaic studies scholars such as Jacob Neusner "very much doubt that rabbinic texts can be used in historical reconstructions of the time of Jesus." That is, the parallels "between the Last Supper and the Passover Seder assume that the Seder ritual we know today was celebrated in Jesus' day. But this is hardly the case." He concludes:

> [P]ractically everything preserved in the early rabbinic traditions concerning the Passover Seder brings us back to the time immediately *following* the Roman destruction of the Temple in 70 C.E. It's not that rabbinic literature cannot be *trusted* to tell us about history in the first century of the Common Era. It's that rabbinic literature—in the case of the Seder—does not even *claim* to be telling us how the Seder was performed before the destruction of the Temple.

In a similar vein, Taylor (1953, 666-67) criticizes the use of Rabbinic material as an apologetic. In his text he also refutes many of Jeremias's arguments:

> Of the inconsistencies alleged in the Synoptic Gospels Jeremias collects ten: (1) The journey to Gethsemane; (2) The carrying of arms; (3) The meeting of the Sanhedrin and the condemnation to death; (4) The rending of the high priest's garments; (5) The participation of the Jews in the Roman trial; (6) The coming of Simon of Cyrene ἀπ᾽ ἀγροῦ; (7) The execution; (8) The purchase of the linen; (9) The taking down of the body, the burial, and the rolling of the stone against the door of the tomb; (10) The preparation of spices and ointments. No one has ever advanced all these objections together and they are not all convincing. Jeremias is justified in saying that No. 1 is erroneous, that No. 6 is based on arbitrary assumptions, and that 5 and 7 concern Roman ordinances; but it is doubtful if he can claim more. Nos. 2, 4, 9, 10 are defended as exceptional circumstances or necessities of life covered by Rabbinical decisions. It is, of course, a moot point how far these later decisions were valid in the time of Christ; and the same uncertainty arises when Rabbinical evidence is held to dispose of Nos. 3 and 8 (*zwei ernst zu nehmende Einwände*). It is not said that the linen cloth was obtained by a fictitious purchase, and, as previously maintained (p. 570), it is doubtful if the examination before the priests was an official session with a verdict amounting to a condemnation. Later Rabbinical decisions about the trial of a "false prophet" on a feast day, in the presence of "the whole people," may therefore not be relevant.

But there is a more pertinent objection. We may recognize a certain force when this or that "irregularity" is defended by an appeal to later Rabbinical decisions, but when this argument is repeated six times over, it wears thin. That arms might be borne by the mob and by the disciples on the day of the Passover, that a session of the Sanhedrin might be held on this day, followed by a condemnation and the rending of the high priest's garments, that the burial can be fitted into rules which, while permitting necessary preparations, enjoined that the limbs of the corpse must not be moved (*Shab.* xxiii. 5; Danby, 120), not to speak of the uncertain tradition concerning spices and ointments (Mk. xvi. 1, Jn. xix. 39 f.)—all this is such a remarkable collection of things to be explained, that it is simpler to believe that the Supper preceded the Passover. Jeremias, 34-7, answers Wellhausen's objections . . . While, therefore, it is right to say that the question is not finally settled, probably most British scholars are justified in holding that the Last Supper and the Crucifixion preceded the Passover.

Finally, Keener (2009a, 297) points out: "That Jesus followed the more common practices regarding Passover cannot be proved especially given the uncertain dating of our extant paschal sources." However, he concludes: "But this proposal is likely, especially in view of the correspondences on points that can be tested."

SPECULATION #12 Hints from Luke

Tabor (2006, 200; cf. Peake 1920, 216) suggests that Luke hints that the last meal was not the Passover meal. "In Luke, for example, Jesus tells his followers at that last meal: 'I earnestly want to eat this Passover with you before I suffer but I won't eat it until it is fulfilled in the kingdom of God'" (Luke 22:14-16). A later copyist of the manuscript inserted the word "again" for the passage to read "I won't eat it again" since the tradition developed that Jesus observed Passover that night and changed its observance to the Christian Eucharist or Mass.

SPECULATION #13 No Family Gathering

Tabor (2006, 201; cf. Theissen and Merz 1998, 426) also rejects the last meal as a Passover meal because Jesus's family was not present for the meal.

The Hebrew Bible unequivocally mandates that the Passover is a time when the family is together:

> Ex 12:3 Speak ye unto all the congregation of Israel, saying, In the tenth day of this month they shall take to them every man a lamb, according to the house of their fathers, a lamb for an house:

> Ex 12:4 And if the household be too little for the lamb, let him and his neighbour next unto his house take it according to the number of the souls; every man according to his eating shall make your count for the lamb.

> Ex 12:5 Your lamb shall be without blemish, a male of the first year: ye shall take it out from the sheep, or from the goats:

> Ex 12:6 And ye shall keep it up until the fourteenth day of the same month: and the whole assembly of the congregation of Israel shall kill it in the evening.

> Ex 12:7 And they shall take of the blood, and strike it on the two side posts and on the upper door post of the houses, wherein they shall eat it.

> Ex 12:8 And they shall eat the flesh in that night, roast with fire, and unleavened bread; and with bitter herbs they shall eat it.

> Ex 12:9 Eat not of it raw, nor sodden at all with water, but roast with fire; his head with his legs, and with the purtenance thereof.

Several verses later, Exodus 12:14 reads: "And this day shall be unto you for a memorial; and ye shall keep it a feast to the LORD throughout your generations; ye shall keep it a feast by an ordinance for ever."

Elaborating on the above, Tabor writes:

> Passover is the most family oriented festival in Jewish tradition. As head of his household Jesus would have gathered with his mother, his sisters, the women that had come with him from Galilee, perhaps some of his close supporters in Jerusalem, and his Council of Twelve. It is inconceivable that a Jewish head of a household would eat the Passover segregated from his family with twelve male disciples. This was no Passover meal.

Jeremias (1966, 46-47) offered two apologetics refuting the above charge. First, it is not possible to assume from the biblical text that the women mentioned in Mark 15:40 and Luke 23:49, 55 were excluded. In addition, the size of the table possibly limited the number of people who could have been part of the Last Supper.

The deficiencies here are obvious. First, the texts were written for the readership and listening audience, those living in the first century. On a literal level there is no reason to expect that the audience—then or today—would assume that women were present at the Last Supper. If the writers of the Gospels knew that there were others present, it is practical to speculate that they "would have been included" in at least one narrative. Jeremias's rationale is an argument based on silence and speculation. In addition, his apologetic about the size and seating capacity of the table is also an argument based on silence and mere speculation.

SPECULATION #14 The Logistics Prior to and Following the Passover Refute the Historicity

THE SYNOPTIC GOSPELS

There are several logistical issues that challenge the historicity recorded in the gospel narratives of the events immediately prior to and following the Last Supper. According to the synoptic Gospels, a great multitude (Mk 14:43; Mt 26:47) participated in the arrest of Jesus on the evening of the Passover Seder. Not only the great multitude but *also* the chief priests, the scribes, and the elders are said to have *directly* participated with the apprehension of Jesus.

> Mk 14:43 And immediately, while he yet spake, cometh Judas, one of the twelve, and with him a great multitude with swords and staves, from the chief priests and the scribes and the elders.

> Lk 22:52 Then Jesus said unto the chief priests, and captains of the temple, and the elders, which were come to him, Be ye come out, as against a thief, with swords and staves?

This text contends that such a scenario is not remotely plausible.

Initially, the priests had just completed their busiest day in the year, the fourteenth of Nisan, presiding over and organizing the slaughter of thousands of lambs in the Temple, to say nothing of the obligation to attend their own paschal meal. That very evening, the evening of the Passover meal, they were to leave their families in the dead of night to assist in the arrest of Jesus.

Second, the synoptic Gospels report that the Sanhedrin held two trials immediately after the arrest of Jesus. It is not plausible that the Sanhedrin would have convened twice, once in the night and once in the morning on the fifteenth of Nisan. Now that the evening had started (i.e., the fifteenth of Nisan) and the Passover Seder had commenced, the chief priests and the elders were supposedly going to leave their families in the dead of night to participate in not one, but two trials. Further, those present at the trial were not just the chief priests and elders, the scribes, and members of the Temple guard were also present. Mark 14:55 went so far as to state that this trial occurred in the presence of "all the council," the entire Sanhedrin: "And the chief priests and all the council sought for witness against Jesus to put him to death; and found none." It is totally implausible to believe that between sixty and up to one hundred people would have left their Passover meal, leaving their families and guests in order to participate in two separate trials.

As a side issue, there is the matter of the illegality of Jesus's trial as recorded in the synoptic Gospels (see Breed 1948; Buss 1906; Chandler 1956; Richards & Aiyar, 1915; Wingo 2011):

1. No process could take place on the Jewish Sabbath or on feast days (Lev 23).
2. No process could be started at night or even afternoon for a trial before a regular Sanhedrin court.
3. No process could be brought in a private home, but only in the legal place: the Beth Din for capital offenses.
4. It was a violation of the Torah to convict a man on the testimony of false witnesses (Deut 17:6).
5. It was a violation of the Torah to convict a man without any witnesses (no witnesses in Luke) (Deut 17:6).
6. It was a violation of the Torah to convict a man without any charge (no charge of blasphemy in Luke) (Deut 17:9-10).
7. It was a violation of the Torah to execute a man without a death sentence: the Sanhedrin did not condemn Jesus to death.
8. A sentence could not be pronounced on the basis of an extorted confession.
9. Death sentences could only be pronounced at least twenty-four hours after the interrogation.

Several additional issues also challenge the contention that Jesus was arrested, questioned, and crucified on the fifteenth of Nisan and during the preparation of the Sabbath. If Jesus were arrested after the Passover meal, this event would be occurring on the fifteenth of Nisan, the Day of the Feast and a holy day that forbade work (Lev 23). Yet

1. the arresting party carried weapons on a Feast Day (Mk 14:43; Mt 26:47; Lk 22:52; Jn 18:3),
2. Peter carried a weapon on a Feast Day (Mk 14:47; Mt 27:51; Lk 22:50; Jn 18:10),
3. Simon the Cyrene was coming out of the country/field, implying he was previously performing work (Mk 15:21; Mt 27:32),
4. Simon the Cyrene was coming out of the country/field; however, on the Day of a Feast, those attending could not leave or enter Jerusalem (Mk 15:21; Mt 27:32), and
5. the high priest tore his clothes during the questioning of Jesus (Mk 14:63; Mt 26:65).

JOHN:

Assuming that John's chronology is correct, his narrative complicates matters even further since Jesus's trial would have been held on the fourteenth of Nisan. Therefore, the high priests and other members of the religious hierarchy would be participating in an arrest and attending a trial on the same day as they would be responsible for presiding over the preparation of thousands of Passover lambs.

Smith (1991, 29n1; cf. Geldenhuys 1951, 650-51), writing for the *Westminster Theological Journal*, attempts to resolve the controversy concerning the chronology of the Last Supper. In the first footnote he writes:

> The following is a partial list of scholars who have concluded that there is no satisfactory way of harmonizing the Johannine chronology with that of the synoptics: G. Dalman, *Jesus-Jeskua* (London: SPCK, 1929); S. Zeitlin, "The Last Supper as an Ordinary Meal in the Fourth Gospel," JQR 42 (1951/52) 251-60; id., "The Time of the Passover Meal," ibid., 45-50, which is a response to P. J. Heawood, "The Time of the Last Supper," ibid., 37-44; G. Ogg, "The Chronology of the Last Supper," in *Theological Collections VI: Historicity and Chronology in the New Testament* (London: SGM, 1965) 75-96; R. Pesch, *Das Markusevangelium* (2 vols.; Freiburg: Herder, 1977) 2.323-28; I. H. Marshall, *Lord's Supper and Last Supper* (Exeter Paternoster, 1980) 57-75; R. Brown, *The Gospel according to John* (2 vols.; AB

29-29A; Garden City, NY: Doubleday, 1970) 2.555-58; C. K. Barrett, *The Gospel according to St. John* (2d ed.; Philadelphia: Fortress, 1978); R. Schnackenburg, *Commentary on the Gospel of John* (3 vols.; London: Burn and Oates, 1982) 3.33-47; L. Morris, *The Gospel according to John* (NICNT; Grand Rapids: Eerdmans, 1971) 774-85; E. Haenchen, Λ *Commentary on the Gospel of John* (2 vols.; Philadelphia: Fortress, 1984) 2.178.

Nevertheless, the controversy has yet to be resolved.

Several years earlier, Fitzmyer (1985, 1382), writing in his *The Gospel according to Luke* (X-XXIV), summarizes the results of his research. He concludes that "the upshot is that we cannot answer the question when the historical Jesus ate the Last Supper or whether he ate it as a Passover meal . . . No attempt should be made to harmonize the Synoptic and Johannine traditions."

ISSUE 5: The Day of the Week Jesus Was Crucified: Wednesday, Thursday, or Friday

1 Cor 15:4	Mk 15:42	Mt 12:40	Lk 23:53	Jn 18:28
And that he was buried, and that *he rose again the third day according to the scriptures.*	*And now when the even was come, because it was the preparation, that is, the day before the Sabbath,* 43 Joseph of Arimathea, an honourable counsellor, which also waited for the kingdom of God, came, and went in boldly unto Pilate, and craved the body of Jesus.	For as Jonas was three days and three nights in the whale's belly; *so shall the Son of man be three days and three nights in the heart of the earth.* Mt 27:62 *Now the next day, that followed the day of the preparation,* the chief priests and Pharisees came together unto Pilate.	And he took it down, and wrapped it in linen, and laid it in a sepulchre that was hewn in stone, wherein never man before was laid. 54 *And that day was the preparation, and the sabbath drew on.* 55 And the women also, which came with him from Galilee, followed after, and beheld the sepulcher, and how his body was laid. 56 And they returned, and prepared spices and ointments; *and rested the sabbath day according to the commandment.*	Then led they Jesus from Caiaphas unto the hall of judgment: and it was early; and they themselves went not into the judgment hall, *lest they should be defiled; but that they might eat the passover.* Jn 19:14 *And it was the preparation of the passover,* and about the sixth hour: and he saith unto the Jews, Behold your King! Jn 19:30 When Jesus therefore had received the vinegar, he said, It is finished: and he bowed his head, and gave up the ghost. 31 The Jews therefore, because it was the preparation, that the bodies *should not remain upon the cross on the sabbath day (for that sabbath day was an high day,)* besought Pilate that their legs might be broken, and that they might be taken away.

There is *no* unanimity that Jesus's arrest, trial, and crucifixion occurred on a Friday, although this is the traditional position maintained by the church fathers and scholars throughout Church history. In contrast, several proponents (Aldrich 1870, 401-29; Frederick 1911, 503-09; Haggard 1912, 664-92; Rusk 1974, 4-6; Tabor 2006, 198-201; Westcott 1881, 343-49) advocate a Thursday crucifixion. However, others (Banks 2005; Bullinger 1914, 181-82, 188; Dake 1961, 13r; Gagne 2007, 411-20; Hailey n.d., 1; Lindsey 2012; Scroggie 1948, 569-77; Stewart 1932, 314; Torrey 1969, 1, 22-23) support a Wednesday crucifixion. A Wednesday crucifixion was also popularized by the late Herbert W. Armstrong (1952), the founder of the Worldwide Church of God.

CONTRADICTION #6 The Day of the Week Jesus Was Crucified

How is it possible that the day of one of the most important events in Church history is disputed? Before analyzing the three contested days proposed by their respective advocates, it would be advantageous to review the biblical chronology of the days before, during, and after Passover:

TABLE 8. The Jewish Passover Chronology Based on Exodus 12, Leviticus 23, and Numbers 28

Nisan 14	Nisan 15	Nisan 15	Nisan 16	Nisan 21
The Passover lambs are being slaughtered in the Temple.	The Festival of Unleavened Bread.	The First Day: 1. A solemn assembly. 2. No work shall be done. 3. Only what everyone must eat, that alone may be prepared by you.	The Second Day.	From the evening of the fourteenth day until the evening of the twenty-first day, you shall eat unleavened bread.
6:00 a.m.- 6:00 p.m.	6:00 p.m.- 6:00 a.m.	6:00 a.m.- 6:00 p.m.	6:00 p.m. (Nisan 15) - 6:00 p.m. (the start of Nisan 16)	

A Friday Crucifixion

Church tradition and the consensus of scholars is that Jesus was crucified on Friday. Among the reasons are:

1. Third-day Rationale:

    a. Jesus predicted that he would die and be raised on the third day (Mk 8:31; 9:31; 10:34; Mt 16:21; 17:23; 20:19; 27:64; Lk 9:22; 13:22; 18:33; 24:6-7, 46).
    b. Jesus's body was laid in the tomb on the evening of the day of preparation, which was a Friday.
    c. Jesus's body was laid in the tomb the day before the Sabbath (Mk 15:4; Mt 27:62; 28:1; Lk 23:54, 56; Jn 19:31, 42).
    d. Jesus walked with two disciples on the road to Emmaus (Lk 24:13), and they told him that their Master was crucified and "now it is the third day since this occurred" (Lk 24:21).
    e. The women returned home and rested on the Sabbath (Lk 23:56).
    f. Early on the first day of the week, Sunday, the women went to the tomb (Mk 16:1-2; Mt 28:1; Lk 24:1; Jn 20:1), which was empty.

2. John 19:31 declared that Jesus's body was taken down from the cross on "the day of preparation" to avoid it being there on the Sabbath.
3. The arguments for Wednesday and Thursday are based almost entirely on one interpretation of an isolated verse (Mt 12:40) rather than on the many statements that Jesus would rise the third day.
4. According to the Jewish custom of inclusive reckoning of time, any part of a day was reckoned as an entire day, including the night. Consequently, part of Friday, all of Saturday, and part of Sunday would have been counted as three days (see Gen 42:17; 1 Kgs 20:29; 2 Chron 10:5, 1 Sam 30:12; *y. Shabbat* 9:3; cf. *b. Pesahim* 4a). Therefore, a Friday burial and Sunday morning resurrection would count as three days.
5. Numerous verses of the Christian scriptures (Acts 10:40; 1 Cor 15:4) prove that Jesus was resurrected on "*the third day*" after his death and burial, not after three literal days.
6. Jesus never stated that he would rise up on the fourth day.

A Thursday Crucifixion

TABLE 9. A Thursday Crucifixion Chronology

Nisan 12	Nisan 13	Nisan 14	Nisan 15	Nisan 15	Nisan 16	Nisan 17
Wednesday morning to Wednesday evening.	Wednesday evening until Thursday morning.	Thursday morning until Thursday evening. The Passover lambs are being slaughtered in the Temple.	Thursday evening. The Passover meal after sunset. This timing is based on the Hebrew mode of determining the start of a day.	Thursday morning until Thursday evening.	From Friday evening until Saturday evening. 1. The weekday Sabbath. 2. The second Sabbath [Two Sabbaths back to back].	From Saturday evening until Sunday evening.
	1. Jesus's Last Supper was **NOT** a Passover Seder. 2. Arrest. 3. Jesus's Interrogation and Trial.	1. Interrogation and trial. 2. Crucifixion started at 9:00 a.m. 3. Darkness from noon till 3:00 p.m. 4. At 3 p.m. Jesus died. 5. Burial before sunset.	1. Jesus never ate the Passover meal. 2. Jesus was in the tomb.	1. The [First] Day of Passover was a Sabbath. 2. A holy day. 3. A day of no work. 4. One can only eat unleavened bread. Jesus was in the tomb.	1. Jesus was in the tomb. 2. No work, the weekly Sabbath.	1. Jesus's resurrection took place. 2. The tomb was discovered empty.
Day 6:00 a.m.- 6:00 p.m.	Night 6:00 p.m.- 6:00 a.m.	Day 6:00 a.m.- 6:00 p.m.	Night 6:00 p.m.- 6:00 a.m.	Day 6:00 a.m.- 6:00 p.m.	Night 6:00 p.m.- 6:00 p.m.	Night 6:00 p.m.- 6:00 p.m.

Proponents of a Thursday crucifixion primarily rest their case on Matthew 12:40: Jesus lay in the heart of the earth for three days *and* three nights. A Thursday crucifixion allows for three full nights, two full days, and a portion of the third day in a tomb. Significantly:

1. Jesus's triumphal entry on Palm Sunday, Nisan 10, fulfills the Old Testament typology of a Passover lamb being selected, namely Jesus himself.
2. The Last Supper was on Wednesday evening. Consequently, this chronology eliminates the silent Wednesday of the traditional Friday view.
3. Jesus, the Passover (paschal) lamb, was crucified on Thursday.
4. Friday, Nisan 15 was the first day of unleavened bread, a day of no work (Lev 23:7) and consequently thought to be "the Sabbath of the Passover." If Nisan 15 fell on any other day than the weekly Sabbath, it would have been called the Sabbath of Passover.
5. In the year that Jesus was crucified, the Passover Sabbath, Nisan 15, fell on Friday, and then the weekly Sabbath followed on the next day. Therefore, there were two Sabbath*s* back to back. Significantly, Matthew 28:1 has the Greek word for Sabbath written in the plural. Therefore, the literal rendering should read "at the end of the Sabbaths."
6. Jesus was buried on Thursday to avoid profaning this "Sabbath," that is, the Passover Sabbath, not the seventh day of the week's Sabbath.

For biblical literalists, Jesus's prophecy, recorded in Matthew 12:40, that he would lie in the heart of the earth for three days *and* three nights rejects any possibility of a Friday afternoon burial and Sunday morning resurrection. Aldrich (1870, 401-02) argues: "He [[Matthew]] foreknew the controversy that would arise in regard to the interval between his death and resurrection; that the term 'three days and three nights' would be understood literally, and that if the period between his death and resurrection did not correspond it would produce scepticism and caviling among the enemies of the truth."

Aldrich (1870, 404-07) also maintains that if Jesus was crucified on a Friday, it would have been impossible to bury him before the start of the Jewish Sabbath and again fulfill the literal three days and three nights of being buried in the tomb:

1. Jesus's death did not take place until after the ninth hour or three o'clock in the afternoon (Matt. xxvii. 46-50).
2. Before Jesus was taken down, Joseph went to Pilate and begged the body of Jesus.

3. Matthew 27:57 and Mark 15:42 reported that Joseph went to Pilate as "the even" was coming. The original word in both these instances, translated "even," *is* ὀψίας. This, in its proper or literal sense, Robinson (New Testament Greek Lexicon) says, signifies "late evening." The Jews reckoned two evenings, one commencing at three o'clock, and the other, it is believed, at five. The word sometimes, we admit, is used to denote the former evening, but it cannot in this instance since Christ did not die until after the first evening had commenced. In Lange's commentary (on Luke, p. 383 of the American edition), it is said: "In all probability we have to understand the late Friday afternoon, between five and six o'clock. Ἐπέφωσκε (the word translated 'drew on') signifies here the dawning, not of the natural, but of the legal Saturday." Joseph then could not have gone to Pilate until five o'clock or after. In going to Pilate, in all probability, they went to the praetorium, or governor's house; and whether this was the palace of Herod, or more probably the fortress Antonia, and whether the place of Christ's crucifixion was that assigned by Christian tradition or not, since it was without the walls of the city, it must have been some distance between the two places. And as Pilate before giving permission called to him (sent for) the centurion, to ascertain if Christ was already dead, this distance must have been traveled over four times: twice by Joseph, in going and returning, once by the messenger sent by Pilate, and once by the centurion. The time thus occupied—and in taking down the body of Jesus, wrapping it in linen with the spices, and laying it in the sepulchre— could not reasonably be supposed to have been less than an hour, and this would bring it to six o'clock, which would have been the beginning of Saturday...

We have shown that the body of our Saviour cannot reasonably be supposed to have been laid in the sepulchre before six o'clock, and this, on the assumption that he was crucified on Friday, would have been the beginning of Saturday. So that, as he rose on the morning of the first day his body could have lain in the grave only on Saturday and a part of Sunday, and hence, he must have risen on the second and not the third, according to the scripture...

In addition, Carl Johnson (2007) posits:

1. Mark 15:34-37 confirms that Jesus was alive in the ninth hour (3 pm). He Died AFTER that, in Mark 15:37. Then Mark 15:42

indicates that the sun has set, which begins the next official Hebrew day. The KJAV is actually more accurate on this point than the NIV, in that the Greek word *ede* (now) is correctly translated "has become, already, even now, by this time." *It even says that THIS new day was the day before the Sabbath.* Mark 15:43 says that Joseph of Arimathea then went into Pilate, and then all the rest. These Scriptures actually prove that the Crucifixion had to occur on Thursday, but the Lord was interred at the very beginning of Hebrew Friday.

2.   There is further biblical support for this view. The original Greek for Mark 15:42 is usually interpreted: *And now when the even was come, because it was the Preparation, that is, the day before the Sabbath,* but the word *epei* (Strong's #1893) actually has a better interpretation than "because," that of "for then" or "thereupon," pointing out that the change of days had occurred. Using this meaning, Mark 15:42 is: *And now when the even was come, for then it was the Preparation, that is, the day before the Sabbath, or, in modern terms:*
And now that the sun sets, Preparation Day begins, that is, the day before the Sabbath.

3.   There would be only three hours and thus insufficient time (between 3:00 p.m. and sunset at 6:00 p.m.) for Joseph of Arimathea to have completed his task.

4.   *Since Jesus was actually interred at the beginning of the Hebrew Friday, it is understandable that Friday became associated with the Crucifixion.* Since the development of modern clocks a few hundred years ago, society came to have an accurate way of identifying the moment of midnight. Most societies chose to change to using midnight as the moment of the change from one day to the next mostly out of convenience because most people were sleeping then and each wakeful period then represented one day for the majority of people.

This alteration on the understanding of when each day begins simplified daily life, but it had a consequence. This means that the evening hours (from sunset to midnight) are now considered to be part of a different day than they were in ancient times. This has caused an element of confusion that affected our understanding of that very important day in Christian history.

For the fifteen hundred years prior to that change, it was correct and proper to honor Good Friday, since He was interred at the beginning of Hebrew Friday; and the rest of the civilized world understood the same day structure (beginning at sunset), so Good Friday became a firmly established tradition. When this alteration of the clock and calendar was instituted a few hundred years ago, those six hours (from sunset to midnight on the beginning of Hebrew Friday) became the LAST six hours of what we now call Thursday! However, the tradition of Good Friday already had around 1,500 years of recognition behind it, and the recognition of it has remained on Friday.

5. It would seem that Hebrew 6-(Friday)—which started at sunset of what is called Thursday and ended at sunset, Friday—and the day before 7-(Sabbath) established so much tradition in the Middle Ages that it was maintained as Friday when the clock technology came into existence. This change caused a slightly different translation of that scripture, which neglected the proper understanding of Mk 15:42 (that of the moment of the change of day) and the potentially confusing fact that the actual Crucifixion had occurred on 5- (Thursday).

Tabor (2006, 199-201) also advocates a Thursday crucifixion. He argues that the last meal Jesus participated in occurred on Wednesday night and was not the Passover meal. By 3:00 p.m., Thursday, he was dead. Tabor writes:

> The confusion arose because all the gospels say that there was a rush to get his body off the cross and buried before sundown because the "Sabbath" was near. Everyone assumed the reference to the Sabbath had to be Saturday—so the crucifixion must have been on a Friday. However, as Jews know, the day of Passover itself is also a "Sabbath" or rest day—no matter what weekday it falls on. In the year AD 30 Friday, the 15th of the Jewish Nisan was also a Sabbath—so *two* Sabbaths occurred back to back—Friday *and* Saturday. Matthew seems to know this as he says that the women who visited Jesus' tomb came early Sunday morning "after the Sabbaths"—the original Greek is plural (Matt 28:1).

Finally, another reason why the Crucifixion could not have taken place on Friday is based on a Jewish principle regarding the Jewish calendar system known as Lo Badu Pesach, which means that the first day of Pesach cannot fall on Monday, Wednesday or Friday. Weiss (1904, 70) writes:

> Another reason why the crucifixion may not have taken place at all is the fact that the first day of Passover never falls on Friday, for the reason that if the first day of Passover would happen on Friday,

Hoshanah Rabbah, or the seventh day of the Feast of Booths, would have to be on Saturday, the Jewish Sabbath, on which day it were forbidden to gather brook willows necessary for the ceremony on that day as prescribed by rabbinic law, hence the almanac system has been so arranged that the first day of Passover never occurs on Friday, whilst the crucifixion has taken place on Friday, which was the first day of Passover. That is evident from the fact that Jesus and his disciples celebrated it the previous night according to Jewish customs, who celebrate their Sabbaths and feasts from eve to eve (see Lev. xxiii., 32, and for Passover Numb. xxviii, 16, 17).

The Torah Learning Resources (2010) further elaborates:

The reason why the Rabbis ordained that Pesach cannot fall on these days is because if Pesach would fall on Monday, Wednesday or Friday, then the first day of Rosh Hashanah would fall on Sunday, Wednesday or Friday. And the Rabbis wanted to prevent these scenarios because of their ramifications regarding Yom Kippur: if the first day of Rosh Hashanah falls on Wednesday, then Yom Kippur falls on Friday, and if Rosh Hashanah falls on Friday, then Yom Kippur falls on Sunday. Either situation—where Yom Kippur falls on Friday or Sunday—would pose considerable difficulty, and the Rabbis therefore arranged the calendar in such a way that this could never happen.

Then, The Torah Learning Resources adds: "It should be noted that these rules took effect only when the Rabbis established the fixed calendar system that we use today. In ancient times, however, when new months were declared based upon testimony to the sighting of the new moon, the Rabbis allowed Pesach to fall on Monday, Wednesday or Friday."

In response to the advocated Thursday crucifixion, Brown (1994a, 2:1351) and Hoehner (1974b, 244-46) note:

1. It is doubtful that anyone would hold to a Thursday timeline if not for Matthew 12:40.
2. There is nothing to prevent Jesus's triumphal entry into Jerusalem to have occurred on Monday.
3. There is no precedent for thinking of Friday as a special Sabbath. "The day of preparation for the Passover" in John 19:31 did not need to refer to the day before Passover. Rather, it could refer to Passover

itself e.g., John 19:31, 42, which speaks of the day of preparation and the Sabbath.

4. New Testament scholar Leon Morris points out in his *The Gospel according to John* (1971, 776-77, 800) that there is no evidence that the phrase indicates the day before the Passover; all clear references to the "day of preparation" refer to Friday.

5. Mark 15:42 exclusively points to "the day of preparation" as being Friday, when he states, "and when the evening had come, because it was the day of preparation, that is, the day before the Sabbath."

6. The term Sabbath is frequently in the plural form (one-third of all its New Testament occurrences) in the New Testament when only one day is in view (p. 245).

A Wednesday Crucifixion

TABLE 10. A Wednesday Crucifixion Chronology Based on John's Nisan 14 Crucifixion

Nisan 11	Nisan 12	Nisan 13	Nisan 14	Nisan 15	Nisan 16	Nisan 17	Nisan 18
Saturday at sunset until Sunday at sunset.	Sunday at sunset until Monday at sunset.	Monday at sunset until Tuesday at sunset.	Tuesday at sunset until Wednesday at sunset.	Wednesday at sunset until Thursday at sunset.	Thursday at sunset until Friday at sunset.	Friday at sunset until Saturday at sunset.	Saturday at sunset until Sunday.
Jesus's triumphal entry into Jerusalem. The lambs were selected on the previous day (Nisan 10).	1. The fig tree incident is recalled. 2. Jesus's prediction (Mt 26: 2) "after two days is the feast of the passover, and the Son of man is betrayed to be crucified"; that is on Thursday the 15th of Nisan.	1. The preparation is made for the observance of the passover. 2. The Supper and the anointing by Mary were probably on this day.	1. There is a Passover meal. 2. The arrest. 3. Interrogation and Trial. 4. Crucified at the sixth hour (12:00 noon?) 5. Darkness from noon till 3:00 p.m. 6. At 3 p.m. Jesus dies. 7. Buried in the tomb before sunset.	1. The day of Passover is a Sabbath. 2. A holy day. 3. A day of no work. 4. Can only eat unleavened bread. 5. In the tomb. 6. Not the weekday Sabbath.	1. The women bought spices to anoint Jesus's body "when the sabbath was past"; that is the Passover Sabbath, not the weekly Sabbath, which was the next day. 2. Nicodemus and Joseph anointed Jesus's body. 3. The tomb is sealed and a guard is set.	1. The Jewish weekly Sabbath. 2. In the tomb.	1. The Resurrection occurs after the sunset on the seventeenth of Nisan. 2. The women discover the empty tomb.
	Night #1 6:00 p.m.– 6:00 p.m.	Night #2 6:00 p.m.– 6:00 p.m.	Night #3 6:00 p.m.– 6:00 p.m.	Night #4 6:00 p.m.– 6:00 p.m.	Night #5 6:00 p.m.– 6:00 a.m.	Night #6 6:00 p.m.– 6:00 a.m.	Night #7 6:00 p.m.– 6:00 p.m.

Proponents of a Wednesday crucifixion primarily rest their case on Matthew 12:40, pointing out that Jesus lay in the heart of the earth for three full nights and three full days in a tomb. Wednesday advocates acknowledge that it is recognized that Jews reckon any part of a day as a whole day. However, when nights are mentioned, as well as days, then the phrase "three days and three nights" ceases to be an idiom. In addition, Wednesday proponents argue:

1. Given a Friday crucifixion, there would be only three hours and thus insufficient time between 3:00 p.m. and sunset at 6:00 p.m. for Joseph of Arimathea to have completed his task.
2. A Wednesday crucifixion would permit the lamb to be selected on the tenth of Nisan.
3. The triumphant entry of Jesus as the Lamb of God would take place in Jerusalem on Saturday, Nisan 10. This would be possible since Bethany was a Sabbath day's journey from Jerusalem (Acts 1:12; cf. Lk 24:50).
4. The Gospels tell us that on the evening before Jesus was condemned and crucified, he kept the Passover with his disciples (Mk 14:16-17; Mt 26:19-20; Lk 22:13-15). This means that Jesus was crucified on the Passover day. According to Leviticus 23:5-6, the day after the Passover is a separate festival, the Feast of Unleavened Bread. Furthermore, the first day of this feast is "a holy convocation" on which "no customary work" is to be done (verse 7). This day is the first of God's annual Sabbaths, and this is the "high day" of which John 19:31 wrote.
5. The Sabbath referred to in Mark 15:42 and Luke 23:54 was the regular weekly Sabbath.
6. Luke 24:21, in the Emmaus episode, is mistranslated and misunderstood in that Sunday was the third day since the Crucifixion. For example:

   KJV: But we trusted that it had been he which should have redeemed Israel; and besides all this, to day is the third day since these things were done.

   NKJV: But we were hoping that it was He who was going to redeem Israel. Indeed, besides all this, today is the third day since these things happened.

NASB: But we were hoping that it was He who was going to redeem Israel. Indeed, besides all this, it is the third day since these things happened.

Wednesday proponents posit:

The Greek word for "since" after "the third day" in Luke 24:21 actually means "away from." Away from is the same as our "after." Yeshua died late on a Wednesday afternoon and was laid in the grave at sundown on Wednesday as Thursday was beginning. He was in the grave 3 days and 3 nights on Wednesday night, Thursday night, and Friday night and Thursday day, Friday day, and Saturday day using our reckoning of days and nights. He rose as the Sabbath was ending. So He was in the grave 3 days and 3 nights and rose after 3 days and 3 nights while the Sabbath was ending. So He rose on the third day. Sunday is therefore the 4th day. The actual literal Greek translation of Luke 24:21 is:

But surely also together with all these things, it brings a third day away from which all these things occurred.

Translators take the cumbersome literal translation and make it flow, taking some liberty with it, but trying to retain accuracy. The 4th day is "away from" the third day. So it is apparent that the verse is literally saying they were walking and talking after the third day, which was Sunday. However, have other translators understood this point too? Yes. Let's look at 3 of them (Luke 24:21).

Moffatt Translation—by James Moffatt but he is dead, and that is three days ago!

The New Berkeley Version in Modern English—Gerrit Verkugl Moreover, three days have already passed, since all these events occurred.

The Syriac New Testament Translated Into English From The Peshitto Version—James Murdock... and lo, three days have passed since all these things have occurred.

The Syriac Reading can be confirmed by 2 of the oldest manuscripts in Estrangelo Aramaic: the Sinaitic Palimpset and the Curetonian Syriac.

There is exceedingly ample evidence that the correct translation for Luke 24:21 is that the KJV should read, "*today is* after the third day *since these things were done.*" As the information above shows, the oldest and multiple original manuscripts show that "away from" is the correct word for since, and shows us that they were talking about Sunday being the 4th day since Yeshua was laid in the grave. That troubled them, because He has clearly said many times that He would rise on the third day, after 3 days and 3 nights. He would fulfill the sign of Jonah, as Jonah was 3 days and 3 nights in the great fish, so Yeshua would be 3 days and 3 nights in the heart of the earth. These two disciples were challenged in their faith, because it appeared that Jesus' many prophecies concerning His being raised from the dead had failed. They were going back to Emmaus in defeat, when a stranger joined them. (Roy A. Reinhold n.d., Jesus [Yeshua] was Crucified on a Wednesday Afternoon)

In support of the notion that Jesus arose on Saturday evening, as stated above, it is relevant to note that "Bishop Gregory of Tours (538-594), although believing in a Sunday resurrection, noted that many believed Jesus rose *on the seventh day of the week*, stating, 'In our belief the resurrection of the Lord was on the first day, and *not on the seventh as many deem*'" (Seiglie 2006).

Yet another set of rationales for a Wednesday crucifixion is based on the idea that there were two Sabbaths; this concept is similar to Thursday proponents. First, there are the regular seventh day Sabbaths; that is, the weekday Sabbath observed from sunset Friday to sunset Saturday. Second, there are seven holy convocations or annual Sabbath days detailed in Leviticus 23.

According to Wednesday proponents,

1. the first Sabbath was a "high day"—the first day of the Feast of Unleavened Bread, which fell on a Thursday; and
2. the second Sabbath was the weekly seventh-day Sabbath.

The Chronology of Jesus's Crucifixion and Resurrection

- Wednesday, the fourteenth of Nisan:

Jesus ate an evening Passover meal with his disciples at the beginning of Nisan 14 (the biblical reckoning: Tuesday evening) and instituted the New Covenant symbols (Mt 26:26-28). Jesus was then betrayed by Judas, arrested, and during the night brought before the high priest Caiaphas. Jesus was crucified and died around the ninth hour or 3:00 p.m. (Mt 27:46-50). This was the preparation day for the annual, not the weekly, Sabbath, which began at sunset (Mk 15:42; Lk 23:54; Jn 19:31). Later, Jesus's body was placed in the tomb just before sunset (Mt 27:57-60).

- Thursday, the fifteenth of Nisan:

This was the high-day Sabbath, the first day of Unleavened Bread (Jn 19:31; Lev 23:4-7). It is described as the day *after* the Day of Preparation (Mt 27:62).

- Friday, the sixteenth of Nisan:

Now that the high-day Sabbath was past, the women bought and prepared spices for anointing Jesus's body before they rested on the weekly Sabbath day, which began at sunset Friday (Mk 16:1; Lk 23:56). On this day Jesus's body was anointed and wrapped by Nicodemus and Joseph. Later, the tomb was sealed and set by a guard.

- Saturday, the seventeenth of Nisan:

The women rested on the weekly Sabbath, according to the fourth commandment based on the Jewish means of reckoning. In contrast, the command to observe the Sabbath is a commandment for Jews (Lk 23:56; Ex 20:8-11). Jesus rose near sunset, exactly three days and three nights after burial, fulfilling the sign of Jonah and authenticating the sign that he gave of his identify.

- Sunday, the eighteenth of Nisan:

The women brought the prepared spices early Sunday morning while it was still dark (Lk 24:1; Jn 20:1). They were informed that Jesus had already risen (Mk 16:2-6; Mt 28:1-6; Lk 24:2-3). Therefore, Jesus did not rise on Sunday morning but near sunset the day before.

Hoehner (1974b, 242-43) rejects the possibility of a Wednesday crucifixion. His arguments include the following:

1. The Wednesday hypothesis is based primarily on one verse of scripture, Matthew 12:40.
2. To the contrary, the three days and three nights are, in fact, employed with any part of a day as a whole day.
3. A literal Wednesday crucifixion would result in Jesus rising from the tomb no later than 6:00 p.m. on Saturday evening. Christians celebrate the Resurrection on the first day of the week (Acts 20:7; 1 Cor 16:2) and not on the Sabbath.
4. A Wednesday crucifixion would mean that Jesus entered Jerusalem on Saturday, the Sabbath. The gospel narratives would have two laws broken: (1) Jesus would be riding on an animal, yet Deuteronomy 5:14 instructs that even animals were not to work on the Sabbath, and (2) the people were cutting down branches from trees (Mk 11:8; Mt 21:8) in violation of the Torah (cf. Num 15:32-36; Deut 5:14).
5. Those who maintain that Jesus was crucified and died on Wednesday and was raised on Saturday violate the literalness of three days and three nights—that is, seventy-two hours—by having four days and three nights.

Sigal (2012, 168-71) presents another set of rationales for refuting the Wednesday crucifixion theory.

1. Why did the women fail to anoint the body on Friday? There was no reason to wait two more days until Sunday.
2. "Had there been a Wednesday crucifixion the women visiting the tomb Sunday morning would have arrived three and one-half days (four days according to Jewish reckoning) after Jesus died."
3. If Jesus died and was buried on Wednesday afternoon, then in accordance with Jewish time reckoning whereby a part of a day is counted as a whole day; he was buried for four days and three nights."
4. If the "three days and three nights" of Matthew 12:40 refers to an exact seventy-two-hour period beginning Wednesday afternoon, Jesus must have risen no later than before sunset on Saturday afternoon. This would allow time on Wednesday afternoon for Joseph of Arimathea to request the body, Pilate to verify that Jesus was dead, and for Joseph to retrieve and bury the corpse before the onset of the festival. Then Jesus would have to rise from the dead exactly at the end of the seventy-two-hour period of time. If the

resurrection occurred any sooner, it could not be a full seventy-two hours; and if it occurred any later, it would have been part of the fourth day after the crucifixion. According to those who hold to a Wednesday crucifixion, the resurrection event would have occurred on the Sabbath, yet Christianity from its inception has celebrated the resurrection on the first day of the week (Acts 20:7; 1 Cor 16:2) and not on the Sabbath. Is the New Testament teaching a false doctrine?

SPECULATION #15 Calendars and Methods of Dating

One broad category of Christian apologetics pertains to the calendars and methods of dating the Last Supper. First, Finegan (1998, 355; and see Beckwith 1989, 199-201) attempts to reconcile the dating contradiction by positing that John used another calendar and agreed with the gospels but just worked out time differently. Such a calendar at Qumran suggests that Wednesday was the first day of Passover.

Second, there was a difference in dating between Palestine and the Diaspora. Therefore, "in Palestine the beginning of the month was determined by observation of the new moon, but perhaps in the Dispersion a fixed calendar was in use" (Finegan 1998, 356 #610).

Third, another possible difference was because of an alternate way of reckoning the day: "Jesus and his disciples, who came from Galilee, followed an old custom and counted the day as beginning at sunrise" (Finegan 1998, 356-57 #611). Elaborating on this point, Mershman, writing in *The Catholic Encyclopedia* (1912, 357), states:

> Jews calculated their festivals and Sabbaths from sunset to sunset: thus the Sabbath began after sunset on Friday and ended at sunset on Saturday. This style is employed by the synoptic Gospels, while St. John, writing about twenty-six years after the destruction of Jerusalem, when Jewish law and customs no longer prevailed, may well have used the Roman method of computing time from midnight to midnight.

The obvious problem with this argument is simple: there is *no* indisputable evidentiary proof that the author of John employed such a rationale; this is another argument based on silence. As a matter of fact, Josephus reports that the Temple followed Pharisee law. In addition, Jocz (1976, 609), writing in *The Zondervan Pictorial Encyclopedia of the Bible*, explains: "There is no evidence that the Sadducees, who had the oversight of the Temple, ever compromised on so important an issue as to allow two different dates." Furthermore, to the contrary, John's "Lamb of God" motif and agenda unmistakably supersedes any such explanation (discussed below). Evaluating the first three theories, Finegan (1998, 357 #613)—former professor emeritus of New Testament and Archeology at the Pacific School of Religion in Berkeley, California, scholar, preacher, and one of the world's foremost experts on biblical chronology— firmly notes, "The foregoing attempts at reconciliation between the Synoptics and the Fourth Gospel are relatively unconvincing."

SPECULATION #16 The Day of Preparation

Another Christian apologetic discussed by Archer (1982, 376) and Beckwith (1989, 203-04) is that John recorded that Jesus died on the Day of Preparation; technically the Day of Preparation was the eve of Passover, which fell on Friday. Therefore, this meant that Jesus died on Thursday. Consequently, the Day of Preparation was just the name for the two feasts together. Thus, Jesus could have died the day after the literal Day of Preparation; the Passover day, Friday, for common usage, fused the two feasts for shortness. However, it should be mentioned that traditional proponents of the Resurrection would reject the notion that Jesus died on Thursday (e.g., Lk 24:21; see Hoehner 1974b, 246). Furthermore, scholars concur that John was writing for non-Jews, and he would have used the calendar which would have plotted Jesus on the cross on Friday.

Akin (1997) posits that a further possibility is that the Day of Preparation does not mean the day of preparing for the Passover. Specifically, it is argued that in the first century, "the day of preparation meant 'the day to prepare for the Sabbath,' in other words, Friday." There are also several problems with this argument:

- There are no means to know what the author of John had in mind.
- There is no proof that the author of John had this intention.
- There is no proof that the phrase "the preparation of the Passover" in John 19:14 refers to words used by first century Jews in reference to the Sabbath (Friday). This again is merely the opinion of the proponent and an argument from silence.
- The text unequivocally explains that the preparation was "of the Passover." What more could the final redactor state to make this idea any clearer or comprehensible?

ISSUE 6: The Hour Jesus Was Initially Crucified

Mk 15:25	Mt 27:33 *And when they were*	Lk 23:33 *And when*	Jn 19:14 *And*
And it was the third hour, and they crucified him.	*come unto a place called Golgotha, that is to say, a place of a skull, 34 They gave him vinegar to drink mingled with gall: and when he had tasted thereof, he would not drink. 35 And they crucified him,* and parted his garments, casting lots: that it might be fulfilled which was spoken by the prophet, They parted my garments among them, and upon my vesture did they cast lots.	*they were come to the place, which is called Calvary, there they crucified him,* and the malefactors, one on the right hand, and the other on the left.	*it was the preparation of the passover, and about the sixth hour:* and he saith unto the Jews, Behold your King!
	Mt 27:45 *Now from the sixth hour there was darkness over all the land unto the ninth hour.*	Lk 23:44 And it was about the sixth hour, and there was a darkness over all the earth until the ninth hour.	

Mark stated that Jesus was crucified at the third hour. Matthew omitted any mention of when the Romans started crucifying Jesus. Luke omitted a direct time reference to the initiation of the Crucifixion. Finally, John too omitted any direct information detailing when the Crucifixion was initiated.

CONTRADICTION #7 John Contradicts Mark

John contradicted Mark regarding the timing of the Crucifixion. Mark specifically declared that Jesus was crucified at the third hour and thus at 9:00 a.m. This timing is based on the fact that the Jewish day started at 6:00 a.m. (i.e., sunrise), which was the first hour. Therefore, 3 (the third hour) plus 6 would be the equivalent of 9:00 a.m. in the modern time frame. Later, Mark 15:33 reports that there was darkness over the whole land from the sixth hour until the ninth hour, when Jesus died. Matthew 27:45 omitted Mark's specification and had noon being his first awareness of the time. He calculated: "Now from the sixth hour" that is, 6 plus 6 equals noon. Similarly, Brown (1994a, 2:961) points out that Luke concurs with Matthew and omits "the third hour."

John 19:14 unequivocally contradicts Mark since he had the court proceedings before Pilate *still* in progress at the noon hour: "And it was the preparation of the passover, and about the sixth hour: and he saith unto the Jews, Behold your King!" Consequently, John has Jesus interrogated on "about the sixth hour" while Mark already had Jesus on the cross for three hours. It is impossible that Jesus was being interrogated while at the same time he was already crucified and hanging from the cross.

TABLE 11. Contradictory Timeline of Jesus's Crucifixion

THE SYNOPTICS	JOHN
Jesus was crucified at 9:00 a.m. on the Day of Passover itself and died by 3:00 p.m. that afternoon (Mk 15:25, 29, 34; Mt 27:45-50; Lk 23:44-46).	*Jesus was condemned to death at the sixth hour on the Day of Preparation before the Passover*; crucifixion and death occurred quickly (Jn 19:14, 31, 42).

A review of the literature by Brown (1994a, 2:1352) finds one hypothesis that attempts to harmonize these conflicting accounts: that John did not start his day and first hour at 6:00 a.m. but rather at midnight. Therefore, the third hour would be 3:00 a.m., the sixth hour 6:00 a.m., and the ninth hour 9:00 a.m. In other words, John employed the Roman civil day, reckoned the day from midnight to midnight, as we do today. For example, Archer (1982, 363-64) writes:

> The simple answer to this is that the synoptic writers (Matthew, Mark and Luke) employed a different system of numbering the hours of day to that used by John. The synoptics use the traditional Hebrew system, where the hours were numbered from sunrise (approximately 6:00 a.m. in modern reckoning), making the crucifixion about 9:00 a.m., the third hour by this system.

> John, on the other hand, uses the Roman civil day. This reckoned the day from midnight to midnight, as we do today. Pliny the Elder (*Natural History 2.77*) and Macrobius (*Saturnalia 1.3*) both tell us as much. Thus, by the Roman system employed by John, Jesus' trial by night was in its end stages by the sixth hour (6:00 a.m.), which was the first hour of the Hebrew reckoning used in the synoptics. Between this point and the crucifixion, Jesus underwent a brutal flogging and was repeatedly mocked and beaten by the soldiers in the Praetorium (Mark 15:16-20).

The crucifixion itself occurred at the third hour in the Hebrew reckoning, which is the ninth in the Roman, or 9:00 a.m. by our modern thinking.

This is not just a neat twist to escape a problem, as there is every reason to suppose that John used the Roman system, even though he was just as Jewish as Matthew, Mark and Luke. John's gospel was written after the other three, around AD 90, while he was living in Ephesus. This was the capital of the Roman province of Asia, so John would have become used to reckoning the day according to the Roman usage. Further evidence of him doing so is found in John 21:19: *"On the evening of that first day of the week."* This was Sunday evening, which in Hebrew thinking was actually part of the second day, each day beginning at sunset.

Brown (1994a, 2:1352-53, also see pp. 961-62), in response to this Christian apologetic, writes:

> In the commentary we have seen that such harmonizations are implausible and unnecessary, so that calculation from 6 A.M. should be accepted throughout, even if that leaves the accounts in conflict. It is not demonstratable that any evangelist had a personal, chronologically accurate knowledge of what happened. Most likely they found a time indication like "the sixth hour" (mentioned by all) in the tradition and attached it to different moments in the passion according to their respective dramatic and theological interests.

Similarly, Finegan (1998, 359), writing in his *Handbook of Biblical Chronology*, bluntly writes:

> Converting these hours to our more familiar manner of speaking: after being brought before Pilate early in the morning, Jesus was condemned by Pilate and sent away to crucifixion at about midday, from which time until three o'clock in the afternoon there was darkness over the land; and at three o'clock Jesus breathed his last, leaving time for Joseph of Arimathea to provide burial before the requisite rest of the Sabbath (Luke 23:54; cf. Luke 4:40). In conflict and incompatible with all of the foregoing is only Mark 15:25, "it was the third hour when they crucified him." This means crucifixion at nine o'clock in the morning rather that at

midday. Even if the reckoning were from either of the two other possible starting points of sunset or midnight it would mean nine o'clock in the evening or three o'clock in the morning and be obviously impossible. Therefore, Mark 15:25 and John 19:14 are "plainly irreconcilable" and Mark 15:35 can even be thought to be an "interpolation."

CHAPTER 3

From Crucifixion to Death

ISSUE 7: Mocking Jesus while on the Cross before His Death

| Mk 15:29 *And they that passed by railed on him, wagging their heads, and saying,* Ah, thou that destroyest the temple, and buildest it in three days, 30 *Save thyself, and come down from the cross. 31 Likewise also the chief priests mocking said among themselves* with the scribes, He saved others; himself he cannot save. 32 Let Christ the King of Israel descend now from the cross, that we may see and believe. And they that were crucified with him reviled him. | Mt 27:39 *And they that passed by reviled him, wagging their heads, 40 And saying,* Thou that destroyest the temple, and buildest it in three days, save thyself. If thou be the Son of God, come down from the cross. 41 *Likewise also the chief priests mocking him, with the scribes and elders, said,* 42 He saved others; himself he cannot save. If he be the King of Israel, let him now come down from the cross, and we will believe him. 43 He trusted in God; let him deliver him now, if he will have him: for he said, I am the Son of God. 44 The thieves also, which were crucified with him, cast the same in his teeth. | Lk 23:35 *And the people stood beholding.* And the rulers also with them *derided him, saying,* He saved others; let him save himself, *if he be Christ, the chosen of God.* | Jn 19:1 Then Pilate therefore took Jesus, *and scourged him.* 2 And the soldiers *platted a crown of thorns,* and put it on his head, and they put on him a purple robe, 3 And said, Hail, King of the Jews! and they *smote him with their hands.* |

THE SYNOPTIC ACCOUNTS reported that there were three groups of mockers of Jesus while he was on the cross: the robbers (Mt 27:38, 44); the passersby (Mk 15:29; Mt 27:39-40); and the Jewish leaders (Mk 15:31; Mt 27:41-43; Lk 23:35). This Jewish hierarchy and elite included the chief priests (Mk 15:31; Mt 27:41), the scribes and elders (Mt 27:41), and the rulers (Lk 23:35). John omitted the mocking actions of any of these specific groups. Significantly, in none of the Gospels are the Pharisees mentioned as being present when Jesus was on the cross.

CONTRADICTION #8 Differing Accounts

Several of the gospel narratives presented differing details about the mocking of Jesus. Mark and Matthew basically reported similar accounts. The passersby (1) hurled insults at Jesus, (2) shook their heads, and (3) challenged Jesus to save himself and come down from the cross. They too reported that the chief priests and the scribes mocked Jesus and challenged him to come down from the cross to prove that he was the Christ, the king of Israel (see Mk 1:1) and the Son of God, a favorite phrase of Matthew (see Mt 4:3, 6; 14:33; 27:40, 54). However, Matthew 27:41 added "and elders" to this group. On the other hand, Luke presented a condensed summary of Mark and Matthew. In direct contrast to the synoptic Gospels, John *omitted* any mocking action of the Jewish leadership at the site of Jesus's crucifixion.

SPECULATION #17 Why John Would Not Mention the Chief Priests

John's account did not include mention of the despicable actions of the chief priests, scribes, elders, and rulers on the eve of the Sabbath and the first day of the Passover as detailed in the synoptic accounts. Yet if these highly significant details did, in fact, occur, it seems implausible that John could have been *un*aware of them or if he deliberately omitted reporting them. In addition, it is noteworthy that according to church tradition and many commentators, John was perhaps present at the cross (cf. Jn 19:26-27; 21:24). Why then would John fail to mention the chief priests' presence at Golgotha during Jesus's crucifixion?

The reason for John's failure to mention the presence of the chief priests is because his timeline is based on a Nisan 14 crucifixion chronology when the paschal lambs were being slaughtered; this substantiates his theological agenda that Jesus was the paschal lamb. (N.T. Wright 1996, 555) Consequently, it would make perfect sense for John to omit the presence of the chief priests at the cross during the day that the lambs were to be slaughtered since it would be illogical for them to leave their posts in the Temple on the busiest day of the year. It must be remembered that for the author of John the issue of the date of the Crucifixion was a concern specifically raised:

Jn 19:31 The Jews, therefore, *because it was the preparation*, that the bodies should not remain upon the cross on the sabbath day, (for that sabbath day was an high day) besought Pilate that their legs might be broken, and that they might be taken away.

In contrast, chronologically, it would make perfect sense for the synoptic Gospels to have the Jewish leaders present and mocking Jesus while he was on the cross. For these writers, this mocking would occur on the fifteenth of Nisan, the day *after* their busiest day in the year. Therefore, in the eyes of the synoptic authors, this date would be viable for the Jewish leadership, the chief priests, scribes, and elders to be present in person during the Crucifixion.

ISSUE 8: The Action of the Thieves on the Cross

Mk 15:27	Mt 27:44	Lk 23:32 And there were also two other, malefactors,	Jn 19:18
And with him they crucify two thieves; the one on his right hand, and the other on his left.	The thieves also, which were crucified with him, *cast the same in his teeth.*	led with him to be put to death. 33 And when they were come to the place, which is called Calvary, there they crucified him, and the malefactors, one on the right hand, and the other on the left. Lk 23:39 *And one of the malefactors which were hanged railed on him, saying, If thou be Christ, save thyself and us. 40 But the other answering rebuked him, saying, Dost not thou fear God, seeing thou art in the same condemnation? 41 And we indeed justly; for we receive the due reward of our deeds: but this man hath done nothing amiss.* 42 And he said unto Jesus, Lord, remember me when thou comest into thy kingdom. 43 And Jesus said unto him, Verily I say unto thee, To day shalt thou be with me in paradise.	Where they crucified him, and two other with him, on either side, one, and Jesus in the midst.

Mark, Luke, and John report that Jesus was crucified between two thieves. Matthew provides no details regarding the positioning of the three condemned. Instead, he only narrates that the two malefactors were crucified with Jesus. Neither Mark nor John reports a dialogue among the three. However, Luke reports that one thief was described as having mocked Jesus while on the cross. In contrast, the second thief (1) rebuked the first thief for mocking Jesus, (2) confessed that both thieves were guilty of their crimes, (3) declared that they were receiving a just reward for their offenses, (4) professed that Jesus was innocent, and (5) requested that Jesus remember him when they entered the kingdom. In reply, Jesus promised that on this very day, the fifteenth of Nisan, based on the synoptic Gospels, they would be in paradise.

CONTRADICTION #9 John 20:17 Contradicts Luke 23:43

John 20:17 raised a significant contradiction with Luke 23:43. This verse narrated by John provides details of a noteworthy conversation between Jesus and Mary Magdalene after her second visit to the tomb on Easter Sunday. Jesus said, "Touch me not; for I am not yet ascended to my Father." In contrast, Luke 23:43 records that while on the cross Jesus promised the thief crucified adjacent to him, "To day shalt thou be with me in paradise." However, now, almost three days later, John 20:17 reported from Jesus's own lips that he declared to Mary Magdalene that he had not *yet* ascended to his Father in heaven. What, then, about his promise to the thief next to him that "to day shalt thou be with me in paradise"? Either Jesus ascended to heaven on the day that he and the thief died or he did not.

Christian apologists Smith, Chowdhry, Jepson, and Schaeffer (2014) argue in their "101 Cleared-Up Contradictions in the Bible!" #54:

> Jesus says to the thief on the cross "Today you will be with me in Paradise." This was indeed true. For the thief was to die that same day on earth; but in paradise "today" is any day in this world, as Heaven is outside of time.

> Jesus says to Mary Magdalene, according to the rendering of the King James translation, that he had not yet "ascended" to his Father. However, this could also be rendered "returned" to his Father.

> Jesus was with God, and was God, before the beginning of the world (John 1 and Philippians 2:6-11). He left all his glory and became fully God, fully man. Later, God did exalt Jesus to the highest place once more, to the right hand of Himself (see Acts 7:56). This had not yet taken place in John 20:17. Jesus saying "for I have not yet returned to the Father" does not rule out the possibility that he was in heaven between his death and resurrection in "our time" (although Heaven is outside of time). By way of parallel (albeit an imperfect one), I do go to my original home and the area where I grew up without returning there. Returning as in myself being restored to what was.

However, a more likely understanding of the text has to do with the context. Another way to say, "Do not hold on to me, for I have not ascended to my Father. Go instead to my brothers…", would be, "Do not hang on to me Mary— I have not left you all yet. You will see me again. But now, I want you to go and tell my disciples that I am going to my Father soon, but not yet."

Both Islam and Christianity believe in the resurrection of the body, and both believe in the intermediate state. In Luke, Jesus dies, and his spirit ascended to Paradise (see vs. 46). In John, Jesus has been bodily resurrected, and in that state, he had not yet ascended to the Father.

The time factor makes this somewhat paradoxical but the texts are not mutually exclusive. There is no contradiction.

The above Christian apologetic is pure speculation. First, it is incorrect to believe that the audience that either heard or read this text would assume or even comprehend the notion that "for the thief was to die that same day on earth; but in paradise *today* is any day in this world, as Heaven is outside of time."

Second, rendering the text to "returned to his Father" is mere speculation and a feeble attempt to rationalize the inconvenient truth that there is an apparent contradiction. In speculation #140, this text will present a survey of the literature that reveals at least seventeen different interpretations that attempt to explain the meaning of this passage. The bottom line is that nobody knows what this passage means.

The third argument that *Jesus is God* is refuted by the Bible. To the contrary, Jesus is not God in the absolute sense. Hosea 11:9 reads, "I will not execute the fierceness of mine anger, I will not return to destroy Ephraim: for I am God, and not man; the Holy One in the midst of thee: and I will not enter into the city" (cf. Num 23:19; 1 Sam 15:29).

Finally, there is no incontrovertible evidentiary proof that Luke and John believed or espoused different views that one writer was talking about the spirit and the other about a bodily resurrection. Again, this is mere conjecture, guesswork, and speculation. How do these Christian apologists know what Luke or John meant? And where is their incontrovertible evidentiary truth? Contradicting Christian apologists, everyday experience demonstrates that the meaning of biblical verses is open to a variety of interpretations. For example, Geddert (1989, 141-43) identified thirty-five interpretations potential meanings of the Temple's veil being torn as Jesus was on the cross (Mk 15:38; Mt 27:51; Lk 23:45).

CONTRADICTION #10 Significant Omissions of Luke's Narrative in Three Gospels

The gospel narratives present significantly differing details about the thieves on the cross. At first appearance, the details in Mark, Luke, and John read virtually the same: there are two thieves being crucified along with Jesus. However, in Matthew an additional and significant fact is provided that *both* thieves also taunted Jesus.

> Mt 27:44 In the same way the robbers who were crucified with him also heaped insults on him. (NIV)

> Mt 27:44 The bandits who were crucified with him also taunted him in the same way. (NRSV)

> Mt 27:44 The robbers who had been crucified with Him were also insulting Him with the same words. (NASB)

Luke's narrative reads like a completely different story: "And one of the malefactors which were hanged railed on him, saying, If thou be Christ, save thyself and us. But the other answering rebuked him, saying, Dost not thou fear God, seeing thou art in the same condemnation?" Now only *one* thief is taunting Jesus whereas before there were two.

However, more importantly, there is the fundamental issue as to why Luke's account differed so much from Mark's and Matthew's. There is a consensus among Christian scholars and theologians that Luke was a historian and was dependent on Mark, Matthew, and other sources to write his gospel. Luke unequivocally stated in his prologue (Lk 1:4) that he investigated everything carefully from the very first. Yet Luke does not agree with Matthew. Matthew stated categorically that *both* thieves taunted Jesus, whereas Luke reported that just *one* thief did. Acknowledging the scholarly consensus that Luke was dependent on Matthew, why did Luke refuse to accept and believe Matthew's account? As will be seen throughout this text, Luke rejected Matthew's historical narratives many times.

Beyond that, Luke reported that part of verses 39 through 43 were found in neither Mark nor Matthew. Where then did Luke obtain his material? On the other hand, given that the event is historical, would it have been possible for Mark, Matthew, and John to be unaware of this tradition? Furthermore, it is not reasonable to expect that three authors would agree to omit such important details from their narratives assuming they knew the tradition.

CONTRADICTION #11 The Viability of the Dialogue

The dialogue between the penitent thief and the unrepentant thief is dubious. Over a century ago, Keim (1873, 157), a liberal German theologian, inquired:

> "How could the robber know anything of the innocence of Jesus or of his return as king?" Jesus was arrested at night and immediately taken for examination by the chief priest, the elders, and the scribes. Afterward, Jesus was brought before Pontius Pilate for an examination. However, Pilate decided to send Jesus off to Herod because Jesus was a Galilean. After Herod interrogated Jesus, he was once again sent back to Pilate. Pilate examined Jesus and eventually proclaimed his innocence. However, at no time were these thieves present at any of the interrogations or trials. Consequently, they did not have any access to the conversations between Jesus and Pilate or the Jewish leadership. Instead, the two thieves were locked up in prison. Therefore, it would have been impossible for Luke's thief to declare (23:41), "But this man hath done nothing amiss."

ISSUE 9: What Did Jesus Say before He Died?

Mk 15:34 And at the ninth hour Jesus cried with a loud voice, saying, Eloi, Eloi, lama sabachthani? which is, being interpreted, My God, my God, why hast thou forsaken me? 35 And some of them that stood by, when they heard it, said, Behold, he calleth Elias. 36 And one ran and filled a spunge full of vinegar, and put it on a reed, and gave him to drink, saying, Let alone; let us see whether Elias will come to take him down. 37 *And Jesus cried with a loud voice*, and gave up the ghost.	Mt 27:46 And about the ninth hour Jesus cried with a loud voice, saying, Eli, Eli, lama sabachthani? that is to say, My God, my God, why hast thou forsaken me? 47 Some of them that stood there when they heard that, said, this man calleth for Elias. 48 And straightway one of them ran, and took a spunge, and filled it with vinegar, and put it on a reed, and gave him to drink. 49 The rest said, Let be, let us see whether Elias will come to save him. 50 Jesus, when *he cried again with a loud voice*, yielded up the ghost.	Lk 23:46 *And when Jesus cried with a loud voice*, he said, Father, into thy hands I commend my spirit: and having said thus, he gave up the ghost.	Jn 19:30 When Jesus therefore had received the vinegar, *he said, It is finished*: and he bowed his head, and gave up the ghost.

Tradition ascribes seven sayings to Jesus while on the cross; that is counting Mark 15:34 and Matthew 27:46 as one saying. However, no gospel records all of them, although each records some of Jesus's sayings. Mark and Matthew had one saying, Luke had three, and John had three. From 9:00 a.m. until about noon, Jesus is recorded to have uttered three sayings. Tables 12 and 13 provide a chronology of the seven sayings, and table 14 presents an analysis of the collected verses recorded in each gospel.

TABLE 12. Chronology of Jesus's Seven Sayings—Morning

Lk 23:34 Father, forgive them; for they know not what they do.
Lk 23:43 Verily I say unto thee, To day thou shalt be with me in paradise.
Jn 19:26-27 Woman, behold thy son . . . Behold thy mother!

From noon to 3:00 p.m. the narratives seem to present two differing accounts of Jesus's last moments. Sequentially, the relevant verses are seen below:

TABLE 13. Chronology of Jesus's Seven Saying—Noon

Mk 14:34 Eloi, Eloi, lama sabachthani? which is, being interpreted, My God, my God, why hast thou forsaken me?
Mt 27:46: Eli, Eli, lama sabachthani? that is to say, My God, my God, why hast thou forsaken me?
Jn 19:28 I thirst.
Jn19:30 It is finished.
Lk 23:46 Father, into thy hands I commend my spirit.

TABLE 14. The Collected Verses of Jesus's Seven Sayings from Each Gospel

Mark	1. Mk 14:34 Eloi, Eloi, lama sabachthani? which is, being interpreted, My God, my God, why hast thou forsaken me?
	2. Mk 14:37 And Jesus cried with a loud voice [Note: *But his words were not recorded.*]
Matthew	1. Mt 27:46 Eli, Eli, lama sabachthani? that is to say, My God, my God, why hast thou forsaken me?
	2. Mt 27:50 Jesus, when he cried again with a loud voice, yielded up the ghost. [Note: *But his words were not recorded.*]

Luke	1. Lk 23:34 Father, forgive them; for they know not what they do.
	2. Lk 23:43 Verily I say unto thee, To day thou shalt be with me in paradise.
John	1. Jn 19:26-27 Woman, behold thy son . . . Behold thy mother!
	2. Jn 19:28 I thirst.
	3. Jn19:30 It is finished.

Smith, Chowdhry, Jepson, and Schaeffer (n.d.), in "Cleared-Up Contradictions in the Bible," state in their contradiction #75:

> What were the last words of Jesus before he died?' is the question asked by Shabbir in this supposed contradiction. This does not show a contradiction any more than two witnesses to an accident at an intersection will come up with two different scenarios of that accident, depending on where they stood. Neither witness would be incorrect, as they describe the event from a different perspective. Luke was not a witness to the event, and so is dependent on those who were there. John was a witness. What they are both relating, however, is that at the end Jesus gave himself up to death.

The often-repeated Christian apologetic of several witnesses to an accident at an intersection is bogus and fallacious. Luke was not a witness, and John's presence is questionable. The narratives were written approximately thirty to seventy years after the event. These gospels are completely different stories, not records or stories by four observers to a common event. These words attributed to Jesus are *not* remembered history. To the contrary of Christian apologists, the "Seven Sayings" attributed to Jesus on the cross are the records of an evolving oral tradition written by non-witnesses approximately thirty to seventy years after the event by non-witnesses.

CONTRADICTION #12 When Jesus Spoke His Last Words

Continuing a constant pattern, the gospel writers present differing narratives of Jesus's final moments before his death. Luke 23:46 and John 19:30 stated that Jesus expired immediately *after* he uttered the final words they narrated.

> Lk 23:46 And when Jesus had cried with a loud voice, he said, Father, into thy hands I commend my spirit: and having said thus, he gave up the ghost.

Jn 19:30 When Jesus therefore had received the vinegar, he said, It is finished: and he bowed his head, and gave up the ghost.

In contrast, Mark 15:34, 37 and Matthew 27:46, 50 implied that Jesus did *not* die after his final words.

Mk 15:34 And at the ninth hour Jesus cried with a loud voice, saying, Eloi, Eloi, lama sabachthani? which is, being interpreted, My God, my God, why hast thou forsaken me?

Mk 15:37 And Jesus cried with a loud voice, and gave up the ghost.

Mt 27:46 And about the ninth hour Jesus cried with a loud voice, saying, Eli, Eli, lama sabachthani? that is to say, My God, my God, why hast thou forsaken me?

Mt 27:50 Jesus, when he had cried again with a loud voice, yielded up the ghost.

The importance of these words has been elaborated by Scroggie (1948, 578):

LAST words are always important and are carefully stored in the memory, especially the last words of the dying, of the martyrs, of people who have been great leaders, inventors, discoverers, writers, and of our own loved ones. But all the greatest last words which have ever been uttered throughout all time are not of comparable significance and value with the Seven Sayings of Jesus on the Cross, and just because no one before or since can be compared with Him, no one before or since has been at once Perfect Man and Very God. It is His Divine-Human Personality that gives all that He ever said its value.

Further, as an additional point, it should be noted that the words recorded in Luke 23:34 ("Father, forgive them; for they know not what they do") are missing from some of the oldest manuscripts: $p^{75}\aleph^1$ B D*ΘW Q 070 1241 579 597 it^{a,d}syr^{s}cop^{sa,bo}. Commenting on these missing words, Whitlark and Parsons (2006, 189) write:

The evidence for the original absence of Luke 23.34a runs from the beginning of the third century to the thirteenth century. Moreover, this reading is found in documents that are characteristically Alexandrian, Western, Byzantine, and Caesarean (if one considers this a legitimate text-type). The fact that the absence of this logion is attested by the three major textual streams from the second century indicates that it appears extremely early in the textual tradition, and that it likely derives from a non-extant exemplar that preceded these textual streams. Also the reading is geographically diverse: Egypt, Europe, Syria, and Byzantium.

Whitlark and Parsons speculate that the addition of Luke 23.34a was based on a numerical motivation to have seven sayings attributed to Jesus as opposed to six. This speculation is based on the idea that the number "seven was clearly a significant number for Jews and Christians in the first and second centuries" whereas the number six, in the early Christian tradition, conveyed a negative connotation." They conclude:

> When the four Gospels were formed into a single collection early on and the narratives read together, the problem of six sayings from the cross emerged and created the 'need' for a seventh saying. The compelling numerical significance of seven influenced the addition of a seventh saying, forming a collection of seven sayings from the cross. Consequently, the text of Luke was modified by a scribe of the Western text in order that the fourfold gospel narrative contained *seven* sayings of Jesus from the cross, thereby 'canonizing' this tradition and Luke 23.34a especially. (p. 201)

Readers are encouraged to read their thought provoking article in its entirety.

SPECULATION #18 What Happened Just before Jesus Died

Mark and Matthew presented a consistent and similar storyline. Significantly, they did not necessarily record Jesus's final words. These narratives suggest that Mark and Matthew knew that Jesus cried out, but seemingly they were not aware of his final words. In contrast, the narratives of Luke and John imply that these authors actually knew and recorded Jesus's last words. That is, perhaps Luke or John wrote the words missing or omitted in Mark and Matthew. Clearly, Luke seemingly knew something that Mark and Matthew did not know.

However, the gospel narratives raise another reason to doubt their reliability and trustworthiness. Mark, Matthew, and Luke reported that Jesus cried out with "a loud voice" prior to his death. This historicity is dubious. Turlington (1969, 398; cf. Beare 1981, 535; O'Reilly and Dugard 2013, 250), writing in *The Broadman Bible Commentary*, points out: "The crucified man who was near death would normally be too weak and exhausted to utter *a loud cry*." At the most, his voice would probably have been nothing more than a whisper. It must be remembered that previous to his crucifixion, Jesus had already been beaten and scourged. In addition, several writers (Casey 1996, 188; Thompson 1995, 61; Tinsley 1965, 204) argue that the Romans did not permit bystanders at the actual place of execution. If this argument is valid, then logically nobody would have been able to hear Jesus's last words. Therefore, it is not realistic to expect that anybody would have been able to hear and thus know what Jesus said before he died. If nobody knew what Jesus said, where did these words attributed to him originate?

SPECULATION #19 Inauthentic Sayings of Jesus on the Cross

Two commentators (Beare 1981, 535; Lüdemann 1999, 58-64) posit that the sayings of Jesus on the cross were inauthentic. An analysis of several of these sayings can be seen in the table 15 below.

> Ps 22 [Title] To the chief Musician upon Aijelth Shahar, A Psalm of David.

> Ps 22:1 My God, my God, why hast thou forsaken me? why art thou so far from helping me, and from the words of my roaring?

TABLE 15. The Sayings of Jesus

VERSE	ANALYSIS
Mk 15:34	1. Beare (1981, 535) raised the point that Jesus's last words as reported by Mark (15:35) and Matthew (27:47) have some bystanders thinking that Jesus was calling for Elias, that is the prophet Elijah. In Mark, the cry of Jesus is in Aramaic, but in Matthew the text printed in most modern editions substitutes the Hebrew *eli* for the Aramaic *eloi*. "How would Jewish bystanders, supposing that they failed to recognize the Psalm [[22:1 AV (2 Hebrew Bible) see below]], ever take either the Hebrew *Ēli* or the Aramaic *Ēloi* for an appeal to Elijah?"
	2. If it was Roman soldiers who heard these words, it is impossible that they would have understood the Aramaic words as a prayer to Elijah.
	3. The primitive Christian needed to adorn the crucifixion scene with borrowing from the Hebrew Bible.
Mt 27:26	Matthew was dependent on Mark (see above).
Lk 23:46	This verse corresponded to Psalm 31:6, which derived from the early Christian tendency to interpret the passion of Jesus in light of the Old Testament psalms.
Lk 23:43	Lüdemann (1999, 60) posits that "evidently the saying represents an attempt to overcome the problem of the delay of the parousia."
Jn 19:30	Lüdemann (1999, 61) maintains that "so the saying derives exclusively from John's overall christological conception and is therefore clearly inauthentic,"

Rabbi Ariel Bar Tzadok (2014) also speculates that the Gospels do not report the authentic words spoken by Jesus while on the cross. His keen and insightful analysis deserves a diligent consideration. First he inquires about Jesus's presumed mentioning of the prophet Elijah. What does Elijah have to do with the Resurrection? According to Malachi 4:5, Elijah will come before the Messiah. Earlier, some people thought that John the Baptist was the prophet Elijah (Mk 6:15; Jn 1:19-21). When pressed on the issue the Baptist declared that he was not that prophet. [NB. Christian apologists contend that John the Baptist came in the spirit of Elijah.] Later, John the Baptist was beheaded by the orders of Herod (Mk 6:16-29; Mt 14:1-12). How then, would people think that John the Baptist could save Jesus unless he too was resurrected?

Second, two gospels (Mk 14:34; Mt 27:46) report that Jesus recited an excerpt from Psalm 22 while on the cross and about to die. It is not the Jewish tradition to recite Psalm 22 when one is about to die.

Finally, Tzadok challenges the last words attributed to Jesus. Presumably, Jesus knew that he is about to die. Unlike Rabbi Akiva and other Jews, Jesus did not say the Shema: "Hear O Israel: the LORD our God is one LORD" (Deut 6:4 AV). "That is, he did *not* die like a Jew would. The Jewish thing is to say the Shema." Why is it not here? Tzadok speculates that Christianity had a problem with the unity of God and by recording the Shema these words would create a challenge to Christian theology.

SPECULATION #20 The Cause of Jesus's Death

There is considerable speculation in medical literature as to the cause of Jesus's early death. According to several opinions, asphyxiation or suffocation was the eventual cause of death associated with crucifixion. This idea was first made by LeBec (1925, 26) and later by Hynek (1936, 85). However, a French surgeon, Barbet (1953, 169-70), is thought to have given this theory widespread currency. Nonetheless, later studies (Edwards, Gabel, and Hosmer 1986; Moedder 1948; Zugibe 1989, 1984) disprove the asphyxiation theory. Instead, Zugibe (1989, 41) is of the opinion: "Shock is unquestionably the cause of Jesus's death on the cross." Later, Zugibe (2005, 135) restated his conclusion: "The Cause of Jesus' Death: If I were to certify the cause of Jesus' death in my official capacity as Medical Examiner, the death certificate would read as follows: Cause of Death: cardiac and respiratory arrest, due to hypovolemic and traumatic shock, due to crucifixion." [[NB. Hypovolemic shock—a condition characterized by low blood pressure and reduced blood flow to the cells and tissues that leads to irreversible cell and organ injury and eventually death.]]

ISSUE 10: The Three Hours of Darkness

| Mk 15:33 And when the sixth hour was come, there was darkness over the whole land until the ninth hour. | Mt 27:45 *Now from the sixth hour there was darkness over all the land unto the ninth hour.* | Lk 23:44 *And it was about the sixth hour, and there was a darkness over all the earth until the ninth hour.* 45 *And the sun was darkened*, and the vail of the temple was rent in the midst. | Jn 19:14 And it was the preparation of the passover, *and about the sixth hour: and he saith unto the Jews, Behold your King!* |

The first unusual phenomenon that occurred during Jesus's crucifixion and death was "darkness." This event occurred between the sixth hour—that is, noon or 6 hours after sunrise—and the ninth hour (that is, 3:00

p.m.), and thus spanned a three-hour period. Here the synoptic writers vary slightly in their wording regarding the initiation and duration of the darkness. According to Mark, the location was "over the whole land" while Matthew narrates that it was "over all the land." In contrast, Luke declares that the darkness was "over all the earth." Only Luke adds the fact that the sun was darkened. This supernatural event appears only in the synoptic Gospels.

CONTRADICTION #13 Source and Lack of Verification

The first unusual phenomenon that occurred during Jesus's crucifixion and death was that darkness fell for a three-hour period during midday. Grant (1977, 201) points out that although this supernatural event appeared in all the synoptic Gospels, it is possible that all are traceable back to a single source. That is, given that Matthew and Luke base their work on Mark, only one witness truly exists. Curiously, John completely omits any description of this miraculous event.

A second issue relates to Luke's statement that there was darkness over all the earth. What would one expect if Luke's statement were literally true? At the minimum there should be some anecdotal evidence confirming if this event were historical. That is, one would expect confirming evidence substantiating that during midday, Jerusalem time, the entire earth went dark. Similarly, one would expect confirming evidence that someone awake in the nighttime during the time of a near full moon experienced a dark earth for a three-hour period. Instead, there is no record of such an event. Significantly, not even John mentions this event in his gospel even though, according to church tradition, John was present during these events.

Third, it would be impossible for Luke to know that at noon, Jerusalem time, there was darkness spanning approximately 12,450 miles to the east and 12,450 miles to the west, given that the earth's circumference is 24,901.55 miles or 40,075.16 kilometers. Obviously, almost half of the earth would have been already dark since it was their evening. It is assumed that the darkness described in Luke's gospel referred to the light reflected by the near full moon. The only way Luke could make such a claim would be if he were positioned in outer space and looking down toward the earth. Given that Luke was using hyperbole, it must be asked: what part of the earth was he talking about, and what was the incontrovertible evidentiary proof for his narrative?

Fourth, John 19:14 sounds odd since in this verse it stated that at the sixth hour Pilate declared to the Jews, "Behold your King!" Here it must be noted that John's sixth hour directly corresponds to Mark, Matthew, and Luke's ninth hour, to noon. Consequently and significantly, this declaration by Pilate occurred simultaneously as the entire earth turned dark:

> Jn 19:14 And it was the preparation of the passover, and about the sixth hour: and he saith unto the Jews, Behold your King!

> Mk 15:33 And when the sixth hour was come, there was darkness over the whole land until the ninth hour.

> Mt 27:45 Now from the sixth hour there was darkness over all the land unto the ninth hour.

> Lk 23:44 And it was about the sixth hour, and there was a darkness over all the earth until the ninth hour.

Yet there is no comment in any of the gospel narratives about a reaction from Pilate or the Jewish people about this simultaneous occurrence.

Furthermore, the interrogation by Pilate occurred after Jesus was arrested, taken to Annas, Caiaphas's father-in-law, then to Caiaphas the high priest, and finally to the judgment hall to be examined by Pilate (Jn 18:28). What immediately followed were at least eight different events detailed by John:

1. Pilate exited the hall of judgment and spoke to the Jewish leadership outside the hall lest they be defiled (18:28-32).
2. Pilate returned inside the hall and personally interrogated Jesus (18:33-37).
3. A second time Pilate went outside the hall and conversed with the Jews (18:38-40).
4. Jesus was ordered scourged, and the command was carried out (19:1-3).
5. Pilate returned a third time to the Jewish leadership outside the judgment hall and again spoke to the Jewish leadership, declaring that he found no guilt in Jesus, yet they declared, "Crucify him, crucify him" (19:4-8).
6. Again Pilate returned inside the judgment hall and spoke to Jesus (19:9-12).
7. Pilate was threatened by the Jews (19:12).
8. Pilate returned a fourth time outside the judgment hall where the crowd demanded that Jesus be crucified (19:13-15).

Yet at this *precise* moment there was darkness over all the earth! And what did the people and chief priest do at this very moment the sky turned dark at midday? They continued to demand the death of Jesus, and Pilate consented (19:14-6). Strange that the request occurred as the whole earth was covered in darkness, yet John mentions nothing. Equally odd, John 19:14 has Jesus ordered taken away in front of the Jewish leadership and the people at noon, which corresponded with the ninth hour in the synoptic Gospels. Sylva (1986, 245n15) comments: "The ninth hour was one of the two times for the incense offerings." Then John detailed that Jesus was further humiliated, crucified, and eventually died, still omitting any mention of worldwide darkness.

How then, do Christian apologists explain the apparent conflict with John's "sixth hour" (Jn 19:14) and the records as found in the synoptic Gospels (Mk 15:33; Mt 27:45; Lk 23:44)? That is, in one instance it was the time of Jesus's trial; in the other the crucifixion. Christian aologists contend that John employed a different system of reckoning hours. Finegan (1998, 359 #614), in response to these apologetics writes:

> In conflict and incompatible with all of the foregoing is only Mark 15:25, "it was the third hour when they crucified him." This means crucifixion at nine o'clock in the morning rather than at midday. Even if the reckoning were from either of the two other possible starting points of sunset or midnight it would mean nine o'clock in the evening or three o'clock in the morning and be obviously impossible. Therefore Mark 15:25 and John 19:14 are *"plain unreconcilable"* [italics mine] and Mark 15:35 can even be thought to be an "interpolation."

Even more noteworthy and significant, there are no incontrovertible primary sources outside the Gospels and thus no external historical verification for this cosmological, metaphysical, and super miraculous worldwide event.

SPECULATION #21 Conflicting Translations

Boring (1995, 492), writing for *The New Interpreter's Bible*, states: "The word translated 'land' (γη gē) can refer either to the 'land' in the national sense (i.e., 'Judea') or the whole earth." The King James Bible and several other Bible translations render Luke's account as "darkness over all the *earth*." In contrast, numerous Bible translations maintain that the verse should read "over the whole *land*" (see table 16). The reason for this conflicting translation is unknown, although the identical Greek term in Mark, Matthew, and Luke is used to describe the locale of the darkness: γη gē (*ghay*). *The Strong Concordance* number for this term is 1093 [Strong 1890, 20].

> 1093 γη **gē** *ghay*; contr. from a prim. word; soil; by extens. **a** region, or the solid part of the whole of the terrene globe (include. The occupants in each application):– country, earth (-ly), ground, land, world.

In contrast, Thayer's *A Greek-English Lexicon of the New Testament* (1886, 114) states:

> 1. *arable land*:…2. *the ground, the earth* as a standing-place,…3. The main *land*, opp. to sea or water:…4. *the earth as a whole, the world* (Lat. terrarium orbis)…

Given that the identical Greek term was employed in all the synoptic Gospels, it is unknown as to why the translators of the AV diverged from their prior translations in Mark and Matthew. Unmistakably, the reading "over all the earth" is much more powerful than "over the whole land."

TABLE 16. English Translations of Part of Luke 23:44

King James Version	and there was a darkness over all the *earth*
New King James Version	and there was darkness over all the *earth*
New Revised Standard Version	and darkness came over all the whole *land* [n Or *earth*]
The New American Standard	and darkness fell over the whole *land*
American Standard	and a darkness came over the whole *land*
New International Version	and darkness came over the whole *land*

SPECULATION #22 Jesus's Death and the Darkness Motif—Symbolism

What then could account for the darkness reported in these narratives during Jesus's passion? According to written accounts, there was an eclipse of the sun at the death of Caesar (Virgil, *Georics* 1, 463-68) and Augustus (*Dio's Roman History* 56, 29). Similarly, Philo wrote: "Eclipses announce the death of kings and destruction of cities (*De Providentia II. 50*; cf. *Plutarch*

Pelopidas xxxi. 2-3; *Diogenes* Laertius IV. 64) (see Culpepper 1978, 586; Plummer 2005, 301-02).

Coincidentally, the earthquake motif and darkness motif are well-known in many other religious traditions, parts of ancient mythology, and even supposed historicity.

1. At the death of the Hindu savior, Krishna, "a black circle surrounded the moon, and the sun was darkened at noon-day; the sky rained fire and ashes; flames burned dusky and livid; demons committed depredations on earth. At sunrise and sunset thousands of figures were seen skirmishing in the air; and spirits were to be seen on all sides" (Doane 1882, 207, 281).

2. At the conflict between Buddha, the "Savior of the World, and the Prince of Evil, a thousand appalling meteors fell; darkness prevailed; the earth quaked; the ocean rose; rivers flowed back; peaks of lofty mountains rolled down; a fierce storm howled around; and a host of headless spirits filled the air" (Doane 1882, 207).

3. On the death of Romulus, the founder of Rome, the sun was darkened for six hours (Doane 1882, 207).

4. "When AEsculapius, the Savior, was put to death, the sun shone dimly from the heavens, the birds were silent, the trees bowed their heads in sorrow, etc." (Doane 1882, 208).

5. "When Hercules died, darkness was on the face of the earth, thunder crashed through the air. Zeus, the god of gods, carried his son home, and the halls of Olympus were opened to welcome the bright hero who rested from his mighty toil. There he now sits, clothed in a white robe, with a crown upon his head" (Doane 1882, 208).

6. When Alexander the Great died, the skies and earth turned dark (Doane 1882, 208).

7. When Atreus of Mycenae murdered his nephews, the sun, "unable to endure a sight so horrible, turned his course backwards and withdrew his light" (Doane 1882, 208).

Furthermore, even the Hebrew Bible detailed and discussed darkness or an eclipse of the sun (often at midday) as a harbinger of judgment (Ex 10:21-23; Isa 13:9-10; 50:3; Jer 13:16; 15:9; Ez 30:18-19, 32:7-8; Joel 2:2, 10, 31; 3:15; Amos 5:20; 8:9; Zeph 1:15; Job 9:7). In addition, Allison (1985, 28) points out that mourning sometimes conjoined with darkness in Jewish texts such as Jeremiah 4:27-28 and 2 Apocalypse of Baruch 10:12.

Yet another explanation from Mark 15:33 was an eschatological tradition. Allison (1985, 29) provides numerous examples: *As. Mos.* 10:5; *Sib. Or.* III,

801-802; V, 344-50; *T. Levi* 4:1; *2 Apoc. Bar.* 10:12; 18:2; 46:2; 77:14; *Liv. Pro. Hab.* 14; *2 Enoch* 34:3; and *b. Sanh.* 99a. Consequently, the darkness motif was well-known to those familiar with the Hebrew Bible, the Apocrypha, the Pseudepigrapha, and the Talmud. The complete failure of these celestial miracles to influence in any way the leadership of the people or the people themselves should be convincing proof of their non-historical character.

Fenton (1963, 442), writing in his *The Gospel of St Matthew*, offers the hypothesis that the darkness was directly related to Matthew's "over all the land." He suggests:

> Mark had *over the whole world* (*eph' holēn tēn gēn*) and Matthew changes this to *over all the land* (*epi pasan tēn gēn*); this apparently unimportant alteration may be due to his recollection of Exod. 10[22], *there was thick darkness in all the land* (*epi pāsan gēn*) *of Egypt three days*. This darkness was the last plague in Egypt before the death of the first born: Jesus' death is parallel to the last plague, so it may be that Matthew saw this three-hour darkness as the fulfillment of the three-day darkness in Egypt. The Jewish expectation that the last days would be like the days of Egypt would predispose him to think so. But we may also compare Amos 8[9], And *on that day, says the Lord God, I will make the sun go down at noon, and darken the earth in broad daylight*.

Finally, Luccock (1951, 8:907), writing for *The Interpreter's Bible*, declares that "Matthew has recorded many strange portents at the time of the Crucifixion. Mark mentions only two: the darkness at noon and the rending of the veil of the Temple. *It seems quite likely that some of these portents found their way into the narrative for their symbolic value, rather than as reports of actual happening*" [italics mine].

SPECULATION #23 An Astral Sign as a Literary Device

Besides serving as a theological agenda, the astronomical incident could also have served as a literary device. It is a curiosity that an astral sign accompanied Jesus's death. Paradoxically, Matthew 2:1-2 and in verses 9-10 recorded another cosmological event on the occasion of Jesus's birth.

> Mt 2:1-2 Now when Jesus was born in Bethlehem of Judaea in the days of Herod the king, behold, there came wise men from the east

to Jerusalem, Saying, Where is he that is born King of the Jews? for we have seen his star in the east, and are come to worship him.

Mt 2:9-10 When they had heard the king, they departed; and, lo, the star, which they saw in the east, went before them, till it came and stood over where the young child was. When they saw the star, they rejoiced with exceeding great joy.

Allison (2004, 533), elaborating on this point, wrote:

Whether due to authorial design or not, the crucifixion narrative nicely balances the infancy narrative. In both chapters 2 and 27 Jesus is called "the king of the Jews," he is passive, and people seek to kill him. Further, whereas in chapter 2 Jesus' birth is signalled by a light in the sky, in chapter 27 his death is accompanied by a heavenly darkness. And if, after Jesus' birth, Gentile foreigners, who otherwise play no role in the story, testify to his messianic status and worship him, after he dies Roman soldiers, who appear only in the crucifixion narrative, attest that Jesus is the Son of God.

Perhaps the author of Matthew was creating a literary bookend. In the birth narrative, Matthew details a special star as if to hint to a rebirth or symbol of life. In contrast, the darkness conceivably symbolizes Jesus's approaching death.

SPECULATION #24 Astronomical and Physical Explanations for the Darkness

According to Christian tradition (Anderson 1969, 19; Bruce 1974, 29-30; Habermas 1996, 196-97; 1984b, 93-94), Julius Africanus (ca. 221), and Origen (ca. 185-254) respectively cited reports by the historian Thallus. According to Habermas, Thallus was a Samaritan-born historian and one of the first Gentiles to mention Jesus's name, writing ca. 52 CE. For Christian apologists this dating is vitally important. For example, Habermas (1996, 1997; idem.1984b, 94) writes:

From this brief statement by Thallus we can ascertain that (1) the Christian gospel, or at least an account of the crucifixion, was known in the Mediterranean region by the middle of the first century AD. This brings to mind the presence of Christian teachings in Rome mentioned by Tacitus and by Suetonius. (2) Unbelievers offered rationalistic explanations for certain Christian teachings or for supernatural claims not long after their initial proclamation, a point to which we will return below. [Note: Habermas is referring to a widespread darkness in the land, implied to have taken place during Jesus's crucifixion.]

Carrier (2011-12, 188n8) wrote in the *Journal of Greco-Roman Christianity and Judaism*: "We do not know when Thallus wrote. Claims are boldly made that it must have been shortly after 52 CE, but that is based solely on a conjectural emendation of a corrupted text." Then in footnote 8, Carrier further elaborated:

The "corroborating" claim that a Thallus is mentioned by Josephus as living in the reign of Tiberius is not only false (the text does not present the name Thallus), it is irrelevant as no mention is made there of this person being a writer. Further, the name Thallus, even if it were included, was common). This has long been known (see Horace Rigg, "Thallus: The Samaritan?" *HTR* 34 [1941], pp. 111-19), so no historian today should still repeat these claims. For further discussion of this problem, see P. Prigent, "Thallos, Phlégon et le Testimonium Flavianum témoins de Jésus?" in Frederick Bruce (ed.), *Paganisme, Judaïsme, Christianisme: Influences et Affrontements dans le Monde Antique* (Paris: Bocard, 1978), pp. 329-34; Ida Miévis, "A propos de la correction 'Thallos' dans les 'Antiquités Judaïques' de Flavius Josèphe," *Revue Belge de Philologie et d'Histoire* 13 (1934), pp. 733-40.

A surviving fragment of Julius Africanus's writing details an eclipse around the time that Jesus was executed.

III.-The Extant Fragments of the Five Books of the Chronography of Julius Africanus. [In Georgius Syncellus, *Chron.*, p. 322 or 256, ed. Paris, 14 Venet.] Ante-Nicene Fathers, Vol VI

XVIII.

On the Circumstances Connected with Our Saviour's Passion and His Life-Giving Resurrection

1. As to His works severally, and His cures effected upon body and soul, and the mysteries of His doctrine, and the resurrection from the

dead, these have been most authoritatively set forth by His disciples and apostles before us. On the whole world there pressed a most fearful darkness; and the rocks were rent by an earthquake, and many places in Judea and other districts were thrown down. This darkness Thallus, in the third book of his *History*, calls, as appears to me without reason, an eclipse of the sun. For the Hebrews celebrate the passover on the 14th day according to the moon, and the passion of our Saviour falls on the day before the passover; but an eclipse of the sun takes place only when the moon comes under the sun. And it cannot happen at any other time but in the interval between the first day of the new moon and the last of the old, that is, at their junction: how then should an eclipse be supposed to happen when the moon is almost diametrically opposite the sun? Let that opinion pass, however; let it carry the majority with it; and let this portent of the world be deemed an eclipse of the sun, like others a portent only to the eye. Phlegon records that, in the time of Tiberius Caesar, at full moon, there was a full eclipse of the sun from the sixth hour to the ninth—manifestly that one of which we speak. But what has an eclipse in common with an earthquake, the rending rocks, and the resurrection of the dead, and so great a perturbation throughout the universe? Surely no such event as this is recorded for a long period. But it was a darkness induced by God because the Lord happened then to suffer. And calculation makes out that the period of 70 weeks, as noted in Daniel, is completed at this time.

There are several problems challenging Habermas's thesis (Price 1985, 147-50). First, there are two different commentators who were known as Thallus. A person, Thallus, was cited by Julius Africanus; and another person was cited by Josephus, a Jewish historian. Josephus (*Antiquities* 18:167 or 18, 6, 4) describes a Thallus who was made a freedman by Tiberius and who loaned money to Herod Agrippa I: "Now there was one Thallus, a freedman of Caesar's, of whom he borrowed a million of drachmæ, and thence repaid Antonia the debt he owed her; and by sending the overplus in paying his court to Caius, became a person of great authority with him." Habermas cites as his source F. F. Bruce's *Jesus and Christian Origins Outside the New Testament* (1974, 29-30). Habermas's citation from Bruce is almost verbatim. However, Habermas acknowledges that "it is debated whether Thallus was the same person referred to by Josephus as a wealthy Samaritan, who was made a freedman by Emperor Tiberius and who loaned money to Herod Agrippa I." Habermas also cites J. N. D. Anderson's *Christianity: The Witness of History A Lawyer's Approach* (1969, 19). In the opinion of Anderson, "there is good reason to believe that this Thallus was a Samaritan historian who wrote about the middle of the first century." Anderson then continues: "If this identification is correct, then from this and other evidence it seems clear that the circumstances surrounding the origin of Christianity were being discussed by non-Christians at a very early date." Significantly, Anderson prefaces his statement with the word *if.* An examination of Anderson's text provides one source for his claim that "there is good reason to believe" that the two are the same Thallus: Roderic Dunkerley's *Beyond the Gospels: An Investigation into the Information on the Life of Christ* found outside the Gospels (1957, 25ff). In response, Dunkerly states, "But the link seems a slender one on which little reliance can be placed" (p. 28).

Second, a third-hand source cites a second-hand source about an event that occurred approximately two hundred years earlier.

Third, astronomers and historians concur that there is no astronomical possibility that this event could be an eclipse. This point is even substantiated by Bruce (*New Testament Documents: Are They Reliable*, 1997, 116) "because a solar eclipse could not take place at the time of the full moon, and it was at the season of the Paschal full moon that Christ died." In addition, the longest period of time a natural eclipse can last is approximately seven minutes (see Meeus. 2003. "The maximum possible duration of a total solar eclipse." *Journal of the British Astronomical Association*, 113(6), 343-348).

Phlegon of Tralles is yet another source cited by Christian apologists in their attempt to support the historicity of the astral event cited in the gospel accounts. Phlegon, a Greek writer, wrote about the Olympic Games for the Roman emperor Hadrian (76-138 CE). Altogether he wrote sixteen books about the Olympic games called the *Olympiads* or *Olympiades*, from the first Olympiad down to the 229th Olympiad (776 BCE to 137 CE). Phlegon's writing on the history of these games is known as *Olympiades*. Reference to an astral event may be found in *Fragmenta Historicum Graecorum* (C. Muller) 1841-1870, volume 3, pages 603-24. In his thirteenth book, he wrote that the 202nd Olympiad was from about June 28, 32 CE, to June 27, 33 CE, and he stated:

> However in the fourth year of the 202nd Olympiad, an eclipse [[*Ekleipsis*]] of the sun happened, greater and more excellent than any that had happened before it; at the sixth hour, day turned into dark night, so that the stars were seen in the sky, and an earthquake in Bithynia toppled many buildings of the city of Nicaea.

Origen also cites Phlegon as follows:

Now Phlegon, in the thirteenth or fourteenth book, I think, of his Chronicles, not only ascribed to Jesus a knowledge of future events (although falling into confusion about some things which refer to Peter, as if they referred to Jesus), but also testified that the result corresponded to His predictions. So that, he also, by these very admissions regarding foreknowledge, as if against his will, expressed his opinion that the doctrines taught by the fathers of our system were not devoid of divine power. ("Against Celsus" 2.14.)

And with regard to the eclipse in the time of Tiberius Caesar, in whose reign Jesus appears to have been crucified, and the great earthquakes which then took place, Phlegon too, I think, has written in the thirteenth or fourteenth book of his Chronicles. (*"Against Celsus"* 2.33.)

Regarding these we have in the preceding pages made our defence, according to our ability, adducing the testimony of Phlegon, who relates that these events took place at the time when our Saviour suffered. (*"Against Celsus"* 2.59.)

However, a total eclipse of the sun occurred in the East on November 24, 29, and the greatest darkness was at was at about eleven in the morning, and the darkness lasted 01m59.2s (Espenak, 2011).

Additional evidence directed against the accounts of darkness reveals that astronomers and historians concur that there is no astronomical possibility that this event was an eclipse or a comet. As the moon was at the full, darkness contradicts an eclipse. Yet some writers such as Humphreys and Waddington (1986, 746; 1985, 5) discuss or speculate that this darkness was caused by a black sirocco, a dust storm. However, a dust storm could not cover the entire earth. The two most obvious possibilities are that the darkness was (1) a miraculous event (that is, a miracle) or (2) a fabrication of its authors to serve a theological agenda. If the darkness was, in fact, a miracle, the silence from history is equally miraculous. Would it not be common sense to expect the Greeks, Romans, the Chinese, or others to have noticed and recorded such darkness occurring at a time of the month when a solar eclipse was impossible? There is no historical evidence that this astronomical event occurred!

ISSUE 11: The Tearing of the Temple's Veil

Mk 15:38 And the vail of the temple was rent in twain from the top to the bottom.	Mt 27:51 *And behold, the vail of the temple was rent in twain from the top to the bottom*; and the earth did quake, and the rocks rent; 52 And the graves were opened; and many bodies of the saints which slept arose, 53 And came out of the graves after his resurrection, and went into the holy city, and appeared unto many.	Lk 23:44 And it was about the sixth hour, and there was a darkness over all the earth until the ninth hour. 45 And the sun was darkened, and *the vail of the temple was rent in the midst.* 46 And when Jesus had cried with a loud voice, he said, Father, into thy hands I commend my spirit: and having said thus, he gave up the ghost.	Jn

The second unusual account related to Jesus's crucifixion and death recorded in the synoptic Gospels was the tearing of the Temple's veil in two from top to bottom (Mark and Matthew). In Luke, the narrative added the fact that the veil was torn in the middle. This "miraculous" event is not reported in John.

CONTRADICTION #14 Contradictory Narratives Regarding the Veil

The Gospel narratives present contradictory information. Mark 15:38 reports that at the ninth hour (3:00 p.m.): "And the vail of the temple was rent in twain from the top to the bottom." Therefore, Mark has the veil tearing *after* Jesus died. Matthew agrees with Mark. In direct contradiction, Luke reports in verse 23:45 the tearing of the veil: "And the sun was darkened, and the vail of the temple was rent in the midst." However, one verse later he significantly writes "And when Jesus had cried with a loud voice, he said, Father, into thy hands I commend my spirit: and having said thus, he gave up the ghost" (Lk 23:46). Significantly, therefore, Luke has the veil tearing *before* Jesus died! The tearing cannot be both ways. Undeniably, one of the two authors must be in error.

SPECULATION #25: Oddities Regarding the Tearing of the Temple's Veil

Josephus's *Jewish Wars* (5.5.4 §§ 212-214) describes the outer veil of the Jerusalem temple as it had appeared since the time of Herod. The outer veil was an enormous curtain, approximately 55 cubits high (82.5 feet) and 16 cubits wide (24 feet). The curtain was approximately one handbreadth thick, made of four kinds of threads (about 4 inches in total), and composed of 72 squares sewn together (see Maimonides 1985, 68). Josephus's *Wars* also details that the veil was a Babylonian tapestry, with embroidery of blue and fine linen, of scarlet also and purple, woven with marvelous skill. The colors and materials associated with the veil were full of mystical meaning. However, significantly, in Josephus, only the fineness of the linen and the embroidery was stressed, not the thickness or strength. Gurtner (2006, 97-114) provides a detailed review of the Temple veil's history and legend.

Given the dimensions of the veil, the materials employed, its profound mystical meaning, and its degree of holiness, the fact that its tearing is *not* reported in any historical records is curious: what is the probability or even plausibility that a four-inch thick curtain of four different kinds of thread spanning approximately 82.5 feet in height and 24 feet in width is torn in two from the top of the veil to the bottom? For the sake of comparison, imagine tearing a cloth fabric the thickness of a good-size telephone directory.

Second, it seems dubious that an earthquake could damage a curtain of flexible material hanging loosely, that is, assuming that the earthquake was the cause of the tear.

In *b. Gittin* 56b, it is reported that none other than Titus, the conquering Roman general, personally entered the Holy of Holies and slashed the curtain: "He took a harlot by the hand and entered the Holy of Holies and spread out a scroll of the Law and committed a sin on it. *He then took a sword and slashed the curtain.* Miraculously blood spurted out, and he thought that he had slain himself." However, Josephus makes no mention of the Temple's veil being cut. Interested readers are referred to Plummer (2005, 301-16) who provides a concise overview of six early nonbiblical sources that reported unusual phenomena in the Temple prior to its destruction.

SPECULATION #26 Symbolism of the Torn Veil

Mark's tearing of the Temple's veil *after* Jesus's death has been subject to two major Christian interpretations that (1) indicates divine judgment and (2) that God now comes to humans from the Holy of Holies behind the curtain, no longer through temple sacrifice but through the death of Jesus (Ehrman 1993, 200-01). In contrast, Luke 23:45 reports that the veil's tearing occurred *before* Jesus died. Therefore, Luke's account "does not show that Jesus's death has opened the path to God; it now symbolizes God's judgment upon his own people who prefer to dwell in darkness" (p. 201).

Motyer (1987, 55-57) points out that there is actually a whole cluster of motifs that occur in Mark 1:9-11 at both the baptism and at the death of Jesus (15:36-39). Ulansey (1991, 123-25), in a concurring opinion, wrote:

> In other words, the outer veil of the Jerusalem temple was actually one huge image of the starry sky! Thus, upon encountering Mark's statement that "the veil of the temple was torn in two from top to bottom," any of his readers who had ever seen the temple or heard it described would instantly have seen in their mind's eye an image of *the heavens being torn* and would immediately have been reminded of Mark's earlier description of the heavens being torn at the baptism. This can hardly be coincidence: the symbolic parallel is so striking that Mark must have consciously intended it.

Below is a modest variety of speculative interpretations of the torn veil. For those interested, Geddert (1989, 141-43) presents a terse listing of thirty-five interpretations!

THE TRINITY

King (1974, 723) suggests that Mark understood the tearing of the veil as part of the factual narrative. "That is, God in person had acted directly at that point, and had done what any devoted Jewish father, standing by the deathbed of a beloved son, would have done: he rent his garments." However, King's interpretation creates two paradoxes for skeptics. First, this Christian apologetic necessitates that there exists three *persons* in the Godhead: the Father, the Son (i.e., Jesus), and the Holy Spirit. Skeptics and detractors of the Resurrection reject the thesis that the Godhead consists of a trinity.

Second, it must be asked, is it to be understood that God is renting His symbolic garment, the veil, because He Himself was dying? Here, too, skeptics and detractors will refute that even metaphorically; a part of "God" is dying.

THE OLD VERSUS THE NEW

Another possible symbolism occurs when Elisha tears his cloak after Elijah's departure in 2 Kings 2:12; he symbolizes the end of his pupilage. Motyer (1987, 156) suggests that "the rending of the veil, like that of Elisha's cloak, indicates the end of the old and the beginning of the new era, in which access to the Holy Place is open to all." However, it has been debated for centuries which veil that Mark referred to: the outer veil, which hung in front of the doors at the entrance to the Temple, or the inner veil, which separated the Holy of Holies from the rest of the Temple? Culpepper (1978, 591) offers the previously stated interpretation: "The rending of the veil indicates that God confirmed Jesus' judgment on the temple. Its destruction was sealed; so attention should focus on the church, the temple not made with hands" (see Jn 2:19-21).

Schleiermacher (1975, 420) also raises the subject of symbolism, specifically of the relationship between the new and old covenant. In his case the tearing of the Temple's veil symbolically represents the end of the *old* covenant, replacing it with a *new* covenant (see Jeremiah 31:31 AV). In Hebrews 8:13, Paul (or its anonymous author) writes about the new covenant superseding the old.

However, Sylva (1986, 250), writing in the *Journal of Biblical Literature*, rejects this notion and those held by the many others previously discussed. "Thus, Luke's purpose in Luke 23:45b, 46a was not to signify the temple's destruction, the abrogation of the temple cultus, or the opening of a new way to God, but rather to present the last moment of Jesus' life as a communion with the God of the temple."

ISSUE 12: The First Earthquake

Mk	Mt 27:51 And behold, the vail of the temple was rent in twain from the top to the bottom; *and the earth did quake, and the rocks rent*; 52 And the graves were opened; and many bodies of the saints which slept arose, 53 And came out of the graves after his resurrection, and went into the holy city, and appeared unto many.	Lk	Jn

The third significant event detailed by Matthew is an earthquake (*seismos*). The narrative unequivocally declared that as a consequence of this quake rocks were split (rent) and, by way of implication, implied that tombs were opened. The earthquake event is unique to Matthew.

CONTRADICTION #15 Historical Evidence

Matthew 27:51 reports: "And, behold, the vail of the temple was rent in twain from the top to the bottom; and the earth did quake, and the rocks rent." The United States Geophysical Survey (USGS) (January 09, 2013a) states that earthquake magnitude classes are defined as follows:

The following table gives intensities that are typically observed at locations near the epicenter of earthquakes of different magnitudes.

Magnitude	Typical Maximum Modified Mercalli Intensity
1.0-3.0	I
3.0-3.9	II-III
4.0-4.9	IV-V
5.0-5.9	VI-VII
6.0-6.9	VII-IX
7.0 and higher	VIII or higher

Abbreviated Modified Mercalli Intensity Scale

I. Not felt except by a very few under especially favorable conditions.

II. Felt only by a few persons at rest, especially on upper floors of buildings.

III. Felt quite noticeably by persons indoors, especially on upper floors of buildings. Many people do not recognize it as an earthquake. Standing motor cars may rock slightly. Vibrations similar to the passing of a truck. Duration estimated.

IV. Felt indoors by many, outdoors by few during the day. At night, some awakened. Dishes, windows, doors disturbed; walls make cracking sound. Sensation like heavy truck striking building. Standing motor cars rocked noticeably.

V. Felt by nearly everyone; many awakened. Some dishes, windows broken. Unstable objects overturned. Pendulum clocks may stop.

VI. Felt by all, many frightened. Some heavy furniture moved; a few instances of fallen plaster. Damage slight.

VII. Damage negligible in buildings of good design and construction; slight to moderate in well-built ordinary structures; considerable damage in poorly built or badly designed structures; some chimneys broken.

VIII. Damage slight in specially designed structures; considerable damage in ordinary substantial buildings with partial collapse. Damage great in poorly built structures. Fall of chimneys, factory stacks, columns, monuments, walls. Heavy furniture overturned.

IX. Damage considerable in specially designed structures; well-designed frame structures thrown out of plumb. Damage great in substantial buildings, with partial collapse. Buildings shifted off foundations.

X. Some well-built wooden structures destroyed; most masonry and frame structures destroyed with foundations. Rails bent.

XI. Few, if any (masonry) structures remain standing. Bridges destroyed. Rails bent greatly.

XII. Damage total. Lines of sight and level are distorted. Objects thrown into the air.

However, the USGS (January 9, 2013b) pointed out that there is not one magnitude above that damage will occur. Other factors related to the amount of earthquake damage include the distance from the quake and the type of soil. "That being said, damage does not usually occur until the earthquake magnitude reaches somewhere above 4 or 5." Therefore, this earthquake registered, at the least between a 4.0 to a 5.9 on the Richter scale. Given the above, the population in many miles in all directions centered from Jerusalem would have perceived by hearing, sight, and kinesthesia an earthquake event.

Finally, it must be remembered that this is *not* just a mere earthquake. This reported geologic phenomenon occurred simultaneously and in conjunction with Jesus's death and other supernatural events. The phenomenon reported included:

1. The sun darkening midday.
2. The tearing of the Temple's veil.
3. The opening of an unknown number of tombs.
4. An unknown number of bodies of saints arose from the dead.
5. These resurrected saints came out of their graves and actually went into the holy city.
6. The resurrected saints appeared to many people in an unknown number.

Therefore, this earthquake, in conjunction with the above, is highly significant.

Nonetheless, an earthquake is *not* recorded by any of the other gospel authors. Why then did Mark and Luke omit such a noteworthy event? Significantly, Luke, writing after Mark and Matthew, reports in the prologue to his gospel that he "carefully investigated everything from the beginning." In other words, he has *multiple* sources. Why then did he omit such an important cosmic event, one that coincided with Jesus's death? In addition, the absence of the earthquake in Luke raises another question: why did Luke prefer Mark as a source over Matthew?

Perhaps Luke's omission, in fact, confirms that the event is an invention of Matthew. Or, as the Catholic scholar McKenzie (1968, 112) wrote in his commentary "The Gospel According to Matthew" in *The Jerome Bible Commentary*: "*51-53. Mt has a number of legendary features peculiar to itself.*" [italics mine] In conclusion, there is no historical verification from even one external source of this remarkable event.

ISSUE 13: The Resurrected Saints Appearing to Many

Mk	Mt 27:51 And behold, the vail of the temple was rent in twain from the top to the bottom; and the earth did quake, and the rocks rent; *52 And the graves were opened; and many bodies of the saints which slept arose, 53 And came out of the graves after his resurrection, and went into the holy city, and appeared unto many.*	Lk	Jn

The fourth significant happening that Matthew describes is actually a combination of events. First, graves are opened, perhaps by the earthquake; and second, many bodies of saints, which slept, a euphemism for were dead, came out the graves. Finally, the resurrected saints went into Jerusalem and appeared to many people.

CONTRADICTION #16 Lack of Corroboration of the Resurrected Saints

The greatest supernatural event, the resurrection of the many saints, appears *only* in Matthew. This is a miracle unsurpassed anywhere else in the Gospels or other books of the Christian scriptures. It makes the post-resurrection appearance of Jesus to the 120 believers cited in Acts 1:15 and "to above five hundred brethren at once" recorded in 1 Corinthians 15:6 appear meek in comparison to the resurrection of many dead saints (*hagioi*) and their appearance to many people in Jerusalem.

> Acts 1:15 And in those days Peter stood up in the midst of the disciples, and said, (the number of names together were about an hundred and twenty,)

> 1 Cor 15:6 After that, he was seen of above five hundred brethren at once; of whom the greater part remain unto this present, but some are fallen asleep.

The exclusion of this stupendous miracle from the other synoptic Gospels demands a rational and sensible explanation. First, it is acknowledged by Christian scholars that Matthew was dependent on Mark. Specifically, Matthew employed almost 600 out of 678 verses (AV) that are found in Mark. However, there is no mention of the resurrected saints in Mark. This omission in Mark raises two questions: (1) what was the source of Matthew's text, and (2) why did Mark deliberately omit such an important event?

Of greater significance, Luke, writing after Matthew, reports in the prologue to his gospel that he "carefully investigated everything from the beginning." Therefore, Luke is claiming that he reviewed numerous sources, including Matthew. Why then did Luke omit such an important event that coincided with Jesus's death? Perhaps his omission is, in fact, a deletion and confirms that the earthquake event is an invention, that is a "myth" developed by Matthew. Moreover, here too there is no historical verification from even one external source for this remarkable event. This omission from sources other than Mark, Luke, or even John should raise the proverbial red flag.

For example, during the Passover and the two additional festival holy days, the primary agenda of the governor and his cohort of troops were to maintain order. Passover was a known time of heightened risk of insurrection. The Passover symbolized the Jewish desire for freedom and liberation, that is, nationalistic hopes. Compounding matters, thousands of Jews were traveling to Jerusalem and swelling its population. Jeremias (1975, 83) estimated that Jerusalem's normal population of 55,000 inhabitants swelled to 180,000, an increase of about 125,000 pilgrims. In contrast, Broshi (1978, 14) estimates that in 70 CE a population of 80,000 lived in Jerusalem prior to its destruction. Josephus indicates that the Roman Legate came to Jerusalem from Syria at such times and greatly increased the number of Roman troops stationed there, compelling the Jews to "carry on their celebration under the watchful eyes of the Roman security forces stationed on the temple porticoes during such festivals" (Martin 1995, 58; also see Brandon 1967, 330). "[F]or when the multitude were come together to Jerusalem, to the feast of unleavened bread, and a Roman cohort stood over the cloisters of the temple, (for they always were armed and kept at the festivals, to prevent any innovation which the multitude thus gathered together might make,)" (Josephus, *Wars of the Jews.* Translated by William Whiston. 2, 12.1. [p. 481]).

As a point of clarification, it should be pointed out that "the main Roman military tower, the Antonia, was adjacent to the Temple." Under these circumstances it is obvious that Pilate would have had numerous soldiers on duty in Jerusalem reporting to him regularly about any possible commotion or disorder. Further, surely Pilate would have had informers keeping him abreast of all relevant information. How then did Roman officials never see or hear about these many resurrected saints? It must be remembered that Matthew employed the word *many* two times: many (πολλὰ, polla) bodies of saints arose and the saints appeared to many (πολλοῖς, pollois).

Wenham (1973, 42-3), a conservative Christian apologist writing in the *Tyndale Bulletin*, also expresses his concern: *"Although arguments from silence are to be treated with the greatest caution, in this case the phenomenon described is so remarkable that some mention of it might be expected in the other gospels or Acts."* [italics mine]

More forcefully, Dale C. Allison (2005b, 127) of the Pittsburgh Theological Seminary, writing in the *Journal for the Study of the Historical Jesus*, states:

> That an earthquake opened the tombs of some long-dead saints, who then awoke from their collective slumber, entered

Jerusalem, and appeared to many—all of which is attested solely by a document coming from perhaps sixty years after the alleged events—does not clearly commend itself as solemn fact to the sober-minded historian. I find Wright's hesitation on this one (in his book, *Resurrection*) hard to fathom. *Mt. 27:51-53 is a religious yarn spawned by the same source that gave us the legend of the seven sleepers of Ephesus and other transparent fictions—the human imagination. It may communicate theology; it does not preserve history.* [italics mine]

In the opinion of Evans (1995, 32-33), he writes:

Not only do we have late and obvious fictions, but in the transmission of the texts of the gospels themselves we are able to observe the infiltration of pious legend and embellishment . . . Another likely candidate, though admittedly there are no extant variants, is the story of the open tombs and the resurrection of saints in Jerusalem (Matt 27:52-53), a tradition, probably based on Ezek 37:12-13 and Dan 12:2, that has been inserted awkwardly into its present context. [italics mine]

Then, seven years later Evans (2012, 466) added, "The peculiar vv. 52-53 are not cited and evidently not alluded to in the writings of the church fathers prior to the Council of Nicaea in 325 A.D."

Similarly, Luz (2005b, 587) declares, *"There is no historical report; it is a polemical legend told by Christians for Christians or, more precisely, a fiction largely created by Matthew for his readers."* [italics mine] R. T. France (1994, 1943), another conservative Christian apologist, writes somewhat cryptically, "The symbolism is fairly clear, but we do not have the resource to determine the status of the story as sober history." Likewise, Anderson (1965, 45) declares: *"What we have here is surely not a historical note, but a theological reminiscence."* [italics mine]

In addition, Donald A. Hagner (1995, 851)—a George Eldon Ladd professor of New Testament, Fuller Theological Seminary—wrote:

I side, therefore, with such recent commentators as Gundry, Senior (*Passion of Jesus*), Gnilka, Bruner, Harrington, D. R. A. Hare (*Matthew*, Interpretation [Louisville: Westminster/ John Knox, 1993]), and R. E. Brown (*Death of the Messiah*) in concluding that the rising of the saints from the tombs in this passage *is a piece of theology set forth as history.* [italics mine]

Sabourin is probably correct when he writes: "Matthew took for historical facts popular reports of what would have taken place at the time of Jesus. He used these stories to convey his own theological message" (919; so too R. E. Brown, *Death of the Messiah*, 1138). It is obvious that by the inclusion of this material Matthew wanted to draw out the theological significance of the death (and resurrection) of Jesus. That significance is found in the establishing of the basis of the future resurrection of the saints. We may thus regard the passage as a piece of realized and historicized apocalyptically depending on OT motifs found in such passages as Isa 26:19; Dan 12:2; and especially Ezek 37:12-14 (though Monasterio, Riebl, Gnilka, and others probably speculate too much in concluding Matthew's dependence on a Jewish apocalyptic text oriented to Ezek 37; contrast Maisch who opts for Matthean composition).

Finally, Michael R. Licona (2010, 552-53) writes in his *Resurrection of Jesus: A New Historiographical Approach*:

> [I]t seems to me that an understanding of the language in Matthew 27:52-53 as "special effects" with eschatological Jewish texts and thought in mind is most plausible. There is further support for this interpretation. If the tombs opened and the saints being raised upon Jesus' death was not strange enough, Matthew adds that they did not come out of their tombs until *after* Jesus' resurrection. What were they doing between Friday afternoon and early Sunday morning? Were they standing in the now open doorways of their tombs and waiting?

> ...It seems best to regard this difficult text in Matthew as a poetic device added to communicate that the Son of God had died and that the impending judgment awaited Israel.

Later, in response to a strong criticism found in two Open Letters by Norman Geisler, Licona (2011) reaffirmed his position: "I proposed that the story of the raised saints in Matthew 27:52-53 should probably be interpreted as apocalyptic imagery rather than literal history." Significantly, numerous conservative writers signed a letter in defense of Licona's position:

> We the undersigned are aware of the above stated position by Dr. Michael Licona, including his present position pertaining to the

report of the raised saints in Matthew 27: He proposes that the report may refer to a literal/historical event, a real event partially described in apocalyptic terms, or an apocalyptic symbol. Though most of us do not hold Licona's proposal, we are in firm agreement that it is compatible with biblical inerrancy, despite objections to the contrary. We are encouraged to see the confluence of biblical scholars, historians, and philosophers in this question.

W. David Beck, Ph.D.
Craig Blomberg, Ph.D.
James Chancellor, Ph.D.
William Lane Craig, D.Theol., Ph.D.
Jeremy A. Evans, Ph.D.
Gary R. Habermas, Ph.D.
Craig S. Keener, Ph.D.
Douglas J. Moo, Ph.D.
J. P. Moreland, Ph.D.
Heath A. Thomas, Ph.D.
Daniel B. Wallace, Ph.D.
William Warren, Ph.D.
Edwin M. Yamauchi, Ph.D.

CONTRADICTION #17 Contradiction about Who Was Raised First

Matthew's account is contradicted by Acts 26:23.

> Acts 26:23 That Christ should suffer, and that *he should be the first that should rise from the dead*, and should shew light unto the people, and to the Gentiles.

Matthew 27:51-53 narrated that the miraculous resurrection of the saints followed immediately *after* Jesus's death on Friday afternoon.

> Mt 27:51 And behold, the vail of the temple was rent in twain from the top to the bottom; and the earth did quake, and the rocks rent;

> Mt 27:52 And the graves were opened; and many bodies of the saints which slept arose,

> Mt 27:53 And came out of the graves after his resurrection, and
> went into the holy city, and appeared unto many.

The NIV translates the opening of verse 51 as "at that moment," referring to the moment immediately following Jesus's death coincided with the renting of the Temple's veil and the splitting of rocks during the earthquake. Therefore, Matthew has the saints resurrecting sometime late Friday afternoon.

The allegation, moreover, that the saints were raised from the dead at that time, and *before* the resurrection of Jesus, also contradicts Revelation 1:5: "And from Jesus Christ, who is the faithful witness, *and the first begotten of the dead*, and the prince of the kings of the earth. Unto him that loved us, and washed us from our sins in his own blood."

In addition, Paul, writing in 1 Corinthians 15, also declares that Jesus was the "first begotten of the dead."

> 1 Cor 15:20 But now is Christ risen from the dead, and *become the firstfruits of them that slept.*

That is, Jesus is "the first fruits of them who had fallen asleep."

SPECULATION #27 Jesus Being the First Fruits of Those That Were Dead

What can explain the seeming contradiction that Jesus is the "first fruits" of those who were previously dead, and the statement in Matthew 27:53 that the saints arose from the grave on Good Friday, three days before Easter Sunday, when church tradition instructs that Jesus was resurrected? A possible Christian apologetic for Jesus being the first to rise from the dead is that he was the "first of importance or priority" and not the first chronologically speaking. Another possible Christian apologetic is that Matthew was reporting a *temporary* resurrection of the saints, which is not the same as Jesus's resurrection to *immortality*. However, these responses are nothing more than apologetic opinions and mere speculations. To summarize, Luke (the assumed author of Acts) has the saints rising three days *after* Jesus's death whereas Matthew has them rising on the *same* day that Jesus was crucified.

SPECULATION #28 Did the Saints Arise Before or After Jesus's Resurrection?

There are additional problems with Matthew 27:52-53. The Greek text states literally that the saints arose from their sleep immediately following Jesus's death but did not come out of their graves until *after* his resurrection. Therefore, Jesus is the first person to come out of a grave and walk around. However, Christian tradition instructs that Jesus did not arise until three days and three nights had passed. Consequently, it must be assumed that the saints did not go into Jerusalem until after Jesus was resurrected.

Problem 1

The first problem is that the precise date and time of Jesus's alleged resurrection is not recorded in the Gospels. Nobody, not even the angels, is recorded in the gospels to have seen Jesus leave the tomb. Yet according to the Christian scriptures, it can only be assumed that the resurrection of these saints took place sometime prior to the following Sunday morning when the women discovered the empty tomb. Reginald Fuller (1988, 980; see Evans 2012, 467), writing in the *Harper's Bible Commentary*, declared: "This is a strange story. One wonders what the resurrected saints were doing between Good Friday and Easter." That is, what were the risen saints doing lingering in their risen states while still in their opened graves from Friday afternoon to Sunday morning (also see Evans 2012, 467; Hill 1985, 78; Licona 2010, 552-53; Osborne 2010, 1046)? Here, Matthew is silent. In addition, these verses raise a related question: what would be the point in raising these saints from the dead just to have them stay in their tombs or near their tombs and then appear in Jerusalem three days later?

Problem 2

Reginald Fuller (1988, 980), writing again in the *Harper's Bible Commentary*, declares: "The story flatly contradicts Paul's teaching that other resurrections will occur only at the parousia" (1 Cor 15:23). The Parousia refers to Jesus's second coming. In other words, Jesus is the first person raised to eternal and everlasting life.

Problem 3

On a literal reading, the Matthew 27 chronology runs from Friday Nisan 15 (1-51) to Sunday Nisan 17 (52-53) and back to Friday, Nisan 15 (see table 17, cf. Evans 2003, 16). Yet if verses 52 and 53 are removed from the gospel, the text reads smoothly.

TABLE 17. A Chart of Matthew's Main Events: Is Matthew Chronological?

DATE	VERSE	EVENTS
Friday, Nisan 15	Mt 27:1-49	Trial, conviction, and execution.
Friday, Nisan 15	Mt 27:50	Jesus cries at the 9th hour and dies.
Friday, Nisan 15	Mt 27:51	1. Temple veil is rent.
	Mt 27:51	2. Earth did quake.
	Mt 27:51	3. Rocks rent.
	Mt 27:52	4. Graves opened.
	Mt 27:52	5. Many bodies of the saints which slept arose.
Sunday, Nisan 17 [Here the text seemingly jumps almost "three" days forward to Easter Sunday unless it is to be understood that the arisen saints remained in their opened graves during those days.]	Mt 27:53	Mt 27:53 And came out of the graves after his resurrection, and went into the holy city, and appeared unto many. [Based on **Acts 26:23;** 1 Cor 15:20; and Rev 1:5 Jesus was the first person resurrected and this occurred three days later on Easter Sunday.]
Friday, Nisan 15 [*Now the text apparently returns to Friday, about the ninth hour.*]	Mt 27:54	The centurion witness.
Friday, Nisan 15	Mt 27:55-56	The women witnesses.
Friday, Nisan 15	Mt 27:57-61	Burial and witnesses to burial.
Saturday, Nisan 16	Mt 27:62-66	The chief priests and Pharisees request a guard; receive a guard; and secure the tomb.

Sunday, Nisan 17		The first-fruits are offered in the Temple (Lev 23:10-12).
Sunday, Nisan 17	Mt 28:1	Women traveled to the tomb.
Sunday, Nisan 17	Mt 28:2-4	Angel, earthquake, and scared guard.
Sunday, Nisan 17	Mt 28:5-6	Angel's message: He is risen.

Wenham (1981, 151), a Christian apologist, is of the opinion that the first two problems can be resolved by analyzing the Greek text. He suggests that a full stop or other strong punctuation be placed after the Greek word *aneōchthēsan* (ανεωχθησαν) for "opened" in verse 52.

TABLE 18. Wenham's Solution

kai	ta	mnēmeia	aneōchthēsan
καὶ	τὰ	μνημεῖα	ἀνεῴχθησαν
and	which	tombs	opened

Consequently, Matthew's account "is parenthetical, breaking into the Good Friday narrative to recount happenings which occurred after Jesus' resurrection, but it does not form a complete and satisfactory parenthesis, because it has no subject." As a result: "Then the succession of events on Good Friday is clearly delineated, and the whole episode of the resurrected saints is placed after the resurrection of Jesus, thus absolving the evangelist from the charge of depicting living saints cooped up for days in tombs around the city."

Hill (1985, 78) argues against Wenham's apologetic. He counters that Wenham's apologetic "is to break an established, eschatological sequence for the sake of solving a modern logical or quasi-historical problem." More forcefully, Evans (2003, 16; cf. Troxel 2002, 36-37) is of the opinion: "The clumsiness of the chronology argues for viewing this strange story as an insertion into the Matthean narrative, an insertion perhaps dating to the second century (though some think it may be older, traditional material, dating to the first century)."

Aarde (2011) offers another apologetic for Matthew's awkward sentence order. He argues that:

> To narrate Jesus' resurrection (*meta tēn egersin* autou—Mt 27:53) *before* it eventually happened (in Mt 28:1ff) should not disturb our logical minds. Matthew was not concerned with what could be reckoned by present-day readers as consequently logical or illogical. He shared imageries that also occur in Ezekiel 37:7, 12, 13-14 and 1 Enoch 51:1-2. Resemblance of the tearing of

the veil can be found in the lives of the prophets (Hab 12:11-12—see Garland 1995:260). The earthquake bears resemblance to Zechariah 14:4 and the 'escorted and communal resurrection' (Crossan 1998:392) to the Gospel of Peter 10:1-5.

The problem with Aarde's hypothesis is that it is nothing more than his opinion. This Christian apologist has no way of knowing whether or not Matthew was "concerned with what could be reckoned by present-day readers as consequently logical or illogical."

However, Hugh Montefiore (1960, 53-54; also see Humphreys 2011, 70, 79; Saarnivaara 1954, 160) suggests that perhaps Paul called Jesus the first fruits in 1 Corinthians 15:20 for a completely different reason unrelated to being the very first person resurrected:

> He uses the word *aparche* because Jesus rose from the dead on the same day as the sheaf of first-fruits was offered in the Temple. As the waving of the first-fruits released the rest of the harvest for reaping and consumption and thus inaugurated the harvest itself, so the resurrection of Jesus inaugurated the New Age in which all shall be made alive, with "Christ as the first-fruits and then them that are Christ's at his coming."

In order to understand this hypothesis, it is necessary to have some understanding of the Jewish calendar. According to Leviticus 23, "the first-fruits were offered in the Temple on the morrow after the sabbath."

> Lev 23:10 Speak unto the children of Israel, and say unto them, When ye be come into the land which I give unto you, and shall reap the harvest thereof, then ye shall bring a sheaf of the firstfruits of your harvest unto the priest:

> Lev 23:11 And he shall wave the sheaf before the LORD, to be accepted for you: on the morrow after the sabbath the priest shall wave it.

> Lev 23:12 And ye shall offer that day when ye wave the sheaf an he lamb without blemish of the first year for a burnt offering unto the LORD.

However, Montefiore cautions that at first sight it might seem that "the phrase 'the morrow after the sabbath' refers to the Sunday in the week of

Passover. As Jesus rose from the dead on this particular Sunday, it has been generally assumed that Paul applied the word 'first-fruits' to Jesus because His resurrection took place on this Sunday."

Montefiore elaborates that for the Sadducees, the Samaritans, and the Karaites, 'the morrow after the sabbath referred to the Sunday which fell during the Festival of Unleavened Bread. In contrast, the Pharisees interpret "the morrow after the sabbath" "not to the seventh day of the week but to the first day of the Festival of Unleavened Bread, which was a 'high day.'"

> Thus, for the Pharisees the offering of the first-fruits was *made not on a fixed day of the week, but on a fixed day of the month* [italics in the original]. The sheaf was waved on the day after Nisan 15 (the first day of the Festival of Unleavened Bread), *i.e.*, on Nisan 16. It was pure coincidence that in the year of Jesus' death Nisan 16 happened to fall on a Sunday.

Montefiore offers three facts in support of this hypothesis.

1. In the New Testament period, the interpretation of the Pharisees usually prevailed in the official calendar over the Sadducees.
2. Philo (*De Sept.*, ii. 20), Josephus *Ant.*, III. x. 5) and the Mishnah (*Menahoth*, x. 3f) agreed that the first fruits were offered on the second day of the festival, i.e., on Nisan 16.
3. Given Paul's Pharisaic upbringing, it is assumed that he would have followed their interpretation of Leviticus 23:10-12.

In conclusion, Montefiore posits: "It may therefore be assumed that Paul called Jesus 'the first-fruits of them that have fallen asleep' not because Jesus was raised from the dead on Sunday during the Festival of Unleavened Bread but because His resurrection took place on Nisan 16."

Problem 4

Evans (2012, 467) raises a fourth problem. He writes, "There are other unanswered questions, too. Who were these saints supposed to be? If they were patriarchs and prophets of old, then how would anyone have recognized them as such? (Remember, there were no photographs or painted portraits for identification!) And further, what happened to them? Did they return to their tombs a few days later?"

SPECULATION #29 A Vindication of Hope as the Source as the Origin of the Resurrected Saints

A final possible explanation of the resurrected saints may also be a basis found outside the scriptures. Here, Senior (1976, 321) suggests that this account was written to serve "as a vindication of hope and as an affirmation of God's saving power in the midst of death" and "as an expression of messianic hope." In contrast, Fales (2001, 29) posits that the purpose of the raised saints is to "command a loyal following of believers even unto martyrdom." Simply put: follow the leader.

ISSUE 14: The Actions of the Roman Soldiers during the Crucifixion and Jesus's Death

| Mk 15:24 And when they had crucified him, *they parted his garments, casting lots upon them, what every man should take.*

Mk 15:39 *And when the centurion, which stood over against him, saw that he so cried out, and gave up the ghost, he said, Truly this man was the Son of God.* | Mt 27:35 *And they crucified him, and parted his garments, casting lots*: that it might be fulfilled which was spoken by the prophet, They parted my garments among them, and upon my vesture did they cast lots. 36 And sitting down they watched him there; 37 *And set up over his head his accusation written,* THIS IS JESUS THE KING OF THE JEWS.

Mt 27:54 Now when the centurion, and they that were with him, watching Jesus, *saw the earthquake, and those things that were done, they feared greatly, saying, Truly this was the Son of God.* | Lk 23:34 Then said Jesus, Father, forgive them; for they know not what they do. *And they parted his raiment, and cast lots.*

Lk 23:36 *And the soldiers also mocked him,* coming to him, and offering him vinegar, 37 And saying, If thou be the king of the Jews, save thyself.

Lk 23:47 Now when the centurion saw what was done, *he glorified God, saying, Certainly this was a righteous man.* | Jn 19:23 *Then the soldiers, when they had crucified Jesus, took his garments, and made four parts,* to every soldier a part; and also his coat: now the coat was without seam, woven from the top throughout. 24 They said therefore among *themselves,* Let us not rend it, *but cast lots for it,* whose it shall be: that the scripture might be fulfilled, which saith, They parted my raiment among them, and for my vesture they did cast lots. These things therefore the soldiers did. |

Mark reports two actions taken by Roman soldiers following Jesus's crucifixion: they divide Jesus's garment, and they cast lots to determine who would obtain possession of it. Later, Mark describes a Roman centurion's reaction to Jesus dying on the cross. Matthew also reports that Jesus's clothes were divided and casting lots determined their future possessors. After watching Jesus on the cross, they placed an inscription over his head stating the specific charge against him: "THIS IS JESUS THE KING OF THE JEWS." Finally, Matthew reports that during the darkness from the sixth hour to the ninth hour, the details of Jesus's death, the tearing of the Temple's veil, the earthquake, the opening of the graves, and the bodies of the saints coming out of their graves and going into the holy city had a collective response on the Roman centurion and those who were with him.

Luke also describes the casting of lots and the dividing of Jesus's clothing. Furthermore, he adds two details: (1) the centurion glorified God by declaring, "Certainly this was a righteous man" and (2) "All the people that came together to that sight, beholding the things which were done, smote their breasts, and returned." Finally, John too details the Roman soldiers dividing Jesus's tunic and casting lots to see who would get it. However, he adds that the observed events were prophetic fulfillment as found in Psalm 22.

CONTRADICTION #18 What the Centurion Saw

Mark is virtually void of any comment about what the centurion saw other than Jesus's death. In contrast, Matthew 27:54 narrates: "Now when the centurion, and they that were with him, watching Jesus, saw the earthquake, and those things that were done, they feared greatly, saying, Truly this was the Son of God." The absence of an earthquake raises two issues: (1) given that an earthquake occurred at the precise moment Jesus died, why did Mark omit such a significant detail from his gospel, and (2) where then did Matthew obtain his source material?

However, it should be pointed out that Oygen (2003, 137; cf. Juel 1999, 146-47) has suggested it is possible that Mark's statement in 15:39 that Jesus was the Son of God was an act of verbal irony or meant as a sarcastic comment: "He is mocking Jesus: "Haha, look at this man. Son of God, is he?!" The ἀληθῶς would in fact mean "not at all"!"

More importantly, Luke 23:47, like Mark, does not provide any facts detailing what the centurion saw: "Now when the centurion saw what was done." Therefore, Luke confirms Mark's narrative. This absence of Matthew's witnesses of the earthquake furthers the argument that challenges the historicity and reliability of Matthew's gospel. Specifically, the earthquake in conjunction with (1) the renting of the Temple's veil, (2) the earth turning dark from 12:00 noon until 3:00 p.m., and (3) Jesus's death is highly significant. It must be reiterated that Luke, writing after Matthew, reported in the prologue to his gospel that he "carefully investigated everything from the beginning." Therefore, Luke is claiming that he reviewed numerous sources, and presumably including Matthew. Why then did Luke omit such a cosmic event? Perhaps Luke's omission is a deletion that confirmed that the event (i.e., "myth") is an invention of Matthew.

CONTRADICTION #19 Topography versus Matthew: The Centurion Could Not View the Tearing of the Temple's Veil

Mark is virtually void of any comment about what the centurion saw other than Jesus's death. In contrast, Matthew 27:54 narrates: "Now when the centurion, and they that were with him, watching Jesus, saw the earthquake, and *those things that were done*, they feared greatly, saying, Truly this was the Son of God." The phrase "and those things that were done" is subject to speculation since no further details are provided. Similarly, Luke 23:47 does not provide any facts detailing what the centurion saw: "Now when the centurion saw what was done." On the other hand, John omits any discussion about what is seen. Instead, he claims that portions of the Crucifixion are prophetic.

Matthew's narrative suggests that the centurion, and perhaps others, standing on Golgotha saw the tearing of the Temple's veil (e.g., Karris 1986, 66). However, Christian scholars and theologians are divided as to which veil is referred to: the inner or outer veil of the Holy of Holies.

Significantly, numerous writers (Brown 1994a, 2:1145-46; Fitzmyer 1985, 1519; France 2007, 1083; 2002, 658; Gundry 1993, 970; Hagner 1995, 852; and Kroll October 2007 "Live From the Holy Land"—aired on October 22-26, 2007; Stein 2008, 718; 1992, 596) point out that the Temple's veil, either inside the Holy of Holies or outside the Holy of Holies, *cannot* be seen from Golgotha, the site of the Crucifixion. Gundry states: "Since the traditional site of Golgotha lies to the west end of the temple whereas only the east end was veiled (not to mention intervening obstacles to view), either tradition has misplaced Golgotha or the centurion's seeing of the veil-rending lacks historical substance."

Gundry's compact sentence requires further elaboration. Josephus (*Wars* 5, 4, 1-5, 5, 8; Whiston pp. 552-56) details how the Temple was originally "built upon two hills which are opposite to one another" and the Temple Mount was built on what David called the citadel. He then goes into detail describing the Temple. Another detailed description of the Temple is vividly described in Ezekiel 40-43. Two significant sections are relevant to this issue:

> Ez 43:1-4 Afterward he brought me to the gate, even the gate that *looketh toward the east*: And, behold, *the glory of the God of Israel came from the way of the east*: and his voice was like a noise of many waters: and the earth shined with his glory. And it was according to the appearance of the vision which I saw, even according to the vision that I saw when I came to destroy the city: and the visions were like the vision that I saw by the river Chebar; and I fell upon my face. And the glory of the LORD came into the house by the way of the gate whose prospect is toward the east.

The key point here is that the Shekinah's glory will enter the Temple compound via the outer eastern gate and go into the most holy place in the Temple to dwell with Israel. In other words, this portion of the Temple is open.

> Ez 41:12 Now the building that was before the separate place at the end toward the west was seventy cubits broad; and the wall of the building was five cubits thick round about, and the length thereof ninety cubits.

Illustration 1. Plan Showing Position of the Temple on Mount Moriah according to the Talmud (Designed by J. D. Eisenstein) "The Temple in Rabbinical Literature," in *The Jewish Encyclopedia*, volume 11, J. D. Eisenstein, p. 94. New York: Funk And Wagnalls, 1906.

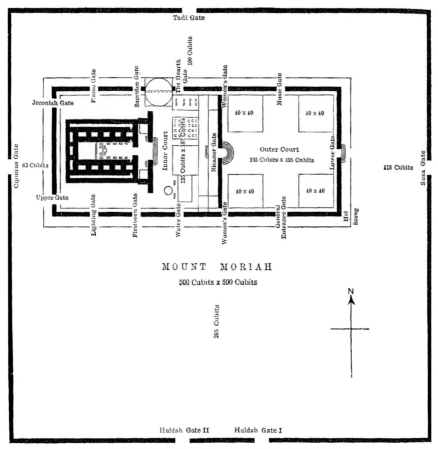

PLAN SHOWING POSITION OF THE TEMPLE ON MOUNT MORIAH ACCORDING TO THE TALMUD.
(Designed by J. D. Eisenstein, New York.)

Illustration 2. Jerusalem in the Time of Jesus. In *The International Bible Commentary*, edited by W. R. Farmer, p. 1,311. Copyright 1998 by Order of Saint Benedict. Published by Liturgical Press, Collegeville, Minnesota. Reprinted with permission.

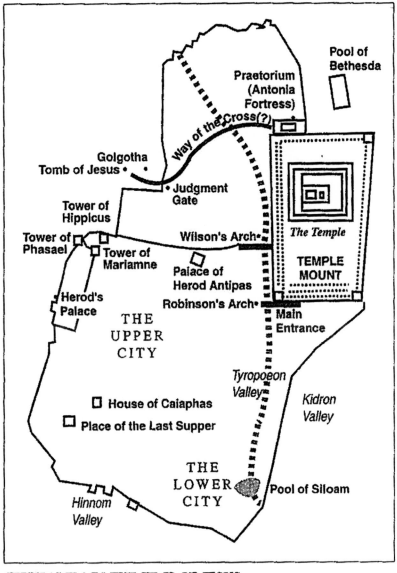

JERUSALEM IN THE TIME OF JESUS

On the map note the locations of Golgotha and the positioning of the Temple, in particular the Holy of Holies. If at that time a person was standing on Golgotha and looking eastward, all that could have been seen was the back wall of the Holy of Holies. The Holy of Holies is enclosed on three sides with its opening on the east side. Consequently, it would have been impossible for the centurion to see the Temple's veil if he had stood west of the Temple.

R. T. France (2002, 658), a conservative Christian apologist, writes:

> The account of the tearing of the curtain intervenes between Jesus' death and the centurion's reaction to that death . . . Many interpreters therefore conclude that Mark intends us to include the tearing of the curtain in what the centurion saw which formed the basis for his exclamation. But Mark does not say that the centurion saw it, and at the narrative level this would be impossible since one would have to be standing east of the temple (and nearer to it than any likely location of Golgotha) in order to see the curtain. The account of the curtain is for the benefit of Mark's readers as they think about the significance of Jesus' death, not in relation to the following mention of the centurion; the centurion's comment is evoked simply by how Jesus died.

In conclusion, the record of the centurion's potentially witnessing the tearing of the Temple's veil is ahistoric.

ISSUE 15: The Actions of Jesus's Followers during the Crucifixion and His Death

Mk 14:50 *And they all forsook him, and fled.* Mk 15:40 *There were also women looking on afar off: among whom was Mary Magdalene, and Mary the mother of James the less and of Joses, and Salome;* 41 (Who also, when he was in Galilee, followed him, and ministered unto him;) *and many other women* which came up with him unto Jerusalem.	Mt 26:56 But all this was done, that the scriptures of the prophets might be fulfilled. Then all the disciples forsook him, and fled. Mt 27:54 Now when the centurion, *and they that were with him, watching Jesus, saw the earthquake, and those things that were done, they feared greatly, saying, Truly this was the Son of God.* 55. *And many women were there beholding afar off, which followed Jesus from Galilee*, ministering unto him: 56 Among which was Mary Magdalene, and Mary the mother of James and Joses, and the mother of Zebedee's children. Mt 27:61 And there was Mary Magdalene, and the other Mary, sitting over against the sepulchre.	Lk 23:47 Now when the centurion saw what was done, he glorified God, saying, Certainly this was a righteous man. 48 *And all the people that came together to that sight, beholding the things which were done, smote their breasts, and returned.* 49 And all his acquaintance, and the women that *followed him from Galilee, stood afar off, beholding these things . . .* Lk 23:56 And they returned, and prepared spices and ointments; and rested the sabbath day according to the commandment.	Jn 19:25 *Now there stood by the cross of Jesus his mother, and his mother's sister, Mary the wife of Cleophas, and Mary Magdalene.* 26 *When Jesus therefore saw his mother, and the disciple standing by, whom he loved,* he saith unto his mother, Woman, behold thy son! 27 Then saith he to the disciple, Behold thy mother! *And from that hour that disciple took her unto his own home.*

Mark 14:50 narrates that all the disciples forsook Jesus, and later, several named women watched from afar as Jesus hung on the cross. Matthew 26:56 also reports that *all* of the disciples had deserted their Master at the time of Jesus's arrest. However, he added that there were many women at a distance from the cross. Later he reports that Mary Magdalene and the other Mary positioned themselves "sitting over against the sepulchre."

Luke 23:49 also supports Mark and Matthew, assuming that the mention of "and all his acquaintance" does not refer to the disciples. Thus, the only followers present during Jesus's crucifixion were the many women followers.

Finally, John 19:25-27 narrates that at least one disciple was present during Jesus's crucifixion: the disciple "whom he loved." In addition, one member of Jesus's family was also in attendance, Mary, Jesus's mother, along with several more women.

CONTRADICTION #20 The Forsaking of the Disciples

The synoptic narratives reports differing details of those present at Jesus's crucifixion and the actions they took. In Mark 14:50, none of the apostles are described as being present during Jesus's crucifixion: "And they all forsook him, and fled." Matthew 26:56 also reports that *all* the disciples had deserted their Master at the time of Jesus's arrest. Luke 23:48 reports: "And all the people that came together to that sight, beholding the things which were done, smote their breasts, and returned." Then, in verse 48, he adds: "And all his acquaintance, and the women that followed him from Galilee, stood afar off, beholding these things." Significantly, Luke fails to identify these acquaintances. Consequently, it is impossible to determine if any of these acquaintances were his disciples.

A contradiction exists, given that Luke's acquaintances include any of the disciples. That is, Luke is known to have been highly dependent upon Mark and Matthew. Yet Luke seemingly rejects something reported by Mark and Matthew. Why then would Luke change such an important fact?

An even greater contradiction appears in John. Contrary to the synoptic Gospels, John had at least one disciple present during Jesus's crucifixion, the disciple "whom he loved."

> Jn 19:25 Now there stood by the cross of Jesus his mother, and his mother's sister, Mary the wife of Cleophas, and Mary Magdalene.
>
> Jn 19:26 When Jesus therefore saw his mother, and the disciple standing by, whom he loved, he saith unto his mother, Woman, behold thy son!
>
> Jn 19:27 Then saith he to the disciple, Behold thy mother! And from that hour that disciple took her unto his own home.

Not only is he the only disciple identified as being present during the Crucifixion, but Jesus also carried on a conversation with him and directed him to care for his mother! In effect, John's narrative reads like a completely different story from the synoptic accounts.

In conclusion, given that Luke's acquaintances included his disciples, Luke and John (John states that at least one disciple was at the cross during Jesus's crucifixion) directly contradicts Mark and Matthew. However, if Luke's "acquaintances" did not include the disciples, now there is a contradiction between John and all of the synoptic Gospels.

CONTRADICTION #21 The Differing Accounts of the Women at the Cross during the Crucifixion

The synoptic narratives reported differing details of those present at Jesus's crucifixion and the actions they took. Mark 14:50 reports that the only people present at the death of Jesus were several women. One chapter later, Mark 15:40 tersely reports a singular action: "There were also women looking on afar off." Mark adds that "among whom where Mary Magdalene, and Mary the mother of James the less and of Joses, and Salome." Consequently, there were also other women present in the vicinity when Jesus died.

Matthew 27:54 narrates: "Now when the centurion, and *they* that were with him, watching Jesus, saw the earthquake, and those things that were done, they feared greatly, saying, Truly this was the Son of God." Given that the women are included in the word *they*, Matthew has them fearing and affirming that Jesus is the Son of God, a significant addition to Mark. In the next two verses, Matthew continues to provide additional information: "And many women were there behold afar off, which followed Jesus from Galilee, ministering unto him." The unknown is how many women comprised this group. However, Matthew categorically states: "Among which was Mary Magdalene and Mary the mother of James and Joses, and the mother of Zebedee's children."

On the other hand, Luke 23:48 slightly differs from Mark's and Matthew's accounts adding: "And all the people that came together to that sight, beholding the things which were done, smote their breasts, and returned." Mark and Matthew provide no such information about the people beating their breasts.

Contrary to the synoptic Gospels, John alone has Jesus's mother present during Jesus's crucifixion. This is the first appearance of Jesus's mother in John. Out of nowhere she suddenly appears. This appearance is striking since there are only a few references to her physical presence in any of the gospels. Chronologically they are the following:

> Luke 1:26-38 detailed Mary's encounter with the angel Gabriel in Nazareth.

Luke 1:39-56 reported Mary traveling to the hill country in Judea and staying with Elizabeth for three months.

Luke 2:1-20 informed his readers that Mary traveled from Nazareth to Bethlehem and gave birth to Jesus in Bethlehem.

Matthew 2:1-6 narrated the visit of the wise men to Jesus (and Mary) in Bethlehem after the birth of Jesus.

Luke 2:22-36 described Jesus's parents presenting Jesus to the Temple.

Matthew 2:21 reported that after Jesus was born Joseph and Mary took the infant Jesus to Egypt.

Luke 2:39-40 detailed the parents returning to Nazareth where Jesus grew and became strong (spanning up to the age of twelve).

Luke 2:41-51 narrated an incident when the twelve year old Jesus visited the Temple.

Consequently, there is no description of the physical presence of Jesus's mother for almost eighteen years, from the age of twelve to the age of thirty. Not only is this physical appearance highly remarkable but John also reports a terse communication Jesus had with his mother while on the cross:

Jn 19:25 Now there stood by the cross of Jesus his mother, and his mother's sister, Mary the wife of Cleophas, and Mary Magdalene.

Jn 19:26 When Jesus therefore saw his mother, and the disciple standing by, whom he loved, he saith unto his mother, Woman, behold thy son!

Jn 19:27 Then saith he to the disciple, Behold thy mother! And from that hour that disciple took her unto his own home.

Yet not one of the synoptic Gospels reports the dying words of Jesus to his mother or even her presence at his death. In particular, it is extraordinary, if not incredible, that Luke did not report these events having examined "all things from the very first" (Lk 1:3) and to have deliberately omitted them.

Finally, John 19:25 contradicted the synoptic Gospels by reporting that the women were positioned close to the cross when Jesus died: "Now there stood by the cross of Jesus his mother, and his mother's sister, Mary the wife of Cleophas, and Mary Magdalene." Yet the synoptic narrative reports that the women were positioned far away.

> Mk 15:40-41 There were also women looking on afar off: among whom was Mary Magdalene, and Mary the mother of James the less and of Joses, and Salome; (Who also, when he was in Galilee, followed him, and ministered unto him;) and many other women which came up with him unto Jerusalem.

> Mt 27:55-56 And many women were there beholding afar off, which followed Jesus from Galilee, ministering unto him: Among which was Mary Magdalene, and Mary the mother of James and Joses, and the mother of Zebedee's children.

> Lk 23:49, 55 And all his acquaintance, and the women that followed him from Galilee, stood afar off, beholding these things . . . And the women also, which came with him from Galilee, followed after, and beheld the sepulchre, and how his body was laid.

Marsh (1908, 44; also see Grassmick 1983, 190; MacArthur 2005, 1259) offers a Christian apologetic that it is possible that some of the women, or even all of them, initially, watched or stood by the cross for a moment as reported in the synoptic Gospels. However, later, the women moved far away from the cross as detailed by John.

Marsh's apologetic is pure speculation without any evidentiary proof. It is an argument based on silence. He had no way of knowing the true intent of the author. Perhaps John directly contradicts the synoptic Gospels to make Jesus's death seem less shameful and more dignified. Of course, this too would be a speculation. Yet another explanation for John's placement of Jesus's mother and the Beloved Disciple at the cross is to enhance the drama and tension. In addition, some scholars speculate that this verse reflects a power struggle within the early church. That is, this episode and others made the Beloved Disciple appear superior to Peter and James. The topic of the conflict between the Petrine community and Johannine community is examined later in this text.

Finally, once more, it must be noted that Luke claims to have reviewed all the existing sources of his day, yet he omits any commentary that the women were present at the cross and then left. The omission of such an important detail does not make sense. That is, unless Christian apologists maintain that Luke knew the women were present and later moved far off, and for some unexplained reason, he deliberately decided to delete these facts.

SPECULATION #30 Those Present during Jesus's Death— the Acquaintances in Luke 23:49

The gospel narratives raise several speculative issues about the presence or nonpresence of those during Jesus's death. The phrase "and (*de*) all (*pas*) his (*autos*) acquaintance (*gnōstoi*, masc.)" has been subject to much debate. Luke incorporates the word "acquaintance" three times: Luke 2:44; 23:49; and Acts 24:23. In a review of the literature, Brown (1994a, 2:1172-173) identifies and elaborates several possible explanations for the specific group of individuals Luke had in mind. These include (1) the Eleven (the Twelve minus Judas); (2) the relatives of Jesus, male and female; and (3) other disciples and/ or friends of Jesus beyond the Twelve. The take-away message is that nobody knows exactly who these onlookers are. Consequently, scholars are only able to offer their best guess, hunch, or speculation.

SPECULATION #31 Improbability of the Presence under the Cross

Christian scholars disagree regarding the probability that Jesus's mother and the disciple whom he loved were near the cross. This skeptical position is based on the rationale that Jesus carried on a conversation with both of them despite being previously beaten, scourged, and crucified. Tinsley (1965, 204; cf. Casey 1996, 188; Corley 2004, 81; 1998, 196n117; Thompson 1995, 61) argues that "The Romans did not permit bystanders at the actual place of execution. John's account is influenced by his symbolic aim. The mother (old Israel) is handed over to the care of the 'beloved disciple' (who represents the new Israel of the Christian Church)."

In contrast, several writers (Keener 2003, 1141; 1993, 313; Köstenberger 2004a, 547; Stauffer 1960, 179n1) contend that it was not likely that women had restricted access to victims on a cross. They argue:

1.   Passages from T. *Gittin* 7.1; *y. Gittin* 7, 48c, 49; *b. Baba Metzia* 83b represent friends of the victims as standing near enough to be within hearing range.

2. The soldiers might not have recognized who among the crowds constituted Jesus's followers.
3. Soldiers would be less likely to punish women present for mourning.
4. The prerogatives of motherhood were highly respected in the ancient world.
5. Women were far less frequently executed than men.

Casey (1996, 188) adds that:

> Another unlikely feature is the group of people besides the cross. Mark has a group of women watching from a long way off (Mk 15.40-1), which is highly plausible. The fourth Gospel's group of people beside the cross includes Jesus' mother and the beloved disciple. It is most unlikely that these people would be allowed this close to a Roman crucifixion. If they had been, and they included people central to Jesus' life and ministry, it is most unlikely that Mark would merely have women watching from a distance. If a major male disciple had approached this close, it is likely that he would have been arrested.

Barrett (1978, 551) refutes these apologetics and argues against the historicity of any presence near the cross. He posits that these citations from the Mishnah and Talmud do not outweigh the military requirements of the execution of a rebel king. Furthermore, he cites Josephus (*Vita*, 420f.) who recorded that with special permission he was able to release three friends who were crucified. One friend actually survived. This incident is significant because it demonstrates that permission would be needed to approach the crosses.

Similarly, Corley (1998, 196n117) writes:

> The rabbinic sources cited by Strack-Billerbeck and others commonly marshaled to support such a contention either deal with such hypothetical situations that they are hardly germane or describe religious, not state executions . . . Commonly cited as evidence are *Y. Gittin* 7:1 (330) or *Baba Metzia* 83b. For example, *Baba Metzia* 83b describes R. Eleazar weeping under the gallows of a man hanged for violating religious law (rape of an engaged woman); *Y. Gittlin* 7:1 describes a wildly hypothetical situation involving divorce.

Holtzmann (1904, 487), a dated source, adds that "the soldiers divided amongst themselves the clothes of the crucified; they then had to keep watch by the cross, lest his sympathising friends should come to the help of the tortured man."

Schnackenburg (1982, 277) offers: "They are standing 'by the cross.' Apparently near Jesus. Whether this is historically probable, since the guard would scarcely allow spectators to approach so close does not worry the evangelist; he is concerned with the deeper meaning of the scene."

SPECULATION #32 The Theological Agenda of John Regarding "the Beloved Disciple"

The synoptic accounts omit mentioning either the absence or presence of the disciples at Jesus's crucifixion. In contrast, the author of John specifically mentions the presence of the "beloved disciple" by whom Jesus's mother would now be cared for. A speculated reason is that the agenda of the author of John was to make "the beloved disciple" superior to Peter and James

> Jn 21:7 Therefore that disciple whom Jesus loved saith unto Peter, It is the Lord. Now when Simon Peter heard that it was the Lord, he girt his fisher's coat unto him, (for he was naked,) and did cast himself into the sea.

> Jn 21:20 Then Peter, turning about, seeth the disciple whom Jesus loved following; which also leaned on his breast at supper, and said, Lord, which is he that betrayeth thee?

> Jn 21:24 This is the disciple which testifieth of these things, and wrote these things: and we know that his testimony is true.

Perhaps more significantly, the author of John is attempting to make the beloved disciple the genuine successor of Jesus by having the dying "son of God" appoint him to be the "guardian of the community represented by Mary." However, this proposition is nothing more than a speculation. Furthermore, this proposal assumes that the "beloved disciple" is John, a point disputed by Charlesworth (1995) and many others.

SPECULATION #33 Could John Have Possessed a Home?

Another curious issue relates to Jesus's disciple, the one "whom he loved," and his taking in of Jesus's mother and bringing her to his own house. John

19:27 reads: "Then saith he to the disciple, Behold thy mother! And from that hour that disciple took her unto his own home." Charlesworth (1995, 127-223; 414-22), in his seminal work, *The Beloved Disciple: Whose Witness Validates the Gospel of John?* offers over twenty speculated theories attempting to identify the Beloved Disciple. Among these included (1) Ananda, (2) an Ideal, Fictitious, or Symbolic Figure, (3) a Symbol of the Apostolic Prophet, (4) a Symbol of the Church, (5) a Real Human Whose Identity is Lost, (6) Matthias, (7) Apollos, (8) Paul or a Paulinist, (8) Benjamin, (9) the Rich Young Ruler, (10) Judas Iscariot, (11) Andrew, Simon Peter's Brother, (12) Philip, (13) Nathanael, (14) Lazarus, (15) John Mark, (16) Judas, Jesus's Brother, (17) John the Apostle, (18) John the Elder, (19) John the Elder Blended with John the Apostle, (20) One of the Two Anonymous Disciples Noted in 21:2, and (21) Thomas.

The issue of who the disciple is engenders deep skepticism and scholarly debate between scholars, theologians, and historians. The issue of skepticism was raised by Bernard (1928, 637; cf. Brown 2:1023), and it relates to the viability of the individual possessing a personal home *if* he was just one of the original twelve apostles. The reason for doubt is that it is questionable that any of the disciples would be able to possess their own home; nonetheless, in Jerusalem, or within its vicinity. All accounts indicate that the disciples were too dependent to possess a house into which to receive Jesus's mother.

For example, in Mark 10:28 Peter declares: "Then Peter began to say unto him, Lo, we have left all, and have followed thee." Given that the disciples "left all" and were nothing more than itinerant disciples of their master, how is it that a disciple owned a home in Jerusalem?

Bernard (1928, 637), commenting on the phrase "to his own home" in John 19:27, writes: "John brought the Virgin Mother to his own lodging (see on 20¹⁰), and she lived with him thereafter; but we cannot build on the phrase εἰς τα ἰδια a theory which would give him a house of residence at Jerusalem (see on 18¹⁵)." A possible Christian apologetic is that one rich or several of Jesus's followers later provided finances for a disciple to obtain a home in Jerusalem. However, this apologetic would be mere speculation without any incontrovertible evidentiary proof.

ISSUE 16: Why the Legs Were Requested to Be Broken

Mk 15:34 *And at the ninth hour* Jesus cried with a loud voice, saying, Eloi, Eloi, lama sabachthani? which is, being interpreted, My God, my God, why hast thou forsaken me?	Mt 27:46 *And about the ninth hour* Jesus cried with a loud voice, saying, Eli, Eli, lama sabachthani? that is to say, My God, my God, why hast thou forsaken me? . . .	Lk 23:44 And it was about the sixth hour, and there was a darkness over all the earth *until the ninth hour.*	Jn 19:30 When Jesus therefore had received the vinegar, he said, It is finished: and he bowed his head, and gave up the ghost. 31 *The Jews therefore*, because it was the preparation, that the bodies should not remain upon the cross on the sabbath day (for that sabbath day was an high day,) *besought Pilate that their legs might be broken, and that they might be taken away.* 32 Then came the soldiers, *and brake the legs of the first, and of the other which was crucified with him.* 33. But when they came to Jesus, and saw that he was dead already, *they brake not his legs.*

John 19:30-31 reports that a group of unnamed Jews sought an audience with Pilate after Jesus had died. They were concerned about the approaching Sabbath. The location and exact time of this meeting is not provided in the narrative. Nevertheless, they requested that Pilate grant permission to have the legs of the condemned thieves broken since they seemingly knew Jesus had earlier died and the bodies of the three taken away. John does not explicitly explain that the purpose of the leg breaking, that is the so-called *crurifragium,* was to facilitate a rapid death. In addition, the narrative does not say that this group of Jews wanted the bodies. Later the narrative describes how the soldiers broke the legs of the first and then the other person crucified with Jesus. However, when they went to break Jesus's legs, he was already dead. Therefore, the soldiers did not break his legs.

CONTRADICTION #22 The Prophetic Fulfillment Is Omitted in the Synoptics

The significant lead-up details in John 19:31 about an unspecified group of Jews appearing before Pilate requesting that the legs of the condemned be broken and the bodies taken away does *not* appear in the synoptic narratives; it is only reported in John: "The Jews therefore, because it was the preparation, that the bodies should not remain upon the cross on the sabbath day, (for that sabbath day was an high day,) besought Pilate that their legs might be broken, and that they might be taken away." Either the information in John was unknown to the synoptic authors, deliberately omitted, or a later fabrication.

How such a significant fact would be unknown to the synoptic authors is incomprehensible and inconceivable. In particular, John claims that the failure to complete the request of the Jews was a prophetic fulfillment of Exodus 12:46. This topic is discussed in issue 17. Even more significantly, Luke 1:3 writes in the prologue to his gospel that he "carefully investigated everything from the beginning." Why then would he have specifically omitted such important details that were later recorded by John?

Luke's omission, in fact, confirms that this episode was a later invention to fulfill the author's theological agenda stated in John 20:31: "But these are written, that ye might believe that Jesus is the Christ, the Son of God; and that believing ye might have life through his name."

SPECULATION #34 John's Purpose of the Crurifragium

The crurifragium entails the crushing of the legs from the hip to the foot with hammers and clubs. In theory, with the legs broken, the victims would be unable to support themselves, which was necessary for breathing. After a brief period of time, the muscles responsible for breathing would fatigue, and the victim would rapidly succumb to death due to asphyxiation. More recently it has been posited that death was more probably due to shock. In either case, the resultant death would rapidly follow.

The rationale given by John for the leg breaking is that the Jews did not want the bodies of the convicted offenders to remain alive on the cross during the Sabbath. Crucified victims were known to survive days on the cross before their final demise. Hence, the group of Jews requested the leg breaking to guarantee a rapid and swift death of the condemned. Another obvious reason for the leg breaking was that John 19:31 had Jesus dying on the fourteenth of Nisan, the eve of the Passover, which was the Day of Preparation. This date is noteworthy because it deliberately coincides with when the lambs were to be slaughtered in the Temple. Therefore, Jesus became the paschal offering. Finally, as a matter of sensibility, it would be desirable to have all the bodies removed prior to the commencing of the Passover Seder.

ISSUE 17: The Bones of the Condemned

Mk	Mt	Lk	Jn 19:31 *The Jews therefore*, because it was the preparation, that the bodies should not remain upon the cross on the sabbath day (for that sabbath day was an high day,) *besought Pilate that their legs might be broken, and that they might be taken away. 32 Then came the soldiers, and brake the legs of the first, and of the other which was crucified with him. 33 But when they came to Jesus, and saw that he was dead already, they brake not his legs.* 34 But one of the soldiers with a spear pierced his side, and forthwith came there out blood and water. 35 And he that saw it bare record, and his record is true: and he knoweth that he saith true, that ye might believe. 36 *For these things were done, that the scripture should be fulfilled, A bone of him shall not be broken.* 37 And again another scripture saith, They shall look on him whom they pierced.

John 19:31 reports that a group of unnamed Jews requested that Pilate order the legs of the crucified men be broken so that the bodies could be removed before the Sabbath. No verbal reply to the request is recorded. In the very next verse, the text detailed that the soldiers then proceeded to break first the legs of the two "thieves" condemned to die with Jesus. When the soldiers came to Jesus, he was already dead, and therefore they did not break his legs. Then in John 19:36, the author unequivocally declares the specific reason that these events previously recorded in verses 31 through 35 occurred: "For these things were done, that the scripture should be fulfilled, a bone of him shall not be broken."

No explicit verse is cited by John as a proof text of the prophetic fulfilment. However, Christian apologists and theologians cite two verses from the Hebrew Bible that they claim points to verse 36, "For these things were done, that the scripture should be fulfilled, A bone of him shall not be broken": Exodus 12:46 and Psalm 34:21 [20 AV].

CONTRADICTION #23 Exodus 12:46 Is *Not* a Prophetic Verse

John falsely claimed in 19:36: "For these things were done, that the scripture should be fulfilled, a bone of him shall not be broken." The scriptural verse referred to in John 19:36 is recorded in the account of the exodus from Egypt. The following are two relevant excerpts from Exodus:

Ex 12:3 Speak ye unto all the congregation of Israel, saying, In the tenth day of this month they shall take to them every man a lamb, according to the house of their fathers, a lamb for an house:

Ex 12:4 And if the household be too little for the lamb, let him and his neighbour next unto his house take it according to the number of the souls; every man according to his eating shall make your count for the lamb.

Ex 12:5 Your lamb shall be without blemish, a male of the first year: ye shall take it out from the sheep, or from the goats:

Ex 12:6 And ye shall keep it up until the fourteenth day of the same month: and the whole assembly of the congregation of Israel shall kill it in the evening.

Ex 12:43 And the LORD said unto Moses and Aaron, This is the ordinance of the passover: There shall no stranger eat thereof:

Ex 12:44 But every man's servant that is bought for money, when thou hast circumcised him, then shall he eat thereof.

Ex 12:45 A foreigner and an hired servant shall not eat thereof.

Ex 12:46 In one house shall it be eaten; thou shalt not carry forth ought of the flesh abroad out of the house; neither shall ye break a bone of it.

Ex 12:47 All the congregation of Israel shall keep it.

Ex 12:48 And when a stranger shall sojourn with thee, and will keep the passover to the LORD, let all his males be circumcised, and then let him come near and keep it; and he shall be as one that is born in the land: for no uncircumcised person shall eat thereof.

Ex 12:49 One law shall be to him that is homeborn, and unto the stranger that sojourneth among you.

Ex 12:50 Thus did all the children of Israel; as the LORD commanded Moses and Aaron, so did they.

Ex 12:51 And it came to pass the selfsame day, that the LORD did bring the children of Israel out of the land of Egypt by their armies.

The problem with Exodus 12:46 as a proof text for Jesus's resurrection is obvious. First, the words recorded in Exodus are *not* prophetic. The words are literally commandments or instructions as to how the paschal lamb had to be prepared. Even the NIV (1978, 77) tersely titled verses 43 through 51 as "Passover restrictions." From the beginning of chapter 12, several examples of instructions regarding the Passover include (1) when the Passover began, (2) how long the Passover was observed, (3) who was not permitted to eat during the Passover, (4) who was permitted to eat during the Passover, and (5) what could not be eaten, seen, or owned during the Passover. Furthermore, the Torah instructs that meat was not to be carried outside the house and that not a bone of it, that is, the paschal lamb, should be broken.

Second, Waetjen (2005, 405-06; cf. Maples 2007, 26) discusses how the author John modified the Hebrew text to fulfill his theological objective:

A bone of it/his shall not be broken. (Ex 12:46b)

They will look upon the one whom they pierced. (Zech 12:10)

It is principally the first of these two fulfillment quotations that implies Jesus' identification as the Paschal Lamb. The author has edited Ex 12:46b in order to change the aorist imperative οὐ συντρίψετε (do not break/smash), the command that God gave Moses and Aaron, into the future passive indicative οὐ συντριβήσεται (it shall not be broken), so that it becomes a directive to future generations for the divinely willed celebration of the Passover. More significantly, however, is the adjustment that the implied readers are required to make, for in the original context of 12:46b the antecedent of the pronoun αὐτοῦ (it/his) is the neuter noun, to τό πάσχα (the Paschal lamb).[64] Because Jesus is signified to be τό πάσχα (the Paschal lamb), it would not be problematic for the implied readers to apply the ambiguous

---

[64] 87 Brawley, 'John 19:28-29,' 429 is quite right to observe that "John 19:36 violates the context of Exod 12:46." But in as far as the implied readers are to infer that Jesus is the Paschal Lamb (τό πάσχα) of Ex 12:27, the contextual violation is theologically legitimate.

pronoun αὐτοῦ of Exodus 12:46b to Jesus instead of the Paschal lamb (τό πάσχα).

Second, nothing in these verses has anything to do with the Messiah and in particular the Messiah's death. To reiterate, the passages are only detailing the requisites for the first Passover and future Passovers. There is no prophetic fulfillment!

CONTRADICTION #24 Psalm 34 Is *Not* a Prophetic Verse

Psalm 34 is the second proof text employed by Christian apologists and theologians for John 19:36. In addition, several Christian Bibles (NIV, NRSV) with footnotes and various Bible guides point to Psalm 34:21 [20 AV as numbered below] as a proof text of John 19:36.

> Ps 34:1 I will bless the LORD at all times: his praise shall continually be in my mouth.

> Ps 34:2 My soul shall make her boast in the LORD: the humble shall hear thereof, and be glad.

> Ps 34:3 O magnify the LORD with me, and let us exalt his name together.

> Ps 34:4 I sought the LORD, and he heard me, and delivered me from all my fears.

> Ps 34:5 They looked unto him, and were lightened: and their faces were not ashamed.

> Ps 34:6 This poor man cried, and the LORD heard him, and saved him out of all his troubles.

> Ps 34:7 The angel of the LORD encampeth round about them that fear him, and delivereth them.

> Ps 34:8 O taste and see that the LORD is good: blessed is the man that trusteth in him.

Ps 34:9 O fear the LORD, ye his saints: for there is no want to them that fear him.

Ps 34:10 The young lions do lack, and suffer hunger: but they that seek the LORD shall not want any good thing.

Ps 34:11 Come, ye children, hearken unto me: I will teach you the fear of the LORD.

Ps 34:12 What man is he that desireth life, and loveth many days, that he may see good?

Ps 34:13 Keep thy tongue from evil, and thy lips from speaking guile.

Ps 34:14 Depart from evil, and do good; seek peace, and pursue it.

Ps 34:15 The eyes of the LORD are upon the righteous, and his ears are open unto their cry.

Ps 34:16 The face of the LORD is against them that do evil, to cut off the remembrance of them from the earth.

Ps 34:17 The righteous cry, and the LORD heareth, and delivereth them out of all their troubles.

Ps 34:18 The LORD is nigh unto them that are of a broken heart; and saveth such as be of a contrite spirit.

Ps 34:19 Many are the afflictions of the righteous: but the LORD delivereth him out of them all.

Ps 34:20 He keepeth all his bones: not one of them is broken.

Ps 34:21 Evil shall slay the wicked: and they that hate the righteous shall be desolate.

Ps 34:22 The LORD redeemeth the soul of his servants: and none of them that trust in him shall be desolate.

There is absolutely no indication that Psalm 34 is intended as prophetic. The reason that Christian apologists believe that Psalm 34 is prophetic is that they presume that it foreshadows (typology) Jesus's crucifixion. Hence, they interpret this psalm as prophetic. Furthermore, there is no indication that Psalm 34 applied to Jesus. The theme of Psalm 34 is that a righteous man is saved from the wicked. When the wicked attempt to impose suffering on this righteous man, they could not break any of his bones because God protected him. Not only was this righteous man protected but also the wicked are slain. In contrast, Jesus was not saved, and the wicked, the Romans, were not slain. Finally, nothing is mentioned about the Messiah being killed. In short, Psalm 34 has nothing to do with Jesus.

In conclusion, Christian apologists and commentators offer two possible verses as references to John 19:36. However, not even one verse in the Hebrew Bible states what John claims. Given that no verse in the Hebrew Bible substantiates John's claim, neither Exodus 12 nor Psalm 34 can serve as examples of prophetic fulfillment.

SPECULATION #35 How Do They Know a Bone Was Not Broken?

John's prophecy that not "A bone of him shall be broken" cannot be proven. All the gospel narratives report that Jesus was brutalized. In addition, the text of John 20 implies that Jesus was nailed to the cross in at least his hands:

> Jn 20:25 The other disciples therefore said unto him, We have seen the Lord. But he said unto them, Except I shall see in his hands the print of the nails, and put my finger into the print of the nails, and thrust my hand into his side, I will not believe.

> Jn 20:27 Then saith he to Thomas, Reach hither thy finger, and behold my hands; and reach hither thy hand, and thrust it into my side: and be not faithless, but believing.

Köstenberger (2004a, 553) states: "Remarkably, not only did Jesus escape the breaking of the legs (unlike those crucified with him), but also his body was pierced by a spear without sustaining bone damage." However, Pennells (1983, 109), writing in the *Journal for the Study of the New Testament*, points out that given this statement to be a fact, "if nails were used it could not be confidently claimed that no bone was broken." Neither can John confidently claim that no bone was broken during Jesus's pre-crucifixion beatings and scourging. John's claim that none of Jesus's bones were broken is a wishful guess. John did not perform an autopsy or have the luxury of an X-ray or MRI to verify his claim. Therefore, the prophecy in John 19:36 is nonvalid and nothing more than pure theology to fulfill his personal theological agenda, that of making Jesus the Paschal lamb.

SPECULATION #36 John's Invented Dubious Details and Theology

John 19:34-6 details (1) the piercing of Jesus's side with a spear, (2) the flowing of blood and water, and (3) fulfilled scripture: "For these things were done, that the scripture should be fulfilled, A bone of him shall not be broken." However, one verse earlier, significantly, the reader is informed as to why these details were presented: "And he that saw it bare record, and his record is true: and he knoweth that he saith true, *that ye might believe*" (Jn 19:35). The goal of John is twofold: propaganda and to fulfill a theological agenda.

Second, Pilate orders that the Roman soldiers break the legs of the crucified men. Nonetheless, these soldiers did *not* execute this specific command in the case with Jesus. It is not reasonable to suppose that Roman soldiers would disregard their orders and potentially subject themselves to severe punishment for disobedience inflicted by Roman military law. Insubordination was a matter not tolerated in the Roman military, and it was meticulously and scrupulously dealt with.

Third, it cannot be argued that the Roman soldiers thought that Jesus was already dead, and therefore, it was not necessary to break his legs. The certainty that Jesus was already dead did not actually exist in the soldiers' minds, except by the centurion mentioned in Mark 15:39 and Luke 23:47.

If the soldiers believed that Jesus was dead, why did one of the soldiers have to pierce his side with a spear? Conceivable motives for doing so would be as an act of brutality and cruelty or to make sure that Jesus was dead (also see Koskenniemi, Nisula and Toppari 2005, 379-91). Given that the Roman soldier had the slightest doubt about Jesus's death, the most effective means of guaranteeing his demise is simply by obeying the order of his superior and breaking the legs.

SPECULATION #37 Dubious Chronology of the Leg Breakings

John's chronology and details describing the breaking of the legs of Jesus's two compatriots on their respective crosses is dubious and unconvincing. Mark and Matthew significantly inform their readers:

> Mk 15:27 And with him they crucify two thieves; the one on his right hand, and another on his left.

> Mt 27:38 Then were there two thieves crucified with him, one on the right hand, and another on the left.

In other words, Jesus was situated in the middle, a position of priority. However, John's narrative reads:

> Jn 19:32 Then came the soldiers, and brake the legs of the first, and of the other which was crucified with him.

> Jn 19:33 But when they came to Jesus, and saw that he was dead already, they brake not his legs.

> Jn 19:34 But one of the soldiers with a spear pierced his side, and forthwith came there out blood and water.

> Jn 19:35 And he that saw it bare record, and his record is true: and he knoweth that he saith true, that ye might believe.

> Jn 19:36 For these things were done, that the scripture should be fulfilled, A bone of him shall not be broken.

> Jn 19:37 And again another scripture saith, They shall look on him whom they pierced.

Significantly, it is important to note the very singular manner in which the leg breaking was performed. The soldiers were said to have broken the legs of the first thief and then of the other (v. 32), thus passing over Jesus in the first instance. Logically the soldiers would have started at one side and work over to the other. Why did the soldiers fail to go in order? John's account has an artificial ring of being written to heighten the literary tension.

SPECULATION #38 The First Breaking of Legs—An Interpolation of John 19:31-38

Cassels (1902, 823), a Christian detractor, posits that John's account of the episode requesting the bodies is an interpolation. John 19:31 narrates that a group of Jews received an audience with Pilate and requested that the legs might be broken and the bodies taken away. In the following three verses (32-34), John details the task being carried out by the soldiers. Therefore, in pursuance of the same order, the bodies would have been taken away. Next, verses 35-37 record the agenda of this episode: "For these things were done, that the scripture should be fulfilled, A bone of him shall not be broken." Then John continues his narration as if it had not been interrupted and proceeds to verse 38 with the appearance of Joseph of Arimathea: "And after this" (*meta tauta*). That is to say after (1) the legs of the crucified thieves had been broken, (2) the side of Jesus pierced, and (3) *the removal of the bodies*, Joseph now appears before Pilate and requests that he might take away Jesus's body. In this same verse (v. 38), Pilate grants permission, and Joseph takes the body of Jesus. But again it must be reiterated that if verses 31-38 are historical, the body of Jesus and the two thieves must already had been taken away.

SPECULATION #39 The Location of the Request

The recorded accounts do not specifically detail where either the group of unnamed Jews or Joseph went to make the request to Pilate. A likely assumption is that they went to the Praetorium (Mk 15:16), which was the seat of office of the Roman prefects. However, Theissen and Merz (1998, 179) suggest that the prefect probably resided in Herod's palace.

ISSUE 18: The Blood and Water

Mk	Mt	Lk	Jn 19:34 But one of the soldiers with a spear pierced his side, *and forthwith came there out blood and water.* 35 And he that saw it bare record, and his record is true: and he knoweth that he saith true, that ye might believe. 36 For these things were done, that the scripture should be fulfilled, A bone of him shall not be broken. 37 And again another scripture saith, They shall look on him whom they pierced.

The next sign mentioned in John is that of the blood and water. John is the only canonical source that specifically mentions blood and water that streamed forth from Jesus when he was stabbed in the side. [Note: "In recent years a view that has gained substantial support is that the epistolary author is making explicit reference to Jn 19:34-35:20. The strength of this view is that Jn 19:34-35 is the only other Johannine passage where water and blood are joined. The flowing of the blood and water from Jesus' side is understood to anticipate, among other things, the gift of the Spirit (note the apparent connection between water and Spirit in 7.37-39" (D. A. Carson 1994, 221).]

CONTRADICTION #25 Lacks Corroboration and a Theological Agenda

John 19:37 states that this piercing event was prophesized in scripture: "And again another scripture saith, They shall look on him whom they pierced." What could explain the omission of this highly significant event from Mark, Matthew, and Luke? In particular, the absence from Luke is curious since in his preface he claims to have examined multiple sources. Luke's omission suggests that either the event was invented by John after Luke had finished his narrative or that he was verifying the narratives of Mark and Matthew that no such event occurred.

CONTRADICTION #26 How Could John Know Blood and Water Exited Jesus's Body?

John 19:34 narrates that "But one of the soldiers with a spear pierced his side, and forthwith came there out blood and water." However, it is doubtful that John could have known that water also "bled" from Jesus's side. Numerous obstacles would make an observance of water flowing from Jesus's side not plausible.

First, when Jesus's side is pierced he is hanging from a cross having previously been scourged. Therefore, it would be difficult to see the water flowing from the side wound as it mixed with the blood from the prior scourging.

Second, given that there is one piercing, the blood and water would be exiting from the same wounded area. Therefore, here too there would be the comingling of blood and water. Assuming this comingling to be correct, how would the witnesses be able to confirm that water also exited this wound area?

Third, there is the issue of sunlight. If Jesus was suspended from the cross several feet off the ground and pierced late in the afternoon, after the three hours of darkness had ended, it is possible that the witnesses would have been looking directly into the sun as it lowered in the western horizon. This looking into the sun could have also impeded their vision.

Finally, it is rejected that the witnesses would have been permitted to get close enough to verify the water flow. Perhaps the presumed "water" was in reality vinegar or white wine. Previously it was discussed as to whether or not it was practical that Jesus could have carried on a conversation in terms of the proximity with his mother and the disciple who he loved. However, this breaking of legs is now a completely different matter. The soldiers were now fulfilling their orders to break the legs of the condemned. This is serious work. At this time it is inconceivable that the Roman soldiers would have displayed any compassion, kindness, or mercy to the witnesses. In fact, it is absolutely impossible that the soldiers would have permitted anyone to be anywhere close to the victims whose knees and legs were literally smashed to smithereens. To repeat, to accomplish this task the soldiers would not have permitted anyone to be in the immediate area and, therefore, be close enough to confirm that water flowed from Jesus's side after he was pierced.

The only alternative is that the soldier who pierced Jesus's side is the source of this information. Such a rationalization would be an argument based on silence to deal with an inconvenient truth that it is impossible for anyone to confirm that water flowed from Jesus's side after he was pierced.

SPECULATION #40 Explanations for the Blood and Water

Several speculated rationales attempting to explain the spearing episode are based on symbolism of the blood and water. Numerous writers (Benoit 1970, 222; Brown 1994a, 2:118-82; Ellis 1984, 276-77; Keener 2003, 1153) discuss the possibility that the "the blood and water" symbolize either the (1) Spirit, which flowed forth from the dead Jesus; (2) the duality of his actions, his baptism of water and his baptism of blood; (3) a new and higher life passes into humanity; (4) the life-giving water that flowed from Ezekiel's new Temple (Ez 47:1-2); or (5) the dispensation of the Temple. Consequently, the "miracle" of the blood and water flowing from Jesus's side is not so much an external fact but a spiritual perception.

Benoit (1970, 222n2)—a Dominican priest, biblical scholar, and expert on the Dead Sea Scrolls—offers a possible rationale based on the *Midrash Leviticus Rabbah*:

> *Leviticus Rabba*, 15 (115c), contains the information that man is made half of water, half of blood: if he is virtuous, the two elements

are in equilibrium; if he is sinful, one element is dominant: if this element is water he becomes dropsical; if it is blood he becomes leprous.

Below additional speculations are detailed.

CHRISTIAN APOLOGETIC

One possible explanation (Brown 1970, 949-52; Köstenberger 2004a, 552) for the blood and the water serve as a proof that Jesus died fully a human being.

APOLOGETIC TO COUNTER THAT JESUS NEVER DIED

A different hypothesis is that John's account of Jesus being speared serves as an apologetic. For example, Watson (1911, 346; cf. Vermes 2008, 145) proposes that the piercing of Jesus's side recorded in John 19:34 is an attempt to reply to the current theory "that Jesus was never really dead." This theory hypothesizes that Jesus was taken from the cross in a state of partial suspension of respiration and circulation, in the tomb he revived and, with or without assistance, removed the stone and so came forth. Later, Jesus had meetings with various friends referred to as "appearances." Eventually, Jesus was supposed to have withdrawn into seclusion and, at some time and place unknown, died a natural death. This theory is discussed later and is "rejected" by this text.

CHAPTER 4

Zechariah 12

PREFACE: ZECHARIAH 12

ZECHARIAH 12 AND Psalm 22:16 [17 AV] are often cited by Christian apologists and missionaries as proof texts for Jesus's messiahship. Specifically, Christians claim that Jesus's crucifixion is foretold in the Hebrew Bible. In general, there are two possible ways to interpret the verses in Zechariah. One possibility is that the events narrated are actual history. That is, the events occurred during the lifetime of Zechariah. In direct contrast, another perspective is to consider as prophetic the words of Zechariah. In other words, the event would take place sometime during the "end of days" and the coming Messianic Era.

ISSUE 19: The Piercing of Jesus's Side to Fulfill Scripture

Mk	Mt	Lk	Jn 19:34 *But one of the soldiers with a spear pierced his side*, and forthwith came there out blood and water. 35 And he that saw it bare record, and his record is true: and he knoweth that he saith true, that ye might believe. 36 For these things were done, that the scripture should be fulfilled, *A bone of him shall not be broken. 37 And again another scripture saith, They shall look on him whom they pierced.*

John alone reports an incident during which Jesus is pierced in his side by a Roman soldier as he hung from the cross. According to John, this piercing fulfills what is recorded in scripture. Below is the entire text of Zechariah 12.

TABLE 19. Zechariah 12 and a Summary

VERSE	KING JAMES TRANSLATION	SUMMARY
Zech 12:1	The burden of the word of the LORD for Israel, saith the LORD, which stretcheth forth the heavens, and layeth the foundation of the earth, and formeth the spirit of man within him.	The chapter begins with praise of God's creative power. It provides a reminder that God is in control and completely able to accomplish what He predicts.
Zech 12:2	Behold, I will make Jerusalem a cup of trembling unto all the people round about, when they shall be in the siege both against Judah and against Jerusalem.	God declares that in a coming day He will astound all the people surrounding Jerusalem. According to Rashi (an eleventh-century Jewish rabbi), "the nations that will siege against Jerusalem will impose upon Judah, for the house of David will be inside and the gentiles will besiege them. And also the children of Judah will come, against their will, to besiege Jerusalem. So did Jonathan render it."
Zech 12:3	And in that day will I make Jerusalem a burdensome stone for all people: all that burden themselves with it shall be cut in pieces, though all the people of the earth be gathered together against it.	Jerusalem will be like a heavy stone, that is, a burden for all those people who besiege Judah and Jerusalem. In the end, God Himself will cut to pieces all those who laid siege against Judah and Jerusalem.
Zech 12:4	In that day, saith the LORD, I will smite every horse with astonishment, and his rider with madness: and I will open mine eyes upon the house of Judah, and will smite every horse of the people with blindness.	God promises that though nations will come against Jerusalem with fury, He will protect the city by imposing their riders with madness. Second: "But upon the [member of the] house of Judah, who are among those gathered against their will, I [God] will open My eyes to protect them from this plague."

Zech 12:5	And the governors of Judah shall say in their heart, The inhabitants of Jerusalem shall be my strength in the LORD of hosts their God.	(1) When the chieftains or princes of Judah see that the others who are gathered are plagued and they (the people of Judah) are saved and (2) the power of Jerusalem will be sufficient to defend them against all enemies, because the LORD is among them.
Zech 12:6	In that day will I make the governors of Judah like an hearth of fire among the wood, and like a torch of fire in a sheaf; and they shall devour all the people round about, on the right hand and on the left: and Jerusalem shall be inhabited again in her own place, even in Jerusalem.	In that day God Himself will intervene and deliver Israel not only through His direct work but also through His blessing and empowering both the governors and inhabitants of Jerusalem. That is, the governors of Judah will return and wage war with those who brought them there. It will be this day of deliverance of Jerusalem that its enemies will be burned up and consumed.
Zech 12:7	The LORD also shall save the tents of Judah first, that the glory of the house of David and the glory of the inhabitants of Jerusalem do not magnify themselves against Judah.	Before the inhabitants of Jerusalem come out of the city, the LORD will save the tents of Judah. That is, Judah will be saved—to return to its tents and homes. Afterward the salvation will come to the inhabitants of the city.
Zech 12:8	In that day shall the LORD defend the inhabitants of Jerusalem; and he that is feeble among them at that day shall be as David; and the house of David shall be as God, as the angel of the LORD before them.	King David is renowned for his fighting ability, courage, and success. God promised a day when the *weakest* in Jerusalem will be as mighty as David.
Zech 12:9	And it shall come to pass in that day, that I will seek to destroy all the nations that come against Jerusalem.	In that day God Himself will seek and destroy all those nations that come against Jerusalem (i.e., the Day of Wrath against the Gentile nations).

Zech 12:10	And I will pour upon the house of David, and upon the inhabitants of Jerusalem, the spirit of grace and of supplications: and they shall look upon me whom they have pierced, and they shall mourn for him, as one mourneth for his only son, and shall be in bitterness for him, as one that is in bitterness for his firstborn.	The concluding verses speak of someone who is "pierced" and died. His death will so shock the nation that the people would be moved to repentance and mourning, an intense mourning of this person who is killed that it will be as if they are mourning for a firstborn son.

The predominant perspective on Zechariah 12:10 among Jewish commentators describe the mourning over those Jews who are slain while defending the Kingdom of Judah and Jerusalem. Those who fall in the battle are the ones described as having been *thrust through* with the swords and spears of soldiers from the attacking nations. In other words, this verse describes a historical event from the biblical times around which this was written. Rashi writes: "And they shall look to Me to complain about those of them whom the nations thrust through and slew during their exile." An alternative explanation is that this text describes a future event. |
| Zech 12:11 | In that day shall there be a great mourning in Jerusalem, as the mourning of Hadadrimmon in the valley of Megiddon. | Commentators offer two interpretations of this verse that deals with mourning. First, this event refers to the mourning of Ahab, the son of Omri, who is slain by Hadadrimmon the son of Tabrimmon in Ramoth Gildead, as it is stated (1 Kgs 22:36): "A cry passed through the camp." Second, This incident refers to the mourning over King Josiah's death (2 Kgs 23:29; 2 Chron 35:20-25): He is such a godly king that the whole nation wept bitterly at his death. |
| Zech 12:12 | And the land shall mourn, every family apart; the family of the house of David apart, and their wives apart; the family of the house of Nathan apart, and their wives apart; | Rashi says of the house of Nathan, the prophet: Some commentators say that it refers to Nathan, the son of David, as it is says (2 Sam 5:14): "Shammua and Shobab, and Nathan and Solomon." |

Zech 12:13	The family of the house of Levi apart, and their wives apart; the family of Shimei apart, and their wives apart;	This verse refers to (1) the priests and the Levites and (2) Shammua, the son of David.
Zech 12:14	All the families that remain, every family apart, and their wives apart.	This verse refers to the house of David.

CONTRADICTION #27 The Distorted Emotional Context of Zechariah 12

Based upon its context, there are three reasons that Zechariah 12 does not refer to Jesus. First, Rabbi Moshe Shulman (cf. Yosef 2001-2011) offers that the emotional reaction of the people in the context of Zechariah refutes any possibility that this chapter could refer to Jesus. That is, do Jesus and the Jewish people as detailed in the Gospels fit the expected picture?

In Zechariah 12, the people are described as mourning, sad, and weeping bitterly:

> Zech 12:11 In that day shall there be a *great mourning* in Jerusalem, *as the mourning of Hadadrimmon* in the valley of Megiddon.

> Zech 12:12 And *the land shall mourn, every family apart; the family of the house of David apart, and their wives apart; the family of the house of Nathan apart, and their wives apart*;

Second, nowhere in the passion narratives or the Resurrection accounts are there any indication that the land of Israel mourned or that every family grieved over the death of Jesus. Only a few people cited in Luke 23:48 seemingly expressed any emotions when Jesus died. As a matter of fact, the Gospels go out of their way reporting that many people seemed not to be the least bit saddened or mournful with the impending death of Jesus. Furthermore, many people such as the chief priests, the scribes, and the elders seemingly delighted in Jesus's approaching death as he hung from the cross:

> Mk 15:29-32 And they that passed by railed on him, wagging their heads, and saying, Ah, thou that destroyest the temple, and buildest it in three days, Save thyself, and come down from the cross. Likewise also the chief priests mocking said among themselves with the scribes, He saved others; himself he cannot save. Let Christ the King of Israel descend now from the cross,

that we may see and believe. And they that were crucified with him reviled him.

Mt 27:39-43 And they that passed by reviled him, wagging their heads, And saying, Thou that destroyest the temple, and buildest it in three days, save thyself. If thou be the Son of God, come down from the cross. Likewise also the chief priests mocking him, with the scribes and elders, said, He saved others; himself he cannot save. If he be the King of Israel, let him now come down from the cross, and we will believe him. He trusted in God; let him deliver him now, if he will have him: for he said, I am the Son of God.

Lk 23:35 And the people stood beholding. And the rulers also with them derided him, saying, He saved others; let him save himself, if he be Christ, the chosen of God.

And even after Jesus's death the Jewish leadership still demonstrated no remorse. That is, on Saturday they went to Pilate, calling Jesus a "deceiver" and worried that his disciples might come and steal his body.

Mt 27:62-64 Now the next day, that followed the day of the preparation, the chief priests and Pharisees came together unto Pilate, Saying, Sir, we remember that that deceiver said, while he was yet alive, After three days I will rise again. Command therefore that the sepulchre be made sure until the third day, lest his disciples come by night, and steal him away, and say unto the people, He is risen from the dead: so the last error shall be worse than the first.

In addition, there was no indication that the disciples mourned. One day later, early on Easter Sunday morning, John 20:1-2 reports that Mary Magdalene found the tomb empty and ran to inform Simon Peter and the other disciple, the one whom Jesus loved, that the body was missing. There is no description of any emotional response. Neither is there an emotional response reported when the two disciples found the tomb empty. In contrast, Luke 24:12 narrates that Peter returned home amazed, but there is no mention of grief or mourning. However, at the same time, this verse is missing in some Greek manuscripts.

When Mary Magdalene returns to the tomb, she encounters two angels. John describes her as weeping. John 20:13 narrates that they asked her why she was weeping. In John 20:14, Mary Magdalene replies: "Because they have taken away my Lord, and I do not know where they have laid him." In others words, she was not weeping because Jesus is dead; instead, she is weeping because she did not know the location of his body. Next, Jesus appears, unbeknownst to her, and asks the same question of the two angels. Again her response indicates no concern about Jesus's death but rather for the location of his body: "Sir, if thou have borne him hence, tell me where thou hast laid him, and I will take him away."

During the next few hours, Luke 24:13-35 reports the conversation of two travelers on the road to Emmaus. Yet not once during this dialogue is there any hint that the people mourned the death of Jesus, not even the two travelers themselves.

Even in the early chapters in Acts, there is not the slightest hint of remorse on behalf of the people or Jewish leadership.

In conclusion, in an emotional context, Zechariah 12:10 does not provide any support for the prophetic fulfillment claimed by Christian apologists. In Zechariah, the land of Israel mourned and every family expressed grief. In direct contrast, the Gospels go out of their way reporting that many people seemed not to be the least bit saddened or mournful with the impending death of Jesus. Nor did Jesus's disciples demonstrate any emotional sense of grief after the Crucifixion.

CONTRADICTION #28 The Distorted Historical Context of Zechariah 12—Israel is Saved

The prophet Zechariah in Zechariah 12 is a fallacious and misleading scriptural chapter in the context of Jesus when it is employed as a proof text of Jesus's calling/prophetic fulfillment commonly cross referenced in Christian bibles and apologetic commentaries (e.g., Lk 1:32-33). Verse 9, declares that God will defend His people: "And it shall come to pass in that day, that I will seek to destroy all the nations that come against Jerusalem." As a matter of fact, Zechariah 12:6 details the utter destruction of Israel's enemies: "In that day will I make the governors of Judah like an hearth of fire among the wood, and like a torch of fire in a sheaf; and they shall devour all the people round about, on the right hand and on the left." In contrast, during the approximate forty years after Jesus's death, the Romans still occupied the Holy Land and Jerusalem was eventually destroyed (70 CE).

Elaborating on this issue, Thomas Ice—the executive director of the Pre-Trib Research Center on the campus of Liberty University in Lynchburg, Virginia—writes (2010. Preterism and Zechariah 12-14):

I noted that Zechariah speaks of "all the peoples" (12:2), "all the nations of the earth will be gathered against it (Jerusalem)" (12:3), and "I will gather all the nations against Jerusalem to battle" (14:2). "This does not sound like the Romans in AD 70," I said. Further, Zechariah goes on to say, "In that day the Lord will defend the inhabitants of Jerusalem" (12:8) and "The Lord will go forth and fight against those nations, as when He fights on a day of battle" (14:3). I concluded that this does not fit with what happened in Jerusalem in AD 70 when the Romans conquered Israel. Finally, it says that the Lord will rescue Israel, in that day (14:3), whereas in AD 70 the Lord judged Israel as Luke 21:20-24 notes.

Then, Ice went on to write:

A preterist cannot give a textual interpretation of Zechariah 12-14 because they believe it is to be equated with God's judgment at the hands of the Romans in a.d. 70 upon Israel—error number one. Greg Beale notes that, "Zechariah 12 does not prophesy Israel's judgment but Israel's redemption." Zechariah 12-14 clearly speaks of a time when Israel is rescued by the Lord from an attack by "all the nations of the earth," not just the Romans—error number two. In this context, Israel must refer to Israel. Since that it true, then the event of Zechariah 12-14 has not yet happened in history. This means that it is a future event.

Below is a modified table based on the work of House and Price (2003, 68; cf. Fruchtenbaum 2003, 251-81; Price 2003, 377-98). This table employs Luke 21:20-24 as a baseline and demonstrates how Zechariah 12-14 *could not* support the belief that Zechariah refers to the events of Jesus's day.

TABLE 20. Contrasts Between Luke 21:20-24 and Zechariah 12-14

Luke 21:20-24	Zechariah 12-14
Past fulfillment—led captive to all nations (v. 24).	Eschatological fulfillment—"in that day" (12:3-4, 6, 8, 11; 13:1-12; 14:1, 4, 6-9).
Day of the desolation of Jerusalem (v. 20).	Day of deliverance of Jerusalem (12:7-8).
Day of vengeance against Jerusalem (v. 22).	Day of victory for Jerusalem (12:4-6).

Day of wrath against Jewish nation (v. 23).	Day of wrath against Gentile nations (12:9; 14:3, 12).
Jerusalem trampled by Gentiles (v. 24).	Jerusalem transformed by God (14:4-10).
Time of Gentile dominion over Jerusalem (v.24).	Time of Gentile submission in Jerusalem (14:16-19).
Great distress upon the Land (v. 23).	Great deliverance for the Land (13:2).
Nations bring the sword to Jerusalem (v. 24).	Nations bring their wealth to Jerusalem (14:14).
Jerusalem destroyed "in order that all things which are written [concerning the Jewish People] may be fulfilled" (in the future), (v. 22).	Jerusalem rescued *and redeemed* that *all things* written (concerning Jewish People) may be fulfilled (13:1-9); cf. Rom 11:25-27.
Jerusalem's desolation is given a time limit: "until the times of the Gentiles be fulfilled" (v. 24). This time limit implies that a time of restoration for Jerusalem will then follow.	The attack on Jerusalem is the occasion for the final defeat of Israel's enemies, thus ending the "times of the Gentiles" (14:2-3, 11).
The Messiah comes into power and glory to be seen by the Jewish People only *after* "these things"— the events of vs. 25-28, which are yet future to the events of vs. 20-24.	The Messiah comes into power and glory *during* the events of the battle (14:4-5).

Christian apologists and missionaries are asked: did God destroy the enemies of Israel or pour out a spirit of grace and supplication toward the house of Israel *after* Jesus was crucified? No! God did not destroy the enemies of Israel after Jesus was crucified. As a matter of fact, the time following Jesus's crucifixion resulted in the opposite of Israel's enemies being destroyed. Approximately forty years after Jesus's crucifixion culminated with the destruction of Jerusalem, the deaths of thousands of Jews, and the enslavement and deportation of the surviving population. Therefore, the historical context of Zechariah has nothing to do with the era in which Jesus lived or the period of time that followed.

In conclusion, Ice declares: "Because of the differences between the above contrasted passages, it is impossible to harmonize with events that have already taken place. Impossible as long as two plus two continues to equal four."

CONTRADICTION #29 The Distorted Historical Context of Zechariah 12—Prophetic Fulfillment

Expanding contradiction #28 and contrary to Christian apologists, Zechariah cannot refer to the period of time immediately following Jesus's death as a fulfillment of scripture. The issue is whether or not the events in first century Israel were fulfilled. There are numerous events described by the prophet Zechariah that are set in the future as compared to his lifetime and specifically at "the end of times." In those days numerous events were to take place. A cursory review of just some of these prophetic events includes the following:

1. God will cut off the names of the idols from the land (13:1).
2. God will remove from the land unclean spirits (13:2).
3. God will cut off and remove from the land two-thirds of the people, who will perish (13:8).
4. God will put one-third of the people left into a fire to be refined (13:9).
5. God will gather all the nations against Jerusalem (14:2).
6. The living waters shall flow out of Jerusalem, half of them to the eastern sea and half of them to the western sea (14:8).
7. It shall continue in summer as in winter (14:8).
8. And the LORD will be one and His name one (14:9).
9. God will strike plague against all the peoples that wage war against Jerusalem (14:12-15).
10. The entire nation of Israel will share in the spoils of war (14:14).
11. All those who survive of the nations that have come against Jerusalem shall go up year after year to worship the King, the LORD of Hosts, and to keep the Festival of Booths (Tabernacles; Succoth) (14:16).
12. God will punish all the nations that do not go up to keep the Festival of Booths (14:20).

The events described in Zechariah do *not* in any way conform to or relate to the events of Jesus's day or the following two thousand years. Therefore, this part of scripture provides no validity as a proof text of Jesus's prophetic calling; to the contrary, it refutes any such claim.

CONTRADICTION #30 The Distorted and Mistranslated Subjects of "They" in Zechariah 12:10

Christian apologists distort the subjects in Zechariah 12:10 in reference to John 19:37. The verse in John 19:37 requires that the word "they" refers to the Roman soldiers: "And again another scripture saith, They shall look on him whom they pierced."

However, firstly, there is *no* reference to Roman soldiers in Zechariah. Secondly, there is no mention of any people being crucified in Zechariah. Thirdly, as previously pointed out, in John's narrative the Romans looked at "him"; that is, they looked at Jesus whom they pierced. In contrast, in Zechariah it is stated that "God" was looked "to":

> Zech 12:10 And I will pour upon the house of David, and upon the inhabitants of Jerusalem, the spirit of grace and of supplications: and they shall **look upon me** whom they have pierced, and they shall mourn for him, as one mourneth for his only son, and shall be in bitterness for him, as one that is in bitterness for his firstborn.

CONTRADICTION #31 The Distorted and Mistranslated Subjects of "HIM" in Zechariah 12:10

Michael L. Brown (2003, 149-50), writing in his *Answering Jewish Objections to Jesus Volume Three: Messianic Prophecy Objections*, concisely puts forth the question of what he describes as a larger issue in reference to Zechariah 12:10: "Are 'they' looking to God or to the one pierced, or is God the one pierced, to whom they are looking?" He writes:

> In answer to the first question, it is clear that the mourners are turning to God, since he is the only one referred to in the first person throughout the chapter, beginning in verse 2, where the Lord declares, "*I* am going to make Jerusalem a cup that sends all the surrounding peoples reeling." Similar expressions are found in all the following verses: verse 3, "*I* will make"; verse 4, "*I* will strike; *I* will keep; *I* will blind"; verse 6, "*I* will make"; verse 9, "*I* will set out to destroy"; and then in verse 10, "And *I* will pour out on the house of David and the inhabitants of Jerusalem a spirit of grace and supplication. They will look on *me*, the one they have pierced." It is perfectly clear, therefore, that the "me" in this verse

is the Lord himself—as rendered in the Jewish translations cited above.

CONTRADICTION #32 The Figurative Subject of "HIM" in Zechariah 12:10

Previously, Brown (2003, 150) agreed that the subject of "**HIM**" in Zechariah 12:10 refers to the Lord himself—"as rendered in the Jewish translations cited above." However, he then added "suggesting the real possibility that the Hebrew text stated that it is the Lord himself who was pierced." Brown went on and posits that from a Messianic Jewish viewpoint "the Messiah is the very image of God, representing his fullness in bodily form on the earth. Thus, piercing the Messiah was equivalent to piercing the Lord, just as rejecting the prophets was equivalent to rejecting the Lord (see, e.g., 2 Chron 36:15-16; for a related New Testament concept, see Matt. 10:14, 40)."

This position is false. It is agreed that the prophet Zechariah is speaking figuratively. However, the difference involves who is this figurative "**HIM**" or what is this figurative "**HIM**"? Nowhere in the Hebrew Bible is there any text stating that God will come to earth in the fullness in a bodily form. To the contrary, the Hebrew Bible refutes any possibility that God can be a man:

> Num 23:19 *God is not a man* that he should lie; neither the son of man, that he should repent: hath he said, and shall he not do it? or hath he spoken, and shall he not make it good?

> Hos 11:9 I will not execute the fierceness of mine anger, I will not return to destroy Ephraim: *for I am God, and not man*; the Holy One in the midst of thee: and I will not enter into the city.

> Job 9:32 *For he is not man, as I am*, that I should answer him, and we should come together in judgment.

> Job 33:12 Behold, in this thou art not just: I will answer thee, *that God is greater than man*.

> 1 Sam 15:29 And also the Strength of Israel will not lie nor repent: for he is not a man, that he should repent.

Instead, Zechariah is referring figuratively to the Jewish people or one person personified as the Jewish people. Sigal (1981, 80-81) elaborates: "God identifies with His people to the degree that He takes part figuratively in the nation's destiny. To attack (pierce) Israel is to attack God. That is why God says: 'Me whom they have pierced' even though it is the people of Israel and not God who is actually pierced." Similarly, Drazin (1990, 163) writes: "Therefore, what befalls Israel is said to have happened to G-d. In this instance, G-d is said to have been 'thrust through' when Israel was in fact the victim." For example, Isaiah 63:9 states: "In all their affliction He was afflicted."

This concept of whoever rises up against Israel is considered as if he rose up against God was stated earlier in Zechariah:

> Zech 2:8 [AV] For thus saith the LORD of hosts; After the glory hath he sent me unto the nations which spoiled you: for he that toucheth you toucheth the apple of his eye.

The "his" in the King James is spelled with a lower case *h*. However, the "his" is referring to "the LORD of host" that is God.

CONTRADICTION #33 The Distorted and Understood PRONOUN "HIM" in Zechariah 12:10

The context of Zechariah 12 does not support the Christian claim that Jesus is the subject being pierced. In fact, it is a different subject who is pierced and mourned. The context of the pronouns refutes any possible relationship to Jesus. To illustrate this point, the second half of Zechariah 12:10 will be analyzed first from the eye of a Christian apologist and then from a traditional Jewish point of view. For point of clarification, the relevant pronouns will be capitalized and followed by an elaboration in brackets (Yosef 2001-2011).

CHRISTIAN PERSPECTIVE

and THEY [*the Jews {or the Romans}*] **shall look upon ME** [*Jesus*] **whom THEY** [*the Romans*] **have pierced; and THEY** [*the Jews*] **shall mourn for HIM** [*Jesus*] **as one mourneth for his only son, and shall be in bitterness for HIM** [*Jesus*] **as one that is in bitterness for his firstborn.**

TRADITIONAL JEWISH PERSPECTIVE

and THEY [*the Jews {or the Romans}*] **shall look upon ME** [*God who has a unique relationship to His servants*] **whom THEY** [*Israel's enemies*] **have pierced; and THEY** [*the Jews*] **shall mourn for HIM** [*the part of God's servant which has been destroyed*] **as one mourneth for his only son, and shall be in bitterness for HIM** [*the part of God's servant that has been destroyed*] **as one that is in bitterness for his firstborn.**

Yosef (2001-2011) commented:

> Grammatically, the "**ME**" and the "**HIM**" *cannot* refer to the same person. The only alternative Christian apologetic is to assume that given God is the speaker, and that Jesus is part of the godhead (the Trinity). However, this raises the question of whether or not the pronouns **ME** and **HIM**, as they appear in this passage, refer to the same person, namely, Jesus? It should be clear that the prophet is speaking here of *not one*, but of *two distinct entities*. Neither can these pronouns, **ME** and **HIM**, refer to the same entity simultaneously! Moreover, there is still the issue of the pronoun **I** as used in the first half of **Zechariah 12:10**. To resolve the issue of the pronoun "I" it is necessary to examine how does God's speaking in the 1st-person in **Zechariah 12:10A** fit in with the rest of the verse, **Zechariah 12:10B**.

Several Jewish commentators (Drazin 1990, 162-63; Moshe 1987, 199; Sigal 1981, 82; Singer 1998, 62; Troki 1970, 181-85) address the previously mentioned issue. However, for sake of clarity and completeness, the commentary of Uri Yosef (2001-2011), a writer with MessiahTruth.Com, is detailed below.

A. The New Testament to the Rescue?

> Evidently, the author of the Gospel of John was familiar with this passage from the Book of Zechariah, and he understood its problematic nature relative to the new religion. To interpret this passage as saying that, at some future time, the Jewish people shall look unto Jesus whom the Romans had pierced, did not appear to him to be what Zechariah had in mind. So he decided

to 'fix' this problem by altering and abridging the passage in the following manner:

> **John 19:37(KJV) - And again another scripture saith, *THEY shall look on HIM whom THEY pierced.***

The RSV translators utilize this version in the New Testament to revise the context of Zechariah's own words in their **Old Testament** version of Zechariah 12:10 (Note: *The Living Bible* has a similar rendition):

> **Zechariah 12:10(RSV) - And I will pour out on the house of David and the inhabitants of Jerusalem a spirit of compassion and supplication, *so that, when THEY look on HIM whom THEY have pierced*, they shall mourn for HIM, as one mourns for an only child, and weep bitterly over HIM, as one weeps over a first-born.**

Although this appears to solve the problem created by the use of two distinct pronouns, "**ME**" and "**HIM**," it does not resolve the identity issue between the two segments of this verse, **Zechariah 12:10A&B**. Moreover, the RSV rendition is a deliberate revision of the prophet's original words designed to "harmonize" this passage and the Christian paradigm. The evidence to support this statement is presented in Table IV.B-1 [[table 21 below]], which shows the Hebrew text, a Jewish translation, and the RSV rendition of **Zechariah 12:10B** broken into three components, with respective terms highlighted.

TABLE 21. Comparing the RSV Translation with the Hebrew Text and Jewish Translation: Zechariah 12:10

Revised Standard Version Translation		Jewish Translation from the Hebrew (reflecting the various Jewish translations)	Hebrew Text
Zechariah 12:10B			
i	so that, when **THEY** look **ON HIM** whom **THEY** have pierced,	and **THEY** shall look **TO ME** because of **HIM/THEY** who **THEY** [the enemy] thrust through.	וְהִבִּיטוּ אֵלַי, אֵת אֲשֶׁר־דָּקָרוּ
ii	**THEY** shall mourn for **HIM**, as one mourns for an only child,	and **THEY** shall mourn **over HIM/THEY** as one mourns over an only son,	וְסָפְדוּ עָלָיו כְּמִסְפֵּד עַל־הַיָּחִיד
iii	and weep bitterly **over HIM**, as one weeps over a first-born.	and be embittered **over HIM/THEM** as one is embittered over a firstborn son.	וְהָמֵר עָלָיו, כְּהָמֵר עַל־הַבְּכוֹר

The significant Hebrew pronouns in the respective phrases that comprise **Zechariah 12:10B** are as follows:

- **Zechariah 12:10B(i)**—Pronoun is אֵלַי (*elai*), **to ME** or **toward ME**.
- **Zechariah 12:10B(ii)**—Pronoun is עָלָיו (*alav*), **over HIM** or **upon HIM** or **for HIM**.
- **Zechariah 12:10B(iii)**—Pronoun is עָלָיו (*alav*), **over HIM** or **upon HIM** or **for HIM**.

The combination of these two terms, אֵלַי (*elai*) and עָלָיו (*alav*), occurring in the same verse is found at Genesis 44:21, a verse that is translated correctly in the RSV:

> **Genesis 44:21(RSV)—Then you said to your servants, "Bring him down TO ME [אֵלַי (*elai*)], that I may set my eyes UPON HIM [עָלָיו (*alav*)]."**

Could there be any doubt that the RSV rendition of Zechariah 12:10B(i) is based on John 19:37 in the New Testament rather than on the text in the Hebrew Bible?

To recap, John 19 reports that Jesus's side is pierced by a Roman soldier. John declares that this action is prophetic fulfillment of "they shall look upon him whom they pierced." This verse is cross referenced to Zechariah 12:9 which says "to Me" (*elai* in Hebrew) and not "upon him (*alav*)." Therefore, the context of Zechariah 12 in reference to the passion is invalid and totally wrong when applied to Jesus.

CONTRADICTION #34 Zechariah 12: Contradictory to the Olivet Discourse

Many Christians (especially those classified as "preterists") believe that Zechariah 12, 13, and 14 represent parallel passages to the Olivet discourse (Mk 13; Mt 24-25; Lk 21:5-36). The term "preterism," which is derived from the Latin *preter* ("past") holds that most, if not all, the prophetic events of the Old and New Testaments have already been fulfilled. Full or extreme preterism contends that all prophecy (including the Second Coming and the bodily resurrection) was fulfilled by 70 CE.

J. Randall Price (2003, 377-98) offers the position that Jesus's Olivet discourses, which is claimed to parallel Zechariah 12, lacks historical agreement with first century fulfillment. An excerpt from Price follows:

> If preterism bases its interpretation of prophecy on the events of AD 70 fulfilling the biblical text, then the historical record should support such details. However, the opposite is the case. For example, such a detail as the direction of Christ's advent [to Jerusalem], in Matthew 24:27 is compared with lightning flashing from *east to west*, whereas the Roman army, which Preterists interpret as fulfilling this prophecy, advanced on Jerusalem from *the west to the east*. Even if we take this simply to mean the Roman army advanced "like lightning" (i.e., quickly), the historical record reveals a very slow assault on Jerusalem, the war being for several years before Jerusalem was even besieged! For this reason in many cases a "correlation" can only be made through the eschatologically biased interpretation of Josephus (such as associating divine signs with the Roman army's impending conquest), reinterpreting the text to fit the preferred historical data (such as taking "the clouds of heaven" as the dust kicked up by the Roman army's advance), or by taking statements that do not fit the historical events of the great Jewish revolt as hyperbole (such as the unprecedented and unsurpassed nature of the Tribulation), in order to claim first-century fulfillment.

In conclusion, Price declares: "If the historical correlation with an AD 70 fulfillment for the Olivet Discourse fails, and preterism depends on such a fulfillment for the maintenance of its eschatological system, then preterism itself fails as a viable eschatological interpretation."

SPECULATION #41 Why the Soldier Speared Jesus's Body

Why did the soldier pierce (spear) Jesus's body if he knew Jesus was already dead? In John's narrative, the soldiers did not know that Jesus was dead until they went to break his legs. In contrast, in Mark 15:39; Matthew 26:54; and Luke 23:47, the centurion seems to know that Jesus was dead right after he cried out. If Jesus died with a *loud* cry, as detailed in Mark 15:37; Matthew 27:50; and Luke 24:46, and if the captain and the watch were astonished at the cry and at his final demise, would the soldiers have been ignorant of Jesus's death until they went up to the cross?

Christian apologists such as Craig (1989a, 165-66) argue that the piercing is in order to fulfill what is spoken in the Hebrew Bible. Classic supposed proof texts include Psalm 22, Isaiah 53, and Zechariah 12:10. However, there is another more likely, practical, and simple explanation: the piercing of Jesus with the spear is nothing more than an act of mere spite, barbarianism, cruelty, and possibly further humiliation performed by a sadistic Roman soldier. Therefore, what the author of John is perhaps attempting is a fast switch, transforming a horrendous action into an evangelizing tool as a biblical proof text that Jesus was prophesied to have suffered the agony of scourging and crucifixion.

Pennells (1983, 99), writing in the *Journal for the Study of the New Testament*, states: "According to both אB, [[NOTE: This is the identification numbering of perhaps the two most significant Greek manuscripts]] in the Matthean gospel Jesus is speared before his death and dies as a result. This contradicts the unanimous Johannine text where the spearing follows the death cry" (19.30). He then provides several examples of this known tradition:

1. Chrysostom. *Hom in Mt* 88.1 [PG LVIII.776]
2. A Pseudo-Cyprian text: *De Montibus Sina et Sion* 8 (G. Hartel, *S. Thasci Caecili Cypriani Opera Omnia*; in *CSEL* III/3, Appendix, p. 112[12])
3. Hippolytus, *Apostolic Tradition* 36.6
4. One manuscript of the *Epitome of the Apostolic Constitutions* 8.24.4 [Text from F.X. Funk, *Didascalia et Constitutiones Apostolorum* (Paderborn, 1905), II, p. 88[24] and *critical apparatus*

5. Tertullian in *Adv Marc* 3.7 (7)
6. *Acts of John* 97
7. *Acts of John* 101
8. εἰς 164-166
9. A report by Abd al'Jabbar in AD 995

CHAPTER 5

Friday Afternoon until Saturday Morning

ISSUE 20: Joseph of Arimathea's Request for Jesus's Body According to John

| Mk 15:42 *And now when the even was come, because it was the preparation, that is, the day before the sabbath* 43 *Joseph of Arimathea*, an honourable counsellor, which also waited for the kingdom of God, came, *and went in boldly unto Pilate*, and craved the body of Jesus. | Mt 27:57 When the even was come, there came a rich man of Arimathea, named Joseph, who also himself was Jesus' disciple: 58 *He went to Pilate*, and begged the body of Jesus. Then Pilate commanded the body to be delivered. | Lk 23:50 And, behold, there was a man named Joseph, a counsellor; and he was a good man, and a just: 51 (The same had not consented to the counsel and deed of them;) he was of Arimathea, a city of the Jews: who also himself waited for the kingdom of God. 52 *This man went unto Pilate*, and begged the body of Jesus. 53 And he took it down, and wrapped it in linen, and laid it in a sepulchre that was hewn in stone, wherein never man before was laid. 54 *And that day was the preparation, and the sabbath drew on.* | Jn 19:38 And after this *Joseph of Arimathea*, being a disciple of Jesus, but secretly for fear of the Jews, *besought Pilate* that he might take away the body of Jesus: and Pilate gave him leave. He came therefore, and took the body of Jesus.

Jn 19:42 There laid they Jesus therefore because the Jews' preparation day for the sepulchre was nigh at hand. |

ALL OF THE gospel narratives record that Joseph visited Pilate sometime between the death of Jesus, approximately 3:00 p.m., and sunset, approximately 6:00 p.m., to ask for his body. This information presupposes that Joseph knew that Jesus was already dead. Mark 15:42 informs the reader of two significant facts: (1) it was even (*opsia*) and (2) it was the day before the Sabbath (i.e., Friday): "Mk 15:42 And now when the even was come, because it was the preparation, that is, the day before the sabbath."

Luke 23:54 also confirms that Jesus died on a Friday, the day before the Sabbath: "And that day was the preparation, and the sabbath drew on." However, Luke did *not* record when Joseph went to Pilate. He merely records that the Sabbath was drawing near ("the sabbath drew on") when Jesus's body was taken down from the cross. In contrast to Luke, Matthew 27:57 did *not* inform his reader that it was the eve of the Sabbath. Instead he stated, "when [*de*] the even [[*opsia*]] was come" [*ginomai*].

SPECULATION #42 The Time of the Request

The Greek word *opsia* occurs eight times in the Christian scriptures: Mk 4:35; 6:47; 15:42; Mt 8:16; 20:8; 26:20; 27:57; and Jn 6:16. According to *Strong's Concordance* (Strong 1890, 53), the Greek word *opsios* (#3798), pronounced op'-see-os, means: "late: fem. (as noun) afternoon (early eve) or nightfall (later eve):- (ing, [-tide])."

Young's Analytical Concordance to the Bible (1970, 309) translated *opsia* for both Mark and Matthew as "*evening*." In his Index-Lexicon to the New Testament, in the appendix section (p. 82), Young states that as a noun *opsia* means "evening." According to J. Weiss in his *Das Urchristentum* as cited by C. G. Montefiore (1968, 1:392), the word *opsios* "never means an earlier moment than sunset." Therefore, the Sabbath had already "begun." Consequently, this action would have violated the very thing that John 19:31 claims that the group of Jews wanted to avoid, having the bodies on the cross during the Sabbath: "The Jews therefore, because it was the preparation, that the bodies should not remain upon the cross on the sabbath day, (for that sabbath day was an high day,) besought Pilate that their legs might be broken, and that they might be taken away." However, according to Jewish law, one is permitted to move a body on the Sabbath with the caveat that it cannot be buried.

The unresolved question is whether or not the narrated accounts are nothing more than minor discrepancies or differences in wording for "late in the afternoon." Another unresolved question is if Matthew states it is, in fact, now evening and already the start of the next day—that is, Saturday, the sixteenth of Nisan. Such an understanding is found in the plain reading in many English translations of this verse (see table 22).

TABLE 22. English Translations of Matthew 27:57

ENGLISH VERSION	TRANSLATION
King James Version [AV]. 1611.	*When the even was come*, there came a rich man of Arimathea, named Joseph, who also himself was Jesus' disciple:
New King James Version. 1982. Thomas Nelson.	*Now when evening had come*, there came a rich man from Arimathea, named Joseph, who himself had also become a disciple of Jesus.
The Holy Bible, English Standard Version. 2001. Crossway Bibles.	*When it was evening*, there came a rich man from Arimathea, named Joseph, who also was a disciple of Jesus.
New American Standard Bible. 1995. Lockman Foundation.	*When it was evening*, there came a rich man from Arimathea, named Joseph, who himself had also become a disciple of Jesus.
Revised Standard Version. 1947, 1952.	*When it was evening*, there came a rich man from Arimathea, named Joseph, who also was a disciple of Jesus.
American Standard Version. 1901.	*And when even was come*, there came a rich man from Arimathea, named Joseph, who also himself was Jesus' disciple:
Robert Young Literal Translation. 1862, 1887, 1898.	*And evening having come*, there came a rich man, from Arimathea, named Joseph, who also himself was discipled to Jesus,
J. N. Darby Translation. 1890.	*Now when even was come* there came a rich man of Arimathea, his name Joseph, who also himself was a disciple to Jesus.

SPECULATION #43 The Logistics and Timing of Joseph's Audience with Pilate

An analysis of the time line presents other problems. Numerous events are needed to transpire during the time between Jesus's death and Joseph's appeal to Pilate. These include the following:

1. Jesus's death needed to be confirmed by those present at the crucifixion site.
2. Joseph needed to receive corroborating information about the death of Jesus. It would take time for this information to reach him. The Gospels do not identify the location of Joseph upon his receiving this information. He could have been home, at the Temple, at the

gathering place of the Sanhedrin, in the court, or somewhere in the city.

3. Joseph needed to prepare himself to see Pilate.

4. Joseph needed to travel to Pilate's locale, make a request to see the procurator, wait for an audience to see him, have a conversation with Pilate, and receive permission for his request.

5. Pilate would probably have had additional time constraints. The city was filled with thousands of pilgrims in celebration of the coming Sabbath and the Passover festival. According to Jeremias (1975, 375), during Jesus's life, Jerusalem had from 25,000 to 30,000 inhabitants; 180,000 celebrants participated at Passover. Consequentially, numerous logistical issues would be his primary focus. At the least, security matters would be a concern for the Roman authorities. Passover was a time at which Jews remembered their salvation by God from subjugation of the Egyptians. The Passover feast also represented a potential silent protest against the Roman Empire's presence in the Holy Land (Kineman 1995, 161, 170; Wylen 1996, 98).

6. Pilate needed to summon a centurion to verify that Jesus was already dead, the centurion had to travel to the site of Jesus's crucifixion and confirm the death, the centurion needed to travel back to Pilate's residence, and then Pilate had to question the centurion.

7. Finally, Joseph needed to be summoned again to Pilate to receive permission to take custody of Jesus's body.

It should be noted that the Gospels are silent about how and when Joseph was informed of Jesus's death.

Was there time to receive, prepare, and bury the body prior to the commencing of the Sabbath after receiving permission from Pilate to take Jesus? All of the Gospels go out of their way to emphasize the urgency of the time factor and to prevent violation of the Sabbath by carrying or burying the body. Clearly, there could not have been hours left; otherwise, the gospel accounts do not make sense. In conclusion, there is reason to doubt that there was sufficient time to complete all the details recorded in the gospel narratives related to the time between Jesus's death and a pre-Sabbath burial.

ISSUE 21: Joseph of Arimathea

Mk 15:43 Joseph of Arimathea, *an honourable counsellor, which also awaited for the kingdom of God,* came, and went in boldly unto Pilate, and craved the body of Jesus.	Mt 27:57 When the even was come, there came *a rich man of Arimathea,* named Joseph, who *also himself was Jesus' disciple.*	Lk 23:50 And, behold, there was a man named Joseph, *a counsellor; and he was a good man, and a just:* 51 *(The same had not consented to the counsel and deed of them;) he was of Arimathea, a city of the Jews: who also himself waited for the kingdom of God.*	Jn 19:38 And after this Joseph of Arimathea, *being a disciple of Jesus, but secretly for fear of the Jews,* besought Pilate that he might take away the body of Jesus: and Pilate gave him leave. He came therefore, and took the body of Jesus.

Mark 15:43 describes Joseph of Arimathea as "an honourable counsellor" [*bouleutēs*]; and waiting for the kingdom of God. Matthew omits two facts from Mark's narrative: (1) Joseph is a "counsellor" and thus a member of the Sanhedrin that had condemned Jesus to death, and (2) he is waiting for the kingdom of God. However, Matthew added two facts not found in Mark: (1) Joseph is rich, and (2) Joseph is a disciple of Jesus. Luke describes Joseph as a plain "counsellor." However, Luke added three important details omitted in Mark and Matthew: (1) he is a good man, (2) he is a just man, and (3) he "had not consented to the counsel and deed of them." Craig (1989a, 174) and Brown (1994a, 2:1213n20) suggested that the word *euschemon* (honourable) meant prominent, influential, noble, or wealthy. Montefiore (1968, 1:391) adds: "So applied [*euschemon*] leads us to infer, a man of high social rank."

CONTRADICTION #35 Luke Contradicts Mark and Matthew

Luke contradicts Mark and Matthew regarding who in the Sanhedrin condemned and did not condemn Jesus. Mark 14:53 states that Jesus was brought before the high priest and all the chief priests and the elders and the scribes after his arrest. Later, Mark 14:64 reports: "And *they all condemned him* to be guilty of death." Finally, in Mark 15:1 there is the added information that "in the morning the chief priests held a consultation with the elders and scribes *and the whole council,* and bound Jesus, and carried him away, and delivered him to Pilate." Therefore, Mark went out of his way to emphasize that *all* members of the council, including Joseph, condemned Jesus and that the *whole* council delivered him to Pilate. Gundry (1993, 980-81; cf. Hanhart 1995, 456) elaborates on this point:

> Rather, he [[Mark]] identifies Joseph as a member of the very Sanhedrin which unanimously condemned Jesus (cf. 14:64 with 14:55). As a "councilor" (βουλευτής), Joseph belongs to that body the whole of which held a "consultation" (συμβουλίου) issuing in the delivery of Jesus to Pilate (15:1; contrast the denial in Luke 23:51 that Joseph consented to their counsel [βουλῇ] and action.)

Twice Matthew reports in his narrative that the council planned and participated in the actions against Jesus:

> Mt 26:59 Now the chief priests, and elders, and all the council, sought false witness against Jesus, to put him to death.

> Mt 27:1 When the morning was come, all the chief priests and elders of the people took counsel against Jesus to put him to death

Therefore, Matthew substantiates Mark's narrative that all members of the Sanhedrin participated in the condemnation of Jesus.

Luke 23:50 reports that Joseph of Arimathea too is described as a *bouleutēs* or a counsellor (AV). Gigot (1910), writing in *The Catholic Encyclopedia*, elaborates: "He is also called by St. Mark and by St. Luke a *bouleutēs*, literally, 'a senator', whereby is meant a member of the Sanhedrin or supreme council of the Jews." Similarly, Brown (1994a, 2:1227) states: "While preserving Mark's *bouleutēs*, which he clearly understands to mean a member of the Sanhedrin responsible for Jesus' death" (v. 51). Yet in the next verse, Luke directly and undeniably contradicts Mark and Matthew by stating, "(The same *had not consented to the counsel and deed of them*;)." Consequently, Luke 23:51 stressed that all members of the council, *except* Joseph, condemned Jesus.

Therefore, according to Luke, Mark 14:64 must have been in error when he narrates: (1) "And they all condemned him to be guilty of death," or (2) it was the whole council except Joseph of Arimathea. Hanhart (1995, 455) points out: "Most exegetes believe it was an oversight on Mark's part not to have mentioned Joseph's absence from the council." Another possible rationalization is that Joseph belonged to a different council. However, Brown (1994a, 2:1228n61) severely criticizes any such interpretations: "There is no need to harmonize historically the Lucan 'all' or 'whole' with this exception by positing that Joseph was not present in the Sanhedrin when the vote was taken. That suggestion runs against Luke's literary intent; clearly he wants to portray Joseph as a man of courage in dissenting."

Finally, it should be noted that if Luke were correct and Joseph was not present or did cast a dissenting vote, it is also possible that other members of the council were also not present, given that it was the night of the Passover meal.

SPECULATION #44 The Significance of the Name Arimathea

An issue subject to speculation is the significance of the name Arimathea. Arimathea has not yet been identified with any guarantee. Hoover (2000, 133) points out: "And we should note one thing more: the location of Arimathea has not (yet) been identified with any assurance; the various 'possible' locations are nothing more than pious guesses or conjectures undocumented by any textual or archaeological evidence."

Richard Carrier (cited by Kirby 2005, 238; 258n22) speculates that the name Arimathea is "a pun on 'best disciple,' *ari{stos} mathe{tes}? Matheia* means 'disciple town' in Greek; *Ari-* is a common prefix for superiority." This hypothesis is based on the notion that the burial of Jesus was by an outsider (i.e., "Joseph of Arimathea as a contrast to the failure of the disciples and intimates of Jesus"). Therefore, we are left with the pun "best disciple town." However, Hays (2006, 195) rejects this hypothesis arguing the need to see lexical evidence that Matheia means "disciple town" and "the word is a Semitic place-name, not a Greek compound."

Craig (1989b, 173) and Hanhart (1995, 420; also see Lyons 2004, 32; MacArthur 2005, 1259) point out another possibility: The epithet "of Arimathea" is a *place* name referring to Ramathaim (LXX, *Harmathaim*), a town near Jerusalem, famous in Hebrew lore as the birthplace of Samuel, who anointed King David (1 Sam 1:1; 16:1). Furthermore, Hanhart (1995, 421) speculates that perhaps Joseph might "be symbolically related to the women who the day after his burial wanted to anoint Jesus."

Aus (2008, 162-65) speculates that the name was based on the site of Moses's death and burial. Deuteronomy 34:5-6 states that Moses died in the land of Moab, opposite Beth-peor. According to tradition, this is the same site as Mount Nebo, "the top of Pisgah." The word "Pisgah," which may mean the "cleft" in a mountain, occurs eight times in the Hebrew Bible. Four times it refers to the slopes of Pisgah: Deuteronomy 3:17; 4:49; and Joshua 3:23; 13:20. "The top of Pisgah" also occurs four times: Numbers 21:20; 23:14; and Deuteronomy 3:27; 34:1.

Targums *Onqelos, Pseudo-Jonathan*, and the *Fragment Targum*
where available always have רמתא for פסגה in the above passages.
Targum Neofiti 1 has the variant רמתה, with an *he* [[ה]] instead of
an *aleph* [[א]] as the final letter...

The Aramaic noun רמא in the singular means "height"...

In light of the above evidence I suggest that the early, Aramaic-
speaking, Palestinian Jewish Christian who first formulated
the narrative of Jesus' burial borrowed the term (Joseph of)
"Arimathea" from Judaic tradition available to him on the site of
the death and burial of Israel's first redeemer, Moses. It was the top
of "Pisgah," in Aramaic the plural רמתא, "Ramatha," "the heights."
It was also the same form employed for the top of "Pisgah" at the
end of the Song of the Well in Num 21:20. As noted above, early
Judaic tradition maintained that the well followed the Israelites to
the site of Moses' death and burial, that is, the Pisgah of Deut 34:1
(with v 6). The author of Jesus' burial probably himself added
an initial *aleph*, often done to place names, as shown in section
A. above, n. 2. The Aramaic ארמתא was then basically correctly
translated into the Greek as Αριμαθαια.

SPECULATION #45 The Council to Which Joseph Belonged

Mark and Luke narrate that Joseph is a counselor. The question is, to
what council did he belong? Mark 15:43 reports that he is a member of the
bouleutēs; however, in 14:55 and 15:1, he is a member of the *synedrion*, that is,
the Sanhedrin, or the "whole council." Crossan (1998, 554) suggests that Mark
wrote "as if there were two councils in charge of Jerusalem, a civil council and a
religious council, with Joseph a member of the former body (*bouleutēs*) but not
in the latter one at all (*synedrion*). There was, of course, no such distinction in
historical life; there was only one council, by whatever name."

In contrast, Matthew 27:57 eliminates any mention of the *synedrion*. It
has been suggested that Matthew made Joseph explicitly a follower of Jesus in
order to solve this problem regarding which council Joseph might have belonged
to. However, in Luke 23:51, Joseph is seemingly Hellenized as a good and
just (upright) man who "had not consented to what the others had planned
and carried out." This significant detail is omitted by Mark and Matthew.
Therefore, Crossan (1998, 554) proposes that Luke's statement that Joseph
"had not consented to the counsel and deed of them" was added to resolve the

specific contradiction in Mark 14:55 where the *synedrion* "sought for witnesses against Jesus to put him to death" and in Mark 15:1 where, in consultation, the *synedrion* "bound Jesus, and carried him away, and delivered him to Pilate."

As previously discussed, it is significant that Luke did not repeat Mark's comment in 14:64 that *all* of the council's judges had condemned Jesus to death. Instead, Luke's description of Joseph directly contradicts Mark 14:64. However, as Crossan (1998, 555) points out, the dilemma remains: "First, if Joseph was in the council, he was against Jesus; if he was for Jesus he was not in the council."

SPECULATION #46 "Waiting for the Kingdom of God" and "Being a Disciple"

Luke is in agreement with Mark's description of Joseph as one who also "waited for the kingdom of God." The relevant question is, what is meant by the phrase "looking for the kingdom of God"? Specifically, did this phrase mean or imply the same as accepting the kingdom of God, entering it, or believing in it?

Obviously, the phrase recorded in Mark did not necessarily mean that Joseph was, in fact, a disciple of Jesus or that he even expected Jesus to bring the "kingdom" about. Rather, Montefiore (1968, 1:391) posits that "there were Pharisees who eagerly expected the Kingdom—and even expected it soon." Such a person was possibly the Joseph recorded here in Mark 15:43. Furthermore, it should be recognized that although Joseph may have been sympathetic toward Jesus and his teachings, this does not necessarily mean that he was a regular disciple, though it was only natural that Mark's words would soon be understood in that sense. Therefore, Myllyoski (2002, 56) suggests that Joseph "seems to be a sort of 'would-be' Christian, an outsider with a positive characterization." In the opinion of Montefiore (1968, 1:391), Mark's description might "only mean that Joseph was a godly Jew who awaited the Messianic coming."

Discipleship is another characterization attributed to Joseph. Curtis (1972, 443) proposed that Matthew deliberately revised Mark's narrative by calling Joseph a disciple. The rationale is that Matthew's gospel "had already written that no rich man (as Joseph had become in Matthew—xxvii. 57, cf. Mark xv. 43) could enter (or presumably, await) the Kingdom of God (xix. 24)." Later, John also describes Joseph as a disciple. Curtis (1972, 443) states: "This implies that John either followed Matthew through dependence upon him, or coincidentally made a similar assessment of Joseph." However, there is no incontrovertible evidentiary proof that Joseph was a follower of Jesus or even sympathetic. (Lyons 2004, 33-37).

SPECULATION #47 The Meaning of "Rich Man" in Matthew 27:57

Only Matthew describes Joseph as being a rich man (*plousios*). Patte (1996, 391) writes: "But the mention that he is rich is necessary to explain why he owns a tomb;" whereas Viviano (1990, 672-73) suggests that the word "rich" is "to explain the enhanced status of the tomb," and then Heil (1991, 93) adds: "Nevertheless, Joseph's status as a 'rich' disciple enables him to request and receive the body of Jesus from Pilate (27:58), which neither the other male disciples who have fled (26:56) nor their substitutes, the women who are helplessly passive (27:55-56), are in a position to do." In contrast, Price (2003, 327) offered the following hypothesis: "It is important that Joseph is rich and buries Jesus in his own, presumably opulent, tomb. This information provides the narrative motivation for tomb robbers to move in and seek the rich funerary tokens they assume have been buried with Joseph, whom they assume must be laid out inside."

Several writers (Barrick 1977, 235; Benoit 1970, 215; Gundry 1994, 580; Filson 1960, 298; Phillips 2002, 334; Senior 1992, 1444) discuss the possibility that this description was an attempt by Matthew to fulfill Isaiah 53:9: "And he made his grave with the wicked, and with the rich in his death; because he had done no violence, neither was any deceit in his mouth." Barrick (1977, 235n2) writes: "This would be consistent with Matthew's fondness for OT correlations to the life and work of Jesus, one example being the star of Bethlehem story" (Mt 2:2-9). Perhaps the only thing missing to lend further credence to this hypothesis is the phrase "as it was foretold in the scripture." The problem with this supposed proof text is that the phrase "buried by a rich man" is hardly equivalent to "buried with the rich." In fact, the accounts in the Christian scriptures are reversed from those stated in the literal sense of the verse in the Hebrew Bible—that is, Jesus died with two thieves at his sides.

Bowen (1911, 247) points out that if one accepted that Mark was the earliest of the four Gospels (as most scholars do), it becomes clear that the gospels have progressively Christianized Joseph of Arimathea. Yet another possibility offered by Hanhart (1995, 182) is that the epithet "a rich man" was in reality a derogatory sneer based on the LXX Isaiah 22:16. Finally, several writers (Lake 1907, 50; Montefiore 1968, 1:392; Swete 1927, 391) suggest that the word "rich" could also have properly meant "of good standing." The important point is that all these explanations about the meaning of "rich" are mere speculation. No one knows with absolute certainty what the author or final editors intended.

SPECULATION #48 An Anti-Jewish Motif

Another related topic of speculation is why Matthew 27:57 seemingly stressed Joseph's Christian rather than Jewish credentials (i.e., "who was a disciple of Jesus"). For example, Gundry (1994, 580) writes that Matthew made Joseph a full-fledged Christian disciple. In addition, numerous scholars and theologians (Cook 2008, 278-88; Levine 2002, 77-88; 1999, 9-36; Luz 2005a, 243-61; and others) discuss a possible anti-Jewish motif, which appears throughout the Gospel of Matthew: (1) usage of the phrase "the Jews" often in a derogatory context and (2) having the Jews respond to Pilate's statement that "I am innocent of the blood of this just person" (Mt 27:24) and "His blood be on us, and on our children" (Mt 27:25).

John 19:38 describes Joseph as "a disciple of Jesus, but secretly for fear of the Jews." This fear motif appears in John 7:13; 9:22; 12:42; and 20:19. Like Matthew, many scholars concur that the Gospel of John contains anti-Jewish polemics (see Peter Richardson 2006. "The Beginnings of Christian anti-Semitism, 70- c. 235." In *The Cambridge History of Judaism*, edited by Steven T. Katz, 244-58. Cambridge: Cambridge University Press; *Faith and Polemic: Studies in Anti-Semitism and Early Christianity*, edited by Craig A. Evans and Donald A. Hager. Minneapolis: Fortress Press, 1992).

John, the last gospel, was written approximately twenty to thirty years after Mark and when the early "Jewish Christians" had split with Judaism. Kysar (1993, 27) cites J. Louis Martyn and Raymond E. Brown, indicating that "the occasion for the writing of the Fourth Gospel was an experience of expulsion of a Christian community from their synagogue home." Kysar, expanding this theme, writes: "The social repositioning of the Christian community was the issue at stake. By being expelled from the synagogue they had experienced the trauma of social dislocation. Their task was now one of making a new place for themselves in a society which appeared to them to be hostile and unaccommodating. Hence the pervasive insider-outsider language of the Gospel."

Here, Matthew 27:57 (Osborne 1997, 39) declares that "one can hardly miss the heightening of Joseph by the various evangelists." Similarly, Benoit (1970, 229) notes: "It is possible that the Christians embellished him and made him out to be more of a Christian than he actually was; there are analogous cases in the gospel, and Pilate [[for example]] is later almost turned into a saint." Likewise, Zangenberg (2007, 877) declares that Joseph was "clearly depicted as a Christian and might very well represent the Christian (Johannine) community who, for fear of repression, does not dare to come out openly."

ISSUE 22: Joseph's Motive in Asking for Jesus's Body

Mk 15:42 *And now when the even was come, because it was the preparation, that is, the day before the sabbath,* 43 Joseph of Arimathea, *an honourable counsellor, which also awaited for the kingdom of God,* came, and went in boldly unto Pilate, and craved the body of Jesus.	Mt 27:57 When the even was come, there came a rich man of Arimathea, named Joseph, who *also himself was Jesus' disciple.* 58 He went to Pilate, and begged the body of Jesus. Then Pilate commanded the body to be delivered.	Lk 23:50 And, behold, there was a man named Joseph, a counsellor; *and he was a good man, and a just*: 51 (The same had not consented to the counsel and deed of them;) he was of Arimathea, a city of the Jews: *who also himself waited for the kingdom of God.* 52 This man went unto Pilate, and begged the body of Jesus. 53 And he took it down, and wrapped it in linen, and laid it in a sepulchre that was hewn in stone, wherein never man before was laid. 54 *And that day was the preparation, and the sabbath drew on.*	Jn 19:38 And after this Joseph of Arimathea, *being a disciple of Jesus, but secretly for fear of the Jews, besought Pilate that he might take away the body of Jesus*: and Pilate gave him leave. He came therefore, and took the body of Jesus.

The synoptic narratives provide several suggestions regarding asking for the body, possibly motivating Joseph's rationale for burying Jesus: (1) the coming of the Sabbath (Mark), (2) Joseph is a disciple of Jesus (Matthew), (3) Joseph's character as a good, honorable, and just man (Mark and Luke), and perhaps (4) Joseph awaited the kingdom of God (Mark and Luke).

In contrast, John presents the notion that Joseph "secretly for fear of the Jews, besought Pilate that he might take away the body of Jesus." Therefore, in Mark and Luke, Jesus's body is requested for altruistic reasons. In the Gospel of John, Joseph went to Pilate in secret "for fear of the Jews." Furthermore, although John does not explicitly state that Joseph was rich, as did Matthew 27:57, he apparently (1) has the ability to have an audience with Pilate, (2) has the ability to have Pilate agree to his request, and (3) has the means to bury Jesus.

Finally, there are several additional unknowns related to Joseph that bear exploration: Specifically, (1) what group of Jews did Joseph fear, (2) why did he fear the Jews, and (3) what did he fear that the Jews might do to him? John does not provide these details.

SPECULATION #49 The Jewish Obligation to Bury the Dead

Luke provides a possible explanation for Joseph's desire to assume responsibility for Jesus's body: Joseph is a good and just man. Expanding on the previous rationale, another reason Joseph might have requested Jesus's body would be to fulfill the obligation or the biblical injunction of all Jews not to leave a body hanging from a tree since it defiled the land, regardless of the day of the week:

> Deut 21:22-23 And if a man have committed a sin worthy of death, and he be to be put to death, and thou hang him on a tree: His body shall not remain all night upon the tree, but thou shalt in any wise bury him that day; (for he that is hanged is accursed of God;) that thy land be not defiled, which the LORD thy God giveth thee for an inheritance.

However, there are several important facts that challenge the Deuteronomy 21:22-23 rationale for Joseph to have removed Jesus's body from the cross: (1) the Deuteronomic verses do not refer to hanging/crucifixion *before* but *after* death, (2) the dead bodies are exposed as a means of humiliation and warning to others, and (3) the display of the bodies must end by nightfall or sunset. The removal by sunset of one crucified *after* death is very different from removal by sunset of one crucified *before* death. (This topic is discussed later.)

An explicit example of the hanging of five kings after death and removal prior to sunset is recorded in Joshua 10:26-27. Remarkably similar to the gospel accounts, these kings are buried in a cave and a large stone is placed over the mouth of the cave. Suffice it to say that the removal by sunset of one crucified after death is very different from removal by sunset of one crucified before death.

The authors of Mark and Luke allude to the fact that Joseph was loyal to the Pharisees or "mainstream" Judaism, being a distinguished member of the Sanhedrin. Failure to bury Jesus would have been an offense against everything decent and good. If Joseph was a Pharisee or even a Sadducee, he would not have violated the Sabbath or *Hag Ha-Matsot*—that is, the Festival of Unleavened Bread—to accomplish the burial.

For example, the book of *Tobias* (1:20 f.; 2:1-9) shows, as G. F. Moore (1971, 71n6) remarks, that the burial of the neglected is regarded as a duty of the highest obligation:

- It took precedence even over study of the Law (Torah).
- It took precedence even over the circumcision of a son.

- It took precedence even over the offering of the paschal lamb.
- Priests—even the high priest—and nazarites were allowed to make themselves [ritually or spiritually] unclean by burying dead person.

However, an unknown is whether Luke based an underlying rationale of Joseph's supposed risk to bury Jesus centered on the tale of Tobit. Here, Tobit buries executed Jews at the risk of his own life.

SPECULATION #50 Did Joseph Care about the Two Crucified Thieves?

If Joseph's only motivation for burying Jesus is merely compliance with Jewish law, surely Joseph would have also complied with the Jewish regulation and must have taken possession of the two *lēstēs* (bandits; cf. Mk 14:48; 15:27; Mt 27:38) or wrongdoers (Lk 23:33).

However, the synoptic narratives go out of their way to indicate that Joseph only cared about Jesus's remains:

> Mk 15:43 Joseph of Arimathea, an honourable counsellor, which also awaited for the kingdom of God, came, and *went in boldly unto Pilate, and craved the body of Jesus.*

> Mt 27:58 He went to Pilate, and *begged the body of Jesus.* Then Pilate commanded the body to be delivered.

> Lk 23:52 This man went unto Pilate, *and begged the body of Jesus.*

There is no indication that Joseph was concerned about the bodies of the two other men crucified with Jesus. As a matter of fact, the Gospels no longer mention any word of these men after their dialog with Jesus while mounted on their respective crosses. Therefore, assuming that Joseph of Arimathea was a pious and observant Jew who carried out the biblical obligations, why is it that he cared only about Jesus's body? (Tilborg and Counet 2000, 177) Why did Joseph fail to ask for the bodies of the two thieves? Craig (1989b, 176) speculated that Joseph obtained all three bodies but placed the bodies of the bandits in a common grave.

Cook (2008, 152) offers an alternative hypothesis:

> The objection that Joseph would then have asked for the other bodies as well (presuming that these, too, were dead) is not

compelling. Even if we assume that the crucified Jesus was indeed flanked by other victims *and* that the Joseph story is genuine history, Gospel tradition could not allow and preserve any inference that Joseph asked for more than one corpse. This would open the possibility that he then buried them all together in his tomb—which would confuse, and compromise, the *empty* tomb story. For example, if on Sunday morning one body of several was missing, skeptics could dispute that the body missing was Jesus. Bodies were already hard to distinguish from each other after sufficient scourging and loss of blood, all the more so the onset of decay and decomposition.

SPECULATION #51 Passover and the Sabbath

Another potential factor for requesting Jesus's body may have been Joseph's interest in maintaining the sanctity of the Passover festival and the upcoming Sabbath. Passover is called *Z'man Cheruteinu*, the Time of Our Liberation. It is a Festival of Freedom. It would be contradictory for Jews to celebrate a time of deliverance, freedom, and liberation from pagan oppression while Jesus and his two compatriots were being crucified by pagans who occupied the Holy Land. In contrast, the Sabbath symbolizes God's day of ordained rest. Here, too, it would be inappropriate for Jews to be observing and remembering the Sabbath, the day of rest, while three men struggled and worked to stay alive. Consequently, at the season of Passover and with the approach of the Sabbath, such sensibilities would have been heightened.

SPECULATION #52 To Humiliate and Bury Jesus in Shame

Byron R. McCane (1999, 451-52; cf. Dijkhuizen 2011, 121-27) also suggests that there was, in fact, another motive in having Jesus buried. However, this motive had *nothing* to do with the Sabbath or sanctity of the upcoming Passover festival. Instead, the purpose of the burial is to *humiliate* and have Jesus buried in *shame*. McCane's hypothesis modifies certain crucial aspects of the gospel narratives. Significantly, the Jewish leaders in Jerusalem are later personified by Christian tradition as Joseph of Arimathea:

> The evidence has further shown that the Jewish leaders who participated in the proceedings against Jesus had strong religious and cultural motives for seeking to bury him in shame. Such

motives came not from any secret allegiance to Jesus, but from observance of traditional law and custom. Finally, the evidence has also shown that the early followers of Jesus described his burial in terms, which were dishonorable. They dignified it as much as possible but did not deny its shame.

On the basis of the evidence, then, the following scenario emerges as a likely course of events for the deposition of Jesus' body: late on the day of his death, *one or more of the Jewish leaders in Jerusalem—later personified by Christian tradition as Joseph of Arimathea—requested custody of the body for purposes of dishonorable burial. These leaders, having collaborated with the Romans in the condemnation of Jesus, had both the means and the motive to bury him in shame: means, in their access to Pilate, and motive, in Jewish law and custom.* [italics mine] Pilate did not hesitate to grant dishonorable burial to one of their condemned criminals. Only the most rudimentary burial preparations were administered—the body was wrapped and taken directly to the tomb, without a funeral procession, eulogies, or the deposition of any personal effects. By sunset on the day of his death, the body of Jesus lay within a burial cave reserved for criminals condemned by Jewish courts. No one mourned.

The shame of Jesus' burial is not only consistent with the best evidence, but can also help to account for an historical fact which has long been puzzling to historians of early Christianity: why did the primitive church not venerate the tomb of Jesus? Joachim Jeremias, for one, thought it inconceivable (*undenkbar*) that the primitive community would have let the grave of Jesus sink into oblivion.[65] Yet the earliest hints of Christian veneration of Jesus' tomb do not surface until the early fourth century CE.[66] It is a striking fact—and not at all unthinkable—that the tomb of Jesus was not venerated until it was no longer remembered as a place of shame.[67]

---

[65] J. Jeremias, *Heilegengraber in Jesu Umwelt* (Gottingen: Vandenhoeck & Ruprecht, 1958) 145.+-9

[66] Eusebius, *Via Constantini* 3.25-32.

[67] I am grateful to my colleague at the Sepphoris Regional Project, Jonathan L. Reed, and to my colleagues at Converse College, Robert J. Hauck and Melissa Walker all of whom read an earlier version of this article and offered constructive criticisms.

However, in a review of McCane's proposal, Craig (2004, 409) opines: "Therefore the probability of Jesus' being dishonourably buried, given the evidence, has not been shown to be higher than the probability that he was honourably buried."

ISSUE 23: Pilate's Reaction, Reply, and Rationale to Joseph's Request

Mk 15:43 Joseph of Arimathea, an honourable counsellor, which also waited for the kingdom of God, came, and went in boldly unto Pilate, and craved the body of Jesus. 44 *And Pilate marvelled if he were already dead: and calling upon unto him the centurion, he asked him whether he had been any while dead.* 45 And when he knew it of the centurion, he gave the body to Joseph.	Mt 27:58 He went to Pilate, and begged the body of Jesus. *Then Pilate commanded the body to be delivered.*	Lk 23:50 And, behold, there was a man named Joseph, a counsellor; and he was a good man, and a just: 51 (The same had not consented to the counsel and deed of them;) he was of Arimathea, a city of the Jews: who also himself waited for the kingdom of God. 52 *This man went unto Pilate, and begged the body of Jesus. 53 And he took it down, and wrapped it in linen,* and laid it in a sepulchre that was hewn in stone, wherein never man before was laid.	Jn 19:38 And after this Joseph of Arimathea, being a disciple of Jesus, but secretly for fear of the Jews, besought Pilate that he might take away the body of Jesus: and *Pilate gave him leave.* He came therefore, and took the body of Jesus.

In Mark, Matthew, and Luke, there is only one appearance before Pilate to request Jesus's body. The request is made by Joseph of Arimathea. In contrast, John reports not one but two appearances before Pilate. First, a group of unnamed Jews approach Pilate and request that the legs of the condemned be broken and that their bodies taken away. Pilate agrees to the first part of this petition for the soldiers to break the legs of the condemned. No information is provided about the second part of the request, "and that they might be taken away." Later, the second appearance has Joseph of Arimathea approaching Pilate and requesting Jesus's body.

Pilate's reaction to Joseph's request appears only in Mark 15:44: "And Pilate marvelled if he were already dead." Mark also provides two details not found in the other gospel narratives: (1) Pilate's questioning the centurion to verify the death and (2) his hesitation in relinquishing Jesus's body.

CONTRADICTION #36 Why Pilate Should Not Have Been Amazed

John 19:30 reports that a nameless group of Jews requests the legs of those condemned be broken: "The Jews therefore, because it was the preparation, that the bodies should not remain upon the cross on the sabbath day, (for that sabbath day was an high day,) besought Pilate that their legs might be broken, and that they might be taken away." In the next verse it appears that Pilate instructs that the legs of the condemned be broken: "Then came the soldiers, and brake the legs of the first, and of the other which was crucified with him." This action conflicts with Mark 15:44 who describes Pilate as being completely unaware of Jesus's death and totally surprised: "And Pilate marvelled if he were already dead: and calling upon unto him the centurion, he asked him whether he had been any while dead."

Why is Mark's Pilate surprised by Jesus's sudden death since he specifically ordered the bones of the condemned to be broken; in addition, that action would have resulted in an almost immediate death. A review of the chronology follows:

1. John 19:31 describes that a group of Jews petition Pilate to have the legs of the condemned broken and the bodies taken away.
2. Apparently, John 19:32-34 reports that Pilate grants permission to break the legs and this is carried out. To quote Brown (1994a, 2:1230): "John indicated implicitly that Pilate ceded the first part of this petition, for the soldiers came and began breaking the legs of those crucified with Jesus (19:32)."
3. Later, after an unknown period of time, John 19:38 narrates that Joseph approaches Pilate and makes his request for Jesus's body. This event corresponds with Mark 15:24; Matthew 27:58; and Luke 23:50.
4. Immediately following, Mark 15:43 reports that Joseph of Arimathea has an audience with Pilate and requests Jesus's body. Obviously Joseph knows that Jesus is dead. One verse later, Mark 15:44 describes Pilate's reaction as being "marvelled" that Jesus is already dead. However, Pilate presumably would have known that Jesus was already dead as earlier recorded in John 19:31-32. That is, the act of breaking the legs was already completed, which would have resulted

in the fast death of the condemned. Why then did Pilate marvel that Jesus was dead? He had after all previously ordered the legs to be broken. It is assumed that the soldiers carried out their orders as they were expected to do. Given this assumption, it is reasonable to assume that Jesus is already dead.

Returning to Mark, the surprised Pilate then orders a centurion to verify Jesus's death. Mark provides no details of how long it took for the centurion to substantiate Jesus's death. Only after Pilate is assured that Jesus is dead did he consent to give the body to Joseph (see Mk 15:45 and Jn 19:38).

SPECULATION #53 Reasons for Pilate's Amazement and Inquiry

Why is Pilate amazed to hear that Jesus died so soon after his crucifixion? Mark's text unmistakably implies that Jesus died sooner than expected. However, crucified victims lasted different lengths of time, depending on their own state of health, the severity of the pre-crucifixion torture, and the way in which they were crucified. John Meier (1991, 280-85) assumes that Jesus, like his father, was a carpenter or, more precisely, "a woodworker" (*tektōn*)—solely based upon Mark 6:3 and Matthew 13:55. Furthermore, there is disagreement as to what this occupation entailed (see Capps 2000, 14). However, here, Meier (1991, 281) adds:

> Thus, while Jesus was in one sense a common Palestinian workman, he plied a trade that involved, for the ancient world, a fair level of technical skill. It also involved no little sweat and muscle power. The airy weakling often presented to us in pious paintings and Hollywood movies would hardly have survived the rigors of being Nazareth's *tektōn* from his youth to his early thirties. (cf. Capps 2000, 14; Powell 1998, 136)

Perhaps here then is a rationale that Pilate is amazed at Jesus's rapid demise on the cross. On the other hand, Myllyoski (2002, 58) posits that perhaps Pilate's amazement and follow-up investigation served "its basic function is to convince the reader that Jesus really died as soon as the crucifixion narrative suggests."

A related rationale is that Luke fails to mention that Jesus is flogged or beaten by Roman soldiers. This lack of violence to Jesus would perhaps make his early death after six hours on the cross seem especially unusual and highly suspicious. Consequently, Brown (1994a, 1:73) writes: "Perhaps, Luke feared that this would cast doubt on the reality of Jesus' death and thus fuel the last-1st-century apologetics against the resurrection that were developing among those opposed to Christianity."

Why then does Luke omit or deliberately delete this incident; that is, the questioning of the guard and Pilate's hesitation in relinquishing Jesus's body, especially if the Gospel of Mark had been part of his source? Such a strategy would be helpful in winning the favor of Rome. However, Lake (1907, 52) suggests that arguments are fairly equally divided that Mark 15:44-45 formed no part of the original Markan document and were an interpolation.

Brown (1994a, 2:1222) offers several additional theories:

- The authors of Matthew and Luke found the scene too scandalous.
- The text was included for apologetic purposes to demonstrate that Jesus was truly dead.
- The text involved antidocetism.
- A redactor added the verses to Mark early enough for them to appear in all known copies but after the authors of Matthew and Luke had drawn upon the gospel.
- The text was purely a decorative narrative embellishment.

Another possible reason for doubt is that Pilate could have thought there was a conspiracy to save Jesus. However, this raises the counter question: who would be behind such a risky venture? This highly speculative topic is discussed later.

SPECULATION #54 Rationales for Pilate Turning Over the Body

Matthew 27:58 reports that Pilate acquiesced and ordered (*ekeleusen*) that Jesus's body be handed over to Joseph of Arimathea "without expressing any hesitation or questioning of Joseph, even though Joseph is a disciple of Jesus" (Brown 1994a, 2:1225-26). One rationale for accepting Matthew's storyline is that Matthew's Pilate is portrayed in a positive light as compared to Mark's description. Some (Brown 1994a, 2:1226; Carson 1991, 629) commentators suggest that Pilate believed Jesus was innocent, was unjustly treated by the Jewish leadership, and, also, recognized that Jesus had no political following.

Second, the Joseph reported in Matthew's narrative is rich and presumably influential. Consequently, Pilate would not wish to offend such a person by refusing his request (1994, 2:1226). Of course, there also could have been an exchange of money (a bribe) to receive permission from Pilate (Kennard 1955, 238). Carson (1991, 629) also posits that the turning over of Jesus's body "may have been a final snub against the Jewish authorities."

King (1995, 5-38) suggests that there are several possible reasons that Pilate agreed to turn Jesus's body over to Joseph:

- It would avoid any further possible disturbance of the peace.
- It would please him and perhaps win Pilate a friendly voice in future dealings with the Sanhedrin.
- It would gall the Jewish leadership without giving them sufficient cause for dangerous action.
- It would have the body securely entombed in Joseph's property.
- It would permit Pilate to know exactly where the body was, and he would have certain custody of it.

Craig (1989b, 177) suggests that the silence of the other gospel accounts may indicate that "they regarded it as superfluous." Craig's rationale is merely his opinion and found wanting. Mark 15:44 reports: "Pilate marvelled if he were already dead." However, this statement makes no sense. Why should Pilate have "marvelled" if Jesus were already dead as previously reported in John 19:31-33; and he had, at the request of the Jews, ordered his soldiers to break the legs of those on the cross—resulting in a rapid death.

Yet another reason that Pilate may have given the body to Joseph is based on Roman law (Digest, XLVIII, 24. *De Cadaveribus Punitorum*) that obliges those in authority to give the body of Jesus to anyone who might request it (Lilly 1940, 102). Specifically, the third legal source cited in #24 from Paul, *Views*, book 1, reads: "The bodies of executed persons are to be granted to any who seek them for burial" (Watson 1998, 2: Book Forty-eight/Dead bodies #24). It is unknown whether this practice was a custom in the first century.

Finally, it must be inquired: Was Pilate's action plausible? Specifically, would Pilate or any other governor have been likely to check on the death of a criminal? This request is possible given that Jesus is executed for being a "rebel rouser," and that his death, in the eyes of Pilate, seemingly did not take long enough time. However, Brown (1994a, 2:1221) writes that, unfortunately, "we know little of the practice of Roman governors pertaining to such an issue."

ISSUE 24: Those Involved in Taking Jesus's Body Down from the Cross

Mk 15:45	Mt 27:59	Lk 23:50 And,	Acts 13:28: And	Jn 19:38 And after this
And when	*And when*	behold, there was a	though they found	*Joseph of Arimathea,*
he knew	*Joseph had*	man named *Joseph,*	no cause of death	being a disciple of
it of the	*taken the*	*a counsellor; and he*	in him, yet desired	Jesus, but secretly
centurion, *he*	*body,* he	*was a good man, and*	they Pilate that he	for fear of the Jews,
gave the body	wrapped it	*a just*: 51 (The same	should be slain.	besought Pilate that
to Joseph.	in a clean	had not consented	29 And when they	he might take away
46 And he	linen cloth.	to the counsel and	had fulfilled all	the body of Jesus: and
bought fine		deed of them;) he	that was written of	Pilate gave him leave.
linen, and		was of Arimathea, a	him, *they took him*	*He came therefore, and*
took him		city of the Jews: who	*down from the tree,*	*took the body of Jesus.*
down, and		also himself waited	*and laid him in a*	39 *And there came also*
wrapped		for the kingdom of	*sepulchre.*	*Nicodemus,* which at
him in the		God. 52 *This man*		the first came to Jesus
linen, and		*went unto Pilate,*		by night, and brought
laid him in		and begged the		a mixture of myrrh
a sepulchre		body of Jesus. 53		and aloes, about
which was		*And he took it down,*		an hundred pound
hewn out of		and wrapped it in		weight. 40 *Then they*
a rock, and		linen, and laid it		*took the body of Jesus*
rolled a stone		in a sepulchre that		and wound it in linen
unto the		was hewn in stone,		clothes with the spices,
door of the		wherein never man		as the manner of the
sepulchre.		before was laid.		Jews is to bury.

Mark 15:46 and Luke 23:53 explicitly mentions that only Joseph took down the body of Jesus from the cross. However, afterward Mark 16:6 narrates that a person described as a young man, who is perhaps an angel, states that as three women arrive at the empty tomb: "Ye seek Jesus of Nazareth, which was crucified: he is risen; he is not here: behold the place where *they* laid him." Mark's later narrative declares that "more" than one person helped to place Jesus's body in the tomb; however, the narrator did not provide support that anyone else assisted Joseph in taking down the body from the cross. In contrast, Matthew and John did not provide any explicit information about Jesus's body being taken down from the cross. Instead, Matthew 27:59 reports that Joseph took the body, whereas John 19:39 narrates that Joseph and, perhaps, Nicodemus took it down. In contradiction, Acts 13:27-29 claims that Jesus's body was taken down from the cross by those who crucified him.

CONTRADICTION #37 Who Took Jesus's Body Down from the Cross?

There is a definite contradiction concerning the removal of Jesus's body from the cross as recorded in Acts. Acts 13:27-29 states that Paul was informed that Jesus was taken down from the cross by the Romans, the *same* people who crucified him.

> Acts 13:27 For they that dwell at Jerusalem, and their rulers, because they knew him not, nor yet the voices of the prophets which are read every sabbath day, they have fulfilled them in condemning him.
>
> Acts 13:28 And though they found no cause of death in him, yet desired they Pilate that he should be slain.
>
> Acts 13:29 *And when they had fulfilled all that was written of him, they took him down from the tree*, and laid him in a sepulchre.

The passage in Acts, attributed to Paul but written by Luke, declares that those who took part in the recovery of Jesus's body were responsible for his execution. Consequently, Paul emphasizes that Jesus was taken down from the cross, not by his followers but by his enemies, the very group who Paul accuses of arranging for his death.

If, however, Christian apologists contend that Acts refers to the Jews and not to the Romans who had engineered Jesus's death, there is yet another contradiction, as previously discussed in Issue 21. Luke 23:51 reports that Joseph was *not* part of the conspiracy. That is, Luke 23:51 stresses that all members of the council *except* Joseph condemned Jesus. If Joseph did not take part in the council's deed to conspire against Jesus, then how could Acts claim "And when they had fulfilled all that was written of him, they took him down from the tree, and laid him in a sepulchre"?

In direct contradiction, the synoptic narratives claim that the action of taking down Jesus's body is carried out by Joseph *alone*. This contradiction seems particularly odd since the author of Acts is also believed to be the writer of Luke, yet he records conflicting accounts. How then is it possible that the Gospel of Luke and the Acts of the Apostles conflict?

Adding to the confusion, John 19:39 states that it was Joseph *and* Nicodemus who take the body, prepare the body, and bury the body: "Then they took the body of Jesus and wound it in linen clothes with the spices, as the manner of the Jews is to bury."

So who prepared and buried the body: (1) those responsible for Jesus's death, (2) Joseph of Arimathea, or (3) Joseph of Arimathea and Nicodemus?

SPECULATION #55 Taking Down Jesus's Body

Nowhere in the Gospels is there any description of the actual removal of the nails or a narration of taking Jesus's body down from the cross. Furthermore, nowhere in the Gospels is there a description of Joseph's age or physical attributes. Therefore, it is, in fact, unknown if Joseph alone had the physical ability to take down Jesus's body from the cross.

Significantly, Brown (1994a, 2:1230n650) points out that it should be noted that there are a number of variant readings in the last periscope of John 19:38. Codex Sinaiticus, Tatian, OL, and some Sahidic have a plural subject: "So *they* came and took away his body." There could have been an officer sent from Pilate who authorized Joseph's actions. However, Craig (1989b, 177) suggests that the taking down from the cross of Jesus's body "does not necessitate that Joseph himself ascended the ladder and pulled out the nails. The Romans may have taken down the body for him; in any case Joseph no doubt had, as a man of authority, servants to help him." Of course, John's narrative of 19:31-34 would make Craig's hypothesis invalid since the body had previously been taken down and discarded. Nonetheless, Matthew Henry, a famous traditional Christian biblical commentator, is of the opinion that Luke implies: "*He took it down, it should seem* with his own hands, and *wrapped it in linen*" (1961, 1499).

Finally, Brown (1994a, 2:1218) points out the importance of Mary Magdalene in the Easter morning tradition and asks an intriguing question: why did the women not help Joseph if he was a fellow disciple instead of planning to come back after the Sabbath when he would not be there? Brown rejects two possible apologetics that "Jewish women were not supposed to talk with men in public, especially strangers" and "sexes were segregated at funerals." His rebuttal is (1) there is no evidence in the Gospels that there is any problem about women talking to men, and (2) Mary Magdalene did not have any difficulty at the tomb addressing a man whom she thinks is a gardener (see n31).

ISSUE 25: When Joseph Took Down Jesus's Body

Mk 15:42 *And now when the even was come*, because it was the preparation, that is, the day before the sabbath, 43 *Joseph of Arimathea*, an honourable counsellor, which also waited for the kingdom of God, came, and *went in boldly unto Pilate*, and craved the body of Jesus.	Mt 27:57 *When the even was come*, there came a rich man of *Arimathea*, named Joseph, who also himself was Jesus' disciple: 58 *He went to Pilate*, and begged the body of Jesus. Then Pilate commanded the body to be delivered.	Lk 23:54 And that day was the preparation, *and the sabbath drew on.*	Jn 19:38 *And after this Joseph of Arimathea*, being a disciple of Jesus, but secretly for fear of the Jews, *besought Pilate* that he might take away the body of Jesus: and Pilate gave him leave. He came therefore, and took the body of Jesus.

None of the Gospels specify when Joseph specifically took down Jesus's body from the cross or the amount of time that transpired between Joseph receiving permission to receive the body, his purchasing the linen, and his arriving at Golgotha. According to Mark 15:34; Matthew 27:45; and Luke 23:44, Jesus died at approximately 3:00 p.m. that is the ninth hour. Then Mark 15:42-43; Matthew 27:57-58; and John 19:38 report that Joseph went to Pilate, requesting Jesus's body during some unknown time between 3:00 p.m. and 6:00 p.m.

Another factor that needs to be considered regarding the time line is the additional time required to move the body to an appropriate place for the ritual cleansing rites. It is assumed that out of respect for the dead, including modesty, this preparation occurred at an appropriate locale. However, the Gospels are silent about the location of Jesus's ritual cleansing prior to his burial. Only Luke provides information, saying that as the task was completed, "the sabbath drew on."

SPECULATION #56 When Jesus's Body Was Removed from the Cross

The translations found in many English Christian Bibles are seemingly misleading regarding when Jesus's body was taken down from the cross. Several writers (Myllykoski, 2002, 71; Ranke-Heinmann 1994, 136; Schreiber 1981, 141-57) maintain that Jesus's body was removed from the cross during the Sabbath. The Greek verb *epiphosko* or *epiphōskein* commonly translated as "drawing near" or "to dawn" appears only twice in the Christian scriptures. In Luke 23:54 the text states "and the sabbath drew on." Similarly, Matthew 28:1 uses the same word *epiphosko* for "to dawn."

Epiphosko is translated in *Young's Analytical Concordance to the Bible* (1970, 271) as "to shine or dawn upon." *Strong's Concordance* (Strong 1890, 32) has number 2020, corresponding to the Greek word *epiphosko* "to begin to grow light:- begin to dawn, X draw on." In other words, Luke is reporting that Jesus's body is laid in the sepulchre (vs. 53) when the Sabbath is beginning. According to the Hebrew Bible (Gen 1:5, 8, 13, 19, 23, 31), a new day starts with evening or darkness. For example, Genesis 1:5 reads: "And God called the light Day, and the darkness he called Night. And the evening and the morning were the first day." Significantly, notice that the order is evening first followed by morning. Therefore, Ranke-Heinemann (1994, 136) reiterates that

> As it was understood back then, the day after the Sabbath, the first day of the week, began immediately after the end of the Sabbath; and the Sabbath ended at sundown on Saturday evening. The new day was said to "shine forth," not with the dawn but when the first stars could be seen.

> Matthew uses the same verb for "shine forth" (*epiphoskein*) that Luke uses at the end of his description of the taking down of Jesus' body from the cross: "It was the day of Preparation, and the sabbath was beginning" (Luke 23:54). The Sabbath began or "shone forth" not on the next morning, but immediately after the day of Preparation, which in turn ended with nightfall. No one would claim here that the Sabbath did not begin until the next morning, and that Jesus must not have been taken down from the cross until the next morning.

In contrast, the late Catholic scholar, Father Raymond Brown (1994a, 2:1256), offers the following apologetic:

> They had to obey the Sabbath rest that was about to begin (23:56b). Luke employs *epiphōskein* in the imperfect 'the Sabbath *was dawning*,' a verb that involves *phos* ('light') and reflects a mind-set where days begin in the morning as the sunlight begins to shine. This verb seems odd in the context of the Jewish calendar where the day begins after sunset and so with the onset

of darkness. Despite efforts to explain the usage in terms of other lights that shine at night [Fitzmyer (*Luke* 2.1529) lists these: the dawning light of the first star, or of the planet Venus, or of the Sabbath candle], surely it merely reflects unthinking customary idiom, which is not always precise.

ISSUE 26: The Provider of the Linen

Mk 15:45 And when he knew it of the centurion, *he gave the body to Joseph. 46 And he bought fine linen*, and took him down, and wrapped him in the linen, and laid him in a sepulchre which was hewn out of a rock, and rolled a stone unto the door of the sepulchre.	Mt	Lk	Jn

Only one gospel details the source of the linen employed in the preparation of Jesus's body; Mark relates that Joseph bought linen. This purchase occurs on the fifteenth of Nisan, the first day of Passover.

CONTRADICTION #38 Joseph's Purchase of the Linen Sheets

Mark 15:46 reports that Joseph purchased linen sheets (a *sindōn*) required for the burial: "And he bought fine linen, and took him down, and wrapped him in the linen, and laid him in a sepulchre which was hewn out of a rock, and rolled a stone unto the door of the sepulchre." The purchase of linen implies that it is new and that he did not just use any cloth that was available.

Mark's sole account of this purchase raises several questions based upon scripture. According to Mark's chronology, and that of Matthew and Luke, this purchase occurs on the first day of Passover. Daube (1984, 312) points out, however, that according to God's instructions it is forbidden to purchase goods on a holy day (festival day).

> Lev 23:6-7 And on the fifteenth day of the same month is the feast of unleavened bread unto the LORD: seven days ye must eat unleavened bread. *In the first day ye shall have an holy convocation: ye shall do no servile work therein.*

> Neh 10:31 And if the people of the land bring ware or any victuals on the sabbath day to sell, *that we would not buy it of them on the*

sabbath, or on the holy day: and that we would leave the seventh year, and the exaction of every debt.

Nonetheless, Mark 15:43 reports that Joseph, a member of the council, purchased linen on a holy day in direct violation of the Law and presumably in full public view. Moreover, who could have sold the linen on the first day of a holy day? No Jew would have sold the linen since it was a holy day. Consequently, the only supposed alternative would be to purchase the merchandise from a non-Jewish merchant.

Davies and Allison (2004, 650) express concern about the time line as compared to Mark 15:46 and Matthew 27:58: "Further, it is no surprise that 'having bought' is absent [[from Matthew 27:58]]: not only is the detail superfluous, but one might ask how Joseph can, if it is by now the Sabbath, buy anything."

On the other hand, if the chronology of John is followed, the purchase occurred on Erev Shabbat, the eve of or transition time just before the Sabbath, and Erev Passover (the eve of or transition time just before the Passover). See John 18:28. In other words, the afternoon Passover offerings were completed. Consequently, John's chronology also raises several problems, the most important being logistics:

1. Would Joseph have purchased linen just before the Sabbath and the Passover meal when he should instead have been preparing for this holy time?
2. Who would be selling linen at this time? All the Jewish vendors would have long closed their shops in preparation of the Passover and upcoming Sabbath.
3. In addition, Joseph could not purchase the merchandise from a non-Jew because of the issue of *tumah*, ritual impurity.
4. By purchasing the linen and subsequently touching Jesus's dead body, Joseph and Nicodemus would not be able to eat the Korban Pesach.

The Korban Pesach—that is, the Passover Offering—is a biblical commandment of the highest order, with the command repeated and amplified in three different places: Exodus 12:3-12; Numbers 9:1-16; and Deuteronomy 16. Among those who cannot offer or eat the Korban Pesach are those in a state of *tumah*, or ritual or spiritual impurity by defilement of contact with a dead body. In Numbers 9:6-12, certain men who were defiled by the dead body of a man approached Moses and Aaron and said: "Why should we be deprived, and not be able to present God's offering in its time, amongst the children of Israel?" (paraphrased) Ten chapters later,

Numbers 19:16 elaborates that this state of ritual impurity lasts seven days: "And whosoever toucheth one that is slain with a sword in the open fields, or a dead body, or a bone of a man, or a grave, shall be unclean seven days." Myllykoski (2002, 71-72; cf. Vermes 2008, 14) points out in reference to the early Christian storytellers that "However, it does not seem likely that they bothered to imagine how Joseph remained impure for seven days after he had buried Jesus. (cf. Num 19:16)."

In response to their plea, God established the fourteenth of Iyar as a Second Passover (Pesach Sheini) for anyone who was unable to bring the offering at its appointed time in the previous month. This day thus represents a "second chance."

> Num 9:6 And there were certain men, who were defiled by the dead body of a man, that they could not keep the passover on that day: and they came before Moses and before Aaron on that day:

> Num 9:7 And those men said unto him, We are defiled by the dead body of a man: wherefore are we kept back, that we may not offer an offering of the LORD in his appointed season among the children of Israel?

> Num 9:8 And Moses said unto them, Stand still, and I will hear what the LORD will command concerning you.

> Num 9:9 And the LORD spake unto Moses, saying

> Num 9:10 Speak unto the children of Israel, saying, If any man of you or of your posterity shall be unclean by reason of a dead body, or be in a journey afar off, yet he shall keep the passover unto the LORD.

> Num 9:11 The fourteenth day of the second month at even they shall keep it, and eat it with unleavened bread and bitter herbs.

> Num 9:12 They shall leave none of it unto the morning, nor break any bone of it: according to all the ordinances of the passover they shall keep it.

The significance of the Korban Pesach must not be overlooked. It is one of the only two positive *miztvot* (plural; i.e., commandments) where the punishment for neglecting to fulfill it is *kareit* or spiritual *excommunication*. The other positive mitzvah is *brit milah* (circumcision). Circumcision is the first commandment imposed on an *individual* Jew when Abraham brought the children of Israel into the covenant as individuals. The commandment of the Korban Pesach is the first commandment imposed on the *Jewish people* as a collective into the covenant as a people. Thus, *the Korban Pesach* is not just a *korban*, that is, an offering. It is actually the first mitzvah, that is, the first commandment and spiritual connection given to *all* of the children of Israel.

Now, one can understand the controversy regarding John's chronology. John has Joseph and Nicodemus becoming spiritually impure through their contact with Jesus's dead body. Consequently, they will be forbidden to partake in the Passover meal and fulfill the Korban Pesach.

Craig (1989a, 177-78) offers the following Christian apologetic: "Joseph himself would probably not have touched the corpse, as he would then have been defiled and could not have eaten the Passover" (Num 19:11). In addition, "as a man of authority" he no doubt had servants available to help him.

Craig's apologetic is fallacious for several reasons. First, following the chronology of the synoptic narratives, Joseph would have already eaten the Passover meal and fulfilled the Korban Pesach on Thursday evening, the previous evening. Therefore, the issue of spiritual defilement will have been irrelevant. Second, following John's chronology, Joseph would have been spiritually defiled before the Passover meal. However, all would not be lost by becoming defiled. As previously mentioned, Joseph could participate in the Passover Sheini, the Second Passover meal, one month later. Third, Joseph is described as a good man, a just man, and an honorable counselor. It must be asked: would Joseph have ordered his servants, given that they were Jewish, to contact a dead body and spiritually defile themselves, and thus not fulfill the *Korban Pesach*, even though they too could partake of it one month later? Such an action would seem to contradict Joseph's description as recorded in Mark and Luke.

> Mk 15:43 Joseph of Arimathea, an *honourable* counsellor, which also waited for the kingdom of God, came, and went in boldly unto Pilate, and craved the body of Jesus.

> Lk 23:50 And, behold, there was a man named Joseph, a counsellor; and he was *a good man, and a just*:

The Christian commentator C. H. Dodd (1963, 139n1) raises another related issue: "Yet the Synoptic accounts are not altogether without difficulties. According to Mark, Joseph had time enough on Friday to buy a winding sheet (xv. 46); why did he not also buy other things necessary for the funeral rites? We are insufficiently informed."

ISSUE 27: The Provider of the Spices Used in the Preparation of Jesus's Body

Mk	Mt	Lk	
			Jn 19:39 And there came also *Nicodemus, which at the first came to Jesus by night, and brought a mixture of myrrh and aloes, about an hundred pound weight.*

Only one gospel details the source of the spices employed in the preparation of Jesus's body. John narrates that Nicodemus, another follower of Jesus, was declared to be the source of the spices without any mention of him actually purchasing them.

ISSUE 28: Nicodemus

Mk	Mt	Lk	
			Jn 3:1 *There was a man of the Pharisees, named Nicodemus, a ruler of the Jews: 2 The same came to Jesus by night,* and said unto him, Rabbi, we know that thou art a teacher come from God: for no man can do these miracles that thou doest, except God be with him. 3 Jesus answered and said unto him, Verily, verily, I say unto thee, Except a man be born again, he cannot see the kingdom of God. 4 Nicodemus saith unto him, How can a man be born when he is old? can he enter the second time into his mother's womb, and be born? 5 Jesus answered, Verily, verily, I say unto thee, Except a man be born of water and of the Spirit, he cannot enter into the kingdom of God.
			Jn 7:50 *Nicodemus* saith unto them, *(he that came to Jesus by night, being one of them,)*
			Jn 19:39 And there came also *Nicodemus, which at the first came to Jesus by night, and brought a mixture of myrrh and aloes, about an hundred pound weight. 40 Then they took the body of Jesus and wound it in linen clothes with the spices,* as the manner of the Jews is to bury.

John 3:1-5 reports that Nicodemus was a Pharisee, a ruler of the Jews, a teacher of Israel, a secret inquirer of Jesus, and a person interested in the kingdom. Furthermore, Nicodemus is implicitly wealthy as demonstrated in the quantity of materials purchased for Jesus's burial preparation. Moreover, John 7:50 reports that the second personage in the shape of Nicodemus was previously introduced: "he that came to Jesus by night, being one of them." Finally, Nicodemus possibly

assists in taking Jesus's body down from the cross and definitely helps in the burial preparation for all to see, and this was done on a holy day.

CONTRADICTION #39 Appearance Only in John

The synoptic accounts do not once mention Nicodemus, either in the narrative of the Passion or in the earlier chapters. Nicodemus appears only in the Fourth Gospel. This remarkable absence casts doubt as to his historical existence.

Significantly, Luke writes in the prologue to his gospel that he "carefully investigated everything from the beginning." Why then did he omit such an important personage and event as the preparation of Jesus's body for burial? Perhaps his omission, in fact, confirms that the event was an invention of John. Keim (1883, 6:263; 1877, 3:274) posits a speculative hypothesis that Nicodemus was a fictitious duplicate of Joseph. That is, there was transference of the official position of Joseph to Nicodemus.

These very issues of doubt aroused Craig (1989b, 178) to argue that "It might be thought that Nicodemus is an unhistorical figure because he does not appear in the Synoptics; but there are other individuals in John who do not appear in the Synoptics, but seem to be nonetheless historical persons." There are at least four possible rebuttals to Craig's apologetic: (1) the other individuals in John who do not appear in the Synoptics may have been an invention, similar to Nicodemus, (2) just because these individuals in John give the impression to be historical persons does not, in fact, make them historical persons, (3) Craig presents nothing more than an argument based on silence, and (4) the rationalization by Craig is merely his opinion.

SPECULATION #57 The Origin of the Name "Nicodemus"

The name Nicodemus is not unique in literature. Researchers have extensively and vigorously attempted to identify this Jewish celebrity. One detailed analysis is presented by Keim (1883, 263-65n4; cf. Bauckham 1996, 1-37). Keim's original text was one extensive paragraph. (This analysis has been divided into several paragraphs to make it more readable.)

> In Jos. *Ant.* 14, 3, 2, an ambassador sent by Aristobulus II. to Pompey is named Nicodemus. In *B.J.* 2. 17, 10 appears a Gorion (Guria, Bux. p. 412, young lion), son of Nicomedes (according to all that follows, this name is the same as Nicodemus), as an

aristocratic head of the Jews in the beginning of the rebellion (summer of 66), from whom is to be distinguished Gorion, son of Joseph, who appears somewhat later (A.D. 68; *B.J.* 4, 3, 9; 4, 6, 1).

The name Nicodemus [[was]] very common among the Greeks, Wetst. p. 850. An Athenian naval commander, *Diod.* 14, 81. In the Talmud, a Nakdimon ben Gorion plays an important part. . . . Indeed, his person is already completely clothed in myth. His proper name is said to have been Bunni) also in Old Test., comp. Bunni, Binnui, Bani, *i.e.* built, in Jos. Banus, and the disciple of Jesus in the Talm. identified by Renan with that Banus, above I, p. 23), *Taan. f.* 19, 2; 20, 1: and he is said to have been the first of the three richest men at the time of Titus's war, *Gitt. f.* 56, 1 (as fourth, a Ben Nakdimon is however introduced). He was rich enough to furnish every inhabitant of Jerusalem with three measures (seah) of meal, *Pirk. Elies.* 2; nay, so rich was he that, like the two others, he could provision Jerusalem for ten years, *Taan. l.c.*, *Kohel. R.* 7, 13. His daughter's bed was strewed with 12,000 denarii, *R. Natan,* 7; and the wise men daily supplied her with 400 gold pieces for spices, *Bab. Chetub.* 66, 2. Her marriage contract spoke of a million golden denarii, Lightfoot, p. 457. He was not only a magnus urbis, but also a disciple of the wise, *Beresh. Rabb.* 42, 1, and counsellor, *Pirk. Elies.* 2, *Echab. Rabb. f.* 64, 1. He was, moreover, so beneficent, that when there was a lack of water at a feast, he would pay twelve talents for the use of twelve wells for the people, *Tann. l.c.* This beneficence made him a favourite of God, who, in answer to his prayer in the sanctuary, sent copious rain, so that on the appointed day he might give back the wells full of water, and when the lenders of the wells derisively told him the sun had already sunk, God renewed the sunshine at his entreaty, *Taan. l. c.* . . . . Though there is here so much that is mythical, we shall not err if we assume that this Nicodemus was at any rate an historical person belonging to the last days of Jerusalem, a Jew and by no means a Christian; wherefore it is quite inadmissible to connect him with Bonai, the disciple of Jesus, a connection which is not found in the Talmud itself.

On the other hand, it is extremely easy to conceive of a fictitious Christian appropriation of this renowned Jew, an appropriation which would be quite analogous to that of Gamaliel (Clem. *Recogn.* 1, 65). . . . It is noteworthy that in Phot. *Cod.* 171 (on the authority of

Eustratius) Nicodemus is made a nephew of Gamaliel, with whom he is baptized by John and Peter (comp. Winer, *Gamaliel*). Significant enough is here (1) the entire ignorance of the earlier Gospels of Nicodemus, who occupied too prominent a position to have been forgotten; (2) the suspicious parallelism of Joseph and Nicodemus; (3) the description of Nicodemus as merely a secret friend (latenter frater) of Christianity, even more retiring than the secret friend Joseph (John xix. 38 sq.); (4) the points of contact between Nicodemus of the Talmud and that of John: a rich man, John xix. 39, also a leader of the Jews, . . . a Sanhedrist, vii. 50, a Pharisee, iii. 1, vii. 50, evidently also an elder in Israel. iii. 4, a teacher, nay, the authority of Israel, iii. 10, one who recognizes the greatest performer of miracles, iii. 2, though himself (in the Talmud) a performer of miracles; at the same time he was still a Jew who, despite his visit—which was only a nocturnal one—to Jesus, remained true to Israel, iii. 10, did not receive the testimony, iii. 11, was not born again from above, iii, 3, therefore did not see the kingdom of God. iii. 3, 5, and in the destruction of Jerusalem and in the loss of his enormous wealth experienced the truth of the principle that what is born of flesh is flesh, iii. 6, and passes away with the flesh, 1 John ii. 16 sq.

From the whole we infer: Nicodemus, like Gamaliel, is a Christian appropriation of the second century, probably not only of the fourth Gospel. The greater the name that was handed down to the second century out of the last history of the falling Jerusalem, the more value would be as a Jewish witness for Christ (and thereby, according to his name, 'victor of popular opinion'), and also as a counter witness against Israel and himself.

ISSUE 29: The Myrrh and Aloes

Mk	Mt	Lk	Jn 19:39 And there came also *Nicodemus, which at the first came to Jesus by night, and brought a mixture of myrrh and aloes, about an hundred pound weight.*

The detail of the spices brought by Nicodemus appears only in John. However, Luke 23:56 later reports that the women prepared spices before the Sabbath. In contrast, Mark 16:1 narrates that several women purchased spices after the Sabbath. The issue of the women and the spices is discussed in issue #44.

John's narrative is the only occurrence of aloe (*aloē*) in the Christian scriptures. In contrast, myrrh is mentioned twice, here and in Matthew 2:11. *Thayer's Lexicon* (#250 and #466) defined aloe and myrrh:

> Aloe is the name of an aromatic tree which grows in eastern India and Cochin China, and whose soft and bitter wood the Orientals used in fumigation and in embalming the dead (as according to Herodotus, the Egyptians did).

> Myrrh is a bitter gum and costly perfume which exudes from a certain tree or shrub in Arabia and Ethiopia, or is obtained by incisions made in the bark: In Matthew 2:11; as an antiseptic it was used in embalming. John 19:39.

SPECULATION #58 The Weight and the Volume of the Spices

According to the *Authorized Version*, the mixture of myrrh (*smurna*) and aloes weighed almost 100 pounds (*hôs litras ekaton*). Of course, a pound as a unit of measurement did not exist in the days of Jesus. In contrast, the NIV (1978, 1224nd) states "Greek a hundred *litrai* (about 34 kilograms/75 pounds)." Here too it should be recognized that use of kilograms as a measure of weight did not exist during the first century of the Common Era.

Also, the hundred *litrai* was an extraordinary amount of spices in terms of its mere volume. To clarify this point, Brown (1994a, 2:1260) points out that such a quantity of myrrh and aloes, "If powdered or fragmented spices are meant, such a weight would fill a considerable space in the tomb and smother the corpse under a mound." Therefore, it must be asked: does this quantity of spices seem realistic? Furthermore, one needs to consider the difficulty of transporting rows of sacks containing the dried or powder form of the spices. Given that the substances were dissolved in wine vinegar or oil, the transportation would have been even more difficult. Commentators are divided as to whether or not oil is present at all. Of course, all this transporting would have been on a holy day, that is, based on Mark's chronology, and a violation of the Torah.

Josh McDowell (1981, 52) argues in his *The Resurrection Factor* that the hundred pounds of spice used to bury Jesus were not unusual for a leader: "One might regard this as substantial, but it was no great amount for a leader." He cited two examples: (1) eighty-six pounds of spices were used when burying the scholar Gamaliel, and (2) a vast amount of spices was used to bury King Herod.

McDowell's apologetic is preposterous. The average man living in first-century Judea was approximately five feet six inches tall and weighed 130 pounds. In first-century Judea, it does not make sense that one hundred pounds of spices would be usual in the preparation and burial of a body. Second, it is disingenuous to compare the amount of spices used to bury Gamaliel and Jesus. Rabbi Gamaliel I was the foremost Jewish scholar and authority of his generation. In the Talmud, Gamaliel bears the title *Rabban*, a rabbinic title given to the Nasi or head of the Sanhedrin; he was the first of seven appointed leaders of the school of Hillel which earned the title. Mishnah *Sotah* 9.15 paid tribute to this quality: "Since Rabban Gamaliel the Elder died, there has been no more reverence for the law, and purity and abstinence died out at the same time."

Comparing Jesus's burial with that of King Herod is hypocritical. Herod had the luxury of having virtually the unlimited resources of his kingship. The state funded his burial. In all accounts, the hundred pounds of spices is extraordinary.

However, one additional point bears consideration. Hakola (2009, 442) writes in *New Testament Studies*: "The abundance of spices is understood as a sign of unbelief because Joseph of Arimathea and Nicodemus regard the burial as final and do not anticipate in any way the following resurrection." Similarly, Rensberger (1988, 40) declares: "Nicodemus shows himself capable only of burying Jesus, ponderously and with a kind of absurd finality, so loading him down with burial as to make it clear that Nicodemus does not expect a resurrection any more than he expects a second birth." Then he adds "Nicodemus, like Caesar's Antony but without his irony, has come to bury Jesus, not to raise him" (50n1).

SPECULATION #59 Monetary Considerations

In terms of its financial value, the purchase of the myrrh and aloes is extraordinary. John 12:5 reports that 300 denarii is equal to a year's wages, and this is the cost of a pound of ointment of spikenard (i.e., the expensive perfume used to anoint Jesus six days prior to the Passover). Therefore, one *denarius* is almost the equivalent of a day's wage, 365 days in a year.

Calculations by Malina and Rohrbaugh (2003, 383) report: "Two denarii (see Luke 10:30-35) would provide 3,000 calories for 5-7 days or 1,800 calories for 9 to 12 days for a family with the equivalent of four adults. Two denarii would provide 24 days of bread ration for a poor indigent. This calculation is for food only; it does not take into account other needs such as clothing, taxation, religious dues, and so on."

The speculative question that needs to be asked is, how much was the financial value of the hundred pounds, seventy-five pounds in modern weights, of spices used to prepare Jesus's body? One obvious problem is that John does not provide specific information regarding the percentage of the hundred pounds that was myrrh and the percentage of the hundred pounds that was aloes or specify the quality of each. Keener (2003, 1163) speculates that Nicodemus's gift "was perhaps worth 30,000 [[denarii]]." This 30,000 denarii amount is also given by Schnelle (2004, 295n35).

Nigel Groom of the British Museum authored "Trade, Incense and Perfume" in the text *Queen of Sheba: Treasures from Ancient Yemen*. His research based on the writing in Pliny's *Natural History* (12.51-70) attempted to determine the value of spices in the Mediterranean between 40 and 70 CE. Pliny wrote that when the incense finally arrived in Rome from the southern Arabian Peninsula, "Roman citizens paid 6 denarii a pound for top quality frankincense, more than most of them could earn in a fortnight [[two weeks or 14 days]], while a pound of myrrh cost the perfumers and apothecaries between 11 and 16 denarii."

Seventy-five pounds of spices times eleven denarii and sixteen denarii respectively creates a range between 825 and 1,200 denarii. Therefore, based on John's one denarii a day, the estimated value of the spices is approximately equal to two and a half years and four years of a worker's wages. In contrast, Pliny's one denarii equals almost two days pay. Therefore, for Pliny the estimated value of the spices would have approximated almost five to eight years of a worker's wages, assuming that the aloes were of the equivalent value.

SPECULATION #60 Historical Precedent

Gamaliel was the grandson of the distinguished Jewish scholar Hillel. Acts 22:3 reports that he was also a contemporary of Jesus who Saul of Tarsus reportedly studied under: "I am verily a man which am a Jew, born in Tarsus, a city in Cilicia, yet brought up in this city at the feet of Gamaliel, and taught according to the perfect manner of the law of the fathers, and was zealous toward God, as ye all are this day." As previously mentioned, when Gamaliel died, approximately eighty-six pounds of spices were used. Gamaliel the Elder was the president of the Sanhedrin and one of the most important scholars of his generation. He represented the Jews before Rome and died approximately eighteen years before the destruction of Jerusalem (52 CE), or about twenty years after the recorded resurrection of Jesus. In addition, approximately eighty pounds of balsam were burned in his honor.

Perhaps the author of John wrote part or all his burial account based on Gamaliel, that is, a copycat attempting one upmanship. The similarities are striking:

TABLE 23. Similarities between the Burials of Gamaliel and Jesus

Gamaliel	Jesus
A Jewish leader.	A Jewish leader.
A rabbi (teacher).	A rabbi (teacher).
Eighty-six pounds of spices were used during his burial.	One-hundred pounds of spices were used during his burial.
Died during a time under Roman rule.	Died during a time under Roman rule.

It should also be recognized that ancient texts often depicted extravagant preparations for the burials of important people.

Finally, C. H. Dodd's (1963, 139n1) comment on the quantity of spices merits consideration: "It seems likely that the somewhat extravagant estimate of the weight of myrrh and aloes provided is a touch introduced by the evangelist, who perhaps is somewhat addicted to numbers, especially large numbers (153 fishes—if the appendix is by the same author)."

In a similar vein, Evans (2005b, 245n22) writes less overtly in the *Journal for the Study of the Historical Jesus*: "Other embellishments are seen, such as the introduction of Nicodemus, a huge amount of spices (fit for a king, evidently), the claim that the tomb was new, rather a criminal's tomb with previous use, etc."

SPECULATION #61 The Myrrh

Myrrh is a fragrant resin used for embalming. Zangenberg (2007, 885) points out:

> This, however, would certainly not help, since resin-like substances like myrrh or odorous wood like aloe can only develop their scent if they are either ground to powder and diluted in a liquid solvent or, if kept in their solid state, burnt (cf. 2 Chr 16, 14). To simply put them between the layers of textile wrappings in pulverized or granulated form would hardly produce the desired effect of subduing unpleasant odours of the decaying corpse (bBer 53a).

As a rule, one can say that if spices were applied *to the body*, they were done so in liquid form (oil or unguent), if they were used in dry form, they were burnt *apart* from the body (there was no cremation in Judaism!). Both John and the Synoptics, however, leave no doubt that the first scenario was envisioned. They also agree on the fact that there was no anointing of the body *between* death and burial.

Mentioning of myrrh occurs only twice in the Christian scriptures. The first occurrence relates to when the *wise men* from the east of Jerusalem came and found the young child Jesus.

> Mt 2:11 And when they were come into the house, they saw the young child with Mary his mother, and fell down, and worshipped him: and when they had opened their treasures, they presented unto him gifts; gold, and frankincense, and myrrh.

The second occurrence took place in conjunction with the preparation of Jesus's body after his death.

> Jn 19:39 And there came also Nicodemus, which at the first came to Jesus by night, and brought a mixture of myrrh and aloes, about an hundred pound weight.

Assuming that John was aware of the tradition of the wise men bringing gifts to the young Jesus, verse 39 may have been written as a literary device, an illusion creating the form of a literary bookend. Or as Goulder (2005, 192) offers, "Matthew invented the gold, myrrh and frankincense in Matthew 2 on the basis of this chapter."

Finally, Lunn (2009, 733) also speculates that there are several passages in which the Ark of the Covenant is alluded to or related with the Johannine burial and resurrection narratives. Altogether he offers ten allusions. In relation to the myrrh he writes:

> Spices are involved in connection with both the ark and Christ's body. In the case of the ark this was anointed with holy oil as an act of consecration: "you shall anoint the tabernacle of meeting and the ark of the testimony" (Exod 30:26). The chief ingredient of this anointing oil was myrrh (Exod 30:23, σμύρνης). As preparation for burial the body of Christ was anointed with spices (cf. John 12:3), the first-mentioned of which was myrrh. (John 19:39, σμύρνης)

ISSUE 30: The Wrapping and Preparation of Jesus's Body

Mk 15:46 And he bought fine linen, and took him down, and *wrapped him in the linen*, and laid him in a sepulchre which was hewn out of a rock, and rolled a stone unto the door of the sepulchre.	Mt 27:59 And when Joseph had taken the body, *he wrapped it in a clean linen cloth.*	Lk 23:53 *And he took it down, and wrapped it in linen*, and laid it in a sepulchre that was hewn in stone, wherein never man before was laid.	Jn 19:40 *Then they took the body of Jesus and wound it in linen clothes with the spices*, as the manner of the Jews is to bury.

The synoptic Gospels report that Joseph alone wrapped the body with a linen shroud or sheet (Greek—*sindōn*). Mark and Luke provide no extra details about the linen used to prepare and bury Jesus. However, Matthew 27:59 alone adds the detail that the sheet was a "clean linen cloth" (*en sindoni kathara*), but it was not purchased at the time as reported in Mark.

John 19:40 does not mention a shroud but speaks in the plural of linen cloths (*othonia*), that is, linen strips and also a *soudarion*, the napkin, which had been on Jesus's head. Later, John 20:7 reports that the napkin was rolled up in a place by itself. In disagreement with the Synoptics, John also asserts that "they"—that is, Joseph and Nicodemus—prepared the body. Furthermore, John alone absolutely declares that the body of Jesus was prepared in "the manner of the Jews." This preparation would have included the ceremonial washing of the body. Here, Gundry (1993, 982) comments on Mark's statement: "The wrapping of Jesus in a linen cloth probably implies that Joseph washed him and anointed him with oil in a characteristically Jewish manner."

The Acts of the Apostles confirm that the New Testament writers knew that washing the body was, in fact, practiced during the first century: "Now there was at Joppa a certain disciple named Tabitha, which by interpretation is called Dorcas: this woman was full of good works and almsdeeds which she did. And it came to pass in those days, that she was sick, and died: whom when they had washed, they laid her in an upper chamber" (Acts 9:36-37).

The importance of washing the body is also stated in the Mishnah:

> *m. Shabbat* 23.5 They may prepare [On Sabbath] all the requirements for a corpse, anoint it and wash [Literally *and rinse*] it, only provided that they do not move any one of its limbs. They may draw away the cushion [Or *mattress*] from under it and lay it on the sand in order that it keeps from decomposition; they may

bind up the chin, not that it should not rise but that it should not fall. And likewise, if a beam were broken, they may prop it up with a bench or with the side pieces of a bedstead, not that it should be raised up but that it should not continue. They may not close the eyes of a corpse on the Sabbath; nor may they do so on a weekday on the departure of the soul, for one that closes the eyes when the soul is still departing is as one who sheds blood. [pp. 91-92]

Craig (1989b, 178; cf. Cohn-Sherbok 1990, 61-63) even confirms and discusses the importance of washing the body. As a matter of fact, he goes so far as to declare that the washing of a corpse prior to burial is considered so necessary that it is even permitted on the Sabbath. On the other hand, the notion of wrapping an unwashed body that has been previously flogged and crucified in clean or pure linen is seemingly counter intuitive.

One final point explained by Zangenberg (2007, 885) is worthy of note. The subject relates to the final preparation of Jesus's body: "The mixing of aromatic ingredients and oil would not have been done at the grave, but in the shop of a spice dealer or at home prior to the burial (Lk 23, 56). Nicodemus very likely would have brought bottles filled with liquid spices in order to pour them out over the body and layers of funeral textiles if we follow the rather condensed phrasing in John 19,40a."

SPECULATION #62 The Purpose of the Body's Preparation— an Apologetic

Mark 15:46 reports: "And he bought fine linen, and took him down, and wrapped him in the linen, and laid him in a sepulchre which was hewn out of a rock, and rolled a stone unto the door of the sepulchre." Matthew 27:59 narrates that "And when Joseph had taken the body, he wrapped it in a clean linen cloth." Luke 23:53 details: "And he took it down, and wrapped it in linen, and laid it in a sepulchre that was hewn in stone, wherein never man before was laid." John 19:40 specifies: "Then took the body of Jesus, and wound it in linen clothes with the spices, as the manner of the Jews is to bury." Collectively, these wrapping narratives are important because they serve as a Christian apologetic. Tenney (1976, 271) elaborates that it would be incredible that at least two men, as reported in John, "should have handled Jesus' body without knowing whether his death were actual or not." Furthermore, Casey (1996, 191) posits, "The fourth Gospel has the further development of the tradition, which functions to exclude the possibility that Jesus' dead and decaying body had been confused with another one.

Nicodemus' spices further exclude that possibility. We must infer that the Johannine developments are entirely secondary."

SPECULATION #63 Paralleling the Manger Episode

Derrett (1982b, 67n20) speculates as to whether or not there was a literary relationship between the stories of Jesus in the manger and his burial? For example, Luke 2:7 reads: "And she brought forth her first-born son, and wrapped him in swaddling clothes, and laid him in a manger; because there was no room for them in the inn." Similarly, Smith (1983, 111) points out this parallel with the birth narrative recorded in chapter 2 of Luke.

The swaddling of linen (i.e., clothes) is found in both texts (Lk 23:53). For instance, Matthew Henry's (1961, 1499) commentary states: "It was the manner of the Jews to roll the bodies of the dead, as we do little children in their swaddling-clothes, so that the pieces of fine linen, which he bought whole, cut into many pieces for this purpose."

Maximus of Turbin, a bishop of Turbin (d. 408/423), posited almost 1,600 years earlier, this identical analysis. Cited in Just (2003, 371): "She wrapped the Lord in swaddling clothes when he was born; he wrapped him in linen cloths when he died." In contrast, Gregory of Nazianzus said that the one who was bound in swaddling clothes at birth was unbound at the resurrection.

Furthermore, Derrett (1982b, 67n20) asks and posits: "Is John referring to the story of Jesus in the manger? The manger was a stone niche resembled a bench grave in a tomb." Therefore, these two passages seemingly created a reminiscent echo and appear to form literary bookends. If so, the unanswerable question remains: Is the description of Jesus's burial a deliberate literary design or, as Cook (2008, 83) delicately termed, "Gospel Dynamics"?

He defines "Gospel Dynamics" as "those skillful techniques—evinced in the gospels—by which early Christians molded their traditions to address their needs decades after Jesus died."

SPECULATION #64 The Burial Shroud

There is another problem regarding the preparation of Jesus's body. The synoptic Gospels report that Jesus is buried in a shroud. However, John 19:40 does not have Jesus being buried in a shroud but rather being bound in "linen clothes," bandages: "Then took they the body of Jesus, and wound it in linen clothes with the spices, as the manner of the Jews is to bury." Derrett (1982b, 51) speculates that John included an embalming of the body without the removal of the internal organs, as practiced by the ancient Egyptians: "The process [[of embalming]] can be easily visualised if you have seen a broken limb being set in plaster of Paris. One starts with clean bandages and these are continuously impregnated with the wet plaster." The absence of a shroud would be contrary to the manner of a Jewish burial.

Fitzmyer (1985, 1527) states: "Since these Johannine details are not mentioned in the Synoptic tradition, which alone speaks of the *sindōn*, one should be wary of harmonizing such disparate data."

SPECULATION #65 Jesus Was Not Brain Dead while on the Cross

Proponents of the Resurrection unequivocally state that Jesus's death is the indispensable prerequisite to his resurrection, the crowning proof that he is both God and the Messiah. Either way, without a death there cannot be a resurrection. Furthermore, proponents of Jesus's resurrection assert that there is overwhelming historical and factual evidence that Jesus died and that he died literally on the cross. (Geisler 2013, 407-08) In contrast, some opponents reject the notion that he literally died on the cross. However, this speculation is not concerned with the presumption that he died or did not die as a result of his crucifixion. To the contrary, speculation #65 postulates that there is insufficient evidence that Jesus was brain dead on the cross *before* his body was removed or prior to his entombment.

Clinical death is commonly characterized by the cessation of breathing (chest does not move), cardiac arrest (no heart beat or pulse), enlargement or lack of change of the pupils, and sometimes release of the bladder or bowel. Other common signs of death are pallor mortis, paleness that happens in the 15-120 minutes after death; livor mortis, a settling of the blood in the lower dependent portion of the body; and algor mortis, the reduction in body temperature. This cooling of the body after death proceeds at a definite rate, influenced by environmental temperature and protection of the body until matching ambient temperature, the temperature in a room, or the temperature surrounding an object; and rigor mortis, the stiffening of the limbs of the corpse (Latin *rigor*) and difficulty in moving or manipulating these limbs. All the gospels validate Jesus's death on the cross by detailing his cessation of breathing (Mk 15:37-39; Mt 27:50-54; Lk 23:46-47; and Jn 19:30-37).

In contrast to clinical death, *Mosby's Medical Dictionary*, eighth edition ©2009, states *brain death* is

> an irreversible form of unconsciousness characterized by a complete loss of brain function while the heart continues to beat. The legal definition of this condition varies from state to state. The usual clinical criteria for brain death include the absence of reflex activity, movements, and spontaneous respiration requiring mechanical ventilation or life support to continue any cardiac function. The pupils are dilated and fixed. Because hypothermia, anesthesia, poisoning, or drug intoxication may cause deep physiologic depression that resembles brain death these parameters must be within normal limits prior to testing. Diagnosis of brain death may require evaluating and demonstrating that electrical activity of the brain is absent on two electroencephalograms performed 12 to 24 hours apart. Brain death can be confirmed with electroencephalograms showing a complete lack of electrical activity (a flat line) or vascular perfusion studies showing a lack of blood flow to the brain.

Consequently, John's record of a spear pierced into Jesus's side is extremely significant because it could possibly demonstrate a state of brain death evinced by his unresponsiveness to stimuli or pain. This affirmative demonstration is based on three assumptions. First, John's account is historical and not a theological invention. Second, the narrative did not fail to omit any significant facts such as a reflex action to the piercing, an argument based on silence. Third, no drug was induced into Jesus while he was on the cross that could cause deep physiologic depression resembling brain death. The covert delivery of a drug to Jesus while on the cross is commonly referred to as a conspiracy theory. The idea of a conspiracy theory is rejected by this text.

Given that the piercing episode was a man-made occurrence, there is no unequivocal proof that Jesus was brain dead while he was still on the cross. Furthermore, the Gospels do not report that any additional neurological tests were recorded that proved Jesus was brain dead: (1) no pupil reaction to light, (2) no response of the eyes to caloric (warm or cold) stimulation, (3) no jaw reflex (the jaw will react like the knee if hit with a reflex hammer), and (4) no gag reflex (touching the back of the throat induces vomiting). Obviously, the existing technology of Jesus's day prohibited verification by an electroencephalogram. Finally, there is no absolute way of knowing whether or not a drug was induced into Jesus while he was on the cross.

However, as mentioned above, there is another possibility explaining how Jesus did not die while he was literally still on the cross. Jesus's body could have been taken down from the cross while he was unconscious, comatose (not perceptibly alive), or clinically dead and he had *not* entered into a state of brain death. Later, he entered into the state of brain death between the time that his body was taken down from the cross to the time the body was prepared for burial. In effect, Jesus would not have died on the cross but *after* being taken down; thus, the death was as a cumulative consequence of his beatings, scourging, and crucifixion.

Carrier (n.d., How Do We Know He was Dead?) wrote:

> Being mistaken for dead is not impossible. Ancient accounts of misdiagnosed deaths exist. Pliny the Elder, writing in the 60s and 70s AD, collects several of them in his *Natural History* (7.176-179): people who were deemed dead, observed as dead all through their funeral, and on the pyre, ready to be set aflame, but who walked away nonetheless (and since all Romans served in the army, one can see from this fact that arguments about the special skills of soldiers are moot). One account includes a wound that would seem almost certainly fatal (a cut throat, 7.176). Alexander the Great himself was impaled by a spear, which punctured one of his lungs, yet he recovered.

Indeed, before the twentieth century this was more common than we would imagine, sometimes causing widespread hysteria. Jan Bondeson's *Buried Alive: The Terrifying History of Our Most Primal Fear* (2001. W. W. Norton & Company) details numerous examples. Even earlier, in 1895, the physician J. C. Ouseley wrote that as many as 2,700 people were buried prematurely each year in England and Wales, although others estimated the figure to be closer to 800. Furthermore, modern accounts of misdiagnosed deaths exist (Internet), proving that even medical experts can be in error.

Below (table 24) is a terse analysis of the augments that Jesus was not brain dead *before* his body was removed from the cross or just prior to the preparation of his body.

Table 24: Did Jesus Die While on the Cross?

Pro-Jesus's Death While on the Cross		Con-Jesus's Death While on the Cross	
Jesus's Death Was Predicted in the Old Testament		**Jesus's Death Was Not Predicted in the Old Testament: Mistranslation/Taken Out of Context**	
Ps 22:16 [AV]	Jesus's hands and feet were "pierced."	Ps 22:17 [16 MT]	The AV translation "they pierced my hands and feet" is not based on the standard Masoretic Text: The Hebrew word translated as "*pierced*" should read "*lion*." Therefore the phrase should read as "like a lion, they are at my hands and my feet" (JPS).
Isa 53:5-10	**The "Suffering Servant" is Jesus**	Isa 53:5-10	1. The suffering servant is Israel (collectively or a righteous remnant).
			2. In verses 5–8, the speaker [is the Gentile nations] confesses that they were the cause of the servant's distress and are more deserving of his afflictions than he was.
			3. Isa 53:7 is contradicted by Jesus's actions. He did *not* remain dumb or silent (Mt 26:39; 27:46; Jn 18:6, 8, 20, 23, 34, 36–37).
			4. Isa 53:8 is contradicted by the Hebrew Bible. There is no indication that Jesus's suffering was to serve as atonement for mankind's sins.
			5. Isa 53:9 is contradicted by Jesus's actions. He acted violently (Mk 11:15–16, Mt 21:12) and advocated violence (**Lk 19:27**).
			6. Isa 53:10 is contradicted by Jesus's words. He did not willingly offer himself as a sacrifice (Mk 15:34; Mt 27:46).
			7. Isa 53:10 is contradicted by Jesus's life. Jesus did not see his seed = *zer'a* (biological children, not spiritual children such as the church) during his life. In scripture, *zer'a* always means a biological or physical offspring.
Dan 9:26	The seventy weeks.	Dan 9:26	1. The punctuation mark *a'tnach* is ignored in Christian translation.
			2. The AV omits the definite article in Dan 9:26, "And after *the* three score and two weeks…

			3. The words *vayn lo* are incorrectly translated by the AV as "but not for himself."
			4. The Christian chronology of Nehemiah is incorrect.
Zech 12:10	Portrays Jesus.	Zech 12:10	[See Issue 19]
			1. The predominant perspective on Zechariah 12:10 among Jewish commentators described the mourning over those Jews who were slain while defending the kingdom of Judah and the city of Jerusalem. Those who fell in the battle were the ones described as having been *thrust through* with the swords and spears of soldiers from the attacking nations. In other words, this verse described a historical event from the biblical times around which this was written. Rashi wrote: "And they shall look to Me to complain about those of them whom the nations thrust through and slew during their exile." An alternative explanation is that this text describes a future event.
			2. After Jesus's death the Jewish leadership still demonstrated no remorse. That is, on Saturday they went to Pilate, calling Jesus a "deceiver" and worried that his disciples might come and steal his body.
			3. The Distorted Historical Context of Zechariah 12: Israel is saved.
			4. The Distorted Historical Context of Zechariah 12: Prophetic fulfillment.
			5. The Distorted and Mistranslated Subjects of "I" in Zechariah 12:10.
			6. The Distorted and Mistranslated Subjects of "*him*" in Zechariah 12:10.
			7. The Figurative Subject of "*him*" in Zechariah 12:10.
			8. The Distorted and Understood *pronoun* "*him*" in Zechariah 12:10.
			9. Zechariah 12: Contradictory to the Olivet Discourse.

Jesus's Death by Crucifixion: Rationale	Jesus's Death by Crucifixion: Doubted/Rejected
1. Jesus had no sleep the night before he was crucified.	1. The Jewish-Palestinian milieu refutes the argument that Jesus had no sleep the night before he was crucified.
	a. A night inquest/ trial on the first evening of Passover held by the chief priests and scribes challenges the historicity and veracity of the gospel accounts.
	b. The conflicting details of the inquest/trial challenges the historicity and veracity of the gospel accounts.
2. Jesus was beaten, scourged, and whipped.	2. Jesus was *not* beaten, scourged, and whipped enough to facilitate his rapid demise while on the cross (a la Mel Gibson's *The Passion*).
	a. The degree of scourging is unknown and subject to speculation.
	b. The length of time that Jesus was scourged is unknown and subject to speculation.
	c. How many times Jesus was struck is unknown and subject to speculation.
	d. The specific implements employed on Jesus during his scourging are unknown and subject to speculation.
	e. The specific type and severity of wounds or injuries resulting from the scourging is unknown and subject to speculation.
	f. Perhaps Pilate let it be known that he wanted a "mild" scourging because (1) he believed that Jesus was innocent or (2) to incense the chief priests.
3. Jesus collapsed while carrying his cross.	3. Jesus did not collapse while carrying his cross.
	a. This presumed episode appears in Mark 15:21 and Matthew 27:32. However, if Matthew's account was solely based on Mark, there was only one source and in reality no multiple attestation.
	b. Neither gospel reports that Jesus literally collapsed while carrying the cross.
	c. No reason is given why the Romans compelled Simon the Cyrene to bear Jesus's cross. Perhaps, Jesus was just walking too slowly for their needs.

4. Jesus bled because "the soldiers platted a crown of thorns, and put it on his head" (Jn 19:2).	4. Jesus did *not* bleed because thorns were placed on his head.
	a. Only John mentioned Jesus's head being platted with a crown of thorns. Therefore this claim does *not* fulfill the criterion of multiple attestations.
	b. There is *no* mention that Jesus's head was bleeding because a crown of thorns was placed on it.
	c. There are *no* facts detailing how the thorns were placed on Jesus's head.
	d. There is *no* description of the type of thorns that were placed on Jesus's head.
5. Jesus was crucified (presumably nailed to a cross by his hands).	5. Jesus was *not* nailed to a cross by his hands.
	a. It is speculated that "the nailing and spearing were derived by John from Psalm 22:17 (16 AV) and Zechariah 12:10 under the erroneous supposition that those passages were prophetically describing the crucifixion of Jesus and under the further assumption that the crucifixion procedures followed those prophecies meticulously.
	b. There exists scholarly opinion that Jesus's hands were not nailed; rather he was fastened or tied with a rope. Recently, Gunnar Samuelsson wrote an extensive thesis (University of Gothenburg) and published *Crucifixion in Antiquity*. He investigated the philological aspects of how ancient Greek, Latin, Hebrew, and Aramaic texts, including the New Testament, depict the practice of punishment by crucifixion. Mohr Siebeck, his publisher, summarized: "The accounts of the death of Jesus are strikingly sparse. Their chief contribution is usage of the unclear terminology in question. Over-interpretation, and probably even pure imagination, have afflicted nearly every dictionary that deals with the terms related to crucifixion as well as scholarly depictions of what happened on Calvary. The immense knowledge of the punishment of crucifixion in general, and the execution of Jesus in particular, cannot be supported by the studied texts."
	c. The two pilgrims on the road to Emmaus did not recognize Jesus despite supposed nail wounds in his hands. This recognition would be expected since Luke 24:30 recorded that Jesus broke bread, blessed it, and handed it to the two travelers.

6. Jesus was crucified (presumably nailed to a cross by his feet).	6. Jesus was not nailed to a cross by his feet.
	a. It is speculated that "the nailing and spearing evidently were derived by John from Psalm 22:17 (16 AV) and Zechariah 12:10 under the erroneous supposition that those passages were prophetically describing Jesus's crucifixion and under the further assumption that the crucifixion procedures followed those prophecies meticulously.
	b. Mohr Siebeck, the publisher of Gunnar Samuelsson's previously mentioned book, summarizes that "the New Testament is not spared from this terminological ambiguity. The accounts of the death of Jesus are strikingly sparse. Their chief contribution is usage of the unclear terminology in question. Over-interpretation, and probably even pure imagination, have afflicted nearly every dictionary that deals with the terms related to crucifixion as well as scholarly depictions of what happened on Calvary. The immense knowledge of the punishment of crucifixion in general, and the execution of Jesus in particular, cannot be supported by the studied texts."
	c. Out of the thousands of crucified victims—only one artifact has been discovered; the crucified man from Giv'at Ha-Mivtar. (Tzaferis 1985, 44–53)
	d. In the Gospel of Matthew (28:8), the women grasped Jesus's feet and worshipped him without mention of his presumed feet wounds.
	e. The two pilgrims on the road to Emmaus did not recognize Jesus despite supposed nail wounds to his feet.
	f. Luke 24:34–43 reports Jesus appearing before the Eleven gathered in Jerusalem. During this encounter Jesus stated in verse 39: "Behold my hands and my feet, that it is I myself: handle me, and see; for a spirit hath no flesh and bones, as ye see me have." This verse does not necessarily support the idea that Jesus's feet were pierced. Perhaps Luke was attempting to substantiate the mere physicality of Jesus's resurrection.

7. Jesus, suspended from the cross from 9:00 a.m. to approximately 3:00 p.m.	7. Jesus, suspended from the cross from 9:00 a.m. (Mk 15:25) to approximately 3:00 p.m., probably would *not* result in his death.
	a. Presumably, Jesus underwent a *typical* crucifixion. Yet Jesus's crucifixion lasted approximately six hours, whereas crucifixions lasted three to six days before death. Supposedly this would mean that Jesus had a very *good* chance of being alive when he was taken down from the cross.
	b. Pilate was amazed that Jesus was dead after such a brief period on the cross.
	c. Jesus's "cross mates" were still alive when he supposedly expired.
	d. Being mistaken for dead is not impossible.
	1) Josephus watched one of three particular victims of crucifixion survive (*Life of Flavius Josephus* § 420–21).
	2) History provides examples of people temporarily surviving after having the most horrible things happen to their bodies. The Coast Guard WWII hero Douglas Munro was pierced a dozen times by Japanese rifle bullets, yet he continued to drive his landing boat, dying only after completing his mission—receiving the Medal of Honor posthumously.
	3) Jan Bondeson's book, *Buried Alive: The Terrifying History of Our Most Primal Fear* provides numerous details of ancient and contemporary mistakes concerning living people assumed to have been dead.
8. The fact that the Roman soldier did not break Jesus's legs, as they did to the other two crucified criminals (Jn 19:31–33), means that the soldier was sure that Jesus was dead.	8. Jesus's legs were *not* broken because he was presumably dead, whereas the legs of his "cross mates" were.
	a. The Roman soldiers directly violated their orders. Pilate ordered that the Roman soldiers break the legs of the crucified. Nonetheless, these soldiers did *not* execute this specific command in the case of Jesus. It is not reasonable to suppose that the Roman soldiers would disregard their orders and potentially subject themselves to severe punishment for disobedience, punishment dictated by Roman military law. Insubordination was a matter not tolerated in the Roman military and was meticulously and scrupulously dealt with.

	b. John reported that a Roman soldier pierced Jesus's side with a spear rather than break his legs on the cross in order not to violate the prohibition found in Exodus 12:46 about breaking the bones of the Passover lamb. Therefore, this account was incorporated for theological reasons.
9. Jesus was pierced with a spear in his side (Jn 19:36–37).	9. The pierced side was an apologetic and theological invention.
	a. Skeptics demand evidence that Jesus was stabbed while suspended from the cross.
	b. Only John directly mentioned Jesus being speared in the side. Therefore, this text does not fulfill the criterion of multiple attestations or that of God's instructions.
	c. Perhaps John's account of Jesus being speared was written as an apologetic that Jesus actually died.
	d. Perhaps the piercing episode was incorporated for theological reasons (Isa 53 or Zech 12:10): "For these things were done, that the scripture should be fulfilled, A bone of him shall not be broken. And again another scripture saith, They shall look on him whom they pierced."
	e. Perhaps the piercing episode was incorporated for theological reasons. That is, a Roman soldier pierced Jesus's side with a spear rather than break his legs on the cross in order not to violate the prohibition found in Exodus 12:46 about breaking bones of the Passover lamb.
	f. Perhaps John's narratives in 20:20 and 20:27 were written to corroborate themselves with details which seemingly created an illusion that the side piercing episode was historical. That is, John was attempting to demonstrate that the risen Jesus and the Jesus who was crucified days earlier were one and the same.
	g. Given that Jesus was stabbed, we do not know with what type of spear he was jabbed.
	h. Given that Jesus was stabbed, we do not know any details describing the spear's tip.
	i. Given that Jesus was stabbed, it cannot be known if the spear was shoved deeply into Jesus's side as opposed to being a poke to see if he would react to painful stimuli.

10. Blood and water came out of Jesus's side after it was pierced.	10. Blood and water coming out of Jesus's side after being pierced was a theological invention and could *not* be confirmed.
	a. Perhaps John wrote the piercing episode in conjunction with the flowing blood and water to serve as a symbol: (1) Spirit, which flowed forth from the dead Jesus, (2) the duality of his actions, his baptism of water and his baptism of blood, (3) a new and higher life passes into humanity, (4) the life-giving water that flowed from Ezekiel's new Temple (Ez 47:1–2), (5) the dispensation of the Temple, and (6) *Leviticus Rabbah*, 15 (115c), contains the information that the man is made of half water, half of blood: if he is virtuous, the two elements are in equilibrium.
	b. There is no means to prove that the fluid that flowed from Jesus's body was 100 percent water. "The source of the water could have been from pleural fluid (that can look like water), which accumulated in the chest cavity" (Lavoie 2000, 164).
	c. See contradiction #26.
	d. Raymond Brown (1994a, 2:1092) in his commentary *The Death of the Messiah* criticizes often-cited medical analyses of Jesus's death. He concludes: "In my judgement the major defect of most of the studies I have reported on thus far is that they were written by doctors who did not stick to their trade and let a literalist understanding of the Gospel accounts influence their judgements." For example, Luke reported that Jesus's "sweat became like blood." Here, Luke is not describing a real medical condition (hematidrosis); rather he is employing the use of a metaphor.
Jesus was confirmed dead when taken down from the cross.	**Jesus was *not* actually confirmed brain dead when taken down from the cross.**
1. The centurion	1. The centurion
	a. Is the centurion's report historical? His final words appear to be embellished over time in the various gospels.
	b. The Gospels themselves admit (see Mk 15:39 and Jn 19:33) that those attending Jesus's crucifixion assumed that he was dead before they even took him down from the cross and had a chance to examine his body. Consequently, detractors question how Jesus's brain death could be determined by the centurion from a distance of quite possibly a few yards.
	c. The narratives do not explain how the centurion confirmed that Jesus was brain dead.

2. The other Roman soldiers:	2. The other Roman soldiers
a. Jesus could not have survived crucifixion. Roman procedures were very careful to eliminate that possibility. Roman law even laid the death penalty on any soldier who let a capital prisoner escape in any way, including bungling a crucifixion. It was never done.	a. The Gospels themselves admit (see Mk 15:39 and Jn 19:33) that those attending the Crucifixion assumed that Jesus was dead before they even took him down from the cross and had a chance to examine his body. Consequently, detractors question how the Roman soldiers could determine that Jesus was brain dead from a distance of quite possibly a few yards.
b. Jesus was crucified by professional Roman soldiers, who performed crucifixions regularly and knew what they were doing. Furthermore, they had greater experience with death than the average citizen due to their profession. Consequently, the signs of death would have been readily identifiable.	b. The narratives do *not* explain how the Roman soldiers confirmed that Jesus was brain dead while he hung from the cross.
	c. It cannot be argued that the Roman soldiers thought that Jesus was already dead and, therefore, that it was not necessary to break his legs. The certainty that Jesus was already dead did not actually exist in the soldiers' minds, except by the centurion mentioned in Mark 15:39 and Luke 23:47.
	d. If the soldiers believed that Jesus was dead, why did a soldier pierce his side with a spear? The only conceivable motives for doing so would be an act of brutality and cruelty or to make sure that Jesus was dead. Given that the Roman soldier had the slightest doubt about Jesus's death, the most effective means of guaranteeing his demise was simply by obeying the order of his superior and breaking the legs.
c. Lastly, if they were unsure, why would they not have broken Jesus's legs as they did to the others that were crucified alongside him? Surely if they were even a little uncertain, they would have done so.	e. It is a fallacious argument that the Roman soldiers: (1) knew what they were doing and (2) would have known when someone was dead. Truth is sometimes stranger than fiction. *No* information is provided regarding the soldiers' age, battle experience, participation in previous crucifixions, or the number of dead bodies they had personally witnessed. Therefore, it is possible that these soldiers were inexperienced or had limited experience with dead bodies.

3. John, an eyewitness, certified that he saw blood and water come from Jesus's pierced side (Jn 19:34–35). This shows that Jesus's lungs had collapsed, and he had died of asphyxiation.	3. There is *no* confirming proof that John saw blood and water exiting Jesus's pierced side (Jn 19:34–35).
	a. It is dubious that John would be able to see any water oozing from Jesus assuming that he was already covered with blood from his prior scourging.
	b. It is dubious that the Roman soldiers would permit John or anyone else to get close enough to examine the crucified body.
	c. The narratives do *not* explain how John confirmed that Jesus was brain dead.
4. The witnesses	4. The witnesses provide *no* support that Jesus literally died on the cross before being taken down.
	a. Luke 23:48 reports that those attending Jesus's crucifixion assumed that he was dead before they even took him down from the cross and had a chance to examine his body. Consequently, detractors question how a man's brain death could be determined from a distance of quite possibly a few yards? Was their interpretation based on the centurion's reactions?
	b. Did Matthew 27:54 imply that "they that were with him" along with the centurion actually knew that Jesus was truly dead or were they reacting to the (1) darkness over the land, (2) renting of the Temple's veil, (3) an earthquake, and (4) opening of the graves and the coming out the saints that slept?
	c. The narratives do *not* explain how the witnesses confirmed that Jesus was brain dead while still on the cross.
5. Pilate's inquiry	5. Pilate's inquiry provides *partial* support for the hypothesis that Jesus did not die on the cross.
	a. Mark 15:44 reported: "And Pilate marvelled if he were already dead: and calling unto him the centurion, he asked him whether he had been any while dead."
	b. Matthew, Luke, and John omit any reference to Pilate's doubt since their agenda requires Jesus's death.

6. Taken down from the cross.
 	
    a. Joseph
    b. Nicodemus
    c. Servants
    d. Roman soldiers?
 	
Jesus was confirmed dead prior to and during his entombment.
	6. Taken down from the cross.

	a. Joseph
	1) It is *unknown* if Joseph of Arimathea himself literally lowered Jesus's body from the cross. Perhaps he employed unidentified servants.
	2) It is *unknown* if Joseph of Arimathea had the physical ability to lower Jesus's body from the cross (no age or physical description is provided).
	3) However, Craig (1989b, 177) suggests that the taking down from the cross of Jesus's body "does not necessitate that Joseph himself ascended the ladder and pulled out the nails. The Romans may have taken down the body for him."
	b. Nicodemus
	1) The historicity and veracity of Nicodemus is *not* multi-attested.
	2) It is *unknown* if Nicodemus helped to lower Jesus from the cross.
	3) It is *unknown* if Nicodemus had the physical ability to lower Jesus's body from the cross (no age or physical description is provided).
	c. Servants
	1) It is *unknown* if any of Joseph of Arimathea's servants helped to lower Jesus from the cross. However, Mark 16:6 narrated that a person described as a young man, who was perhaps an angel, stated to the three women who had arrived at the empty tomb: "Ye seek Jesus of Nazareth, which was crucified: he is risen; he is not here: behold the place where *they* laid him." Thus, Mark's narrative declared that "more" than one person (i.e., they) helped to place Jesus's body in the tomb and possibly assisted in taking it down from the cross.
	2) It is *unknown* if any of Joseph of Arimathea's servants were present when Jesus was lowered from the cross.
	d. Roman soldiers?
	1) According to the Gospels, it is *unknown* if any Roman soldiers helped lower Jesus from the cross.
	2) According to the Gospels, it is *unknown* if any Roman soldiers observed Jesus's body being lowered from the cross.

	3) However, Acts 13:27–29 claimed that Jesus's body was taken down from the cross by those who crucified him.
Jesus was literally dead prior to or during his burial.	**Jesus was *not* actually confirmed brain dead prior to or during his burial.**

1. His body was handled/prepared for burial.
 	
    a.   Joseph
    b.   Nicodemus
    c.   Servants
	1. His body was handled/prepared for burial.

	a. Joseph:
	1) Perhaps the entire body preparation and burial narrative was an invention (i.e., Jesus's body was dumped in a ditch) to protect Jesus's honor or provide a proof that he was, in fact, dead.
	2) Presumably, if Joseph handled/prepared the body (wrapped the body in a cloth or linen shroud), he would know if Jesus was dead unless he was part of a conspiracy (rejected by this text).
	b. Nicodemus:
	1) Perhaps the entire body preparation and burial narrative was an *invention* (i.e., Jesus's body was dumped in a ditch) to protect Jesus's honor or to provide proof that he was, in fact, dead.
	2) Perhaps Nicodemus is an *invention*. His name is not multi-attested.
	3) Presumably, if Nicodemus helped Joseph to handle/prepare the body (wrapped the body in a cloth or linen shroud), he would know if Jesus was dead unless he was part of a conspiracy.
	c. Servants:
	1) Perhaps the entire body preparation and burial narrative was an *invention* (i.e., Jesus's body was dumped in a ditch) to protect Jesus's honor or to provide proof that he was, in fact, dead.

	2) Presumably, if any servants helped handle/prepare the body (wrapped the body in a cloth or linen shroud), they would know if Jesus was dead unless they were part of a conspiracy.
2. Jesus was buried in a tomb with one hundred pounds of spices.	2. Jesus's burial in a tomb with one hundred pounds of spices was a legendary embellishment/invention.
	a. The historicity and veracity of Nicodemus's purchase of the one hundred pounds of "myrrh and aloes" is *not* multi-attested.
	b. Contrary to John's assertion, packing bodies in spices was *not* a Jewish practice. Instead, this was an Egyptian custom. Perhaps the mention of spices was an invention meant to link the burial of Jesus with that of Israel (Jacob) and Joseph (Gen 50:2, 26).
	c. The historicity and veracity of Nicodemus's purchase of the one hundred pounds of "myrrh and aloes" has the sounds of legendary embellishment. C. H. Dodd's (1963, 139n1) comment on the quantity of spices merits consideration: "It seems likely that the somewhat extravagant estimate of the weight of myrrh and aloes provided is a touch introduced by the evangelist, who perhaps is somewhat addicted to numbers, especially large numbers (153 fishes—if the appendix is by the same author)."
	d. Perhaps the author of John wrote part or all of his burial account based on Gamaliel the Elder (i.e., a copycat) as an attempt of one upmanship.
	e. Assuming that John was aware of the tradition of the wise men bringing gifts to the young Jesus, verse 39 may have been written as a literary device (illusion) creating the form of a literary bookend.
Jesus had no food or water for approximately twelve hours (since his last meal) between the Last Supper and his crucifixion.	**It is generally agreed that Jesus probably would have died if he received no food or water for approximately twelve hours (since his last meal) and after previously having been severely scourged and crucified.**
Jesus had no medical treatment before, during, or after being scourged and crucified.	**It is postulated by conspiracy theorists that Jesus received some type of medical treatment before, during, or after being beaten, scourged, and crucified.**

	a. It is generally agreed that Jesus probably would have died if he did not receive adequate medical assistance either prior to, during, or thirty-six hours after previously having been scourged and crucified.
	b. Those advocating a conspiracy [Rejected by this text] posit that Jesus received some type of drug while he was on the cross. Specifically, there was a mysterious sponge that contained vinegar which was given to Jesus just before he allegedly "gives up the ghost" (see Mk 15:36; Mt 27:48; Jn 19:29).
	c. Conspiracy theorists challenged; how could any of the Gospel writers know what was soaked into this mysterious sponge? Each writer claimed it was vinegar. Again, how could they know that it was vinegar? Even if it is assumed that the gospel writers themselves witnessed Jesus's crucifixion (and there is good reason not to accept this position), would they have gone up to the person who put the sponge to Jesus's lips and asked what was in the sponge? Perhaps the sponge was filled with vinegar; but that does not preclude it from being filled with other substances as well. Conspiracy theorists suggest that this mysterious sponge was laced with opium. Opium was available in Judea in those days, and Jesus could very easily have procured it.

ISSUE 31: The Time Required for Preparing and Transporting the Body for Burial

Mk	Mt	Lk 23:54 And that day was the preparation, *and the sabbath drew on.*	Jn

The Gospels are silent regarding the length of time required to prepare the body and transport it and to transport the approximate hundred pounds of myrrh and aloes to the tomb. The distance between the traditional site of Jesus's crucifixion and burial site is approximately fifty meters. It must be remembered that Taylor (1998, 185; see the map) postulates that the distance was actually almost two hundred meters. However, Luke points out that there was not much time remaining since the Sabbath was about to begin.

ISSUE 32: The Garden

Mk	Mt	Lk	Jn 19:41 Now in the place where he was crucified *there was a garden*; and in the garden a new sepulchre, wherein was never man yet laid.

Only the Gospel of John reports that a garden (*kēpos*) is at the place where Jesus is crucified. In contrast, the synoptic Gospels omit any details about the immediate area surrounding the site of the Crucifixion.

CONTRADICTION #40 Archaeological Rebuttal to an Existing Garden at the Garden Tomb

The Gospel of John reports (1) Jesus is buried in a sepulchre, (2) the sepulchre is located in a garden, and (3) the garden is located in the place where Jesus was crucified. John 19:17 specifies that the garden and the sepulchre have to be located in Golgotha: "And he bearing his cross went forth into a place called the place of a skull, which is called in the Hebrew Golgotha."

In contrast, Mark, Matthew, and Luke omit any details about the location of the tomb. However, Matthew 27:60 adds that the tomb personally belongs to Joseph: "And laid it in his own new tomb, which he had hewn out in the rock: and he rolled a great stone to the door of the sepulchre, and departed." On the other hand, Mark 15:22 and Matthew 27:33 confirm that Jesus was crucified at a place called Golgotha (i.e., the Skull).

Currently there is no consensus on the exact location of the burial site. Instead, two sites contend for recognition of Jesus's burial place: (1) the Holy Sepulchre, currently located within the walled Old City, and (2) the Garden Tomb, a burial cave located outside the Old City walls, north of the Damascus Gate.

In addition, contrary to the Gospel of John, archaeological research challenges the notion that Jesus was buried in the area of a garden tomb. Barkay (1986, 4053, 56-57), writing in *Biblical Archaeology Review*, pointed out several facts that challenge the traditional view that Jesus was buried in a Garden Tomb and specifically what is known today as the Garden Tomb.

The Garden Tomb was found in 1867 by a peasant. In 1874, Conrad Schick published a report that was followed by a second more detailed account in 1892. In 1883, General Charles George Gordon arrived in Jerusalem and "identified the hill in which the Garden Tomb is located as the hills of Golgotha, mentioned in the Gospels as the site of the crucifixion" (Barkay p. 44). "Even before Gordon identified the hill as Golgotha, other scholars had mentioned this possibility" (p. 46).

In the 1970s, Barkay and Kloner conducted archaeological investigations of burial chambers located in Jerusalem, north of the Garden Tomb. In addition, a review of earlier excavation findings and publications (James E. Hanauer 1924; unpublished data of the 1937 excavations) was reexamined. Barkay (1986, 56-57) summarizes: "On the basis of all evidence, it seems clear that the Garden Tomb burial cave was first hewn in Iron Age II, the First Temple period, the eighth to seventh centuries BC. It was not again used for burial purposes until the Byzantine period. So it could not have been the tomb in which Jesus was buried."

Reinforcing the findings of Barkay, Viviano (1990, 673), writing for the *New Jerome Biblical Commentary*, points out that archaeological research challenges John's description of Jesus's burial site. He writes: "These magnifying details lack verisimilitude, since according to recent excavations the tomb was undoubtedly in an abandoned quarry, i.e., not a splendid location (→ Biblical Archaeology, 74:150). Mark's more modest account fits the site better." Similarly, Keener (2003, 1166) writes "…the traditional Protestant "Garden Tomb" is a much later site and cannot represent the site of Jesus' burial…"

SPECULATION #66 A Literary Device

Another possible explanation of the garden is that John employs a literary device creating a type of bookend paralleling Jesus's earlier arrest in a garden and his burial in a garden (Cole 2007, 167; Zimmerman 2008, 227): "When Jesus had spoken these words, he went forth with his disciples over the brook Cedron, where was a garden, into the which he entered, and his disciples" (Jn 18:1).

Coincidentally, as previously discussed, John is the only gospel that mentions a garden (*kēpos*) associated with Jesus's arrest. Christian apologists often argue that the omission or deliberate deletion of this significant detail in the synoptic Gospels is due to either the audience or agenda of its authors. A more probable explanation is that the synoptic authors did not record this detail because John invented it.

SPECULATION #67 Reenactment of Genesis

Mackay (1963, 293-94; cf. Lunn 2009, 733; Ramsey 1946, 33) suggests that the Resurrection is an act akin to creation and a reenactment of Genesis. Therefore, just as Adam, the first man, is in a garden, so too is Jesus, the Second Man or last Adam. Furthermore, he points out how such a garden ambience recalled plant symbolism:

1. Israel shall blossom and bud, and fill the face of the world with fruit (Isa 27:6).
2. It shall bring forth boughs, and bear fruit, and be a goodly cedar: and under it shall dwell all fowl of every wing (Ez 17:23).
3. As the earth brings forth shoots, and as a garden causes what is sown in it to spring up, so the Lord God will cause righteousness and praise to spring forth before all nations (Isa 61:11).
4. I will be as the dew to Israel; he shall blossom as the lily, he shall strike root as the popular; his shoots shall spread out; his beauty shall be like the olive. . . . They shall flourish as a garden; they shall blossom as the vine (Hos 14:5 ff).

SPECULATION #68 Alternative Explanations for the Garden

It is also suggested that the garden tomb had another possible function. The purpose of the garden scene is to provide the author of John 20:15 an opportunity to have Mary Magdalene mistake the risen Jesus for a gardener: "Jesus saith unto her, woman, why weepest thou? She saith unto them, Because they have taken away my Lord, and I know not where they have laid him." Brown (1970, 1009) posits that this is another instance of the Gospels' tendency or motif to make the post-resurrection Jesus hard to recognize:

> Mk 16:12 After that he appeared in another form unto two of them, as they walked, and went into the country.

> Lk 24:15-16 And it came to pass, that, while they communed together and reasoned, Jesus himself drew near, and went with them. But their eyes were holden that they should not know him.

Another hypothesis is that the garden episode prepares the way for a dramatic recognition scene. Perkins (1992, 39) and Nicholas (1990, 21-38) offer an alternative explanation for the garden. Perkins writes: "Some exegetes have suggested that the unusual setting of the tomb in a garden was also derived from paradise imagery." Yet another speculation is that the brutality of Jesus's death has been sublimated through hope and imagination into its opposite, a victory over death (Crossan 1994, 174).

ISSUE 33: The Tomb

Mk 15:46 And he bought fine linen, and took him down, and wrapped him in the linen, and laid him *in a sepulchre which was hewn out of a rock*, and rolled a stone unto the door of the sepulchre.	Mt 27:60 *And laid it in his own new tomb, which he had hewn out in the rock*: and he rolled a great stone to the door of the sepulchre, and departed.	Lk 23:53 And he took it down, and wrapped it in linen, *and laid it in a sepulchre that was hewn in stone, wherein never man before was laid.*	Jn 19:41 Now in the place where he was crucified there was a garden; and in the garden *a new sepulchre, wherein was never man yet laid.*

The first time the burial place itself is mentioned, the translators of the AV employ two words: Mark employs "sepulchre" twice, Matthew uses "tomb" and "sepulchre," and Luke and John utilizes only the term "sepulchre." Hence, the Gospels are basically reporting the same description. In terms of the building material, both Mark and Matthew mention that it was hewn (*latomeo*) out of a rock (*petra*). In contrast, Luke has the sepulchre hewn out of stone. Luke and John declare that no man was ever previously laid in the tomb, and hence it was new (Brown 1994a, 2:1252-53). Matthew adds the fact that it was Joseph's "own" tomb.

Later, the Gospels provide additional information to help identify the type of tomb used to bury Jesus. Luke 24:3-4 narrates that at least five people could stand inside the tomb; in addition, two gospels (Lk 24:12; Jn 20:5, 11) indicate that it was necessary to stoop down to look inside the sepulchre; and John 20:12 reports that two angels were sitting inside the tomb where the body of Jesus had lain.

SPECULATION #69 The Type of Tomb

Three types of tombs were in use during the time of Jesus. The more common type of tomb is the *kokim* tomb (pl.), which features *loculi* or long narrow niches cut horizontally at right angles into the chamber of a burial cave in order that the body could be placed inside headfirst. Each niche is large enough to hold a single body. These burial shafts or niches are called *loculi* graves in Latin and *kokim* graves in Hebrew. Harrington (1991, 407) describes them as "bunk-like" platforms cut out of the sides of the cave. The body would remain in the niche for approximately one year, after which the bones would be gathered and placed in a stone box (ossuary) (see Evans 2003, 21-22n2; Fine 2000, 69-76).

The other type of tomb popular during the first century is known as the *acrosolia* tomb or semicircular niche, so-called for its arched or overhanging vault. In contrast, the *quadrosolia* is rectangular, with a straight top. The acrosolia tomb features (1) shallow niches that are cut parallel to the wall to the chamber, (2) an arch-shaped or semicircular top over the recess that is at the most two feet high, and (3) a shelf or trough for the body.

A third type of tomb is the bench tomb. These contain a bench around the inner walls of the tomb that serve as a resting place for the body. Such tombs are generally reserved for individuals of a higher socio-economic class.

The type of tomb used as the burial place for the body of Jesus cannot be identified with certainty. Brown (1994a, 2:1248-49) states that "no Gospel account tells us what type of burial accommodation was envisaged; but the story of the women at the empty tomb in Mark 16:5 may suppose an anteroom with a bench since it describes a young man sitting inside on the right." However, Craig (1989b, 187) and others are of the opinion that the details in the gospel accounts preclude a *kokim* sort of tomb. Instead, he states: "It is evident from the gospels' description of the empty tomb that it was either of the *acrosolia* [[niches 2½ feet above the floor and two or three feet deep containing either a flat shelf or a trough for the body]] or bench type of tomb with a roll-stone for the door." Craig also argues:

1. Such tombs were scarce in Jesus' day and were reserved for the very wealthy (Mt 27:57).
2. Both Luke 24:12 and John 20:5, 11 mention the necessity of stooping in order to enter or look through the low door of the tomb.
3. The angels were seen sitting at both Jesus' head and feet (Jn 20:12).

Brown (p. 1249; cf. O'Rahilly 1941, 152) too states that "reconstruction of Jesus' tomb based on knowledge of the venerated site in the Church of the Holy Sepulchre point to an arcosolium."

However, Kloner (1999, 29) challenges this view: "The gospel text also indicates that Jesus was not laid on a quadrosolium or arcosolium. In John 20:12 Mary sees two angels "sitting where the body of Jesus had lain, one at the head and the other at the feet." This would have been impossible (or unlikely) if the body had been laid in a burial niche because arcosolia and quadrosolia were at most two feet high. In contrast, Kloner believes: "Most likely Jesus' tomb was a standard small burial tomb, with a standing pit and burial benches alone three sides." He further suggests that "the body was simply and hastily covered with a shroud and placed on a burial bench in a small burial cave." His rationale is that "this is the context in which should understand John 20:11, in which we are told that Mary 'bent over to look into the tomb,' and saw two angels sitting at the head and foot of where Jesus' body had lain."

Yet, another argument against an arcosolia design is that the tomb is large enough for Jesus's followers to enter. For example, Luke 23:3-4 reports that several women, along with two men (i.e., presumably angels) stood inside the tomb. In contrast, John 20:6-8 provides details discussing Peter and the other disciple entering the sepulchre.

> Mk 16:5 And entering into the sepulchre, they saw a young man sitting on the right side, clothed in a long white garment; and they were affrighted.

> Lk 24:3-4 And they entered in, and found not the body of the Lord Jesus. And it came to pass, as they were much perplexed thereabout, behold, two men stood by them in shining garments.

> Jn 20:6 Then cometh Simon Peter following him, and went into the sepulchre, and seeth the linen clothes lie.

> Jn 20:8 Then went in also that other disciple, which came first to the sepulchre, and he saw, and believed.

Again, the height of the inside chamber will have precluded an arcosolia type of tomb with these people standing there.

SPECULATION #70 Interpretations of "No Man Was Ever Laid"

Mark 15:46 states that Jesus is buried in a "sepulchre which is hewn out of rock," and he omits any discussion about it previously having been used or not used. Matthew's narrative states that the tomb is *new* and thereby implies that it was never used. However, Luke 23:53 and John 19:41 explicitly state that Jesus's burial occurred in a tomb "wherein no man was ever laid." Price (1989, 17) raises the notion that perhaps their comments are meant to parallel Mark 11:2, which describes the colt Jesus is to ride upon entering Jerusalem on Palm Sunday: "ye shall find a colt tied, whereon never man sat; loose him, and bring him." Similarly, in 1 Samuel 6:7 it records where the Ark of the Covenant is borne by cattle "on which there hath come no yoke." However, Brown (1994a, 2:1268n71) is of the opinion that these claims are farfetched.

On the other hand, Brown (1970, 959) maintains that the claim in John 19:41 that Jesus is buried in "a new tomb where no one had ever been laid" more likely "reflects apologetics—there was no confusion in the report of the empty tomb, for Jesus was not buried in a common tomb where his body might have been mixed with others, and the tomb was in an easily identifiable place near the well-known site of public execution."

Finally, Don Allen (1893, 42n) speculates:

> The evangelist is very particular in telling us that this was a new tomb, "wherein never man before was laid." The object of being thus precise in this detail is to keep us from thinking that the resurrection of Jesus might have been brought about by the body of Jesus coming in contact with bones of some old prophet that would bring it to life, as the Moabite was brought to life from coming in contact with Elisha's bones, in the days of old. (2 Kings xiii, 20, 21)

SPECULATION #71 Joseph's Motivation for Burying Jesus in His Personal Tomb

Craig (1989b, 175), citing Blinzler (1974, 97) writes: "It has been suggested that Joseph laid Jesus there only because time was short and his tomb was close, and he intended to later transfer the body to the criminals' common graveyard." More forcefully, Magness (2005, 147) states: "When the Gospels tell us that Joseph of Arimathea offered Jesus a spot in his tomb, it was because Jesus' family did not own a rock-cut tomb and there was no time to prepare a grave—that is, there was no time to *dig* a grave, *not* hew a rock-cut tomb (!)—before the Sabbath."

In contrast, Abogunrin (1981, 58) summarized the work of Buchler (1930, 87) who challenged the traditional belief that Jesus was buried in Joseph's tomb:

> According to Buchler, the fourth gospel lends support to the idea of a twofold burial by implying that Joseph's sepulcher was not the one visited by the women. The place of Jesus' burial was chosen because it was close to Calvary and because it was the Jewish day of preparation. Joseph's own tomb must have been somewhere else. He says further that no Jew of Joseph's distinction would have chosen a location near the Roman place of execution for his family tomb. His piety would be inclined to locate his tomb on the slopes of the Kidron valley.

However, in reality, nobody knows with certainty Joseph of Arimathea's motivation to bury Jesus. All that commentators can offer are assumptions, guesses, and suppositions of possible motives. Of course, in addition, these speculations presume that the burial episode is historical.

ISSUE 34: The People Who Buried Jesus

| Mk 15:43 *Joseph of Arimathea*, an honourable counsellor, which also waited for the kingdom of God, came, and went in boldly unto Pilate, and craved the body of Jesus.

Mk 15:46 *And he* bought fine linen, and took him down, and wrapped him in the linen, and laid him in a sepulchre which was hewn out of a rock, *and rolled a stone unto the door of the sepulchre.*

Mk 16:5 And entering into the sepulcher, they saw a young man sitting on the right side, clothed in a long white garment; and they were affrighted. 6 And he saith unto them, Be not affrighted: Ye seek Jesus of Nazareth, which was crucified: he is risen; he is not here: behold the place where *they* laid him. | Mt 27:57 When the even was come, there came a rich man of Arimathea, named *Joseph*, who also himself was Jesus' disciple:

Mt 27:60 And laid it *in his own new tomb*, which he had hewn out in the rock: *and he rolled a great stone to the door of the sepulchre, and departed.* | Lk 23:50 And, behold, there was *a man named Joseph*, a counsellor; and he was a good man, and a just: 51 The same had not consented to the counsel and deed of them;) he was of Arimathea, a city of the Jews: who also himself waited for the kingdom of God. 52 This man went unto Pilate, and begged the body of Jesus. 53 *And he* took it down, and wrapped it in linen, *and laid it in a sepulchre* that was hewn in stone, wherein never man before was laid. | Acts 13:27 For they that dwell at Jerusalem, and their rulers, because they knew him not, nor yet the voices of the prophets which are read every sabbath day, they have fulfilled them in condemning him. 28 *And though they found no cause of death in him*, yet desired they Pilate that he should be slain. 29 And when they had fulfilled all that was written of him, *they took him down from the tree, and laid him in a sepulchre.* | Jn 19:38 And after this *Joseph of Arimathea*, being a disciple of Jesus, but secretly for fear of the Jews, besought Pilate that he might take away the body of Jesus: and Pilate gave him leave. He came therefore, and took the body of Jesus. 39 And there came also *Nicodemus*, which at the first came to Jesus by night, and brought a mixture of myrrh and aloes, about an hundred pound weight.

Jn 19:42 *There laid they Jesus* therefore because of the Jews' preparation day; for the sepulchre was nigh at hand. |

The synoptic Gospels indicate that Joseph alone buried Jesus. In contrast, John states that Joseph *and* Nicodemus laid Jesus's body in the sepulchre. However, the Acts of the Apostles declares that his enemies, in fact, buried Jesus.

Acts 13:27-29 For they that dwell at Jerusalem, and their rulers, because they knew him not, nor yet the voices of the prophets which are read every sabbath day, they have fulfilled them in condemning him. And though they found no cause of death in him, yet desired they Pilate that he should be slain. And when they had fulfilled all that was written of him, they took him down from the tree, and laid him in a sepulchre.

CONTRADICTION #41 John and Acts versus the Synoptics

John and Acts directly contradict the synoptic Gospels regarding who buried Jesus. The synoptic Gospels report that Joseph alone buried Jesus.

Mk 15:46 And *he* bought fine linen, and took him down, and wrapped him in the linen, and laid him in a sepulchre which was hewn out of a rock, and rolled a stone unto the door of the sepulchre.

Mt 27:60 And laid it in his own new tomb, which *he* had hewn out in the rock: and *he* rolled a great stone to the door of the sepulchre, and departed.

Lk 23:53 And *he* took it down, and wrapped it in linen, and laid it in a sepulchre that was hewn in stone, wherein never man before was laid.

To the contrary, John and Acts report that a *plurality* of people buried Jesus. John 19:42 claims that Joseph *and* Nicodemus buried Jesus: "There laid *they* Jesus therefore because of the Jews' preparation day; for the sepulchre was nigh at hand." In addition, Acts 13:29 reports that a plurality of people buried Jesus: "And when *they* had fulfilled all that was written of him, *they* took him down from the tree, and laid him in a sepulchre." Thus, there is a glaring and incontrovertible contradiction.

Proponents of Jesus's resurrection could refer to one possible exception in Mark 16:6, where a young man gave a message to the three women visiting the tomb: "And he saith unto them, Be not affrighted: Ye seek Jesus of Nazareth, which was crucified: he is risen; he is not here: behold the place where *they* laid him." By employing the word *they*, Mark implies that more than one person was involved. However, this sentence contradicts what he said earlier in 15:46 and what appears in the other synoptic Gospels.

This verse then raises the previously stated question: Given that Luke investigated "all things" and expressed his goal (Lk 1:4) to write an account so that those reading his narrative "mightiest know the certainty of these things," why did he declare in his gospel that Joseph alone buried Jesus?

CONTRADICTION #42 Acts versus the Synoptics and John

The burial narrative of the writer of the Gospel of Luke is assumed also to be the author of Acts, yet he records conflicting accounts. Luke 23:52-53 declares that Joseph *alone* buried Jesus: "This man went unto Pilate, and begged the body of Jesus. And he took it down, and wrapped it in linen, and laid it in a sepulchre that was hewn in stone, wherein never man before was laid." In agreement, Mark 15:46 states: "And he bought fine linen, and took him down, and wrapped him in the linen, and laid him in a sepulchre which was hewn out of a rock, and rolled a stone unto the door of the sepulchre"; and Matthew 27:60 reports: "And laid it in his own new tomb, which he had hewn out in the rock: and he rolled a great stone to the door of the sepulchre, and departed." Both report that Joseph buried Jesus *singularly*.

To the contrary, Acts 13:29: records the word *they* (plural), referring to those who had culpability, who had participated in Jesus's guilty verdict and execution and who had also assisted in his burial: "And when they had fulfilled all that was written of him, they took him down from the tree, and laid him in a sepulchre." In his preface, Luke claims to have investigated all the sources of his day. Yet the narrative in Acts contradicts Luke. How then could these works be by the same person?

Finally, John 19:42 reports that a plurality of two men buried Jesus, Joseph of Arimathea and Nicodemus: "There laid they Jesus therefore because of the Jews' preparation day; for the sepulchre was nigh at hand."

CONTRADICTION #43 Luke versus Luke

Earlier it was discussed that if Christian apologists maintain that the passage in Acts refers to the Jews and not the Romans who had engineered his death, there is yet another contradiction. According to Luke 23:51, Joseph is not part of the conspiracy. That is, Luke 23:51 stresses that *all* members of the council *except* Joseph, condemned Jesus: "The same had not consented to the counsel and deed of them;) he was of Arimathea, a city of the Jews: who also himself waited for the kingdom of God." Thus Luke exonerates Joseph of any complicity in the plot of the Sanhedrin.

Luke 23:51 creates an obvious contradiction. If Joseph did not, in fact, take part in the council's deed to conspire against Jesus, then how could Acts 13:28-29 claim "And though they found no cause of death in him, yet desired they Pilate that he should be slain. And when they had fulfilled all that was written of him, they took him down from the tree, and laid him in a sepulchre"? By using the word *they*, the narrative includes Joseph in the conspiracy against Jesus. Once more, here, there is a plain and incontrovertible contradiction.

ISSUE 35: The Stone

| Mk 15:46 And he bought fine linen, and took him down, and wrapped him in the linen, and laid him in a sepulchre which was hewn out of a rock, and *rolled a stone* unto the door of the sepulchre. | Mt 27:60 And laid it in his own new tomb, which he had hewn out in the rock: *and he rolled a great stone* to the door of the sepulchre, and departed. | Lk 24:1 Now upon the first day of the week, very early in the morning, they came unto the sepulchre, bringing the spices which they had prepared, and certain others with them. 2 *And they found the stone rolled away from the sepulchre.* | Jn 20:1 The first day of the week cometh Mary Magdalene early, when it was yet dark, unto the sepulchre, *and seeth the stone taken away from the sepulchre.* |

All the gospel narratives mention a stone used at the sepulchre. Mark reports the presence of a stone, whereas Matthew adds one detail that the stone is "great." Luke 24:2 and John 24:1 omit any description of a stone used to seal the opening of the tomb, although they later mention a stone being found rolled or taken away from the sepulchre.

ISSUE 36: Rolling the Stone to Wedge the Door

Mk 15:46 *And he* bought fine linen, and took him down, and wrapped him in the linen, and laid him in a sepulchre which was hewn out of a rock, *and rolled a stone unto the door of the sepulchre.*	Mt 27:60 And laid it in *his own new* tomb, which he had hewn out in the rock: *and he rolled a great stone to the door of the sepulchre, and departed.*	Lk	Jn

Mark and Matthew report that Joseph of Arimathea alone rolled the stone to wedge the door of the tomb. Luke and John omit any discussion about how or by whom the stone is wedged at the tomb's entrance.

SPECULATION #72 Historical Accuracy of the Stone to Close Joseph's Tomb

A speculated controversy relates to the accuracy of the stone's description. This issue is explored in Amos Kloner's (1999) article "Did a Rolling Stone Close Jesus' Tomb?" found in the journal *Biblical Archaeology Review*. Kloner discusses the archaeological evidence of Jewish tomb burial practices in antiquity. He observes that more than 98 percent of the Jewish tombs from this period, called the Second Temple period (ca. first century BCE to 70 CE), were closed with *square* blocking stones.

Kloner reports that only four *round*, disc-shaped blocking stones out of nine hundred burial caves in and around Jerusalem are known prior to the Jewish War. The four exceptions are blocking entrances to elaborate tomb complexes of the extremely rich. However, the Second Temple period ended with the Roman destruction of Jerusalem in 70 CE. "In later periods the situation changed, and round blocking stones became much more common" (p. 25). Carrier (2005), based on the research of Kloner, suggests that the gospel accounts could be a fabrication.

> Why is this significant? Three of the four Gospels repeatedly and consistently use the word 'roll' to describe the moving of the tomb's blocking stone ("rolled to" *proskylisas*, Matthew 27:60; "rolled away" *apekylisen*, Matthew 28:2; "rolled to" *prosekylisen*, Mark 15:46; 'roll away' *apokylisei* Mark 16:3; "rolled away" *apokekylistai* Mark 16:4; "rolled away" *apokekylismenon* Luke 24:2). The verb in every case here is a form of *kyliein*, which always means to roll: *kyliein* is the root of *kylindros*, i.e., cylinder (in antiquity a "rolling stone" or even a child's marble). For example, the demon-possessed boy in Mark 9:20 'rolls around' on the ground (*ekylieto*, middle form meaning "roll oneself," hence "wallow"). These are the only uses of any form of this verb in the New Testament.
>
> Kloner argues that the verb could just mean "moved" and not rolled, but he presents no examples of such a use for this verb; I have not been able to find any myself in or outside the Bible, and such a meaning is not presented in any lexicon. His argument

is based solely on the fact that it "couldn't" have meant rolled because the stone couldn't have been round in the thirties CE. But he misses the more persuasive point: if the verb can only mean round, then the gospel authors were not thinking of a tomb in the thirties CE but of one in the latter part of the century. *If* the tomb description *is* flawed, this would also put Mark as having been written after 70 CE and would support the distinct possibility that the entire tomb story is fiction.

Even so, there is nothing decisive about this. There could still be a core truth about a tomb burial, with the details being added from the imaginations of the authors or their sources, as often happened when even reliable historians described scenes in such vivid detail. There was a kind of acceptable license when painting scenes this way, provided that the historian did not contradict any known facts or propose the implausible. So the fact that the story was told in terms familiar to the writers, though historically inaccurate, would not entail that the story did not originally involve sliding a square stone instead. But the incongruity would still lend some support to an overall case against the authenticity of the story.

In opposition to the above, Glenn Miller (2002), a Christian apologist argues:

1. There is the obvious possibility that the rich Joseph/Nicodemus couple could have been wealthy enough to use the circular, disc-shaped stone anyway (as per the qualification of Kloner). The value of the spices used would certainly argue for this possibility.
2. The lexical data indicates that "roll" does not imply "circularity of shape" but rather "end over end" movement (e.g., the tumbling of boulders down a hillside or cliff). Accordingly, it is general enough a term to describe *both* the cases above *and* cases of rotation of a cylinder along its circular circumference.

There are several rebuttals to Miller's apologetic that Joseph is wealthy enough to use a circular disc-shaped stone.

First, as previously discussed, the word *rich* does not literally need to mean monetarily rich or wealthy. It could mean a man of "good standing" (Lake 1907, 50; Montefiore 1968, 1:392; Swete 1927, 50) or a derogatory sneer (Hanhart 1995, 182).

Second, several writers (Barrick 1977, 235-39; Benoit 1970, 215; Bowen 1911, 247) suggest that the word *rich* may have been a deliberate invention to serve as a proof text of Isaiah 53.

Third, the entire Joseph of Arimathea personality may be an invention.

Fourth, hypothetically assuming that a rich Joseph actually existed, it again bears repeating: archaeological research only found four circular stones out of nine hundred burial stones used before the destruction of the Second Temple. Therefore, statistically speaking, it would be extremely doubtful that Joseph owned such a tomb door.

Last, if the door stone was "not" round, it seems odd that the Gospels continually describe the stone as being "rolled out" of the way (Mk 16:3, 4; Mt 27:60; 28:2; and Lk 24:2).

SPECULATION #73 The Practicality of Joseph Rolling the Stone

Mark and Matthew report that Joseph *alone* rolled the stone (*lithon*) to wedge the door (*thyra*). In contrast, Luke and John omit any discussion regarding how the stone is wedged to the door. Could one person by himself be capable of moving such a stone? Research by McDowell (1981, 67) claims that a stone needed to roll against an approximate five-feet doorway would have to weigh a minimum of one and one-half to two tons. In further support of his opinion, McDowell (1981, 53) points out: "In the Mark 16:4 portion of the Bezae manuscripts in the Cambridge Library in England, a parenthetical statement was found that adds: '20 men could not roll away.'" Elaborating on this parenthetical comment, McDowell states:

> The significance of this is realized when one considers the rules for transcribing manuscripts. It was the custom that if a copier was emphasizing his own interpretation, he would write his thought in the margin and not include it within the text. One might conclude, therefore, that the insert in the text was copied from a text even closer to the time of Christ, perhaps, a first-century manuscript. The phrase, then, could have been recorded by an eyewitness who was impressed with the enormity of the stone which was rolled against Jesus' sepulcher.

How then could Joseph move the stone into position if he did it alone? McDowell posits that the stone was held in place by a wedge as it rested in a groove or trench that sloped down to the front of the tomb. Therefore, when the wedge is removed, the heavy circular stone just rolled into position.

There are a number of problems with his theory. First, McDowell's apologetic is an argument based on silence. Second, McDowell's apologetic is nothing more than his mere opinion. Third, there is *no* incontrovertible evidentiary proof or justification to conclude (1) the Bezae manuscript was copied from a text even closer to the time of Jesus, perhaps a first-century manuscript, and (2) an eyewitness could have recorded the phrase. These rationales are the wishes of a non-objective Christian apologist arguing from silence. Instead, it must be asked, is there a greater likelihood that the scribe was embellishing the text with his parenthetical statement?

Another reason that the scribe might have embellished the Codex Bezae was to make sure that no one could argue that people stole Jesus's body.

Fifth, there is *no* proof that the stone at Joseph of Arimathea's tomb was held in place by a wedge as it sat in a groove or trench that sloped down. This Christian apologetic is mere wishful thinking to explain the narratives of Mark and Matthew. Sixth, there has been discussion by Kloner (1999, 28-29) as to whether or not the stone was actually round. Given that the stone is not round, it is doubtful that it was "rolled" into place or later rolled away from the sepulchre. Finally, Levitan (2006), in a personal communication points out that McDowell's hypothesis that the stone weighed one to two tons supports the contention that the *they* in Acts 13:27-29 was a large crew and certainly not only one or two people; this hypothesis then undermines the credibility of all four gospels.

ISSUE 37: When the Tomb Was Closed

Mk	Mt	Lk 23:54 And that day was the preparation, *and the sabbath drew on.*	Jn 19:42 There laid they Jesus therefore because of the Jews' preparation day; for the sepulchre was nigh at hand.

Only one of the gospel's authors provides general information as to when the tomb was finally closed. According to Luke, the tomb was closed as "the sabbath drew on." Therefore, sunset had to be approaching. In contrast, only John reports that Jesus was buried on the day of preparation.

ISSUE 38: The Gospels' Witnesses Who Saw the Body Placed in the Tomb

Mk 15:47	Mt 27:61 *And*	Lk 23:55 *And*	Jn 19:39 And there came *also Nicodemus*,
And Mary	*there was Mary*	*the women, also,*	which at the first came to Jesus by night,
Magdalene and	*Magdalene, and*	*which came with*	and brought a mixture of myrrh and
Mary the mother	*the other Mary,*	*him from Galilee,*	aloes, about an hundred pound weight.
of Joses beheld	sitting over	followed after,	40 *Then took they the body of Jesus*, and
where he was	against the	and beheld the	wound it in linen with the spices, as the
laid.	sepulchre.	sepulchre, and	manner of the Jews is to bury. 41 Now
		how his body was	in the place where he was crucified there
		laid.	was a garden; and in the garden a new
			sepulchre, wherein was never man yet
			laid. 42 *There laid they Jesus* therefore
			because of the Jews' preparation day; for
			the sepulchre was nigh at hand.

Issue 15 provides details that several people are present at the moment of Jesus's death. At a later period of time, the Gospels name several people present at the burial, and thus capable of providing potential witnesses to this significant event. All the evangelists mention Joseph since he was the one who buried Jesus. Mark 15:47 identifies two women, Mary Magdalene and Mary, the mother of Joses. He specifically declares that they "beheld where Jesus was laid" without any mention of their location. Matthew 27:61 has Mary Magdalene accompanied by the "other Mary," with the added fact that they are positioned "sitting over against the sepulchre." Luke 23:55 reports that unspecified women (plural) witnessed Jesus's burial, but there was no discussion of their locale. These women are described as those "which came with him (i.e., Jesus) from Galilee."

Finally, John mentions that Nicodemus assisted with the burial and, therefore, had to be included as a witness. It must be noted that earlier John 19:25 identifies several women and one disciple at the cross when Jesus died. However, John does not provide any information about their presence during the burial. Instead, prior to Jesus's death it is recorded in verse 27: "Then saith he to the disciple, Behold thy mother! And from that hour that disciple took her unto his own home." Therefore, it is unknown if Mary the wife of Cleophas and Mary Magdalene remained at the scene or left before Jesus was placed in the tomb.

TABLE 25. The Witnesses of Jesus's Burial Excluding Joseph of Arimathea

GOSPEL	WITNESSES	NUMBER of WITNESSES (Excluding Joseph of Arimathea)	THE LOCATION of the WITNESSES
Mark	Mary Magdalene and Mary the mother of Joses.	2	The women "beheld where Jesus was laid" without details to their location.
Matthew	Mary Magdalene and the other Mary.	2	The women are "sitting over against the sepulchre."
Luke	The women who came with Jesus from Galilee.	Unspecified number of women.	No details about the location of the women.
John	Nicodemus.	Insufficient information to determine a number.	No mention about any female witnesses to Jesus's burial. However, Nicodemus participates in the burial process.

CONTRADICTION #44 Conflicting Accounts

The details provided in the gospel narratives present conflicting data. A quick look at table 25 shows a clear conflict in that each account differs. They report different names of those present at the tomb, different numbers of those present at the tomb, and different locations of the witnesses at the tomb.

SPECULATION #74 The Purpose of the Numerous Witnesses

Why do the synoptic Gospel authors provide multiple witnesses for Jesus being laid in the tomb? First, the collective witnesses could serve as an answer to potential enemies who might allege that Jesus did not die on the cross. Second, the witnesses could counter any charges that Jesus's tomb had been mistakenly identified when visitors later returned and found an empty sepulchre. In brief, Jesus is dead and the witnesses did *not* go to the wrong tomb. Finally, the multiple witnesses provide the minimum of two needed to confirm a legal testimony:

> Deut 17:6 At the mouth of two witnesses, or three witnesses, shall he that is worthy of death be put to death; but at the mouth of one witness he shall not be put to death.

> Deut 19:15 One witness shall not rise up against a man for any iniquity, or for any sin, in any sin that he sinneth: at the mouth of two witnesses, or at the mouth of three witnesses, shall the matter be established.

ISSUE 39: The Action Taken by the Women Immediately after the Tomb Was Sealed

Mk	Mt	Lk	Jn
Mk 15:47 And Mary Magdalene and Mary the mother of Joses *beheld where he was laid.* Mk 16:1 And when the sabbath was past, Mary Magdalene, and Mary the mother of James, and Salome, *had bought sweet spices*, that they might come and anoint him.		Lk 23:56 *And they returned, and prepared spices and ointments*; and rested the sabbath day according to the commandment.	

Mark 15:47 reports that after the sepulchre was sealed, Mary Magdalene and Mary the mother of Joses saw where Jesus's body was laid. The next verse starts chapter 16 and commences over twenty-four hours later: "And when the sabbath was past." Mark narrates that three women purchased some sweet spices to anoint Jesus's body. This purchase means that the women did not have the ingredients for the ointments in their possession. Therefore, Mark 16:1 has the women purchasing spices after the Sabbath was over.

Luke 23:56 narrates that on Friday afternoon, after witnessing all that took place, the women returned, prepared spices and ointments, and rested on the Sabbath day. This scenario follows the synoptic chronology with Jesus being executed and dying on the fifteenth of Nisan. No details are provided by either Matthew or John regarding the action taken by the women after the tomb is sealed prior to their Sunday morning visitation.

TABLE 26. The Synoptic Accounts of the Spices

GOSPEL	WHO OBTAINED SPICES	HOW THE SPICES WERE OBTAINED	WHEN THE SPICES WERE OBTAINED
Mark	Mary Magdalene, Mary the mother of James, and Salome.	Bought.	After the Sabbath.
Matthew	No mention of spices.	No mention of spices.	Omitted.
Luke	An unknown group of women who followed Jesus from Galilee.	No mention how the spices were obtained.	Omitted.

CONTRADICTION #45 Luke Contradicts Mark

Luke directly contradicts Mark's account of the women preparing the spices. Mark 16:1 explicitly reports that Mary Magdalene, Mary, the mother of James, and Salome bought sweet spices *after* the Sabbath. The verse reads: "And when the sabbath was past, Mary Magdalene, and Mary the mother of James, and Salome, had bought sweet spices, that they might come and anoint him."

Luke 23:56 claims that the women prepared their spices *before* the Sabbath: "And they returned, and prepared spices and ointments; and rested the sabbath day according to the commandment." Therefore, the women had possession of the spices *prior* to the Sabbath.

The obvious problem is the impossibility for Luke's women to prepare spices *before* the Sabbath if they did not purchase them until *after* the Sabbath, as reported in Mark 16:1: "And when the sabbath was past, Mary Magdalene, and Mary the mother of James, and Salome, had bought sweet spices, that they might come and anoint him."

In addition, Christian apologists might contend that some of the women prepared additional spices before the Sabbath, whereas others had to purchase spices after the Sabbath. However, here, too, there is no incontrovertible evidence to support such a thesis.

In conclusion, Brown (1994a, 2:1257) admits that "useless are the ingenious attempts to harmonize Luke, where the women had the spices before the Sabbath began, with Mark, where the women did not buy the spices until the Sabbath was over."

CONTRADICTION #46 Luke Violates the Yom Tov

According to Luke's depiction, the women violated a commandment of God, although not the commandment referring to abstaining from work on the Sabbath. Luke 23:56 narrates: "And they returned, and prepared spices and ointments; and rested the sabbath day according to the commandment." Therefore, Luke has several women *preparing* burial unguents on late Friday afternoon just *before* the Sabbath. Luke omits to inform his readership that Friday, the fifteenth of Nisan and the first day of Passover, is also a Yom Tov, a holy day; work is *forbidden* as it is in direct violation of God's instructions:

> Lev 23:7: In the first day ye shall have an holy convocation: *ye shall do no servile work therein.*

> Neh 10:31 And if the people of the land bring ware or any victuals on the sabbath day to sell, *that we would not buy it of them* on the sabbath, *or on the holy day*: and that we would leave the seventh year, and the exaction of every debt.

Therefore, although the women are not violating the Sabbath they are in fact violating God's instructions not to work on a Yom Tov (i.e., a holy day) by preparing the spices and ointment.

There is no mention in Luke of the women purchasing any spices; instead, Luke 23:56 has the women preparing the spices *prior* to the Sabbath "according to the commandment." Although the women observe the law of the Sabbath, as specified in Exodus 20:8-11, they directly contradict the commandment that forbids work on a Yom Tov, a holy day. The work carried out by these women includes "preparing the spices." Scroggie (1948, 572) clarifies the point that preparing the spices specifically entailed grinding and cooking them. Both of these actions, despite their noble cause, are a violation of working on a Yom Tov.

CONTRADICTION #47 The Gospels' Violations of the Yom Tov

In direct contradiction to God's instructions, Mark, Matthew, and Luke record numerous violations of the Yom Tov, which are specified in Leviticus 23:7 and Nehemiah 10:31. This scenario follows the chronology of the synoptic Gospels. These violations include the following:

Mt 26:47 A great multitude carried swords and staves from none other than the chief priests and elders of the people to arrest Jesus.

Mt 26:65 The high priest tore (rented) his clothes.

Lk 22:55 A fire was lit in the house of the chief priest.

Mt 26:56-64 A trial was held at the high priest's palace.

Mk 15:21 Simon the Cyrenian had "passed by, coming out of the country" where he had obviously been working (McNeile 1915, 377-78; Ricciotti 1947, 563 and rejected by Keener 2009b, 635n205; 1993, 180).

Mk 15:46 Joseph of Arimathea purchased fine linen.

Lk 23:56 The women prepared spice and ointments before the Sabbath.

Significantly not only are the chief priests, and the multitude are violating the Yom Tov. So too is Joseph of Arimathea, a respected member of the council, and Nicodemus, a Pharisee. Last, even the pious women followers of Jesus are reported to have violated the Holy Day.

Further, casting doubt about these narratives is John 13:29, in which Jesus orders Judas to purchase goods during the Last Supper: "For some of them thought, because Judas had the bag, that Jesus had said unto him, Buy those things that we have need of against the feast; or, that he should give something to the poor." The collective numbers of people who openly violate the Yom Tov refute the reliability of the gospel narratives.

SPECULATION #75 Why Luke Modified Mark

Luke 23:56 narrates: "And they returned, and prepared spices and ointments; and rested the sabbath day according to the commandment." To the contrary, Mark 16:1 states: "And when the sabbath was past, Mary Magdalene, and Mary the mother of James, and Salome, had bought sweet spices, that they might come and anoint him." Either Luke contradicts or seemingly corrects Mark because he knew that purchasing goods on Saturday evening or Sunday morning before sunrise was not probable. Therefore, he had the women preparing the spices and ointments before the Sabbath. Then in the first verse of chapter 24, he declares: "Now upon the first day of the week, very early in the morning, they came unto the sepulchre, bring spices which they had prepared, and certain others with them."

SPECULATION #76 Luke's Women Obtaining Their Spices

Wenham (1992, 68), a Christian apologist, offers the hypothesis that possibly Luke refers to Joanna and Susanna who obtain the spices. He posits that Joanna and Susanna were wealthy and "were able to prepare their share of the burial ointments from their own resources on Friday evening without having recourse to the Saturday market." This hypothesis is based on Luke 8:3: "And Joanna the wife of Chuza Herod's steward, and Susanna, and many others, which ministered unto him of their substance."

Wenham's hypothesis is entirely speculative. He has no evidentiary proof that these women, in fact, obtained the spices and ointments. However, even if the women purchased the spices on Friday, they completed their work on a Yom Tov (a holy day), which is still in violation of God's instructions. In addition, Mark and Matthew do not mention at any time either the name Joanna or Susanna in their gospel narratives.

SPECULATION #77 The Plausibility of Luke's Timeline

Luke 23:55 reports that the women saw the tomb and how Jesus's body was laid in it: "And the women also, which came with him from Galilee, followed after, and beheld the sepulchre, and how his body was laid." Therefore, the time had to be extremely close to sunset. Luke continues his narrative stating that the women traveled back to their home and prepared spices and ointments and rested on the sabbath day in obedience to the commandment. Scroggie (1948, 572) declares that preparing the spices would entail grinding and cooking them, which will obviously require more time.

Where the women lived would be an important factor. One possibility is that the women lived in Bethany. At Bethany, Jesus often received hospitality in the house of his friends, Mary, Martha, and Lazarus; near this village Jesus ascended into heaven. This village is located fifteen furlongs or almost two miles east of Jerusalem, at the base of the southwestern slope of the Mount of Olives. Given that their home is in Bethany, the distance would be approximately two miles from the site of Golgotha.

If they walk at a brisk pace, the time to travel from Bethany to Golgotha would take the women at least one hour. Even if the location is elsewhere and just a mile away, it would still have required approximately thirty minutes for the women to reach their home. Fitzmyer (1985, 1530), also troubled by this timeline, writes: "When the women could have done this, after what has been said in v. 54b [["and the sabbath drew on"]], is a mystery; it may reveal something about Luke's understanding."

In conclusion, there was insufficient time for the women to travel back to their homes, prepare the spices and ointments, and prepare a meal before the commencement of the Sabbath.

ISSUE 40: The Visit to Pilate after Jesus Had Been Buried

Mk	Mt 27:62 *Now the next day, that followed the day of the preparation,* the *chief priests* and *Pharisees* came together unto Pilate.	Lk	Jn

Only Matthew records that several people went to visit Pilate the day after Jesus's crucifixion to request a guard. These people included the chief priests and an unknown number of Pharisees. Therefore, these members of the Jewish leadership met with Pilate on the Sabbath, the day following the preparation day. When did this visitation occur: Friday evening or Saturday morning? Allen (1893, 44) speculates: "As the Jewish day began at sundown, or some time Friday night. It is not reasonable that the chief priests allowed the grave to go unguarded during the night, and demanded the guard in the morning." Most commentators presume that the visit was held on Saturday morning.

CONTRADICTION #48 Christian Apologists Doubt Its Historicity

It is most noteworthy that even Christian apologists with impeccable credentials doubt the historicity of the visit to Pilate and the request of a guard. For example, Craig (1989b, 211) writes: "Matthew's account has been nearly universally rejected as an apologetic legend" but then adds a personal apologetic, "though the reasons for this assessment are of unequal worth." Jumping forward almost twenty years, Craig (1998, 211-12) was interviewed and specifically questioned about the controversy related to the guard at the tomb. His full comment bears sensible and thoughtful consideration:

> "Only Matthew reports that guards were placed around the tomb," he replied. "But in any event, I don't think the guard story is an important facet of the evidence for the Resurrection.

> For one thing, it's too disputed by contemporary scholarship. I find it's prudent to base my arguments on evidence that's most widely accepted by the majority of scholars, so the guard story is better left aside."

Similarly, John Wenham (1992, 79) openly and candidly admits that Matthew's story of the Roman guard "bristles with improbabilities at every point."

Plainly, these two Christian apologetic scholars raise doubt as to the veracity of Matthew's account.

CONTRADICTION #49 Historical Reliability

The visit of the Jewish leadership to Pilate on the Sabbath is doubtful. First, Matthew is the *only* gospel to record this remarkable event. In the eyes of Christian apologists, omission of facts by three of the four gospel narrators is considered to be a weak position by opponents of Jesus's resurrection since it is an argument based on silence. Carson (2010b, 654) further argues that "Matthew has regularly given information in the passion narrative that the other evangelists omit (e.g., vv.19, 34-35, 62-63); and it is methodologically wrong to doubt the historicity of all details that lack multiple attestation—not least because such 'multiple attestations' may sometimes go back to one literary source."

Craig also offers: "This may be the reason why the other evangelists omit it. In the circles they were writing for, the report circulated by the Jews may not have been current, so no explanation was necessary." However, Craig's apologetic is nothing more than an argument based on silence. First, it is impossible for detractors to provide evidence that the set of verses detailing the guard at the tomb is a piece of "creative writing" designed to provide "witnesses" to the Resurrection or that Jesus's body had not been stolen *if* the event never occurred. Second, making matters more difficult for opponents of Matthew's narrative, the account of the guard at the tomb was written approximately forty to fifty years after the supposed event occurred—Jerusalem had been destroyed and the population murdered, deported, and enslaved, and the remnants scattered over vast areas of geography.

Consequently, arguments of silence are, in fact, usually invalid. However, in this instance, the omitted details are exceptional. This event is uniquely significant because it serves as a strong proof text of Jesus's resurrection. That is, the tomb is guarded and, consequently, it is virtually impossible for anybody to have taken away the body. Therefore, the only way for the body to have left the tomb is by a miraculous resurrection.

Second, Christian apologetic texts that claim the historical reliability of the Christian scriptures often praise the accuracy and reliability of the author of Luke and Acts. Yet this highly significant event is omitted from these two works. Nonetheless, the apostle Luke is commonly referred to as a historian. As a matter of fact, the author of Luke claims in his preface to have investigated and had "a perfect understanding of all things from the very first." In addition, he unequivocally stated that his objective was to set right what others had declared. However, doubt is raised when the author of Luke/Acts who claims to have "had perfect understandings of all things from the very first" and who was writing in order that Theophilus might "know the certainty of those things" fails to mention that the chief priests and Pharisees went to Pontius Pilate on the Sabbath to request a guard at the tomb.

Craig (1984a, 276) offers the following Christian apologetic:

> Since the guard played virtually no role in the events of the discovery of the empty tomb - indeed the Matthean account does not exclude that the guard had already left before the women arrived -, the pre-Markan passion story may simply omit them. If the slander that the disciples stole the body was restricted to certain quarters ("the story has been spread among Jews [*para Ioudaiois*] to this day"), then it cannot be ruled out that Luke or John might not have these traditions. And the evangelists often inexplicably omit what seem to be major incidents that must have been known to them (for example, Luke's great omission of Mk 6:45-8:26) so that it is dangerous to use omission as a test for historicity.

Craig's last words bear careful decoding: Although "it is dangerous to use omission as a test for historicity," nonetheless, it should not be excluded as a factor in the totality of evaluating the historicity of an event. Contrary to Craig's apologetic, perhaps the author of Luke is, in fact, setting the record straight and stating that the events recorded in Matthew did not occur.

SPECULATION #78 The Apocrypha Supports the Guards at the Tomb

To counter the argument against the historicity of the visit to Pilate on the Sabbath, perhaps proponents of Matthew's narrative could argue that the story of the guard requested by Jewish leadership is attested by two of the apocryphal gospels of the second century: the *Gospel of the Hebrews* and the *Gospel of Peter*. Here, several scholars (Schaeffer 1991, 499 cited J. D. Crossan 1988; J. Denker 1975; Johnson 1965; and Koester 1980) posit and/or discuss the idea that the *Gospel of Peter* is older than Matthew and is essentially the source used by Matthew.

There are several obvious problems with this theory:

1. These texts belong to the Apocrypha and are not even recognized as part of scripture by the Protestant Church and hence are rejected by evangelical Christian fundamentalists.
2. The authorship of these works is unknown.
3. The source of their information is unknown.
4. Their details are possibly based on Matthew's text.
5. These noncanonical texts are estimated to have been published approximately ca. 80-150 CE and ca. 70-160 CE respectively, well after the commonly established date of Matthew.

SPECULATION #79 Matthew Writing for a Jewish Audience

The Christian apologists Ankerberg and Weldon (2005) posit that Matthew's account of the Sabbath visit to Pilate is absolutely logical. They state: "Writing for a Jewish audience, it would be perfectly consistent with Matthew's purpose to include an account of Jewish actions."

Despite the claims of Ankerberg and Weldon, there is absolutely no evidentiary proof that Matthew was written exclusively or primarily for a Jewish audience. Ankerberg and Weldon are challenged to provide incontrovertible evidentiary proof that it is likely the author of Matthew is dealing with *only* a Jewish audience to the exclusion of others. This Christian apologetic of Ankerberg and Weldon is nothing more than their *opinion*.

Richard Bauckham (1998, 9-48; 249-53; cf. Carson 2007, 49-50), in direct opposition, has vigorously challenged the scholarly "consensus" that each of the four gospels is written and addressed to a specific local church community. Specifically, is the Gospel of Matthew written for Matthew's own church, the so-called Matthean community. Instead, Bauckham contends that the Gospels are really intended for more general circulation throughout all the early churches and, hence, are written for all Christians. This hypothesis is shared by his colleagues Loveday Alexander, Stephen C. Barton, Richard Burridge, Michael B. Thompson, and Francis Watson.

SPECULATION #80 The Unusual Wording in Matthew

It is speculated that Matthew employed unusual wording in 27:62 to deliberately obscure the fact that he would have the Jewish leadership violating the Sabbath. According to the synoptic accounts, Saturday—the seventh day of the week, the sixteenth of Nisan—is the day that followed Jesus's crucifixion and is the second day of Passover. Matthew 27:62 states: "Now the next day, the day that followed the preparation, the chief priests and the Pharisees came to meet Pilate."

Numerous Christian commentators themselves are puzzled and ask, why then did Matthew write this sentence in such a bizarre manner? For example, Craig (1984a, 274) points out that "Matthew strangely circumnavigates the issue by calling it the day after the day of Preparation," and Giblin (1975, 412) "rendered somewhat ambiguous." More forcefully, Fuller (1971, 72) writes: "The opening phrase is curiously worded in a way that obscures the fact that the 'next day,' the day after the Preparation, was actually the Sabbath!" Similarly, Gundry (1994, 583) discusses the possibility that "the failure of the word 'Sabbath' to appear forestalls our thinking that he is portraying the chief priests and Pharisees as breaking the Sabbath by going to Pilate." Then Gundry adds: "Rather, he is compensating for omitting the reference to preparation in v 57 (cf. Mark 15:42)." In addition, it will be on the Sabbath, God's holy day of rest, when the chief priests and Pharisees would be traveling to visit Pilate to carry out their sinister plan.

ISSUE 41: The Chief Priests and Pharisees' Request That Pilate Secure the Sepulchre

Mk	Mt 27:63 Saying, sir, we remember that that *deceiver* said, while he was yet alive, After three days I will rise again. 64 Command therefore that the sepulchre be made secure until the third day, *least his disciples come by night, and steal him away, and say unto the people. He is risen from the dead: so the last error shall be worse than the first.*	Lk	Jn

Matthew was the only gospel that provides details of the chief priests and Pharisees presenting a request to Pilate. A plain meaning and natural reading of the text provides no indication that the Jewish leadership believed in a physical, bodily resurrection of Jesus or is convinced of any miracles that are attributed to him. Instead, according to Matthew 27:63, the Jewish leadership requests that the sepulchre containing the body of Jesus be made secure because they feared the disciples would (1) come by night and steal the body and (2) then they would declare to the people that Jesus had risen from the dead. The author of this narrative adds a clarification and elaboration as to why this request was made, to prevent "so the last error shall be worse than the first." Thus, as Morison (1930, 95) succinctly points out, "what the Priests are said to have sought of Pilate was not permission to remove the body, but to prevent it from being removed or stolen." Finally, it must be understood that to converse directly with Pilate without the use of a translator, the chief priests and Pharisees would have to speak in Greek or Pilate's ability to comprehend and respond to the Jewish leadership implies that he had the ability to speak Aramaic.

ISSUE 42: Pilate's Reply to the High Priests and Pharisees

Mk	Mt 27:65 Pilate said unto them, *Ye have a watch: go your way, make it as sure as ye can.*	Lk	Jn

The plain language of the dialogue here, and in the preceding verses, indicates that Pilate told them to secure the tomb: (1) the high priests and Pharisees request permission for the tomb to be secure (v. 64) and (2) it is your business, so take care of it yourself. Pilate thus accedes to the high priests and the Pharisees by granting permission for them to take a detachment of soldiers and make the tomb as secure as they knew how.

SPECULATION #81 The Meaning of Verse 65

A controversial and significant problem with Matthew's narrative is interpreting the meaning of verse 65: who would be guarding the tomb: Roman soldiers or Jewish guards from the Temple? For example, examine table 27:

TABLE 27. Translations of Matthew 27:65

VERSION	TRANSLATION	FOOTNOTES
AV	Pilate said unto them, *Ye have a watch*: go your way, make it as sure as ye can.	
NIV	*"Take a guard,"* Pilate answered. "Go, make the tomb as secure as you know how."	
NRSV	Pilate said to them, *"You have a guard*[j] of soldiers;* go, make it as secure as you can."[k]	[j] Or *Take a guard* [k] Gk *you know how*

The first question here is whether or not Pilate is saying to them "Take a guard" or "You have a guard." The second question is, does the former rendering imply that Pilate is placing Roman soldiers under Jewish control, or is he maintaining control but placating the wishes of the high priests and the Pharisees? If the former, the pertinent question is, would a Roman governor permit the Jewish leadership to control a Roman contingent of soldiers? Christian apologists, scholars, and theologians are divided on this matter. For example, Morison (1930, 155) is of the opinion that "Pilate *refused this request*" to send Roman soldiers. France (2007, 1095; cf. Carson 1984, 590-91; Cornfeld 1982, 178; Lee 1969, 173) offered: "But the fact that the guard will subsequently report back not to Pilate but to the priests (28:11), and that the governor's hearing of their failure is mentioned only as a possibility (28:14), makes it more probable that it was the temple guards that were used." Nonetheless, France adds in footnote 19, that "the majority of recent commentators suppose the troops to be Roman." In contrast to Morison, others (Allison 2004, 537; Brown 1994a, 2:1294-95; 1990a, 161; Craig 1984a, 273-81; Fowler 1985, 897; Gundry 1994, 592; McDowell 1981, 55; A. T. Robertson 1930a, 239; Turner 2005, 367) are convinced that a Roman guard was placed at the grave.

SPECULATION #82 The Sanhedrin Ordering Non-Jews to Work on the Sabbath

It is written in Exodus 20:8-10: "Remember the sabbath day, to keep it holy. Six days shalt thou labour, and do all thy work: But the seventh day is the sabbath of the LORD thy God: in it thou shalt not do any work, thou, nor thy son, nor thy daughter, thy manservant, nor thy maidservant, nor thy cattle, nor thy stranger that is within thy gates." Nonetheless, according to Christian apologists, members of the Sanhedrin, *perhaps* all of them, are now going to order non-Jews to work on the Sabbath in direct violation of God's instruction and in full public view. Such a blatant and deliberate violation of the Torah in public refutes the historicity of this legendary episode.

SPECULATION #83 Pilate's Cooperation with the Jewish Leadership

Pilate's willingness to enter into a scheme with members of the Sanhedrin, especially in view of his friendly attitude to Jesus at the trial, is dubious. For example, Sparrow-Simpson (1905, 98) cites Réville (1897), who states that he "does not think that Pilate would have been so condescending as to send the guards after his recent defeat by the Sanhedrin." It must be noted that in the Gospel of John (19:12), the Jews virtually threaten Pilate, implying that they would inform Rome and charge the governor with treason for seeking to release Jesus: "And from thenceforth Pilate sought to release him: but the Jews cried out, saying, If thou let this man go, thou art not Caesar's friend: whosoever maketh himself a king speaketh against Caesar." Even Craig (1984a, 274) writes: "If one might mention a psychological consideration, Pilate would probably be by this point so disgusted with the Jews that he might well rebuff them."

Another pertinent question is, why would Pilate grant a guard for something he surely would have found to be absurd? Caine (1938, 975-76) raises another point bearing consideration:

> Besides, that the story is incredible is apparent in the fact that it asks Pilate to enter into consideration of the *religious* issues concerned in Jesus's case. He knew nothing of such religious issues at the trial, while Jesus was alive. That these issues are now forced upon him in the story after Jesus is dead shows that it is a fabrication of Christian-Jewish minds, to whom the religious alone is present.

SPECULATION #84 Privileged Communication

Matthew's account involves reporting privileged conversations between the chief priests, the Pharisees, and Pilate that no Christian would have known. Where Matthew obtains his information is unknown and subject to speculation. Significantly however, Luke omits any mention of this event in his narrative. Further, Luke claims that he examined all of the oral and written traditions. Assuming that this statement is factual is remarkable if not extraordinary! That Luke deliberately omits such an important detail that could serve as a strong proof of Jesus's resurrection (i.e., that the tomb was guarded), if indeed he knew it to be true, is extraordinary. On the other hand, it makes perfect sense that Luke deliberately omits this event as a part of his narrative if, in fact, he doubts Matthew's sources.

ISSUE 43: Making the Sepulchre Secure

Mk	Mt 27:66 *So they went, and made the sepulchre sure, sealing the stone, and setting a watch.*	Lk	Jn

Matthew records that the high priests and Pharisees made the sepulchre secure. A two-step process achieved this securing of the tomb. First, the tomb is sealed with a stone. Second, a detachment of soldiers is set to watch the tomb.

CONTRADICTION #50 The Sanhedrin Performing Work on the Sabbath by Sealing the Tomb

Matthew 27:66 reads: "So they went, and made the sepulchre sure, sealing the stone, and setting a watch." As the text is literally read at face value in the AV, the high priests and the Pharisees themselves (i.e., "they," in person) accompany the soldiers and make the tomb secure, seal the stone, and set the watch. This action of sealing the tomb is taking place on the Sabbath. However, this action is work and in direct violation of God's command and deserves the death penalty:

> Ex 20:8-11 Remember the sabbath day, to keep it holy. Six days shalt thou labour, and do all thy work: But the seventh day is the sabbath of the LORD thy God: in it thou shalt not do any work, thou, nor thy son, nor thy daughter, thy manservant, nor thy maidservant, nor thy cattle, nor thy stranger that is within thy gates: For in six days the LORD made heaven and earth, the sea, and all that in them is, and rested the seventh day: wherefore the LORD blessed the sabbath day, and hallowed it.

> Ex 35:2 Six days shall work be done, but on the seventh day there shall be to you an holy day, a sabbath of rest to the LORD: whosoever doeth work therein shall be put to death.

> Num 15:32-36 And while the children of Israel were in the wilderness, they found a man that gathered sticks upon the sabbath day. And they that found him gathering sticks brought him unto Moses and Aaron, and unto all the congregation. And they put him in ward, because it was not declared what should be done to him. And they put him in ward, because it was not

declared what should be done to him. And all the congregation brought him without the camp, and stoned him with stones, and he died; as the LORD commanded Moses.

Deut 5:12-15 Keep the sabbath day to sanctify it, as the LORD thy God hath commanded thee. Six days thou shalt labour, and do all thy work: But the seventh day is the sabbath of the LORD thy God: in it thou shalt not do any work, thou, nor thy son, nor thy daughter, nor thy manservant, nor thy maidservant, nor thine ox, nor thine ass, nor any of thy cattle, nor thy stranger that is within thy gates; that thy manservant and thy maidservant may rest as well as thou. And remember that thou wast a servant in the land of Egypt, and that the LORD thy God brought thee out thence through a mighty hand and by a stretched out arm: therefore the LORD thy God commanded thee to keep the sabbath day.

Jer 17:21-22 Thus saith the LORD; Take heed to yourselves, and bear no burden on the sabbath day, nor bring it in by the gates of Jerusalem; Neither carry forth a burden out of your houses on the sabbath day, neither do ye any work, but hallow ye the sabbath day, as I commanded your fathers.

According to Matthew, this blatant, overt, and unabashed offense is literally taking place in the eyes of the public. It must be remembered that at this time the population of Jerusalem would have expanded from an estimated thirty thousand to over one hundred thousand people. Not only the population within the walled city of Jerusalem would have swollen, but so too would the area surrounding the hills of Jerusalem. Consequently it seems impossible for the public not to know about the violation of the Sabbath by the Jewish religious leadership.

The notion that the entire Jewish leadership blatantly transgressed the Sabbath in such an overt manner refutes its historicity (cf. Lachs 1987, 437).

SPECULATION #85 Rationale for Invention of the Guard Episode—Proof of the Resurrection

One of the foremost objectives of the Gospel of Matthew is to prove Jesus's resurrection. In order to fulfill this objective its author invented the episode of the guard at the tomb. Matthew 27:64 narrates that the purpose of the guard is to secure the tomb "least his disciples come by night, and steal him away, and say unto the people. He is risen from the dead: so the last error shall be worse than the first." However, this uniquely written episode is nothing more than a clever façade of the author.

Having a guard at the tomb suggests that Jesus's body could not have been stolen. Given that the body has not been stolen or the tomb mistaken for another, there is one explanation for it being empty: Jesus's miraculous resurrection from the dead. The presence of the guard is irrelevant. The issue of concern for Matthew is to create a fail-proof set of circumstances to prove that Jesus resurrected from the tomb.

SPECULATION #86 Rationale for Invention of the Guard Episode—Politics

What could possibly explain Matthew's invention of the guard at the tomb? Numerous explanations are possible, but for sake of space, this text will explore what is considered the most practical rationale. Pagels (1995, 81) posits that Matthew was written approximately between the years 80 and 90 CE. Therefore, the writing of this legendary episode is approximately ten to twenty years *after* the destruction of the Temple. The author of Matthew is now in direct competition with the new Jewish leadership, the Pharisees (i.e., the rabbis and sages), who now rival his teachings about Jesus.

For Matthew's author, Jesus embodied and fulfilled true righteousness as found in the Torah and the prophets. It is Jesus who "practices a greater righteousness, not a lesser one." Consequently, here and other places in the Gospels, the agenda is obvious: the Pharisees are represented as "hypocrites" and vilified for their evilness. It is the Pharisees who the Gospels constantly portray as obsessed with following the "letter of the law" as opposed to the "spirit of the law." In these few verses spanning 27:62-66, the author of Matthew ingeniously weaves an account in which the Pharisees are shown to openly and flagrantly violate a multiple of God's teachings. In direct contrast, Jesus's disciples and followers are reported as diligently observing the letter of "the law" by not working on the Sabbath.

> Mk 16:1 And when the sabbath was past, Mary Magdalene, and Mary the mother of James, and Salome, had bought sweet spices, that they might come and anoint him.

> Lk 23:56 And they returned, and prepared spices and ointments; and rested the sabbath day according to the commandment.

Finally, it is instructive to note that the author of Matthew employs the word Pharisee(s) thirty times. However, significantly, its author mentions the Pharisees only here (27:62) and nowhere else in the entire passion or postpassion accounts. Pagels's rationale (1995, 75-76) again bears repeating: the Pharisees become adversaries of the Christian communities only in the time of Matthew. Therefore, they are inserted here because they are the chief opponents of Matthew's church and surely skeptical about the claims of Jesus's resurrection.

SPECULATION #87 The Means of Securing the Tomb

Matthew reports that the high priests and Pharisees, perhaps all the members of the Sanhedrin, make the sepulchre secure by first sealing the stone. Details related to the stone were previously discussed in issues 35 and 36. The pertinent fact is that the stone is large.

Second, the tomb is secured by placing a guard or watch detachment at the tomb. Strong's number G2892 (Strong 1890, 43) matches the Greek κουστωδίας (*kŏustōdia*) for "a Roman *sentry*: — watch" which occurred three times in three verses in the Greek concordance of the KJV: Matthew 27:65, 66, and 28:11. Later Matthew 28:12 utilizes the Greek term στρατιώταις, *stratiōtēs*, for "(common *warrior* (lit. or fig.): — soldier" (Strong 1890, 67 #4757). No specific number of soldiers is presented by Matthew.

The single source of the episode definitely makes clear that there are more than two soldiers present at the tomb. This rationale is evident from Matthew 28:11, which reads: "Now when they were going, behold, some of the watch came into the city, and shewed unto the chief priests all the things that were done." Consequently, Matthew's statement about *some* of the watch means that others remained while still others, not "one of the guards," went into the city. In the opinion of Anthony Horvath (April 6, 2009), a Christian apologist, "for this to work it seems you would need at least *four* guards. If these are, in fact, Roman guards, then four is, in fact, the minimum that protocol would dictate, with each man taking three hours out of the night."

However, Horvath suggests that "if we begin to look at the matter from the basis of the evidence rather than from art work and conventional presentation I think it becomes clear that there were likely much more than four." For example, Matthew 27:64 reports that the Pharisees approach Pilate for guards because "otherwise, his disciples may come and steal the body and tell the people that he has been raised from the dead. This last deception will be worse than the first." Here, scholars admit the ambiguity in the Greek text. However, most Bible exegetes believe that the context affirms the reading that

Roman soldiers are dispatched. Horvath continues: "Please keep in mind that by 'a guard' it would be like saying a 'squad,' where the singular implies a plurality. Eg, if he had said 'Take a Legion' we wouldn't foolishly believe Pilate appointed just one man."

Horvath continues:

> Pilate then tells them to make the tomb as "secure as they know how." How many guards might we imagine they would decide to send if they were afraid of Jesus' disciples stealing the body? Well, at the minimum, you know there are 11 disciples out there, so I imagine if you are trying to thwart them that you would have at least as many soldiers as you had people you feared were coming. If you had half a brain (and I believe the Romans did in such affairs) you would send twice or thrice the amount. If you said twenty Roman guards here I think that would be a conservative but safe estimate.

> One of the other often forgotten dimensions is that this all occurred during the Passover, when Jerusalem becomes flooded with pilgrims. There are so many that they certainly cannot all fit inside the city walls. The hills are likely packed with people camping out (and since they are all dressed the same in accordance with purification rites, you see the need for Judas to lead the way and then kiss Jesus). Just a few days earlier all of Jerusalem was singing "Hosannah!" as Jesus entered the city. In other words, the Romans and chief priests both knew that Jesus didn't have only 11 disciples, but 11,000. Or more. How many guards would *you* send?

> Now we see coming into focus why when the facts roll in it becomes really difficult to believe the story that was circulated that Jesus' body was stolen. There were probably dozens of guards about. Even if sleeping the guards would have heard something. Rolling a heavy stone away (remember the women wondered how it was going to be done) would have required lots of grunting and probably the use of some tools. This is not a quiet endeavor. Then the disciples would have to slip away—with everyone of the guards remaining fast asleep—and not be spotted by any of the thousands of people camped out in the hillside. Imagine going to a July 4th festival and smuggling a dead body out without being spotted by anyone.

So it becomes more important than we may have realized to understand the real situation of the moment. It was the Passover. There were hundreds of thousands of pilgrims in town. Many of these were fans of Jesus. The Romans knew this. The Chief Priests knew this. *They would have posted guards proportional to the perceived threat.* [italics mine.]

How many? I am not going to get bogged down into trying to give a firm number. The Greek word here "custodian" seems to have a variety of uses and may or may not refer to a specific Roman military unit. In Acts 12:4 Herod dispatches "four squads of four soldiers each" to guard *one* man: Peter. If it was perceived that sixteen men were needed to watch just one of the disciples, one can only guess how many they thought were necessary to guard against a minimum of eleven. If pressed, I personally suspect that thirty to fifty guards were present; but even if there were only sixteen (per the Acts 12:4 model), it is virtually impossible to believe, seriously, that they *all* fell asleep and *remained* so as a bunch of disciples were slinking about, clawing at a honking big tombstone, and then extracting the body. We are talking about Roman soldiers here, after all.

Numerous writers (Dobson 1934, 68-69; Jeremiah 2013, 1332; Kane 1971, 8; MacArthur 1989, 322; McDowell 1981, 56; Muncaster 2000a, 18; 2000b, 20-21) maintain that a Roman guard unit is a four- to sixteen-man security force. This opinion is perhaps based on Acts 12:4. Bullinger (1914, 1379) writes: "a watch = a guard: the word being a transliteration of the Latin custodia, consisting of four soldiers" (Acts 12:4). In contrast, several writers (Cambron 1954, 105; Horne 1856, 243; Ralston 1924, 643; Wakefield 1869, 87) are of the opinion that the watch consists of sixty soldiers. However, Maas (1898, 310) points out: "The gospel of Nicodemus [I. B. 12] makes the number of soldiers 500; but the apocrypha usually exaggerate facts."

Third, the tomb is secured by placing the governor's seal on its entrance. McDowell (1981, 59) speculates that "after the guard inspected the tomb and rolled the stone in place, a cord was stretched across the rock. This was fastened at either end with sealing clay. Finally, the clay packs were stamped with the official signet of the Roman governor."

Matthew did not report whether or not the guards inspected the tomb and checked for the body before they put a seal on the closed tomb. Nolland (2005, 1239) assumes that the Jewish leadership and guard will have checked for the body on the other side of the stone before sealing it. Here the Gospel of Matthew is silent. Furthermore, it is instructive that Henten (2001, 159) points out: "Matthew's description of the grave's protection did not match any practice attested by archaeological or epigraphical sources."

ISSUE 44: The Women's Acquisition of Spices

Mk 16:1	Mt	Lk 23:55	Jn 19:39
And when the Sabbath was past, Mary Magdalene, and Mary the mother of James, and Salome, *had bought sweet spices*, that they might come and anoint him.		Lk 23:55 *And the women also, which came with him from Galilee,* followed after, and beheld the sepulchre, and how his body was laid. 56 *And they returned, and prepared spices and ointments; and rested the sabbath day* according to the commandment.	Jn 19:39 And there came also *Nicodemus*, which at the first came to Jesus by night, *and brought a mixture of myrrh and aloes,* about an hundred pound weight. 40 Then took they the body of Jesus, *wound it in linen clothes with spices*, as the manner of the Jews is to bury.

Mark 16:1 provides information that three women purchased sweet spices when the Sabbath had passed. Matthew omits any discussion of spices. In contrast, Luke has several unnamed women preparing the spices before sunset on Friday, the fifteenth of Nisan, the first day of Passover. Then, Luke 23:56 reports that on the Sabbath day (the sixteenth of Nisan), they "rested according to the commandment." Finally, John 19:39-40 omits any discussion of women. Instead he mentions that Nicodemus brought several spices which are used in preparing Jesus's body (see issue 29).

CONTRADICTION #51 Contradictory Historical Background

Mark's narrative declares that several women bought sweet spices after the Sabbath. In other words, as Hendriksen (1978, 1044) states, "The bazaars were open again." The first-century environment of Judea refutes any such possibility.

First, most people in the Ancient Near East go to sleep after it becomes dark and then awake in the morning at sunrise. Jeremias (1966, 44-46) elaborates that "in fact, it was customary to have two meals a day: a very simple breakfast between 10 and 11 a.m. and *the main meal in the late afternoon*." Jeremias (45n1) clarifies through various sources that the phrase *in the late afternoon* is meant "in the hours before evening," "toward evening," or "before evening." Later, when it becomes dark, people go to sleep. The notion that people will then go to their local merchants (bazaar, convenience store, or shopping center) during the evening simply does not occur in first-century Palestine. That is, twenty-four-hour convenience stores did *not* exist.

Second, this purchase is occurring after the Sabbath has past, and therefore it is now dark. Consequently, these women will now need to travel by night to find a merchant with a store that had reopened after the Sabbath. Again, merchants, like everyone else, will be sleeping at this time. Furthermore, there is another problem associated with the merchants: insufficient lighting to illuminate their merchandise. Merchants at this time did not have the convenience and luxury of modern electrical lighting. To the contrary of Mark's scenario, two thousand years ago such a purchase would not be plausible.

Craig's (1989b, 201) apologetic requires a completely different reading of Luke. He writes:

> Luke is the only other evangelist to mention the spices, and he also states that they had been prepared prior to the visit on the first day of the week (Lk. 24:1). The insertion of 23:56b gives the impression that the women prepared the spices on Friday night, but this is probably unintentional, since in v. 54 the sabbath was already beginning and Luke says in v. 56b they did not work on the sabbath. So there was no time to buy and prepare spices on Friday night. Rather v. 56b is probably to be taken as a parenthetical remark, not the narration of a chronologically successive event. The preparation of v. 56a was probably understood by Luke as taking place Saturday night, since Mark is quite clear. But by inserting his parenthetical remark on the pious behavior of the women he generates an apparent contradiction.

Craig's speculative and wishful thinking requires deconstruction:

1. The argument that the insertion of 23:56b gives the impression that the women prepared the spices on Friday night is "probably unintentional," is subjective, and avoids several unattractive alternatives: (1) Luke is deliberately writing a contradiction for unknown reasons, (2) Luke is deliberately recording a conflated

oral tradition, or (3) Luke or his redactor includes an error in the narrative.

2. Craig's claim that verse 56b is a parenthetical remark is pure speculation. To the contrary, it is, in fact, possible that Luke or his redactor meant that the narration is a chronological succession of events.

3. Contrary to Craig's apologetic, the preparation recorded in 56a is not meant by Luke to be understood as taking place Saturday night. Rather, Luke deliberately corrects and thus contradicts Mark. Therefore, Luke is declaring that the preparation did, in fact, occur on Friday.

CONTRADICTION #52 Mark Provides No Time to Purchase the Spices

Mark's chronology provides no time for the women to have purchased the spices. Mark 16:1 states: "And when the sabbath was past, Mary Magdalene, and Mary the mother of James, and Salome, had bought sweet spices, that they might come and anoint him." Technically, the Sabbath ends at sunset. Several writers (Geddert 2001, 392; Williams 1920, 12; Yeager 1982, 497) maintain that the shops would "reopen on Saturday evening." However, in first-century Jerusalem, during the evening, the markets and shops would have been closed. Unlike today, first-century merchants did not have the luxury of electrical lighting. Therefore, the only time to purchase these goods would have been early in the morning (cf. Driver 1965, 329) but no earlier than sunrise. This would be the first day of the work week. However, Mark 16:2 reported: "And very early in the morning the first day of the week, they came unto the sepulchre at the rising of the sun." Therefore, Mark's time line makes it impossible to have had sufficient time to purchase the spices.

CHAPTER 6

Saturday Evening until Sunday Morning

PREFACE: INCREASING CONTROVERSY OVER THE TIMELINES

The chronologies of the gospel narratives are in general agreement up until the sealing of the tomb and the women returning home to rest for the Sabbath. From this point on, there is increasing controversy over the timeline. Numerous biblical scholars, New Testament historians, theologians, and others openly acknowledge the impossibility of harmonizing the accounts found in the Christian scriptures.

First, this text will follow the general chronology of the synoptic accounts. Next, it shall examine John's narrative with Mary Magdalene's visit to the tomb and her encounter with the risen Jesus. Later, it will incorporate a chronology, attempting to harmonize 1 Corinthians 15:3-11, Acts 1, and the closing pericopes of the synoptic narratives.

In today's modern world with the conveniences of electrical lighting and clocks, the importance of sunrise and sunset is often overlooked. In ancient times, people were more attuned to nature. For these ancient people, the times of sunrise and sunset are highly significant. At approximately sunset, people went to sleep. In contrast, at sunrise people woke up to go to the fields to works. In addition, the notion that women were up in the middle of the night or before sunrise and traveling without male companions in the dead of dark was not typical of the time period.

ISSUE 45: When the Women Started Traveling to the Sepulchre

Mk 16:1 And when the *sabbath was past*, Mary Magdalene, and Mary the mother of James, and Salome, had bought sweet spices, that they might come and anoint him. *2 And very early in the morning the first day of the week, they came unto the sepulchre at the rising of the sun.*	Mt 28:1 In the end of the sabbath, *as it began to dawn toward the first day of the week,* came Mary Magdalene, and the other Mary to see the sepulchre. 2 And behold, there was a great earthquake: for the angel of the Lord descended from heaven, and came and rolled back the stone from the door, and sat upon it.	Lk 24:1 Now upon the first day of the week, *very early in the morning,* they came unto the sepulchre, bringing the spices which they had prepared, and certain others with them.	Jn 20:1 The first day of the week cometh Mary Magdalene early, *when it was yet dark,* unto the sepulchre, and seeth the stone taken away from the sepulchre.

None of the gospel narratives provide any facts detailing the exact moment that the women started traveling toward the tomb.

SPECULATION #88 When the Women Set Off for the Tomb

Mark declares that the women arrive at the sepulchre at the rising of the sun. Therefore, they had to have been traveling when it was dark. Matthew provides confusing details about the time the women were traveling: (1) the end of the Sabbath, which is post-Saturday at sunset, and (2) as the day (sun) began to dawn. The unknown is whether the women started traveling just after 6:00 p.m. Saturday or between 3:00 and 6:00 a.m. Sunday.

Carlton (2001, 326n839), writing in his *The Translator's Reference Translation of the Gospel of Matthew*, states: Since Jewish days began in the evening around

6:00 p.m., this translation would mean that the women are going to the tomb as it is *getting dark*." Similarly, Newman and Stine (1988, 876) writing in the United Bible Societies' *A Handbook on the Gospel of Matthew* writes:

> If this interpretation is accepted, then the events took place in the evening following the Sabbath day, and the scene is that of two women traveling in the darkness to visit the tomb. Thus Matthew's account would contrast with Mark's, according to which the three women purchased spices at the end of the Sabbath day, but did not actually take them to the tomb until early the next morning. This suggests that in this part of his narrative Matthew represents the earliest tradition, which was later succeeded by the more popular account of the early Sunday morning visit.

Luke narrates that several women came to the sepulchre very early in the morning. Hence, they had to start traveling when it was still dark, perhaps between 4:00 and 5:00 a.m. Finally, John reports that Mary Magdalene was traveling while it was still dark and thus approximately prior to 5:00 a.m.

ISSUE 46: When the Women Arrived at the Sepulchre

Mk 16:1 And when the *sabbath was past*, Mary Magdalene, and Mary the mother of James, and Salome, had bought sweet spices, that they might come and anoint him. 2 *And very early in the morning the first day of the week, they came unto the sepulchre at the rising of the sun.* 3 And they said among themselves, *Who shall roll us away the stone from the door of the sepulchre?* 4 And when they looked, they saw that the stone *was rolled away*: for it was very great.	Mt 28:1 In the end of the sabbath, *as it began to dawn toward the first day of the week*, came Mary Magdalene, and the other Mary to see the sepulchre. 2 And behold, there was a great earthquake: for the angel of the Lord descended from heaven, and came and rolled back the stone from the door, and sat upon it.	Lk 24:1 Now upon the first day of the week, *very early in the morning*, they came unto the sepulchre, bringing the spices which they had prepared, and certain others with them.	Jn 20:1 The first day of the week cometh Mary Magdalene early, *when it was yet dark*, unto the sepulchre, and seeth the stone taken away from the sepulchre.

The gospel narratives unanimously agree that several women went to the tomb on the first day of the week. John records Mary Magdalene's arrival at the tomb early Sunday "when it was yet dark." In contrast, Matthew describes the visitation at the tomb as the day began to dawn. On the other hand, Luke only declares that it was "very early in the morning" when the women arrive at the sepulchre. In agreement with Luke, Mark records that visitors arrive very early in the morning but adds that simultaneously there is "the rising of the sun."

TABLE 28. Chronological Order of the Time of Arrival

GOSPEL	DESCRIPTION of the WOMEN'S TIME of ARRIVAL
John	Early, when it was yet dark.
Matthew	As it began to dawn (sunlight begins lighting the sky).
Luke	Very early in the morning.
Mark	Very early in the morning at the rise of the sun (i.e., the sun itself becomes visible).

The National Oceanic and Atmospheric Administration's (NOAA) (2009) Relevant Astronomical Terms, Illustrated Terms and Specific Times in Order from Darkness to Light state:

Nautical Twilight

> The time after civil twilight, when the brighter stars used for celestial navigation have appeared and the horizon may still be seen. It ends when the center of the sun is 12 degrees below the horizon, and it is too difficult to perceive the horizon, preventing accurate sighting of stars.

Sunset

> The phenomenon of the sun's daily disappearance below the western horizon as a result of the earth's rotation. The word [[sunset]] is often used to refer to the time at which the last part of the sun disappears below the horizon in the evening at a given location.

Astronomical Dusk

> This is the time at which the sun is 18 degrees below the horizon in the evening. At this time the sun no longer illuminates the sky.

Astronomical Dawn

The time the sun is 18 degrees below the horizon in the morning. Astronomical dawn is that point in time at which the sun starts lightening the sky. Prior to this time during the morning, the sky is completely dark.

Nautical Dawn

The time in which the sun is 12 degrees below the horizon in the morning. Nautical dawn is defined as that time at which there is just enough sunlight for objects to be distinguishable

Civil Dawn

The time of morning in which the sun is 6 degrees below the horizon. At this time, there is enough light for objects to be distinguishable and that outdoor activities can commence.

Sunrise

The phenomenon of the sun's daily appearance on the eastern horizon is a result of the earth's rotation. The word [sunrise] is often used to refer to the time at which the first part of the sun becomes visible in the morning at a given location.

Illustration 3. Types of Twilight

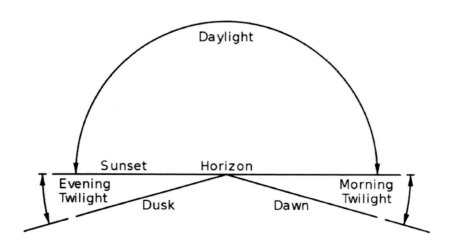

TABLE 29. Thursday, April 1, 2010 [The Third Day of Passover Corresponding to the Women's Traveling and Arrival at the Tomb]

NOAA Terminology	Thursday, April 1, 2010
Astronomical twilight (=starts at Astronomical Dawn)	Begins at 5:06 a.m.
Nautical twilight (=starts at Nautical Dawn)	Begins at 5:35 a.m.
Civil twilight (=starts at Civil Dawn)	Begins at 6:04 a.m.
Sunrise	Starts at 6:28 a.m. in direction 84° East

CONTRADICTION #53 Contradictory Arrival Time

The gospel narratives present contradictory information about the *arrival* time of the women at the tomb. John 20:1 reports: "The first day of the week cometh Mary Magdalene early, *when it was yet dark*, unto the sepulchre, and seeth the stone taken away from the sepulchre." Therefore, John has an arrival at the tomb early Sunday when it is "yet dark" (*prōi skōtias eti ousēs*). In other words, it is still prior to what is technically termed "astronomical dawn," or the point in time at which the sun starts lightening the sky.

Matthew's narrative in 28:1 states: "In the end of the sabbath, as *it began to dawn* toward the first day of the week, came Mary Magdalene, and the other Mary to see the sepulchre." Boyarin (2001, 688), on philological grounds favors at different reading: "at the end of the Sabbath, at the beginning of the first day of the week." However, Mann (1986, 664) succinctly identifies a problem with this text:

> Matt 28:1 has *opse de Sabbatōn, te epi phōskouse eis mia Sabbatōn* (after the Sabbath, and toward dawn on the first day of the week). The problem with Matthew's text is that *opse* can mean "after" and equally can mean "late," though presumably when followed by *epi phōskouse* it means "after." But what is the "first day of the week"? Does Matthew follow the Jewish calendar (in which case the "first day of the week" will be after about 6:00 p.m. on Saturday) or the Roman calendar—which would then give us 3-6 a.m. on Sunday?

Keeping in mind just the morning scenario, it is clearly no longer dark and sunrise has not yet occurred. [NB. The Hebrew term '*alot ha-shahar* (the rising of the morning) denotes the period immediately before sunrise (comp. Gen 19:15, 23.)]

Mark 16:2 narrates: "And *very early in the morning the first day* of the week, they came unto the sepulchre *at the rising of the sun.*" This narrative clarifies for Mark's readers that the moment the women arrive at the tomb is *later* in the morning than Matthew reported since it refers to the *rising* of the sun. The key point is that the sun has *already* risen. Technically, Mark declares that the women arrive at the tomb when it is *sunrise* and *part of the sun is visible*. Therefore, at this time, there is enough light for objects to be distinguishable and outdoor activities to commence [NB. For comparison, the sunrise in Jerusalem on Nisan 17 = April 1, 2010 was at 6:28 a.m. in direction 84° East].

Commenting on this timeline, Mann (1986, 664) writes: "*Lian prōi (very early)* would seem to suggest something between 3 a.m. and 6 a.m., with preference being given to the earlier hours (cf. 1:35). But this is contradicted by *just after (or at) sunrise* (Greek *anateilantos tou hēliou)*." Similarly, Lane (1974, 585) writes: "Normally 'very early' refers to the earlier part of the period 3:00-6:00 a.m., prior to sunrise (cf. Ch. 1:35)" as did Edward's (2002, 492) "the time between 3 and 6 a.m., but here it is qualified by 'just after sunrise.'" Also, Brooks (1991, 269) states: "The words translated 'very early' usually refer to the two or three hours before sunrise (3:00 a.m. to 6:00 a.m.: cf. 1:35) but they cannot do so in conjunction with 'just after sunrise.'" Finally, Evans (2001, 534) opts for the women having "set out for the tomb around 5:00 a.m. Since it is so early in the morning, the women must have bought their spices Saturday evening 'when the sabbath was past'" (v 1).

Luke 24:1 makes no mention of the sun. Instead, Luke reports that it is *very early in the morning*" when the women came to the sepulchre. Mann (1986, 664) renders Luke's 24:1 *orthrou batheōs* as "at first light." Consequently, Luke is implying or referring to either sunrise or sometime *after* sunrise, approximately 6:30 to 8:00 a.m.

Therefore, the gospel narratives contain at least four contradictions:

- Mark cannot be John because "at the rising of the sun" contradicts "when it was yet dark."
- Luke cannot be John because at very early in the morning contradicts "when it was yet dark."
- Matthew contradicts John because "as it began to dawn" is not the same thing as "when it was yet dark."
- Matthew contradicts Mark and Luke because "as it began to dawn" is not the same thing as "very early in the morning."

In *Answers to Tough Questions Skeptics Ask about the Christian Faith*, the Christian apologists Josh McDowell and Don Stewart (1980, 53) attempt to answer the question as to when the women arrive at the tomb:

> One of the seeming contradictions that bothers people concerns the time the women came to the tomb, related differently by John and Mark. Mark's account has the women coming to the tomb at the rising of the sun, while John states that Mary Magdalene came to the tomb when it was dark.
>
> This difficulty is solved when it is realized that the women had to walk quite some distance to reach the grave, since they stayed in Jerusalem or Bethany. It was dark when they left the place in which they were staying, but when they arrived at the tomb the sun was beginning to shine. Therefore, Mark is speaking of their arrival, while John refers to their departure.

Also, addressing these contradictions, the Christian apologists Ankerberg and Weldon (2005 Pt 1) write:

Further, if the women lived different distances from the tomb, then when they each started their journey, the time factor would have been slightly different. Notice, each writer was free to report the time the women left their homes and started their journey, the time during any part of the journey itself, or the time when they arrived at the tomb.

Finally, each Gospel writer could have received the information from which he wrote his account from one or more of the women. Each woman would naturally tell the event from her perspective, mentioning the details that seemed relevant to her and omitting the others. [Bold in the original.]

However, R. T. France (2002, 677), a conservative Christian apologist, challenges the above apologetic rationales:

But Mark's additional phrase ἀνατείλαντος τοῦ ἡλίου assures us that it was already light, so that they could see clearly;[25] even John has Mary 'seeing' the stone on her arrival.

25. The suggestion that λίαν πρωΐ describes the time when they set out (before dawn) and ἀνατείλαντος τοῦ ἡλίου the time when they reached the tomb (just after the sun rose) is plausible in itself, but is not what Mark actually says. For Mark's habit of adding a second clause to define a statement of time cf. 1:32, 35; 14:12; 15:42.

Finally McDonald and Porter (2000, 183) analyze two explanations that Lilly (1940, 99-111) offers for the difference between Mark and John. They write:

First, he says it is possible that while the women were on their way to the tomb, they needed to purchase the spices. Mary Magdalene left this task to the other women and went to the tomb by herself, and the others came later, 'when the sun had risen,' to join her. His second explanation is derived from a possible translation of ἔρχεται πρωΐ σκοτίας ἔτι οὔσης (*erchetai prōi skotias eti ousēs*) in John 20:1. If Mary 'is on her way before daylight,' then, according to Lilly, the emphasis is on the *beginning* of the journey to the tomb, while it was still dark. Lilly's first explanation, however, is foreign to Mark, who writes that the women went (3rd per.

pl. ἔρχονται, *erchontai*, here 'they went') to the tomb when the sun had risen. Mark makes no room for a separation or parting of the women. Lilly's second explanation which emphasizes the present tense of ἔρχουται (John 20:1), fails to consider that such a literalistic translation, even if possible in this context, would demand that he translate ἔρχουται in Mark 16:2 with the same present force. If this were done, the women in Mark would begin their trip 'when the sun had risen' and Mary in John would begin her journey 'while it was still dark.' Such explanations are not convincing: they do not seem to make a coherent explanation of the differences or allow them to stand in the text.

To recapitulate, Mark 16:2 reads: "And very early in the morning the first day of the week, they came unto the sepulchre at the rising of the sun." In contrast, John 20:1 states: 'The first day of the week cometh Mary Magdalene early, when it was yet dark, unto the sepulchre, and seeth the stone taken away from the sepulchre." Clearly both accounts are referring to the time of the women's arrival; their time of departure is of no consequence. Thus, the apologetics of McDowell and Stewart and Ankerberg and Weldon is worthless. There are definite and incontrovertible contradictions between the Gospel narratives. Either it is dark or not dark when the women *arrive* at the tomb.

SPECULATION #89 An Evening Visit to the Tomb

An analysis of the Vulgate Bible and various concordances (Strong's, Young's) and standard lexicons (Bauer's, Lindell and Scott, Mounce, Thayer's) substantiates the possible hypothesis that Matthew is, in fact, talking about an evening visit by the women to the tomb. For example, Ranke-Heinemann (1994, 136) writes:

> As it was understood back then, the day after the Sabbath, the first day of the week, began immediately after the end of the Sabbath; and the Sabbath ended at sundown on Saturday evening. The new day was said to "shine forth," not with the dawn but when the first stars could be seen.
>
> Matthew uses the same verb for "shine forth" (*epiphoskein*) that Luke uses at the end of his description of the taking down of Jesus' body from the cross: "It was the day of Preparation, and

the sabbath was beginning" (Luke 23:54). The Sabbath began or "shone forth" not on the next morning, but immediately after the day of Preparation, which in turn ended with nightfall. No one would claim here that the Sabbath did not begin until the next morning, and that Jesus must now have been taken down from the cross until the next morning...

Jerome understood Matt. 28:1 correctly and translated it in the Vulgate, "Vespere autem sabbati" (on the eve of the Sabbath), but today the passage is falsely translated almost everywhere else as "Now after the sabbath, toward the dawn of the first day of the week, Mary Magdalene and the other Mary went to see the sepulchre." In the original Greek text, however, there is not the least mention of dawn.

However, an evening visit creates a problem. The Jewish day begins at sunset, which would mean that the women bought the spices as soon as the shops opened in the evening, planning to do the anointing in the morning when it was light. In the opinion of Williams (1920, 12), shops would "reopen on Saturday evening." So too Brooks (1991, 268) declares that "the shops reopened briefly after the conclusion of the Sabbath." However, shops could not be open at that time for business because there is no sufficient lighting. Besides, evening time is when people go to sleep. Furthermore, traveling at night to a shop would entail the women carrying a torch to light their way to and from the shop. However, the specific detail that it was "late on the sabbath would mean just before sunset, not shortly before dawn. The Jewish day began and ended at sunset" (Beare 1981, 541-42).

Similarly, Winger (1994, 285), writing in *New Testament Studies*, points out: "The difficulty is that in their primary meanings, Matthew's two temporal clauses have inconsistent senses: *opse* means 'late,' and *epiphoskein* means 'to grow light,' so that v. 1 reads: 'Late on the sabbath, as it was becoming light on the first day of the week . . .' But, assuming that the Jewish day is here in view, this is impossible: the Jewish day begins at sunset."

Finally, Gundry (1994, 585-86) concludes:

Mark 16:2 goes on to indicate that after purchasing the spices on Saturday evening, the women came to the tomb early the next morning. Matthew obliterates this temporal shift. For the time being the names of Mary Magdalene, Mary the mother of James, and Salome drop out, and their buying spies and intending to anoint Jesus vanish permanently. Furthermore, Mark's, καὶ λίαν πρωῖ τῇ μιᾷ τῶν σαββάτων, "And exceedingly early on the first [day] of the week," becomes . . ., "as [the day] was developing into the first [day] of [the] week." Since the first day of the week started at sunset on Saturday, the women come and discover the empty tomb at the time initially indicated, viz., Saturday evening. Matthew's advancing their discovery of the empty tomb from early Sunday morning to Saturday evening is confirmed by his omitting "when the sun had risen" at the close of Mark 16:2...

SPECULATION #90 Why the Women Left Early for the Tomb

The gospel narratives (Mk 16:1-2; Mt 28:1; Lk 24:1; Jn 20:1) unmistakably report that the women left for the tomb or arrived "early in the morning." The question is, why did the women leave so early? There are at least two speculative explanations as to why the women are described as having left so early in the morning to reach the tomb.

First, all the gospel authors want to demonstrate the women's reverence and devotion to Jesus. (Edwards 2002, 491) Second, these authors have the women mimicking a common Biblical motif of arising early in the service of God or arising because of an issue of pressing concern. These and other examples of arising early can be found in table 30.

TABLE 30. Arising Early Motif

VERSE	PERSON ARISING EARLY	TEXT
Gen 20:8	Abimelech	Therefore, Abimelech rose early in the morning, and called all his servants, and told all these things in their ears: and the men were sore afraid.
Gen 22:3	Abraham	And Abraham rose up early in the morning, and saddled his ass, and took two of his young men with him, and Isaac his son, and clave the wood for the burnt offering, and rose up, and went unto the place of which God had told him.
Ex 34:4	Moses	And he hewed two tables of stone like unto the first; and Moses rose up early in the morning, and went up unto mount Sinai, as the LORD had commanded him, and took in his hand the two tables of stone.

| Josh 6:12 | Joshua | And Joshua rose early in the morning, and the priests took up the ark of the LORD. |
| Dan 6:19 | King Darius | Then the king arose very early in the morning, and went in haste unto the den of lions. |

ISSUE 47: The Women Who Specifically Went to the Tomb

Mk 16:1	Mt 28:1 In the end	Lk 24:1 Now upon the first day	Jn 20:1 The first
Mary Magdalene, and Mary the mother of James, and Salome, had bought sweet spices, that they might come and anoint him.	of the sabbath, as it began to dawn toward the first day of the week, came *Mary Magdalene, and the other Mary* to see the sepulchre.	of the week, very early in the morning, *they came* unto the sepulchre, bringing the spices which *they had prepared, and certain others with them.* Lk 24:10 *It was Mary Magdalene, and Joanna, and Mary the mother of James, and other women that were with them,* which told these things unto the apostles.	day of the week *cometh Mary Magdalene early,* when it was yet dark, unto the sepulchre, and seeth the stone taken away from the sepulchre.

Mark 16:1 specifically names three women who travel to the tomb: Mary Magdalene, Mary, the mother of James, and Salome. In contrast, Matthew 28:1 reduces the number of women from three to two, Mary Magdalene and the "other" Mary. However, Luke 24:10 specifically names three women who are present, Mary Magdalene, Joanna, and Mary, the mother of James. In addition, Luke adds the phrase "and other women that were with them." Therefore, there had to have been a minimum of two additional women accompanying the three named visitors since the phrase "and other women that were with them" denotes a plurality. Consequently, Luke has at least five women visiting the tomb and possibly more. Why Luke omits the name of Salome is unknown. On the other hand, John specifically names only one person who went to the tomb, Mary Magdalene.

CONTRADICTION #54 Contradictory Testimony

The gospel writers present contradictory facts regarding the women visitors at the tomb: the number of visitors as well as the names of the visitors (see table 31 below). Christian apologists often present two rationales, attempting to explain the divergent testimony: (1) omission of facts is not a contradiction and (2) the narratives exemplify four witnesses of a car accident (see topic 9).

As previously discussed, these apologetics are deceptive, erroneous, and fallacious. First, the authors of the narratives are recognized only as anonymous writers. Consequently, their testimony is invalid. Second, it is acknowledged by scholars (Boring and Craddock 2009, 105; Burkett 2002, 121; deSilva 2004, 194; Hurtado 2006, 27; Perrin and Dulling 1982, 42; Pregeant 2009, 111) that the anonymous authors are not witnesses to the events they record. Third, the narrators are either recorders of evolving oral traditions that spanned approximately thirty to seventy years after the event (or, in the eyes of Christian apologists, actual firsthand eyewitnesses). Yet another explanation is that the gospel writers were writing a legendary account. Gundry (1994, 623-40) has termed these legendary accounts as "Midrash." Fourth, the accounts, especially John's as compared to the synoptic Gospels, read like entirely different stories. Fifth, the Hebrew scriptures and Jewish law required confirmation of details in a court of law. Collectively, these facts refute the accounts recorded in the Gospel narratives.

TABLE 31. The Visitors to the Tomb

GOSPEL	THE NUMBER OF VISITORS	THE NAMES OF THE VISITORS
Mark	3	Mary Magdalene, Mary the mother of James, and Salome.
Matthew	2	Mary Magdalene and the other Mary.
Luke	At least five women.	Mary Magdalene, Joanna, and Mary the mother of James.
John	1	Mary Magdalene.

SPECULATION #91 The Women's Names

What can explain the varying accounts of the named women who came to the tomb as narrated in the Gospels? There is an explanation based on the work of Allison (1985, 27). He points out that Mark's narrative is characterized by triadic patterns as exemplified in list of female witnesses (15:40-41, 47; 16:1). Previous examples of his triadic patterns include: the three denials of Peter (Mk 15:68, 70); the three scenes of mockery (14:65; 15:16-20, 29-32); the three questions of Pilate (15:9-14); the three utterances of the high priest (15:60, 61, 63); the three pericopes concerning the activity of Judas (14:10-11, 17-21, 43-47); and perhaps the three times of prayer in Gethsemane (14:35, 36, 39). Therefore, perhaps, Mark's narrative is based on a literary style.

Another explanation for two of the names of the women is also seen through a literary lens: Mary Magdalene and Salome. Mary Magdalene is a name subject to speculation. Who was she and where did she come from? According to the Gospel narratives, she is the most prominent Galilean female follower of Jesus. In fact, Mary Magdalene is mentioned in five out of six gospel narratives and, when mentioned, is always the first person named (O'Collins and Kendall 1987, 634; also see Fitzmyer 1985, 2:1535-37). In Aramaic, Magdalene refers to "one from Magdala." However, Blair (1969, 221), writing for *The Interpreter's Dictionary of the Bible*, states that "Magdala is not mentioned in the gospels or in Josephus (Magdala' in Matt 15:39 KJV should read 'Magadan' as in אBD; so RSV). In the Talmud, Magdala is located near Tiberias and is called Migdal Nunya' ('fish tower'); Pes[[ahim]] 46a." Furthermore, Goulder (1976, 211) points out that "women in the NT world were identified by their fathers' name or their husbands' name." On the other hand, Richard Fellows (n.d.) argues that Magdalene was rather a nickname signifying that she is a tower of strength.

Another speculation by Goulder (1976, 212) is that Mary Magdalene's name may perhaps be based on an account in Exodus: "Where did the Israelites cross the Red Sea? 'Speak to the children of Israel, and let them turn and encamp before the village, between Magdolos and the sea . . .' (Exod. 14.2) It was at Magdolos, Migdol, the Tower: Mary will have come from Migdol, the Tower, Magdala-by-the-sea in Galilee."

Goulder (1976, 211) suggests another possible connection with Moses's sister, Miriam, and the two Marys in Mark 15:40. The question that arises is, are the similarities between the two *Miriams* a mere coincidence or a deliberate literary creation?

TABLE 32. Parallels between Mary Magdalene and Moses's Sister Miriam

MIRIAM	MARY
Miriam, who, when Moses was earlier consigned to the water in his ark, watched from afar, to learn what had happened to him (Ex 2:4).	The witnesses of Jesus's death, burial, and resurrection must have been women watching from afar, and one of them must have been called Miriam.
[Another] great type of resurrection is the crossing of the Red Sea at the first Passover, and the great work of Yahweh was then celebrated by the prophetess Mariam who answered the women, "Sing ye to the LORD for he hath triumphed gloriously" (*ga'oh ga'ah*, Ex 15:21).	The post-resurrected Jesus and the empty tomb.

However, Stecchini and Sammer (1996) raise another point regarding the name of Mary Magdalene.

> The name Mary Magdalene means "Mary, a native or a resident of Magdala"—but it must be emphasized that the word Magdalene has a Latin ending. Only in Latin is it possible to derive from the noun Magdala an adjective Magdalena, meaning "woman from Magdala." This evident fact has not been called to attention by commentators, because for *a priori* reasons they have not considered the possibility that the gospels drew on a source written in Latin.

Another rationale for these names is based on their Hebrew meaning. Derrett (1991, 213; cf. Opočenská 1997, 44) adds that "the Hebrew *Miryam* (if not Egyptian) derives from the root MRR (*Pesiqta Rabbati* 15.11), which implies 'bitterness.'" *Thayer's Lexicon* defined the Hebrew name of Miriam (i.e., Mary) as "obstinacy" and "rebelliousness." In contrast, the name Salome extracted from the Hebrew *shalom* means "peaceful." Therefore, these names are possibly a literary device employed by the author.

Yet Goulder (1976, 212) offers another rationale, saying that the name Salome may be related to an earlier biblical account:

> Who in the Bible is the great bringer of spices to Israel? It is Solomon (1 Kgs 10:25), Solomon the author of the Song which is still recited at Passovertide, of whom it is said, "Thine ointments have a goodly fragrance; thy name is ointment poured forth" (Cant 1.3)? Will not one of the women then have borne Solomon's name, and be called Shelomith, Salome? But she is a late arrival on the scene, and has no patronymic. Matthew makes her the mother of the sons of Zebedee, who was perhaps known to have been so called.

ISSUE 48: Why the Women Went to the Sepulchre

Mk 16:1 And when the sabbath was past, Mary Magdalene, and Mary the mother of James, and Salome, had bought sweet spices, *that they might come and anoint him.*	Mt 28:1 In the end of the sabbath, as it began to dawn toward the first day of the week, came Mary Magdalene, and the other Mary *to see the sepulchre.*	Lk 24:1 Now upon the first day of the week, very early in the morning, they came unto the sepulchre, *bringing the spices which they had prepared,* and certain others with them.	Jn 20:1 The first day of the week cometh Mary Magdalene early, when it was yet dark, unto the sepulchre, and seeth the stone taken away from the sepulchre.

Why did the women go to the sepulchre? What was their errand? Mark 16:1 plainly states that the purpose of their visit is to anoint Jesus's body. Therefore the women *did not* bring spices to reduce or eliminate the odor of Jesus's decomposing body in order to make it bearable to be within the tomb. In contrast, Matthew 28:1 claims that the women came to see or view the sepulchre. The author of Luke 24:1 mentions that the women came to the tomb with the spices they had earlier prepared. However, Luke does not state the explicit reason that the women brought the spices with them. Finally, the author of John provides no explanation for the visit of Mary Magdalene.

CONTRADICTION #55 Contradictory Testimony

The gospel writers present contradictory facts regarding the women's purpose to visit the tomb (see table 33).

TABLE 33. Why the Visitors Went to the Tomb

GOSPEL	WHY THE VISITORS WENT TO THE TOMB
Mark 16:1	The visitors came "that they might come and *anoint him.*"
Matthew 28:2	The visitors came "to *see the sepulchre.*"
Luke 23:56	No explicit reason. However, Luke's mentioning of spices indicated that he probably understood and agreed with Mark.
John	No reason.

Christian apologists often present two rationales, attempting to explain the divergent narratives: (1) the omission of a fact is not a contradiction and (2) the narratives exemplify four witnesses of a car accident. Once again it bears repeating that their apologetics are not sustainable.

First, omission of facts by a later writer or witness could have been a deliberate effort to contradict or correct an earlier source. The problem here is that this argument is based on silence. Second, the authors of these narratives are recognized as anonymous writers. Consequently, their testimony is invalid. Third, it is recognized that the anonymous authors are not witnesses to the events. Instead, they are recorders of evolving oral traditions that grew approximately thirty to seventy years after the event. Fourth, the accounts, especially John's as compared to the synoptic Gospels, read like entirely different stories. Fifth, the Hebrew scriptures and Jewish law requires confirming details of at least two witnesses in a court of law. Collectively, these arguments refute the narratives that are recorded in the Gospels.

SPECULATION #92 The Women's Purpose

Commentators vary in their explanation of why the women went to the sepulchre. Mark thinking that it is to *anoint* Jesus's body directly parallels the agenda of its author as openly declared in the very first sentence of his gospel (Mk 1:1): "declaring the good news that Jesus is the Christ and the Son of God." Significantly the word *Christ* is a translation from the Hebrew word *Mashiach* (or in English the Messiah) which means *anointed*!

Gundry (1994, 582, 586) speculates that Matthew's claim that the women coming to *see* or *gaze* at the sepulchre demonstrates their continuing vigil and exemplifies true discipleship: "In Mark the women merely observe the location of Jesus' burial" whereas "In Matthew they sit opposite the grave in vigil." However, Gundry (p. 586) points out that Matthew setting a guard at the tomb and the sealing of its stone necessitates this change from Mark. According to Gundry, "The concern has switched from the state of Jesus' corpse to the state of the tomb. Since the Jewish authorities had taken precautions to make the tomb secure, the resurrection of Jesus again looks all the more impressive in Matthew."

Although Luke did not specifically state the reason the women brought the spices with them, it can be speculated that he too is *implying* that they came to anoint the body. Therefore, both Mark and Luke seemingly have their purpose for completing the burial rites (i.e., anointing Jesus's body).

The intention to anoint a body that had already been anointed and one that had been dead for two nights and one day has been questioned. For example, Taylor (1953, 604; cf. Elliott 1982, 79; Hooker 1991, 383) writes that "it is hard to credit the women with the intention of going to anoint the body a day and two nights after death."

Another problem with the purpose of anointing relates to the issue of the linen. According to the Gospels, Jesus's body is washed (Jn 19:40; cf. Acts 9:37), wrapped in fine linen (Mk 15:46) and clean linen cloth (Mt 27:59), and the cloth mixed with the spices (Jn 19:40). *It does not make sense for the women to unwrap a previously properly prepared body, anoint it, and then re-wrap the body with the now unclean and used (stained) linen.* Furthermore, there is no indication that the women brought new linen with them to complete the burial process.

Christian apologists offered two common defenses. First, Craig (1989b, 204) and Gundry (1993, 997) point out that, coupled with its elevation, the temperature in Jerusalem during the evening is cool. However, the temperature inside Jesus's tomb may have been much warmer than sixty-five degrees Fahrenheit. Therefore, Lowder (2005, 289) writes: "Unfortunately, given the lack of meteorological records from the time, one can only speculate on what the temperature would have been inside Jesus' tomb." Furthermore, Lowder points out that the decomposition of the body was known to occur after several days. For example, he cites Midrash Rabbah Genesis C:7 (994) that states that facial features of a corpse become disfigured in three days.

Second, Cranfield (1959, 464) offers that to anoint a body after such a length of time "is not incredible, since love often prompts people to do what from a practical point of view is useless." Similarly, Brooks (1991, 268; cf. Carmichael 1980, 49) declares "but love often causes irrational actions." However, this is a speculation based on silence.

Another possible reason the women brought their spices is to reduce the odor of the decomposing body in order to complete their undeclared task. Here Gundry (1993, 997) mentions that "in fact, the buying of aromatics, not oils, implies the purpose of counteracting a stench, as in the use of aromatics to counteract the stench of Alexander's corpse."

Finally, John's lack of an explanation for a visit made perfect sense since he reported in 19:40 that Jesus's body had already been properly prepared by Joseph and Nicodemus in the manner of the Jews: "Then took they the body of Jesus, and wound it in linen clothes with the spices, as the manner of the Jews is to bury."

ISSUE 49: The Question in Mark the Women Asked Themselves on the Way to the Sepulchre

Mk 16:3 And they said among themselves, *Who shall roll us away the stone from the door of the sepulchre?*	Mt	Lk	Jn

A question asked by the women as they approach the tomb appears only in Mark. The question is "Who shall roll us away the stone from the door of the sepulchre?"

SPECULATION #93 Why the Women Did Not Bring People with Them

Matthew 27:61 reports that the women were literally "sitting over against the sepulcher" after the tomb was closed. Therefore, it would be impossible for them *not* to know the size of the stone and not be cognizant of the impracticality of the women to move it. Therefore, Moiser (1995, 237) writes: "if the women were aware beforehand of the difficulty of removing the stone, why did they not summon some male disciples to accompany them? The presence of the latter in Jerusalem is implied in v. 7": "But go your way, tell his disciples and Peter that he goeth before you into Galilee; there shall ye see him, as he said unto you." Yet it can also be asked: why did the women fail to have their brothers or sons or husbands or even servants (if they had any) to come along to assist them and serve as protection? Consequently, the question asked by the women is proof that they did not go to the sepulchre. The question also implies that the women would need assistance to complete their mission to anoint Jesus's body.

First, Christian apologists will argue that assistance from the disciples is impractical since Mark 14:50 reports that they had previously fled or were in hiding: "And they all forsook him, and fled." However, this Christian apologetic is defeated by John, who reports that Mary Magdalene knew exactly where Simon Peter and the other disciple who Jesus loved are residing:

> Jn 20:2 *Then she runneth, and cometh to Simon Peter, and to the other disciple*, whom Jesus loved, and saith unto them, They have taken away the Lord out of the sepulchre, and we know not where they have laid him.

> Jn 20:3 Peter therefore went forth, and that other disciple, and came to the sepulchre.

Also, Luke's two visitors on the road to Emmaus obviously knew precisely where the eleven disciples were located when they returned Sunday evening to inform them that Jesus was alive:

> Lk 24:33 And they rose up the same hour, and returned to Jerusalem, and found the eleven gathered together, and them that were with them.

Therefore, the Christian apologetic argument that assistance from the disciples would be impractical since they had previously fled or were in hiding is fallacious.

Second, some Christian apologists might also put forward the defense that the women did know of the guard at the tomb or of the tomb being sealed. However, collectively the gospel narrators identified at least five and probably more women traveling to the tomb. First, the events occurred visibly and in public. That is, Matthew narrates that the chief priests and an unknown number of Pharisees (perhaps the entire Sanhedrin) went together to ask Pilate to furnish a guard. Then many of the seventy plus members of the Jewish elite, along with Roman soldiers, went from Pilate's presence, presumably walked through the packed streets of Jerusalem, went out through the gates and into a cemetery, sealed the tomb, placed a guard there, and then returned to the city. Surely this must have been a public spectacle. It is *not* probable or even plausible that this matter could have been kept secret from *all* the women.

Third, there is another more practical and rational explanation as to why Matthew did not have the women ask the question. Jarvis (1988, 64) suggests: "For to add guards to the cast of characters means that the narrative must change in order to maintain its inner logic. No longer can the women come with spices to anoint the body, for they know that the guards would never let them near the tomb. The question, 'Who will roll away the stone for us?' could not be asked because that is the very thing the guards are there to prevent."

Similarly, Gundry (1994, 586) offers: "The women's wondering who will roll back the stone and finding it already rolled away (Mark 16:3-4) drops out because inserting the sealing of the stone and the guarding of the tomb makes their question senseless. Nobody would dare unseal the stone and roll it away for them. Because of the guard, nobody could." On the other hand, Jonge (2008, 127) posits: "The suggestion of the story is that no one was expected to be there at that time of the day."

The possibility of the guard or strangers assisting the women to remove the stone is analyzed in speculations #94 and #95.

SPECULATION #94 Practicalities of Receiving Assistance from the Guard

If, as the author of Mark 15:47 relates, Mary Magdalene had already seen where Jesus was buried, and also how his body was prepared, it makes no sense that she and other women would set off to anoint Jesus. Furthermore, it is even more doubtful that along the way they would begin to wonder and ask their question: "Who shall roll us away the stone from the door of the sepulchre?" However, Osiek (1993, 98) suggests that the question is a "literary embellishment to heighten the sense of amazement in v. 4 when they find the stone already rolled back." But it must be asked, why is this question only found in Mark? Obviously the three following gospel authors deliberately changed the text of Mark because they understood the inappropriateness between the women's intention to anoint Jesus's body and their initial oblivion to the problem of moving the large stone.

Next, it must be asked, was it practical or even plausible for the women to have expected assistance from the guard in disinterring Jesus's body, assuming that the women knew of its presence? It is the opinion of this text that the disinterment of a once buried body in a tomb guarded by a detachment of Roman soldiers is inconceivable for the following reasons:

1. It was not realistic or reasonable for the women to expect the soldiers to violate the governor's seal on a tomb.
2. It was not realistic or reasonable for the women to expect the soldiers to contradict a direct command from the commanding officer and to face execution.
3. It was not realistic or reasonable for the women to expect the soldiers to assist some unknown women in their errand to disinter a body that had been in a grave for two nights and one day.

The notion that the guard will assist the women is absurd.

SPECULATION #95 Practicalities of Receiving Assistance from a Stranger

There are two issues that must be examined regarding the practicality of receiving assistance from a stranger. First, there is the practicality of finding a stranger on the road at sunrise. As previously mentioned, people living in Judea during the first century would have normally been asleep at this time.

Second, the disinterment of a once buried body in a tomb by a passerby seems inconceivable, even assuming that the women knew there was no presence of a guard but only a royal seal on the stone.

1. It is not normal or natural that a passerby, as a matter of accommodation, will accede to the request of a group of strange women that he open a tomb to disinter a body that had been in a grave for two nights and one day, especially since he was not related to the deceased.
2. It is not normal or natural that a passerby will accede to the request of a group of strange women to disinter a body of a man that has been publically condemned to death by the Roman government and executed by crucifixion.
3. It is not normal or natural that a passerby, as a matter of accommodation, will accede to the request of a group of strange women that he open a closed grave for them, one that has a royal seal of the Roman governor on the tomb.
4. It is not normal or natural that a passerby, as a matter of accommodation, will accede to the request of a group of strange women that he open a closed grave for them, one that is the private property of another person.

Finally, even assuming that the women were, on their own, capable of moving the large stone or able to receive assistance, poses at least two remaining problems: (1) how could they have moved the stone back to its original position and (2) how could they replaced the torn seal?

ISSUE 50: The Second Earthquake

Mk	Mt 28:1 In the end of the sabbath, *as it began to dawn toward the first day of the week*, came Mary Magdalene, and the other Mary to see the sepulchre. 2 And, behold, *there was a great earthquake*: for the angel of the Lord descended from heaven, and came and rolled back the stone from the door, and sat upon it.	Lk	Jn

Matthew's narrative details an earthquake on Easter Sunday. This is the second recorded earthquake that had occurred in almost three days. However, it was of a larger magnitude than the previous earthquake since Matthew describes this latter geological event as a *great* earthquake. Therefore, this is not a mere earthquake or weaker after shock.

CONTRADICTION #56 Absence from Sources

First, Matthew is the only author who reports an earthquake: "And, behold, there was a great earthquake: for the angel of the Lord descended from heaven, and came and rolled back the stone from the door, and sat upon it." Yet the author of John, who proponents claim is presumably an eyewitness to the events of that day, did *not* even mention this extraordinary event.

Second, and equally noteworthy, Luke 1:1-4 declares that he examined all of the oral and written sources available to him: It is inexplicable that he would omit such an important and vital detail if he knew it. Given then that Luke heard and knew about the oral tradition of a second earthquake, it must be concluded that he too doubts this tradition and obviously contradicts Matthew's narrative. If this supposition is correct, there is no reason that we should accept Matthew's account.

Last, it is significant to note that no record of such an event occurs in any Jewish or Roman writing.

SPECULATION #96 What Time the Second Earthquake Occurred

The second earthquake described by Matthew raises the question as to specifically when this momentous event occurred. Matthew 28:1 declares that second earthquake occurred "as it began to dawn." Therefore, the time of the earthquake is after the sky is completely dark although it is not yet sunrise.

The Christian apologist Glenn Miller (1997) points out:

> This interpretation depends on the Greek word (*ginomai*) rendered "There was" in verse two. The verb is the standard one rendered "at it came to pass" or "it came to be." The issue is that it is in the *aorist tense*—a rather undifferentiated verbal structure that pushes attention away from itself. The verb is generally *not used* by itself to make a point of chronological sequence; the gospel writers depend on other additional words to make sequence clear (as we would use constructions like "and then" or "subsequently" or "after this").
>
> So, the aorist can be translated "was" and can *also* be translated by an English pluperfect ("had been").

John Wenham (1992, 78), writing in his apologetic, *Easter Enigma: Are the Resurrection Accounts in Conflict?* speculates: "We may thus conclude that the earthquake took place before the arrival of any women and that the terrified guards had already left by the time they arrived. It was presumably a recurrence of the earth tremors which had caused the rending of the massive curtain which divided the Holy Place from the Holy of Holies at the time of the crucifixion." Therefore, Matthew's legendary earthquake probably occurred between 3:00 and 5:00 a.m.

However, several writers (France 2007, 1100; Hagner 1995, 876; Newman and Stine 1988, 881) maintain or suggest that the guard left the tomb and traveled to the chief priests while the women were attempting to make their report to the disciples. This topic is examined in issues 53 and 54.

SPECULATION #97 Why Matthew Called the Second Earthquake "Great"

Matthew 27:51-53 provides numerous facts that occur during the first earthquake that are seemingly interrelated: (1) The Temple's veil is rent from top to bottom, (2) "the earth did quake and the rocks rent," and (3) graves were opened. Because of these events, Matthew 27:54 reports: "Now when the centurion, and they that were with him, watching Jesus, saw the earthquake, and those things that were done, they feared greatly, saying, truly this was the Son of God." Given that the first quake actually rented rocks, it probably ranged from a category 4.0-5.9.

However, Matthew 28:1 states that this second earthquake (*seismos*) was a *great* earthquake. This narrative raises several unanswerable questions. Why is the second quake described as a *great* quake, given there was no report of damage? And why is substantial damage mentioned in the first quake while the second geologic event is referred to as a *great* earthquake? One possibility is that the great earthquake is fully or partly responsible for removing the great stone sealing the tomb. At the same time, the problem is that Matthew can also be interpreted as stating that it was the angel who moved the stone.

ISSUE 51: The Angel of the Lord Descending from Heaven

Mk	Mt	Lk	Jn
	Mt 28:1 In the end of the sabbath, *as it began to dawn toward the first day of the week*, came Mary Magdalene, and the other Mary to see the sepulchre. 2 And, behold, there was a great earthquake: *for the angel of the Lord descended from heaven*, and came and rolled back the stone from the door, and sat upon it. 3 His countenance was like lightning, and his raiment white as snow. 4 And for fear of him the keepers did shake, and become as dead men.		

The episode of the angel of the Lord descending from heaven occurs only in Matthew. No description is provided of this descent. Only later are the angel's appearance and the consequences of his arrival discussed.

SPECULATION #98 Witnessing the Descent

Matthew is the only person presumably aware of this miraculous account of the angel of the Lord (*angelos gar Kuriou*) descending from heaven. This narrative raises an obvious question: Given that Matthew's account in 28:1-2 is indeed to be understood in the perfect tense: who was or were the specific eyewitnesses who saw the angel descending from heaven?

Johnson (1992b, 59) states that Matthew alone described the removal of the stone, apparently in the "presence" of the women and presumably by an angel of the Lord. Therefore, it is perhaps the angel who removed the stone. However, this explanation lacks corroboration and verification.

In the opinion of Waters (2005, 296), "there is no real indication that they had actually arrived *before* the earthquake and the angelophany." Similarly, D. A. Carson (1984, 588), writing in *Matthew* (*Expositor's Bible Commentary 8*), states: "There is no evidence that the women witnessed the earthquake and the first descent of the angel."

Shamoun (n.d. Responses to Understanding-Islam), elaborating on the position that the events occur before the women's arrival, writes: "The verb *egeneto*, is an aorist tense and comes from the verb *ginomai*. It can mean, 'it came to pass,' 'it came to be,' or 'there had been.' This implies that the earthquake, the descent of the angel, and the flight of the guards had already taken place before the women had arrived."

Finally Allison (2004, 541) writes: "Commentators are divided over whether the women witness the descent of the angel and its consequences or only come along later." Nonetheless he offers: "Given the introduction of the women before v. 2, it may be best to think of them seeing everything."

In summary, Matthew did not incontrovertibly, indisputably, and unequivocally detail who witnessed the descent of the angel.

ISSUE 52: When the Stone Was Removed

Mk 16:4	Mt 28:1 In the end of the	Lk 24:2 And	Jn 20:1 The first
And when	sabbath, *as it began to dawn*	*they found the*	day of the week
they	*toward the first day of the week,*	*stone rolled*	cometh Mary
looked,	came Mary Magdalene, and the	*away from the*	Magdalene early,
they saw	other Mary to see the sepulchre.	*sepulchre.*	when it was yet
that the	2 And, behold, there was a great		dark, *unto the*
stone *was*	earthquake: *for the angel of the*		*sepulchre, and seeth*
rolled away:	*Lord descended from heaven*, and		*the stone taken away*
for it was	came and rolled back the stone		*from the sepulchre.*
very great.	from the door, and sat upon it.		

Only Matthew described the removal of the stone after the women arrived, "as it began to dawn." In contrast, Mark, Luke, and John record that the stone was already removed prior to the arrival of the women. Therefore, the stone had to have been removed prior to sunrise when it was still dark.

CONTRADICTION #57 Matthew's Chronological Contradiction

Reimarus posits that Matthew 28:2 is self-contradictory: "And, behold, there was a great earthquake: for the angel of the Lord descended from heaven, and came and rolled back the stone from the door, and sat upon it." Specifically, Reimarus (1971, 183) makes the claim that if Matthew's report is true that "the stone had been rolled away by an angel in the presence of the women, then it must be untrue that the women became aware from a distance that the stone had been rolled away and that it was gone." The NIV translation (1978, 1151) of Mark 16:2-3 supports Reimarus's interpretation that from a distance (i.e., "they were on their way to the tomb") the women observed that the tomb's entrance was not blocked.

> Mk 16:2 Very early on the first day of the week, they were on their way to the tomb. It was just after sunrise. They asked each other, "Who will roll the stone away from the entrance to the tomb?"

> Mk 16:3 Then they looked up and saw that the stone had been rolled away. The stone was very large.

To recapitulate, Mark has the women viewing from a distance as the stone was being rolled away just prior to their physical arrival at the tomb. Therefore, Reimarus maintains that the chronological order of the text in Matthew is switched since he narrates (1) the women came to the sepulchre, (2) the angel descended from heaven, (3) there was an earthquake, and then (4) the stone was rolled away.

SPECULATION #99 How the Stone Was Removed

The three synoptic accounts record that the stone was already rolled away *prior* to the arrival of the women. How was this great stone removed? To answer this question it is necessary to determine who saw the event occurring with their own eyes. Matthew alone describes the removal of the stone, perhaps in the presence of the women and, perhaps, by an angel of the Lord. Therefore, it is perhaps the angel who removes the stone. However, this explanation lacks corroboration and verification. In contrast, Gundry (1994, 587) is of the opinion that Matthew's angel of the Lord descends from heaven and rolls away the stone. Yet he states: "In fact, Mark and the other evangelists never do say who rolled it away."

In the opinion of Waters (2005, 296), "there is no real indication that they had actually arrived *before* the earthquake and the angelophany." Similarly, D. A. Carson (1984, 588), writing in *Matthew* (*Expositor's Bible Commentary 8*) states: 'There is no evidence that the women witnessed the earthquake and the first descent of the angel."

In contrast, McDonald and Porter (2000, 187) states that the angel and the removal of the stone were witnessed. They write: "Matthew says that the women and guards (28:4) saw an 'angel of the Lord' descend from the heaven and roll back the stone" (28:2).

Shamoun (n.d.), elaborating on the position that the events occur before the women's arrival, writes: "The verb *egeneto*, is an aorist tense and comes from the verb *ginomai*. It can mean, 'it came to pass', 'it came to be', or 'there had been', This implies that the earthquake, the descent of the angel, and the flight of the guards had already taken place before the women had arrived."

Obviously there is no consensus among Christian scholars and theologians as to whether or not the women witness the angel's descent or the manner in which stone was removed. Given that nobody saw the stone being removed, it is impossible to definitely explain how the tomb's entrance was cleared and opened.

SPECULATION #100 Why the Stone Was Removed

A pertinent question that must be asked is why was the stone removed? Christian commentators and apologists posit that the reason for an open tomb was to permit the women to see inside, *not* to allow Jesus to leave. Or as Stagg (1969, 250), writing in *The Broadman Bible Commentary*, states: "So understood, the stone was not rolled away to let Jesus out but to let the women in." Similarly, Wenham (1981, 152) writes: "the stone was not removed to let Jesus out, but to let the witnesses in." Likewise, Turner (2005, 370) states: "Either way, the stone was rolled aside, not to let Jesus out, but to show the women that the tomb was empty because the resurrection had already occurred."

Almost 1,500 years earlier, Peter Chrysologus presents the identical rationale, quoted in Simonetti (2002, 306): "An angel descended and rolled back the stone. He did not roll back the stone to provide a way of escape for the Lord but to show the world that the Lord had already risen. He rolled back the stone to help his fellow servants believe, not to help the Lord rise from the dead." Undoubtedly, without the empty tomb there could not be a resurrection legend. That is, if the tomb remained closed, the populace would still believe that Jesus's body remained in the tomb. Nonetheless, given the empty tomb and missing body, there must be an explanation.

However, it is patently *untrue* that the stone was removed to permit the women or the disciples in the sepulchre to serve as witnesses that Jesus's body was gone. Why would it be necessary to verify that Jesus's body was not in the tomb to serve proof that he was physically resurrected from the dead?

Mark reports that three women enter the tomb and receive a message from a young man dressed in white, presumably an angel. The angel reports that Jesus is risen and not physically present. The message just as easily could have been conveyed by the messenger outside of the tomb. Besides, the message and the absence of the body does not provide any unequivocal evidentiary proof that Jesus has risen from the dead. All that Mark presents is a statement by a young man that Jesus's body was missing from the tomb.

Read literally, Matthew 28:1-8 states that neither the women nor the angel of the Lord entered the tomb. Therefore, the stone's removal provides no proof for Jesus's resurrection. The only information provided is an unconfirmed and unsubstantiated statement by an angel. As a matter of fact, there is no weakness to Matthew's storyline if the first eight verses are omitted. That is, Matthew narrates that Jesus physically appears to the women as they are on their way back to the disciples. Matthew alone refutes the apologetic that the stone needs to be removed to let the women in to serve witness to the missing body.

Similar to Mark, if Luke 24:1-11 is omitted, there would be no loss. In these verses Luke reports that several women enter the tomb and receive a message from two men while inside the tomb. These men, also presumably angels, inform the women that Jesus has risen and is not physically present. The message just as easily could have been conveyed by the messengers outside of the tomb. Besides, the message and the absence of the body do not provide any evidentiary proof that Jesus has risen from the dead. All that Luke presents is a statement by two men that Jesus's body is missing from the tomb. The visitation of Peter detailed in Luke 24:12 also fails to provide any support for the claim that Jesus has risen from the dead. Luke merely reports that Peter "departed, wondering in himself at that which was come to pass."

Immediately following, Luke narrates in 24:13-33 the Emmaus episode. Eventually after a daylong encounter with Jesus, and as dinner approached, he is finally recognized by the two travelers. Consequently, this recognition also eliminates the need for the stone to be removed and exploration of the tomb. More significantly, Luke 24:33-53 reports Jesus physically appears to the disciples on Easter Sunday evening. At this time he speaks, eats in their presence, and offers them the opportunity to handle his body. This appearance to the disciples alone suffices for eliminating any need that the stone had to be removed and that the women need to investigate the empty tomb to prove that Jesus was resurrected.

Finally, John 20 and 21 provides no support for the apologetic that the removed stone permits Mary Magdalene, Simon Peter, or "the other disciple whom Jesus loved" to verify that Jesus has been physically resurrected. Mary Magdalene states three times that she believes some group of unknown people have taken Jesus away. In addition, the subsequent investigation by the two disciples provides no support for the risen Jesus. To the contrary, Luke 24:8 reports that the other disciple sees and believes after he too enters the tomb. It is the position of several scholars that the other disciple believes Mary Magdalene's report that some unknown group of people have taken away Jesus's body and it is unknown where it is currently located—not that Jesus has been physically resurrected or that he has fulfilled his resurrection predictions.

Later that evening Jesus physically appears to the ten disciples (cf. Luke 24:33-53) while they are hiding behind closed doors. This appearance negates any need for removal of the stone to permit an examination and verification that Jesus's body is not buried in the tomb. Jesus's appearance Easter evening is proof enough that he has physically resurrected. Waiting approximately twelve extra hours after the women's initial discovery of the empty tomb does not changes anything. It would make no difference if Jesus was witnessed at approximately sunrise or roughly about sunset. His appearance Easter evening is proof enough that he resurrected from the tomb. Furthermore, eight days later Jesus makes another physical appearance to the disciples in Jerusalem followed by yet another appearance at the Sea of Tiberias (John 21). Collectively John 20 and 21 refutes the claim that removal of the stone is necessary for there to be an investigation of the empty tomb.

In conclusion, it is *false* to assume that the stone is removed to permit the women or the disciples into the sepulchre to serve as witnesses that Jesus's body is gone.

CHAPTER 7

The Guard's Report and the Bribe

PREFACE: THE GUARD AT THE TOMB

A T THIS POINT this text now jumps to Sunday morning. Once again, Matthew provides information not found in any other gospel. He narrates that the Jewish leadership received a report from the guard at the tomb informing them that there was an earthquake, an angel descended from heaven, and that the stone was rolled away.

ISSUE 53: The Report of the Guard to the Chief Priests and the Elders

Mk	Mt	Lk	Jn
	Mt 28:4 And for the fear of him the keepers did shake, and become as dead as men.		
	Mt 28:11 Now when they were going, behold, some of the watch came into the city, and shewed unto the chief priests all the things that were done.		

Matthew 28:4 reports that because of the guards' fear of the angel, they "became as dead men." After a seven-verse interlude, Matthew's narrative returns to the "guard episode," and he has them recover from their fright. Presumably after the women have left the tomb, then some of the watch go into the city of Jerusalem and, specifically to the chief priests, in order to explain the events that took place. The exact number of men who went to the chief priests is unknown. In addition, it is significant that nowhere in Matthew does the text state that the guard actually witnessed Jesus coming forth from the tomb. In addition, Matthew never records that the Jewish

leadership question the report of the guards or went to the tomb to verify their report.

ISSUE 54: The Conspiracy of the Chief Priests and Elders

Mk	Mt 28: 12 And when they were assembled with the elders, and had taken counsel, *they gave large money* unto the soldiers. 13. Saying, *Say ye, His disciples came by night, and stole him away while we slept.* 14 And if this come to the governor's ears, *we will persuade him, and secure you.* 15 So they took the money, and did as they were taught: and this saying is commonly reported among the Jews until this day.	Lk	Jn

After receiving information from the soldiers about the earthquake and angel, the chief priests met with the elders and decided to devise a plan. The Jewish leadership's plan gave the soldiers a large sum of money in exchange for them reporting that the disciples had stolen Jesus's body during the night while they were sleeping. In addition, the Jewish leadership told the soldiers that they could keep them out of trouble if the report was to reach Pilate. The soldiers took the money as they were instructed. Finally, Matthew declares that, as a consequence, this story has been widely circulated among the Jews to this very day.

CONTRADICTION #58 Apologetic Christian Sources Do Not Believe the Veracity of the Guard Episode

Numerous Christian scholars doubt or outrightly refute Matthew's account of the guard. First, the renowned Christian scholar C. H. Dodd (1963, 146n2) writes:

> The statement that it was while the women were on their way that the guard from the tomb made their report, and took a bribe to spread a false rumour, *is clearly a piece of artificial composition.* There is no essential connection between 9-10 and 11-15, or again between this passage and 16-20, which begins as abruptly as any narrative *pericope* in the earlier part of the gospels. [italics mine]

Father Raymond Brown, writing in *Death of the Messiah* (1994a, 2:1312n60), challenges fundamentalists and specifically discusses W. L. Craig's position regarding the historicity of the guard:

W. L. Craig has written very perceptively on the resurrection of Jesus and has deflated some of the presuppositions that underlie facilely repeated arguments against its reality. *In his attempt (unsuccessful in my judgment) to defend the historicity of the guard story, it is disappointing that he seems to see worthless legend as the alternative to a historical account* ("Guard" 274). The Bible is a collection of literature of many different genres, and *we devalue it if we emphasize history in a way that would demean other types of biblical literature.* Jonah is an OT book of extraordinary value even if no man bearing that name was ever swallowed by a large fish or put a foot in Nineveh [italics mine]

Third, Robert H. Gundry (1994, 585) writes: "At the very least—i.e., *even though we suppose complete invention of the story by Matthew*—the insertion of vv 62-66 presupposes Jewish admission that Jesus' grave was empty. Otherwise, the story lacks a reason for being." [italics mine]

Fourth, even standard reference sources seriously question the historicity of the guard. For example, the *New Catholic Encyclopedia* (Ceroke 2003, 152) states:

Therefore the payment of the guards to secure their silence (Mt 28:11-15) *cannot be understood as historical data.* Since this material, however, is taken seriously in Mt, the possibility suggests itself that *neither the Christian story of the guarding of the tomb, nor the Jewish story of the payment of the guards were originally historical assertions but forms of theological debate,* probably (but not necessarily) over the religious significance of the open-empty tomb. But what precisely such a theological debate might have centered upon is not presently ascertainable. [italics mine]

Similarly, *The New Jerome Biblical Commentary* (Viviano 1990, 673) concedes that Matthew's guard was "motivated by late apologetics" and "reflects the apologetics and polemics of the 80's or 90's." And the previously cited *Interpreter's Bible* (Buttrick 1951, 7:613), states:

Even conservative commentators are obliged to admit that these verses are probably legend. Thus, *The Expositor's Greek Testament* says that this story is "among the less certain elements of the passion history." [I, 334, note on vss. 62-66] . . . *We have here the echo of a great controversy between the synagogue and*

the early church. The strife raged through several generations.
[italics mine]

Allison (2005a, 311) discusses in his text *Resurrecting Jesus: The Earliest Christian Tradition and its Interpreters* the possibility that Matthew's account was an invention. He writes: "Its force is all the greater when we add that Christians were quite capable not just of making up stories about Jesus but also making up stories about his resurrection. Surely, for instance, the guard of Matt 27:62-66 and the earthquake of Matt 28:2 *are sheer fiction.*" [italics mine]

Boring (1995, 501), writing for *The New Interpreter's Bible*, also supports the previously stated positions. He writes: "The fact that Roman soldiers would report to the chief priests is one of the indications that *the story is not literal history* but part of Matthew's understanding of the resurrection." [italics mine]

In addition, Fuller (1988, 981) raises another issue: "The reference to the Pharisees involvement in the plot, and the statement that the slanderous story was current among the Jews until Matthew's day, betrays its origin: it is an apologetic legend designed to counter the Torah-Israel's slander about the origin of the Easter faith."

Even William Lane Craig (in Strobel 1998, 211-12) agrees that the majority of scholars question the authenticity of Matthew's narrative regarding the watch at the tomb.

"Only Matthew reports that guards were placed around the tomb," he replied. "But in any event, I don't think the guard story is an important facet of the evidence for the Resurrection. *For one thing, it's too disputed by contemporary scholarship. I find it's prudent to base my arguments on evidence that's most widely accepted by the majority of scholars, so the guard story is better left aside.*" [italics mine]

Finally, a point of contention and discussion of several New Testament scholars, theologians, and historians (Collins 1993, 120-31; Crossan 1995, 160-68; 1991, 391-94; Fuller 1971, 52-57; Gardner-Smith 1938, 12-13; Goulder 1996, 57; Hamilton 1965, 415-21; Küng 1976, 361-63; Lampe 1966, 41-47, 57-59; Lindar 1993, 118, 129; 1986, 90; Mack 1991, 308-09; McCane 1999, 431-52; Myllykoski 2002, 68; Perrin 1977a, 80; Pokorný 1987, 152-53; Ranke-Heinemann 1994, 131) is whether or not there even was an actual tomb in which Jesus was buried. Given that there was no tomb, there was no guard.

CONTRADICTION #59 Craig's Apologetic

Craig and other Christian apologists are wrong when they contend that it would have been impossible for anyone to clandestinely remove Jesus's body from the tomb because there was a guard that would have prevented such an occurrence. Christian apologists are also wrong when they argue that, without any possibility for the body to have been covertly carried away, the only other logical conclusion is that Jesus must have truly been raised from the dead.

Amplifying this Christian apologetic, Craig (1984a, 278; cf. Dudrey 2000, 75) writes:

> Matthew fails to say that the sepulchre was opened and checked before it was sealed, so that it is possible that the disciples had removed the body and replaced the stone Friday night after Joseph's departure. Of course we would regard such a ruse as historically absurd, but the point is that if the guard is a Christian invention aimed at refuting the Jewish allegation that the scheming disciples had stolen the body, *then the writer has not done a very good job.* [italics mine]

To recapitulate Craig's position, "if the guard is a Christian invention aimed at refuting the Jewish allegation that the scheming disciples had stolen the body, then the writer has not done a very good job." In other words, Craig argues that if Matthew wanted to have created a better story, he could have done so by fabricating a bigger lie. Since Matthew did not fabricate a bigger lie, this proves that he is not lying regarding the details about the guard episode as found in his narrative.

This defense is an argument based on silence. Matthew is working with Mark's narrative written ca. 70 CE as well as with an evolving oral tradition approximately fifty years after Jesus's crucifixion. At this time, Matthew is faced with a dilemma: there are no cameras, no video recorders, and no other technological means to verify that the tomb is sealed for two evenings and one day time prior to Jesus's resurrection. All Matthew can rely upon is the testimony of several women visiting a tomb. Yet Mark 16:8 reports that the women say nothing to anyone after their visit.

In addition, at the time Matthew is being written an increasing number of people doubted the empty tomb accounts. An obvious argument by doubters is that anyone could have removed the body before the tomb is discovered early Sunday morning by the several women. To circumvent this argument, Matthew is forced to invent a guard at the tomb. However, the presence of a guard will require a rational explanation. Consequently, Matthew is forced to invent the account of the Jewish leadership going to Pilate. But when is it possible for this visitation to have occurred? The earliest possible day would have been on the Jewish Sabbath. However, a visit by the Jewish leadership on the Sabbath will have seemed highly unlikely to most knowledgeable readers or listeners to the text. Consequently, Matthew 27:62 obscures from its readers and listeners that this visitation occurs on the Sabbath: "Now the next day, that followed the day of the preparation, the chief priests and Pharisees came together unto Pilate." This lie is necessitated because of Mark's chronology (Mk 15:47; cf. Lk 54-56). That is, there is not enough time for the Jewish leadership to return to Pilate before the Sabbath and request a guard.

But why did the Jewish leadership need to see Pilate? There has to be a reason. Consequently, the previous lie necessitates Matthew inventing the idea that the Jewish leadership knew about Jesus's prophecy that he will rise again after three days, "Saying, Sir, we remember that that deceiver said, while he was yet alive, After three days I will rise again" (Mt 27:63). How the Jewish leadership knew about this prophecy is not provided by Matthew.

Up to now, Matthew has explained why a guard is at the tomb, and he also provides information for his readers and listening audience that the guard stayed there for an undetermined length of time until the women arrive. This scenario now creates an even bigger problem. How can the women examine the tomb and verify that the tomb is empty if it is guarded by a Roman watch? Somehow these Roman soldiers must be eliminated from the scene. To resolve this problem, figuratively speaking, the angel descending from heaven and removing the stone, thus terrifying the guard into a state of paralysis, kills two birds with one stone. Matthew has now explained how the tomb is open for the women to verify that Jesus's body is missing and how the guard became immobilized to permit the women's investigation at the tomb.

However, Matthew has now dug an even bigger hole for himself. Given that there is a guard at the tomb, why is it that there is no record of what they saw? That is, why is there no record that the guard saw both the angel descending from heaven and the removal of the stone? To take care of this problem, Matthew invents the bribe: "And when they were assembled with the elders, and had taken counsel, they gave large money unto the soldiers" (Mt 28:12). However, this bribe creates yet another loophole. Would all the guards accept such a bribe knowing that, if they were found out, it would mean their certain execution? Consequently, Matthew needs to invent another lie to protect his narrative. Thus, Matthew 28:14 states that the Jewish leadership will come to their assistance: "And if this comes to the governor's ears, we will persuade him, and secure you." [Note: Cassels (1902, 828), posits, "The large bribe seems to have been very ineffectual, since the Christian historian is able to report precisely what the chief priests and elders instruct them to say."]

In brief, Matthew could have created a better lie. Every time he tells a lie it requires another and bigger lie to cover up the problem created by the previous lie. All these lies are ingeniously interwoven.

There is however yet another possibility to challenge Craig's claim that "then the writer has not done a very good job." That is, the writer did an excellent job *not* writing a lie but narrating a legendary account to further his theological agenda based on the Hebrew Bible. Specifically, Matthew creatively and skillfully weaves a legendary account incorporating passages from Joshua 10 and Daniel 6 that are supposedly fulfilled by Jesus.

CONTRADICTION #60 It Is Possible that the Body Could Have Been Removed before the Stationing of the Guard

Christian apologists are wrong when they contend that it would have been impossible for anyone to have clandestinely removed Jesus's body from the tomb because there were guards posted at the tomb who would have prevented such an occurrence. Christian apologists are also wrong when they argue that without any possibility of the body being covertly carried away, the only other logical conclusion is that Jesus must have truly been raised from the dead.

Even William Lane Craig refutes this Christian apologetic several times. First he states (1984a, 277): "For example, if the story is an apologetic fiction designed to preclude the theft of the body by the disciples, then the story is not entirely successful, for there is an obvious time period during which the disciples could have stolen the body undetected, namely between six o'clock Friday night and sometime Saturday morning." So unequivocally, Craig acknowledges and concedes that it is possible that the tomb could have been violated prior to the arrival of the guard.

Further rejecting this Christian apologetic, Craig (1984a, 278) writes: "Matthew fails to say that the sepulchre was opened and checked before it was sealed, so that it is possible that the disciples had removed the body and replaced the stone Friday night after Joseph's departure." Craig goes on to state: "Of course, we would regard such a ruse as historically absurd." However, the bottom line is that it *is* possible for Jesus's body to have been removed from the tomb prior to a guard being stationed there.

Second, the Gospel of John nullifies the argument that without any possibility of Jesus's body being removed from the tomb, the only other logical conclusion is that he must have been resurrected from the dead. According to John's narrative, that is precisely what Mary Magdalene thought had happened. Mary Magdalene clearly did *not* think that the scenario of Jesus's body being removed was unlikely, for twice she states that only logical conclusion. First, in John 20:2, she tells Simon Peter and the other disciple: "Then she runneth, and cometh to Simon Peter, and to the other disciple, whom Jesus loved, and saith unto them, They have taken away the Lord out of the sepulchre, and we know not where they have laid him." And then, after Mary Magdalene returns to the tomb a second time, she encounters two angels. Here, in John 20:13, this second time Mary Magdalene states unequivocally to the two angels that she believes someone or some group has absconded with Jesus: "And they say unto her, Woman, why weepest thou? She saith unto them, Because they have taken away my Lord, and I know not where they have laid him." Therefore, even John's narrative refutes the claim that it is impossible that the body could have been removed before the stationing of the guard.

CONTRADICTION #61 Luke versus Matthew—"Until This Day"

The closing words of Matthew 28:15 in the style of an appendix or parenthesis read: "And this saying is commonly reported among the Jews until this day." Therefore, according to Matthew, the story is general knowledge among the Jews of his time. However, it defies common sense as to how Luke, the highly acclaimed historian, omits this event from his gospel. Significantly it must be noted that Luke is writing after Mark and Matthew, and he claims to have surveyed "all things." Why then did Luke reject or omit such an important and well known detail?

Finally, the closing words of verse 15 bear careful consideration insofar as what the author omits to inform his readership. Three omissions identified by Evans (1970, 86) includes (1) where the controversy begins, (2) at what time the controversy begins, and (3) "whether by the time the controversy began any possibility of investigation into the historical details had disappeared."

SPECULATION #101 Argumentum Ad Hominem (An Attack on the Jews versus Pointing Out the Facts)

In his gospel, Matthew employs an *argumentum ad hominem*. An argumentum ad hominem is a general category of fallacies in which a claim or argument is rejected on the basis of some irrelevant fact about an opposing group or individual. Specifically, this tactic involves replying to an argument or assertion by attempting to discredit the group or person offering the argument or assertion. In reality, this Christian apologetic is nothing more than an attempt to deflect attention from the real matters: the fabrication of the entire event of the guard at the tomb, the invention of the guard's report, and the Jewish leadership's concoction of the false report.

The episode of the guards at the tomb is, in part, artificially created to serve a dual agenda: as an apologetic and as an *ad hominem* against the Jewish leaderships. The entire episode presents the Jewish leaders in the worst possible light:

- They refuse to listen to the soldiers' report.
- They create a false explanation for the empty tomb.
- They bribe the soldiers to present false testimony.

Furthermore, Senior (1998, 343) points out: "The generic reference to 'the Jews' rather than to a specific leadership group is unusual in Matthew and seems to imply a growing distance between his own mixed community of Jews and Gentiles and other Jewish groups." More forcefully, Perry (1986, 652), crediting Schweizer (1977, 526), writes: "Finally, in 28:15 the *narrator* refers to the 'Jews,' but this is the only place in Matthew's Gospel where the term is not found on the lips of a Gentile (2:27 [sic]; 27:11, 29, 37) and suggests that its author lived after the split between the church and synagogue had become pronounced."

SPECULATION #102 Plausibility of the Jewish Leadership Bribing the Guard

The plausibility of the Jewish leadership bribing the guard is highly doubtful. The pertinent question that must be asked is why would the Jewish leadership have bribed the guard?

First, bribing the soldiers to lie is in direct violation of the Torah.

Second, the high priests and elders would be risking their own lives by bribing the Roman soldiers, of which only one is needed to reveal their plan.

Third, not only the bribe makes no sense, but it is also illogical and irrational:

- The high priests and elders are to bribe the guards to accuse themselves of falling asleep on their watch, not one or two of them but *all* of them and at the *same* time. Numbers vary, but several proponents suggest that the guard totaled four; others suggest sixteen in number who worked in shifts of four; and others propose as many as sixty total soldiers.

- The high priests and elders are to instruct the guards that they are to accuse themselves that not even one of them awoke to wake up his fellow sentries during the disturbance.
- The guards are to accuse themselves, saying that *all* of them slept so soundly that the disciples came to the tomb, break the seal, remove the seal, move a one to two ton stone, strip the clothes off a dead body, ignore any difference in odor either from a decaying body or the presence of spices, and then carry away the body without a single guard being awakened.
- The guards are to accuse themselves saying that all of them slept so soundly that not even one of them was awakened by a major earthquake.
- Then the guards ultimately are to declare that when they awoke and found the stone lying flat and the body gone, yet they knew precisely what took place during their extraordinary sleep. In reality it would be impossible for them to prove that the disciples stole Jesus's body since they were asleep.
- The guards are to accuse themselves of all of the above, despite the penalty for this being inverted crucifixion (upside down) for dereliction of duty.

Fourth, it would have made more sense for the Sanhedrin to have told the soldiers to say nothing at all or report that everything was in order and that they had left at the proper time (Schleiermacher 1975, 430).

Fifth, Allen (1893, 75) inquires: "Then what was to prevent the rest of the watch who did not go into the city, and were not bribed, from telling such a wonderful occurrence?"

Sixth, Allen (p. 76) writes:

> Had it been true that the guards ran away on account of the earthquake, then the story of the chief priests would have been like this—"that owing to the earthquake the guards became alarmed and ran away. The disciples took advantage of their absence and stole the body, and that is how it came to be missing" Then the priests would have had the fact of the earthquake, which the people also experienced, to assist their story. This story would have been more credible to the guards than that they had been asleep on post, and more reasonable to the people who knew of the earthquake. Whereas it seems to me those priests were too intelligent to pay large money to the guards to say they were asleep while a great earthquake was in progress, when the other story

would have answered their purpose much better, and also had
been more credible to the guards—in fact, would have excused
them from punishment if it were shown that the earthquake was
so frightful that any reasonable men would have done as they did.

Another rationale that Allen offers is why didn't the guards, as soon as
they got their money, go back to the tomb, resume their posts, and pretend
to guard it the best they could? (p. 79) Later, the guards could claim that
the earthquake moved the stone and was responsible for the tearing of the
seal.

SPECULATION #103 No Effect of the Supernatural Events on the Jewish Leadership

The guard at the tomb then raises another matter. Bowen (1911, 272)
writes: "But most incredible of all are the statements of xxviii:12-15. The
guards report earthquake, angel, and resurrection, *and the Sanhedrists believe
them!* None the less they hope to defeat God's plan, in the face of this
tremendous and direct attestation to Jesus' Messiahship, by bribing the guard
to tell a false story! And what a story."

Given that the high priests and elders were convinced of the reality of
this miracle (plus the darkness over *all* the land, the multiple earthquakes, the
tearing of the Temple veil, and the resurrection of the many saints), it would
be expected that they should have recognized that Jesus was the Messiah, and
they should have united with him in working to deliver their nation from the
yoke of the infamous Roman idolaters. Yet the supernatural manifestation
of the angel as reported in Matthew 28, in conjunction with the additional
supernatural events made no impression on either the chief priests or other
members of the Jewish leadership.

This point is demonstrated in Acts 4 and 5 which reports what occurs
more than fifty days after Easter Sunday. In Acts 4:18, the Jewish leadership
ordered Peter and John "not to speak at all nor teach in the name of Jesus."
Later, Acts 5 reports that the apostles, after being imprisoned, were brought
before the council and high priest to explain why they did not follow the
earlier stated command. Eventually, Acts 5:40 narrates that it was decided
to free the apostles after a beating and again give them the command "not to
speak in the name of Jesus." Here the Acts of the Apostles provides definitive
proof that the earlier supernatural events made no impact on the Jewish
leadership.

SPECULATION #104 No Effect of the Supernatural Events on the Roman Guard

Wenham (1973, 50), writing in the *Tyndale Bulletin*, states: "Perhaps the most difficult problem is the psychological one: would the guards—would anyone—have agreed to the deception if they had just witnessed the angelic intervention?" Remember that the guard(s):

1. Experience an earthquake (Mt 28:2).
2. Witness an angel descending from heaven, with a countenance like lightning (Mt 28:3).
3. Presumably watch an angel—by himself—roll back the stone blocking the door estimated to weigh well over one ton.
4. Almost two days earlier the guard experience an earthquake and see the whole earth turned dark at midday. In all probability, they too would have also heard about or perhaps seen the supposed raised bodies of saints in their opened graves!

Although the soldiers are pagans, nonetheless, it seems dubious if not unbelievable that a previously terrified person who saw all these wonders would now have declared for a sum of money that he was asleep and saw nothing. What else could have accounted for soldiers becoming virtually unimpressed by the miracles and wonders they had just witnessed after just a few hours earlier or the previous day? It just does not seem plausible that these soldiers, *all* of them, would now have had the courage to tell lies about something supernatural that they witnessed with their own eyes.

Furthermore, it does not seem sensible to assume that these soldiers, *all* of them, after having witnessed such an amazing and remarkable event, could be reliably expected to keep silent about it. Nor did it make any sense that the soldiers, *all* of them, would have accepted money for reporting a falsehood for which the angel of the Lord might very properly have punished them. Instead, it would be another miracle if the guard actually remained silent. Given that the Roman soldiers "had" observed such a fantastic scene, what more would be necessary to convince them to accept the "Christian faith"?

Wenham (1973, 50-51) responds to his previous rhetorical question: "But although this argument is at first sight plausible, it is dangerous to place too much weight on arguments about what people might or might not have done in a situation, when we have very little detailed information about it."

Of course, there is at least one major problem with Wenham's strategy, the synonymous "domino theory" or "slippery slope" phenomenon. This response could be used to counter the commentary of virtually every Christian apologist, biblical commentator, or theologian regarding portions of the Resurrection narratives.

SPECULATION #105 Turning in the Soldiers

Another obvious point relates to the issue of the Jewish leadership and the Roman guard. Cassels (1902, 828; cf. Ordal 1923, 91-92) writes: "And if they [[i.e., the chief priests and elders]] did not believe it, would not the very story itself have led to the punishment of the men, and to the confirmation of the report they desired to spread, that the disciples had stolen the body?" Therefore, the priests had *no* need to invent such an incredible story. As a matter of fact, the Jewish leadership would have been delighted to have the soldiers arraigned before Pilate to see them punished and found guilty of sleeping on duty and letting Jesus's body be stolen, for that gave the perfect cover. That was why the soldiers would not have gone to the chief priests, for they would have had to expect this. The Jews knew that the people would think that the Roman authorities were covering something up if the soldiers could go around freely saying that they let the body be stolen and were not punished. Obviously they would have drawn the conclusion that Jesus had risen. Therefore, Matthew has the Jews doing exactly what they did not want to do!

SPECULATION #106 Paradox of a Nonarrest

If the guards had made an accusation that they knew it was Jesus's disciples who carried off his body, they would have had to make some arrests. Yet there are no arrests or trial for this supposed crime. Furthermore, the guard would have needed some false witnesses to convict the accused body snatchers. Since these events never happened, it demonstrates that Matthew made up the entire episode.

SPECULATION #107 The Roman Failure to Investigate

The breaking of the governor's seal had to be known, given the empty tomb. Yet the Roman government failed to investigate who broke the seal. Breaking a seal issued by a governor was equivalent to sedition. This act of defiance would hardly have been overlooked least of all by the very governor whose orders were violated. It was Pilate, after all, who had allowed Joseph of Arimathea to receive Jesus's body for burial. What is inexplicable and enigmatic is why Pilate failed to summon Joseph of Arimathea and Nicodemus to ask them what had happened to the body. Moreover, it is baffling why Pilate did not employ force to get the truth out of his soldiers once he questioned them.

SPECULATION #108 Privileged Communication

It must be asked: How did the author of Matthew 28:12 know what the chief priests and elders said in their private counsel? "And when they were assembled with the elders, and had taken counsel, they gave large money unto the soldiers." This was information that no Christian could have known unless perhaps one of the soldiers divulged it at a risk to himself and his compatriots. A Christian apologetic is that one of the guards later converted to Christianity and provided the details. However, this explanation requires one to assume that there was at least one soldier who converted and forwarded the information. Furthermore, there is no record that Pilate or even the chief priests ever tried to find Jesus's body.

CHAPTER 8

Easter Sunday: Travels, Angelic Encounters, and an Appearance of Jesus

PREFACE: ISSUES 55 to 67 WILL FOLLOW THE ORDER OF the SYNOPTIC GOSPELS

IN GENERAL, ISSUES 55 to 67 follows the accounts recorded in the synoptic Gospels that relate several women's visit to the tomb and what they encountered. Starting with Issue 68, this text will investigate in more detail John's narrative detailing Mary Magdalene's visit to the tomb, and her eventual encounter with the risen Jesus. The reason for this strategy is that, from this point of the Easter day chronology, the gospel narratives continue to go off on divergent tangents. Since John is so completely different from the synoptic Gospels, its chronology cannot be harmonized with them. Numerous biblical commentators, historians, and scholars candidly admit that these accounts cannot be harmonized.

ISSUE 55: Who Was at the Tomb?

| Mk 16:5 And entering into the sepulchre, they *saw a young man* sitting on the right side, clothed in a long white garment; and they were affrighted. | Mt 28:2 And, behold, there was a great earthquake: for *an angel of the Lord* descended from heaven, and rolled back the stone from the door, and sat upon it. 3 *His countenance was like lightning, and his raiment white as snow.* | Lk 24:3 And they entered in, and found not the body of the Lord Jesus. 4 And it came to pass, as they were much perplexed, thereabout, behold *two men* stood by them in shining garments. | Jn 20:1 The first day of the week cometh Mary Magdalene early, when it was yet dark, unto the sepulchre, and seeth the stone taken away from the sepulchre. 2 Then she runneth, and cometh to Simon Peter, and to the other disciples whom Jesus loved.

Jn 20:12 *And, seeth two angels* in white sitting, the one at the head, and the other at the feet, where the body of Jesus had lain. |

Table 34 provides details regarding the women's encounter at the tomb upon their arrival: (1) their number, (2) their classification, (3) their description, (4) their location, and (5) how they were situated. Significantly, John's narrative provides details of Mary Magdalene's second visit to the tomb.

TABLE 34. The Messengers at the Tomb

GOSPEL	NUMBERS PRESENT AT the TOMB	CLASSIFICATION of THOSE PRESENT at the TOMB	DESCRIPTION of the MESSENGER(S)	LOCATION	SITUATED
MARK	1	A young man.	Clothed in a long white garment.	Inside the tomb in the right side.	Sitting.
MATTHEW	1	An angel.	His countenance was like lightning and his raiment as white as snow.	Outside the tomb sitting on the stone.	Sitting.
LUKE	2	Men.	In shining garments.	Inside the tomb.	Standing.
JOHN (non-Synoptic)	2	Angels.	Dressed in white.	Inside the tomb with one at the head and the other at the feet where the body of Jesus had lain.	Sitting.

CONTRADICTION #62 Contradictory Facts

The gospel narratives present similar and yet significantly contradictory details regarding those who were present at the tomb. Luke and John contradict Mark and Matthew. The former had two people at the tomb when the women arrived, whereas the latter detailed the presence of only one person. However, the presence of Matthew's "one person" does not include the comatose guard still at the tomb. The descriptions of those present at tomb also contradicts each other. Mark reports that a young man (*neaniskos*) was at the tomb prior to the women's arrival, whereas Luke describes them as men, implying their maturity. In contradiction to Mark and Luke, Matthew describes the person as an angel (*anggelos*) while John reports two angels. However, it is recognized that in the Hebrew Bible angels can come in the form of men. Nonetheless, there are Christian writers who challenge the notion that the young man in Mark was an angel. This topic is explored below.

Another area of contradiction is the location of these men. Matthew describes his stranger as being located outside the tomb. In contradiction Mark, Luke, and John have their strangers located inside the tomb. Furthermore, only Mark locates his young man inside the sepulchre and sitting on the right side. Miller (2004, 80) points out that this location "is associated with the place of honour, and it recalls the prophecy of Jesus at his trial that the Son of Man will appear sitting on the right hand of power (14.62)." Finally, Luke contradicts Mark, Matthew, and John by having his visitors in a standing position, whereas the other gospel narrators have their visitors sitting.

Christian apologists maintain that there is nothing that prohibits the writers from mentioning that after the women found the person or people outside the tomb, he/they later moved inside the sepulchre. This argument is precluded by the text recorded in Matthew. Matthew provides no opportunity for his angel to have later moved into the tomb. That is, Matthew 28:5-7 details the angel's message to the women who immediately left the tomb to inform the disciples about what they heard and saw.

SPECULATION #109 The Young Man Is Not an Angel

Matthew 28:2 refers to the person who appeared to the women as an angel (*aggelos*) of the Lord: "And, behold, there was a great earthquake: for the angel of the Lord descended from heaven, and came and rolled back the stone from the door, and sat upon it." To the contrary, Mark 16:5 calls him a young man (*neaniskos*): "And entering into the sepulchre, they saw a young man sitting on the right side, clothed in a long white garment; and they were affrighted." In Luke 24:4, however, two (*duo*) men (*aner*) are present: "And it came to pass, as they were much perplexed thereabout, behold, two men stood by them in shining garments."

Much speculation has centered on the identity of Mark's young man. Perhaps he was the same young man identified in Mark 14:51 who followed Jesus on the night of his arrest: "And there followed him a certain young man, having a linen cloth cast about his naked body; and the young men laid hold on him." This view is rejected by Black (2011, 343) who posits that this young man triggers "a reader's imagination of how 'the Son of Man has gone as it has been written of him' (14:21 AT)—both in accord with Scripture and in alignment with characters and episodes *within Mark itself.*" Significantly, Jenkins (1983, 239) points out that the author of Mark used the same word (*neaniskos*) in these two instances only.

Jenkins (1983, 237) states that the consensus of scholarly opinion is that *neaniskos* undoubtedly refers to an angelic being. He writes: "The grounds that are universally adduced are parallels in Hellenistic and Jewish literature to angels appearing as young men, and 'white robes' as conventional language indicating heavenly beings." In addition, Hays (2006, 150-51) identified five clues in Mark pointing to an angelophany:

a) In biblical angelology, angels took the form of men, and since they're ageless, they presumably took the form of young men.

b) In Jewish usage (Josephus, *Ant.* 5.8.2-3; 2 Macc 3:26, 33; Tobit 5:5-10.), this is a traditional designation for angels.

c) The young man is arrayed in white, and in biblical iconography, white is a symbolic color often associated with heavenly beings. I've already documented this practice.

d) The women were afraid, and fear is a standard reaction in numinous encounters.

e) The young man clearly plays the role of a divine messenger.

Then Jenkins (cf. Villers 2010, 31) proceeds to destroy the opinion that the young man was an angel.

1. Had Mark wanted to plainly and unambiguously imply or infer angels, he could have said so since he employed the word angels in 1:13, cf. 8:38; 12:25, 32. [[cf. Villers 2010, 3]]

2. It must be asked, if we did not know the other gospels, would there be any question of assuming the young man to be an angel?

3. There were no other references in the OT of angels appearing as youths.
4. Only in 2 Macc. 3:26 and Josephus, *Antiquities*, v. 8.2 are any parallels found to supernatural beings appearing in such a guise.
5. The young man dressed in a "robe" (*stolē*) was unremarkable and the robe referred to an ordinary item of dress (Mk 12:38; Lk 15:22).
6. The description of "white" (*leukē*) does not, in and of itself, indicate a supernatural being.
7. The most frequent reference to white robes is found in the book of Revelation, where it described the dress of martyrs in heaven (Rev 6:11; 7:13).
8. All other uses of *neaniskos* in the NT were of clearly human figures (Mt 19:20, 22; Lk 7:14; Acts 5:10; 1 Jn 2:13).

Collectively Jenkins (1983, 239) hypothesizes:

> It has been argued that if Mark is read in its own right without reference to the other gospels the evidence for suggesting that by 'young man he meant 'an angel' is far from conclusive. Rather, it is more likely that an association is intended to be made with the unknown disciple of 14:^{51f}, and that the imagery of a white robe is suggestive of a heavenly state of a martyr. The appearance of the young man in the empty tomb would be a challenge to the follower of Jesus in Mark's day not to flee, but to face death if necessary in the faith that he 'who loses his life for Jesus' sake and the gospel's (8:^{35}) will also "through the grave and gate of death pass to his joyful resurrection."

Another speculation is that the *young man* in Mark 16:5 could be an adaptation based on Tobit 5:13 where the angel Raphael was called *a young man*: "And the young man said to him, 'Be steadfast in soul. Your cure from God is near.'" Therefore, there is a lack of unanimity as to the nature of the person or people the women encountered: man/men or angel/angels.

Assuming that the person described in Mark was really a young man (*neaniskos*) and nothing more; this raises several questions. Among these are the following:

1. Where did the young man come from and how long was he in the tomb?
2. What is the probability that a young man would sit in the defiling ground of a tomb?

3. What is the probability that a young man would sit in the area of a private tomb in violation of Roman law?
4. What is the probability that a young man would sit in the precincts of a tomb that contained the body of a man condemned to death by the prefect and executed by crucifixion for the high crime of treason?

SPECULATION #110 The Young Man is the Illegitimate Son of Mary Magdalene

Wolfe (1989, 12-18) offers the hypothesis that the young man at the tomb was John Mark, the gospel writer and the "the illegitimate son of Mary Magdalene's preconversion days." In part this hypothesis is based on Acts 12:12: "And when he had considered the thing, he came to the house of Mary the mother of John, whose surname was Mark; where many were gathered together praying."

His highly speculative scenario runs as follows:

1. Mary Magdalene and Mark had a home within the walled city of Jerusalem.
2. Mark attended the Last Supper and was the young man in Mark 14:50-52 who fled naked.
3. On Easter Sunday, Mark's mother informed him that she and two other women were going to the tomb to anoint Jesus's body.
4. Mary left the house to pick up the other two Marys.
5. John Mark, wearing the same clothes worn the prior night, decided to go to the tomb but found the stone rolled away.
6. The Roman centurion at the crucifixion was the one who said, "Truly this man was the Son of God" (Mk 15:39) and "Certainly this was a righteous man" (Lk 23:47); and he had earlier rolled away the stone and found Jesus alive.
7. He unbound Jesus and helped him to escape.
8. Jesus requested that the centurion tell any of his disciples who might come to the tomb "that he goeth before you into Galilee: there shall ye see him, as he said unto you (Mk 16:7)."
9. The centurion relayed the message to John Mark, who was the first to reach the tomb, and then he departed on his way.
10. John Mark decided to enter the tomb to examine it.
11. Soon, thereafter, the women arrived and John Mark relayed the message to them.

How then did the women fail to recognize John Mark? Here too Wolfe has an explanation: (1) the women were not expecting to see him at the tomb, (2) the women did not see the speaker with any distinctiveness since their eyes had not yet adjusted from the bright sunshine outside the tomb to the relative darkness inside it, (3) the tomb's chamber distorted John Mark's voice to the point of unnaturalness, and (4) "the women were so excited at hearing the astounding news, and finding the body gone, that they scarcely heard what the speaker was saying and were therefore in no shape to form any proper judgment as to whom they were hearing. (p. 23)."

SPECULATION #111 The Parallels with Daniel

Curiously, Matthew's description of his angel, as well as the reaction of the guard, distinctly parallels the vision in Daniel 7:9 (Fuller 1971, 24; Gundry 1994, 587; Leske 1998, 1328); Daniel 7:13-14 (Allison 2001, 885; Evans 2005a, 352; Fuller 1971, 83, 128); and Daniel 10:6-7 (Gundry 1994, 588; Leske 1998, 1328):

> Dan 7:9 I beheld till the thrones were cast down, and the Ancient of days did sit, whose garment was white as snow, and the hair of his head like the pure wool: his throne was like the fiery flame, and his wheels as burning fire.

> His body was like chrysolite, his face like lightning, his eyes like flaming torches, his arms and legs like the gleam of burnished bronze, and his voice like the sound of a multitude. Daniel was the only one who saw the vision; the men with me did not see it, but such terror overwhelmed them that they fled and hid themselves.

> I fell prone on the ground in a trance.

> - Daniel 10:6-7, 9 LXX

Was this similarity a coincidence, or did the author of Matthew deliberately borrow from Daniel to write his narrative?

SPECULATION #112 Angels as a Literary Device

In Matthew, an "angel of the Lord" serves as a heavenly messenger. Reid (2005, 143) posits that "In the opening chapters an angel conveyed to Joseph the divine interpretation of the puzzling events surrounding Jesus' birth. Similarly, an angel communicates the meaning of the extraordinary aftermath of Jesus' death." Likewise, Senior (1998, 340) points out, "In the infancy narrative an 'angel of the Lord' had appeared to Joseph in dreams to interpret the meaning of Mary's pregnancy and to give Joseph his charge to protect the mother and child (1:20-23; 2:13, 19). The angel will perform a similar function for the women at the tomb." Smith (1983, 111; cf. Chouinard 1997, 505; Harrington 1991, 409; Hill 1972, 359) also earlier raised this identical point that "the resurrection narrative seems to echo some elements of the birth narrative: an angel or angels appeared (*epestē/epēstēsan*, 2:9, 13; 24:4)."

Was this episode the deliberate creation as a literary bookend by a creative writer?

ISSUE 56: The Women Entering the Tomb

Mk 16:5 *And entering into the sepulchre they* saw a young man sitting on the right side, clothed in a long white garment; and they were affrighted.	Mt 28:6 He is not here: for he is risen, as he said. Come, see the place where the Lord lay.	Lk 24:3 *And they entered in*, and found not the body of the Lord Jesus. 4 And it came to pass, as they were much perplexed thereabout, behold, two men stood by them in shining garments	Jn 20:1 The first day of the week cometh Mary Magdalene early, when it was yet dark, unto the sepulchre, and seeth the stone taken away from the sepulchre. Jn 20:11 But Mary *stood without at the sepulchre* weeping: and as she wept, she stooped down, and looked into the sepulchre.

Mark narrates that the women (plural) found the stone rolled away, entered the tomb, received a message from a young man, but did not bother to investigate the tomb any further. It is unknown who the reference to "they" includes. Palmer (1974, 212) points out: "Thus in Mk the women do not find an empty tomb, but an open tomb with an angel, whose message . . ., included the empty tomb." In contrast, Matthew, did not describe any women (plural) entering the sepulchre. Instead, he reports that the angel sat on upon the stone that had been rolled away from the tomb's entrance. From there the angel spoke to the women and then they departed quickly with "fear and joy." Hence, the women did not enter the tomb.

However, Luke 24:4 not only unequivocally declares that the women entered the tomb but that they also explored it and "behold, two men stood by them in shining garments"; and they vouched for its emptiness. Finally, the Gospel of John reports that in neither the first (Jn 20:1-2) nor the second visit (Jn 20:11) was Mary Magdalene recorded to have entered the tomb. Therefore, Matthew seems more in line with John's narrative, omitting entry into the tomb.

CONTRADICTION #63 Matthew Contradicts Mark and Luke Contradicts Matthew

Matthew contradicts Mark regarding whether or not the women entered the tomb. Mark 16:5 reads: "And entering into the sepulchre, they saw a young man sitting on the right side, clothed in a long white garment; and they were affrighted." To the contrary, Matthew 28:6 reports that the women were instructed by the angel to see where Jesus's body laid: "He is not here: for he is risen, as he said. Come, see the place where the Lord lay." Two verses later Matthew 28:8 informs the readers that the women ran away: "And they departed quickly from the sepulchre with fear and great joy; and did run to bring his disciples word."

Matthew's narrative precludes any possibility of the women entering the tomb. He reports an angel of the Lord (1) descended from heaven, (2) rolled back the stone from the door, and (3) sat upon it. After the guard became immobilized the angel communicated with the women and issued them a command. Most noteworthy, during this communication the angel was still *outside* the tomb and sitting on the stone. And, presumably, the guard was still present at the tomb, although incapacitated during this communication with the women. After the angel's command to go quickly to the disciples and convey his message, the women, in fact, departed quickly. Therefore, Matthew's narrative absolutely ruled out any chance or possibility that the women went inside the tomb in contrast to Mark and Luke. Here, we have two completely different stories. Consequently, there was no reason for the women to enter the tomb since they were already informed that Jesus's body was not there.

Gundry (1994, 590), elaborating on this episode, points out that Matthew's narrative is directly the opposite of Mark's narrative. He writes "in Mark 16:5 the women were *in* the tomb and now go *out*, in Matthew they did *not* go in (but were only invited to peer in v 6) and therefore now go *away*, just as Joseph 'went away.'" [italics are in the original]

Lastly, Luke contradicts Matthew in that he has the women entering the sepulchre. Entering the tomb was possible because Luke did not have the women impeded by Matthew's angel who was sitting outside and on top of the stone. To the contrary, Luke had his two men already standing inside the tomb greeting the women after they entered it; they then conveyed their message. Furthermore, Luke's narrative that omitted the presence of a guard reported in Matthew would make it viable for the women to enter and inspect the tomb. However, Bode (1970, 53) offers another rationale for the presence of the guard:

> It seems more likely that Matthew intends the angel's action to have been witnessed by the women for the action interrupts the narrative about the women and the words to the women are immediately joined to the angel's effect upon the guard by the particle *de*. Moreover, this interpretation seems to shore up further the apologetic intention evidenced in the guard narrative—thus the tomb would have been guarded until the arrival of Christian witnesses and there would have been no time when the tomb remained open but unobserved. Recall that in Mark the women find the tomb already open upon their arrival.

SPECULATION #113 Would the Women Enter the Tomb Illegally?

There are several practical problems that challenge the assumed authenticity and historicity of Luke's narration with the women entering the tomb. First, this tomb contained the body of a man who had been condemned to death by the State and executed by crucifixion.

Second, the women were entering the personal tomb of Joseph of Arimathea. Connick (1974, 402) maintains that based on the tomb's prior description, it would be obvious that the sepulchre where Jesus lay was the private property of a wealthy Jew and a member of the Sanhedrin. Furthermore, as reported in John 19:41, Jesus's burial tomb was in a garden, a location presumably available only to the wealthy. Reinforcing this position, Mark 15:47 and Luke 23:55 detailed that the women actually beheld the sepulchre where Jesus's body was laid. Matthew 27:61 went even further stating that the women, in point of fact, were sitting over against the sepulchre.

Third, the women would have been subject to Roman law because Judea was under Roman authority. Under Roman law, entering the tomb of someone else without permission would have been an act of sacrilege and an extremely serious crime [Gaius, *Institutes* 2.2-10; Marcian, *Institutes* 14]. The punishment for such a crime was severe, ranging from "deportation to an island" to execution [Ulpian, *Duties of the Proconsul* (7; D. 48.13.7)].

Fourth, Matthew's gospel reports that an unknown number of guards were incapacitated when the angel descended and the stone was rolled away. It must be asked, given that the guard was still present at the tomb when the women arrived, would they have taken the added risk to enter the tomb not knowing when the soldiers would recover from their state of unconsciousness?

Finally, while it seems reasonable to believe that the women would not have been afraid of the consequences of punishment once they had come to believe that Jesus had risen from the dead, the story portrays the women as entering the tomb *before* they came to believe that Jesus was resurrected.

Collectively the weight of the cumulative details precludes the probability that the women would have entered Joseph of Arimathea's personal tomb and the burial place of Jesus.

ISSUE 57: The Women's Initial Reaction to Finding the Tomb Empty and Meeting the Messenger(s)

Mk 16.5	Mt 28:2 And,	Lk 24:4 *And*	Jn 20:1 The first day of the
And entering into the sepulchre, they saw a young man sitting in the right side, clothed in a long white garment; *and they were affrighted.*	behold, there was a great earthquake: for an angel of the Lord descended from heaven, and rolled back the stone from the door, and sat upon it. 3 His countenance was like lightning, and his raiment white as snow: 4 And for fear of him *the keepers did shake, and became as dead men.* 5 And the angel answered and said unto the women, *Fear not ye: for I know that ye seek Jesus, which was crucified.*	*it came to pass, as they were much perplexed thereabout,* behold, two men stood by them in shining garments: 5 *And as they were afraid, and bowed down their faces to the earth,* they said unto them, Why seek ye the living among the dead?	week cometh Mary Magdalene early, when it was yet dark, unto the sepulchre, and seeth the stone taken away from the sepulchre. 2 *Then she runneth, and cometh to Simon Peter, and to the other disciples whom Jesus loved and said unto them, They have taken away the Lord out of the sepulchre, and we know not where they have laid him....* Jn 20:12 And seeth two angels in white sitting, the one at the head, and the other at the feet, where the body of Jesus had lain. 13 And they say unto her, Woman why weepest thou? *She saith unto them, Because they have taken away my Lord, and I know not where they have laid him.*

Mark and Luke report that the women initially expressed fear after meeting the young man sitting outside the tomb. Matthew does not describe an initial emotion of the women. Instead, he implies that the women were afraid because of the statement of the angel of the Lord. In contrast, Luke narrates two emotions: confusion and perplexity. Numerous texts testify that humans are often incapacitated by awe and fear (e.g., Ez 1:28; 3:23-24; Dan 8:17-18; 10:7-12, 15-19; 1 Enoch 14:14, 24-25; 15:1; 60:3-4; 71:2; Mt 17:6-8; Rev 1:17). Finally, John reports that during Mary Magdalene's second visit to the tomb she was sad and disturbed.

CONTRADICTION #64 **Contradictory Emotions**

The gospel narratives present contradictory descriptions of the women's emotions while at the tomb. In Mark 16:5 there is *no* comment about the women's first reaction after seeing an empty tomb. Technically, however, the women did *not* discover an empty tomb; a young man was there and nowhere is the reader told that the tomb is empty. Swain (1993, 16) points out that "nowhere does Mark state that the women noticed that Jesus' body or corpse *was* missing from the tomb." Instead, Mark reports that the women were frightened because of the appearance of the young man clothed in white.

Matthew 28:5 implies that the women were afraid because of the angel of the Lord stating: "Fear ye not." In contrast, Luke 24:4-5 reports that the women were *perplexed* and *afraid*: "And it came to pass, as they were much perplexed thereabout, behold, two men stood by them in shining garments: And as they were afraid, and bowed down their faces to the earth, they said unto them, Why seek ye the living among the dead?" Furthermore, he adds that the women "bowed down their faces to the earth." Thus, the authors of Mark and Luke narrate that the women's initial reaction to the stranger(s) appearance at the tomb was *phobos*. *Thayer's Lexicon* defined the Greek word *phobos* as fear, dread, terror, and that which strikes terror. Since Mark and Luke provide no details about an earthquake as narrated in Matthew, the women's fear could only be in response to the appearance of the angel(s).

John narrates that Mary Magdalene made two visits to the tomb. Reading John 20:1 at its face value and in isolation reveals that during her initial visit she was the first to come to the tomb and discover that the stone covering the tomb's entrance was already taken away. Therefore, Mary Magdalene concluded that someone had removed the body from the grave, although she did not look into the tomb until verse 11. Nonetheless she ran to Simon Peter and to "the other disciple whom Jesus loved" saying: "They have taken (*êran*) away the

Lord out of the sepulchre, and we know not (*ouk oidamen*) where they have laid (*ethêkan*) him."

During her second visit to the tomb, John 20:13 describes Mary Magdalene as weeping. However, John provides *no* description of Mary Magdalene's initial reaction to meeting the two angels. As a matter of fact, she did *not* seem to know that the two men were angels, as the reader does. Instead, her weeping was because she believed that Jesus's body had been taken away, and she did not know where it was now located.

In the gospel narratives different feelings or reactions were recorded for the same event. Significantly, it should be noticed that before Jesus's resurrection, the synoptic Gospels were in general agreement with each other but differed with John. However, after Jesus's resurrection, all the gospel narratives conflict with each other.

ISSUE 58: The Messengers' Initial Words to the Women

Mk 16:6 And he said unto them, *Be not affrighted*: Ye seek Jesus of Nazareth, which was crucified: he is risen; he is not here: behold the place where they laid him.	Mt 28:5 *Fear not ye*: for I know that ye seek Jesus, which was crucified. 6 He is not here: for he is risen, as he said. Come, see the place where the Lord lay.	Lk 24:5 And as they were afraid, and bowed down their faces to the earth, they said unto them, *Why seek ye the living among the dead?* 6 He is not here, but is risen: remember how he spake unto you when he was yet in Galilee, 7 Saying, the Son of man must be delivered into the hands of sinful men, and be crucified, and the third day rise again.	Jn 20:13 *And they say unto her, Woman why weepest thou?* She saith unto them, Because they have taken away my Lord, and I know not where they have laid him. 14 And when she had thus said, she turned herself back, and saw Jesus standing, and knew not that it was Jesus.

Mark and Matthew report that the women were explicitly instructed not be afraid. In contrast, Matthew reports that the sentinels at the tomb had previously reacted in fear (cf. Witherup 1987, 583). In Luke the angels responded with a question: "Why seek ye the living among the dead?" It is unknown whether or not the question raised by the angel was asked sarcastically. The idea that the question was stated sarcastically is based on the notion that the women should have remembered as they evidently did not the time when Jesus was still in Galilee and instructed that he would rise on the third day. Finally, John's angels initially asked a question of a weeping Mary Magdalene, however, this was only after her second visit to the tomb.

CONTRADICTION #65 Contradictory Facts

Luke reports contradictory facts that contrast with Mark and Matthew. Mark 16:6 and Mathew 28:5 are in agreement with each other and report essentially the same initial words spoken to the women that they should not be afraid.

> Mk 16:6 And he said unto them, Be not affrighted: Ye seek Jesus of Nazareth, which was crucified: he is risen; he is not here: behold the place where they laid him.

> Mt 28:5 Fear not ye: for I know that ye seek Jesus, which was crucified.

In contradiction, Luke 24:5 reports that the women were spoken to, not by one but *simultaneously* by two men, both of whom offered no comment to alleviate the women's fear. Instead, the two men responded to the women's presence in the tomb with a question: "And as they were afraid, and bowed down their faces to the earth, they said unto them, Why seek ye the living among the dead?"

John 20:13, however, reads like a completely different story from the synoptic Gospels. A weeping Mary Magdalene returned to the tomb after a second visit and was received by two angels. Since John did not have Mary Magdalene afraid (she was weeping), the two angels made no inquiry as to why she was afraid. Instead, they simultaneously responded with a question: "And they say unto her, Woman why weepest thou? She saith unto them, Because they have taken away my Lord, and I know not where they have laid him." The only similarity was that both Luke and John had two messengers talking simultaneously and conveying basically the same message to Mary Magdalene.

One additional point of contradiction requires additional fleshing out. Luke and John report that the angels ignored the human emotional response of the women. Here the angels seem to be cold and distant and offer a strange response. In contradiction, the narratives in Mark and Matthew appear to have the angels comforting the women. It is one thing to have different words appearing in the narratives, but it is another to have completely different emotions being reported. For the sake of analysis, assume that there was a car accident with several witnesses. It is one thing for these witnesses to present different wording describing the accident. However, it would be a completely different matter if two witnesses reported that several women inside a car hit at a high speed responded by laughing, yet two other witnesses testified that the women were terrified.

ISSUE 59: What the Women Were Told by the Messenger(s)

Mk 16:5 And entering into the sepulchre, they saw a young man sitting on the right side, clothed in a long white garment; and they were affrighted. 6 And he said unto them, Be not affrighted: *Ye seek Jesus of Nazareth, which was crucified: he is risen; he is not here: behold the place where they laid him.* 7 *But go your way, tell his disciples and Peter that he goeth before you into Galilee: there shall ye see him,* as he said unto you.	Mt 28:5 And the angel answered and said unto the women, Fear not ye: *for I know that ye seek Jesus, which was crucified. 6 He is not here: for he is risen, as he said. Come, see the place where the Lord lay.*	Lk 24:5 And as they were afraid, and bowed down their faces to the earth, they said unto them, *Why seek ye the living among the dead?* 6 *He is not here, but is risen: remember how he spake unto you when he was yet in Galilee,* 7 Saying, the Son of man must be delivered into the hands of sinful men, and be crucified, and the third day rise again.	Jn 20:13 *And they say unto her, Woman why weepest thou?* She saith unto them, Because they have taken away my Lord, and I know not where they have laid him. 14 And when she had thus said, she turned herself back, and saw Jesus standing, and knew not that it was Jesus.

In Mark 16:6 and Matthew 28:5, the messengers seemingly have knowledge of the women's purpose. In both accounts the person speaking to the women essentially state the same words that they seek Jesus, who was crucified. Then the messenger informs the women that Jesus was risen and not in the tomb. However, the time of Jesus's resurrection is not mentioned. In Luke 24:5 there is a question asked by the angels: "Why seek ye the living among the dead?" followed by a statement that Jesus spoke to them while in Galilee prophesying his arrest, crucifixion, and resurrection. Finally, in John 20:13, during Mary Magdalene's second visit, the angels inquire, "Why weepest thou?"

ISSUE 60: The Message for the Disciples

Mk	Mt	Lk	Acts	Jn
Mk 16:6 And he saith unto them, Be not affrighted: *Ye seek Jesus of Nazareth*, which was crucified: he is risen; he is not here: behold the place where they laid him. 7 *But go your way, tell his disciples and Peter that he goeth before you into Galilee: there shall ye see him*, as he said unto you.	Mt 28:6 He is not here: for he is risen, as he said. Come, see the place where *the Lord lay*. 7 And *go quickly, and tell his disciples that he is risen from the dead*; and, behold, *he goeth before you into Galilee; there shall ye see him:* lo, I have told you.	Lk 24:6 He is not here, but is risen: remember how he spake unto you when he was yet in Galilee, 7 Saying, the Son of man must be delivered into the hands of sinful men, and be crucified, and the third day rise again.	Acts 1:4 And, being assembled together with them, *commanded them that they should not depart from Jerusalem, but wait for the promise of the Father,* which, saith he, ye have heard of me.	

Mark and Matthew reports that the women were instructed to tell the disciples that Jesus was going before them to Galilee and that there they would see him as he had said to them. However, in Mark's narrative, Peter of all the disciples was specifically singled out. Significantly it should also be noted that the message did *not* call the disciples to the tomb or even to its vicinity. And notably, the young man or angel knew that without the message and testimony from the women, Peter and the disciples would never be looking for Jesus in Galilee.

In contrast, Luke reminds the women that Jesus foretold that he would be (1) delivered into the hands of sinful men (high priests and Pharisees), (2) crucified, and (3) resurrected on the third day. On the other hand, Luke does not directly state that Jesus was going before them to Galilee or that he would be seen there. Neither did the two men directly commission a message to be delivered to the disciples. However, in Acts 1:4 the disciples are told by Jesus not to depart Jerusalem. In John, there is no message given by the two angels Mary Magdalene encountered during her second visit to the tomb.

TABLE 35. Contradictory Commands for the Disciples to Go to the Galilee and Meet Jesus

VERSE	TEXT	COMMANDS and CONTRADICTIONS
Mark 16:7	*But go your way, tell his disciples and Peter that he goeth before you into Galilee: there shall ye see him*, as he said unto you.	An explicit command to go to the Galilee and there the disciples and Peter would meet Jesus.
Matthew 28:7	And *go quickly, and tell his disciples* that he is risen from the dead; and, behold, he goeth before you into Galilee; there shall ye see him: Lo, I have told you.	An explicit command to go to the Galilee and there the disciples would meet Jesus.
Luke 24:49	And, behold, I send the promise of my Father upon you: but tarry ye in the city of Jerusalem, until ye be endued with power from on high.	No explicit command to meet Jesus in the Galilee. To the contrary Luke explicitly contradicts Matthew and Mark.
Acts 1:4	And, being assembled together with them, *commanded them that they should not depart from Jerusalem, but wait for the promise of the Father*, which, saith he, ye have heard of me.	No explicit command to meet Jesus in the Galilee. To the contrary, Acts explicitly contradicts Matthew and Mark.
John		No explicit command to meet Jesus in the Galilee.

CONTRADICTION #66 Luke Contradicts Mark and Matthew

Luke contradicts Mark and Matthew regarding the instructions as to where the disciples were to travel and meet Jesus. Mark 16:7 narrates that a young man commanded the women: "But go your way, tell his disciples and

Peter that he goeth before you into Galilee: there shall ye see him, as he said unto you." Similarly, Matthew 28:7 reports that the women were instructed by an angel of the Lord to inform the disciples that they were to meet Jesus in Galilee: "And go quickly, and tell his disciples that he is risen from the dead; and, behold, he goeth before you into Galilee; there shall ye see him: lo, I have told you." Therefore, it is understood that the disciples were being told to go to the Galilee. Not much later Matthew 28:10 reports that Jesus himself commanded the women, saying, "Then said Jesus unto them, Be not afraid: go tell my brethren that they go into Galilee, and there shall they see me." Consequently, Mark and Matthew are in general agreement that the disciples were to go on to the Galilee and there they would meet Jesus.

Contrary to Mark and Matthew, in Luke and John there is no command for the disciples to go to the Galilee and there meet Jesus. In contradiction, on Easter Sunday evening, Luke 24:43-48 reports that Jesus himself actually visited the disciples in Jerusalem. Luke 24:34 also reports that Jesus was earlier seen by Simon. Fifteen verses later Luke 24:49 narrates that Jesus commanded them to stay in Jerusalem: "And, behold, I send the promise of my Father upon you: but tarry ye in the city of Jerusalem, until ye be endued with power from on high." Furthermore, Luke, the presumed author of Acts 1:4, also has Jesus commanding his disciples to stay in Jerusalem: "And, being assembled together with them, commanded them that they should not depart from Jerusalem but wait for the promise of the Father, which, saith he, ye have heard of me." In other words, Jesus commanded his disciples to remain in Jerusalem and not travel elsewhere, which would include Galilee. Therefore, Jesus's instructions recorded in Luke directly contradicts the message to the women narrated in Mark and Matthew.

SPECULATION #114 Why Peter's Name Is Included in Mark's Message

Contrary to Matthew and Luke, Mark notably adds the words: "and to Peter." The Christian apologists Ankerberg and Weldon suggest that the words "and to Peter" were added because "Mark was Peter's friend and traveling companion." Even if Mark was Peter's friend and traveling companion, this is no guarantee that the recorded text is accurate. All that Ankerberg and Weldon offer is their own opinion and mere speculation. Another speculated explanation is that this passage was written after James had died (ca. 62 or 63) and Peter had become a claimant to the headship of the church. Consequently, the verse reinforces Peter's claim to head the church.

ISSUE 61: The Empty Tomb

Mk 16.5 *And entering into the sepulchre, they saw a young man sitting in the right side,* clothed in a long white garment; and they were affrighted. 6 *And he said unto them, Be not affrighted: Ye seek Jesus of Nazareth, which was crucified: he is risen; he is not here: behold the place where they laid him.*	Mt 28:2 And, behold, there was a great earthquake: for an angel of the Lord descended from heaven, and rolled back the stone from the door, and sat upon it. 3 His countenance was like lightning, and his raiment white as snow: 4 And for fear of him the keepers did shake, and became as dead men. 5 *And the angel answered and said unto the women, Fear not ye: for I know that ye seek Jesus, which was crucified. 6 He is not here: for he is risen, as he said. Come, see the place where the Lord lay.*	Lk 24:3 *And they entered in, and found not the body of the Lord Jesus.* 4 And it came to pass, as they were much perplexed thereabout, behold, two men stood by them in shining garments: 5 And as they were afraid, and bowed down their faces to the earth, *they said unto them, Why seek ye the living among the dead? 6 He is not here, but is risen:* remember how he spake unto you when he was yet in Galilee, 7 Saying, the Son of man must be delivered into the hands of sinful men, and be crucified, and the third day rise again.	Jn 20:1 The first day of the week cometh Mary Magdalene early, when it was yet dark, unto the sepulchre, and *seeth the stone taken away from the sepulchre. 2 Then she runneth, and cometh to Simon Peter, and to the other disciples* whom Jesus loved and said unto them, They have taken away the Lord out of the sepulchre, and we know not where they have laid him.... Jn 20:12 *And seeth two angels in white sitting, the one at the head, and the other at the feet, where the body of Jesus had lain.* 13 And they say unto her, Woman why weepest thou? She saith unto them, Because they have taken away my Lord, and I know not where they have laid him.

Mark and Matthew report that only after receiving a message did the women seemingly notice the empty tomb. Therefore, in a strict sense, the women did not discover the emptiness of the tomb; the messenger pointed out that the tomb was empty after his proclamation of Jesus's resurrection. To the contrary, Luke 24:3-7 reverses the order: first the women discover that the tomb is empty and *then* they hear the announcement.

In contrast, John 20 reports that Mary Magdalene arrives at the tomb when it is still dark. Nonetheless she is able to see that the stone blocking the entrance to the tomb has been removed. Without any further explanation, she runs to the disciples and informs them that some unknown people have removed Jesus's body. Mary's evaluation that Jesus's body has been removed is not based on an actual entry of the tomb or on a peeking into the tomb from outside or even a message from any angels.

SPECULATION #115: Significance of the Empty Tomb

Up to this point, neither Jesus's prior teachings, his miracles, the empty tomb, nor the angel's message demonstrated any proof that Jesus was resurrected in the eyes of his followers. Numerous commentators and theologians (Heil 1992b, 354; Hendrickx 1984, 16; O'Collins 1999, 17; 1993, 20; Plevnik 1980, 500; Schlier 2008, 34; Smith 1971, 40; Stein 1996, 263; 1977, 125; Wright 2003, 688-89) have recognized and discussed this fact. A concise summary is found in Sheehan (1986, 143-44):

> First: *The empty tomb is not a proof of the resurrection.* The angel does not say that the tomb is empty and therefore Jesus has been raised, but that Jesus has been raised and consequently the tomb is empty. It is the resurrection that explains the tomb, not vice versa. Of itself the empty tomb leads to confusion rather than faith.

> Second: Not just the empty tomb but *even the angel's announcement that Jesus has been raised does not bring about faith.* Having heard the proclamation and seen the empty tomb, the women simply flee without believing that Jesus has been raised. As listeners, we are expected to understand that if the angel's kerygma did not bring the women to believe, neither will it instill faith in us. That is, if one does not have faith already, neither the pronouncements of angels nor the emptiness of tombs can provide it. The source of Easter faith must lie elsewhere.

> Third: The listener is therefore meant to understand that *the women's confused flight and subsequent silence is in fact the appropriate response to the scene at the tomb.* It is rhetorically understandable that the women tell no one what they have heard and seen, for the point of the story is that angels' words do not effect faith (they did not for the women in the legend, and they will not for the listeners) and that empty graves of themselves say

nothing about a resurrection. The women's flight in disbelief is not an embarrassment to Christian faith but rather is the very point of the story: Those who go looking for Jesus in a tomb (be it empty or occupied) are left in the dark.

Consequently, *all that the empty tomb proves is that it was empty.* That is, Jesus's body was not inside the confines of the tomb. Therefore, in itself, the empty tomb provides no proof of how the tomb became empty. To quote Thiselton (2000, 1197; cf. Edward 2002, 494), "The empty tomb could never in itself constitute a "proof," for it could be explained in a variety of ways."

Finally, the words of Gilmour (1965, 12-13), written approximately fifty years ago, are deserving of thoughtful consideration:

> There is no indication in Paul's letters that the apostle had any knowledge of the doctrine of the empty tomb. It has frequently been argued that the doctrine is implied in his words that Christ died, was buried, and was raised, but to assume that the verb "was raised" must refer to a physical resurrection seems to me a non sequitur. To the other argument occasionally employed, that Paul makes no reference to the empty tomb because he took knowledge of it for granted, the answer is that an argument from silence is a poor tool. How illogical the claim that, because Paul makes no mention of an empty tomb, he must have been familiar with the doctrine!
>
> Even if Paul had heard the story of the empty tomb, I do not believe he could have accepted it. It is clear from the apostle's argument in 1 Corinthians 15 that he believed that our resurrection body will not be the body of this flesh. He asserts (1) that Christ rose from the dead; (2) that our Lord's resurrection is the assurance that those who belong to him will also be raised at his second coming; and (3) that the resurrection body will not be the body that is laid in the grave but a spiritual body that differs from the physical as the plant differs from the seed that is sown. In 2 Corinthians 5:1-5 Paul describes this spiritual body as "a building from God, a house not made with hands, eternal in the heavens." It follows, therefore, that, just as we are to be clothed at our resurrection with a spiritual body, so the Risen Christ has a "body of God's splendor," not a resuscitated corpse.

ISSUE 62: The Women's Final Disposition to the Message They Received

Mk 16:8 *And they went out quickly, and fled from the sepulchre; for they trembled and were amazed:* neither said they any thing to any man; *for they were afraid.*	Mt 28:8 And they departed quickly from the *sepulchre with fear and great joy*; and did run to bring his disciples word.	Lk 24:8 And they remembered his words. 9 *And returned from the sepulchre,* and told all these things unto the eleven, and to all the rest.	Jn

The synoptic writers describe a variety of emotions and reactions in response to the women having met the messenger(s) and received their message. Mark 16:8 reports that the women fled the tomb, "trembling and bewildered." Matthew 28:8 records that the women were filled with both fear and great joy. Luke 24:8 narrates: "And they remembered his words" and "return" to Jerusalem in order to inform the apostles. John's narrative omits Mary receiving a message from the two angels and, consequently, there cannot be a reaction.

CONTRADICTION #67 The Gospels Report Contradictory Emotional Reactions

The final reactions of the women to the messenger(s) reads like four completely different stories and are not comparable to four witnesses reporting what they saw at a car accident. Mark 16:8 declares that the women Mary Magdalene, Mary the mother of James, and Salome fled from the tomb trembling and amazed: "And they went out quickly, and fled from the sepulchre; for they trembled and were amazed: neither said they any thing to any man; for they were afraid." Four times the word *they* in the English appears in the verse pointing to the group as a whole.

Contrary to Mark, Matthew 28:8 declares that the women left the tomb with fear and great joy: "And they departed quickly from the sepulchre with fear and great joy; and did run to bring his disciples word." In other words, the women in Matthew left the tomb with a mixture of contrasting, distinct, and unrelated attitudes. Collectively there are at least five women leaving the tomb in a mixture of incongruent attitudes: Mary Magdalene, Mary the mother of James, the other Mary, Joanna (detailed in Luke), and Salome. However, *joy* has no similarity to trembling or amazed.

Luke 24:8 totally drops the women's trembling and amazement as detailed in Mark. Therefore, Luke's narrative reads completely different from Mark's. Similarly, Luke omits any of the descriptive emotions of the women portrayed in Matthew. Instead, Luke changes Matthew's reportedly confused flight from the tomb into a simple: "And they remembered his words. And returned from the sepulchre, and told all these things unto the eleven, and to all the rest." Again, Luke's narrative reads like a completely different account.

Finally, John 20 does not report that Mary Magdalene received any message from the two angels while at the tomb. Consequently no emotional response is reported.

PREFACE: A LITERARY DEVICE

The next four speculations relates to several texts in Mark and Matthew, serving as a literary device.

SPECULATION #116 The Relationship between Mark 10:32 and Mark 16:8

Mark is the only gospel that describes the women as *afraid*. A careful analysis of Mark 10:32 parallel the message of Mark's young man in chapter 16:

TABLE 36. The Linguistic Issue between Mark 10 and Mark 16

Mark 10	Mark 16
Mk 10:32 And they were in the way going up to Jerusalem; and Jesus *went before* [*proago* #4254] them: and they were *amazed* [*thambeo* #2284]; and as they followed, they were *afraid* [*phobeo* #5399]. And he took again the twelve, and began to tell them what things should happen unto him,	Mk 16:7 But go your way, tell his disciples and Peter that *he goeth before* [*proago* #4254] *you* into Galilee: there shall ye see him, as he said unto you.
	Mk 16:8 And they went out quickly, and fled from the sepulchre; for they trembled [*tromos* #5156 and were *amazed* [*ekstasis* # 611]: neither said they any thing to any man; for they were *afraid* [*phobeo* # 5399].

Mark 10:32 describes Jesus as leading his disciples. Further, they were amazed, and those who accompanied him were afraid. Similarly, in Mark 16:8 these concepts are implied, with the verses employing the identical Greek words. Only the Greek word translated in English as "amazed" differs: *thambeo* versus *ekstasis*. Nonetheless the images portrayed by the author are unmistakable.

SPECULATION #117 The Relationship between Mark 6:50-52 and Mark 16:8

Another relationship located in the conclusion of Mark is found in the sixth chapter of his testament. Naluparayil (2000, 423-24) writes unequivocally: "There exists a total parallelism between the two accounts (6:50-52//16:5-8) except for the concluding narrative comment regarding the incomprehension of the disciples (6:52)."

TABLE 37. The Parallel Sequence in Mark 6 and Mark 16 (modified from Naluparayil)

Mark 6:50-52	Mark 16:5-8
1. The disciples are terrified: 6:50b.	1. The women are amazed: 16:5b.
2. Jesus says, "*I am*": 6:50f.	3. The *resurrection* [he is risen]: 16:6c-f.
3. There is a command not to fear: 6:50eg.	2. There is a command not to be amazed [affrighted]: 16:6b.
4. There is a failure of the command and the astonishment of the disciples: 6:51c.	4. There is failure of the command, and the fear and astonishment of the women: 16:8bd.

SPECULATION #118 The Relationship between Mark 1:27 and Mark 16:8

O'Collins (1988b, 502) posits that from the onset of Mark's gospel and Jesus's ministry there was the repeated motif of *amazement* or *astonishment*. In the first chapter the people are described as *astonished* at Jesus's teaching (Mk 1:22) and *amazed* at his power over unclean spirits (Mk 1:27). Hence these words may have been deliberately incorporated into the text to form a type of literary bookend.

TABLE 38. Mark 1:22, 27, and 16:8

Mark 1:22	And they were *astonished* at his doctrine: for he taught them as one that had authority, and not as the scribes.	*Ekplesso* [Strong #1605].
Mark 1:27	And they were all *amazed*, insomuch that they questioned among themselves, saying, What thing is this? what new doctrine is this? for with authority commandeth he even the unclean spirits, and they do obey him.	*Thambeo* [Strong #2284].
Mark 16:8	And they went out quickly, and fled from the sepulchre; for they trembled and were *amazed*: neither said they any thing to any man; for they were afraid.	*Ekstasis* [Strong #1611].

SPECULATION #119 The Relationship between Matthew 2:10 and Matthew 28:8

Another speculative literary bookend can be found in the Magi's visit to the infant Jesus. For example, Gundry (1994, 590) points out the parallel presence of the phrase *great joy*.

Mt 2:10 When they saw the star, they rejoiced with exceeding *great joy*.

Mt 28:8 And they departed quickly from the sepulchre with fear and *great joy*; and did run to bring his disciples word.

In direct contrast, Buchanan (1996, 1021) writes:

Do not be afraid. This statement was literally designed to form an inclusion of the entire gospel. In the first chapter the angel of the Lord removed Joseph's anxiety by telling him not to be afraid (Matt 1:20). Before Jesus was born the angel announced to Joseph that he should not be afraid, and the, after his death, the angel appeared again to offer the same comfort.

ISSUE 63: Delivering the Message of the Angels

Mk 16:8 And they went out quickly, and fled from the sepulchre; for they trembled and were amazed: *neither said they any thing to any man; for they were afraid.* 9 Now when Jesus was risen early the first day of the week, he appeared first to Mary Magdalene, out of whom he had cast seven devils. 10 And she went and told them that had been with him, as they mourned and wept. 11 And they, when they had heard that he was alive, and had been seen of her, believed not.	Mt 28:8 And they departed quickly from the sepulchre with fear and great joy; *and did run to bring his disciples word.*	Lk 24:9 And returned from the sepulchre, *and told all these things unto the eleven, and to all the rest.*	Jn

Mark 16:8 narrates that the women said nothing to any man about that which the young man instructed them to deliver. Therefore, the women did not carry the message to the disciples. Nonetheless, two verses later Mark reports that Mary Magdalene informed the disciples that she had seen Jesus. Matthew 28:8 declares that even though the women fled from the tomb, it was to tell the disciples what they had seen along with the message of the angel. However, Matthew failed to unequivocally mention that the women actually carried out the commission one way or another. He tersely narrates that the women "did run to bring his disciples word." Similarly, Luke 24:9 reports that Mary Magdalene and the women ran to bring word to the disciples. This time the message was successfully transmitted to the eleven disciples and other unnamed people possibly present in the room.

John 20:2 states that only Mary Magdalene is mentioned as bringing a message to the disciples. However, her first message was *not* based on any communication. Instead, it was based on seeing the stone taken away and the assumption that Jesus's body was gone. Thus, accordingly, there was *no* angelic message. After having returned to the tomb a second time, Mary Magdalene encountered two angels and the risen Jesus. Immediately following, John 20:18 had Mary Magdalene's second report to the disciples specifying that she had seen the risen Jesus and reported the things he spoke.

CONTRADICTION #68 The Contradictions and Issues Related to the Women's Silence

Mark 16:7-8 narrates that the women fled the tomb in terror and amazement and said nothing to anyone about what the angel instructed them to deliver. Therefore, the women did *not* carry the message to the disciples.

Nonetheless, two verses later Mark reports that Mary Magdalene found the disciples mourning and weeping and informed them that Jesus was in fact alive. However, Mark did not provide any suggestion that the message of the angel was transmitted or that Jesus himself had sent a message for the disciples.

In the Gospel of Matthew (28:8) the women fled from the tomb in order to tell the disciples what they had seen as well as to give the message of the angel. They were described with conflicting emotions: with fear and great joy. However, before they could reach the disciples they were intercepted by the risen Jesus. Immediately the women grasped Jesus's feet and worshipped him. Then Jesus proceeded to essentially repeat the command of the angel for the women to tell his disciples to go to the Galilee and there they would see him. Significantly Matthew failed to provide any incontrovertible evidence that the women actually carried out the commission one way or another. However, five verses later Matthew described the eleven disciples at Galilee having an encounter with Jesus after an unknown period of time following Easter Sunday.

In the Gospel of Luke the women did not receive a command or message from an angel to convey to the disciples. However, Luke 24:9 reports that Mary Magdalene and the women "returned from the sepulchre" and attempted to bring word of what they experienced to the disciples. This time the women were successful and the message transmitted to the eleven disciples and others possibly present in the room. However, their report was not believed. On the same day, two travelers heading for Emmaus, encountered an unrecognized and risen Jesus. During their conversation, it was mentioned that some of those who were with these two travelers found the tomb empty, just as some women had reported. However, the two disciples did not see Jesus.

Finally, John reports that Mary Magdalene came to the tomb when it was dark and discovered that the stone was removed. She ran back and found Peter and the other disciple whom Jesus loved. There was a race to the tomb, an investigation, a failure to understand what had occurred, and a return to their homes. Then, Mary Magdalene returned and encountered two angels. Immediately, the angels asked her why she was crying. After she responded and turned around, Jesus was standing there. However, she did not know that it was him. Jesus asked why she was crying. Mary Magdalene responded with a question. Eventually Mary Magdalene recognized Jesus, and he told her, "Touch me not; for I am not yet ascended to my Father: but go to my brethren, and say unto them, I ascend unto my Father, and your Father; and to my God, and your God." Then Mary Magdalene went back to Jerusalem and transmitted to the disciples what had occurred.

At this point it is important to review the numerous contradictions related and unrelated to the women. Mark 16:7 and Matthew 28:7 confirms that an angel gave a message to several women about the disciples meeting Jesus in the Galilee. Although, Luke 24:23 contradicts their narrative: "And when they found not his body, they came, saying, that they had also seen a vision of angels, which said that he was alive." Significantly, Luke's narrative is known to be based on Mark and Matthew, yet this gospel omits any discussion about the women being commanded to inform the disciples of continuing on to Galilee and there meet Jesus. Similarly, John omits any mention about angels giving a command or message to Mary Magdalene about the disciples meeting Jesus in Galilee. Instead, in John 20:13 the two angels merely ask one question and then disappear: "And they say unto her, Woman, why weepest thou?" So Luke and John contradict Mark and Matthew.

The next topic of contradiction is the transmission of the angel's message. Mark 16:8 reports unequivocally that no message was delivered: "And they went out quickly, and fled from the sepulchre; for they trembled and were amazed: neither said they any thing to any man; for they were afraid." However, in Mark 16:11 it is unknown if Mary Magdalene transmitted the angel's command: "And they, when they had heard that he was alive, and had been seen of her, believed not." All that Mark states is that Jesus was alive. In contrast, Matthew 28:16 possibly intimates that a message was delivered since the disciples eventually met Jesus in Galilee: "Then the eleven disciples went away into Galilee, into a mountain where Jesus had appointed them." In contrast, with Luke 24:1-9 there is no specific message assigned to the women for transmission. They were merely reminded by two angels what Jesus previously instructed. Furthermore, Luke 24:22-23 also provides no specific facts that the women received a command from angels or delivered a message: "Yea, and certain women also of our company made us astonished, which were early at the sepulchre; And when they found not his body, they came, saying, that they had also seen a vision of angels, which said that he was alive." Finally, John 20:13 did not report that either a command or a message from the two angels was given to Mary Magdalene: "And they say unto her, Woman, why weepest thou?" Consequently, there was no command or message to forward to the disciples.

A third issue of contradiction is whether or not one or several women had a physical encounter with the risen Jesus on Easter Sunday. Mark 16:9 and Matthew 28:9 report actual encounters. So too does John 20:14: "And when she had thus said, she turned herself back, and saw Jesus standing, and knew not that it was Jesus." However, Luke 24:22-24 reports: "Yea, and certain women also of our company made us astonished, which were early at the sepulchre; And when they found not his body, they came, saying, that they had also seen a vision of angels, which said that he was alive. And certain of them which were with us went to the sepulchre, and found it even so as the women had said: but him they saw not."

The fourth area of contradiction relates to whether or not Jesus gave a message to one or several women on Easter Sunday morning for the disciples to meet him in the Galilee. Matthew 28:9 narrates a definite encounter with Jesus with actual physical contact: "And as they went to tell his disciples, behold, Jesus met them, saying, All hail. And they came and held him by the feet, and worshipped him." In the next verse Matthew recorded: "Then said Jesus unto them, Be not afraid: go tell my brethren that they go into Galilee, and there shall they see me." John 20:14-17 also substantiates that Jesus met with Mary Magdalene. Perhaps here, too, physical contact was made with Jesus with the enigmatic verse: "Jesus saith unto her, Touch me not; for I am not yet ascended to my Father: but go to my brethren, and say unto them, I ascend unto my Father, and your Father; and to my God, and your God." In contradiction, Mark and Luke omit any information that provides support that Jesus gave a specific message for the women to transmit.

Another topic of contradiction is whether or not Jesus's command or a communiqué on Easter Sunday morning was forwarded to the disciples. Since no command appears in Mark and Luke, it would be impossible for them to forward a message. John has a message for the disciples; however, it has nothing to do with the disciples going on to the Galilee and meeting Jesus. In contrast, Matthew 28:1d implies that some type of communication was forwarded since here it was reported that at some unknown time in the future the disciples went to the Galilee: "Then the eleven disciples went away into Galilee, into a mountain where Jesus had appointed them." However, it is also possible that just the angel's message in Matthew 28:7 was transmitted: "And go quickly, and tell his disciples that he is risen from the dead; and, behold, he goeth before you into Galilee; there shall ye see him: lo, I have told you."

The final issue of contradiction deals with the transmission of a *related experience* with Jesus or the angels on Easter Sunday morning. In Mark 16:11 there is reported a related experience that was transmitted: "And they, when they had heard that he was alive, and had been seen of her, believed not." However, what the nature of the transmission was remains unknown. In Matthew, it is unknown if there was the transmission of a related experience with Jesus or the angels. Yet in Luke 24:9-10 and 23 there is definitely a transmission of a related experience:

> Lk 24:9 And returned from the sepulchre, and told all these things unto the eleven, and to all the rest.

> Lk 24:10 It was Mary Magdalene and Joanna, and Mary the mother of James, and other women that were with them, which told these things unto the apostles.

Lk 24:23 And when they found not his body, they came, saying, that they had also seen a vision of angels, which said that he was alive.

Finally, John 20:18 definitely reports a related experience: "Mary Magdalene came and told the disciples that she had seen the Lord, and that he had spoken these things unto her."

TABLE 39. Contradictions Related to the Women's Silence on Easter Sunday Morning

The Gospel	An Angel (or two Angels) Gave a Message to a Woman or Several Women about the Disciples Meeting Jesus in the Galilee	Transmission of the Angel's Message on Easter Sunday Morning about Meeting in the Galilee	One Woman or Several Women Met Jesus on Easter Sunday Morning	Jesus Gave a Message to One Woman or Several Women about Meeting in the Galilee on Easter Sunday Morning	Transmission of Jesus's Message to the Disciples About Meeting in the Galilee on Easter Sunday Morning	Transmission of a RELATED Experience with Jesus or the Angels on Easter Sunday Morning
Mark	YES: Mk 16:7	NO: Mk 16:8 UNKNOWN: Mk 16:11	YES: Mk 16:9	NO	NO	YES: Mk 16:11 but UNKNOWN what she transmitted.
Matthew	YES: Mt 28:7	POSSIBLY INTIMATED: YES Mt 28:16	YES: Mt 28:9	YES: Mt 28:10	UNKNOWN BUT MAYBE IMPLIED by Mt 28:16	UNKNOWN
Luke	NO: Lk 24:23	UNKNOWN	NO: Lk 24:24	NO	NO	YES: Lk 24:9-10, 23
John	NO	NO	YES: Jn 20:14	YES: Jn 20:17	NO	YES: Jn 20:18

TABLE 40. Contradictions Related to the Appearances to the Women on Easter Sunday (Modified from William Thomas Kessler. Peter as the First Witness of the Risen Lord: An Historical and Theological Investigation (Roma: Editrice Pontificia Universita Gregoriana, 1998), 59)

JESUS	MARK	MATTHEW	LUKE	JOHN
TO	Mary Magdalene	Mary Magdalene and Mary	No appearance	Mary Magdalene
MESSAGE	No message.	Fear not.	No appearance.	Woman, why weepst thou? Whom seekest thou? Touch me not; for I am not yet ascended to my Father. But go to my brethren, and say unto them, I ascend unto my Father, and your Father; and to my God, and to your God.
MISSION/ TASK	No mission/ task.	Fear not.	No appearance.	Tell Jesus's brethren that he would ascend to his Father.
RESULT	She went and told the disciples. The disciples mourned and wept.	No account was provided.	No appearance.	Mary Magdalene went and told the disciples. The disciples still remained afraid (i.e., assembled with fear).

CONTRAST	Jesus's message added nothing to the angel's message.	Jesus, unlike the young man was silent.	No appearance.	Jesus joined an appearance with two angels. Jesus repeated the angels' question.
ANALYSIS	The disciples did not believe.	No mention of faith.	The disciples did not believe.	The disciples did not respond.

SPECULATION #120 Commentaries on the Women's Silence

There are a number of speculations concerning the women's silence after having received their message as recorded in Mark. Bode (1970, 39-44; cf. Topel 2012, 79-96) suggests five possible interpretations of the women's silence scenario:

1. The silence explains why the legend of the empty tomb remained so long unknown.
2. The silence is an instance of Mark's Messianic secret motif.
3. The silence is temporary.
4. The silence served the apologetic purpose of separating the apostles from the empty tomb.
5. The silence is the paradoxical human reaction to divine commands as understood by Mark.

Several of these interpretations, along with others, are examined below.

First, Christian apologists (Allison 2005, 130; Bode 1970, 40; Catchpole 1977, 3-10; Craig 1989b, 229-30; Jonge 2008, 128; Moule 1965,133; Witherington 2001, 415) argue that 16:8 only means that the women never told any man what they saw as they left the tomb, not that they never informed anyone about their experience. Waterman (2006, 175) posits three possible options when the women broke their silence: "(1) before Jesus' appearance to the disciples, (2) after Jesus' appearance to the disciples, and (3) after decades—say, after Peter and Paul's death."

On the other hand, Jonge (2008, 127) posits: "The suggestion of the story is that no one was expected to be there at that time of the day." Or as Jonge (2008, 129) questioned, "Otherwise, how could the news of the empty tomb have become known?" Given that Mark ended at 16:8 and was the only gospel or the only surviving gospel, read at face value, the only honest interpretation is that the women did not speak to anyone about their experience. The above Christian apologetic is an explanation based on silence and nothing more than pure speculation.

Second, Wilhelm Bousset, as cited by Adela Yarbo Collins (1993, 120), suggests that "the statement in verse 8, 'and they said nothing to anyone' referred originally to the discovery of the empty tomb (v. 6) and not to the command that they give the disciples the message about Galilee (v. 7)." Yet Allison (2005, 130) mentions that 16:8 could plausibly mean that the women said nothing to anyone "except his disciples."

Third, another possible explanation could be that the motive of the author was self-serving. By suggesting that the women failed to relay the message of Jesus's resurrection, Mark implicitly identified himself as the first to proclaim the story of the empty tomb.

Fourth, O'Collins (1988b, 490-91), in a review of the literature, identifies another reason for the women's silence. On historical grounds, it has been argued that "the story of the empty tomb was unknown before the appearance of Mark's Gospel" (Badham and Badham 1982, 23-24; cf. Alsup 1975, 88) and its author invented the entire story. Therefore, "his final words ('they said nothing to anyone, for they were afraid') show him trying to cover his tracks and hide from the reader the fact that 'the generally received traditions about Jesus contained no story about the discovery of the empty tomb" (also see Alsup 1975, 90n26; Hamilton 1965, 415-21).

Fifth, and in contrast with the above, there are at least three broad theological explanations: (1) the women's fearful silence is based on William Wrede's 1901 work *Das Messiassgeheimnis in den Evangelien* (in this work, the *Messianic Secret* refers to a motif primarily in the Gospel of Mark in which Jesus is portrayed as commanding his followers to hide his identity from his enemies by commanding the disciples to keep silent about his Messianic mission on earth and the miracles that he performed), (2) the women failed their master and failed their trust by not delivering the message Jesus entrusted to them (Perrin 1977b, 32-33), and (3) the women's silence was a result of the "fear" caused by the revelation which produced the women's amazement, flight, trembling, and astonishment (Hare 1996, 225; Heil 1992a; Hooker 1991; Lane 1974, 590; Lightfoot 1950, 88). In support of this position, O'Collins (1988b, 500n20) points out: "In Mark's Gospel the theme of 'amazement' ('which ranges from 'astonishment' through 'trembling' to 'fear') occurs 34 times. The last few verses of Mark speak six times of various forms of 'amazement' (Mark 16:5-8)" i.e., a primordial terror at a divine intervention in our world (p. 502). Collins (1993, 120) suggests that stated another way, "the silence of the women is not to be taken literally, but is a conventional expression of the human reaction to the numinous."

Cook (2001, 8) challenges the hypothesis of Wrede's so-called Messianic Secret in Mark that Jesus instructed his disciples to conceal his identity until after the Resurrection: "And as they came down from the mountain, he charged them that they should tell no man what things they had seen, till the Son of man were risen from the dead" (Mk 9:9). However, Cook points out that "this motif is curious since it contradicts other traditions, in Mark itself, that assert Jesus' fame already during his ministry."

> Mk 1:28 And immediately his fame spread abroad throughout all the region round about Galilee.

> Mk 1:45 But he went out, and began to publish it much, and to blaze abroad the matter, insomuch that Jesus could no more openly enter into the city, but was without in desert places: and they came to him from every quarter.

> Mk 2:13 And he went forth again by the sea side; and all the multitude resorted unto him, and he taught them.

> Mk 3:7-9 But Jesus withdrew himself with his disciples to the sea: and a great multitude from Galilee followed him, and from Judaea, And from Jerusalem, and from Idumaea, and from beyond Jordan; and they about Tyre and Sidon, a great multitude, when they had heard what great things he did, came unto him. And he spake to his disciples, that a small ship should wait on him because of the multitude, lest they should throng him.

> Mk 4:1 And he began again to teach by the sea side: and there was gathered unto him a great multitude, so that he entered into a ship, and sat in the sea; and the whole multitude was by the sea on the land.

> Mk 5:24 And Jesus went with him; and much people followed him, and thronged him.

> Mk 7:36-37 And he charged them that they should tell no man: but the more he charged them, so much the more a great deal they published it; And were beyond measure astonished, saying,

> He hath done all things well: he maketh both the deaf to hear, and the dumb to speak.

Unequivocally the "Messianic secret" in Mark was no secret. What then was the rationale for this contradiction? Cook elaborates:

> But the "Secret" becomes more intelligible as a Markan device to explain away an otherwise glaring anomaly, namely: if "the Messiah" originated as a Jewish concept, and if Jesus were genuinely that Messiah, then why had so few Jews ever acknowledged him? As a stratagem, the suggestion that Jesus' identity was initially hidden would render more comprehensible why the vast majority of Jews, beginning already with Jesus' own day, had not accorded him appropriate recognition-if indeed they had ever known of him at all. (p. 8)

Sixth, Hinrich (1998) posits that another explanation for Mark's awkward and abrupt ending at verse 8 may be due to the rest of the manuscript being lost because the oldest manuscripts end at verse 8. However, these writers have omitted at least one other possibility: the entire episode was a fabrication and invention by its author or final redactors.

Seventh, Dewey (2006, 28) makes a comment that could perhaps suggest a literary rationale for the women's silence: "Here Mark continues the pattern of irony seen throughout the Gospel. When Jesus has instructed people to keep silent, they have repeatedly gone and told (e.g., 1:45; 7:36-37). Now, the women are to tell, but instead they keep silent. Thus Mark's Gospel ends." Consequently, the theme of silence forms literary bookends.

Eighth, Goulder (1996, 57-58) offers another possible answer as to why the women failed to report what they heard and saw. It could be argued that Mark 16:8 was, in fact, an apologetic:

> But now Mark thinks of a difficulty. What are people going to say who hear this story for the first time in 70—especially Jewish Christians holding the opposition view in 1 Corinthians 15:12, who will be deeply skeptical of physical resurrection stories? Will they not say, "I've been a Christian for forty years, and it is the first time I have heard such a tale? Why have I never heard this before? It is a pack of lies." So Mark thinks of an answer to this problem. He ends the tale, "And [the women] went out and fled from the tomb, for trembling and astonishment seized upon them; and they said nothing to anyone, for there were afraid" (16:8). You know

what women are like, brethren: they were seized with panic and hysteria, and kept the whole thing quiet. That is why people have not heard all this before.

Later, of course, an unknown redactor of Mark added the final eleven verses not found in the original to cover up the discrepancy of Matthew 28:8 and Luke 24:9, which had the women going forth to tell the disciples.

Ninth, there is the issue of discipleship and faithfulness. That is the lack of action as narrated by Mark on the women's part and as demonstrated by their silence; this effectively repeated the example of the disciples' faithlessness. Williams (1994, 197) elaborates on the negative reaction of the women in 16:8:

> Every aspect of the women's response in Mk 16:8 is negative. The flight (ἔφυγον) of the women from the tomb is similar to the cowardly flight of the disciples after the arrest of Jesus in the garden (ἔφυγον, 14:50). The trembling and terror that causes the women to flee is also an inappropriate response. Earlier, the young man commanded the women not to be amazed after their initial response of the astonishment at the miraculous events at the tomb. Instead of setting aside their amazement in obedience to the young man's command, the women increase their level of emotion to trembling and terror. In addition, the silence of the women is an act of disobedience to the young man's command, and this silence is clearly negative because it arises out of fear. In Mark's gospel, fear is related to a lack of trust and an unwillingness to face suffering and self-sacrifice. This unbelief and lack of self-denial is especially evident in the fear of the disciples (4.41; 6.50; 9.32; 10.32). Out of fear, the women say nothing to anyone, with the result that they disobey the command of the young man and fail to pass on the message to the disciples. This disobedient and fearful silence, along with the women's flight and amazement, is part of a wholly negative response on their part.

In contradiction, Culpepper (1978, 596) suggests that the women's silence is *not* an example of failed discipleship. Rather, "Jesus often commanded those who had witnessed the disclosure of his power in a mighty act to tell no one. Ironically here for the first time the command is obeyed." It is only later in Mark 16:11 that a message is transmitted to the disciples: "And they, when they had heard that he was alive, and had been seen of her, believed not." Obviously the reason for the women's silence is a matter of extensive debate and open speculation.

Finally, Mark's account of the women's silence creates two further problems: How could anybody know what the women had witnessed if they had not, in fact, communicated that information to anybody? In other words, how do we know that the women said nothing? Furthermore, why would an angel give the women a message which they could not deliver? Christian apologists have argued that the women ran to the disciples without speaking to anyone "along the way," not that they ran off and never told anyone. Here even the conservative Christian apologist R. T. France (2002, 684n39) tactfully differs: "This is all very plausible in a real-life situation, but unfortunately Mark does not say that."

Moiser (1995, 237) inquires if Mark's statement that the women said nothing to anyone was credible: "How, amongst other things, would they explain their quick return from the tomb, even presuming they had dropped the spices in their panic and so returned empty-handed? And how would they explain their breathlessness and agitation?"

Moiser's comment alludes to another problem that is often ignored by commentators: what did the women do with the spices that they brought to the tomb? The synoptic Gospels do not mention a single word about their final whereabouts after the women left the tomb: (1) did they leave the spices at the tomb, or (2) did they take the spices with them after leaving the tomb?

In closing, the various Christian apologetics discussed attempt to explain the women's silence are nothing more than explanations based on silence and pure speculation.

ISSUE 64: The Women Grasping the Feet and Worshipping Jesus

Mk	Mt	Lk	Jn
	Mt 28:8 And they departed quickly from the sepulchre with fear and great joy; and did run to bring his disciples word. 9 And as they went to tell his disciples, *behold, Jesus met them, saying, All hail. And they came and held him by the feet, and worshipped him. 10 Then said Jesus unto them, Be not afraid: go tell my brethren that they go into Galilee, and there shall they see me.*		

Matthew 28:8 reports that Mary Magdalene and the other Mary met Jesus on their way to deliver the message of the angel. Jesus appears and greets them: "All hail." Next, the women grasp hold of Jesus by his feet and then they worship him.

CONTRADICTION #69 Luke Contradicts the Other Synoptic Narratives

Matthew's account reports that Jesus met the women after leaving the tomb. Here several women meet the resurrected Jesus. In a similar manner, Mark 16:10 reports that Mary Magdalene was the first to see the risen Jesus: "Now when Jesus was risen early the first day of the week, he appeared first to Mary Magdalene, out of whom he had cast seven devils."

Luke, in his preface, claims to have examined all of the evidence, and yet, he, too, did not record this episode. Even John omits mention of this significant meeting.

Finally, it must be noted that Matthew's narrative enhances the possibility and viability of the claimed Resurrection by documenting additional witnesses.

ISSUE 65: Jesus's Message to the Women

Mk 16:8. And they went out quickly, and fled from the sepulchre; for they trembled and were amazed: neither said they any thing to any man; for they were afraid. 9 Now when Jesus was risen early the first day of the week, he appeared first to Mary Magdalene, out of whom he had cast seven devils. 10 And she went and told them that had been with him, as they mourned and wept. 11 And they, when they had heard that he was alive, and had been seen of her, *believed not*.	Mt 28:9 And as they went to tell his disciples, behold, Jesus met them, saying, All hail. And they came and held him by the feet, and worshipped him. 10 Then said Jesus unto them, *Be not afraid: go tell my brethren that they go into Galilee, and there shall they see me.*	Lk 24:49 And, behold, I send the promise of my Father upon you: but tarry ye in the city of Jerusalem, until ye be endued with power from on high.	Jn 20:17 Jesus saith unto her, Touch me not; for I am not yet ascended to my Father: but go to my brethren, and say unto them, I ascend unto my Father, and your Father; and to my God, and your God.

Mark relates no message from Jesus given to any women. Instead, Mark 16:10-11 reports that Mary Magdalene informed the disciples that Jesus had been with her but they did not believe her. Matthew 28:9 reports an introductory communication from Jesus to the women. One verse later Matthew 28:10, quotes Jesus speaking to the women: "Be not afraid; go, tell my brethren that they go into Galilee, and there they shall see me." Therefore, the women were specifically commissioned to tell Jesus's followers to (1) go into the Galilee and (2) see Jesus there. In contrast, Luke narrates that Jesus instructed his disciples to stay in Jerusalem. Finally, John reports that Jesus instructed Mary Magdalene to say: "I ascend unto my Father, and your Father; and to my God, and your God."

CONTRADICTION #70 Luke 24:49 Contradicts Matthew 28:10

Luke 24:49 unequivocally declares that Jesus saw his disciples in Jerusalem and orders them to stay there: "And behold, I send the promise of my Father upon you: but tarry ye in the city of Jerusalem, until ye be endued with power from on high." In contradiction, Matthew 28:10 reports that Jesus commanded the women to inform his disciples that he would meet them in Galilee: "Be not afraid: go tell my brethren that they go into Galilee, and there shall they see me." In addition, Jesus had previously instructed his disciples that they were to meet him in Galilee. This message to go to Galilee was also stated earlier in Mark and Matthew during the Last Supper.

> Mk 14:28 But after that I am risen, I will go before you into Galilee.

> Mt 26:32 But after I am risen again, I will go before you into Galilee.

One point should be very clear: Jesus's order to go into Galilee and the statement that at that locale he would first appear to the disciples is unmistakable, repeated, and peremptory. In conclusion, Luke contradicts Matthew.

ISSUE 66: The Disciples' Reaction to the Women's Report

Mk	Mt	Lk	Jn
Mk 16:8. And they went out quickly, and fled from the sepulchre; for they trembled and were amazed: neither said they any thing to any man; for they were afraid. 9 Now when Jesus was risen early the first day of the week, he appeared first to Mary Magdalene, out of whom he had cast seven devils. 10 And she went and told them that had been with him, as they mourned and wept. 11 And they, when they had heard that he was alive, and had been seen of her, *believed not.*		Lk 24:11 And their *words seemed to them as idle tales, and they believed them not.* 12 Then arose Peter, and ran unto the sepulchre; and stooping down, he beheld the linen clothes laid by themselves, and departed, wondering in himself at that which was come to pass.	Jn 20:3 *Peter therefore went forth, and that other disciple, and came to the sepulchre.* 4 *So they ran both together:* and the other disciple did outrun *Peter, and came first to the sepulchre.*

Mark 16:8 reports that the women did not transmit the message of the young man because of their fear. Later, in 16:10-11, Mark narrates a different episode in which Mary Magdalene meets Jesus. At this later time she transmitted information about having seen Jesus, but the disciples "believed not." In Matthew there is no confirmation that the message of either the angel or Jesus was transmitted. Therefore, there is no record of the women being believed or disbelieved.

Luke 24:11 reports that the group of women was not believed. Bock (1994, 381) states that "*Lēeros* (NIV *nonsense*), used here for 'idle tale,' was used in everyday Greek to refer to the delirious stories told by the very sick as they suffer in great pain or to tales told by those who failed to perceive reality (4 Macc 5:11; Josephus *Jewish Wars* 3.8.9 §405)." In the next verse Luke reports that Peter arose and ran to the tomb after receiving the report of the women's encounter with the two men. So either Peter believed the women or, in doubt, he went to the tomb to verify their report.

Finally, in John 20:3-4, Peter and the disciple who Jesus loved ran to the tomb after being told that Jesus's body was missing. Here, too, it was possible that both Peter and the other disciple believed the women, or in doubt, they went to the tomb to verify the report.

ISSUE 67: The Race to the Tomb

	Mt		
Mk 16:8. And they went out quickly, and fled from the sepulchre; for they trembled and were amazed: neither said they any thing to any man; for they were afraid. 9 Now when Jesus was risen early the first day of the week, he appeared first to Mary Magdalene, out of whom he had cast seven devils. 10 And she went and told them that had been with him, as they mourned and wept. 11 *And they, when they had heard that he was alive, and had been seen of her, believed not.*		Lk 24:11 And their words seemed to them as idle tales, and they believed them not. 12 *Then arose Peter, and ran unto the sepulchre; and stooping down, he beheld the linen clothes laid by themselves, and departed, wondering in himself at that which was come to pass.*	Jn 20:3 *Peter therefore went forth, and that other disciple, and came to the sepulchre. 4 So they ran both together*: and the other disciple did outrun *Peter, and came first to the sepulchre.*

Only John reports a race to the tomb. Luke 24:11 states that the group of women was not believed. Nonetheless, in the next verse, Luke reports that Peter alone arose and ran to the tomb and inspected it. In contrast, John 20:3-4 describes a race to the tomb between Peter and the disciple who Jesus loved after they were informed that Jesus's body was missing.

SPECULATION #121 **The Purpose of Peter's Investigation**

Several writers (Bonney 1983, 240; Brown 1994a, 2:1004-07; Charlesworth 1995, 390-410; O'Day 1995, 840; Quast 1989, 7; Tobin 1968, 27-70; Wolfe 1989, 117) discuss the narrative's possible depiction of an ecclesial rivalry between Petrine and Johannine Christianity. Skinner (2008, 105) refers to this rivalry as the *community-conflict hypothesis.* For example, Wolfe posits that "the race to the tomb reflects the rivalries between the Petrine and Johannine factions of the Early Church in graphic manner, showing how human nature and favoritism for preferred church leaders became woven even unto the fabric of the Easter tapestry." John 19:27 reintroduces the rivalry between Peter and the disciple who Jesus loved, and this competition was repeated in John 21:7, 24. Luke 24:12 records that Peter ran to the tomb but did *not* go into the sepulchre. Why would Peter or the other disciple be running to the tomb to examine it if, in the previous verse, Luke said, "Their words seemed to them as idle tales, and they believed them not"?

In a similar vein, Bonney (1983, 240n45) states: "Most commentators regard the race to the tomb as a polemic regarding the relationship between John's community and the rest of the Church."

Lorenzen (1995, 169) suggests that Peter's investigation served a twofold purpose:

- It enhances the authority of Peter and the beloved disciple in their respective communities by linking them with this important tradition.
- Since male witnesses were considered to be superior to female witnesses, the credibility of the empty tomb tradition was enhanced.

SPECULATION #122 **Peter's Impulsive Behavior**

A speculated rationale that Luke reported Peter ran to the tomb immediately after being informed by the women was to emphasize his impulsive behavior as recorded earlier in Luke 22:54: "Then took they him, and led him, and brought him into the high priest's house. And Peter followed afar off" and possibly 22:50: "And one of them smote the servant of the high priest, and cut off his right ear." Once again, this hypothesis is in part based on the notion that there existed a rivalry between the Eastern communities and Western communities.

Throughout the Gospels, Peter is projected as quick, hasty, impulsive, and rash. Sometimes he speaks without thinking and at other times he acts before thinking. Of course, what some think to be an impulsive behavior others could consider to be trust. Examples of Peter's impulsive behavior are illustrated in table 41:

TABLE 41. Examples of Peter's Impulsive Behavior

THE SOURCE	THE VERSE	SYNOPSIS
Mt 14:30	But when he saw the wind boisterous, he was afraid; and beginning to sink, he cried, saying, Lord, save me.	Peter immediately proceeded to walk on water after Jesus's request.
Mt 15:15	Then answered Peter and said unto him, Declare unto us this parable.	Peter asked Jesus to explain a parable.
Mk 8:29; Mt 16:15-16; Lk 9:20	And he saith unto them, But whom say ye that I am? And Peter answereth and saith unto him, Thou art the Christ.	Peter was the first to answer Jesus's question to the disciples and he declared that Jesus was the Messiah.
Mk 8:32; Mt 16:22	And he spake that saying openly. And Peter took him, and began to rebuke him.	Peter rebuked Jesus for predicting his death.
Mk 9:5; Mt 17:4; Lk 9:33	And Peter answered and said to Jesus, Master, it is good for us to be here: and let us make three tabernacles; one for thee, and one for Moses, and one for Elias.	Peter was the first to talk at Jesus's Transfiguration: he wanted to build three tabernacles.
Jn 13:8	Peter saith unto him, Thou shalt never wash my feet. Jesus answered him, If I wash thee not, thou hast no part with me.	Peter would not let Jesus wash his feet.
Mk 14:29; Mt 26:33; Lk 22:33; Jn 13:37	But Peter said unto him, Although all shall be offended, yet will not I.	Peter promised that he would never desert Jesus.
Jn 18:10	Then Simon Peter having a sword drew it, and smote the high priest's servant, and cut off his right ear. The servant's name was Malchus.	Peter cut off a servant's ear while Jesus was arrested.

Mk 14:68; Mt 26:70; Lk 23:57; Jn 18:17	But he denied, saying, I know not, neither understand I what thou sayest. And he went out into the porch; and the cock crew.	Peter's first denial of Jesus.
Mk 14:70; Mt 26:72; Lk 23:58; Jn 18:25	And he denied it again. And a little after, they that stood by said again to Peter, Surely thou art one of them: for thou art a Galilaean, and thy speech agreeth thereto.	Peter's second denial of Jesus.
Mk 14:71; Mt 26:74; Lk 23:60; Jn 18:27	But he began to curse and to swear, saying, I know not this man of whom ye speak.	Peter's third denial of Jesus.
Lk 24:12; Jn 20:3	Then arose Peter, and ran unto the sepulchre; and stooping down, he beheld the linen clothes laid by themselves, and departed, wondering in himself at that which was come to pass.	Peter ran to the tomb at the report of the women.
Jn 20:6	Then cometh Simon Peter following him, and went into the sepulchre, and seeth the linen clothes lie,	Peter was first to enter the tomb although he was second to arrive there.
Jn 21:7	Therefore, that disciple whom Jesus loved saith unto Peter, It is the Lord. Now when Simon Peter heard that it was the Lord, he girt his fisher's coat unto him, (for he was naked,) and did cast himself into the sea.	Peter jumped immediately overboard and swam to Jesus once he was informed that the voice belonged to Jesus.
Jn 21:11	Simon Peter went up, and drew the net to land full of great fishes, an hundred and fifty and three: and for all there were so many, yet was not the net broken.	Peter alone pulled 153 fish to shore after Jesus requested that the disciples bring him some fish.
Jn 21:21	Peter seeing him saith to Jesus, Lord, and what shall this man do?	Peter asked Jesus what would eventually happen to the disciple who Jesus loved.

ISSUE 68: The Result of the Investigation by Peter and the Other Disciple

1 Cor 15:5	Mk	Mt	Lk 24:12 Then	Jn 20:2 Then she runneth, and
And that he was seen of Cephas, then of the twelve:			arose Peter, and ran unto the sepulchre; and stooping down, *he beheld the linen clothes laid by themselves, and departed, wondering in himself at that which was come to pass.*	cometh to Simon Peter, and to the other disciple, whom Jesus loved, and saith unto them, They have taken away the Lord out of the sepulchre, and we know not where they have laid him. 3 Peter therefore went forth, and that other disciple, and came to the sepulchre. 4 So they ran both together: and the other disciple did outrun Peter, and came first to the sepulchre. 5 *And he stooping down, and looking in, saw the linen clothes lying; yet went he not in. 6 Then cometh Simon Peter following him, and went into the sepulchre.* And seeth the linen clothes lie. *7 And the napkin, that was about his head, not lying with the linen clothes, but wrapped together in a place by itself.* 8 Then went in also that other disciple, which came first to the sepulchre, *and he saw, and believed.* 9 For as yet they knew not the scripture, that he must rise again from the dead. 10 Then the disciples went away again unto their own home.

Luke 24:12 reports that Peter alone ran to the tomb but he did not enter it. Upon his arrival, he (1) stooped down, (2) looked in, (3) saw the linen clothes, (4) departed, and (5) wondered what had occurred. In contrast, John 20:3-6 states that Peter and the other disciple whom Jesus loved ran to the tomb. Although the other disciple arrived first, he did not enter the tomb. On the other hand, Peter entered the tomb and explored it. Only afterward, in John 20:8 did the other disciple also enter the tomb.

John 20:5-7 adds that Simon Peter and the other disciple saw "the napkin, that was about his head, not lying with the linen clothes, but wrapped together in a place by itself." Then John 20:8 reports that the other disciple "saw and believed." In the following verse the narrator added: "For as yet they knew not the scripture, that he must rise again from the dead." Finally, the disciples returned to their respective homes.

CONTRADICTION #71 Four Different Stories

The gospel narratives present several internal contradictions. Mark and Matthew say nothing about Peter or anyone else investigating the tomb. Luke states that Peter *alone* ran to the tomb and explored it from *outside*. He omits any statement about anyone else going to the tomb. John's text seemingly contradicts Luke and declares that *two* people raced to the tomb, namely, Peter and the disciple who Jesus loved. Then John adds that it was the other disciple who Jesus loved who entered the tomb only *after* Peter first entered it. Remarkably, Mark, Matthew, and Luke omit the fact that Peter *entered* Jesus's burial place.

SPECULATION #123 What the Other Disciple Believed

It is a fallacious claim that the other disciple believed that Jesus rose from the tomb. John 20:8 records that the other disciple went *into* the sepulchre, saw, and believed: "Then went in also that other disciple, which came first to the sepulchre, and he saw, and believed." Of course, Christian apologists claim that other disciple believed that Jesus had risen from the tomb.

To the contrary, John does *not* inform his readers of what the other disciple actually believed. For example, Conway (1997, 189; cf. Koester 1989, 344) writes: "The most obvious problem is that the text does not state what it is the disciple sees and believes. It simply assumed that the reader will be able to fill in the object of these verbs." More specifically, Minear (1976, 127) rejects the position that the other disciple believed that Jesus was resurrected. Minear declares that "the context wholly fails to support that answer." A sensible explanation was that grave robbers had taken the body or that it was reburied elsewhere for reasons unknown. This still raises the question of exactly what scripture was being referred to that Jesus "must rise again from the dead"? Here John is silent and only subject to speculation.

Minear (1976, 127) suggests that there is a more obvious explanation for what the other disciple saw and believed. *"They now 'believed' in Mary's report and thus joined in her confession of ignorance, 'we don't know where he is'"* [italics mine] This position is also discussed by others (Bonney 1998, 73n51; Brown 1970, 987; Bryant 2001, 268; Bultmann 1971, 658-87; De Boer 2004, 169;

Meacham 2009, 322-36; Neirynck 1972, 552; Grant 1997, 245; O'Day 1995, 841; Waterman 2006, 30).

John Wesley states in his *Explanatory Notes upon the New Testament* (London: William Bowyer, 1755) that he unequivocally rejects the notion that the disciple believed Jesus had been resurrected. He writes:

> "He saw": That the body was not there, and "believed"—that they had taken it away as Mary said.

> "For as yet": They had no thought of his rising again.

In addition, John Peter Lange (*Commentary on the Holy Scriptures*. Grand Rapids: Zondervan, 1862; 1954, 605 reprint) points out that Erasmus and Luther had similar views on the passage.

Furthermore, this issue was questioned almost 1600 years earlier by Saint Augustine. In Tractate CXX he writes:

> 9. "Then went in also that other disciple who had come first to the sepulchre." He came first, and entered last. This also of a certainty is not without a meaning, but I am without the leisure needful for its explanation. "And he saw, and he believed." Here some, by not giving due attention, suppose that John believed that Jesus had risen again; but there is no indication of this from the words that follow. For what does he mean by immediately adding, "For as yet they knew not the scripture, that He must rise again from the dead"? He could not then have believed that He had risen again, when he did not know that it behoved Him to rise again. What then did he see? What was it that he believed? What but this, that he saw the sepulchre empty, and believed what the woman had said, that He had been taken away from the tomb?

This excerpt comes from "St. Augustin: Lectures Or Tractates on the Gospel According to St. John." In *The Nicene And Post-Nicene Fathers of the Christian Church. volume 7. The Homilies on the Gospel of John. Homilies on the First Epistle of John. Soliloquies.* Edited by Philip Schaff and translated by John Gibb and James Innes. (New York: The Christian Literature Company. 1888. p. 436).

However, Saint Augustine is not finished. Literally, in the next Tractate (CXXI) he opens his next homily by repeating the same point:

> 1. MARY MAGDALENE had brought the news to His disciples, Peter and John, that the Lord was taken away from the sepulchre;

and they, when they came thither, found only the linen clothes wherewith the body had been shrouded; and what else could they believe but what she had told them, and what she had herself also believed? . . .

Minear offered the following support for this conclusion:

1. Verse 9 ["For as yet they knew not the scripture, that he must rise again from the dead."] made no sense if the beloved disciple saw and believed in the Resurrection since this was clearly said *after* the notice of the disciple's belief.
2. Verse 10 ("then the disciples went back to their homes") excluded the possibility of faith in the resurrection.
3. "John proceeds to tell the later episodes in chapter as though they were the first instances of appearances of the risen Lord, and the origin of faith in his living presence (vs. 16, 20, 25)." (pp. 128-130)

Conway (1997, 189-90) raises yet another reason to doubt that John came to resurrection faith. "The eventful conclusion of the scene in verse 10 confirms this, as the disciples simply return to their homes. Indeed, those who argue that the beloved disciple came to faith in the resurrection must explain why he did not communicate his understanding to anyone else, especially Peter."

As a side issue, significantly, perhaps it was this event that enabled the beloved disciple rather than Mary Magdalene to be the *first* to believe in Jesus's resurrection. Unmistakably, the accounts of Luke and John provide *no* support for believing that Jesus was resurrected.

SPECULATION #124 Embellishment of the Grave Clothes

For Christian apologists the orderly arrangement of the clothes is clearly proof that neither grave robbers or anyone else had not taken away the body. For example, Watson (1987, 368-69) raises the question: "For what tomb-robbers would have taken the body and left the clothes and spices behind?"

However, there is a natural explanation for these narratives. The evolution of the clothes is apparent: (1) from no clothes (Mark and Matthew), (2) to clothes lying about (Luke), and finally (3) to clothes orderly arranged (John). Thus, the Gospels are clearly and unmistakably embellished. A second possibility advocated by detractors is that the entire burial and Resurrection narratives are ahistoric and written for evangelical and theological reasons.

SPECULATION #125 The Grave Clothes as an Apologetic against Theft

Numerous scholars (Bonney 1983, 240n16; Lindnars 1982, 601; O'Day 1995, 841; Robinson 1993, 20; Schnackenburg 1990, 311-12; Talbert 1992, 24) posit that the author of John could also have invented the left over clothes to serve as an apologetic or polemic; the linen clothes lying by themselves argues against theft. A thief would have taken not only the body but *also* the expensive clothes. Furthermore, the clothes and burial shroud also offers a potential apologetic to identify the tomb as Jesus's. Therefore, Watson (1987, 369) raises the possibility that the details of the tomb narratives may have been originally intended to *exclude* any rational arguments against Jesus's death, burial, and resurrection.

However, Allen (1893, 68) conjectures that the clothes were left behind "to prevent tracing and identification in the future, after decomposition was far advanced, should anybody find it at that time." It must be remembered how the preparation of Jesus's body was described. Mark 15:46 reports that Joseph of Arimathea "bought fine linen, and took him down, and wrapped him in the linen." In addition to this report Matthew 27:59 states that Jesus was wrapped in clean linen cloth. At the same time, Luke 23:53 too reports that Jesus's body was wrapped in linen. Finally, John 19:40 narrates how Joseph of Arimathea and Nicodemus wrapped Jesus's body "in linen clothes with spices, as the manner of the Jews is to bury." Therefore, at the absolute least, it could be assumed that Joseph of Arimathea, Nicodemus, or any other possible assistants would have been able to identify the burial clothes that Jesus was buried in, not the body. Thus, if Jesus's body was reburied elsewhere and eventually discovered it might have been possible to identify the body via its burial clothes. Consequently, the original burial clothes were left behind.

SPECULATION #126 Jesus Withdrew from the Grave Leaving His Clothes Behind

Many Christian apologists claim that another miracle of sorts occurred in relation to Jesus's resurrection: Jesus's body mysteriously "withdrew" from the clothes, leaving them "collapsed" as they were. For example, Shafto (1930, 21) writes: "But the grave-cloths are not only in the tomb; they are in the actual position and folds in which they would have been if the body were still within them—they were not just a heap of discarded wrappings." Hall (1933, 205) declares: "Our Lord's clothes were found lying in the empty tomb in positions suggestive of His body having exhaled from them, so to speak, without disturbing them except by causing them to collapse." Likewise, Chafer (1948, 81) writes: "The grave clothes which were left behind, retaining the form they had when He occupied them." A year later Goodier (1949, 43) describes the scene: "It was as if the body within the cloths had melted away, the cloths themselves falling in accordingly." Then a few years later Cambron (1954, 106) writes: "Peter discovered that the grave clothes were unmolested; the clothes appeared as though they were still wrapped around the body—but there was no body."

Two years later, Barclay (1956, 310) writes:

> And then something else struck John—the grave clothes were not disheveled and disarranged; they were lying there *still in their folds*—that is what the Greek means—the clothes for the body where the body had been; the napkin where the head had lain. The whole point of the description is that the grave clothes did not look as if they had been put off or taken off; they were lying there in their regular folds as if the body of Jesus had simply evaporated out of them and left them lying.

Similarly, Anderson (1968a, 8) surmises: "as though the body had simply withdrawn itself."

Stott (1971, 53), more elaborately writes:

> It would have "vaporized," being transmuted into something new and different and wonderful. It would have passed through the grave clothes, as it was later to pass through closed doors, leaving them untouched and almost undisturbed. Almost, but not quite. For the body cloths, under the weight of 100 lbs. of spices once the support of the body had been removed, would have subsided or collapsed, and would now be lying flat. A gap would have appeared between the body cloths and the head napkin, where his face and neck had been. And the napkin itself, because of the complicated criss-cross patterns of the bandages, might well have retained its concave shape, a crumpled turban, but with no head inside it.

> Third, this same napkin was "not lying . . . but wrapped together." This last word has been translated "twirled." The Authorized Version "wrapped together" and the Revised Standard Version 'rolled up' are both unfortunate translations. The word aptly describes the rounded shape which the empty napkin still preserved."

So too, Ryrie (1976, 1595) states: "Despite the absence of the body, the clothes retained the same shape and position they had when it was there." Similarly, Salvoni (1979, 76) writes that "it seemed that the corpse of Jesus had evaporated, passing to a new existential dimension not existing before. Jesus' body had become a spiritual body and passed through the linen and the napkins without moving them from their position."

Finally, N. T. Wright (2003, 689) declares: "The fact that the grave-clothes were left behind showed that the body had not been carried off, whether by foes, friends or indeed a gardener (verse 15). Their positioning, carefully described in verse 7, suggests that they had not been unwrapped, but that the body had somehow passed through them, much as, later on, it would appear and disappear through locked doors (verse 19)."

We have devoted considerable space to the notion espoused by numerous Christian writers that Jesus miraculously exited his burial cloth. And this text could have identified additional minded writers who support this view (Barrett 1967, 468; Blair 1973, 267; Bruce 1983, 385; Cranfield 1998, 147; 1990, 171; Ellis 1984, 284; Kysar 1986, 296-97; MacArthur 1997, 1626; Stone 2010, 104). However, are these claims accurate? Below is cited several writers, primarily conservative, who have rejected any such notion that Jesus seemingly passed through his burial clothes.

William Lane Craig (1989b, 242) discusses the idea that "the clothes were still in their wrapped-up shape, and the body had passed through them, leaving them like an unbroken, though collapsed, cocoon." However, then he rejects this idea: "But there is no evidence that the Jews wrapped their dead like mummies, and if the burial were in a shroud, the jaw band should have been found *inside* the shroud, not in a place by itself."

D. A. Carson (1991, 637), a conservation Christian evangelist, writes:

> Some have thought that the burial cloth still retained the shape of Jesus' head, and was separated from the strips of linen by a distance equivalent to the length of Jesus' neck. Others have suggested that, owing to the mix of spices separating the layers, even the strips of linen retained the shape they had when Jesus' body filled them out. *Both of these suggestions say more than the text requires.* What seems clearest is the contrast with the resurrection of Lazarus (11:44). Lazarus came from the tomb wearing his grave-clothes, the additional burial cloth still wrapped around his head. Jesus' resurrection body apparently passed through his grave-clothes, spices and all, in much the same way that he later appeared in a locked room (vv. 19, 26). The description of the burial cloth that had been around Jesus' head *does not suggest that*

it still retained the shape of the corpse, but that it had been neatly rolled up and set to one side by the one who no longer had any use for it. [italics mine]

Similarly this imagery may be appealing; however, as Bostock (1994, 202) points out: "It also leaves us with the problem that the *original Greek does not readily suggest* that the clothes lay 'collapsed as they were'" (italics mine).

However, more extensively Morris (1995, 735), another conservative Christian, writes:

In recent years this has often been taken to mean that the grave clothes were just as they had been when placed around the body. That is to say, Jesus' body rose through the grave-clothes without disturbing them. *This is not inconsistent with the language, but we should bear in mind that John does not say this.* That the headcloth was not with the others scarcely supports the view, for had this been the case it would have been right alongside them, with no more than the length of the neck (if that) between them. *Moreover "folded up" does not look like a description of the way it would have appeared if the head simply passed through it.* [italics mine]

Hendricksen (1953, 450) also refutes any idea that Jesus's body just passed through the clothing:

Just what did all this mean? It is necessary to stress at this point that not more must be read into the text than is actually there. Ideas such as these, namely, that the headband was lying there as if it had not been removed from the head, and that the bandages were lying there just as if the limbs of Jesus were still enclosed by them, or as if the body had been abstracted from them, are foreign to the text. We do not even know exactly *where* the linen bandages and the sweat-band were lying. Neither John nor Luke (in his Gospel, 24:12) says anything about such matters. What Luke emphasizes is that the bandages were lying there by *themselves.* Which, again, does not mean that they were being held in position mysteriously and in violation of the laws of gravity; but simply indicates that they were lying there *without the body.*

Likewise, John A. T. Robinson declares in his *The Priority of John* (1985, 293): "For John never actually suggests that the body had simply passed through the clothes leaving them undisturbed. In fact this is a typically twentieth century picture of the relation of spirit to matter.[275] In footnote 275, Robinson goes on to demolish the theory that Jesus's body materialized through his clothing.

> Brown (*John* II [[*The Gospel According to John XIII-XXI*. Anchor Bible. 1970]], 1007) traces it back to Ammonius of Alexandria in the fifth century, and no doubt it recurs, but it is notably absent from the classical commentators. Thus, Chrysostom [[*In Jo. Hom.* LXXXV 4; PG 59:465]] makes the point that the arrangement of the grave-clothes argues not that they had not been moved but that it could not have been the work of robbers, who would either have taken them with the body or left them in disarray. . . . Westcott too, comments: 'There were no traces of haste. The deserted tomb bore the marks of perfect calm . . . It was clear, therefore, that the body had not been stolen by enemies.' It is interesting that between the sentences his son and editor added in brackets 'The grave-clothes lay as the body had withdrawn from them', thus introducing Bishop Westcott's later conviction derived from H. Latham's book *The Risen Master*, Cambridge 1901, of dematerialization through the undisturbed clothes (*John* II, 339f.). The influence of this book seems to have been decisive in changing popular presumptions.

In the following page, Brown (1970, 1008) demolishes any possibility that burial cloth retained the shape of Jesus's body:

> Moreover, the *soudarion* (=sindōn), a large cloth that had been around the whole body *inside* the bindings, was now carefully folded in the corner on the left-hand side of the tomb . . . If the Johannine writer described the position of the burial clothes in such a way as to imply that Jesus' body had passed through them and left them undisturbed, would he have waited until later to hint subtly at such an unexpected power? Moreover, a translation, such as ours, whereby the *soudarion* is not with the other wrappings, militates against such a theory—Jesus would have passed through all the burial clothes at the same time, leaving them in the one place. Finally, such a theory demands that Peter also should have come to believe; for if the position of the clothes miraculously preserved the image or location of the body, Peter could scarcely have missed the import. Yet Luke XXIV 12 reports that Peter "saw

the cloth wrappings lying there, and he went home wondering at what had happened."

SPECULATION #127 Did Jesus Leave the Tomb Naked?

Luke and John detail in their narratives that linen clothes were left behind in the tomb. However, these claims raise a simple issue: Christian fundamentalists maintain that Jesus was physically resurrected as a corporeal body and not as a ghost, phantom, or spirit. This belief then raises the obvious issue of whether or not Jesus left the tomb naked. It must be remembered that prior to Jesus's crucifixion the Roman soldiers *took* his clothes:

> Mk 15:24 And when they had crucified him, they parted his garments, casting lots upon them, what every man should take.

> Mt 27:35 And they crucified him, and parted his garments, casting lots: that it might be fulfilled which was spoken by the prophet, They parted my garments among them, and upon my vesture did they cast lots.

> Jn 19:23-24 Then the soldiers, when they had crucified Jesus, took his garments, and made four parts, to every soldier a part; and also his coat: now the coat was without seam, woven from the top throughout. They said therefore among themselves, Let us not rend it, but cast lots for it, whose it shall be: that the scripture might be fulfilled, which saith, They parted my raiment among them, and for my vesture they did cast lots. These things therefore the soldiers did.

Consequently, it must be asked, was Jesus naked when he left the tomb and appeared before Mary Magdalene (Mk 16:9; Jn 20:14-17) and Mary Magdalene and the other Mary after receiving the angel's instructions at the tomb (Mt 28:9-10)?

SPECULATION #128 Petrine and Johannine Rivalry

O'Day (1995, 840) points out that some scholars have elaborate theories about verses 4-6 as a narrative depiction of ecclesial rivalry between Petrine and Johannine Christianity (cf. Brown 1994b, 1004-07; Koester 2003, 70; Quest 1989, 7; Schneiders 1983, 94-97; Wolfe 1989, 117). Therefore, perhaps by having the beloved disciple win the race with Peter, the author of Luke was simply asserting his priority over Peter. Not only does the narrator have Peter losing the race but Grant (1997, 229) also points out "three times that the beloved disciple arrives at the tomb ahead of Peter (i.e., vv. 4, 6, and 8.).""

Significantly, mention of the Beloved Disciple appears only in John; Peter is cast in a negative light whereas the Beloved Disciple is portrayed in a positive light.

TABLE 42. John's Positive Accounts of the Beloved Disciple and Negative Views of Peter

Positive View of the Beloved Disciple	Negative View of Peter
One of this disciples was specifically described as the one "whom Jesus loved" (Jn 13:23).	Peter was never called or described as the one who Jesus loved.
It was the Beloved Disciple who asked Jesus during the Last Supper who it was that would betray him (Jn 13:23).	Peter asked second who it was that would betray him (Jn 13:25).
It was the Beloved disciple who was reclining next to Jesus during the Last Supper (Jn 13:23).	Peter did not apparently sit at the right hand (the side symbolic of favoritism) of Jesus during the Last Supper (Jn 13:23).
	Peter rashly declared that he would lay down his own life for Jesus (Jn 13:37).
	Peter was rash in cutting off the ear of the high priest's slave during Jesus's arrest (Jn 18:10).
	Peter denied Jesus three times (Jn 18:17, 25, 27).
The Beloved Disciple followed Jesus to the cross (19:26).	Peter did not follow Jesus to the cross (Jn 19:25-26).
While being crucified, Jesus told his mother "Woman, here is your son"; that he indicated the Beloved Disciple was to be her son. Then to the Beloved Disciple he said: "Here is your mother" implying Mary was to be his "mother." Finally, the author of John declared that from that hour the disciple took her into his own home (Jn 19:26-7).	Peter was not made responsible for taking care of Jesus's mother (Jn 19:27).

When Mary Magdalene discovered the empty tomb, she ran to tell the Simon Peter *and* the Beloved Disciple of her discovery (Jn 20:2).	
The Beloved Disciple was the first to reach the empty tomb, but Simon Peter was the first to enter (Jn 20:4).	Peter was the first to enter the tomb demonstrating his brashness (20:6).
The Beloved Disciple was the first to believe (Jn 20:8).	Peter did not believe after seeing and entering the empty tomb (Jn 20:6-10).
	Peter did not at first recognize the resurrected Jesus (Jn 21:4-6).
	Peter was rash diving naked into the Sea of Tiberias (Jn 21:7).

SPECULATION #129 Why John Has Two Witnesses

Mark and Matthew omit mention of any examination of the tomb by male witnesses. Luke 24:12 had just one witness, Peter examining the tomb and from outside: "Then arose Peter, and ran unto the sepulchre; and stooping down, he beheld the linen clothes laid by themselves, and departed, wondering in himself at that which was come to pass." However, John 20:8 increases the number of witnesses from one to two, and they actually went inside the tomb and examined it: "Then went in also that other disciple, which came first to the sepulchre, and he saw, and believed."

Talbert (1992, 24) speculates that "the second empty-tomb story in Luke furnishes a second witness that is needed for a valid testimony under Jewish law."

> Num 35:30 Whoso killeth any person, the murderer shall be put to death by the mouth of witnesses: but one witness shall not testify against any person to cause him to die.

> Deut 17:6-7 At the mouth of two witnesses, or three witnesses, shall he that is worthy of death be put to death; but at the mouth of one witness he shall not be put to death. The hands of the witnesses shall be first upon him to put him to death, and afterward the hands of all the people. So thou shalt put the evil away from among you.

> Deut 19:15 One witness shall not rise up against a man for any iniquity, for any sin, in any sin that he sinneth: at the mouth of

two witnesses, or at the mouth of three witnesses, shall the matter be established.

SPECULATION #130 Plausibility of the Disciples Entering the Tomb

There are several practical problems that challenge the authenticity and historicity of Peter and the other disciple entering the tomb (similar to the women) on Easter Sunday.

1. According to Matthew's narrative, Peter and the other disciple would be entering a tomb previously sealed by the Roman guard and under the direct orders of Pilate. Presumably the seal and cord could still be visible, although this is not an absolute given, even if the stone were rolled aside.
2. Compounding matters, this tomb contained the body of a man who had been condemned to death by the State and executed by crucifixion.
3. Peter and the other disciple would be entering the personal tomb of Joseph of Arimathea. Based on the tomb's prior description, it would have been obvious that the sepulchre where Jesus's body lay was the private property of a wealthy and perhaps powerful Jew.
4. Peter and the other disciple would have been subject to Roman law because Judea was under Roman authority. Under Roman law, entering the tomb that belonged to someone else without permission would have been an act of sacrilege and an extremely serious crime [Gaius, *Institutes* 2.2-10; Marcian, *Institutes* 14.]. The punishment for such a crime was severe, ranging from "deportation to an island" to execution [Ulpian, *Duties of the Proconsul* (7; D. 48.13.7)].

Therefore, it is doubtful that Peter or the other disciple would have entered Joseph's tomb.

SPECULATION #131 The Hundred Pounds of Spices

Mark, Matthew, and Luke omit any discussion about the "hundred pound weight" of myrrh and aloes being employed during the preparation of Jesus's body or his burial. John 19:39 alone reports: "And there came also Nicodemus, which at the first came to Jesus by night, and brought a mixture of myrrh and aloes, about an hundred pound weight." One-hundred pounds of plant leaves would occupy a substantial volume even larger than Jesus himself.

Earlier, Mark 16:5 reports that three women entered the tomb and found a young man inside. However, there is no mention of Jesus's clothes or the "hundred pound weight" of myrrh. Matthew 28:6 has two women offered the opportunity by an angel to explore the tomb: "He is not here: for he is risen, as he said. Come, see the place where the Lord lay." However, there is no indication that the women accepted the offer. Consequently, Matthew omits any comment about either the myrrh or aloes in the tomb. Luke 24:3 confirms that several women entered the tomb: "And they entered in, and found not the body of the Lord Jesus." Instead they encountered two men who spoke to them. The women exited the tomb without any comment about the contents or lack of contents. However, Luke 24:12 narrates that Peter ran to the tomb and looked inside only to find some linen clothes: "Then arose Peter, and ran unto the sepulchre; and stooping down, he beheld the linen clothes laid by themselves, and departed, wondering in himself at that which was come to pass." John 20:5-10 discusses Peter and the other disciple who Jesus loved entering the tomb. John 20:7 specifies only two things were reported to be visible: "And the napkin, that was about his head, not lying with the linen clothes, but wrapped together in a place by itself."

What happened to these valuable spices? Here the gospel accounts are silent. However, several possible speculations include the following:

1. The entire tomb burial narrative was an invented tradition.
2. The burial in the tomb occurred but the "hundred-pound weight" of myrrh and aloes was an invention or embellishment.
3. Joseph and Nicodemus retrieved the spices that were not used after the preparation of the body. However, this raises several issues: (1) would the wealthy Joseph and Nicodemus have cared about retrieving the spices, (2) would Joseph and Nicodemus have the time to complete this action, and (3) would Joseph and Nicodemus have risked transporting materials on the Sabbath as it was virtually upon them? Of course, they were already in violation of working on a festival.
4. Joseph and Nicodemus left the unused spices at the site where Jesus's body was prepared.
5. The authors or final redactors did not think that this was an important detail to record and therefore omitted it.

SPECULATION #132 Legitimizing Faith in Jesus's Resurrection

John 20:8 reports that the other disciple who ran with Peter was the first to believe: "Then went in also that other disciple, which came first to the sepulchre, and he saw, and believed." Significantly the text does not explicitly declare what the other disciple believed. In the following verse John 20:9 reports that neither Peter nor the other disciple knew the scripture that predicted Jesus would rise from the dead: "For as yet they knew not the scripture, that he must rise again from the dead."

In a doctoral dissertation, Bonney (1997, 242-43) analyzed the phrase "to know." He writes:

> If one takes the form of the verb "to know" (ἤδεισαν) in 20:9 in the sense of the imperfect, the line says that they "did not know the scripture, that he must rise from the dead." Such a reading would clearly indicate that the beloved disciple's faith is somehow inadequate. If one takes the verb to be a pluperfect, however, the verse conveys the sense that up until the point where they saw the tomb 'they had not understood the scripture.' But, once having seen the tomb, they did understand.

> Whether one reads the pluperfect or the imperfect, the text indicates that the sight of the tomb *alone* was not adequate to arouse the proper sort of faith. For it either arouses a faith that presupposes (or includes) an understanding of the scriptures (cf. 20:8). Clearly, however, John wishes his readers to understand that the beloved disciple had a special insight into the scene of the tomb, an insight that surpassed that of either Peter or Mary. And, in this context, the pluperfect reading flows more easily.

Then Bonney (p. 242) adds in footnote 49: "Several copyists have tried to eliminate this difficulty by either changing the verb to a plural in 20:8 or by changing the verb to a singular in 20:9. See Brown, *John XIII-XXI*, 987. The majority of commentators (Brown, Schnackenburg, Lindars, Barrett, Beasley-Murray etc.) and the majority of English translations (RSV, NAB, JB, etc.) read the imperfect."

Crossley (2005, 183) suggests that there is a practical reason the author of John incorporated verse nine into his narrative. He hypothesizes that

John 20.8-9 involves the historically dubious beloved disciple and legitimizes faith prior to scriptural justifications, something no doubt necessary for Gentiles with little knowledge of Jewish scriptures entering the Christian community and indeed for those struggling to find exactly where the scriptures might mention Jesus' bodily resurrection . . . [[Therefore]] It can be cautiously suggested then that a possible reason for a lack of scriptural reference in the resurrection narratives was that such knowledge was not a prerequisite for scripturally ignorant Gentile believers who only had to believe in this central aspect of early Christian belief.

SPECULATION #133 The Historicity of Peter's Lack of Faith

Peter was personally instructed multiple times that Jesus would die and return (e.g., Mk 8:31; 9:31; 10:33-34; Mt 16:21; 17:22-23; 20:18-19; Lk 9:22; 18:31-33). However, Luke 24:7 narrates that after Peter "beheld the linen clothes laid by themselves" (AV), "he went away, wondering to himself what had happened." (NIV) These words are remarkable.

The Gospels report that during Peter's discipleship he saw, experienced, heard, and learned from his Master and others the following:

- Jesus drove out an evil spirit from a man at Capernaum (Mk 1:23-27).
- Jesus healed Simon's mother-in-law (Mk 1:30).
- Jesus healed many and drove out many demons (Mk 1:34).
- Jesus drove out demons throughout the Galilee (Mk 1:39).
- Jesus healed a man with leprosy (Mk 1:42).
- Jesus healed a paralytic man (Mk 2:10-12).
- Jesus healed a man with a shriveled hand (Mk 3:3).
- Jesus calmed a storm, i.e., wind and waves (Mk 4:39).
- Jesus gave permission for evil spirits to enter about two thousand pigs, and then they rushed down a steep bank into a lake and drowned (Mk 5:11-14).
- Jesus healed a woman subject to bleeding for a twelve year period (Mk 5:25-29).
- Jesus healed a dead girl, the daughter of Jairus (Mk 5:35-42).
- Jesus fed five thousand with five loaves and two fish (Mk 6:38-44).
- Jesus walked on the lake (water) (Mk 6:48).
- Jesus empowered Peter to walk on water (Mt 15:29).

- Jesus calmed the wind (Mk 6:51).
- Jesus healed all those who touched him (Mk 6:56).
- Jesus healed a girl possessed by an evil spirit (Mk 7:30).
- Jesus healed a deaf and dumb man (Mk 7:32-37).
- Jesus fed about four thousand men with seven loaves (Mk 8:5-9).
- Jesus healed a blind man at Bethsaida (Mk 8:22-25).
- Jesus was transformed on a high mountain before Peter, James, and John (Mk 9:3).
- Jesus was seen by Peter, James, and John talking to Elijah and Moses (Mk 9:2-4) and later both were seen enveloped by a cloud and suddenly disappeared (Mk 9:7-8).
- Jesus healed a boy with an evil spirit (Mk 9:17-28).
- Jesus healed the blind Bartimaeus (Mk 10:52).
- Jesus cursed a fig tree and it became withered (Mk 11:20-21).
- Jesus predicted Peter would disown Jesus three times (Mk 14:66-72).
- Jesus healed the ear that was cut off of the high priest's servant by touching it (Lk 22:50-51).
- Jesus's death coincided with darkness over the whole of the land (Mk 15:33).
- Jesus's death coincided with the curtain of the Temple being torn in two from top to bottom (Mk 15:38).
- Jesus's death coincided with an earthquake (Mt 27:51).
- Jesus's death coincided with bodies of raised saints coming out of their tombs, traveling into the holy city, and appearing to many people (Mt 27:52-53).

The obvious problem is that Peter seems to not realize that he was just seeing the evidence that Jesus had promised his disciples would transpire. Therefore, it must be asked: if Peter believed that Jesus said he would rise again on the third day, why was he at all amazed at seeing the burial cloths in an empty tomb?

In conclusion, it is dubious that Peter was (1) told before by Jesus that he was going to be arrested, crucified, and resurrected multiple times (Mk 8:31; 9:31; 10:33-34; Mt 16:21; 17:22-23; 20:18-19; Lk 9:22; 18:31-33 and perhaps 24:6 by the women) and (2) Jesus performed multiple supernatural and miraculous events in Peter's presence on almost a daily occurrence, and yet he did not believe. Rather than being historical, these events were written to serve a theological intent to demonstrate that faith was more important than seeing or witnessing miracles and signs.

SPECULATION #134 Why Luke 24:12 Is Missing in Many Old Manuscripts

Luke 24:12 is missing from a number of important early Greek manuscripts. *The Interpreter's Bible* (1981, 7:420) declares: "In KJV; RSV mg. Missing from Codex Bezae and the O.L. MSS, and no doubt an interpolation based on John 20:3-10." Even the NRSV (1989, 88n*w*) states: "Other ancient authorities lack verse 12." The question that must asked is, why does verse 12 appear in a number of less important manuscripts?

Ehrman (2003, 226), a New Testament scholar speculates:

> In fact, the verse that reports it is not found in some of our important textual witnesses. And when one looks at the verse carefully, it contains a disproportionate number of words and grammatical characteristics not otherwise found in Luke's Gospel (or in Acts). Moreover, it looks very similar to an account found in John 20:3-10, almost like a summary or synopsis of that story. How does one account for all this? Probably the easiest explanation is that the verse was an addition to Luke's original account. In considering reasons for a scribe to have added it, we should not overlook how the verse could serve the proto-orthodox cause. Here Jesus is raised bodily from the dead; this is not some kind of spiritualized resurrection as some docetists would have it. The proof is who sees them? Not just women telling a silly tale, but Peter, the chief of the apostles, eventually the bishop of Rome, the head of the proto-orthodox church. This appears, then, to be a proto-orthodox change of the text, made to counter a docetic understanding of Jesus.

[Note: The proto-orthodox "may be considered the forebears of Christian orthodoxy" and "eventually came to dominate the religion toward the middle of the third century" (ibid.). In contrast, Docetism "denied the reality of Christ's suffering and death." Therefore, "Jesus was not really a-flesh-and-blood human but only 'appeared' to be so (the Greek word for "appear" or "seem" is *doceo*, hence the terms *docetic/docetism*). For these docetists, Jesus' body was a phantasm (ibid. p. 15)]." Another speculation is that perhaps this interpolation was designed to gloss over the previous scene and rescue Peter's honor when he rejected Jesus three times or when he did not believe the women's testimony that they had seen the risen Jesus.

However, Ross (1987, 108), in defense of the genuineness of Luke 24:12, argues "many whole verses of the New Testament are lacking in one or a few manuscripts (e.g., John 21:25), having been omitted either through carelessness or for other reasons. [Therefore] To prove genuineness of such a verse it is not necessary to give a reason for the omission." The weakness with this Christian apologetic should be obvious. Just because some verses of the Christian Bible are lacking in a few manuscripts because they have been omitted either through carelessness or for other reasons does not mean this defense is necessarily applicable to Luke 24:12. It is the burden of the Christian apologist to prove that this verse is genuine.

SPECULATION #135 The Viability of the Disciples' Homes

John 20:10 reports that after having explored the tomb, "Then the disciples went away again unto their own homes." This again raises a previously explored issue of home ownership (speculation 34, issue 15. See Bernard 1928, 637): (1) when did Peter and the other disciple who Jesus loved obtain a personal home, and (2) was it viable for them to possess their own homes in Jerusalem or its vicinity while all accounts indicated that they lacked adequate means?

Mark 10:28 reports Peter, declaring, "Then Peter began to say unto him, Lo, we have left all, and have followed thee." Given that the disciples "left all" and were nothing more than itinerant disciples of their master, it seems unlikely that they would have had the means to *own* a home in the vicinity of Jerusalem.

Based on Luke 8:3, Christian apologists posit that Jesus and the disciples were financially supported by women followers. However, the degree of financial support is unknown. At the least, this Christian apologetic is a speculation offered to explain how twelve itinerant men possessed homes in Jerusalem or its vicinity.

CHAPTER 9

Mary Magdalene's Travels

PREFACE: MARY MAGDALENE IN JOHN 20:11-18

Jesus's appearance to Mary Magdalene is detailed only in John 20:11-18. John starts off with Mary Magdalene reaching an empty tomb while it is still dark. Prior to this time, commentators differ whether or not Matthew's guard fled the tomb. However, the historicity of the guard is refuted by this text. Numerous unsuccessful efforts have been attempted to harmonize the conflicting resurrection accounts. As previously stated, numerous Bible scholars, historians, and theologians candidly admit the inability to harmonize these recorded accounts.

ISSUE 69: John's Mary Magdalene Message to the Disciples and Encounter with Two Angels

Mk	Mt	Lk	
			Jn 20:1 The first day of the week cometh Mary Magdalene early, when it was yet dark, unto the sepulchre, and seeth the stone taken away from the sepulchre. 2 *Then she runneth*, and cometh to Simon Peter, and to the other disciples whom Jesus loved *and said unto them, They have taken away the Lord out of the sepulchre, and we know not where they have laid him.*
			Jn 20:12 And seeth two angels in white sitting, the one at the head, and the other at the feet, where the body of Jesus had lain. 13 And they say unto her, Woman why weepest thou? *She saith unto them, Because they have taken away my Lord, and I know not where they have laid him.*

JOHN'S NARRATIVE HAS Mary Magdalene making two visits to the tomb. During her initial visit detailed in John 20:1 she is the first to come to the tomb, discovering that the stone covering the entrance had been taken away. She concludes that someone removed the body from the grave, although she does not look inside the tomb until verse 11. Nonetheless, she runs to Simon Peter and to "the other disciple whom Jesus loved" saying: "They took (*êran*) the Lord out of the sepulchre, and we [[plural]] know not (*ouk oidamen*) where they laid (*ethêkan*) him."

During the second visit to the tomb Mary Magdalene meets two angels but seemingly does not know that they are angels, although the reader does. In this gospel account, the angels do not deliver to Mary the message of the Resurrection or the news of Jesus's resurrection. Instead, simultaneously, they simply question her: "Woman why weepest thou?" She responds a second time that Jesus has been taken away and she does not know where he has been laid.

CONTRADICTION #72 The Conflicting Chronology

A significant controversy about the Mary Magdalene account relates to the time line and the statement that she made to Simon Peter and the other disciple who Jesus loved. In the first verse of chapter 20, John narrates that: "The first day of the week cometh Mary Magdalene early, when it was yet dark, unto the sepulchre, and seeth the stone taken away from the sepulchre." In the following verse Mary Magdalene runs to and informs the two disciples that (1) she did not know who took away Jesus's body and (2) she did not know where Jesus's body had been laid. However, this response makes no sense when read in conjunction with the Synoptic accounts.

Mark relates that Mary Magdalene, Mary the mother of James, and Salome arrive at the tomb just after sunrise and find the stone rolled away. They enter the tomb and encounter a young man dressed in white. He tells them not to be alarmed, and that Jesus was risen and not here; he offered them the opportunity to examine the tomb where Jesus's body was laid and to go tell the disciples and Peter that Jesus was going ahead of you into the Galilee; there they would see him, just as he told you. Consequently, Mary Magdalene knew that Jesus was risen and not in the tomb.

Matthew narrates that Mary Magdalene and the other Mary traveled to the tomb. There was an earthquake, an angel descended from heaven, and the stone rolled away. In addition, an unknown number of guards at the tomb were so terrified that they became like dead men. Then, the angel assures the women not to be afraid. Next, he instructs them that Jesus is not present and that he has risen, and he invites the women to come see where Jesus previously laid. Finally, the angel instructs the women to tell the disciples that Jesus had risen from the dead, that he was going ahead of them into the Galilee, and that there they would see him. At no time is there any indication that the women entered the tomb. Later and presumably following the guards' recovery the soldiers left the tomb after Mary Magdalene and the other Mary departed to convey the angel's message to the disciples. Again, Mary Magdalene is informed that Jesus was risen and not present in the tomb.

Luke reports that Mary Magdalene and several women arrived at the tomb, found the stone rolled away, and entered it. Here there is no mention of Matthew's incapacitated guard. There, they met two men. These two men informed them that Jesus was not here and that he had risen. Then the women were reminded that Jesus had told them that he would be delivered into the hands of sinful men, crucified, and on the third day be raised. Once more, Mary Magdalene knew that Jesus was not in the tomb; instead, he had previously risen.

Later, and based on a plain and simple reading of Matthew 28:1-9, Mary Magdalene and the other Mary literally encounter Jesus after having left the empty sepulchre. During this encounter they "held him by the feet" and "worshipped him." According to Matthew's chronology, all this occurred before she ever saw the disciples. Why then, in John's narrative, is Mary Magdalene totally oblivious to and unaware of where Jesus's body was moved, when according to Matthew 28:9-10, she had already heard from two reliable sources, the angel at the tomb and none other than Jesus himself that Jesus had risen from the dead?

Collectively, based on the Synoptic accounts, Mary Magdalene's statement in John makes absolutely no sense. In the synoptic Gospels, Mary Magdalene had been informed that not only Jesus had "risen from the dead" but that he had also gone to Galilee and "there shall ye see him." Consequently, the tomb was empty. Therefore, it is illogical to think that someone had moved Jesus's body, given that Mary Magdalene had been informed of his resurrection and where he ultimately would be seen.

Stated another way, the late Farrell Till (n.d., the Mary Magdalene problem), a well-known atheist posed what he called the Mary Magdalene problem:

> The Mary Magdalene problem is simple. Mary M was presented in the synoptic Gospels as having seen an angel or angels at the tomb, and heard him or them announce the resurrection of Jesus, after which she actually encountered Jesus and worshiped him as she was running from the tomb to tell the disciples what had happened. In John's gospel, however, Mary Magdalene is presented as having found the tomb empty, after which she ran

to Peter and the disciple 'whom Jesus loved' and told them that the body had been stolen. So the problem is: Why Mary would have told the disciples that the body had been stolen if she had seen and heard everything that the synoptic gospels claim that she saw and heard?

CONTRADICTION #73 Mary Magdalene Refutes that She Believed Jesus Was Going to Be Resurrected

Mary Magdalene's message to Peter and the other disciple in John 20:2 that "they have taken away the Lord out of the sepulchre, and we do not know where they have laid him" and her similar communication with the two angels recorded in John 20:13: "And they say unto her, Woman, why weepest thou? She saith unto them, Because they have taken away my Lord, and I know not where they have laid him" proves that she did *not* initially believe that Jesus was raised from the dead or was to be raised from the dead. Obviously, it would make no sense to bury Jesus a second time if he was resurrected. Unequivocally, Mary Magdalene did not believe that Jesus had been resurrected or was to be resurrected.

Significantly too, neither the disciples nor the two travelers believed or expected that Jesus would be resurrected. Mark 16:10 reports that Jesus first appeared to Mary Magdalene and she informed them that he was alive. Mark 16:11 describes the disciples' reaction: "And they, when they had heard that he was alive, and had been seen of her, believed not."

Matthew did not report that the women transmitted their experience at the tomb. Therefore, no reaction of the disciples' response to the women was possible. However, later Matthew 28:17 reports a meeting in the Galilee with his eleven disciples. Here it was detailed: "And when they saw him, they worshipped him: but some doubted."

Luke 24:11 narrates a response that when several women told the disciples the message of the two angels with whom they conversed inside the tomb and who declared that Jesus was risen: "And their words seemed to them as idle tales, and they believed them not." In the next verse Luke reports that nonetheless Peter ran to examine the tomb. He looked inside the tomb and found some linen clothes. His response was that he wondered what happened: "Then arose Peter, and ran unto the sepulchre; and stooping down, he beheld the linen clothes laid by themselves, and departed, wondering in himself at that which was come to pass."

Later that same morning, Luke 24:22-24 narrates a conversation between two travelers on the road with an unrecognized Jesus. They told Jesus of the previous episode. Immediately Jesus (vv 25-26) criticized the two travelers for their lack of understanding: "Then he said unto them, O fools, and slow of heart to believe all that the prophets have spoken: Ought not Christ to have suffered these things, and to enter into his glory?"

Compounding matters, later that evening when Jesus appeared to the eleven disciples they still did not believe. Luke 24:41 emphatically states: "And while they yet believed not for joy, and wondered, he said unto them, Have ye here any meat?" In every instance of Luke's gospel up until this point, the disciples were totally clueless about Jesus's resurrection.

Finally, John 20:6-10 expands on an episode reported in Luke 24:12-16. This time, however, there were two disciples and they both entered the tomb. John 20:8 stated: "Then went in also that other disciple, which came first to the sepulchre, and he saw, and believed." The problem is that John did not inform his readers of what that other disciple believed. On a literal reading, he believed what Mary Magdalene had reported: *the tomb was empty and the whereabouts of Jesus's body was unknown.* Then John 20:9 adds: "For as yet they knew not the scripture, that he must rise again from the dead." This editorial comment verified that these two disciples did *not* believe in Jesus's prophesied resurrection.

SPECULATION #136 The "We" Controversy

John 20: 2 details that Mary Magdalene report to the disciples: "They have taken away the Lord out of the sepulchre, and *we* do not know where they have laid him." This statement creates a puzzling question: Who are the "*we*" mentioned by Mary Magdalene? A literal reading of the text infers that she was not alone. New Testament commentators are divided as to whether or not Mary Magdalene traveled alone.

However, Mary Magdalene traveling alone raises a serious dilemma. Would a woman living in the proximity of Jerusalem during the first century have traveled alone while it was still dark? Blomberg (2001, 259) states:

> John mentions only Mary Magdalene by name (20:1), but her first-person plural language in verse 2 is best taken as her speaking for more than one person: "we don't know where they have put him." For safety reasons alone, it is historically improbable that a single woman would have gone out by herself at this time of day to a graveyard in the environs of Jerusalem. (Morris 1995: 734, cf. Bruce 1983: 384)

Even John Wenham (1994, 91), a Christian apologist, is of the opinion that "a woman would scarcely have ventured unaccompanied." So was Mary Magdalene alone or not when she first visited the tomb? If not, who was with her and why did John fail to clearly elaborate this important detail? Here the author of John is silent and commentators are only able to offer their speculations.

SPECULATION #137 The Number of Visits to the Tomb

Sheppard (1929, 187), writing in *The Expository Times*, speculates that "at least six different visits were paid to the tomb by five various sets of people." Sequentially, these visits include:

TABLE 43. Sheppard's Speculated Six Visits to the Tomb

VERSES	VISIT OF	WHEN
Jn 20:1-2	The visit of Mary Magdalene (alone).	When it was yet dark.
Mt 28:1, 5	The visit of Mary Magdalene and the other Mary.	At the beginning of dawn when Mary Magdalene had run to tell her news to the two apostles.
Jn 20:3-10	The visit of John and Peter.	After Mary Magdalene gave her report.
Jn 20:11-18	The return of Mary Magdalene.	After John and Peter left the tomb.
Lk 24:1-9	The visit of Mary Magdalene, Joanna, Mary the mother of James, and all the others with them.	At early dawn.
Mk 16:1-8	The visit of Mary Magdalene, Mary the mother of James, and Salome.	When the sun was rising.

Sheppard (pp. 185-87) explains how the Greek text, when properly understood, substantiates that six different visits were made to Jesus's burial place by five various sets of people; "none of them met each other either when going or returning" (p. 187). In defense of this hypothesis, Sheppard argues:

1. The dimness of the light in the hour immediately before the dawn.
2. The six visits were of very short duration; "they were spread over a period of about one and a half hours, thus leaving plenty of time for intervening intervals."
3. The nearness of the tomb to the city and the fact that there were probably half a dozen or more different winding streets which led from or near Jerusalem's gate and the disciples were scattered in different quarters of Jerusalem.

There are several shortfalls with Sheppard's arguments:

- First, Sheppard had all these people coming and going is quite unusual, especially at that time of day. During the first century, people usually awakened at sunrise.
- Second, Easter Sunday morning would have been the third day after a full moon. Consequently, assuming that the sky was clear, there would have been illumination from the near full moon. However, if it was cloudy, it would probably be dark and difficult to see.
- Third, he has Mary Magdalene making five trips in total either to or from the tomb in approximately a one hour period. The notion that Mary Magdalene ran back and forth to the tomb five times is not only strange but ridiculous.
- Fourth, assuming that those involved lived inside Jerusalem, city walls were normally closed at night and not reopened until sunrise.
- Fifth, although the tomb may have been near the city, Sheppard is not taking into consideration the city's topography. Jerusalem's roads are built on many hills that are physically demanding to transverse. Although women may have been hardier back in the first century, there are no descriptions of Mary Magdalene's age or physical condition.
- Finally, John has Mary Magdalene traveling alone and in dark at approximately 3:00 a.m. In the first century, this action would have been rather unusual.

SPECULATION #138 Mary Magdalene and the Guard

John's account of Mary Magdalene's visit to the tomb raises an issue commonly ignored by commentators. Matthew reports that there were an unknown number of sentinels guarding the tomb. Commentators often speculate that the numbers ranged from four to sixteen or as many as sixty-four. When Mary Magdalene arrived it was still dark. Presumably this was when Matthew's angel descended on to the tomb and the earthquake occurred, since John 20:1 reports that the stone was already removed: "The first day of the week cometh Mary Magdalene early, when it was yet dark, unto the sepulchre, and seeth the stone taken away from the sepulchre." Yet Matthew 28:2-5 reports that because of these occurrences, the guards became "as dead men." Therefore, it had to have been after these events that John's Mary Magdalene saw "the stone taken away from the sepulchre" (Jn 20:1), and she ran to the disciples to tell them what had occurred.

The question is, how close did John's Mary Magdalene get to the tomb's entrance? That is, did she literally walk up to the tomb's entrance without looking inside, or did she observe that the stone was rolled away from a distance? If Mary Magdalene indeed went up to the tomb's entrance, did she have to tippy-toe around and over the guards assigned to secure the tomb? If so, why did she fail to report to Peter and the other disciple the presence of the guard and their state of incapacitation? Plainly the guards had to have left the garden after Mary Magdalene left the tomb and before Peter arrived.

On the other hand, there remains the problem of harmonization. If Mary Magdalene and the other women—as reported in Mark 16:2-8; Matthew 28:5; and Luke 24:18—arrived while the guards were still incapacitated, this would mean that a group of women, potentially at least five in number (Mary Magdalene, Mary the mother of James, Joanna, Salome, and other women), not only looked inside the tomb from the outside but actually went inside the tomb and explored it (Mk 16:5; Lk. 24:3). This too would have required the women to have tippy-toed around and over the guards assigned to securing the tomb. However, there is no account of the sentinels being walked over or around. After receiving their angelic message, the women left the tomb. It would have been after this time that the guards regained consciousness and some of them returned to the Jewish leadership. This chronology is supported by several commentators. For example, Long (1997, 324; cf. Craig 1984a, 276; Gundry 1994, 592; Hagner 1995, 876) writes, "As the women leave the tomb with their mission of truth, the guards also leave the tomb, but to become embroiled in a mission of lies." Similarly, Montague (2010, 357; cf. Bode 1970, 52; Parambi 2003, 186) declares, "The guards posted to watch the tomb were left unconscious; now they rouse themselves only to discover the tomb open and empty." And Craig (1984a, 276; *idem*. 1989b, 214-15) writes: "Since the guard played virtually no role in the events of the discovery of the empty tomb – *indeed the Matthean account does not exclude that the guard had already left before the women arrived* –, the pre-Markan passion story may simply omit them." (italics mine)

ISSUE 70: The Identity of the Direct Witnesses to Jesus's Resurrection

| 1 Cor 15:5 And that he was seen of Cephas, then of the twelve: 6 After that he was seen by over five hundred brethren at once, of whom the greater part remain to the present, but some have fallen asleep. 7 After that he was seen by James, then by all the apostles. 8 Then last of all he was seen by me also, as by one born out of due time. | Mk 16:6 And he said unto them, Be not affrighted: Ye seek Jesus of Nazareth, which was crucified: *he is risen; he is not here: behold the place where they laid him.* 7 But go your way, tell his disciples and Peter that he goeth before you into Galilee: there shall ye see him, as he said unto you. | Mt 28:5 Fear not ye: for I know that ye seek Jesus, which was crucified. 6 *He is not here: for he is risen, as he said. Come, see the place where the Lord lay.* 7 And go quickly, and tell his disciples that he is risen from the dead; and, behold, he goeth before you into Galilee; there shall ye see him: lo, I have told you. | Lk 24:5 And as they were afraid, and bowed down their faces to the earth, they said unto them, Why seek ye the living among the dead? 6 *He is not here, but is risen*: remember how he spake unto you when he was yet in Galilee, 7 Saying, the Son of man must be delivered into the hands of sinful men, and be crucified, and the third day rise again.

Lk 24:34 Saying, The Lord is risen indeed, and *hath appeared to Simon.* | Jn 20:1 The first day of the week cometh Mary Magdalene early, when it was yet dark, unto the sepulchre, and seeth the stone taken away from the sepulchre. 2 Then she runneth, and cometh to Simon Peter, and to the other disciples whom Jesus loved, *and said unto them, They have taken away the Lord out of the sepulchre, and we know not where they have laid him.* |

Who directly witnessed Jesus's resurrection from the tomb? Paul reports in 1 Corinthians 15:5-8 a list of six events during which the post-resurrected

Jesus was seen. However, there is no mention of a direct witness of Jesus's post mortem resurrection. According to Mark and Luke, the young man or two men at the tomb state that Jesus was not present and that he had risen. In other words, Jesus's resurrection had already occurred before anyone arrived at the sepulchre.

Matthew 28:1-2 perhaps reports that upon arrival at the tomb the women witnessed the actual removal of the stone. However, Matthew 28:6 informs its readers that the angel only declared: "He is not here, for he was raised (*êgerthê gar*)," and then he invited the women to see the place where Jesus had lain. Thus, here, too, the actual resurrection is spoken of as a thing which had taken place before.

In the Fourth Gospel, the author of John 20:2 reports that Mary Magdalene visited the tomb, saw that the stone was removed, and then ran to the disciples exclaiming: "They have taken away the Lord out of the sepulchre, and we know not where they have laid him." Therefore, in the eyes of John, Jesus's resurrection had also already occurred.

Consequently, there is *not* a single direct eyewitness of Jesus's physical, bodily resurrection. Rather, the empty grave, coupled with the narrated subsequent appearances of Jesus, is the only evidence of Jesus's resurrection. On this point, Phillips (1975, 420; cf. Binz 1989, 67; Denaux 2002, 128; MacQuarrie 1977, 288; McBride 1996, 261; McDonald and Porter 2000, 181) tersely writes: "Nowhere in the New Testament is the actual process of the raising of Jesus described."

In conclusion, there was not a single direct eyewitness to Jesus's resurrection from the tomb mentioned in the entire Christian Bible. The only accounts provided in the Christian scriptures describe Jesus's postmortem resurrection appearances.

CONTRADICTION #74 When Jesus Was Supposed to be Raised

The Christian scriptures *never* report even one direct eyewitness to Jesus's resurrection. To the contrary, the Christian scriptures only provide limited and often contradictory details of who witnessed Jesus's post-resurrection appearances. Given that Jesus's resurrection was not directly eye witnessed, it cannot be known or attested as to when Jesus was supposedly resurrected in order to fulfill his three day prophecy.

The three day prophecy was first discussed by Paul in his epistle to the Corinthians. In 1 Corinthians 15:3-4 he writes: "For I delivered unto you first of all that which I also received, how that Christ died for our sins according to the scriptures; And that he was buried, and that he rose again the third day according to the scriptures." Novakovic (2012, 116) states:

> The claim that Jesus "was raised on the third day in accordance with the Scriptures" (1 Cor 15:4) belongs to the earliest Christian attempts to interpret the resurrection of Jesus in the light of Scripture. Yet the formulation is so terse and enigmatic that a consensus has yet to emerge concerning its origin, scriptural reference, and underlying theology . . . The testimony of Scripture can refer either to Jesus' resurrection alone or to the entire claim that he was raised on the third day.

The pertinent issue is whether or not Jesus fulfilled what was "according to the scriptures."

This question is complicated because the Christian scriptures present four descriptions of the "three days" in reference to Jesus's resurrection. These descriptions are: (1) the third day, (2) three days, (3) three days and three nights, and (4) after three days (see table 44).

Table 44. Three-Day References to Jesus's Resurrection

REFERENCE	VERSE
The third day.	Mk 9:31 For he taught his disciples, and said unto them, The Son of man is delivered into the hands of men, and they shall kill him; and after that he is killed, he shall rise *the third day*.
	Mk 10:34 And they shall mock him, and shall scourge him, and shall spit upon him, and shall kill him: and *the third day* he shall rise again.
	Mt 16:21 From that time forth began Jesus to shew unto his disciples, how that he must go unto Jerusalem, and suffer many things of the elders and chief priests and scribes, and be killed, and be raised again *the third day*.
	Mt 17:23 And they shall kill him, and *the third day* he shall be raised again. And they were exceeding sorry.
	Mt 20:19 And shall deliver him to the Gentiles to mock, and to scourge, and to crucify him: and *the third day* he shall rise again.
	Mt 27:64 Command therefore that the sepulchre be made sure *until the third day*, lest his disciples come by night, and steal him away, and say unto the people, He is risen from the dead: so the last error shall be worse than the first.

	Lk 9:22 Saying, The Son of man must suffer many things, and be rejected of the elders and chief priests and scribes, and be slain, and be raised *the third day.*
	Lk 18:33 And they shall scourge him, and put him to death: and *the third day* he shall rise again.
	Lk 24:7 Saying, The Son of man must be delivered into the hands of sinful men, and be crucified, and *the third day* rise again.
	Lk 24:21 But we trusted that it had been he which should have redeemed Israel: and beside all this, to day is *the third day* since these things were done.
	Lk 24:46 And said unto them, Thus it is written, and thus it behooved Christ to suffer, and to rise from the dead *the third day*:
	Acts 10:40 Him God raised up the *third day*, and shewed him openly;
	1 Cor 15:4 And that he was buried, and that he rose again *the third day* according to the scriptures:
Three days [Note: Earlier, John 2:19-21 explained that the phrase "the temple" referred to Jesus and his resurrection. Therefore, when Mark and Matthew mention "the temple" they are in fact referring to Jesus's resurrection.]	Mk 14:58 We heard him say, I will destroy this temple that is made with hands, and within *three days* I will build another made without hands.
	Mk 15:29 And they that passed by railed on him, wagging their heads, and saying, Ah, thou that destroyest the temple, and buildest it in *three days*.
	Mt 26:61 And said, This fellow said, I am able to destroy the temple of God, and to build it in *three days*. [Note: This was the testimony provided by two false witnesses before the chief priest.]

	Mt 27:40 And saying, Thou that destroyest the temple, and buildest it in *three days*, save thyself. If thou be the Son of God, come down from the cross.
	Jn 2:19 Jesus answered and said unto them, Destroy this temple, and in *three days* I will raise it up. 20 Then said the Jews, Forty and six years was this temple in building, and wilt thou rear it up in *three days*? 21 But he spake of the temple of his body.
Three days *and* three nights.	Mt 12:40 For as Jonas was three days and three nights in the whale's belly; so shall the Son of man be *three days and three nights* in the heart of the earth.
After three days.	Mk 8:31 And he began to teach them, that the Son of man must suffer many things, and be rejected of the elders, and of the chief priests, and scribes, and be killed, and *after three days* rise again.
	Mt 27:63 Saying, Sir, we remember that that deceiver said, while he was yet alive, *After three days* I will rise again.

Given that Jesus was buried on Friday afternoon and before the start of the Sabbath, the consequence of these four "three day" references to Jesus's resurrection will be analyzed. The statement "the third day" could possibly support an Easter Sunday morning resurrection, given that a *portion* of Friday afternoon, Saturday, and a portion of Sunday morning each counted as a whole day. Similarly, the reference to "three days" could possibly support an Easter Sunday morning resurrection for the same reason with each *part* of a day counting as an *entire* day.

However, the reference to "three days *and* three nights" and "*after* three days" precludes an Easter Sunday morning resurrection. Obviously the statement "*after* three days" would force a Monday resurrection at the earliest (and as many as weeks later).

TABLE 45. Three-Day Scenario with Part of a Day Counting as an Entire Day

DAY 1	DAY 2	DAY 3	DAY 4 [AFTER 3 DAYS]
Friday	Saturday	Easter Sunday	Monday

However, Matthew 12:40 is the time reference of most importance. Here Jesus likened his burial and resurrection to Jonah being swallowed by the giant fish: "For as Jonas was three days and three nights in the whale's belly; so shall the Son of man be three days *and* three nights in the heart of the earth."

The reason that this reference is so critical is because what Matthew reports in chapter 27. Matthew describes the chief priests and the Pharisees coming to see Pilate the day after Jesus was crucified and buried. Consequently, they were visiting Pilate on the Sabbath. What they wanted from Pilate was a guard for the tomb. The rationale given to Pilate is narrated in verse 63: "Saying, Sir, we remember that that deceiver said, while he was yet alive, *After* three days I will rise again." This statement explicitly means that the guard would need to be at the tomb at the least until Monday morning.

However, the specific request was delivered in the following verse: "Command therefore that the sepulchre be made sure *until the third day,* lest his disciples come by night, and steal him away, and say unto the people, He is risen from the dead: so the last error shall be worse than the first." When did Jesus ever make such a claim that they would have such knowledge? To answer this question it is necessary to examine Matthew 12:38-40.

Jesus was having an encounter with some scribes and Pharisees. They posed a challenge to him and he responded. This episode is often referred to as the sign of Jonah (Jonas in the AV). It is because of this "three day" reference that the Jewish leadership would possibly have known Jesus's claim.

> Mt 12:38 Then certain of the scribes and of the Pharisees answered, saying, Master, we would see a sign from thee.

> Mt 12:39 But he answered and said unto them, An evil and adulterous generation seeketh after a sign; and there shall no sign be given to it, but the sign of the prophet Jonas:

> Mt 12:40 For as Jonas was three days and three nights in the whale's belly; so shall the Son of man be three days and three nights in the heart of the earth.

Now the chief priests and the Pharisees requested of Pilate a guard for *until the third day.* This request would have been based on Jesus's prophecy that he would have been in the heart of the earth for *three days and three nights.* Therefore, they would require a guard at least until Monday. In addition, the chief priests and the Pharisees knew that Pilate was neither a Jew nor a Torah scholar. Being a Roman, for him there was no such concept that a part of a day counted as an entire day. Consequently, the Jewish *inclusive reckoning* of time that *part* of a day was considered a *whole* day would be nonsense. It is the burden of Christian apologists to prove that Pilate clearly understood that the request of the Jewish leadership was for a guard to watch the tomb until

Sunday. As a result for Pilate too, the request from the Jewish leadership would entail keeping a guard at the tomb at least until Monday.

Nolland (2005, 1237) raises additional insight regarding the three day prophecy recorded in Matthew 27:64. He inquires:

> The critical window created by the remembered prediction will be open for three days. (Actually "until the third day" [ἕως τῆς τρίτης ἡμέρας] here is quite ambiguous. Where does the count start from, the day of the crucifixion or the day of the present speaking? Is ἕως ["until"] inclusive or exclusive of the third day? And if the third day is to be included, is only its beginning included or the whole day through to its end? Not the immediate language but the larger sense and particularly "after three days" in the previous verse must control the choice.)

TABLE 46. Three Full Days and Three Full Nights

FRIDAY	SATURDAY	EASTER SUNDAY	MONDAY
Night 1	Night 2	Night 3	XXXXXXXXXXXXXXXXXXXXXXXXXXXXXXXXXX
XXXXXXXXXXXXX	Day 1	Day 2	Day 3

For the chief priests, the Pharisees, and Pilate, there had to have been a mutual understanding that Jesus was talking about a Monday resurrection given a Friday afternoon crucifixion. Consequently, the entire notion of an Easter Sunday morning resurrection is impossible if Jesus were to fulfill his resurrection prophecy. At the same time, the notion of an Easter Sunday morning resurrection to fulfill a three-day prophecy is a matter of tradition, not historicity.

Finally, and most noteworthy, it is impossible to know undeniably when Jesus was resurrected, given that there were no eyewitnesses to the event. Furthermore, it is also impossible to know whether or not Jesus's body was previously removed (or resurrected) from the tomb, even if it was guarded as exclusively mentioned in Matthew. What Matthew's narrative unequivocally presents was an unguarded tomb from approximately some unknown time spanning from late Friday afternoon until Saturday when a guard was deployed. However, Schaeffer (1991, 506) is of the opinion that "it seems highly implausible that the guard would seal an empty tomb." However, life is oftentimes stranger than fiction. Given that no person actually witnessed

Jesus's resurrection from the tomb, it would be impossible to unequivocally proclaim that he fulfilled that which was "according to the scriptures."

ISSUE 71: Mary Magdalene's First Words to Jesus after Recognizing Him

Mk	Mt	Lk	
			Jn 20:14 And when she had thus said, she turned herself back, and saw Jesus standing, and knew not that it was Jesus. 15 And when she had thus said, she turned herself back, and saw Jesus standing, and knew not that it was Jesus. 16 Jesus saith unto her, Mary. She turned herself, and saith unto him, *Rabboni*; which is to say, Master.

John's narrative states that during Mary Magdalene's second visit to the tomb she encountered two angels. After they disappeared she saw Jesus; however, at first she did not recognize him. Next, Jesus addressed her and she finally recognized him. Then, Mary Magdalene said to Jesus: *Rabboni*.

CONTRADICTION #75 Which Women Saw the Post-resurrected Risen Jesus on Easter Sunday?

The books and epistles found within the Christian scriptures that relate to Jesus's resurrection read like completely different stories, not several people witnessing the same event from different vantage points. In the Epistles of Paul there is *no* mention of any women witnesses. Christian apologists have offered various explanations for this omission.

Mark 16:1-8 records *no* witnesses. Only later Mark 16:9-11 discusses the *sole* witness of Mary Magdalene. In contrast, Matthew 28:1 and 28:9 report that *two* women, Mary Magdalene and the other Mary, witnessed a post-resurrected Jesus. Luke narrates that *no* women saw the risen Jesus. The only exception might have been the second pilgrim on the way to Emmaus. However, the gender of this person is unknown and subject to speculation. Conversely, Luke 24:34 later reports that Jesus had an earlier appearance with Simon, i.e., Peter. Finally, John 20:16-18 narrates that Mary Magdalene *alone* witnessed the resurrected Jesus.

These conflicting accounts, along with those discussed throughout this text, prove that the Christian scriptures are unreliable.

SPECULATION #139 "Which Is To Say Master" Shows John Was Written to a Non-Jewish Audience

After the two angels talked to Mary Magdalene, they seemingly vanished, and she turned around and saw Jesus standing there. However, she did not recognize him. Jesus asked her a question, to which Mary Magdalene responded. John 20:16 narrates a terse conversation between the two: "Jesus saith unto her, Mary." Afterward: "She turned herself, and saith unto him, *Rabboni*; which is to say, Master." John's phrasing, "which is to say, Master" demonstrates that these words were written many years after the supposed event. Evidently the text was *not* written in Judea and most significantly *not* for a Jewish audience. Any Jewish ignoramus would have known that the word *rabboni* meant "teacher." Even earlier, John 1:38 presented a similar clarification for his readership. Here, John discusses the first disciples' meeting Jesus: "Then Jesus turned, and saw them following, and saith unto them, What seek ye? They said unto him, Rabbi, (which is to say, being interpreted, Master,) where dwellest thou?"

Collectively these two clarifications by the author of John strongly suggest that his text was written for a gentile readership.

ISSUE 72: Touching Jesus after His Resurrection

Mk 16:11 And they, when they had heard that he was alive, and had been seen of her, believed not.	Mt 28:9 And as they went to tell his disciples, behold, Jesus met them saying, All hail. *And they came and held him by the feet*, and worshipped him.	Lk 24:39 Behold my hands and my feet, that it is I myself: *handle me*, and see; for a spirit hath not flesh and bones, as ye see me have.	Jn 20:17 Jesus saith unto her, *Touch me not*; for I am not yet ascended to my Father: but go to my brethren, and say unto them, I ascend unto my Father, and your Father; and to my God, and your God.

Mark 16:1-8 contains no mention of Jesus meeting anyone. However, in Matthew's narrative, the women not only meet Jesus, but they actually grasp hold of his feet. Here also there was no mention of Jesus granting permission to the women to make bodily contact. Unlike Mark, Luke reports that the disciples were not only granted permission to touch Jesus but that they were also actually encouraged to do so.

In contrast, John narrates that "Jesus saith unto her [[i.e., Mary Magdalene]], *Touch me not*; for I am not yet ascended to my Father: but go to my brethren, and say unto them, I ascend unto my Father, and your Father; and to my God, and your God." Eight days later, John 20:27 strongly suggests that Jesus was handled or touched during the Doubting Thomas episode.

CONTRADICTION #76 John Versus Matthew and Luke

The Gospel of John directly contradicts Matthew and Luke. The original Mark 16 omits any mention of women meeting a resurrected Jesus. Consequently, there was no bodily contact with Jesus or even a message proffered. Based on a literal reading of the text, instead, the women met a young man, received a message, subsequently fled the tomb, and spoke to nobody.

Matthew 28:9 reports that several women left the tomb after meeting an angel and having received a communication. On their way to the disciples, they encountered the resurrected Jesus. Then, the women grasped hold of Jesus by his feet and worshiped him: "And as they went to tell his disciples, behold, Jesus met them saying, All hail. And they came and held him by the feet, and worshipped him."

Luke 24:13-33 extensively details Jesus traveling with two pilgrims on their way to Emmaus during most of the day. Later, Luke 24:34-43 had Jesus appearing before the Eleven gathered in Jerusalem as well as the two travelers previously mentioned. During this encounter Jesus states in verse 39: "Behold my hands and my feet, that it is I myself: handle me, and see; for a spirit hath no flesh and bones, as ye see me have." Therefore, here, Jesus encouraged his disciples to touch him. It is unknown if the offer was accepted.

In direct contradiction, John 20:14 has Mary Magdalene alone meeting Jesus on Easter Sunday morning after her second visit to the tomb. After recognizing Jesus, she addressed him, saying, "Rabboni." Then, John 20:17 reports that Jesus told Mary Magdalene, "Touch me not."

John's narration completely contradicts the synoptic accounts.

CONTRADICTION #77 Failure to Harmonize the Chronology

Mary Magdalene's encounter with Jesus in John 20:14-17, after returning to the tomb the second time, cannot be reconciled with Matthew. John 20:17 narrates that Mary Magdalene was told by Jesus not to touch or cling on to him: "Jesus saith unto her, Touch me not; for I am not yet ascended to my Father: but go to my brethren, and say unto them, I ascend unto my Father, and your Father; and to my God, and your God." However, not much earlier that same morning, Matthew 28:8 has Mary Magdalene and the other Mary meeting Jesus after departing the tomb after having received instructions from an angel. Now, Matthew 28:9 has Mary Magdalene grasping Jesus by the feet: "And as they went to tell his disciples, behold, Jesus met them, saying, All hail. And they came and held him by the feet, and worshipped him."

However, Mark 16:1 states that there were two additional women who traveled to the tomb on Easter Sunday, Mary the mother of James and Salome: "And when the sabbath was past, Mary Magdalene, and Mary the mother of James, and Salome, had bought sweet spices, that they might come and anoint him." On the other hand, Luke 24:10 adds that Joanna and other women (at least two) in addition to those identified by Mark and Matthew seemingly saw the resurrected Jesus: "It was Mary Magdalene, and Joanna, and Mary the mother of James, and other women that were with them, which told these things unto the apostles."

According to Christian apologists (Hinks 1999; Lee 1991, 161; Thomas and Gundry 1988, 237; Wenham 1992, 82-83, 91-99) who attempt to harmonize the resurrection chronology, it was only after Mary Magdalene's initial meeting in John 20:14-17 that the other women returned to Mary in the garden or started to go to the disciples. It was at this later time, Matthew 28:9 records that the women actually "came and held him by the feet."

The problem with this attempt to harmonize the text is that a plain and simple reading of Matthew 28:5-8 has Mary Magdalene and the other Mary earlier meeting and receiving an instruction from an angel and then departing the tomb. And if Luke 24:10 is to be reconciled with Matthew, there must have been other women present during the initial meeting with the angel. In addition, Luke 24:4 has the one angel transformed into two men. Here, the events cannot be reconciled.

SPECULATION #140 The Meaning of the Phrase "Touch Me Not"

Hook (1978, 11-22), as part of his master's thesis at Dallas Theological Seminary, surveyed seventeen different views demonstrating that "there was no unanimity of opinion as to what Jesus meant" by the phrase "Touch me not; for I am not yet ascended to my Father." These seventeen interpretations include the following:

1. Jesus did not want to be touched because his wounds were still sore.
2. "Having heard of the Eucharistic meal on Thursday evening, Magdalene sees Jesus risen and is holding onto him, pleading that he give her holy communion."
3. "Jesus cautioning Magdalene against ritual defilement incurred in touching a dead body."
4. "Do not sullen him [[Jesus]] with ordinary contact."
5. "Jesus is asking Mary to show more respect for his glorified body."
6. Since Jesus had risen naked, it would be inappropriate for Mary's ministrations "until she too would have ascended to heaven and no longer be in danger of temptation."
7. Emend the text (translate the text in an unusual way) to read: "Don't fear."
8. Emend the text to read: "Touch me."
9. Emend the text to read: "No need to cling to me, for I am not leaving immediately, but will be around a short time (forty days) before I ascend."
10. "Don't (fear to) touch me."
11. "Do not insist on touching me; it is true that I have yet ascended to the Father, but I am about to do so."
12. The original read: "Don't touch me, but go to my brothers; for my part I am ascending."
13. "The idea appears to be that of 'holding,' in the desire to retain, and not of 'touching' with a view to ascertain the corporal reality of the presence."
14. The command "Touch me not" symbolically means "The earthly relationship with the Jews ceases and a new relationship, heavenly with the Jewish remnant, resumed at our Lord's return, He will be bodily present in the kingdom; but in the heavenly relationship He is bodily absent and believers are in a heavenly union with the risen Christ."
15. Mary thought this return to be the one He promised to the disciples (Jn 14:3), but this was not His second coming. "That would have to be preceded by the ascension and the sending of the Spirit. In the interim Jesus could not be retained on earth by Mary or the others. He had another function to perform in heaven, ministering on behalf of all believers."
16. "He [[Jesus]] could be telling Mary (who has begun to move toward Him in order to touch), to cease what she has started to."
17. "He [[Jesus]] could be telling Mary (who has already grasped Him), to stop what she is doing."

McGehee (1986, 301) suggests that one reason "[C]ommentators have not been able to approach a consensus on what Jesus's supposed explanation to Mary means" is because "the traditional rendering does not make sense grammatically." He further posits that "in general, these efforts [[to explain verse 17]] have been flawed by being overly complex in assumptions and by resorting to arcane explanations of what John was attempting to express."

The bottom line is that nobody knows for sure what Jesus meant by the phrase "Touch me not; for I am not yet ascended to my Father."

ISSUE 73: Jesus's Message and Command to Mary Magdalene

Mk	Mt	Lk	Jn 20:17 Jesus saith unto her, *Touch me not; for I am not yet ascended to my Father: but go to my brethren, and say unto them,* I ascend unto my Father, and your Father; and to my God, and your God. 18 Mary Magdalene, came and told the disciples that she had seen the Lord, and that he had spoken these things unto her.

Jesus's sole message to Mary Magdalene occurs only in the Gospel of John. Jesus's initial command to Mary Magdalene of "Touch me not" (*Mê mou aptou*) was immediately followed be an explanation and a command: "For I have not yet ascended to the Father: but go to my brethren, and say unto them: I ascend unto my Father and your Father, and my God and your God."

John 20:18 provides details that Mary Magdalene successfully carried out Jesus's instructions. "Mary Magdalene came and told the disciples that she had seen the Lord, and that he had spoken these things unto her." However, the narrator does not provide any information detailing how the disciples reacted to Mary's words. Furthermore, John does not provide any information as to whether the disciples accepted or rejected her words.

ISSUE 74: What Mary Magdalene Did on Easter Sunday

Mk 16:1 And when the sabbath was past, Mary Magdalene, and Mary the mother of James, and Salome, had *bought sweet spices*, that they might come and anoint him. 2 And very early in the morning the first day of the week, *they came unto the sepulchre at the rising of the sun. 3 And they said among themselves, Who shall roll us away the stone from the door of the sepulchre? 4 And when they looked, they saw that the stone was rolled away:* for it was very great. 5 And entering into the sepulchre, they saw a young man sitting on the right side, clothed in a long white garment; and they were affrighted… Mk 16:8 And they went out quickly, and fled from the sepulchre; for they trembled and were amazed: neither said they any thing to any man; for they were afraid. 9 Now when Jesus was risen early the first day of the week, he appeared first to Mary Magdalene, out of whom he had cast seven devils. 10 And she went and told them that had been with him, as they mourned and wept.	Mt 28:1 In the end of the sabbath, as it began to dawn toward the first day of the week, *came Mary Magdalene and the other Mary to see the sepulchre.* Mt 28:8 *And they departed quickly* from the sepulchre with fear and great joy; *and did run to bring his disciples word. 9 And as they went to tell his disciples,* behold, Jesus met them saying, All hail. *And they came and held him by the feet, and worshipped him.* 10 Then said Jesus unto them, Be not afraid: go tell my brethren that they go into Galilee, and there shall they see me. 11 Now when they were going, behold, some of the watch came into the city, and shewed unto the chief priests all the things that were done.	Lk 24:1 Now upon the first day of the week, very early in the morning, *they came unto the sepulchre, bringing the spices which they had prepared,* and certain others with them. 2 *And they found the stone rolled away from the sepulcher. 3 And they entered in, and found not the body of the Lord Jesus.* Lk 24:5 And as they were afraid, *and bowed down their faces to the earth,* they said unto them, Why seek ye the living among the dead? Lk 24:8 *And they remembered his words, 9 And returned from the sepulchre, and told all these things* unto the eleven, and to all the rest. 10 It was Mary Magdalene, and Joanna, and Mary the mother of James, and other women that were with them, which told these things unto the apostles.	Jn 20:1 The first day of the week *cometh Mary Magdalene* early, when it was yet dark, unto the sepulchre, *and seeth the stone taken away from the sepulchre. 2 Then she runneth, and cometh to Simon Peter, and to the other disciple, whom Jesus loved, and saith unto them, They have taken away the Lord out of the sepulchre, and we know not where they have laid him.* Jn 20:11 But *Mary stood without at the sepulchre weeping: and as she wept, she stooped down, and looked into the sepulchre, 12 And seeth two angels* in white sitting, the one at the head, and the other at the feet, where the body of Jesus had lain. 13 And they say unto her, Woman, why weepest thou? *She saith unto them, Because they have taken away my Lord, and I know not where they have laid him.* 14 And when she had thus said, *she turned herself back, and saw Jesus standing,* and knew not that it was Jesus. 15 Jesus saith unto her, Woman, why weepest thou? whom seekest thou? She, supposing him to be the gardener, saith unto him, Sir, if thou have borne him hence, tell me where thou hast laid him, and I will take him away. 16 Jesus saith unto her, Mary. She turned herself, and saith unto him, Rabboni; which is to say, Master. 17 Jesus saith unto her, Touch me not; for I am not yet ascended to my Father: but go to my brethren, and say unto them, I ascend unto my Father, and your Father; and to my God, and your God. 18 Mary Magdalene came and told the disciples that she had seen the Lord, and that he had spoken these things unto her.

Mary Magdalene's' actions on Easter Sunday are recorded in the four gospel narratives. In the synoptic Gospels she was with others while in John she seemingly traveled alone. Some of the actions attributed to her are found in more than one gospel, whereas, some of her actions are unique just to one narrative.

CONTRADICTION #78 Conflicting Details and the Impossibility to Harmonize the Chronology

The gospel narratives present conflicting details that report numerous actions taken by Mary Magdalene on Easter Sunday. Christian apologists contend that these accounts and others differ because of omissions of the gospel narrators, not contradictions. However, numerous scholars and theologians acknowledge that it is impossible to harmonize these narratives. An examination of table 47 reveals that the Mary Magdalene [MM] of the Gospels was a busy lady on Easter Sunday morning.

TABLE 47. Mary Magdalene's (MM) Actions on Easter Sunday Morning Exclusive of Other Women

MARK 16:1-20	MATTHEW 28:1-20	LUKE 24:1-13	JOHN 20:1-18	ANALYSIS
And when the sabbath was past, Mary Magdalene, and Mary the mother of James, and Salome *bought sweet spices* so that they might come and anoint him (16:1).				When the Sabbath was completed [Saturday evening after 6:00 p.m. which would be Sunday by the Jewish mode of counting] MM *purchased* some spices to anoint Jesus. Implied in the text, MM needed to *travel* to a merchant's shop to purchase the goods.

				The first day of the week cometh Mary Magdalene early, when it was yet dark, *unto the sepulchre*, and *seeth* the stone taken away from the sepulchre (20:1).	MM *traveled* to the tomb and she arrived while it was *still dark*. Upon her arrival, she *saw* the stone that had formerly blocked the entrance of the tomb had been removed (20:1).
				Then she runneth, and cometh to Simon Peter and the other disciple, whom Jesus loved, *and saith unto them*, "They have taken the Lord out of the sepulchre, and we know not where they have laid him (Jn 20:2).	Afterwards, MM *ran* to Peter and the other disciple and *informed* them that Jesus's body had been taken away (Jn 20:2). Given that the disciples were inside the city, the distance traveled ranged from two hundred to five hundred yards.
				But Mary *stood* without at the sepulchre *weeping*: and as she *wept*, she stooped down, and *looked* into the sepulchre (Jn 20:11).	Immediately following, MM *traveled* back to the tomb and arrived there after the two disciples had departed.

			And *seeth* two angels in white sitting, the one at the head, and the other at the feet, where the body of Jesus had lain. And they *say* unto her, Woman, why weepest thou? She *saith* unto them, Because they have taken away my Lord, and I know not where they have laid him (Jn 20:12-13).	Then, MM *met* two angels and had a terse *conversation*.
Now when Jesus was risen early the first day of the week, *he appeared* first to Mary Magdalene, out of whom he had cast seven devils (Mk 16:9).			And when she had thus said, she turned herself back, and *saw* Jesus standing, and knew not that it was Jesus. Jesus *saith* unto her, Woman, why weepest thou? whom seekest thou? She, supposing him to be the gardener, *saith* unto him, Sir, if thou have borne him hence, tell me where thou hast laid him, and I will take him away. Jesus *saith* unto her, Mary. She turned herself, and *saith* unto him, Rabboni; which is to say, Master. Jesus *saith* unto her, Touch me not; for I am not yet ascended to my Father: but go to my brethren, and say unto them, I ascend unto my Father, and your Father; and to my God, and your God (Jn 20:14-17).	Immediately following, MM *saw* Jesus and they had a brief *conversation*. Mark 16:9 confirmed that MM was the first person to see Jesus.

And she *went* and *told* them that had been with him, as they mourned and wept (Mk 16:10).			Mary Magdalene *came* and *told* the disciples that she had seen the Lord, and that he had spoken these things unto her (Jn 20:18).	Next, MM *returned* (running?) presumably to the city to find the disciples and *transmitted* Jesus's message.
And very early in the morning the first day of the week, *they came unto the sepulchre* at the rising of the sun (16:2).	In the end of the sabbath, as it began to dawn toward the first day of the week, came Mary Magdalene and the other Mary to see the sepulchre (28:1).	Now upon the first day of the week, very early in the morning, they *came* unto the sepulchre, *bringing the spices* which they had prepared, and certain others with them (Lk 24:1).		In contrast, Mark has MM *traveling* early in the morning and arriving at the tomb at sunrise. However, Matthew narrates that MM *traveled* to the tomb and arrived as it began to dawn (i.e., before sunrise). On the other hand, Luke has MM *traveling* very early while *transporting spices* that were prepared on Friday before the start of the Sabbath.
And they said among themselves, *Who shall roll us away the stone from the door of the sepulchre?* (16:3).				Just prior to her arrival at the tomb, MM *asked a question.*

	And, behold, there was a *great earthquake*: for the angel of the Lord descended from heaven, and came and rolled back the stone from the door, and sat upon it (Mt 28:2).			Presumably, MM *experienced* a *great earthquake*, although Matthew does not state that this was a fact. The distance between Golgotha and MM's location was probably no more than a few hundred yards.
And when *they looked*, they *saw* that the stone was rolled away: for it was very great (16:4).	And, behold, there was a great *earthquake*: for the angel of the Lord descended from heaven, and came and rolled back the stone from the door, and sat upon it (Mt 28:2).	And they *found the stone rolled away* from the sepulchre (Lk 24:2).		Then, MM *looked* and discovered that the stone blocking the tomb's entrance was rolled away. Commentators are undecided if she directly witnessed ("saw") (1) the stone being rolled away or (2) an angel descended from heaven.

And entering into the sepulchre, they *saw* a young man sitting on the right side, clothed in a long white garment; and they were affrighted (16:5).	And, behold, there was a great earthquake: for the angel of the Lord descended from heaven, and came and rolled back the stone from the door, and sat upon it. His countenance was like lightning, and his raiment white as snow: (Mt 28:2-3).	And they entered in, and found not the body of the Lord Jesus. And it came to pass, as they were much perplexed thereabout, behold, two men stood by them in shining garments: (Lk 24:3-4).		According to Mark, MM *saw* a young man (an angel) inside the tomb. In contrast, Matthew reports that MM *saw* the angel sitting upon the stone (outside the tomb) which was rolled back away from the tomb's entrance. In conflict, Luke reports MM saw two men inside the tomb. Note: Some writers attempt to coincide this viewing with John 20:11-12. However, this interpretation cannot be harmonized with all of the gospel narratives.
And entering into the sepulchre, they saw a young man sitting on the right side, clothed in a long white garment; and they were affrighted (16:5).		And they *entered* in, and found not the body of the Lord Jesus. And it came to pass, as they were much perplexed thereabout, behold, two men stood by them in shining garments: (Lk 24:3-4).		Next, Mark reports that MM *entered* the tomb. In contrast, Matthew's narrative indicates that MM *never entered* the tomb. On the other hand, Luke declares that MM *entered* the tomb.

And he *saith* unto them, Be not affrighted: Ye seek Jesus of Nazareth, which was crucified: he is risen; he is not here: behold the place where they laid him. But go your way, tell his disciples and Peter that he goeth before you into Galilee: there shall ye see him, as he said unto you (16:6-7).	And the angel *answered* and *said* unto the women, Fear not ye: for I know that ye seek Jesus, which was crucified. He is not here: for he is risen, as he said. Come, see the place where the Lord lay. And go quickly, and tell his disciples that he is risen from the dead; and, behold, he goeth before you into Galilee; there shall ye see him: lo, I have told you (Mt 28:5-7).	And as they were afraid, and bowed down their faces to the earth, they *said* unto them, Why seek ye the living among the dead? He is not here, but is risen: remember how he spake unto you when he was yet in Galilee, Saying, The Son of man must be delivered into the hands of sinful men, and be crucified, and the third day rise again (Lk 24:5-7).		Here, MM *received a message* from as many as two angels.
		And they *remembered* his words (Lk 24:8).		Luke reports that MM *remembered* the words of Jesus.
And they *went out* quickly, and *fled* from the sepulchre; for they trembled and were amazed: neither said they any thing to any man; for they were afraid (16:8).	And they departed quickly from the sepulchre with fear and great joy; and did *run* to *bring his disciples word* (28:8).	And *returned* from the sepulchre, and told all these things unto the eleven, and to all the rest. It was Mary Magdalene and Joanna, and Mary the mother of James, and other women that were with them, which told these things unto the apostles (Lk 24:9-10).		Later, Mark, Matthew, and Luke confirm that MM *ran* away after she received the message.

	And as they went to tell his disciples, behold, Jesus met them, saying, All hail. And they came and held him by the feet, and worshipped him (Mt 28:9).			Following, MM *met* Jesus while she *traveled* to Jerusalem. She *bowed down* to Jesus, *held* him by his feet, and *worshipped* him.
	Then *said* Jesus unto them, Be not afraid: go tell my brethren that they go into Galilee, and there shall they see me (Mt 28:10).			Then, MM *received* a message from Jesus.
And they went out quickly, and fled from the sepulchre; for they trembled and were amazed: *neither said they any thing to any man*; for they were afraid (16:8).				Presumably, at first Mark does *not* report that MM *delivered* a message.
		It was Mary Magdalene and Joanna, and Mary the mother of James, and other women that were with them, which *told* these things unto the apostles (Lk 24:10).		Later, Mark reports that MM *delivered* the message. However, Matthew does not report if the message was delivered. Nonetheless, perhaps Mt 28:16 implies that the message was delivered. The *delivery* of the message was definitely confirmed by Luke.

CHAPTER 10

The Judas Episodes

PREFACE: THE JUDAS EPISODES

FOLLOWING THE ARREST and execution of Jesus, Christian writers were faced with several dilemmas. Chief among these was, how was it that God's chosen servant met his final demise? Acknowledging the fact that Jesus was executed, who could have engineered and planned such a devious scheme? Equally important, what was the motivation of the conspirators. Finally, why would God permit such a thing to happen, least of all to His "beloved Son, in whom I am well pleased" (Mk 1:11)? Woven throughout the gospel narratives are several episodes related to Judas Iscariot that were attempts of its authors to deal with these questions.

> The next few issues will deal with the complicated topic of Judas Iscariot. Among the topics that will be examined are (1) Judas's conspiracy and betrayal, (2) the alleged Jeremiah prophecy claimed by Matthew, (3) Judas's repentance, (4) Judas's suicide, and (5) Judas and the Potter's Field.
>
> Judas Iscariot was one of the original apostles and his name appears in all the Gospels and in Acts. In the synoptic narratives, Judas traveled to the Jewish leadership and offered to betray Jesus. After Judas betrayed Jesus, he repented and later committed suicide.
>
> The Christian scriptures present conflicting reports in many important details. The major issues of concern in the Judas episodes are (1) the internal contradictions found within the Christian scriptures, (2) the false prophecies declared in Matthew, (3) the growing amplifications and embellishments of the storyline, and (4) the literary or theological agenda of each gospel author and the author of Acts.

ISSUE 75: Judas's Conspiracy and Betrayal

Mk 14:10 And Judas Iscariot, one of the twelve, *went unto the chief priests, to betray him unto them.* *11 And when they heard it, they were glad, and promised to give him money. And he sought how he might conveniently betray him.*	Mt 26:14 Then one of the twelve, called Judas Iscariot, *went unto the chief priests,* *15 And said unto them, What will ye give me, and I will deliver him unto you? And they covenanted with him for thirty pieces of silver.* *16 And from that time he sought opportunity to betray him.*	Lk 22:3 *Then entered Satan into Judas surnamed Iscariot, being of the number of the twelve. 4 And he went his way, and communed with the chief priests and captains, how he might betray him unto them.* *5 And they were glad, and covenanted to give him money. 6 And he promised, and sought opportunity to betray him unto them in the absence of the multitude.*	Jn 13:2 And supper being ended, *the devil having now put into the heart of Judas Iscariot, Simon's son, to betray him;*

Mark 14:10-11 narrates that (1) Judas went to the chief priests to betray Jesus, (2) they were glad to hear his offer, (3) they promised to give him money to complete the deed to betray Jesus, and (4) from that time on, Judas watched for an opportunity to betray Jesus. Significantly, the chief priests offers Judas money only after he offered to betray Jesus. Mark omits two important details from his narrative: (1) what it was, exactly, that Judas had agreed to betray and (2) the specific motive for Judas's betrayal.

Matthew's narrative makes two additions to Mark: (1) Judas asks the chief priests what he would receive in exchange for delivering Jesus and (2) the chief priests counts out thirty silver coins. The text implies that the coins were given to Judas at this time. Similar to Mark, from this time on Judas sought an opportunity to betray Jesus.

Luke 22:3-6 adds three additional facts that do not appear in the other synoptic accounts: (1) *Satan entered Jesus*, (2) Judas communed with the chief priests *and captains* ("officers of the temple guard" NIV), and (3) Judas sought an opportunity to betray Jesus *"in the absence of the multitude"* (i.e., "when no crowd was present" NIV). Bock (1996, 1706) clarifies this statement, thus making "a 'safe' arrest possible." Luke also omits numerous details cited by Mark and Matthew. From both earlier gospels, Luke omits Judas's full name.

John's narrative adds two facts: (1) the statement that "the devil having now put *into the heart* of Judas Iscariot" and (2) Judas Iscariot *was Simon's son*.

CONTRADICTION #79 Matthew Contradicting Mark-Luke When Judas Was Paid

Matthew directly contradicts Mark (and also Luke) by reporting the time *when* Judas was paid by the chief priests. Mark narrates that Judas specifically went to the chief priests to betray Jesus. When the Jewish leadership heard from Judas, they were pleased and promised to give him an undisclosed amount of money. Therefore, *no money was received in advance.*

> Mk 14:10 and Judas Iscariot, one of the twelve, went unto the chief priests, to betray him unto them.

> Mk 14:11 And when they heard it, they were glad, and promised to give him money. And he sought how he might conveniently betray him.

Similar to Mark, Luke's Judas did *not* receive any money up front:

> Lk 22:4 And he went his way, and communed with the chief priests and captains, how he might betray him unto them.

> Lk 22:5 And they were glad, and covenanted to give him money.

In contradiction, Matthew reports that Judas *received his money up front*:

> Mt 26:14 Then one of the twelve, called Judas Iscariot, went unto the chief priests,

> Mt 26:15 And said unto them, "What will you give me, and I will deliver him unto you?" And they covenanted with him for thirty pieces of silver.

Several Bible translations make clear and shed light on the point that Matthew had Judas being paid *before* he carried out his deed:

> Mt 26:15 and asked, "What are you willing to give me if I hand him over to you?" So they counted out for him thirty silver coins. (New International Version © 1984)

> Mt 26:15 and said, What are ye willing to give me, and I will deliver him unto you? And they weighed unto him thirty pieces of silver. (New Revised Standard Version ©1989)

Mt 26:15 and asked, "What are you willing to give me if I hand him over to you?" So they counted out for him thirty silver coins. (New American Standard Bible ©1995)

Davies and Allison (1997, 450) offer a rationale for Matthew's Judas being paid in advance. They suggest that "this prepares for the repentance of 27:3-10: Judas must be paid before he can return the money."

In conclusion, in Mark and Luke, Judas did *not receive any money up front*; the chief priests only agreed to enter into an agreement and give him money. In contradiction, Matthew's Judas *was paid in advance*. Matthew incontrovertibly and indisputably contradicted Mark and Luke.

CONTRADICTION #80 Satan Being Judas's Motivation for Betraying Jesus

The gospel narratives present contradictory information regarding Judas's motivation for betraying Jesus. Mark 14:10 reads: "And Judas Iscariot, one of the twelve, went unto the chief priests, to betray him unto them." Consequently, Mark provides *no* explanation as to why Judas betrayed Jesus. Instead, Mark 14:11 declares that upon receiving Judas's offer to betray Jesus, then and only then did the chief priests promise to give him money for his action: "And when they heard it, they were glad, and promised to give him money. And he sought how he might conveniently betray him." Consequently, a plain reading of the text reveals that Judas did *not* go to the chief priests with the forethought of receiving money.

Matthew 26:14-15 presents important details omitted in Mark: "Then one of the twelve, called Judas Iscariot, went unto the chief priests, And said unto them, What will ye give me, and I will deliver him unto you? And they covenanted with him for thirty pieces of silver." Therefore, unlike Mark, Matthew had Judas specifically going to the chief priests and bargaining for how much they would pay him to deliver Jesus. The amount agreed upon was thirty pieces of silver. As a result, Matthew reports that Judas's motivation was money (i.e., perhaps covetousness).

Contrary to Mark and Matthew, Luke 22:3 reports that the rationale for Judas's action was that Satan had entered into him *before* the Last Supper: "Then entered Satan into Judas surnamed Iscariot, being of the number of the twelve. And he went his way, and communed with the chief priests and captains, how he might betray him unto them." Significantly, Luke omits any preconceived notion of Judas desiring money to betray Jesus or expecting to receive compensation for his deed. The action was seemingly the result of Satan entering Judas. Bock (1996, 1704) writes: "Judas acts and is responsible, but Satan is the impetus."

Expanding Luke's narrative, John 13:26-27 has Satan entering into the heart of Judas *during* the Last Supper.

> Lk 22:3 Then entered Satan into Judas surnamed Iscariot, being of the number of the twelve.

> Lk 22:4 And he went his way, and communed with the chief priests and captains, how he might betray him unto them.

> Lk 22:5 And they were glad, and covenanted to give him money.

> Lk 22:13 And they went, and found as he had said unto them: and they made ready the Passover.

> Lk 22:14 And when the hour was come, he sat down, and the twelve apostles with him.

> Lk 22:15 And he said unto them, With desire I have desired to eat this passover with you before I suffer.

> Jn 13:26 Jesus answered, He it is, to whom I shall give a sop, when I have dipped it. And when he had dipped the sop, he gave it to Judas Iscariot, the son of Simon.

> Jn 13:27 And after the sop Satan entered into him. Then said Jesus unto him, That thou doest, do quickly.

Therefore, only Luke and John charge that the devil (i.e., Satan) made Judas do it. Two highly significant facts of information are not provided to the reader by these writers: (1) how did Luke and John know that Satan made Judas do it, and (2) where was their incontrovertible evidentiary proof to their claim? A review of the literature located an explanation as to how Luke and John knew so positively when Satan made these entrances. Morris (1943, 950) writes: "The answer that they saw it in the countenance of Judas is unsatisfactory, for this could not apply to Luke. The other answer that Luke and John arrived at 'a psychological certainty' is too vague and subjective. Both Luke (22:4) and John have the immediate acts of Judas as grounds for their assertions and also the guidance of the Spirit in what they say about Judas." Unequivocally, Morris's response is pure speculation guided by his personal theological convictions. Here, there is no incontrovertible evidentiary proof.

In a response to an opponent, the Christian apologist James Patrick Holding (n.d. Response to "1001 Errors in the Bible") offers a possible explanation for the contradictory narratives presented by various gospel writers. In issue #431 he sarcastically refutes his opponent stating: *"Doh!* 😊 *Guess Wally still doesn't get that ancient writers felt free to exclude, include, or rearrange material according to their purposes. Not that again, Luke's Gentile readers would make much of anointing requirements in the OT."*

Then, in issue #433, Holding once again repeats his apologetic:

> Luke 22: (KJV) 5 "And they were glad, and covenanted to give him money." Compare to Matthew 26: (KJV) 15 "and said unto them, What will ye give me, and I will deliver him unto you? And they covenanted with him for thirty pieces of silver." The KJV's "covenanted" for Matthew is a mistranslation and should be "paid." Almost every other major, modern Christian translation says the equivalent of "paid." Even the NKJV says "paid." So Luke's Judas didn't receive money up front but Matthew's Judas did. *No, Matthew just left out, per normal freedom of composition in the day, the details Luke includes. Wally will never get over this hump because he's stuck in Funda-literal Land.*

This text absolutely agrees one hundred percent with Holding's statement; the gospel narrators probably lied in the *modern* sense of the word. When a witness in a court of law deliberately excludes, includes, or rearranges material according to his purposes, he is committing perjury. The authors and final redactors of the gospel narratives were liars in a modern sense.

The second problem with Holding's apologetic is that it is an argument based on silence. What Holding will not declare openly and unambiguously is the impossibility for him to know in any way that John was not adding to Luke or Luke was not adding to Mark. What Holding is stating is what Holding wants to believe. His explanation is not a reason; it is an excuse. Here, there is absolutely no historicity.

CONTRADICTION #81 Contradictory Chronology When Judas Concocted His Plan

John's chronology contradicts the synoptic narratives as to when Judas formed or first conceived his plan to betray Jesus. Matthew 26:14-15 reads: "Then one of the twelve, called Judas Iscariot, went unto the chief priests, And said unto them, What will ye give me, and I will deliver him unto you?

And they covenanted with him for thirty pieces of silver." Matthew thus states that Judas designed his plan immediately *after* the incident which took place in the house of Simon the leper at Bethany.

The episode of Simon the leper anointing Jesus while he was in Bethany is recorded in Matthew 26:6-13. This event occurred on Tuesday, two days *before* the Passover meal preparation. During this episode Jesus was anointed with a very expensive ointment of alabaster. Matthew 26:8 narrates: "But when his disciples saw it, they had indignation, saying, To what purpose is this waste? For this ointment might have been sold for much, and given to the poor." In reply, Jesus proceeded to criticize them. It was now, immediately *after* this rebuking incident recorded in verses 14 and 15 that Matthew states that Judas went to the chief priests and asked what he would receive in exchange for delivering Jesus. Therefore, Matthew had Judas concocting his plan to betray Jesus *before* the Last Supper.

Mark 14:3-9 records the same incident. However, Mark differs from Matthew in several details: (1) the ointment was identified as spikenard, (2) some of the disciples were described as indignant, and (3) the value of the ointment was declared to be "more than three hundred pence." After Jesus spoke to the disciples, Mark 14:10 substantiates Matthew's text: "And Judas Iscariot, one of the twelve, went unto the chief priests, to betray him unto them." Therefore, Mark 14:10-11 also has Judas arranging to betray Jesus on Tuesday, two days *before* the Last Supper.

Luke 22:1 narrates: "Now the feast of unleavened bread drew nigh, which is called the Passover." Therefore, Passover was approaching. A few verses later, Luke 22:3-4 stated that Satan entered into Judas and he then went to the chief priests and captains "how he might betray him [[i.e., Jesus]] unto them." Therefore, Luke 22:3-6 also records that Judas's arrangement to betray Jesus occurred on Tuesday. Again, the Passover meal had *not* yet occurred.

John 12:1-8 substantially embellishes the text, making Judas appear progressively more heinous and odious than the synoptic narratives: (1) he had Judas being the *solitary* disciple who challenged the anointment with three hundred pences worth of spikenard, and (2) he editorialized that Judas's opposition to the anointing by Mary was not by any love for the poor but because he was at one time a thief and the purse bearer of the society, which had gathered around Jesus. In addition, John 11:1 and 12:3 identifies the previous anonymous anointer as Mary of Bethany, the sister of Lazarus.

In the next chapter, John 13:1 reports that now it was "before the feast of the passover, when Jesus knew that his hour was come that he should depart out of this world." Consequently, John is stating that it was now the day "*before* the feast of the passover." Then, John 13:2 declares: "And supper being ended, the devil having now put into the heart of Judas Iscariot, Simon's son, to betray him." Therefore, following Mark's chronology, it was now Thursday evening and the Passover meal had concluded. However, according to John's timeline, this would not be a Passover meal.

Up to this exact moment John's Judas had *not* held a conference with the chief priests and the Pharisees. As a matter of fact, John 13:27-30 narrates that it was none other than Jesus who told Judas during this meal to go and buy some things for the feast or that he should give something to the poor:

> Jn 13:27 And after the sop Satan entered into him. Then said Jesus unto him, That thou doest, do quickly.

> Jn 13:28 Now no man at the table knew for what intent he spake this unto him.

> Jn 13:29 For some of them thought, because Judas had the bag, that Jesus had said unto him, Buy those things that we have need of against the feast; or, that he should give something to the poor.

> Jn 13:30 He then having received the sop went immediately out: and it was night.

Then Jesus's command was fulfilled by Judas. In the next four chapters (Jn 14-17) Jesus delivered his farewell discourses. It was during this time that Judas developed his scheme with the chief priests to betray Jesus. John 18:3 then had Judas receiving "a band of men and officers from the chief priests and Pharisees" to arrest Jesus. If this truly was the night of the Passover, "a band of men and officers from the chief priests and Pharisees" would be leaving their home the night of the Passover to arrest Jesus. Compounding matters, the arrest and following trial would be taking place on the first day of Passover, and that was a holy day, a day in which work was not permitted.

Finally, John unequivocally demonstrates that his gospel contradicted the Synoptics. John 18:28-29 narrated that the arrested Jesus was brought before Pilate. Presumably, as a matter of civility or consideration, Pilate left the judgment hall to meet the Jewish leadership and Jesus. John explains the reason that the Jewish leadership would not enter the judgment hall: "Then led they Jesus from Caiaphas unto the hall of judgment: and it was early; and they themselves went not into the judgment hall, lest they should be defiled; but that they might eat the passover." In other words, if the Jewish leadership entered the judgment hall, they would have been defiled (i.e., made themselves ritually unclean) and would not be able to partake of the passover. It makes no sense that the Jewish leadership would have been concerned about becoming ritually unclean and consequently disqualified from eating the passover if the Passover meal had already occurred.

TABLE 48. A Harmonized Sunday through Thursday Chronology Based on a Friday Crucifixion

DESCRIPTION OF THE EVENT	MARK	MATTHEW	LUKE	JOHN
PREPARATION FOR THE PASSOVER	PREPARATION FOR THE PASSOVER	PREPARATION FOR THE PASSOVER	PREPARATION FOR THE PASSOVER	PREPARATION FOR THE PASSOVER
Jesus Predicted His Death.	14:1–2	26:1–5	22:1–2	XXXXXXXXXXXX
Anointing of Jesus by Mary of Bethany.	14:3–9	26:6–13	XXXXXXXXXXXX	12:2–8
TUESDAY	TUESDAY	TUESDAY	TUESDAY	TUESDAY
Judas Planned His Betrayal.	14:10–11	26:14–16	22:3–6	XXXXXXXXXXXX
THURSDAY	THURSDAY	THURSDAY	THURSDAY	THURSDAY
Preparation for the Paschal Meal.	14:12–16	26:17–19	22:7–13	**XXXXXXXXXXX**
THURSDAY EVENING: FRIDAY IN THE JEWISH CALENDAR	THURSDAY EVENING: FRIDAY IN THE JEWISH CALENDAR	THURSDAY EVENING: FRIDAY IN THE JEWISH CALENDAR	THURSDAY EVENING: FRIDAY IN THE JEWISH CALENDAR	THURSDAY EVENING: FRIDAY IN THE JEWISH CALENDAR
The Passover	14:17	26:20	22:14–16	XXXXXXXXXXXX
John declared that it was before the feast of the Passover.	XXXXXXXXXX	XXXXXXXXXX	XXXXXXXXXXXX	13:1
The Betrayer was Pointed Out.	14:18–21	26:21–25	XXXXXXXXXXXX	13:21–30
Institution of the Lord's Supper.	14:22–25	26:26–30	22:14–23	XXXXXXXXXXXX
Jesus Rebuked the Apostles' Jealousy.	XXXXXXXXXX	XXXXXXXXXX	22:24–30	XXXXXXXXXXXX
Judas "Was Sent" to Purchase food.	XXXXXXXXXX	XXXXXXXXXX	XXXXXXXXXXXX	13:29–30
The New Commandment.	XXXXXXXXXX	XXXXXXXXXX	XXXXXXXXXXXX	13:31–35
Jesus Foretold Peter's Denial and the Apostles' Desertion.	14:26–31	26:31–35	22:31–38	13:31–38
Jesus's Farewell Discourse.	XXXXXXXXXX	XXXXXXXXXX	XXXXXXXXXXXX	14:1–31
Jesus Prayed in Gethsemane.	14:32–42	26:36–46	22:39–46	18:1

The Betrayal and Arrest.	14:43–51	26:47–56	22:47–54	18:2–11
The Jews would not enter the hall of judgment in order not to be defiled so that they might be able to eat the Passover.	XXXXXXXXXX	XXXXXXXXXX	XXXXXXXXXXXX	18:28

In conclusion, the synoptic narratives have Judas taking almost three days (Tuesday, Wednesday, and Thursday) to find an opportunity to betray Jesus. To the contrary, John reports that Judas betrayed Jesus on Thursday evening and immediately *after* the Passover meal. It must be reiterated that this scenario is based on Mark's chronology of a Thursday evening Last Supper and Friday crucifixion. Unequivocally, John contradicts the synoptic Gospels.

SPECULATION #141 Judas as a Thief

For several reasons John's addition that Judas was a one-time thief seems like an artificial embellishment. First, this highly significant fact that Judas was a thief is omitted from the earlier gospels. Second, this information has the ring of a literary design to entertain the reader by making Judas a more contemptible and despicable person. Third, this fact is dubious, given that "that the group included at least two former tax collectors (Levi and Matthew)" (Osler 2009, 35). That is, why were these more qualified men not given the responsibility to maintain the group's finances? Finally, it was peculiar that Jesus would have selected this one time thief to have been put in charge of the group's finances, given that Jesus was omniscient and knew in advance that he would also betray the group.

SPECULATION #142 The Existence of Judas

Some scholars and skeptics speculate that Judas never existed. Raymond Brown (1994a 2:1394-96), one of the foremost Catholic scholars, disputes this position but identifies several arguments advanced for this thesis:

1. The paucity of evidence in the Christian scriptures,
2. John (the brother of James) was named more frequently (thirty times) than was Judas, compared to twenty-two mentions of Judas,

3. the staged nature of the scenes as at the Last Supper where each disciple was asked if he was the one who would betray Jesus, and then Judas spoke last (Mt 26:21-25),
4. Judas appeared in a setting in which an earlier gospel did not have him, e.g., the anointing at Bethany (Jn 12:4-5), and
5. the conflicting accounts of Judas's death in the Gospel of Matthew and Acts.

Significantly, Paul, writing before Mark, seemingly knows *nothing* of Judas. Nonetheless Paul mentions in 1 Corinthians 15:3-5, which predated the Gospels, an appearance of Jesus to "the Twelve." But 1 Corinthians 15 unequivocally indicates that neither Judas nor anyone else had yet been identified or removed in the early years in the writings of Paul. Evidently, the betrayal of Judas was a later developed tradition with which Paul was unfamiliar. Only later did Matthew 28:16 and Luke 24:33 talk about "to the Eleven."

On the other hand, there is another relevant fact to consider. Brown (1994a, 2:1394) points out that Judas's name is mentioned twenty-two times in the Christian scriptures: Mark 3, Matthew 5, Luke-Acts 6 (i.e., numerous scholars consider that Luke and Acts were written by the same author), and John 8: "If that listing of NT works is correct chronologically, interest in Judas was progressive."

A further important factor arguing against the existence of Judas is found in Mark, the oldest gospel. Consider how much of Judas's story is lacking in the earliest account of Mark:

- Mark omitted the thirty pieces of silver paid to Judas.
- Mark omitted the description of Judas as a thief.
- Mark omitted Judas's name at the Last Supper.
- Mark omitted Judas's repentance.
- Mark omitted Judas's death by suicide.

SPECULATION #143 What Judas Actually Did

Traditionally, Judas is accused of betraying Jesus. But how did Judas betray Jesus? Stein (1996, 219) declares that the "Messianic secret" can be outright eliminated as an explanation. According to this theory, Judas betrayed to the chief priests that Jesus was secretly teaching his disciples that he was the Messiah. Some wrongly suggest that if such a fact was true, the Sanhedrin would have had grounds to arrest Jesus. However, Stein posits that this argument was not viable since Judas was not present at the trial when the Sanhedrin sought evidence to condemn Jesus: "If Judas had been paid to betray Jesus by revealing that he claimed to be the Jewish Messiah, then he would have been present at the trial as a witness of this."

Mark 14:1-2 presents the answer: "After two days was the feast of the passover, and of unleavened bread: and the chief priests and the scribes sought how they might take him by craft, and put him to death. But they said, Not on the feast day, lest there be an uproar of the people." Therefore, the betrayal was Judas making available information to the Jewish leadership of how, when, and where Jesus could be arrested without risking a riot. That is, information was needed as to how Jesus could be arrested in secret and away from the crowds.

Besides providing this information, Judas also participated in the arrest and he personally identified Jesus with a kiss (Mk 14:44-45; Mt 26:47-49; Lk 22:47-48; Jn 18:2-5).

SPECULATION #144 Reasons for Judas's Betrayal

The topic of Judas's betrayal has been subject to much scholarly discussion. Judas's betrayal of Jesus is commonly explained on several grounds. [Note that the topic of Judas's nonbetrayal is examined in speculation #146.]

1. *Money.* Label this "avariciousness," "covetousness," or "greed." This motive is hinted in the Gospels. Matthew 26:15 reports that Judas specifically went to the chief priests stating: "And said unto them, What will ye give me, and I will deliver him unto you?" Reinforcing this notion, John 12:6 states that Judas was: (1) a thief, (2) a keeper of the money bag, and (3) he used to help himself to what was put into it: "This he said, not that he cared for the poor; but because he was a thief, and had the bag, and bare what was put therein." Osler (2009, 35) posits:

> John 12 describes Judas as the keeper of the purse for the apostles, the one who maintained the finances for the group of thirteen. Given that the group included at least two former tax collectors (Levi and Matthew), it seems odd that Judas received the task, and it could well be that he sought it out, establishing a money nexus that defined his relationship with Jesus from the start to the last.

In addition, Enslin (1972, 127) points out that earlier in John 12:4-8, Judas "had protested the lavish waste of money at the anointing by Mary." Money was clearly one of Judas's weaknesses.

2. *Disillusionment* with Jesus's ministry and cause. This theory is based on the name Iscariot as derived from the Latin *sicarius*, which means "dagger man," a word applied to members of the Zealot movement. The implication was that Judas was a political zealot who believed that Jesus was the true Messiah who would free the Jewish homeland from Roman occupation. But he was disappointed that Jesus seemed to be pursuing a spiritual and educational agenda rather than one who would lead to a conflict with the Romans.

3. *Hurt* by some rebuke by Jesus that Judas did not accept and which grew and turned into hatred. This motive could perhaps be classified as rebellion and attributed to pride.

4. *Jealousy* of other disciples who were more prominent than he. Therefore, perhaps the betrayal was a way to do something historically important, if only for a moment. It could also be that Judas's jealousy mingled with a low self-image and an extreme self-absorption.

5. *Humiliation.* Fosdick (1949, 185) discusses the notion that Judas thought Jesus was the Messiah. Eventually doubt crept in: "He had been made a fool of by this Galilean, and by as much as he had believed with ardent hope in Jesus' messiahship, but so much he now resented and was determined to destroy the one who had let him down."

6. *Sociology.* France (2007, 976) points out that "it may be worth noting that Judas *may* have been the only non-Galilean member of this provincial movement, and thus, in addition to perhaps resenting the leading role of Galilean fishermen, would have found himself in an awkward position when they came south and found themselves in confrontation with the Judean authorities."

7. *Religious*: N.T. Wright (1992, 555) offers that Judas betrayed to the chief priests was "that Jesus had performed a scandalous counter-Temple act in celebrating his own supper as a new and radical alternative."

8. On a lighter side, Davies and Allison (1997, 452) point out that "tradition (Coptic Gospel of Bartholomew; Hennecke I, p. 505) has also offered that he was moved by his wife's nagging."

Brown (1994a, 2:1400) tersely identifies several additional theories along with a list of their proponents:

1. that Jesus claimed that he would destroy the sanctuary (Goguel),
2. that Jesus claimed to be God's Son (Grundmann),
3. that Jesus claimed to be the Messiah, thus breaking the Messianic secret (Bacon, Bornhäuser, A. Schweitzer, Seitz),
4. that Jesus hoped to inaugurate the kingdom of God immediately after the Last Supper (Bacon, Preisker; see Mk 14:25; Lk 22:28-30 [Ps 122:5]),
5. that Jesus had let himself be anointed (Bacon; see Mk 14:4, 8 [1 Sam 16:13]),
6. that Jesus celebrated the Passover at an illegal time or in an illegal way (M. Black), and
7. that Jesus had approved the use of the sword (Stein-Schneider; see Lk 22:36-38; Isa 53:12).

In conclusion, extensive theories have been proposed to explain why Judas betrayed Jesus. These theories are nothing more than guesses, hunches, and speculations. In fact, no historian, scholar, or theologian knows why Judas acted the way he did. Only Judas would ultimately know why he betrayed Jesus, assuming that this episode is historical.

SPECULATION #145 The Value of Thirty Pieces of Silver

What was the *real value* of thirty pieces of silver in the days of Jesus and what would be its equivalent value in today's world? Various writers have posited a wide range of responses. Examples of these responses include the following:

1. Stein (1996, 218) writes: "Yet thirty pieces of silver was not a great sum of money; it was the price of a slave (compare Ex 21:32 and Zech 11:13).
2. R. T. France (2007, 978) states that "this is something like a month's wages."
3. Santiago Bovisio (n.d. The Valley of Jesus) writes: "Those thirty pieces of silver paid for Jesus, updated in our days, would be equal to the three-month salary of an ordinary worker, approximately."

4. Davies and Allison (1997, 452) estimate that "if they are Tyrian shekels, as the use of Zech 11.12-13 implies, Judas gains the equivalent of about four months of minimum wage."

5. Jeremias (1975, 138-40) substantiates that the price of an average field was approximately 120 denarii, which was the equivalent of 30 shekels.

6. Erica Reiner (1988, 189), writing in *The Journal of the American Oriental Society*, offers the hypothesis that the thirty shekels reflected an idiomatic Sumerian expression, namely "a trifling amount."

7. Fuljenz (2009), writing in *Coin News Today* ("Rare Coins: The Tyre Shekels' Connection To History"), states:

In Jesus' time, the most universally recognized circulated coin was the Greek silver *tetradrachm*, which literally means 'four drachms' (pronounced drams). For almost two hundred years, the historic coin was minted in Tyre by the Phoenicians. From 126 BC until AD 70, the silver *tetradrachm* became the universal currency accepted throughout the Roman Empire. In currency terms, the silver *tetradrachm* is the equivalent of the American dollar in today's global economy. In value terms, one of these coins roughly equaled a week's wages for a skilled laborer in those days.

The Jewish moneychangers of the time called them shekels. The temple in Jerusalem accepted only the Tyre shekels as currency. Although it has never been definitively proven, it is a virtual certainty that Judas received Tyre shekels for his traitorous complicity. At the time, thirty shekels equaled over half a year's wages for skilled laborers. Viewed another way, thirty shekels purchased a slave.

SPECULATION #146 Judas's Nonbetrayal

In comparatively recent times, Klassen (1999, 396-410; 1996, 47-61; cf. Briskin 2004, 194-97; Ehrman 2012, 122; Fredriksen 1999, 117-18; Winter 1998, 147-50) posits the hypothesis that Judas did *not* betray Jesus. Based on the Greek word *paradidomi*, Klassen's text *Judas: Betrayer or Friend of Jesus* offered the thesis that Judas did not betray Jesus. The word translated as *betray* in the entire gospel narratives is *paradidomi*, corresponding to Strong's number 3860 (Strong 1890, 54). The full breadth of the word included *betray, bring forth, cast, commit, deliver (up), give (over, up), hazard, put in prison*, or *recommend*. "Not one ancient classical Greek text . . . has the connotation of treachery. Any lexicon that suggests otherwise is guilty of theologizing rather than assisting us to find the meaning of Greek words through usage" (1996, 48). Therefore, the Greek word employed in the Gospels that is commonly translated as "betray" does not actually have that negative meaning that is associated with betrayal in English.

In support of this position, Robinson (2006, 42-43) writes:

> In the standard Greek-English dictionary of the New Testament that all scholars use, the first meaning is listed neutrally as "hand over, turn over, give up" a person. But it has also the decidedly positive meaning "give over, commend, commit," for example, to commend a person "to the Grace of God" (Acts 14:26; 15:40). It often means "hand down, pass on, transmit, relate, teach" the oral or written tradition. It is in fact most familiar to us in the liturgy of the Lord's Supper, "For I received from the Lord what I also *handed on* to you" (1 Cor 11:23), and in the way Paul introduced a list of resurrection appearances: "For I *handed on* to you as of first importance what I in turn had received" (1 Cor 15:3). It is consistent with this double meaning of the verb that the noun means a *handing over* or a *handing down* both in the sense of an *arrest* and in the sense of the *transmission* of *tradition*. It is clear from the use of this verb that Judas *handed* Jesus *over*. The etymology of the Greek word is neutrally *give over*, which I hence use in what follows. But what that *giving over* actually meant is the question at issue.

Brown (1994a, 2:1399; also see 1: 211-13), writing earlier, also offers support to Robinson. He too points out that the verb *paradidonai* applied to Judas means "to give over," not to betray. Brown adds in footnote 4: "The classical verb for betraying is *prodidonai*. The only time a word from that stem is applied to Judas in the NT is Luke 6:16 (*prodotēs*). Did the overwhelming preference for *paradidonai* stem from usage in Isa 53:13 [LXX]: "He was given over for our sins"?

An additional argument raised against a "betrayal" motif includes Mark's lack of even a single element of a story of betrayal.

Brown (1994a, 2:1402-04) identifies several additional non-betrayal hypotheses. These included the following:

1. Judas, a faithful disciple, hoped to stop a revolt that Jesus' actions had caused and, with money, sought to get the chief priests to let him go (Stein-Schneider "Recherche" 415-20).
2. Judas was only obeying the orders of Jesus (Jn 13:27) to give him over to Caiaphas who was known to Judas (the unnamed disciple of John 18:15b). The morsel of bread given to Judas by Jesus at the supper

was a gesture of thanks, and Judas' kiss was a gesture of farewell as in Ruth 1:14 (G. Schwarz *Jesus* 12-31).

However, in contrast, Gosling (1999, 117-26), writing in *Evangelical Quarterly* refutes the thesis proposed by Klassen. His review of the literature concluded that the Greek word *paradidomi* does carry the negative nuance of betray rather than to simply "hand over, deliver."

SPECULATION #147 Evolution and Embellishment of Judas's Life

The Gospels and the Acts of the Apostles present an ever-increasing evolution and embellishment of Judas's life. In order to demonstrate this phenomenon it is necessary to examine seven parallel episodes reported in the Gospels and Acts: (1) the identity of the twelve disciples, (2) the crisis at Capernaum, (3) the Bethany affair, (4) the betrayal, (5) the Last Supper, (6) the arrest of Jesus, and (7) Judas's death.

1. THE IDENTITY OF THE TWELVE DISCIPLES

Mk 3:14 *And he ordained twelve*, that they should be with him, and that he might send them forth to preach, 15 And to have power to heal sicknesses, and to cast out devils: 16 And Simon he surnamed Peter; 17 And James the son of Zebedee, and John the brother of James; and he surnamed them Boanerges, which is, The sons of thunder: 18 And Andrew, and Philip, and Bartholomew, and Matthew, and Thomas, and James the son of Alphaeus, and Thaddaeus, and Simon the Canaanite, 19 And *Judas Iscariot*, which also betrayed him: and they went into an house.	Mt 10:1 And when he had called unto him his *twelve disciples*, he gave them power against unclean spirits, to cast them out, and to heal all manner of sickness and all manner of disease. 2 Now the names of the twelve apostles are these; The first, Simon, who is called Peter, and Andrew his brother; James the son of Zebedee, and John his brother; 3 Philip, and Bartholomew; Thomas, and Matthew the publican; James the son of Alphaeus, and Lebbaeus, whose surname was Thaddaeus; 4 Simon the Canaanite, and *Judas Iscariot*, who also betrayed him.	Lk 6:13 And when it was day, he called unto him *his disciples: and of them he chose twelve*, whom also he named apostles; 14 Simon, (whom he also named Peter,) and Andrew his brother, James and John, Philip and Bartholomew, 15 Matthew and Thomas, James the son of Alphaeus, and Simon called Zelotes, 16 And Judas the brother of James, and *Judas Iscariot*, which also was the traitor.	Jn

The first mention of Judas comes from the list of the twelve apostles. Mark and Matthew mention "one" Judas. In contrast, Luke identifies "two" people who shared the name Judas. In each of the synoptic narratives Judas was named Judas Iscariot. However, in Mark and Matthew, Judas Iscariot was identified to the reader as the one who "also betrayed him." In both of these narratives, the Greek root word *paradidomi* translated in the AV is "betrayed" and corresponds to 3860 in Strong's numbering (Strong 1890, 54). In contrast, Luke declares that Judas was also a *prodotes* (Strong's list number 4273) or "betrayer, traitor." Therefore, in the English language, Luke employs a stronger negative connotation. Finally, John omits a list of Jesus's disciples.

2. THE CRISIS AT CAPERNAUM

Mk	Mt	Lk	Jn 6:68 Then Simon Peter answered him, Lord, to whom shall we go? thou hast the words of eternal life. 69 And we believe and are sure that thou art that Christ, the Son of the living God. 70 Jesus answered them, Have not I chosen you twelve, *and one of you is a devil?* 71 *He spake of Judas Iscariot the son of Simon: for he it was that should betray him, being one of the twelve.*

Sequentially, the next specific reference to Judas occurs in John following the death of John the Baptist (Mk 6:14-2; Mt 14:1-12; Lk 9:7-9) and during the crisis at Capernaum.

TABLE 49. Time Line from the Death of John the Baptist to the Discourse on the Tradition of Men

DETAILS	MARK	MATTHEW	LUKE	JOHN
The death of John the Baptist.	Mk 6:14-29	Mt 14:1-12	Lk 9:7-9	
The Twelve returned and retired with Jesus for rest.	Mk 6:30-32	Mt 14:13	Lk 9:10	
The miraculous feeding of five thousand.	Mk 6:33-34	Mt 14:31-21	Lk 9:11-17	Jn 6:1-13
The disciples and multitude were sent away, and Jesus retired for prayer.	Mk 6:45-46	Mt 14:22-23		Jn 6:14-15

Jesus walked on the sea.	Mk 6:47-52	Mt 14:24-33		Jn 6:14-15
The reception at Gennesaret.	Mk 6:53-56	Mt 14:34-36		
The discourse on the bread of life.				Jn 6:22-71
The discourse on the tradition of men.	Mk 7:1-23	Mt 15:1-20		

The episode of the discourse of bread was only reported in John. John 6:53-54 had Jesus teaching: "Then Jesus said unto them, Verily, verily, I say unto you, Except ye eat the flesh of the Son of man, and drink his blood, ye have no life in you. Whoso eateth my flesh, and drinketh my blood, hath eternal life; and I will raise him up at the last day." When many of Jesus disciples heard this, they complained: "Many therefore of his disciples, when they had heard this, said, This is an hard saying; who can hear it? When Jesus knew in himself that his disciples murmured at it, he said unto them, Doth this offend you?" (Jn 6:60-61).

John declares that from the very first Jesus knew two significant facts: (1) the ones who did not believe and (2) the person who would betray him: "But there are some of you that believe not. For Jesus knew from the beginning who they were that believed not, and who should betray him" (Jn 6:64). It was from this moment that many disciples left Jesus: "From that time many of his disciples went back, and walked no more with him" (Jn 6:66).

Next, Jesus asked his twelve remaining disciples if they would remain with him. This mention of "the Twelve" in John 6:67 was the first time this reference appeared in John. John 6:68-69 reported Peter's reply by stating their loyalty and declaring that Jesus was "the Christ (i.e., Messiah) and the Son of the living God."

Immediately, John 6:70 has Jesus explicitly and unequivocally declaring that he was the one who chose the Twelve and that one of them was the devil: "Jesus answered them, Have not I chosen you twelve, and one of you is a devil?" Finally, the author of John, as if with a footnote, adds a closing remark: "He spake of Judas Iscariot the son of Simon: for he it was that should betray him, being one of the twelve" (Jn 6:71). Here, John has raised the tension. Jesus had full foreknowledge that Judas would betray him and yet designated him to be one of his apostles. Here, Judas was seemingly evil or wicked from the start.

3. THE BETHANY AFFAIR

Mk 14:3 And being in Bethany in the house of Simon the leper, as he sat at meat, there came a woman having an alabaster box of ointment of spikenard very precious; and she brake the box, and poured it on his head. 4 And there were some that had indignation within themselves, and said, Why was this waste of the ointment made? 5 For it might have been sold for more than three hundred pence, and have been given to the poor. And they murmured against her. 6 And Jesus said, Let her alone; why trouble ye her? she hath wrought a good work on me. 7 For ye have the poor with you always, and whensoever ye will ye may do them good: but me ye have not always. 8 She hath done what she could: she is come aforehand to anoint my body to the burying. 9 Verily I say unto you, Wheresoever this gospel shall be preached throughout the whole world, this also that she hath done shall be spoken of for a memorial of her.	Mt 26:6 Now when Jesus was in Bethany, in the house of Simon the leper, 7 There came unto him a woman having an alabaster box of very precious ointment, and poured it on his head, as he sat at meat. 8 But when his disciples saw it, they had indignation, saying, To what purpose is this waste? 9 For this ointment might have been sold for much, and given to the poor. 10 When Jesus understood it, he said unto them, Why trouble ye the woman? for she hath wrought a good work upon me. 11 For ye have the poor always with you; but me ye have not always. 12 For in that she hath poured this ointment on my body, she did it for my burial. 13 Verily I say unto you, Wheresoever this gospel shall be preached in the whole world, there shall also this, that this woman hath done, be told for a memorial of her.	Lk 7:37 And, behold, a woman in the city, which was a sinner, when she knew that Jesus sat at meat in the Pharisee's house, brought an alabaster box of ointment, 38 And stood at his feet behind him weeping, and began to wash his feet with tears, and did wipe them with the hairs of her head, and kissed his feet, and anointed them with the ointment. 39 Now when the Pharisee which had bidden him saw it, he spake within himself, saying, This man, if he were a prophet, would have known who and what manner of woman this is that toucheth him: for she is a sinner. Lk 10:38 Now it came to pass, as they went, that he entered into a certain village: and a certain woman named Martha received him into her house. 39 And she had a sister called Mary, which also sat at Jesus' feet, and heard his word. 40 But Martha was cumbered about much serving, and came to him, and said, Lord, dost thou not care that my sister hath left me to serve alone? bid her therefore that she help me. 41 And Jesus answered and said unto her, Martha, Martha, thou art careful and troubled about many things: 42 But one thing is needful: and Mary hath chosen that good part, which shall not be taken away from her.	Jn 12:1 Then Jesus six days before the passover came to Bethany, where Lazarus was which had been dead, whom he raised from the dead. 2 There they made him a supper; and Martha served: but Lazarus was one of them that sat at the table with him. 3 Then took Mary a pound of ointment of spikenard, very costly, and anointed the feet of Jesus, and wiped his feet with her hair: and the house was filled with the odour of the ointment. 4 Then saith one of his disciples, Judas Iscariot, Simon's son, which should betray him, 5 Why was not this ointment sold for three hundred pence, and given to the poor? 6 This he said, not that he cared for the poor; but because he was a thief, and had the bag, and bare what was put therein.

The third incident in which Judas appears is the Bethany affair. The story seemingly is a conflation of two other accounts recorded in the Gospels. The first episode occurred in Bethany. In the first story, Mark, Matthew, and Luke report that an unnamed woman poured a very precious ointment of spikenard on the head of Jesus. Mark reports that this ointment was valued at 300 pence. Mark 14:4 has several people present and complaining about this waste, which could have helped the poor: "And there were some that had indignation within themselves, and said, Why was this waste of the ointment made?" In contrast, Matthew 26:8 reports that the indignation was by the "disciples." Then, Mark and Matthew report that Jesus rebuked those who criticized the woman, commending the woman for her actions.

Luke's story in chapter seven is altogether different. In Luke's narrative, the criticism came from a group of Pharisees. However, in contrast to Mark and Matthew, these Pharisees did not complain about the waste of money. They directed their complaint directly to Jesus since he permitted a sinful woman to have contact with him. Specifically, this woman (1) bathed Jesus's feet with her tears, (2) dried his feet with her hair, (3) kissed his feet, and (4) anointed Jesus's feet (unlike the head in Mark and Matthew). From Luke 7:40 to 7:48, Jesus carried on a dialogue with Simon. The bottom line is that Jesus rebuked Simon and forgave the sins of the unnamed woman.

Luke 10:38-42 narrates a completely different story as compared to chapter seven. After the previous anointing episode, Jesus met two sisters in an unnamed village. A woman named Mary sat at Jesus's feet, figuratively drinking his words. While Mary was listening to Jesus's words, it was her sister Martha who served Jesus and performed numerous tasks. Martha complained to Jesus that she was doing all the work and requested that he tell Mary to help with the work. Instead, Jesus rebuked Martha and complimented Mary.

In all three of the stories Judas Iscariot's name was *not* mentioned.

In direct contrast, in the Fourth Gospel, Judas's name was specifically mentioned. John 12:4 stated: "Then saith one of his disciples, Judas Iscariot, Simon's son, which should betray him." Thus, the criticism evolved from Mark's generic "some that had indignation" to Matthew's "his disciples" to Luke's the Pharisees or "Martha" to John's "Judas Iscariot, Simon's son." Not only was Judas named but John 12:4 also castigated and pre-labeled him as the one "which should betray him."

Not stopping here, John 12:6 adds three significant editorial remarks: "This he said, not that he cared for the poor; but because he was a thief, and had the bag, and bare what was put therein." That is: (1) Judas did not really care about the poor, (2) Judas was a thief, and (3) Judas kept the purse and used to steal what was put into it. Here, in John 6:71, the narrations evolved Judas into a contemptible, despicable, and loathsome person.

4. THE BETRAYAL

Mk 14:10 And Judas Iscariot, *one of the twelve, went unto the chief priests, to betray him unto them.* 11 And *when they heard it, they were glad,* and promised to give him money. And he sought how he might conveniently betray him.	Mt 26:14 Then one of the twelve, called Judas Iscariot, *went unto the chief priests,* 15 And said *unto them, What will ye give me, and I will deliver him unto you?* And they covenanted with him for thirty pieces of silver. 16 And from that time he sought opportunity to betray him.	Lk 22:3 Then entered Satan into Judas surnamed Iscariot, being of the number of the twelve. 4 *And he went his way, and communed with the chief priests and captains, how he might betray him unto them.* 5 And they were glad, and covenanted to give him money. 6 And he promised, and sought opportunity to betray him unto them in the absence of the multitude.	Jn

The fourth episode continues the negative embellishment of Judas as he made his plan to betray Jesus. This arrangement only occurred in the synoptic Gospels. Since this episode was analyzed earlier, only the growing embellishments are discussed.

Mark reports (1) Judas went to the chief priests on his own initiative to betray Jesus, (2) they were glad to hear his offer, (3) they promised to give him money to complete the deed, and (4) from that time on, Judas watched for an opportunity to betray Jesus. No mention was given as to why Judas turned against Jesus. Matthew expands Mark's narrative, making Judas appear worse by asking the chief priests what he would receive in exchange for delivering Jesus. It was agreed that Judas would be paid thirty pieces of silver. Seemingly, Judas was paid up front to complete his mission.

Luke adds three pieces of information not recorded in the earlier synoptic Gospels: (1) *Satan entered Judas*, (2) Judas communed with the chief priests *and captains* ("officers of the temple guard" NIV), and (3) Judas sought an opportunity to betray Jesus "*in the absence of the multitude*" (i.e., "when no crowd was present" NIV). The significant embellishment of Luke was that Judas had now become a Satan-inspired character.

John's narrative adds a final coup de'grâce. However, this would need to wait until the Last Supper. But to recap, Mark provides no motive for Judas's betrayal, Matthew reports that the motivation was money, and Luke had Satan being the impetus. Here, too, there is a definite embellishment of the text.

5. THE LAST SUPPER

Mk 14:17 And in the evening he cometh with the twelve. 18 And as they sat and did eat, Jesus said, Verily I say unto you, One of you which eateth with me shall betray me. 19 And they began to be sorrowful, and to say unto him one by one, Is it I? and another said, Is it I? 20 And he answered and said unto them, It is one of the twelve, that dippeth with me in the dish.	Mt 26:20 Now when the even was come, he sat down with the twelve. 21 And as they did eat, he said, Verily I say unto you, that one of you shall betray me. 22 And they were exceeding sorrowful, and began every one of them to say unto him, Lord, is it I? 23 And he answered and said, He that dippeth his hand with me in the dish, the same shall betray me. 24 The Son of man goeth as it is written of him: but woe unto that man by whom the Son of man is betrayed! it had been good for that man if he had not been born.	Lk 22:14 And when the hour was come, he sat down, and the twelve apostles with him. Lk 22:19 And he took bread, and gave thanks, and brake it, and gave unto them, saying, This is my body which is given for you: this do in remembrance of me. 20 Likewise also the cup after supper, saying, This cup is the new testament in my blood, which is shed for you. 21 But, behold, the hand of him that betrayeth me is with me on the table. 22 And truly the Son of man goeth, as it was determined: but woe unto that man by whom he is betrayed!	Jn 13:2 And supper being ended, the devil having now put into the heart of Judas Iscariot, Simon's son, to betray him; Jn 13:21 When Jesus had thus said, he was troubled in spirit, and testified, and said, Verily, verily, I say unto you, that one of you shall betray me. 22 Then the disciples looked one on another, doubting of whom he spake. 23 Now there was leaning on Jesus' bosom one of his disciples, whom Jesus loved. 24 Simon Peter therefore beckoned to him, that he should ask who it should be of whom he spake. 25 He then lying on Jesus' breast saith unto him, Lord, who is it? 26 Jesus answered, He it is, to whom I shall give a sop, when I have dipped it. And when he had dipped the sop, he gave it to Judas Iscariot, the son of Simon.

21 The	25 Then Judas,	23 And they began	27 And after the sop Satan entered
Son of man	which betrayed	to enquire among	into him. Then said Jesus unto him,
indeed	him, answered and	themselves, which	That thou doest, do quickly. 28 Now
goeth, as it	said, Master, is it I?	of them it was that	no man at the table knew for what
is written of	He said unto him,	should do this	intent he spake this unto him. 29 For
him: but woe	Thou hast said. 26	thing. 24 And there	some of them thought, because Judas
to that man	And as they were	was also a strife	had the bag, that Jesus had said unto
by whom the	eating, Jesus took	among them, which	him, Buy those things that we have
Son of man	bread, and blessed	of them should	need of against the feast; or, that he
is betrayed!	it, and brake it,	be accounted the	should give something to the poor. 30
good were it	and gave it to the	greatest.	He then having received the sop went
for that man	disciples, and said,		immediately out: and it was night.
if he had	Take, eat; this is		31 Therefore, when he was gone out,
never been	my body.		Jesus said, Now is the Son of man
born.			glorified, and God is glorified in him.

The fifth episode entails the Last Supper. Mark 14:18 has Jesus announcing that one of his disciples would betray him. Consequently, they asked who the betrayer was. Jesus responded in Mark 14:20: "It is one of the twelve, that dippeth with me in the dish." In Mark, there is no mention of Judas.

Matthew 26:21 also has Jesus announcing that one of them would betray him. When they too inquired who the betrayer was, Jesus responds in Matthew 26:23 by declaring: "He that dippeth his hand with me in the dish, the same shall betray me." Next, Matthew 26:25 embellishes Mark when it narrates: "Then Judas, which betrayed him, answered and said, Master, is it I? He said unto him, Thou hast said." Only Judas's words and Jesus's reply were reported. Once again, Jesus knew in advance that Judas would betray him. Then the dinner continued.

Luke's account of the Last Supper did not explicitly identify Judas by name although his role as a betrayer was strongly suggested. Similar to Mark and Matthew, Luke 22:21 had Jesus announcing that one of them would betray him: "But, behold, the hand of him that betrayeth me is with me on the table." Luke 22:23 also has the disciples inquiring as to who was the traitor was. This lead to Jesus's disciples raising the question who among them was the greatest. Jesus responded with a rebuke.

John's narrative is the longest and most detailed, and it contains the most serious negative embellishment of Judas. John 13:2 declares, in no uncertain words, that Judas was in league with Satan: "And supper being ended, the devil having now put into the heart of Judas Iscariot, Simon's son, to betray him." Here we now have the ultimate motive, Satan and the forces of darkness and evil. Adding further to the narrative, John is the only gospel that employed a biblical quotation (the second half of Psalm 41:9) prophesying the role of Judas: "I speak not of you all: I know whom I have chosen: but that the scripture may be fulfilled, He that eateth bread with me hath lifted up his heel against me" (Jn 13:18).

Like the synoptic Gospels, John has Jesus announcing (1) one of the disciples would betray him, (2) an inquiry who was the betrayer, and (3) a mention of sop. However, John continues with his embellishment: "And after the sop Satan entered into him. Then said Jesus unto him, That thou doest, do quickly." This relevant portion of the Last Supper ended with Judas leaving the room, although none of the disciples knew why. John 13:29-30 adds an editorial comment: "For some of them thought, because Judas had the bag, that Jesus had said unto him, Buy those things that we have need of against the feast; or, that he should give something to the poor. He then having received the sop went immediately out: and it was night." What John has ingeniously supplied was an explanation how Judas was able to leave the Last Supper and lead the arrest party to Jesus.

6. THE ARREST OF JESUS

Mk 14:43 And immediately, while he yet spake, cometh Judas, one of the twelve, and with him a great multitude with swords and staves, from the chief priests and the scribes and the elders. 44 And he that betrayed him had given them a token, saying, Whomsoever I shall kiss, that same is he; take him, and lead him away safely. 45 And as soon as he was come, he goeth straightway to him, and saith, Master, master; and kissed him.	Mt 26:47 And while he yet spake, lo, Judas, one of the twelve, came, and with him a great multitude with swords and staves, from the chief priests and elders of the people. 48 Now he that betrayed him gave them a sign, saying, Whomsoever I shall kiss, that same is he: hold him fast. 49 And forthwith he came to Jesus, and said, Hail, master; and kissed him. 50 And Jesus said unto him, Friend, wherefore art thou come? Then came they, and laid hands on Jesus, and took him. 51 And, behold, one of them which were with Jesus stretched out his hand, and drew his sword, and struck a servant of the high priest's, and smote off his ear.	Lk 22:47 And while he yet spake, behold a multitude, and he that was called Judas, one of the twelve, went before them, and drew near unto Jesus to kiss him. 48 But Jesus said unto him, Judas, betrayest thou the Son of man with a kiss? 49 When they which were about him saw what would follow, they said unto him, Lord, shall we smite with the sword? 50 And one of them smote the servant of the high priest, and cut off his right ear. 51 And Jesus answered and said, Suffer ye thus far. And he touched his ear, and healed him.	Jn 18:2 And Judas also, which betrayed him, knew the place: for Jesus ofttimes resorted thither with his disciples. 3 Judas then, having received a band of men and officers from the chief priests and Pharisees, cometh thither with lanterns and torches and weapons. 4 Jesus therefore, knowing all things that should come upon him, went forth, and said unto them, Whom seek ye? 5 They answered him, Jesus of Nazareth. Jesus saith unto them, I am he. And Judas also, which betrayed him, stood with them. 6 As soon then as he had said unto them, I am he, they went backward, and fell to the ground.

46 And they laid their hands on him, and took him. 47 And one of them that stood by drew a sword, and smote a servant of the high priest, and cut off his ear. 48 And Jesus answered and said unto them, Are ye come out, as against a thief, with swords and with staves to take me? 49 I was daily with you in the temple teaching, and ye took me not: but the scriptures must be fulfilled. 50 And they all forsook him, and fled. 51 And there followed him a certain young man, having a linen cloth cast about his naked body; and the young men laid hold on him: 52 And he left the linen cloth, and fled from them naked. 53 And they led Jesus away to the high priest: and with him were assembled all the chief priests and the elders and the scribes.	52 Then said Jesus unto him, Put up again thy sword into his place: for all they that take the sword shall perish with the sword. 53 Thinkest thou that I cannot now pray to my Father, and he shall presently give me more than twelve legions of angels? 54 But how then shall the scriptures be fulfilled, that thus it must be? 55 In that same hour said Jesus to the multitudes, Are ye come out as against a thief with swords and staves for to take me? I sat daily with you teaching in the temple, and ye laid no hold on me. 56 But all this was done, that the scriptures of the prophets might be fulfilled. Then all the disciples forsook him, and fled. 57 And they that had laid hold on Jesus led him away to Caiaphas the high priest, where the scribes and the elders were assembled.	52 Then Jesus said unto the chief priests, and captains of the temple, and the elders, which were come to him, Be ye come out, as against a thief, with swords and staves? 53 When I was daily with you in the temple, ye stretched forth no hands against me: but this is your hour, and the power of darkness. 54 Then took they him, and led him, and brought him into the high priest's house. And Peter followed afar off.	7 Then asked he them again, Whom seek ye? And they said, Jesus of Nazareth. 8 Jesus answered, I have told you that I am he: if therefore ye seek me, let these go their way: 9 That the saying might be fulfilled, which he spake, Of them which thou gavest me have I lost none. 10 Then Simon Peter having a sword drew it, and smote the high priest's servant, and cut off his right ear. The servant's name was Malchus. 11 Then said Jesus unto Peter, Put up thy sword into the sheath: the cup which my Father hath given me, shall I not drink it? 12 Then the band and the captain and officers of the Jews took Jesus, and bound him, 13 And led him away to Annas first; for he was father in law to Caiaphas, which was the high priest that same year.

TABLE 50. An Analysis of the Total Number of Verses, Total Number of Words (AV), and Total Number of Words Spoken by Jesus (AV)

ANALYSIS	MARK	MATTHEW	LUKE	JOHN
Total number of Verses	11	11	8	12
Total Number of Words	220	263	177	243
Total Number of Words Spoken by Jesus	37	120	62	62

The sixth episode deals with the arrest of Jesus. Mark reports numerous significant pieces of information up to the arrest of Jesus:

1. that along with Judas came "a great multitude with swords and staves, from the chief priests and the scribes and the elders" to arrest Jesus,
2. Mark, along with Matthew and Luke explain to the reader the purpose of the kiss,
3. Judas spoke to Jesus two words: "Master, master",
4. Judas gave the sign of a kiss to those arresting Jesus,
5. upon grasping Jesus, an unknown person with Jesus drew his sword and cutoff the ear of the high priest's servant,
6. Jesus complained to the arresting crowd,
7. the reader was informed that all of his disciples forsook Jesus and fled him,
8. a young man who fled the arrest scene naked left behind a linen cloth, and
9. Jesus was taken to the house of Caiaphas, the high priest, where all the chief priests, the elders, and the scribes had gathered.

Matthew narrates at least ten significant facts from the time of Judas's arrival until the time Jesus was brought to Caiaphas:

1. along with Judas came a "great multitude with swords and staves, from the chief priests and elders of the people,
2. the writer explained to the reader the purpose of the kiss,
3. Judas said to Jesus two words "Hail, master",
4. Judas gave the sign of a kiss to those arresting Jesus,
5. Jesus responded to the kiss with a question "Friend, wherefore art thou come?",
6. upon grasping Jesus, an unknown person with Jesus drew his sword and cutoff the ear of the high priest's servant,
7. Jesus responded to the sword wielder,
8. Jesus declared that this action was fulfillment of scripture,
9. Jesus complained to the arresting crowd, and
10. Jesus was taken to the house of Caiaphas, the high priest, where the scribes and elders had gathered.

Matthew embellishes Mark in several ways. Matthew's narrative contained 43 extra words and Jesus speaks 83 extra words (i.e., AV translation). Second, Matthew had Jesus responding to Judas's kiss with a question: "Friend, wherefore art thou come?" Third, Brown (1994a, 1:267) states that Matthew went beyond Mark in making the sword-wielder a disciple. Fourth, Jesus responds to the sword-wielder, demonstrating that he was in control.

Luke's narrative was shorter than Mark's and Matthew's. However, Fritzmyer (1985, 1448) concisely states: "No one will deny that the story has grown under Luke's pen." (1) "Judas then, having received a band of men and officers from the chief priests and Pharisees, cometh thither with lanterns and torches and weapons" (Jn 18:3), (2) Jesus preempted any words by Judas and asked him a question, (3) those with Jesus asked him if they should use the sword against the arresting party, (4) an unknown person with Jesus drew his sword and cut off the right ear of the high priest's servant, (5) Jesus healed the servant's ear, (6) Jesus complained to the arresting party, and (7) Jesus was taken to the house of the high priest.

In Luke, there were several significant differences:

1. Judas was leading the arresting party,
2. the reader was never informed if Judas actually kissed Jesus,
3. Jesus's preemptive question to Judas about the kiss only appeared here,
4. Jesus knew why Judas had come, and the asked a question that demonstrated he was in control,
5. Luke's disciples took a more pro-active stance and were seemingly willing to fight whereas Mark 14:50 and Matthew 26:56 had the disciples fleeing the scene,
6. similar to Matthew, Luke went beyond Mark in making the sword-wielder a disciple,
7. during the sword-wielding incident the servant's "right" ear was specified and Jesus miraculously healed it with a mere touch! Brown's (1994a, 1:271-72) review of the literature perhaps provided a reason for the specification of the ear: "Yet Rostovtzeff cites an Egyptian papyrus of 183 BC (Tebtunis III, 793, xi. 10 where cutting off the right ear is a deliberate choice to render a shameful lesson to someone and points out that damage to an organ on the right side was considered more serious than damage to an organ on the left (see Mishna, *Baba Qamma* 8:6 for the general principle that dignity increases the offense)", and
8. Luke identified the three groups in the arresting crowd as the chief priests, captains of the temple, and the elders.

John embellishes the synoptic Gospels by adding and expanding numerous details:

1. Judas "knew the place: for Jesus oft times resorted thither with his disciples."
2. Judas was portrayed as leading two arresting groups. First, there was a band of men. Brown (1994a, 1:248) pointed out that a Roman cohort—that is, six hundred soldiers—went to arrest Jesus. Bullinger (1914, 1564) explained that the word cohort "means the tenth part of a legion, therefore 600 men." The notion of six hundred Roman soldiers plus a group made up of the chief priests and Pharisees seems ahistorical. Bullinger suggested that "the term was probably used with some latitude." Brown's review of the literature (1994a, 1:250) raised the issue "that there were too few Roman soldiers in Jerusalem for a cohort or any sizable number to have been sent out against an unarmed man. Others contend that Roman soldiers would never have delivered a prisoner to a Jewish high priest" (as reported in Jn 18:13).
3. John embellished the text with an editorial comment that "Jesus knew all things," thus reinforcing the idea that he was in total control.
4. John had Jesus preempting the arresting party with a question: "Whom seek ye?" again, demonstrating his control over the situation;
5. The arresting party identified who they wanted and Jesus identified himself as "I am."
6. This gospel embellished the synoptic Gospels by have the arresting party withdraw backward and falling to the ground.
7. Again, Jesus asked the arresting party who they wanted and again Jesus replied "I am he." These actions too demonstrated his total control over the scene.
8. Simon Peter was identified as the sword-wielding disciple who cut off the right ear of the high priest's servant. Therefore, the Gospels evolved from an unnamed person, to an unnamed disciple, and to Peter Simon being identified as the assailant.
9. The servant whose ear was cut off was now given a name: Malchus.
10. After being apprehended, John further embellished the synoptic Gospels that not only Jesus was taken but that they also "bound him." In *no* previous gospel was Jesus described as being bound.
11. The final embellishment of the arrest was Jesus being transported to Annas: "And led him away to Annas first; for he was father in law to Caiaphas, which was the high priest that same year."

7. JUDAS'S DEATH

Mk	Mt	Lk	Acts	Jn
	Mt 27:5 And he cast down the pieces of silver in the temple, and departed, *and went and hanged himself.*		Acts 1:18 Now this man purchased a field with the reward of iniquity; *and falling headlong, he burst asunder in the midst, and all his bowels gushed out.*	

The seventh and final embellishment is the death of Judas. Mark provides no commentary about the final whereabouts of Judas. In contrast, Matthew has Judas committing suicide by hanging himself. In total contradiction, the author of Luke-Acts has Judas dying after having his intestines spilled out. Finally, John omits any discussion about the final demise of Judas.

In conclusion, the Gospels and Acts present an obviously ever increasing evolution and embellishment of Judas's life that portrayed him in an ever growing negative light.

ISSUE 76: An Examination of the Alleged Jeremiah Prophecy Claimed by Matthew

Mk	Mt	Lk	Acts	Jn
	Mt 26:14 Then one of the twelve, called Judas Iscariot, went unto the chief priests, 15 And said unto them, What will ye give me, and I will deliver him unto you? And they covenanted with him for thirty pieces of silver. 16 And from that time he sought opportunity to betray him. Mt 27:3 Then Judas, which had betrayed him, when he saw that he was condemned, repented himself, and brought again the thirty pieces of silver to the chief priests and elders, 4 Saying, I have sinned in that I have betrayed the innocent blood. And they said, What is that to us? see thou to that. 5 And he cast down the pieces of silver in the temple, and departed, and went and hanged himself. 6 And the chief priests took the silver pieces, and said, It is not lawful for to put them into the treasury, because it is the price of blood. 7 And they took counsel, and bought with them the potter's field, to bury strangers in. 8 Wherefore that field was called, The field of blood, unto this day. 9 Then was fulfilled that which was spoken by Jeremy the prophet, saying, And they took the thirty pieces of silver, the price of him that was valued, whom they of the children of Israel did value; 10 And gave them for the potter's field, as the Lord appointed me. And gave them for the potter's field, as the Lord appointed me.			

Matthew's narrative explains that Judas's actions were all part of prophecy. Specifically, Matthew 27:9 declares: "Then was fulfilled that which was spoken by Jeremy the prophet." Specifically it is the prophet Jeremiah.

CONTRADICTION #82 Matthew's False Citation of Jeremiah's Name

Matthew 27:9 is in error when it cites the prophet Jeremiah as the source of a supposed prophecy: "Then was fulfilled that which was spoken by Jeremy the prophet, saying, And they took the thirty pieces of silver, the price of him that was valued, whom they of the children of Israel did value." Nowhere in Jeremiah does any such statement appear.

Many writers (Allison 2001, 883; Brown 1994a, 1:651; Bullinger 1914, 184-86; Gundry 1994, 557-58; 1975, 125; Menken 1984, 5-24) discuss the issue as to whether or not the writer had confused (conflagulated) his memory with the potter passage of Jeremiah 18:2, with a field purchase detailed in Jeremiah 32:9 and the text of Zechariah 11:12-13. Such an interpretation is implied in the NIV (1978, 124n10a "Jer 32:6-9") and supported by the NRSV (1989, 31nu). These three texts are analyzed below.

MacArthur (2005, 1181) offers the following apologetic for Matthew 27:9 citing the prophet Jeremiah: "Jeremiah came first in the order of prophetic books, so the Prophets were sometimes collectively referred to by his name." The problem with this apologetic is simple: Jeremiah does not come first in the order of prophetic books. The actual order is Isaiah, Jeremiah, and Ezekiel; who are then followed by the Minor Prophets.

Triestman (1997, 183; cf. Johnson 1896, 311), a Jewish-Christian apologist, also acknowledges a difficulty here. He posits that this conflagulation is simply due to "a scribal error." However, Triestman concedes that this is an argument from silence since "there is no evidence of such an error." Therefore, he goes on to say: "it is easier to assume that an earlier copyist erred than to assume that the evangelist did." How does Triestman know that it was easier for the scribe to have made an error than Matthew? This action is a classic example in which a Christian apologist finds it convenient not to deal with the obvious.

In contrast, Bullinger (1914, 184-85), clerical secretary of the Trinitarian Bible Society, offers seven suggestions to deal with the difficulties connected with Matthew 27:9-10.

1. That "Matthew quoted from memory" (Augustine and others).
2. That the passage was originally in Jeremiah, but the Jews cut it out (Eusebius and others), though no evidence for this is produced.

3. That it was contained in another writing by Jeremiah, which is now lost (Origen and others).

4. That Jeremiah is put for the whole body of the prophets (Bishop Lightfoot and others), though no such words can be found in the other prophets.

5. That it was "a slip of the pen" on the part of Matthew (Dean Alford).

6. That the mistake was allowed by the Holy Spirit on purpose so that we may not trouble ourselves as to who the writers were, but receive all prophecy as direct from God, who spake by them (Bishop Wordsworth).

7. That some annotator wrote Jeremiah in the margin, and it "crept" into the text (*Smith's Bible Dictionary*).

Obviously Christian apologists are attempting to rationalize this obvious error in Matthew.

By understanding this verse, it will be unequivocally apparent that Matthew's citation is either erroneous or a deliberate embellishment to serve as a proof that the Hebrew Bible foreshadowed (typology) Judas's heinous crime. First, in Matthew's eyes, the Messiah was going to be sold for thirty pieces of silver. Second, the money to pay for the Messiah was later to be returned to its original owner. In Matthew 27:10, a third prophecy is visualized in the mind of Matthew that this money would eventually be used to pay for a potter's field. This third component is, in fact, based on Jeremiah 18. However, none of these claimed prophecies is a prophecy.

For the sake of clarity, it is necessary to examine both the content and context of Jeremiah 18, Jeremiah 32, and Zechariah 11. The relevant portions of Jeremiah 18 are seen below:

JEREMIAH 18:1-6

Jer 18:1 The word which came to Jeremiah from the LORD, saying,

Jer 18:2 Arise, and go down to the potter's house, and there I will cause thee to hear my words.

Jer 18:3 Then I went down to the potter's house, and, behold, he wrought a work on the wheels

Jer 18:4 And the vessel that he made of clay was marred in the hand of the potter: so he made it again another vessel, as seemed good to the potter to make it.

Jer 18:5 Then the word of the LORD came to me, saying,

Jer 18:6 O house of Israel, cannot I do with you as this potter? saith the LORD. Behold, as the clay is in the potter's hand, so are ye in mine hand, O house of Israel.

Jeremiah 18:1-6 reports that the prophet received the Word from the LORD. The *Word* is both a declaration and teaching of God's ways in dealing with nations and kingdoms. Here, God was instructing that He could easily do what He willed with Israel, as easily as the potter could with clay. What Matthew did was transform Jeremiah's metaphor written hundreds of years earlier to the priests in Jesus's day purchasing a potter's field in order to bury Judas. However, the prophet Jeremiah was *not* making a prophecy. Instead, through a metaphor he was teaching the people a truth that the nations and kingdoms were to God as a lump of clay was to a potter. God could do with nations and kingdoms as He desired. Again, here there is no prophecy. Instead, Matthew took Jeremiah 18 out of its context to serve as his theological agenda.

JEREMIAH 32:1-14

Jer 32:1 The word that came to Jeremiah from the LORD in the tenth year of Zedekiah king of Judah, which was the eighteenth year of Nebuchadrezzar.

Jer 32:2 For then the king of Babylon's army besieged Jerusalem: and Jeremiah the prophet was shut up in the court of the prison, which was in the king of Judah's house.

Jer 32:3 For Zedekiah king of Judah had shut him up, saying, Wherefore dost thou prophesy, and say, Thus saith the LORD, Behold, I will give this city into the hand of the king of Babylon, and he shall take it;

Jer 32:4 And Zedekiah king of Judah shall not escape out of the hand of the Chaldeans, but shall surely be delivered into the hand of the king of Babylon, and shall speak with him mouth to mouth, and his eyes shall behold his eyes;

Jer 32:5 And he shall lead Zedekiah to Babylon, and there shall he be until I visit him, saith the LORD: though ye fight with the Chaldeans, ye shall not prosper.

Jeremiah 32:1-5 reports that Jeremiah receives the Word from the LORD foretelling the destruction of Jerusalem by the Babylonians and the captivity of King Zedekiah. The king would be taken to Babylon and remain captive there until God would visit him. That is, God would put an end to his life by a natural death.

> Jer 32:6 And Jeremiah said, The word of the LORD came unto me, saying,
>
> Jer 32:7 Behold, Hanameel the son of Shallum thine uncle shall come unto thee saying, Buy thee my field that is in Anathoth: for the right of redemption is thine to buy it.
>
> Jer 32:8 So Hanameel mine uncle's son came to me in the court of the prison according to the word of the LORD, and said unto me, Buy my field, I pray thee, that is in Anathoth, which is in the country of Benjamin: for the right of inheritance is thine, and the redemption is thine; buy it for thyself. Then I knew that this was the word of the LORD.

Jeremiah 32:6-8 reports that once again Jeremiah had received the Word of the LORD. At this time Jeremiah was in a Babylonian prison. The prophet was instructed that his nephew Hanameel would come to visit him and request that Jeremiah purchase a piece of land in Anathoth. This land was located in the land of the tribe of Benjamin.

> Jer 32:9 And I bought the field of Hanameel my uncle's son, that was in Anathoth, and weighed him the money, even seventeen shekels of silver.
>
> Jer 32:10 And I subscribed the evidence, and sealed it, and took witnesses, and weighed him the money in the balances.
>
> Jer 32:11 So I took the evidence of the purchase, both that which was sealed according to the law and custom, and that which was open:
>
> Jer 32:12 And I gave the evidence of the purchase unto Baruch the son of Neriah, the son of Maaseiah, in the sight of Hanameel mine uncle's son, and in the presence of the witnesses that subscribed

the book of the purchase, before all the Jews that sat in the court of the prison.

Jer 32:13 And I charged Baruch before them, saying,

Jer 32:14 Thus saith the LORD of hosts, the God of Israel; Take these evidences, this evidence of the purchase, both which is sealed, and this evidence which is open; and put them in an earthen vessel, that they may continue many days.

Jeremiah 32:9-14 details that Jeremiah purchased the land for seventeen shekels of silver. No information is provided as to how Jeremiah was in possession of money to purchase this land while he was in prison. A description of the transaction follows: (1) the transaction was performed before witnesses (i.e., before all the Jews that sat in the court of the prison), (2) one copy was sealed up, (3) the other was open, and (4) Baruch, one of the witnesses, was instructed to put the evidence of the transaction in an earthen vessel.

In context, Jeremiah 32 has nothing to do with Judas. The context describes an event that occurred almost six hundred years before Judas's death. Second, the purchase price for the land was seventeen shekels, not thirty. Third, the transaction occurred in a prison, not in a similar locale where Judas carried out his transaction with the chief priests. This locale was probably in the Temple or the chief priests' home. Fourth, the evidence of the transaction was sealed in an earthen vessel; no such sealing in an earthen vessel occurred in Matthew. Fifth, the money Hanameel received was not used to pay for a potter's field. Sixth, there was no returning of the silver shekels as detailed in Matthew 27:5.

ZECHARIAH 11:1-13

Zech 11:1 Open thy doors, O Lebanon, that the fire may devour thy cedars.

Zech 11:2 Howl, fir tree; for the cedar is fallen; because the mighty are spoiled: howl, O ye oaks of Bashan; for the forest of the vintage is come down.

Zech 11:3 There is a voice of the howling of the shepherds; for their glory is spoiled: a voice of the roaring of young lions; for the pride of Jordan is spoiled.

Zechariah 11:1-3 foretold the destruction of the Temple and the nation in figurative expressions. Lebanon contained a mountain boundary between Judea and its neighbors on the north. From here, Judah [Judea] would be invaded. The cedars, shepherds, and the lions possibly referred to the rulers or leading men of the doomed nation. Others suggest that the cedars, oaks of Bashan, and the young lions were symbols of great power. The mention of cedars may also have referred to the Temple, since it was constructed of cedars of Lebanon: "And say, Thus saith the Lord GOD; A great eagle with great wings, longwinged, full of feathers, which had divers colours, came unto Lebanon, and took the highest branch of the cedar" (Ez 17:3).

The shepherds have been interpreted as referring either to (1) the native rulers (kings) and spiritual guides (cf. Jer 2:8; 16:16; 23:1-4; Ez 34:2; etc.), (2) God (Isa 40:11; Ez 34:11-16), (3) representing the "ideal servant" (Ez 11:4-7), or (4) "the Prophet was now commanded to personate God in this His office of Shepherd, and to feed (i.e., to protect and take care of His flock) the house of Israel, whom their foreign rulers (their owners, sellers, and shepherd) were grinding down" (Lowe 1892, 100).

> Zech 11:4 Thus saith the LORD my God; Feed the flock of the slaughter;

The prophet was directed by God to act the role of a shepherd. The prophet pastured his doomed flock, indicating that he would do his job. Nonetheless, the flock (i.e., Israel) was destined for slaughter.

> Zech 11:5 Whose possessors slay them, and hold themselves not guilty: and they that sell them say, Blessed be the LORD; for I am rich: and their own shepherds pity them not.

Verse 5 pictures the helpless plight of the people. The foreign nations traffic with them remorselessly and without impunity. The concluding part of the sentence reads: "their own shepherds pity them not." That is, the Jewish rulers who should have guarded, protected, and safeguarded the interests of the people, provided them with no protection.

> Zech 11:6 For I will no more pity the inhabitants of the land, saith the LORD: but, lo, I will deliver the men every one into his neighbour's hand, and into the hand of his king: and they shall smite the land, and out of their hand I will not deliver them.

> Zech 11:7 And I will feed the flock of slaughter, even you, O
> poor of the flock. And I took unto me two staves; the one I called
> Beauty, and the other I called Bands; and I fed the flock.

The phrase "For I will no more pity the inhabitants of the land" provided a reason for the need of a new shepherd. The prophet acted the part of God, whose sovereign pastoral charge he had, as it were taken upon himself. But Israel did *not* appreciate or understand the benefits God wanted to confer on them. Here, the prophet was portrayed as a good shepherd rejected by his sheep. But because the people despised him, God permitted the Israelites to be abused by their rulers. The references to those who buy and sell were the overlords and their own shepherds (i.e., the Jewish-ruling people).

The concept of protection is symbolized in verse 7 where it states: "And I took unto me two staves." Shepherds carry a rod and a staff (Ps 23:4). The function of the rod was to ward off attacks of wild beasts. In contrast, the staff (the crook) was used by the shepherd to guide the flock. The rod (Beauty) represented God's favor and good will in His protective care of Israel against outside foes. On the other hand, the binders, representing the staff, denoted God's desire to promote unity in Israel.

> Zech 11:8 Three shepherds also I cut off in one month; and my
> soul lothed them, and their soul also abhorred me.

Commentators are divided and speculate the meaning of "the three shepherds." Some think they were contemporary officials or three classes of rulers in Israel made up of the kings, the priests, and the prophets, all who were unfaithful. Others posited that they were three successive kings or high priests. The bottom line is that either allegorically or literally God eliminated three shepherds in one month. If one takes this verse to represent Israel's literal history, then the three shepherds might have represented the successive removal of the final three wicked kings of Judah with one month representing their short reigns (2 Kgs 23:34-24:20).

> Zech 11:9 Then said I, I will not feed you: that that dieth, let it
> die; and that that is to be cut off, let it be cut off; and let the rest
> eat every one the flesh of another.

> Zech 11:10 And I took my staff, even Beauty, and cut it asunder,
> that I might break my covenant which I had made with all the
> people.

> Zech 11:11 And it was broken in that day: and so the poor of the
> flock that waited upon me knew that it was the word of the LORD.

Verse 10 is thought to represent the prophetic indictment of the Judean leadership. The term "beauty" is thought to signify some sort of protection for God's people from attacks. However, the breaking of the staff of favor allowed the nations to oppress the Israelites again. Therefore, God's special providence over them was at an end. Others interpret this phrase to mean that the union was broken, signifying disunity between Israel and Judea.

> Zech 11:12 And I said unto them, If ye think good, give me my
> price; and if not, forbear. So they weighed for my price thirty
> pieces of silver.

Now, for his efforts the shepherd asked the people for his wages to compensate him for the services he had rendered. However, he left it to the people to determine the value of the services he had provided. What followed was that the nation loathed the shepherd so much that they paid him an insulting thirty pieces of silver. This amount equaled the value of a slave gored by an ox under the Torah (Ex 21:32). Half of the same price was given by Hosea for an adulteress (Hos 3:2). This phrase was also an ancient idiom for a trifling amount. Consequently, the shepherd sarcastically called the amount magnificent (handsome or lordly) (see the NRSV translation).

> Zech 11:13 And the LORD said unto me, Cast it unto the potter:
> a goodly price that I was prised at of them. And I took the thirty
> pieces of silver, and cast them to the potter in the house of the
> LORD.

Then God said to the shepherd/prophet to cast it, the thirty pieces of silver, into the potter that the shepherd's work was appraised. The phrase the "goodly price" is said sarcastically. Then, as God instructed, the shepherd took the thirty pieces of silver and threw them to the potter in the House of the Lord. Potters were essential to the Temple services since they made jars for ceremonial worship (Lev 6:28; cf., Jer 18:6; 19:1). However, by throwing the thirty pieces of silver to the potter rather than into Temple treasury (Josh 6:24; Ezra 2:69; Neh 7:70), which would support the priests, the shepherd demonstrated the demeaning value of the payment. To put the money into the treasury would have supported the corrupt shepherds of Israel. In contrast, to throw the money at the potter demonstrated how pitiful the payment was since it seems to be equated with the work of a potter. In other words, to make clay vessels in no way compared with shepherding God's people; thus, the shepherd threw the money to the potter because the people had truly demonstrated their lack of thankfulness.

> Zech 11:14 Then I cut asunder mine other staff, even Bands, that I might break the brotherhood between Judah and Israel.

Then the prophet shatters his staff, denoting breaking and dissolution of all unity and harmony between Israel and Judah. This action also could have symbolized the historical breaking of the bond of union between Judah and Israel's ten tribes under Rehoboam. With the breaking of the staff, the people were now left to their fate, a prey to evil.

> Zech 11:15 And the LORD said unto me, Take unto thee yet the instruments of a foolish shepherd.

> Zech 11:16 For, lo, I will raise up a shepherd in the land, which shall not visit those that be cut off, neither shall seek the young one, nor heal that that is broken, nor feed that that standeth still: but he shall eat the flesh of the fat, and tear their claws in pieces.

What follows was that God permitted the people to now be abused by foolish shepherds as a punishment for having rejected the good shepherd. Now, in contrast to the faithful shepherd earlier described in the chapter, this person was told to play the role of the shepherd again, but this time his role was that of the foolish shepherd (Zech 11:15). This foolish shepherd would not miss those of his flock that had gone astray. Furthermore, not only would this shepherd not spare his flock but he would also exploit, devour, and destroy the people (Zech 11:16).

In conclusion, here, too, a contextual reading of Zechariah 11 proves that this chapter has nothing to do with Judas. The context describes an event that occurred almost six hundred years prior to Judas's death. Second, the shepherd has nothing in common with Judas: (1) Judas never served as a good shepherd to the people of Israel, (2) the good shepherd never betrayed Israel, whereas Matthew's Judas betrayed Jesus, (3) Judas was never commanded by God to return the silver, (4) Judas never severed the harmony between Israel and Judah, (5) the mention of the potter in this story has no relationship with the account of Judas, and (6) the shepherd in Zechariah did not commit suicide.

As stated earlier, Matthew mistakenly conflated the prophet Jeremy (i.e., Jeremiah) with Zechariah. However, here, the concern is with the translation and an understanding of the text (see Keim 1883, 6:191; Senior 1972, 399).

TABLE 51. Translations of Zechariah 11:13 (AV)

ZECHARIAH 11:13 (AV)	ALTERNATIVE TRANSLATION
And the LORD said unto me, Cast it *unto the potter*: a goodly price that I was prized at of them.	And the LORD said unto me, Cast it (the wage) *into the treasury*, the splendour of the worth at which I am valued by them.
And I took the thirty pieces of silver, and *cast them to the potter* in the house of the LORD.	Then I took the thirty pieces of silver, and cast them *into God's house*, into the treasury.

In the original Zechariah, *no field was purchased with the money.* God simply told Zechariah *to throw the money "to the potter,"* and Zechariah threw the pieces into the house of God "for the potter." Question: Since when is a potter a potter's field? In effect, Matthew and its translation have transformed a non-transaction into a financial transaction to purchase a field.

> NRSV (p. 871) Then the LORD said to me, "Throw it *into the treasury*"—this lordly price at which I was valued by them. So I took the thirty shekels of silver and threw them into the treasury in the house of the LORD.

Again, Jeremiah presents *no* prophecy or typology relevant to the times and events detailed of Judas's life. Instead, Matthew took Jeremiah 18 out of context to serve his theological agenda.

CONCLUSION: THE FALSE PROPHECY OF JEREMIAH CLAIMED BY MATTHEW

Several conclusions can be formulated having analyzed the relevant excerpts from Jeremiah 18, Jeremiah 32, and Zechariah 11. First, Matthew states that it was the prophet *Jeremiah* who discusses the topic of "thirty pieces of silver" whereas it was the prophet *Zechariah* in verse 11:13 who discusses the matter of "thirty pieces of silver." Second, *nowhere* in the entire book of Jeremiah does the phrase "thirty pieces of silver" appear; instead, there does appear in Jeremiah 38:10 a statement about "thirty men": "Then the king commanded Ebedmelech the Ethiopian, saying, Take from hence thirty men with thee, and take up Jeremiah the prophet out of the dungeon, before he die." One has to stretch his imagination to the limits to see any connection between the events recorded by Zechariah and the payment of thirty pieces of silver to Judas as a payment for his betrayal of Jesus.

The only similarity in Jeremiah relates to the type of money, specifically in *silver* as opposed to *gold*. Here, one possible explanation for the number thirty is a conflation with the number *thirty* in Exodus 21:32: "If the ox shall push a manservant or a maidservant; he shall give unto their master thirty shekels of silver, and the ox shall be stoned." In this verse, an owner pays "thirty shekels of silver" in compensation to a slaveholder if his ox gores a slave.

This text speculates that the number thirty was a deliberate decision of Matthew. The name Judas is a Greek transliteration of the Hebrew name Judah. Judah was the fourth son of Jacob and arranged to deliver his younger brother Joseph into the hands of foreigners by selling him into slavery for twenty pieces of silver (Ex 37:27). Consequently, "the first Judah/Judas betrayed the designated leader of the nation of Israel by handing him over to foreigners and received money for his actions, just like the disciple Judas." In addition, "the name corresponds to the political entity of Judea that rejected Jesus and turned him over to the Romans" (Greenberg 2007). But why then did the author of Matthew incorporate the number thirty into his narrative? It is speculated that the numerical value of the Hebrew name Judah/Judas is thirty [(Y = 10) + (H = 5) + (W = 6) + (D = 4) + (H = 5)], and this number corresponds to the thirty pieces of silver recorded in Matthew.

Matthew 27:9 falsely declares that the events associated with Jesus's betrayal by Judas fulfilled that which was spoken by the prophet Jeremiah. It must be recognized that the passages in Jeremiah 18 and 32 are *not* Messianic, prophetic, or reflect typology. Instead, they are historical events recorded in the Hebrew Bible. Therefore, Matthew's inferences that Jeremiah's words are prophetic are fallacious and utterly wrong. In no way does the Gospel of Matthew demonstrate how the Judas episode served as a continuation and a fulfillment of the Old Testament (Hebrew Bible).

Below, an examination of table 52 illustrates how Matthew erroneously combined two portions from the writings of Jeremiah and one from Zechariah. Stringing together three verses from scripture out of their original context does not prove fulfillment of a prophecy; rather, it demonstrates a theological agenda to attest to and provide evidence that Jesus is the Messiah.

TABLE 52. A Comparison of Matthew 27, Jeremiah 18, Jeremiah 32, and Zechariah 11

MATTHEW 27	JEREMIAH 18	JEREMIAH 32	ZECHARIAH 11	EVALUATION
27:9 *Then was fulfilled that which was spoken by Jeremy the prophet, saying, And they* took the thirty pieces of silver, the price of him that was valued, whom they of the children of Israel did value;	18:1 *The word which came to Jeremiah from the LORD, saying,*	32:6 *And Jeremiah said,* The word of the LORD came unto me, saying,	11:13 And the LORD said unto *me,* Cast it unto the potter: a goodly price that *I* was prised at of them. *And I took* the thirty pieces of silver, and cast them to the potter in the house of the LORD.	1. The common theme was *the name of Jeremiah speaking in the name of the LORD as His prophet.* 2. Matthew transformed the *"I"* in Zechariah into *"they,"* referring to the chief priests and elders who took the pieces of silver.
27:3 Then Judas, which had betrayed him, when he saw that he was condemned, repented himself, and brought again the *thirty pieces of silver* to the chief priests and elders,		32:9 And I bought the field of Hanameel my uncle's son, that was in Anathoth, and weighed him the money, *even seventeen shekels of silver.*	11:12 And I said unto them, If ye think good, give me my price; and if not, forbear. So they weighed for my price *thirty pieces of silver.*	1. The similar thread was the mentioning of *silver.* 2. The common thread in Zechariah was the *thirty pieces of silver.*
27:3 Then Judas, which had betrayed him, when he saw that he was condemned, repented himself, and brought again the thirty pieces of silver *to the chief priests and elders,*	18:2 Arise, and *go down to the potter's house,* and there I will cause thee to hear my words.	32:7 Behold, Hanameel the son of Shallum thine uncle *shall come unto thee, saying,* Buy thee my field that is in Anathoth: for the right of redemption is thine to buy it.		*The shared motif was that the purchaser would go to a place or person* to deliver a sum of silver.

27:3 Then Judas, which had betrayed him, when he saw that he was condemned, *repented himself,* and brought again the thirty pieces of silver to the chief priests and elders,		32:7 Behold, Hanameel the son of Shallum thine uncle shall come unto thee, saying, Buy thee my field that is in Anathoth: *for the right of redemption* is thine to buy it.		The common issue was the idea of *repentance and redemption.*
27:4 Saying, I have sinned in that I have betrayed the innocent blood. And they said, What is that to us? see thou to that.				
27:5 *And he cast down the pieces of silver in the temple,* and departed, and went and hanged himself.		32:9 And I bought the field of Hanameel my uncle's son, that was in Anathoth, and weighed him the money, *even seventeen shekels of silver.*		The common topic was the pieces of *silver.*

27:5 *And he cast down the pieces of silver in the temple,* and departed, and went and hanged himself.	18:3 *Then I went down to the potter's house,* and, behold, he wrought a work on the wheels.	32:8 So Hanameel mine uncle's son came to me in the court of the prison according to the word of the LORD, and said unto me, Buy my field, I pray thee, that is in Anathoth, which is in the country of Benjamin: for the right of inheritance is thine, and the redemption is thine; buy it for thyself. Then I knew that this was the word of the LORD. 32:14 Thus saith the LORD of hosts, the God of Israel; Take these evidences, this evidence of the purchase, both which is sealed, and this evidence which is open; *and put them in an earthen vessel,* that they may continue many days.		The shared theme was *placing the silver in a specific place* (although misconstrued by the author of Matthew).
27:6 And the chief priests took the silver pieces, and said, It is not lawful for to put them *into the treasury,* because it is the price of blood.	18:4 And the vessel that he made of clay was marred in the hand of the potter: so he made it again another vessel, as seemed good to the potter to make it.	32:14 Thus saith the LORD of hosts, the God of Israel; Take these evidences, this evidence of the purchase, both which is sealed, and this evidence which is open; *and put them in an earthen vessel,* that they		Again, the common theme was *placing the silver in a specific place* (although misconstrued by the author of Matthew).

27:7 And they took counsel, and *bought with them the potter's field*, to bury strangers in.		32:14 Thus saith the LORD of hosts, the God of Israel; Take these evidences, this evidence of the *purchase*, both which is sealed, and this evidence which is open; *and put them in an earthen vessel*, that they may continue many days.		The mutual subject was *purchasing*. The mistaken motif was where the silver was placed.
27:8 Wherefore that field was called, The field of blood, unto this day.				
27:9 *Then was fulfilled that which was spoken by Jeremy the prophet,* saying, And they took the thirty pieces of silver, the price of him that was valued, whom they of the children of Israel did value;	18:5 *Then the word of the LORD came to me, saying,* 18:6 O house of Israel, cannot I do with you as this potter? *saith the LORD.* Behold, as the clay is in the potter's hand, so are ye in mine hand, O house of Israel.	32:14 *Thus saith the LORD of hosts, the God of Israel;* Take these evidences, this evidence of the purchase, both which is sealed, and this evidence which is open; and put them in an earthen vessel, that they may continue many days.		The common theme was *the name of Jeremiah speaking in the name of the LORD as His prophet.*

| 27:10 And gave them for *the potter's field*, as the Lord appointed me. | 18:6 O house of Israel, cannot I do with you as this potter? saith the LORD. Behold, as the clay is *in the potter's hand*, so are ye in mine hand, O house of Israel. | 32:14 Thus saith the LORD of hosts, the God of Israel; Take these evidences, this evidence of the purchase, both which is sealed, and this evidence which is open; *and put them in an earthen vessel*, that they may continue many days. | 11:13 And the LORD said unto *me*, Cast it unto the potter: a goodly price that *I* was prised at of them. And *I* took the thirty pieces of silver, *and cast them to the potter in the house of the LORD.* | 1. The mutual topic was the related but misconstrued words: *potter's field, potter's hand, and earthen vessels (i.e., pots).* |
| | | | | 2. Matthew transformed the "*I*" or "*me*" in the first part of the verse in Zechariah into an implied "*they*," referring to the chief priests and elders who gave the silver to purchase the field. |

Scroggie (1948, 267-70) identifies 129 references from the Hebrew Bible employed by Matthew, of which fifty-three are citations and seventy-six are allusions. The paralleled texts of Jeremiah 18, Jeremiah 32, and Zechariah 11 employed in Matthew 27 are readily evident. The reason Matthew states that the verse from Zechariah, which is misidentified as from Jeremiah, should be obvious. This citation in Matthew reflects the theological agenda of its author. This agenda is to illustrate how Jesus experienced what was in fact a fulfillment of the prophecies recorded in the Hebrew Bible. This agenda is exemplified multiple times. [NB: Christian apologists will argue these events are an example of biblical typology (or typological symbolism/foreshadowing; see Osborne 2006, 328-29). This is a Christian form of biblical interpretation that proceeds on the assumption that God placed anticipations of Jesus in the laws, events, and people of the Old Testament.]

TABLE 53. Matthew's Explicit Fulfillment: Quotations or Citations from Scripture

VERSE	FULFILLMENT CLAUSE	CITATION, QUOTATION OR REFERENCE IN MATTHEW	CLAIM	REBUTTAL
Mt 1:22-23	Now all this was done, that it might be fulfilled which was spoken of the Lord by the prophet, saying,	Behold, a virgin shall be with child, and shall bring forth a son, and they shall call his name Emmanuel, which being interpreted is, God with us.	Jesus being born of a virgin was a fulfillment of Isaiah 7:14.	This prophecy does not refer to a virgin *but to a young woman*, living at the time of the prophecy. Furthermore Gundry (1975, 195) points out "Isa 7:14 was not interpreted Messianically in Judaism."
Mt 1:22-23	Now all this was done, that it might be fulfilled which was spoken of the Lord by the prophet, saying,	Behold, a virgin shall be with child, and shall bring forth a son, and they shall call his name Emmanuel, which, being interpreted, is God with us.	Jesus being called Emmanuel was a fulfillment of Isaiah 7:14.	In his lifetime, Jesus was *never* called Emmanuel or Immanuel. The prophecy in Isaiah 7:14 was that a specific child would be given the name Immanuel, *not that he would be one who was described or represented "God is with us."*

Mt 2:5-6	And they said unto him, In Bethlehem of Judaea: for thus it is written by the prophet,	And thou Bethlehem, in the land of Juda, art not the least among the princes of Juda: for out of thee shall come a Governor, that shall rule my people Israel.	Jesus being born in Bethlehem was a fulfillment of Micah 5:2: "But thou, Bethlehem Ephratah, though thou be little among the thousands of Judah, yet out of thee shall he come forth unto me that is to be ruler in Israel; whose goings forth have been from of old, from everlasting."	1. Mark is silent about Jesus's birth place. In contrast, John 7:42 related that some people believed that the Messiah would come from Bethlehem, yet he *never took advantage of the opportunity to demonstrate that Micah's prophecy was fulfilled by claiming that Jesus was actually born there.* 2. Why then did *John fail to challenge the assertion that Jesus was really of Galilean origin* (Jn 1:46, 7:41)? 3. Many people were born in Bethlehem.
Mt 2:5-6	And they said unto him, In Bethlehem of Judaea: for thus it is written by the prophet,	And thou Bethlehem, in the land of Juda, art not the least among the princes of Juda: for out of thee shall come a Governor, that shall rule my people Israel.	Jesus being called King of the Jews was a fulfillment of Micah 5:2: "But thou, Bethlehem Ephratah, though thou be little among the thousands of Judah, yet out of thee shall he come forth unto me that is to be ruler in Israel; whose goings forth have been from of old, from everlasting."	1. Jesus *never* was a ruler of Israel. 2. The Jewish people *rejected* Jesus. 3. The title "King of the Jews" that was ordered by Pilate to be placed *on the cross was an act of ridicule and sarcasm.* 4. Contextually, this leader is to *be a military leader* as discussed in Micah 5:6 and *he would defeat the Assyrians, which, Jesus never did.*

Mt 2:15	And was there until the death of Herod: that it might be fulfilled which was spoken of the Lord by the prophet, saying,	Out of Egypt have I called my son.	Jesus's preservation in Egypt was a sign of divine sonship" and a fulfillment of Hosea 11:1: "When Israel was a child, then I loved him, and called my son out of Egypt."	1. In the following verse, Hosea 11:2 describes Israel worshipping idols. *When did Jesus worship idols?* Hosea 11:3 *depicts Israel as a rebellious son; this view is in direct contradiction to Christian tradition.* 2. The phrase "Out of Egypt have I called my son" is addressed to Joseph (cf. 2:19, 21) whereas in Hosea 11:1, God referred to the Jewish people (and in Exodus 4:10 God spoke to Moses).
Mt 2:17-18	Then was fulfilled that which was spoken by Jeremy the prophet, saying,	In Rama was there a voice heard, lamentation, and weeping, and great mourning, Rachel weeping for her children, and would not be comforted, because they are not.	Matthew quoted Jeremiah 31:15: "Thus saith the LORD; A voice was heard in Ramah, lamentation, and bitter weeping; Rahel weeping for her children refused to be comforted for her children, because they were not." He claimed that it was a prophecy related to King Herod's slaughter of the children in and around Bethlehem after the birth of Jesus.	1. Jeremiah 31:15 refers to the Babylonian captivity. This is understood by reading Jeremiah 31:16 and 17. Consequently, it has nothing to do with Herod's massacre. 2. Jeremiah 31:16 *omits any mention of children being killed.* On the contrary, it states: "Thus saith the LORD; Refrain thy voice from weeping, and thine eyes from tears: for thy work shall be rewarded, saith the LORD; *and they shall come again from the land of the enemy.*" 3. Matthew 2:16 states that Herod ordered that all of the children under two years old to be slaughtered in Bethlehem which was part of Judah and consequently, Rachel was weeping over their death (v. 18). However, as members of Judah's tribe they were Leah's children, not Rachel's. Therefore, *Leah should be weeping for the children, not Rachel.*
Mt 2:23	And he came and dwelt in a city called Nazareth: that it might be fulfilled which was spoken by the prophets,	He shall be called a Nazarene.	Matthew claimed that this prophecy was fulfilled when Jesus dwelt in Nazareth.	1. *No such prophecy exists in the Hebrew Bible.* 2. *Nowhere in the Hebrew Bible does it state the Messiah will take the Nazarite vow.* 3. *The spellings of the words* Nazarite, נזיר (*nazir*) and Nazarene נצרי (*notsri*) are *not the same in Hebrew.*

Mt 4:13-14	That it might be fulfilled which was spoken by Esaias the prophet, saying,	And leaving Nazareth, he came and dwelt in Capernaum, which is upon the sea coast, in the borders of Zabulon and Nephthalim:	1. Jesus dwelt in Capernaum, which is adjacent the sea coast, in the borders of Zabulon and Nephthalim was a fulfillment of Isaiah 9:1-2.	1. *Jesus leaving Nazareth and traveling to Capernaum proves nothing.* Thousands of people transverse that route.
			2. The verses read: "Nevertheless the dimness shall not be such as was in her vexation, when at the first he lightly afflicted the land of Zebulun and the land of Naphtali, and afterward did more grievously afflict her by the way of the sea, beyond Jordan, in Galilee of the nations.	2. *The prophet Isaiah is describing historical events.* The king of Assyria had at first attacked only the lands of Zebulun and Nephthalim, and therefore, it is described as being a relatively light affliction. Afterward, the affliction became more severe when another king of Assyria, Sennacherib, marched against Judea and captured all its strongholds so that he came to attack Jerusalem as seen in 2 Kings 19. There in verse 35, it relates that an angel of the LORD destroyed 185,000 of Sennacherib's men.
			3. The people that walked in darkness have seen a great light: they that dwell in the land of the shadow of death, upon them hath the light shined."	3. Thus, the statement "The people that walked in darkness have seen a great light; they that hath dwelt in the shadow of death upon them the light hath shown" *refers to the light of deliverance caused by the severe blow to Sennacherib's army.* It has nothing whatsoever to do with the alleged light brought by Jesus to the people living in his time. 4. *The word "light" used in the context of Isaiah meant a physical deliverance*, not an enlightenment.

Mt 8:17	That it might be fulfilled which was spoken by Esaias the prophet, saying,	Himself took our infirmities, and bare our sicknesses.	Matthew claimed that when Jesus healed Peter's mother and many others he fulfilled Isaiah 53:4: "Surely he hath borne our griefs, and carried our sorrows: yet we did esteem him stricken, smitten of God, and afflicted."	1. Healings and miracles do not prove anything. Deuteronomy 13:1-10 [AV] expressly *warns*: "If there arise among you a prophet, or a dreamer of dreams, *and giveth thee a sign or a wonder, And the sign or the wonder come to pass, whereof he spake unto thee, saying, Let us go after other gods, which thou hast not known, and let us serve them; Thou shalt not hearken unto the words of that prophet, or that dreamer of dreams: for the* LORD *your God proveth you, to know whether ye love the* LORD *your God with all your heart and with all your soul.* 2. *Healings are common in many cultures.*
Mt 11:10	For this is he of whom it is written,	Mal 3:1 For this is he of whom it is written, Behold, I send my messenger, which shall prepare thy way before thee.	Matthew claimed that Jesus was a fulfillment of Malachi 3:1 "Behold, I will send my messenger, and he shall prepare the way before me: and the LORD, whom ye seek, shall suddenly come to his temple, even the messenger of the covenant, whom ye delight in:	In Matthew, *the personal pronoun "me" has been changed to "thee" thus distorting the prophecy and giving the false impression that God was speaking to Jesus about a messenger.* 1. In Matthew, *the personal pronoun "me" has been changed to "thee" thus distorting the prophecy and giving the false impression that God was speaking to Jesus about a messenger.* 2. Malachi 3:1 states that the prophet Elijah must return prior to the coming of the Messiah and the ushering in of the Messianic Era. Therefore, Matthew claims that John the Baptist is the reincarnated prophet Elijah sent to prepare the way for Jesus. This claim is also restated in Mark 9:13. However, in the Fourth Gospel, John the Baptist was literally asked if he was Elijah. In John 1:21 his reply was stated unequivocally: "And he answered, No."

			behold, he shall come, saith the LORD of hosts."	In the source, "me" is obviously referring to God. In reality, the AV of Malachi reads: "Behold, I will send my messenger, and he shall prepare the way before *me*: and the LORD, whom ye seek, shall suddenly come to his temple, even the messenger of the covenant, whom ye delight in: behold, he shall come, saith the LORD of hosts."
Mt 12:17-18	That it might be fulfilled which was spoken by Esaias the prophet, saying,	Behold my servant, whom I have chosen; my beloved, in whom my soul is well pleased: I will put my spirit upon him, and he shall show judgment to the Gentiles.	The servant was supposed to be Jesus with God's spirit based on Isa 42:1-4 (LXX).	1. *The pronoun "him" of Isaiah 40:1 is God's servant Israel (see 41:8-10; 43:1, 10, 21; 44:1).* It should be noted that God has already put His spirit upon "him" so that Israel would be a light to the nations (42:6). 2. For those who insist that the servant in Isa 42:1 is Jesus, Isaiah 42:19 *provides a further description, which is not flattering*: "Who is blind, but my servant? or deaf, as my messenger that I sent? who is blind as he that is perfect, and blind as the LORD's servant?" *Do Christians believe that these words also apply to Jesus?*

Mt 12:17-21	That it might be fulfilled which was spoken by Esaias the prophet, saying,	Behold my servant, whom I have chosen; my beloved, in whom my soul is well pleased: I will put my spirit upon him, and he shall show judgment to the Gentiles. He shall not strive, nor cry; neither shall any man hear his voice in the streets. A bruised reed shall he not break, and smoking flax shall he not quench, till he send forth judgment unto victory. And in his name shall the Gentiles trust.	Jesus's behavior fulfilled the divine intention that was written in Isaiah 42:1-4 (LXX).	*Contrary to Isaiah 42:2*: "His voice not being heard in the open street," *Jesus spoke to multitudes and to great crowds which followed him* (e.g., Mt 4:24; 13:2; Lk 4:14-15).
Mt 12:40	For as Jonah was three days and three nights in the whale's belly, so shall the Son of Man be three days and three nights in the heart of the earth.	For as Jonah was three days and three nights in the whale's belly, so shall the Son of Man be three days and three nights in the heart of the earth.	Matthew reported that like Jonah, Jesus would be buried three days and three night and then return was a fulfillment of Jonah 1:17 "Now the LORD had prepared a great fish to swallow up Jonah. And Jonah was in the belly of the fish three days and three nights."	1. Jesus did not duplicate Jonah's feat: Jonah went inside a great fish's belly *alive*, stayed *alive* in the fish's belly for three days and three nights, and was spit out *alive* from inside the fish's belly. In contrast, Jesus went into the tomb *dead, stayed dead for one day and two nights*, and came out alive. 2. Jesus was not in the tomb for 72 hours whereas Jonah was actually inside the fish's belly for 72 hours

Mt 13:14-15	And in them is fulfilled the prophecy of Esaias, which saith	By hearing ye shall hear, and shall not understand; and seeing ye shall see, and shall not perceive: For this people's heart is waxed gross, and their ears are dull of hearing, and their eyes they have closed; lest at any time they should see with their eyes and hear with their ears, and should understand with their heart, and should be converted, and I should heal them.	Matthew claimed that Jesus taught in parables because of the hardened nature of the Jewish people's hearts as prophesied in Isaiah 6:9-10: "And he said, Go, and tell this people, Hear ye indeed, but understand not; and see ye indeed, but perceive not. Make the heart of this people fat, and make their ears heavy, and shut their eyes; lest they see with their eyes, and hear with their ears, and understand with their heart, and convert, and be healed."	This prophecy can be dated by the fact that it was *a message Isaiah brought to his own generation*. Verse 8 says: *Here I am; send me.* Gundry (1975, 197) pointed out that "the fulfillment-citation in verses 14, 15 is obviously an editorial expansion of the allusive quotation in verse 13 and parallels."
Mt 13:34-35	That it might be fulfilled which was spoken by the prophet, saying	I will open my mouth in parables; I will utter things which have been kept secret from the foundation of the world.	Jesus spoke many parables to the people was a fulfillment of Psalm 78:2: "I will open my mouth in a parable: I will utter dark sayings of old."	1. There is *nothing in this psalm that is prophetic*. 2. Nothing in the psalm can refer to Jesus's parables because *none of his parables mentioned the Law*. Whereas the aim of this psalm was to bring the knowledge of the Law to each generation. This becomes obvious when the Psalm is read in its entirety.

Mt 15:7-9	Ye hypocrites, well did Esaias prophesy of you, saying,	This people draweth nigh unto me with their mouth, and honoureth me with their lips; but their heart is far from me. But in vain they do worship me, teaching for doctrines the commandments of men.	These verses fulfilled Isaiah 29:13: "Wherefore the Lord said, Forasmuch as this people draw near me with their mouth, and with their lips do honour me, but have removed their heart far from me, and their fear toward me is taught by the precept of men."	*Isaiah was not prophesying about the people of Jesus's time* as the New Testament writer suggests. When the words of the prophet are examined it can be clearly seen *that they were intended for his generation.* The use of the phrase "this people" meant the people of Isaiah's time, *not* those of the time of Jesus some seven hundred years later.
Mt 21:4-7	All this was done, that it might be fulfilled which was spoken by the prophet, saying,	Tell ye the daughter of Sion, Behold, thy King cometh unto thee, meek, and sitting upon an ass, and a colt the foal of an ass. And the disciples went, and did as Jesus commanded them, And brought the ass, and the colt, and put on them their clothes, and they set him thereon.	Jesus's preparation and entering Jerusalem were fulfilled in Isaiah 62:11 and Zechariah 9:9: "Behold, thy King comes victorious and humble for he is riding upon an ass, and upon a colt the fole of an ass."	1. Matthew's text read *literally had Jesus riding simultaneously two animals "rodeo" style.* 2. *Traveling on an ass was the common mode of travel* in first-century Roman-occupied Jerusalem. 3. Jesus was *never anointed as king of Israel.* 4. Given that Jesus or the writer of Matthew knew Zechariah 9:9, the command to the disciples made the "prophecy" self-fulfilling.

Mt 21:12-13	And said unto them, It is written,	And Jesus went into the temple of God, and cast out all them that sold and bought in the temple, and overthrew the tables of the moneychangers, and the seats of them that sold doves, And said unto them, It is written, my house shall be called a house of prayer. But ye have made of it a den of thieves.	Matthews cited Jesus's claim that the moneychangers in the Temple fulfilled Isaiah 56:7: "Even them will I bring to my holy mountain, and make them joyful in my house of prayer: their burnt offerings and their sacrifices shall be accepted upon mine altar; for mine house shall be called an house of prayer" and Jeremiah 7:11: "Is this house, which is called by my name, become a den of robbers in your eyes? Behold, even I have seen it, saith the LORD."	1. Matthew had *Jesus culling two completely separate and unrelated half verses from the Hebrew Bible* to fulfill his theological agenda. 2. The moneychangers provided a necessary and ordained function for pilgrims (Deut 14:22-26).
Mt 26:54	But how then shall the scriptures be fulfilled, that thus it must be?	"He was oppressed, and he was afflicted, yet he opened not his mouth: he is brought as a lamb to the slaughter, and as a sheep before her shearers is dumb, so he openeth not his mouth.	Jesus's arrest and eventual execution on the cross were fulfilled in Isaiah 53:7.	Jesus opened his mouth before Pilate (Mt 27:10; Lk 23:3; Jn 18:34, 36-37).

		He was taken from prison and from judgment: and who shall declare his generation? for he was cut off out of the land of the living: for the transgression of my people was he stricken. And he made his grave with the wicked, and with the rich in his death; because he had done no violence, neither was any deceit in his mouth."	Christians claim that Jesus made his grave with the wicked and that his death was with the rich. And he made his grave with the wicked, and with the rich in his death.	Here, there can only be *speculation since Matthew does not cite the scriptures or the prophets.* However, it is falsely claimed that Jesus fulfilled the statement that he "made his grave with the wicked and that his death with the rich: 1) Jesus was not buried with anyone who was wicked (e.g., the two thieves); rather the Gospels state that he was presumably buried in the tomb of a righteous man who was one of his disciples, 2) detractors reject the belief that Jesus was buried in a grave, 3) the Gospels report that Jesus died between two thieves and therefore his death was not with the rich, 4) Christian translators change the plural word "deaths" (in Hebrew) into a singular "death" thereby concealing the identity of the Suffering Servant – the people of Israel, and 5) the reference to "they" refers to Gentiles who robbed rich Jews by falsely accusing them of wrongdoings. Later, the Gentiles killed these affluent Jews and buried them with common criminals.

Mt 26:56	But all this was done, that the scriptures of the prophets might be fulfilled.	Then all the disciples forsook him, and fled.	The disciples forsook and fled from Jesus. Consequently, the disciples' rejection guaranteed Jesus's death in fulfillment perhaps in Zechariah 13:7: "Awake, O sword, against my shepherd, and against the man that is my fellow, saith the LORD of hosts: smite the shepherd, and the sheep shall be scattered: and I will turn mine hand upon the little ones."	Here, too, there can only be *speculation since Matthew does not cite the scriptures or the prophets.* Jewish detractors reject the idea that this verse has any relationship to Jesus. Instead, God promises to inspect the "shepherds" and bring them close to Him. Then God will punish them for oppressing His flock, the people of Israel.
Mt 27:9	Then was fulfilled that which was spoken by Jeremy the prophet, saying, And they took the thirty pieces of silver, the price of him that was valued, whom they of the children of Israel did value;	I told them, "If you think it best, give me my pay; but if not, keep it." So they paid me thirty pieces of silver. And the LORD said to me, "Throw it to the potter"—the handsome price at which they priced me! So I took the thirty pieces of silver and threw them into the house of the LORD to the potter.	Matthew claimed that Judas received thirty pieces of silver fulfilled the words spoken by the prophet Jeremiah.	There is *no such prophecy in the book of Jeremiah.*

Mt 27:35	And they crucified him, and parted his garments, casting lots: that it might be fulfilled which was spoken by the prophet,	They parted my garments among them, and upon my vesture did they cast lots.	The soldiers casted lots and divided Jesus's garments fulfilled (typology) Psalm 22:18: "They part my garments among them, and cast lots upon my vesture."	This statement is *not* a prophecy.

What then can explain Matthew's phrasing in 27:9b-10? Lachs (1987, 243) offers an intriguing explanation that Matthew's phrasing was based on an extant text cited in Saint Jerome's (ca. 320-420) commentary. Jerome on Matthew 27:9, citing the *Gospel According to the Hebrews*, comments: "I read not long ago in a certain Hebrew book, which a Jew of the Nazarene sect gave me, an apocryphal book on Jeremiah in which I found this [i.e., Matt. 27.9b-10] written word for word."

It is argued that some of the verses in Matthew could have been based on an erroneous text not attested to and thus their inclusion is flawed, invalid, and unfounded incorporation into his text. However, most of the fulfillment quotations found in Matthew are incorporated to fulfill his theological agenda—that Jesus was the Messiah.

CONTRADICTION #83 The Words of Jeremiah Were Not Prophetic

Matthew 27:9 falsely declares that the events associated with Jesus's betrayal by Judas fulfilled that which was spoken by the prophet Jeremiah. It must be recognized that the events in Jeremiah 18 and 32 were *not* Messianic or prophetic. [Note: Christian apologists claim that this event is an example of "typology"—the interpretation of some characters and stories in the Hebrew Bible as allegories foreshadowing the New Testament.] Instead, they were historical events recorded in the Hebrew Bible. Therefore, Matthew's inferences that Jeremiah's words were prophetic are fallacious and utterly wrong.

In addition, Matthew is still in error, even if he meant to reference Zechariah, because his statement was an incorrect application of the passage. Keim (1883, 6:190-91n3), a liberal German theologian, writes: "in Zechariah

God disdainfully returns the wretched wage of the pastoral office exercised in Ephraim by the prophets, whilst here it is the *betrayer* of the sent of God that does this." Here, there is no prophecy related to Jesus.

CONTRADICTION #84 The Prophecy Attributed to Jeremiah Could Not Really Be Zechariah 11:10-13

One Christian apologetic for Matthew 27:9 is that the prophecy was mistakenly attributed to Jeremiah but was really written in Zechariah 11:10-13. However, this apologetic cannot be the solution for multiple reasons. A detailed explanation can be found in Bullinger's *The Companion Bible*. The purchase of "the potter's field" (1914: appendix 161, 185):

1. Zechariah 11:10-13 contains no reference either to a "field" or to its *purchase*. Indeed, the word "field" (*shadāh*) does not occur in the whole of Zechariah except in 10:1, which has nothing to do with the subject at all.

2. As to the "thirty pieces of silver," Zechariah speaks of them with approval, while in Matthew they are not so spoken of. "A goodly price" (*'eder hay^kar*) denotes *amplitude, sufficiency*, while the Verb *yakār* means *to be priced, prized, precious;* and there is not the slightest evidence that Zechariah spoke of the amount as being paltry, or that the offer of it was in any sense an insult. But this latter is the sense in Matthew 27:9, 10.

3. The *givers* were "the poor of the flock." This enhanced the value. "The worth of the price" was accepted as "goodly" on that account, as in Mark 12:43, 44 and 2 Corinthians 8:12.

4. The *waiting* of "the poor of the flock" was not hostile but friendly, as in Proverbs 27:18. Out of above 450 occurrences of the Heb. *shāmar*, less than fourteen are in a hostile sense.

5. In the disposal of the silver, the sense of the Verb "cast" is to be determined by the context (not by the Verb itself). In Zechariah 11, the context shows it to be in a good sense, as in Exodus 15:25; 1 Kings 19:19; 2 Kings 2:21, 4:41, 6:6; and 2 Chronicles 24:10, 11.

6. The "potter" is the fashioner and his work was not necessarily confined to fashioning "clay," but it extended to *metals*. Cp. Genesis 2:7, 8; Ps 33:15; 94:9; Isaiah 43:1, 6, 10, 21; 44:2, 9-12, 21, 24; 45:6, 7; 54:16, 17. Out of the sixty-two occurrences of the Verb (*yāzar*), more than three-fourths have nothing whatever to do with the work of a "potter."

7. A "potter" in connection with the Temple, or its service, is unknown to fact or to Scripture.

8. The *material* "silver" would be useless to a "potter" but necessary to a fashioner of metallic vessels, or for the payment of artizans who wrought them (2 Kings 12:11-16; 22:4-7; 2 Chronicles 24:11-13). One might as well cast *clay* to a silversmith as *silver* to a potter.

9. The prophecy of Zechariah is rich in reference to metals; and only the books of Numbers (31:22) and Ezekiel name as many. In Zechariah we find Gold, six times (4:2, 12; 6:11; 13:9; 14:14); Fine gold, once (9:3); Silver, six times, (6:11; 9:3; 11:12, 13; 13:9; 14:14); Brass, once (6:1, margin); Lead, twice (5:7, 8); Tin, once (4:10, margin). Seventeen references in all.

10. Zechariah is full of refs to what the prophet *saw* and *said*, but there are only *two* refs to what he *did*; and both of these have references to "silver" (6:11; 11:13).

11. The Septuagint, and its revision by Symmachus, read "cast them (i.e., the thirty pieces of silver) *into the furnace*" (Greek *eis* to *chŏneutērion*), showing that, before Matthew was written, *yōtzēr* was interpreted as referring not to a "potter" but to a fashioner of metals.

12. The *persons* are also different. In Matthew we have "they took," "they gave," "the price of him"; in Zechariah we read "I took," "I cast," "I was valued."

13. In Matthew the money was given "for the field," and in Zechariah it was cast "unto the fashioner."

14. Matthew names *three* parties as being concerned in the transaction; Zechariah names only *one*.

15. Matthew not only quotes Jeremiah's *spoken* words but names him as the speaker. This is in keeping with Matthew 2:17, 18. Jeremiah is likewise named in Matthew 16:14 but nowhere else in all the New Testament.

The conclusion: From all this we gather that the passage in Matthew (27:9, 10) cannot have any reference to Zechariah 11:10-13.

ISSUE 77: Judas's Repentance

Mk	Mt	Lk	Acts	Jn
	Mt 27:3 Then Judas, which had betrayed him, when he saw that he was condemned, repented himself, and brought again the thirty pieces of silver to the chief priests and elders, 4 Saying, I have sinned in that I have betrayed the innocent blood. And they said, What is that to us? see thou to that. 5 And he cast down the pieces of silver in the temple, and departed, and *went and hanged himself.*		Acts 1:16 Men and brethren, this scripture must needs have been fulfilled, which the Holy Ghost by the mouth of David spake before concerning Judas, which was guide to them that took Jesus. 17 For he was numbered with us, and had obtained part of this ministry. 18 Now this man purchased a field with the rewards of iniquity; *and falling headlong, he burst asunder in the midst, and all his bowels gushed out.* 19 And it was known unto all the dwellers at Jerusalem; insomuch as that field is called in their proper tongue, Aceldama, that is to say, The field of blood. 20 For it is written in the book of Psalms, Let his habitation be desolate, and let no man dwell therein: and his bishoprick let another take.	

Mark, Luke, and John omit any discussion about Judas's repentance. Matthew alone reports that Judas repented his betrayal of Jesus but only after he saw that he was condemned. Consequently, Judas brought to the chief priests and elders the thirty pieces of silver that he had received for his task. Then Judas confessed, saying that he had sinned in betraying innocent blood. The chief priests and elders responded that this was no concern of theirs and that instead "that's your responsibility." (NIV) Afterward, Judas threw down the pieces of silver in the Temple; he departed and finally hanged himself. In Acts there was no mention of repentance. Instead, Judas purchased a field with the silver he had received from the chief priests and later died with his bowels bursting.

CONTRADICTION #85 Acts Contradicts Matthew—Judas's Repentance

The account of Judas's nonrepentance reported in Acts directly contradicts Matthew. This narration is perhaps one of the simplest and yet strongest arguments supporting the thesis that their respective authors wrote completely different stories. Unequivocally, these two stories demonstrate *no* resemblance to each other. In addition, they neither compliment nor supplement each other. To the contrary, the author of Acts refutes Matthew's narrative that

Judas remorsefully committed suicide by hanging. To support this thesis, it is necessary to carefully examine the supporting details in each narrative.

Matthew 27:3-5 reports that after Jesus was arrested: "Then Judas, which had betrayed him, when he saw that he was condemned, repented himself, and brought again the thirty pieces of silver to the chief priests and elders, Saying, I have sinned in that I have betrayed the innocent blood. And they said, What is that to us? see thou to that. And he cast down the pieces of silver in the temple, and departed, and went and hanged himself." In other words, *Judas acted out his own free will and committed suicide*. Nowhere in Matthew is there the slightest hint or suggestion that Judas was coerced or forced by any person, angel, demon, or the devil himself to commit suicide.

Matthew's storyline spanning 27:3-10 is very simple and can be broken down into eight distinct details. These facts include

1. Judas recognized that he was condemned,
2. Judas repented (i.e., felt remorseful),
3. Judas returned to the chief priests,
4. Judas openly declared that he had sinned,
5. Judas received a reply from the chief priests and elders stating that this issue was not a matter of their concern,
6. Judas threw down in the Temple the thirty pieces of silver that he previously received from the chief priests,
7. Judas left the Temple, and
8. Judas hanged himself.

A careful analysis of Matthew's Judas reveals a repentant and remorseful Judas. Allison (2001, 883) elaborates on this point: "This, and the depiction of Judas throughout much of church history as infamy embodied, have led most to see in Matthew's Judas an everlasting failure, doomed for destruction. This accords with 26:24. On the other hand, the verb translated here by 'he repented' is used in Mt 22:29 and 32 of authentic repentance."

Thus, Judas was so remorseful that he wanted nothing to do with the money that he had received for betraying Jesus. Instead, he returned to his co-conspirators and attempted to return the payment for the "innocent blood" that he had helped to shed. Here, Judas received no contentment, happiness, or gain for the thirty pieces of silver. To the contrary, Matthew described an anguished, guilt-ridden, and depressed person who hanged himself in an unidentified location. This Judas is portrayed as a pathetic and pitiful person, not to be despised but pitied. Unable to deal with reality, in the only way he knew how to cope, he tried to make amends for what he has done: He committed suicide.

Acts 1:16-20 reports:

> Men and brethren, this scripture must needs have been fulfilled,
> which the Holy Ghost by the mouth of David spake before
> concerning Judas, which was guide to them that took Jesus. For
> he was numbered with us, and had obtained part of this ministry.
> Now this man purchased a field with the rewards of iniquity; and
> falling headlong, he burst asunder in the midst, and all his bowels
> gushed out. And it was known unto all the dwellers at Jerusalem;
> insomuch as that field is called in their proper tongue, Aceldama,
> that is to say, The field of blood. For it is written in the book
> of Psalms, Let his habitation be desolate, and let no man dwell
> therein: and his bishoprick let another take.

Thus, Acts omits any explicit details how Judas specifically died. Not
only does the author of Acts omit discussion of a suicide but he also failed
to hint, imply, or even insinuate anything about a means of death. In direct
contradiction to Matthew, Acts 1:18 implies that Judas *died by an act of God.*
That is, Judas's death was a result of God's wrath and fury is a fulfillment of
scripture, God's word. This fulfillment of God's wrath is graphically detailed
with Judas's bowels bursting out.

In the Acts of the Apostles, a totally different story is presented, and it is a
different Judas from the one portrayed in Matthew. Contrary to Matthew, Acts
1:16-20 presents five significant details omitted from Matthew's narrative:

1. Judas purchased a field for betraying Jesus,
2. Judas died but not from a suicide,
3. Judas fell headlong or swelled up for some unexplained reason,
4. Judas burst open in the middle, and
5. Judas's bowels gushed out.

Furthermore, Acts 1:16 prefaces the Judas episode with a prophetic fulfillment:
"Men and brethren, this scripture must needs have been fulfilled, which the
Holy Ghost by the mouth of David spake before concerning Judas, which was
guide to them that took Jesus."

Acts 1:18 states that Judas acquired a field with the reward of his
wickedness. Here, there is no repentance. Instead, Judas has consciously
decided to purchase a field with his blood money. Research by Jeremias (1975,
138-40) substantiates that the price of an average field was approximately
120 denarii, which was the equivalent of 30 shekels. However, Timothy Luke
Johnson (1992a, 36) posits that the translation of the word *chōrion* as "a field"

is misleading: "But the imagery of 'falling headlong' and of a 'dwelling-place' suggests something more of a farm or country estate with buildings on it rather than simply a bare 'field.'" Others have also supported this reading of a farm (e.g., Barrett 1994, 98; Haenchen 1971, 160; Krodel 1986, 65; Meyer 1883, 34; Talbert 1997, 32).

Up until this time, Judas, who had been one of the followers of Jesus, was obviously a poor man, as the other apostles were. The significance of Matthew's declaration that Judas purchased some land, especially if it is a farm or county estate, is monumentally important. Today, people commonly associate wealth with stocks, bonds, or money. However, in the Ancient Near East (ANE), a major determinant of wealth was land. Davids (1992, 702-03), writing in the *Dictionary of Jesus and the Gospels*, succinctly elaborates: "Those without land (and without the skills of an artisan), the hired laborers and the beggars were truly the poor. Their hand-to-mouth existence was considered hardly worth living. . . . However defined, the poor lived on the edge of existence even in the best of times, for to be in an agricultural economy without owning sufficient productive land to provide security is to be economically marginal." Hanson and Oakman (1998, 112) also point out a significant factor often overlooked by moderns of the twenty-first century: "Land and labor were not readily available for sale in the ancient world. Land, as the primary productive factor and requirement for survival, was held by families as hereditary patrimony (inherited) or taken by conquest."

By purchasing the land (= a "small farm") Judas perhaps had raised his status in Palestinian society (i.e., "into a higher social class"; see Wall 2002, 49). Land ownership in an agrarian society (such as first century Judea) was vital for several reasons. Kuhnen (1992: See 1.1.1.1 Systems of Land Ownership) succinctly states: "Rights in land bring with them work and income, prestige, and influence. Anyone without rights in land is dependent in an agrarian society. He is forced to work on someone else's land in order to earn his livelihood." Thus, becoming a landowner was something extremely significant for people in the ANE. However, France (2007, 979) dissents and he posits that the thirty pieces of silver were "surely not enough by itself to alter the direction of a person's whole life."

Acts 1:18 states that Judas took his blood money (i.e., the thirty pieces of silver previously received from the chief priests and elders for betraying Jesus) and invested it in real estate: "Now this man purchased a field with the reward of iniquity; and falling headlong, he burst asunder in the midst, and all his bowels gushed out." This action made him a landowner in an agrarian society with all the benefits that it would entail, money, prestige, and a livelihood. Acts thus likens Judas to a heartless entrepreneur who purchased a field with "the rewards of iniquity." Danker (1988, 343) amplifies this point and wrote that Judas could have done his deed on principle (i.e., for free, but he does it for money). Contrary to Matthew, in Acts there is no repentance, no remorse, and no sense of guilt. Furthermore, Acts seemingly described a cold and calculating businessman.

In conclusion, Acts directly contradicts Matthew. Acts unequivocally refutes and repudiates any notion that Judas (1) recognized that he was condemned, (2) repented or felt remorseful, (3) openly declared that he had sinned, and (4) returned to the chief priests and cast down in the Temple the thirty pieces of silver previously received from them. Acts also has no indication that Judas committed suicide by hanging.

SPECULATION #148 **Why Judas Was Considered So Heinous**

Several writers (Hanson and Oakman 1998, 101-12; Malina 2001, 89-105; 1993; Neyrey 1993, 122-27) raise additional noteworthy insights related to the Judas episode and perhaps provide a further understanding as to why his deed was so dastardly and reprehensible in the eyes of a first-century ANE Judean. Malina (2001, 89-105) elaborates:

> [In life] all goods exist in limited amounts that cannot be increased or expanded, it follows that individuals, alone or with their families, can improve their social positions only at the expense of others. Hence any apparent relative improvement in someone's position with respect to any good in life is viewed as a threat to the entire community. Obviously, others are being deprived and denied something that is theirs, whether they know it or not.

Malina (2001, 90) posits that therefore "most people would be interested in maintaining things just the way they are." Honorable people could do this by (1) developing personal defensive strategies toward each other with whom they do not want to get involved and (2) developing alliances with those with whom they do not want to get involved.

Malina (p. 97) suggests that "most people in the first-century Mediterranean world worked to maintain their inherited status, not to get rich." Consequently, "the honorable persons would strive to avoid and prevent the accumulation of capital, since they would see it a threat to the community and community balance." Remember, "a person could not accumulate wealth except through the loss and injury suffered by another" (p. 97). Therefore, Judas's misdeed was heinous on several grounds.

ISSUE 78: Judas's Death

| Mk 14:21 The Son of man indeed goeth, as it is written of him: but woe to that man by whom the Son of man is betrayed! good were it for that man if he had never been born. | Mt 27:5 And he cast down the pieces of silver in the temple, and departed, and *went and hanged himself.* | Lk | Acts 1:16 Men and brethren, this scripture must needs have been fulfilled, which the Holy Ghost by the mouth of David spake before concerning Judas, which was guide to them that took Jesus. 17 For he was numbered with us, and had obtained part of this ministry. 18 Now this man purchased a field with the rewards of iniquity; *and falling headlong, he burst asunder in the midst, and all his bowels gushed out.* | Jn |

Mark 14:21 reports nothing specific about Judas's fate other than Jesus pronouncing woe on the one who would betray the Son of man (i.e., him). Unlike Mark, Matthew 27:5 explicitly declares that Judas committed suicide by hanging himself. However, the specific date of this suicide was not provided. No additional reference to Judas hanging himself appears anywhere in the Gospels. In direct contrast to Matthew, Acts 1 provides *no* hint or even the faintest suggestion of a suicide. Instead, Acts 1:18 reports that Judas "falling headlong, he burst asunder in the midst, and all his bowels gushed out." Acts concludes that this event fulfilled what David spoke.

SPECULATION #149 Means of Judas's Death

ALTERNATIVE 1: SUICIDE

Matthew 27:5 reports that Judas hanged himself as an act of suicide. In order to reconcile Matthew and Acts, Christian apologists (Archer 1982, 344; Geisler and Howe 1992, 361; Keener 2012, 762-63; McDowell and Stewart 1980, 84; Triestman 1997, 184) maintain that Judas hanged himself on something such as a branch, and the branch broke, thus resulting in his "falling headlong." What then about his bowels bursting?

Another apologist, Darrell Cline (n.d., Is the Bible Full of Contradictions?), suggests the following scenario:

> If you hanged yourself by tying a rope to a rather high branch
> of a tree and then tied the other end to your neck and stepped
> out into the empty space beneath the limb, you would be pretty

much hanged. Then if you hung there for several hours during the hot part of the day, you would swell up like a balloon from the gases within. Then if the rope gave way, or someone cut it, when your body fell to the ground while it was stretched to its limits by internal gases, it wouldn't be a big thing for the skin that holds your guts in to pop like an over stressed piece of fabric. Then your insides would spill out.

James Patrick Holding (n.d. The Death of Judas Iscariot) took this apologetic one step further:

> The **standard explanation** given by harmonists is that Judas hung himself, and then his body fell and broke open. This has some promise: Judas hanged himself on Passover and before a Sabbath, and no Jew was going to touch the hanging corpse (touching a dead body caused defilement; it would have been work to take it down on the Sabbath; added to that, death by hanging was especially a disgrace; and hoisting a dead body isn't an attractive vocation if it isn't on your property), so it is safe to assume that Judas hung himself and that the branch or rope eventually broke.

At least six obvious problems exist with the above Christian apologetics:

1. Judas committed suicide by hanging; therefore, his head and upper torso would have been closest to the tree limb that he was hanging from and his feet nearest to the ground. Consequently, from a hanging position, Judas would be falling feet first. Yet Acts reports that Judas fell head first without any mention of a hanging. It would seem that Judas would need to be hanging from a substantial height for his body to have adequate time to rotate or tumble into a head first position. The physics of such a scenario is open to speculation.
2. Even if Judas were assumed to be falling head first, he would have presumably split open his head, not his guts.
3. Judas's exploding guts could be a literary metaphor. Perhaps Acts was describing how Judas spiritually died by falling from the grace of God. Therefore, Judas's falling was a metaphor for sinning against God, and his body bursting open meant losing all His mercy and kindness as a result of his traitorous conduct.
4. There is no incontrovertible evidentiary proof that the temperature was hot on the day Judas committed suicide. Temperatures vary widely from day to night, and Jerusalem evenings are typically cool

even in the summer. However, the Weather Channel Interactive (2008) reports that the average monthly "high" temperature in Jerusalem in April is 77° F. Furthermore, Mark 14:54 and 67 implied that during the morning hours of Jesus's detention, the weather was cold since Peter and the servants had to warm themselves by a fire. This point is made even more direct in John 18:18: "And the servants and officers stood there, who had made a fire of coals; for it was cold: and they warmed themselves: and Peter stood with them, and warmed himself." In addition, Jerusalem's elevation is approximately 2,500 feet or 700 m [meters] above sea level (cf. Craig 1989b, 204).

5. In reference to Holding's apologetic, he is only stating a personal speculated opinion. Holding offers no incontrovertible evidentiary proof to support his hypothesis.

6. "There is also a possibility that the Greek expression *prenes genomenos* in v. 18 means 'swelling up' instead of 'falling headlong,' in which case we can imagine his corpse becoming bloated in the heat and bursting open while still hanging" (Peterson 2009, 124).

ALTERNATIVE 2: AN ACCIDENT

In contrast to Matthew, Acts 1:18 presents an alternative explanation: Judas died a sudden horrible death, falling head first and afterward his bowels gushed out. However, details are lacking that describe the time, place, and nature of this fall. Several writers (Gundry 1994, 553; Johnson 1992a, 36; Zweip 2004, 17) offer that the death was apparently an accident. Johnson adds: "We are to think of him falling from a height, perhaps from a building; certainly we should not try to harmonize this with the version of Judas' suicide by a hanging in Matt 27:5."

ALTERNATIVE 3: AN ACT OF DIVINE JUDGMENT

However, there is another possible way to explain Judas's death. Acts strongly suggested that Judas's death was like an *act of divine judgment* for his infamous betrayal of Jesus and for fulfilling scripture. Or as Allison (2001, 882; cf. Keener 2012, 760-61; Myllyokoski 2006, 156; Oropeza 2010, 354, 58; Schnabel 2012, 99) writes, "the accounts in Acts and Papias have Judas die by the hand of Heaven." The particular scripture that was fulfilled was Psalm

69:25, as Acts 1:20 quoted. "For it is written in the book of Psalms, Let his habitation be desolate, and let no man dwell therein: and his bishoprick let another take."

On a superficial reading, Acts seemingly wants the reader to believe that verse 25 related to Judas being buried in a field that he had purchased. That is, Judas was buried in a desolate field. An alternative interpretation is that Judas invested his "reward of iniquity" to get rich; instead he died a horrible death. Johnson (1992a, 36) comments: "What is odd in this application to Judas is that he is the evildoer but it is the property that is cursed!" Furthermore, nowhere in the text did it state that Judas was actually buried in this field.

However, this explanation too is contrary to the context of Psalm 69 read in its totality. Kraus (1993, 60) developed a useful analysis of this psalm:

TABLE 54. An Analysis of Psalm 69

Verse(s)	Theme
2a	A call to petition or cry of supplication.
2b-4	A description of distress or plight introduced by *ki*.
5	A confession to God.
6	A petitionary prayer.
7-12	Resumption of the lament, again introduced by *ki*.
13-15	Petitions and desires.
19-21	A lamenting description of disgrace and humiliation at the hands of the enemies.
22-28	Petition for God's judgment of wrath upon the enemies.
29	A self-portrayal as *ani* and a final petition.
30-37	Vows of thanksgiving.

If the context of these verses is carefully examined, it appears that the author of Acts is comparing King David to Jesus and King David's enemies to Judas. Just as enemies made King David suffer, Judas made Jesus suffer. Just as King David clearly requested that God intercede on his behalf and take His wrath on his enemies, so too Acts described the fulfillment of this verse with God punishing this evil man Judas (cf. Marshall 1980, 65). The Judas of Acts was cold, calculating, and unsympathetic. He got what he deserved.

TABLE 55. Psalm 69

Psalm	God's Wrath on David's Enemy	
69:23	Let their eyes be darkened, that they see not;	
	and make their loins continually to shake.	
69:24	Pour out thine indignation upon them,	
	and let thy wrathful anger take hold of them.	
69:25	Let their habitation be desolate;	
	and let none dwell in their tents.	
69:26	For they persecute him whom thou hast smitten;	
	and they talk to the grief of those whom thou hast wounded.	
69:27	Add iniquity unto their iniquity:	
	and let them not come into thy righteousness.	
69:28	Let them be blotted out of the book of the living,	
	and not be written with the righteous.	

SPECULATION #150 Judas's Demise Parallels the Deaths of Other Wicked People

Christian commentators (Allen 1997, 38-65; Johnson 1992a, 36; Keener 2012, 761; Kokkinos 2002, 28-31, 34-35, 62; Lake 1933, 29; Talbert 1997, 32; Wall 2002, 50) point out and discuss the fact that terrible deaths were well-known in antiquity and that perhaps Judas's descriptive demise was in part based on any of a number of these events. For example, Whiston's translation (1981, 365) of Josephus's *Antiquities* (17, 6, 5) vividly describes the death of Herod:

> But now Herod's distemper greatly increased upon him after a severe manner, and this by God's judgment upon him for his sins; for a fire glowed in him slowly, which did not so much appear to the touch outwardly, as it augmented his pains inwardly; for it brought upon him a vehement appetite to eating, which he could not avoid to supply with one sort of food or other. His entrails were also exulcerated, and the chief violence of his pain lay on his colon; an aqueous and transparent liquor also settled itself about his feet, and a like matter afflicted him at the bottom of his belly. Nay, farther, his privy member was putrefied, and produced worms; and when he sat upright he had a difficulty of breathing, which

was very loathsome, on account of the stench of his breath, and the quickness of its returns; he had also convulsions in all parts of his body, which increased his strength to an insufferable degree. It was said by those who pretended to divine, and who were endued with wisdom to foretell such things, that God inflicted this punishment on the king on account of his great impiety.

Johnson (1992a, 36) adds: "A similar sequence is found in *bTHullin* 56b: 'A gentile once saw a man fall from the roof to the ground so that his belly burst open and his entrails protruded.' A pitching headlong of the wicked is found in Wis 4:19, and a splitting of the bowels in the killing of Amasa in 2 Sam 20:10."

Derrett (1981, 132) also reports a curious counterpart of Acts 1:18 recorded in the *Seder Rabbah di-Bereshit* § 30, ed. S. A. Wertheimer, 1st ed., 1893, p. 20 = 2nd ed. Ibid., p. 38. The excerpt reads: "In Hell there are scorpions of gigantic size in a cave, bearing very many rings, and if a man handles a ring...he splits (or bursts) and every single limb in him drops off from his trunk and his belly is burst open and (his bowels) drop out before his face."

Coincidentally, later, Herod Agrippa I, the grandson of Herod I, also died by a sudden illness in which he was eaten by worms after executing James, the son of Zebedee:

> Acts 12:1 Now about that time Herod the king stretched forth his hands to vex certain of the church.

> Acts 12:2 And he killed James the brother of John with the sword.

> Acts 12:3 And because he saw it pleased the Jews, he proceeded further to take Peter also. (Then were the days of unleavened bread.)

> Acts 12:4 And when he had apprehended him, he put him in prison, and delivered him to four quaternions of soldiers to keep him; intending after Easter to bring him forth to the people.

> Acts 12:5 Peter therefore was kept in prison: but prayer was made without ceasing of the church unto God for him.

> Acts 12:20 And Herod was highly displeased with them of Tyre and Sidon: but they came with one accord to him, and, having

made Blastus the king's chamberlain their friend, desired peace; because their country was nourished by the king's country.

Acts 12:21 And upon a set day Herod, arrayed in royal apparel, sat upon his throne, and made an oration unto them.

Acts 12:22 And the people gave a shout, saying, It is the voice of a god, and not of a man.

Acts 12:23 And immediately the angel of the Lord smote him, because he gave not God the glory: and he was eaten of worms, and gave up the ghost.

In conclusion, Lake writes:

> Early narratives as to the death of men distinguished either for good or bad qualities are always liable to be colored by the literal tradition as to similar persons. This fact certainly has its bearing on the story of the death of Judas. From the complete contradiction between the three narratives, which do not fully agree in any point and differ sharply on most, it is clear that we have not much real recollection of fact.

SPECULATION #151 Theological Agenda of Acts

One of the agendas and motifs of Acts, along with Matthew, was theological. For example, (Conzelman 1987, 11; Gundry 1994, 553, 557; Keener 2012, 763-64; Parsons 2008a, 33; Talbert 1988, 45) posit that these verses demonstrated how God punished those who opposed Him or His servants. In other words, Acts and Matthew were stating that God's wrath would fall on those people who betrayed or rejected Jesus just as God's wrath fell on those who opposed or rejected King David. If you too betray Jesus, the same will happen to you.

SPECULATION #152 Copyist's Errors

Maccoby (1992, 180) in his *Judas Iscariot and the Myth of Jewish Evil* and Polhill's *Acts* (1992, 92n59) speculates that a discrepancy in the Judas narrative was the possibility of a copyist's error. In other words, there was an error in the finished copied manuscript, not the original manuscript. Specifically, in Acts 1:18, the phrase translated "becoming headlong" (*prenes genomenos*) was translated as "falling headlong" in the Authorized Version (King James) and was a mere transcription error away from being "becoming swollen" (*presthes genomenos*). The latter may well be what was originally written and as such might describe Judas's body swelling up after hanging for a while. This reading is found in later Syriac, Georgian, and Armenian manuscripts.

SPECULATION #153 Judas Did Not Commit Suicide

Another hypothesis offered by the skeptic Joseph Francis Alward is that Judas did *not* commit suicide. This hypothesis is based on the notion that the word "hanged" did not refer to a method of execution.

> The Greek word translated "hanged himself" is the word apanchomai which is used in Greek literature to mean choking or squeezing one's self as with great emotion or grief. In English we have a similar expression when we say that someone is "all choked up." We do not mean that they have died. We mean that they are overcome with emotion. Judas cast down the pieces of silver in the temple and left doubling himself over with grief.

James Patrick Holding (n.d. The Death of Judas Iscariot), a Christian apologist, elaborating on this hypothesis writes: "A check of the lexicons shows that such a meaning is indeed *possible*, but I found only one actual example listed -- the vast majority of the meanings given were for a physical hanging; there was only one example of a figurative meaning as described. So I would say that this is a possible solution, but not likely."

SPECULATION #154 The Bursting Bowels as a Metaphor

Alward (2003) also speculates that Judas's exploding intestines was not a literal, historic event. Rearranging his presentation, he points out:

> If the Acts author wanted his audience to understand that Judas' swelling was the result of his hanging himself and being left to rot on the tree for days, then why in the world did he not have the good sense to say so? It makes no sense for the author to tell us that

Judas' guts burst without telling us why it happened. One's guts bursting out is such a rare event that surely if Luke believed that this extraordinary thing is what actually happened to Judas, he would have made certain to provide the extraordinary explanation for its occurrence. The fact that he didn't do this is strong evidence that Luke didn't believe Judas' guts literally burst open.

So what then is the meaning of the bursting intestines? Alward advances that the author of this passage "in Acts was using literary license to construct a fictional spiritual death scene in which Judas' 'bursting guts' were not literally bursting guts, but were represented his failure to accept the new teachings of Jesus, which to Luke evidently was like the spiritual death he alluded to in his gospel." For example, he cites Luke 5:37: "And no one pours new wine into old wineskins. If he does, the new wine will burst the skins, the wine will run out and the wineskins will be ruined." He goes on to explain that "Old skins cannot expand to accommodate the gases released from still-fermenting new wine, while new ones are still elastic enough to accommodate the release of gas." Accordingly, Alward opines that "Luke expected his readers would see that Judas was holding on to the old law, the old way of thinking, and was unable to accommodate the new teachings of Jesus and thus 'burst open' just as does an old wineskin filled with new wine." Consequently, Alward postulates that "Luke clearly never meant for his readers to take his description of Judas literally."

Finally, Alward offers in support of his hypothesis the following points:

> The only place in the New Testament (NIV) where the words "burst" are used are in the three parallel verses dealing with wineskins, and the *one* place in the rest of the New Testament where the word is used to describe what happened to Judas. Here are the references:

> Mark 2:22 And no one pours new wine into old wineskins. If he does, the wine will burst the skins, and both the wine and the wineskins will be ruined. No, he pours new wine into new wineskins.

> Matthew 9:17 Neither do men pour new wine into old wineskins. If they do, the skins will burst, the wine will run out and the wineskins will be ruined. No, they pour new wine into new wineskins, and both are preserved.

Luke 5:37 And no one pours new wine into old wineskins. If he does, the new wine will burst the skins, the wine will run out and the wineskins will be ruined.

Acts 1:18 With the reward he got for his wickedness, Judas bought a field; there he fell headlong, his body burst open and all his intestines spilled out.

SPECULATION #155 Judas Committed Suicide to Shame the Jewish Leadership

Why it must be asked did Judas hang himself? The Authorized Version of Matthew 27:3-4 states that Judas "saw that he was condemned, repented himself and brought again the thirty pieces of silver pieces to the chief priests and elders." This part of Matthew rendered by the NRSV (1989, 31) reads: "When Judas, his betrayer, saw that Jesus [ˢ Gk *he*] was condemned, he repented and brought back the thirty pieces of silver to the chief priests and elders. He said, 'I have sinned by betraying innocent blood.' Then he went and hanged himself."

Reed's (2005, 57) review of recent literature by scholars points out "that Judas never repents but only 'regrets' his actions." So why then did he commit suicide? Employing a cross-cultural analysis he argued in *Biblical Theology Bulletin*:

1. Judas's suicide was not a shameful act but an honorable one that atoned for Judas's "sin" of betraying Jesus's innocent blood.
2. Judas's act of hanging himself was a vehicle designed to place blame on the Jewish leaders.
3. Judas's suicide was a well-calculated process intended to publicly humiliate the authority figures (i.e., Judas's suicide was not meant to shame Judas but to shame the Jewish leaders).

Audrey Conrad (1991, 158-68) also emphasizes the position that it is the chief priests and elders who are responsible for Jesus's execution.

ISSUE 79: What Judas Did with the Money

Mk	Mt 27:3 Then Judas, which had betrayed him, when he saw that he was condemned, repented himself, and brought again the thirty pieces of silver to the chief priests and elders, 4 Saying, I have sinned in that I have betrayed the innocent blood. *And they said, What is that to us? see thou to that. 5 And he cast down the pieces of silver in the temple, and departed, and went and hanged himself. 6 And the chief priests took the silver pieces, and said, It is not lawful for to put them into the treasury, because it is the price of blood. 7 And they took counsel, and bought with them the potter's field, to bury strangers in. 8 Wherefore that field was called, The field of blood, unto this day. 9 Then was fulfilled that which was spoken by Jeremy the prophet, saying, And they took the thirty pieces of silver, the price of him that was valued, whom they of the children of Israel did value; 10 And gave them for the potter's field, as the Lord appointed me.*	Lk	Acts 1:18 *Now this man purchased a field with the rewards of iniquity;* and falling headlong, he burst asunder in the midst, and all his bowels gushed out	Jn

Matthew's narrative states that after Judas hanged himself the "chief priests" took the silver he left behind at the Temple and bought with it a potter's field to bury strangers. Matthew concludes that this event fulfilled what the prophet Jeremiah spoke. In contrast, Acts records that "Judas himself" purchased the field. Here, there is an incontrovertible contradiction.

CONTRADICTION #86 Acts 1:18 Contradicts Matthew 27:7 Regarding the Action Taken by Judas

Acts 1:18-19 contradicts Matthew's 27:3 report of the action taken by Judas concerning his money. Matthew had a remorseful Judas *returning* the thirty pieces of silver whereas the author of Acts had Judas himself *purchasing* the field with his "reward of iniquity" (i.e., blood money that he received for the betrayal of Jesus). Did Judas return his silver or use his silver to purchase the potter's field? Without a doubt, the texts read at face value contradict each other.

Furthermore, Lachs (1987, 423) points out that it should be noted that the Hebrew word *leshashlikh* does not necessarily mean to "cast down" as translated in the AV. The AV translation implied "to throw something down violently" but "rather it can mean 'to abandon' cf. Gen 21:15."

TABLE 56. Comparing Matthew 27:5a and Acts 1:18

Mt 27:5 *And he cast down the pieces of silver in the temple, and departed*, and went and hanged himself.	Acts 1:18 *Now this man purchased a field* with the reward of iniquity; and falling headlong, he burst asunder in the midst, and all his bowels gushed out.

CONTRADICTION #87 Acts 1:18 Contradicts Matthew 27:7 Regarding Who Purchased the Field

Acts 1:18 contradicts Matthew 27:7. Matthew, the earlier of the two accounts, straightforwardly reports that it was the chief priests (i.e., they; them = plural) who purchased the field with money: "And they took counsel, and bought with them the potter's field, to bury strangers in." In contradiction, Acts 1:18 unequivocally declared that it was Judas (i.e., this man = in singular) who bought the field with his bounty money: "Now this man purchased a field with the reward of iniquity; and falling headlong, he burst asunder in the midst, and all his bowels gushed out." Therefore, it must be asked, Who purchased the field, one person or several people, Judas or the chief priests? Here, there is an incontestable contradiction.

Longenecker (1981, 263) offers a contrived Christian apologetic that attempts to harmonize Matthew and Acts. He posits that "The chief priests bought the potter's field in Judas' name with the thirty silver coins belonging to him." But there is absolutely no textual proof to support this apologetic.

As a side issue, Krodel (1986, 65) points out that "the Hebrew text would not have been suitable to score the point of Luke's text and connect Judas' fate with this psalm." The reason is that the Hebrew Bible reads plural in Psalm 69:25: "Let *their* habitation be desolate; and let none dwell in *their* tents." Therefore, "Luke had to change the plural of the LXX 'their habitation' into singular 'his habitation' to make the quotation fit the occasion." Dillion and Fitzmyer (1968, 170) and Johnson (1992a, 36) also point out that Acts changed the pronoun from plural to singular; that is the Masoretic text has the plural possessive "their" instead of the singular "his." Pervo (2009, 54) bluntly states: "Acts alters the subject of the citation from Psalm 69 from plural to singular, by adjusting a pronoun and removing a clause (n42. 'In it' ἐν αὐτῇ refers to the 'homestead' ἔπαυλις, rather than to 'their tents.'). Otherwise is could scarcely be applied to Judas."

TABLE 57. Comparing Matthew 27:7 and Acts 1:18

Mt 27:7 And *they* took counsel, and bought with *them* the potter's field, to bury strangers in.	Acts 1:18 Now *this man* purchased a field with the reward of iniquity; and falling headlong, *he* burst asunder in the midst, and all *his* bowels gushed out.

SPECULATION #156 Naming of the Field

The phrase "field of blood" is one detail shared with Matthew 27:9 and Acts 1:19. Matthew claims that the purchased field (*agros*) was named "The field of blood" because the chief priests purchased it with the blood money Judas received for turning in Jesus (i.e., the betrayal of innocent blood). In direct contradiction, Acts states unequivocally that the field was called the field of blood because the man who purchased the field (i.e., Judas) met his bloody demise there with Judas bursting open. Here, an isolated and literal reading of the text indicated that there was no hanging or suicide as detailed in Matthew.

To the contrary, Judas's exploding intestines seemingly were a direct act of God as a just retribution for his heinous misdeeds (Allen 1997, 143-45; Keener 2012, 761). Christian apologists may argue that Matthew and Acts were each merely mentioning one reason for the naming of the field; however, in reality both events occurred. That is Judas hung himself and then the branch upon which he was hanging snapped or the rope tore and resulted in his fall. However, this hypothesis is merely a speculation. For all that we know, perhaps the authors of Matthew and Acts were, in fact, writing what they considered to be the historical facts or to fulfill their theological agenda.

Zwiep (2004, 74), in a review of the literature (Benoit, *Exegise* 1: 341-43 and Conzelman *Apg* 29), posits that the legend of Judas's death was a name aetiology, that is, a story to explain the origin of a popular name in usage. Johnson (1992a, 36) adds: "For a similar aetiological account, see Plutarch, *On the Malice of Herodotus* 15 (Mor. 858B)."

Finally, Yadin (1985, 134) offers an alternative explanation for the origin of the phase "field of blood." Yadin writes:

> Aceldama, which the field was called, according to Acts, in the language of "all the inhabitants of Jerusalem," is simply the Greek transliteration of two Aramaic words which mean "field of blood." It seems to me that that was the traditional name of the area of

the field of the potter in the Kidron valley because it was fertilized by the mixture of water and blood from the Temple sacrifices. The "blood money" explanation in Matthew seems to have been added in order to tie the name of the place to the act of Judas. And this explanation was given greater force by the sophisticated recognition that the Hebrew word for "blood" in the plural is also one of the words for "money."

ISSUE 80: The Theological Agenda of the Gospels and Judas

Mk 1:1 The beginning of the gospel of Jesus Christ, the Son of God;	Mt 1:22 Now all this was done, that it might be fulfilled which was spoken of the Lord by the prophet, saying,	Lk See tables 58 & 59 below.	Jn See table 60 below.

The gospel narratives were written to highlight the theological point(s) that each author sought to emphasize. In part, perhaps this agenda also reflects the time and place the respective gospel was written and the audience to whom it was written.

SPECULATION #157 Jesus's Role in the Judas Episode

The agenda of Mark is to portray Jesus as the Messiah. This agenda is unabashedly declared in the opening verse of Mark 1:1: "The beginning of the gospel of Jesus Christ, the Son of God." The word "Christ" is from the Greek work *Christos*, which is derived from the Hebrew *maschiah* or messiah. Therefore, the name *Jesus Christ* literally means "Jesus Messiah." Brown (1994a, 2: 992n21) elaborates: "Of seven Marcan uses of *Christos* ('Messiah') four are followed by a title in apposition: Son of God/Blessed (1:1; 14:61), son of David (12:35), king of Israel (here [[15:32]])."

Mark's narrative continued to emphasize that Jesus was the Son of God. During his baptism it was recorded in 1:11: "And there came a voice from heaven saying, Thou art my beloved Son, in whom I am well pleased." In Mark 3:11, even the demons knew the identity of Jesus: "And unclean spirits, when they saw him, fell down before him, and cried, saying, Thou art the Son of God." Later, Mark 8:29 reported that Peter declared that Jesus was the Messiah: "And he saith unto them, But whom say ye that I am? And Peter answereth and saith unto him, Thou art the Christ." In the next verse, Jesus commanded his disciples to remain silent on this matter. Finally, Mark presented the reason for Jesus's death, that he was destined to die in order to usher in the kingdom of God:

> Mk 9:31 For he taught his disciples, and said unto them, The Son of man is delivered into the hands of men, and they shall kill him; and after that he is killed, he shall rise the third day.

> Mk 10:33 Saying, Behold, we go up to Jerusalem; and the Son of man shall be delivered unto the chief priests, and unto the scribes; and they shall condemn him to death, and shall deliver him to the Gentiles:

> Mk 10:34 And they shall mock him, and shall scourge him, and shall spit upon him, and shall kill him: and the third day he shall rise again.

Matthew's agenda is to demonstrate that Jesus is the fulfillment of the Hebrew Bible (cf. Kaider, Davids, Bruce, and Brauch 1996, 511). For example, he combined Zechariah 11:12-13 and Jeremiah 32:6-12 and with perhaps overtones of Jeremiah 18:1-4. Consequently, Matthew employs numerous citations and allusions in his text. As a result, Jesus's death was not the design of men. It was predicted and fulfilled exactly as scripture declared. Therefore, everything that happened was a direct part of God's plans. The earliest example of these fulfillment designs can be found in Matthew 1:22: "Now all this was done, that it might be fulfilled which was spoken of the Lord by the prophet, saying."

Luke's gospel contains at least three important agendas in reference to the Judas episodes. First, the betrayal and ultimate crucifixion of Jesus was a diabolical plot of Satan. The theme of Satan was woven throughout Luke, starting with the Temptation of Jesus (4:1-13) while in the wilderness. The last verse reads: "And when the devil had ended all the temptation, he departed from him for a season." In Luke 10:18, there were again the terse reminders of Satan's presence: "And he said unto them, I beheld Satan as lightening falling from heaven" as well as Luke 13:16: "And ought not this woman, being a daughter of Abraham, whom Satan hath bound, lo, these eighteen years, be loosed from this bond on the Sabbath day." Finally, Luke 22:3 reports that it was Satan himself who was responsible for the plot to do away with the Son of God: "then entered Satan into Judas surnamed Iscariot, being of the number of the twelve." Fitzmyer (1985, 1374) adds: "Luke is the only Synoptic evangelist who makes evil 'enter' Judas as 'Satan.'"

Luke's second agenda is to demonstrate that Jesus was completely in control from beginning to end. Details are provided by several writers (Bock 1996, 1709; Ehrman 2006, 31-33; Fitzmyer 1985, 1363, 1377-78; Pagels and King 2007, 20-31):

Table 58. Jesus is in Control

VERSE	SYNOPSIS
Lk 22:3	Satan entered Judas in order to bring about God's plan for fulfillment.
Lk 22:47-48	Judas came up to kiss Jesus but Jesus stopped him.
Lk 22:49-51	During the arrest, the servant of the high priest's ear was cut off; Jesus rebuked the arresting party, and he healed the servant's ear.
Lk 22:66-71	Jesus, before the council, did not remain silent; he challenged them.
Lk 23:3	Jesus before Pilate did not remain meek or silent. Instead he responded defiantly to Pilate.
Lk 23:9	In contrast, Jesus before Herod remained defiantly silent while being interrogated.
Lk 23:27-31	While on the cross, Jesus told a group of women not to weep for him but for their children, demonstrating that he was more concerned about their fate than he was about his own.
Lk 23:34	While on the cross, Jesus prayed for those who were for his crucifixion.
Lk 23:39-43	While on the cross, Jesus carried on an intelligent conversation with one of the thieves and even gave him calm and reassuring words that on this very day both of them would be in paradise.
Lk 23:46	Contrary to Mark's cry in 15:34, "My God, my God, why hast thou forsaken me?" Jesus declared willingly, "Father, into thy hands I commend my spirit."

Third, Luke also demonstrates that all that occurred was prophesied in scripture. A cursory review of events starting with Luke chapter 19 and Acts 1 include the following:

TABLE 59. Luke/Acts Demonstrated all that Occurred was Foretold in the Hebrew Scriptures

LUKE/ACTS	SCRIPTURE
Lk 19:38	Psalm 118:26
Lk 19:46	Isaiah 56:7; Jeremiah 17:11
Lk 20:17	Psalm 118:22

Lk 21:25	Isaiah 13:10; Ezekiel 32:7; Joel 2:31
Lk 21:27	Daniel 7:13
Lk 22:20	Jeremiah 31:31-34
Lk 22:21	Psalm 41:9
Lk 22:37	Isaiah 53:12
Lk 23:30	Hosea 10:8
Lk 23:34	Psalm 22:18
Lk 23:35	Psalm 22:7
Lk 23:46	Psalm 31:5
Acts 1:20	Psalm 69:25
Acts 1:20	Psalm 109:8

Fourth, Kaiser, Davids, Bruce, and Brauch (1996, 511) posit that Luke had another concern, "that Judas got what he deserved, a horrible death."

Finally, John continues Luke's agenda, by portraying that Jesus was directing all events, even his own betrayal (see Pagels and King 2007, 31). For many evangelicals and conservative fundamentalists, John also believes that Jesus is divine.

TABLE 60. Jesus Directing All Events

VERSE	SYNOPSIS
Jn 1:1-4	Jesus came from heaven.
Jn 1:47	Jesus could identify his disciples and tell them things about their lives, despite having never previously known them.
Jn 6:53-54	Jesus declared that those wanting an eternal life must eat his flesh and drink his blood.
Jn 6:71	Jesus knew in advance that one of his disciples would betray him.
Jn 8:58	"Jesus said unto them, Verily, verily, I say unto you, Before Abraham was, I am."
Jn 10:11-18	Jesus declared that it was he laying down his own life on his own accord, not that someone else was taking his life away from him.
Jn 13:20	Jesus knew in advance that one of his disciples would betray him.
Jn 13:29-30	Jesus had Judas leave the Last Supper, knowing full well that he was going to betray him.

Based on these agendas, Kaiser et al. (1996, 511) suggest: "But the accounts are not necessarily contradictory." Instead, they offered the following rationale: "Acts is concerned that Judas' money and name were connected to a field. Whether or not the chief priests actually purchased it, perhaps some time after Judas' death, would not be a detail of concern to the author. His point was the general knowledge that Judas' money went to the purchase, which resulted in the title 'Field of Blood' being attached to the field" (pp. 511-12).

The former apologetic has numerous deficiencies. First, there is no way we can know whether or not something was a detail of concern to the author. All that Christian apologists can offer is a guess. Second, there is no way to know that there existed general knowledge that Judas's money went to the purchase of the land, which became known as the field of blood. Scholarly consensus posits that Acts was written after the destruction of the Temple and when most of its population were murdered or sold into slavery. Under these conditions, there would be virtually no means to verify the assumed "general knowledge" that the Judas episode was a legendary development that evolved many years after the events were reported to have occurred.

SPECULATION #158 To Serve as a Warning to Those Who Renounce Jesus

In contradiction to Matthew, the author of Acts was writing to fulfill a theological agenda demonstrating how God punished those who opposed Him. In other words, Acts was stating: See God's wrath on the person who betrayed Jesus. If you too betray Jesus, the same will happen to you.

In addition, Acts (and Matthew) also potentially served as a theological warning to others: do not betray or reject Jesus. Gundry (1994, 553) elaborates: "professing Christians who renounce Jesus to avoid persecution and professing Christians who betray others in the church to persecutors in order to save their own necks. Both carry the same point: do not do it—you will be sorry!" Acts was *not* a call for the person to kill himself because of his mental anguish, as described in Matthew.

SPECULATION #159 Explanation of the Concept "Apostle" and Judas's Replacement

Assuming that there was an historical Judas and somehow or other he was no longer one of the twelve disciples, it would be necessary to explain how it came to be that he was no longer a disciple of Jesus and how his replacement was selected. Acts 1:21-26 fulfills this theological agenda. It defined who was an apostle and how it came to be that Matthias replaced Judas as one of the twelve apostles.

> Acts 1:21 Wherefore of these men which have companied with us all the time that the Lord Jesus went in and out among us,

> Acts 1:22 Beginning from the baptism of John, unto that same day that he was taken up from us, must one be ordained to be a witness with us of his resurrection.

> Acts 1:23 And they appointed two, Joseph called Barsabas, who was surnamed Justus, and Matthias.

> Acts 1:24 And they prayed, and said, Thou, Lord, which knowest the hearts of all men, shew whether of these two thou hast chosen,

> Acts 1:25 That he may take part of this ministry and apostleship, from which Judas by transgression.

> Acts 1:26 And they gave forth their lots; and the lot fell upon Matthias; and he was numbered with the eleven apostles.

One final point discussed by Pervo (2009, 54) that relates to the eventual replacement of Judas as one of the Twelve must be added here. In Acts 1:20d, the text in the AV reads "*Let* someone else take his position." Part d of verse is derived from Psalm 109. However, Psalm 108:8b LXX reads "*May* someone else take his position." Pervo writes: "The verb in Psalm 109 (108):8 has been changed from optative, which may denote a mere wish, to imperative, thus coordinating the two verbs (γενηθήτω/λαβέτω) and necessitating action."

ISSUE 81: Two Contradictory Texts on the Death of Judas—Matthew versus Acts

Mk	Mt	Lk	Acts	Jn
	Mt 27:3 Then Judas, which had betrayed him, when he saw that he was condemned, repented himself, and brought again the thirty pieces of silver to the chief priests and elders, 4 Saying, I have sinned in that I have betrayed the innocent blood. And they said, What is that to us? see thou to that. 5 And he cast down the pieces of silver in the temple, and departed, and went and hanged himself. 6 And the chief priests took the silver pieces, and said, It is not lawful for to put them into the treasury, because it is the price of blood. 7 And they took counsel, and bought with them the potter's field, to bury strangers in. 8 Wherefore that field was called, The field of blood, unto this day. 9 Then was fulfilled that which was spoken by Jeremy the prophet, saying, And they took the thirty pieces of silver, the price of him that was valued, whom they of the children of Israel did value; 10 And gave them for the potter's field, as the Lord appointed me.		Acts 1:16 Men and brethren, this scripture must needs have been fulfilled, which the Holy Ghost by the mouth of David spake before concerning Judas, which was guide to them that took Jesus. 17 For he was numbered with us, and had obtained part of this ministry. 18 Now this man purchased a field with the rewards of iniquity; and falling headlong, he burst asunder in the midst, and all his bowels gushed out. 19 And it was known unto all the dwellers at Jerusalem; insomuch as that field is called in their proper tongue, Aceldama, that is to say, The field of blood.	

Matthew reports that Judas repented when he recognized that he was condemned. Consequently, Judas attempted to return his "blood money," but it was not accepted. In despair, Judas threw down the pieces of silver into the Temple and departed. Later, Judas committed suicide by hanging. Afterward, the chief priests took the money and purchased a potter's field to bury strangers in. As a result, it was called the field of blood.

In contrast, Acts reports that Judas took his "blood money," and he alone purchased a field. Later, he fell head first, he burst open in the middle, and his bowels gushed out. No explanation was given as to where, when, or under what conditions this event occurred. However, in no way does a literal and plain face reading of the text imply that Judas committed suicide. Finally, it was stated that because of this event, a field was named the "field of blood."

CONTRADICTION #88 Acts and Matthew—Two Different Stories

The Acts of the Apostles directly contradicts Matthew. Acts unequivocally refutes and repudiates any notion that Judas (1) recognized that he was condemned, (2) repented or felt remorseful, (3) openly declared that he had sinned, (4) returned to the chief priests, and (5) cast down in the Temple the thirty pieces of silver previously received from them. Acts also provided no indication that Judas committed suicide by hanging.

Furthermore, Acts 1:18 declares in direct contradiction to Matthew and in no uncertain words that it was *Judas* who purchased the field with the money he earned for betraying Jesus. In contrast, Matthew 27:9 states that the *chief priests* purchased the field.

On a literal and plain reading, Matthew 27:5 succinctly declares that Judas died by hanging himself, that is, *his own free will*. Yet Acts omits any specific details of how Judas precisely died. Not only did the author of Acts omit discussion of a suicide but he also failed to indicate anything about a death by hanging. In direct contradiction to Matthew, Acts 1:18 implies that Judas *died by an act of God*.

Matthew states unequivocally that Judas committed suicide. Therefore, Matthew implies that Judas was acting out his own free will. Contrary to Matthew, Acts does *not* provide any notion of free will on Judas's behalf for his ultimate demise. Judas's death was a result of God's wrath and fury being a fulfillment of scripture, God's word. This fulfillment of God's wrath is graphically detailed with Judas's bowels bursting out.

If one were to rewrite with dummy lines and compare Acts and Matthew, nobody would think that we were talking about the same story. For example, in Matthew substitute the name Matthew for Judas:

> Then Matthew, which had betrayed him [Jesus], when he [Matthew] saw that he [Matthew] was condemned, repented himself [Matthew], and brought again the thirty pieces of silver to the chief priests and elders, Saying, I [Matthew] have sinned in that I [Matthew] have betrayed the innocent blood. And they said, What is that to us? see thou to that. And he [Matthew] cast

down the pieces of silver in the Temple, and departed, and *went and hanged himself* [Matthew].

Next, substitute the name Luke for Judas in Acts:

> Now this man [Luke] purchased a field with the rewards of iniquity; and falling headlong, he [Luke] burst asunder in the midst, and all his [Luke's] bowels gushed out. And it was known unto all the dwellers at Jerusalem; insomuch as that field is called in their proper tongue, Aceldama, that is to say, The field of blood. For it is written in the book of Psalms, Let his [Luke's] habitation be desolate, and let no man dwell therein: and his [Luke's] bishoprick let another take.

Except for the same names employed in Acts and Matthew, it would be *impossible* to know that these two stories were about the same person. In no way does Acts complement or supplement Matthew. Neither do Matthew and Acts record witnesses of the same event as often likened to an auto accident. Matthew and Acts are two completely different and contradictory stories.

Zweip (2004, 17; cf. Oropeza 2010, 345) concludes:

> From early days on attempts have been undertaken to harmonize these two accounts, for example by advancing the thesis that Judas hanged himself on a tree (= Matthew), but that either the branch or the rope broke, so that he fell forward on the ground and his entrails gushed out (= Acts). Or that his attempted suicide failed and that he continued to live on his own property, until he died by an unfortunate fall or in otherwise unknown circumstances. However from a modern perspective these harmonizations, creative and ingenious as they may be, are unconvincing and superficial on several grounds. First, the integrity of both stories as complete narratives in themselves is seriously disrespected when these two separate stories are being conflated into a third, harmonized version. Neither story was ever meant to be read in the light of the other. Second, in addition, to the two canonical stories, there was a third, allegedly independent account of Judas' death in early Christian sources. Apollinaris of Laodicea, who lived around 390, attributes to Papias, who was active in the first decade of the second century (!), the story that after the betrayal Judas continued to live, but that at a given time his body swelled to such immense proportions "that where a wagon could go through

easily, he could not go through" and when he finally came to die 'after many trials and sufferings, he died in his own place, which because of the stench has remained deserted and uninhabitable to the present day. Until today, no one can pass by that place without holding his nose." Significantly, such conflicting traditions on the death of Judas were passed on in Christian circles even in conscious competition with the existing canonical stories, as, for example, the various fragments from Apollinaris make clear (*intra* chapter 5). In light of the wild and early expansion of these traditions the conclusion that the early Christians were divided on the exact details how and when Judas died is unavoidable. The process of legendary embellishment of the Judas tradition has started at a very early age already, so it seems, in NT times.

The Judas episodes in the Gospels and Acts do not reflect historicity. On the contrary, in reference to Judas's repentance, death, and the purchase of a field, they exemplify two different writers relating two completely different stories.

Finally, it is more than interesting to note that the problem of contradictory accounts of Judas's death was one of the points that caused the great Christian apologist C. S. Lewis to reject the view "that every statement in Scripture must be historical truth." Lewis received a letter raising questions related to inerrancy, inspiration, and historicity of Scripture. In a letter to Clyde S. Kilby, 7 May 1959, quoted in Michael J. Christensen, *C. S. Lewis on Scripture* [Abingdon, 1979, Appendix A], he states:

Whatever view we hold of the divine authority of Scripture must make room for the following facts:

1. The distinction which St. Paul makes in 1 Cor vii between *ouk ego all' ho kurios* [not myself but the Lord] (v. 10) and *ego lego oux ho kurios* [I myself say, not the Lord] (v. 12) [Modified from the original since Lewis only supplied the Greek.].
2. *The apparent inconsistencies between the genealogies in Matt. i and Luke ii; with the accounts of the death of Judas in Matt. xxvii 5 and Acts i 18-19.*
3. St. Luke's own account of how he obtained his matter (i. 1-4)
4. The universally admitted unhistoricity (I do not say, of course, falsity) of at least some of narratives in Scripture (the parables), which may well also extend to Jonah and Job.
5. If every good and perfect gift comes from the Father of Lights, then all true and edifying writings, whether in Scripture or not, must be *in some sense* inspired.

6. John xi. 49-52 Inspiration may operate in a wicked man without his knowing it, and he can then utter the untruth he intends (propriety of making an innocent man a political scapegoat) *as well as* the truth he does not intend (the divine sacrifice).

    It seems to me that 2 and 4 rule out the view that every statement in Scripture must be historical truth. And 1, 3, 5, and 6 rule out the view that inspiration is a single thing in the sense that, if present at all, it is always present in the same mode and the same degree. Therefore, I think, rules out the view that any one passage taken in isolation can be assumed to be inerrant in exactly the same sense as any other: e.g., that the numbers of O.T. Armies (which in view of the size of the country, if true, involve continuous miracle) are statistically correct because the story of the Resurrection is historically correct. That the over-all operation of Scripture is to convey God's Word to the reader (he also needs his inspiration) who reads it in the right spirit, I fully believe. That it *also* gives true answers to all the questions (often religiously irrelevant) which he might ask, I don't. The very *kind* of truth we are often demanding was, in my opinion, not even envisaged by the ancients. [italics mine]

CHAPTER 11

The Two Travelers on Their Way to Emmaus

PREFACE: THE TWO TRAVELERS on THEIR WAY to EMMAUS

THE NEXT CHAPTER opens for examination the episode detailing two travelers on their way to Emmaus. This chapter will then dovetail directly into Luke 24:33ff and John 20:19ff when Jesus met his eleven disciples in Jerusalem on Easter Sunday at dinnertime.

ISSUE 82: The Travelers on the Road to Emmaus

1 Cor 15:5	Mk 16:12	Mt	Lk 24:13	Jn
And that he was seen of Cephas, then of the twelve.	After that he appeared in another form unto *two of them*, as they walked, and went into the county.		And, behold, *two of them* went same day to a village called Emmaus, which was from Jerusalem about threescore furlongs. 14 And they talked together of all these things which had happened. 15 And it came to pass, that, while they communed together and reasoned, Jesus himself drew near, and went with them. 16 But their eyes were holden that they should not know him. 17. And he said unto them, What manner of communications are these that ye have one to another, as ye walk, and are sad? 18 And the one of them, whose name was *Cleopas*, answering said unto him, Art thou only a stranger in Jerusalem, and hast not known the things which are come to pass there in these days?	

The emergence of Jesus on the road to Emmaus is an event thought to have occurred after the appearance to the women in Jerusalem. This episode is tersely recorded in Mark 16:12 and substantially detailed in Luke 24:13-33. Luke presents two pilgrims or travelers whose purpose for their journey is unknown. McGlynn (2012, 285) adds, "Why did they set off when everyone else was staying around Jerusalem?" Significantly, this is the first appearance of Jesus recorded by Luke. Presumably, the two travelers are not members of the Twelve but *of all the rest* mentioned in 24:9: "And returned from the sepulchre, and told all these things unto the eleven, and to all the rest." Only one of the travelers is named: Cleopas (spelled Cephas in the NIV and NRSV). The identity of Cleopas mentioned in verse 18 has been subject to much speculation, as had his companion, without any consensus.

SPECULATION #160 The Location of Emmaus

Luke 24:13 states that Emmaus "which was from Jerusalem about threescore furlongs." The NIV translation reads this distance as "about seven miles." The NIV's footnote (1978, 1194 n. 13a) reads: "Greek *sixty stadia* (about 11 kilometers)." A Greek *stadion* equaled 600 Greek feet, 625 Roman feet, 607 English feet, or 185 meters (BAGD, 764). Hence, 60 stadia would equal roughly 6.8 miles and 160 stadia roughly 18.4 miles.

TABLE 61. Furlong Conversion Chart Distance and Length: British (Imperial) and U.S. System

One furlong is equal to

Metric	
kilometer	0.201168
meter	201.168
Ancient Greek	
stadium olympic	1.046279
stadium attic	1.087512
stadium ptolemey	1.087395
thousand of orgium	0.1086807
mile	0.1449076

Several writers (Fitzmyer 1985, 1561; Marshall 1973, 86n122; Reece 2001, 262-66; Shanks 2008, 42-44) point out that "some MSS of Luke 24:13 have 160 stadia instead of 60." Fitzmyer elaborates:

> *Stadious hexēkonta*, "60 stadia," is the reading in mss. P[75], A, B, D, K[2], L, W, X, Δ, Ψ, 063, 0124, $f^{1, 13}$ and many others, as well as in most of the ancient versions. However, mss. ℵ, K*, θ, π, 079, 1079*, and some patristic writers (Eusebius, Jerome, Sozomen) read *studious hexaton hexēkonta*, "160 stadia." The better reading is clearly 60 stadia.

Marshall also adds, "but this looks like a correction" to the reading of "160" to which he cited B. M. Metzger 1971, 184 *"A Textual Commentary on the Greek New Testament."* In contrast, Shanks points out that three prominent Israeli scholars support Emmaus-Nicopolis, located 160 stadia away, as the Emmaus mentioned in Luke (S.v. "Colonia, Emmaus, Moza," Yoram Tsafrir, Leah Di Segni and Judith Green, *Tabula Imperii Romani Judaea-Palaestina*. Jerusalem: Israel Academy of Sciences and Humanities, 1994, 105.) According to Shanks (2008, 42), Emmaus-Nicopolis is the leading contender. Obviously, however, there is a significant difference between traveling sixty stadia or one hundred and sixty stadia.

Josephus, in his *Jewish Wars* (Whiston 7, 6, 6; p. 597), details a site called Emmaus for a colony of eight hundred Roman soldiers after the fall of Jerusalem. Josephus states that it was "distant from Jerusalem threescore furlongs." In Maccabean times, Amwâs, about fifteen miles from Jerusalem on the Jaffa road, was also known as Emmaus (later Nicopolis). Emmaus was mentioned for the first time in 166-165 BCE, when Judas Maccabeus defeated there the army of Gorgias (1 Macc 3:40; 4:25). However, the *Jerome Bible Commentary* (1968, 163) contended that this is "too far for the 'sixty stadia' (7 miles) mentioned here [[i.e., in Luke 24]." Others have calculated this distance at 153 stadia or 18.6 miles from Jerusalem via the Kiriath-Jearim Ridge Route. Additional proposed sites include the following:

A. The modern village of el-Quebeibeh, located 65 stadia from Jerusalem.

B. Abu-Ghosh, located about 83 stadia or 9 miles from Jerusalem.

C. Qaloniyeh (ancient Colonia; modern Motza), located approximately 35 stadia or 4 miles from Jerusalem.

Illustration 4 The Nine Contenders for Emmaus [From Hershel Shanks. 2008. "Emmaus: Where Christ Appeared." *Biblical Archaeology Review* 34(2): 42. Permission Biblical Archaeology Society, Washington, DC (*www.biblicalarchaeology.org*)

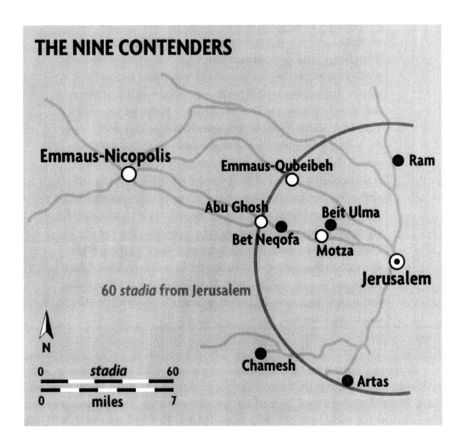

Price (2003, 339) offers another alternative for Emmaus. He suggests that the name is actually a pun: "My guess is that Luke intends a punning reference to the name from the Odyssey, that of Eumaeus, the faithful servant to whom Telemachus and Odysseus reveal their secret identities, as Jesus does to the Emmaus disciples."

In conclusion, the identification of Emmaus has been a problem for most church theologians, historians, and scholars since the early church historian Eusebius. And, as Shanks (2008, 44) aptly states: "Modern scholars are just as divided as the ancient sources."

ISSUE 83: The Conversation on the Road to Emmaus

Mk	Mt	Lk 24:17 And he said unto them, What manner of communications are these that ye have one to another, as ye walk, and are sad? 18 And the one of them, whose name was *Cleopas*, answering said unto him, Art thou only a stranger in Jerusalem, and hast not known the things which are come to pass there in these days? 19 And he said unto them, What things? And they said unto him, Concerning Jesus of Nazareth, which was a prophet mighty in deed and word before God and all the people: 20 And how the chief priests and our rulers delivered him to be condemned to death, and have crucified him. 21 But we trusted that it had been he which should have redeemed Israel: and beside all this, to day is the third day since these things were done. 22 Yea, and certain women also of our company made us astonished, which were early at the sepulchre; 23 And when they found not his body, they came, saying, that they had also seen a vision of angels, which said that he was alive. 24 And certain of them which were with us went to the sepulchre, and found it even so as the women had said: but him they saw not. 25 Then he said unto them, O fools, and slow of heart to believe all that the prophets have spoken: 26 Ought not Christ to have suffered these things, and to enter into his glory? 27 And beginning at Moses and all the prophets, he expounded unto them in all the scriptures the things concerning himself.	Jn

As two travelers were talking to each other on their way to Emmaus, Jesus suddenly appeared, but they were kept from recognizing him. After a request from Jesus, they informed him of the previous events. Then, Jesus rebuked the pilgrims for their lack of faith. Hays (2003, 229) points out that "Jesus scolds them for their failure to believe the *prophets* (interestingly not for their failure to believe Jesus' own predictions of his death and resurrection) and begins to instruct them all over again."

CONTRADICTION #89 Why the Pilgrims Failed to Recognize Jesus during the Daylight

The failure of the two disciples to recognize Jesus refutes his claimed physical appearance. From the morning until almost evening, in plain daylight, Jesus was in full view of the travelers. In addition, during this multihour journey the pilgrims not only heard Jesus's voice but they also saw his gestures and mannerisms. Yet they did not recognize him, although they had *apparently* previously known him well.

Furthermore, they did not even recognize any physical signs of trauma that Jesus was subjected to prior to his crucifixion. Chronologically, Jesus was

1. beaten after his arrest and while in custody of the chief priests (Mk 14:65; Mt 26:67; Lk 22:63; Jn 18:22),
2. ordered flogged and scourged by Pilate, which were carried out by the Roman soldiers (Mk 15:15; Mt 27:26; Jn 19:1),
3. plaited with a crown of thorns onto his head (Mt 27:29; Jn 19:5), and
4. struck prior to his crucifixion (Mk 15:19; Mt 27:30).

As a side issue it should be noted that Luke had Jesus predicting that he would be scourged, but he never was in the third Gospel. This missing fact perhaps explains why the third Gospel did not mention this type of trauma being potentially visible to the two travelers or later (Lk 24:36-49) on Easter Sunday evening to the disciples in Jerusalem.

Moreover, the two pilgrims did not recognize Jesus despite supposed nail wounds in his hands or feet as a result of his crucifixion, yet later, these wounds were shown to "the eleven gathered together" in Jerusalem:

Lk 24:39 Behold my hands and my feet, that it is I myself: handle me, and see; for a spirit hath not flesh and bones, as ye see me have.

Jn 20:20 And when he had so said, he shewed unto them his hands and his side. Then were the disciples glad, when they saw the Lord.

Jn 20:27 Then saith he to Thomas, Reach hither thy finger, and behold my hands; and reach hither thy hand, and thrust it into my side: and be not faithless, but believing.

The fact that the two travelers did not recognize Jesus demonstrates that he had no nail wounds in his hands. Unmistakably, it would have been impossible for the travelers not to have seen the approximate thirty-six-hour nail wounds virtually any time during their excursion. This would be especially true when Luke 24:30 records that Jesus broke bread, blessed it, and handed to them: "And it came to pass, as he sat at meat with them, he took bread, and blessed it, and brake, and gave to them." The only other possible explanations are that Jesus wore a pair of gloves, his wounds healed miraculously, the travelers' eyes were supernaturally blocked, or the account is legendary. Danker (1988, 391), writing in his *Jesus and the New Age*, posits that "Luke's use of the passive verb, *were kept*, points to God as the agent . . . Seeing Jesus after his resurrection is therefore more than a matter of ocular recognition. What the mind does not anticipate it does not believe, and in the absence of faith the eye is blind."

Franklin (2001, 958), writing for *The Oxford Bible Commentary* (2001, 958), succinctly inquires: "[H]ow two people could walk 7 miles without recognizing someone who was not only familiar to them, but was also at the same time in the forefront of their concerns." Then the commentary provides a speculative answer, stating that it "is to misread the nature of Luke's story, which is told, not so much as to describe a past encounter, as to show how the Eucharistic meals of his church unite them to the living presences of the risen Lord." In other words, the narrative is theological, not historical!

How then was it possible that the two pilgrims did not recognize Jesus? Luke 24:16 explains the answer to this latter question: "But their eyes were holden that they should not know him." Therefore, according to Luke, a miracle occurred which was responsible for the pilgrims' inability to recognize Jesus. Expanding on this point, Tolbert (1970, 9:184) offers the opinion that this "was part of a divine plan," and their blindness and ignorance provided Jesus an opportunity "to expound the meaning of the experiences about which they had been talking." However, this explanation is mere speculation. Specifically it must be asked, how did Luke know that "their eyes were holden that they should not know him"? What was the source of this claim? Where was the incontrovertible evidentiary proof for the source of this claim? Because Luke is stating his opinion, it is merely that and nothing more. An obvious and more practical alternative explanation, as discussed above, is that this episode was written by Luke to serve a theological agenda.

ISSUE 84: Eating and Disappearing

1 Cor	Mk 16:14	Mt 28:16	Lk 24:28 And they drew nigh unto	Jn 20:19 Then
15:5 And	Afterward	*Then the*	the village, whither they went:	the *same day at*
that he	he appeared	*eleven*	and he made as though he would	*evening, being*
was seen	unto the	*disciples went*	have gone further. 29 But they	*the first day of*
of Cephas	eleven as they	*away into*	constrained him, saying, Abide	*the week, when*
then of the	sat at meat,	*Galilee, into*	with us: for it is toward evening,	*the doors were*
twelve . . .	*and upbraided*	*a mountain*	and the day is far spent. And he	*shut where the*
	them with	where Jesus	went in to tarry with them. 30 *And*	*disciples were*
	their unbelief	had appointed	*it came to pass, as he sat at meat with*	*assembled* for
	and hardness	them. 17 And	*them, he took bread, and blessed it,*	fear of the
	of heart,	when they	*and brake, and gave to them. 31*	Jews, came
	because they	saw him, they	*And their eyes were opened, and they*	Jesus and
	believed not	worshipped	*knew him; and he vanished out of*	stood in the
	them which	him: but	*their sight.* 32 And they said one to	midst, and
	had seen him	some	another, Did not our heart burn	saith unto
	after he was	doubted.	within us, while he talked with us	them, Peace be
	risen.		by the way, and while he opened to	unto you.
			us the scriptures? 33 And they rose	
			up the same hour, and returned to	Jn 20:24
			Jerusalem, and found the eleven	*But Thomas,*
			gathered together, and them that	*one of the*
			were with them, 34 Saying, The	*twelve, called*
			Lord is risen indeed, and hath	*Didymus, was*
			appeared to Simon. 35 And told	*not with them*
			what things were done in the way,	*when Jesus*
			and how he was known of them in	*came.*
			breaking of bread.	

Luke 24:29 reports that as the two travelers and Jesus approached Emmaus it was "toward evening and the day is spent." Then, the two travelers asked Jesus to stay with them and he agreed. Following, Jesus sat down with the two travelers at a table and took some bread, blessed and broke it and gave it to them to eat. At that moment the two travelers recognized Jesus and he vanished. That same hour the two travelers rose up and started returning to Jerusalem where they eventually found the Eleven gathered together, only to be informed that Jesus had previously appeared to Simon.

CONTRADICTION #90 When and Where the Gathering Occurred

The gospel narratives present contradictory reports about when and where Jesus's gathering with the Eleven occurred. Mark 16:14 has Jesus appearing to eleven disciples without specifying the locale or time of the meeting when they sat at a meal: "Afterward he appeared unto the eleven as they sat at meat, and upbraided them with their unbelief and hardness of heart, because they believed not them which had seen him after he was risen."

On the other hand, Matthew 28:16 reports: "Then the eleven disciples went away into Galilee, into a mountain" where Jesus appointed them to go and meet him. Here, too, Matthew did *not* provide any details about the precise location (i.e., what mountain) or time of this meeting; nor was there any mention of a meal. However, the event had to have taken place at least several days after the Crucifixion since Galilee is located roughly 100 to 130 kilometers (65 to 85 miles) away, depending upon whether the location was near the south shore or the north shore of the Sea of Galilee (Waterman 2006, 164), a three- to four-day journey.

In direct contradiction, Luke has the two pilgrims breaking bread with Jesus late Easter Sunday afternoon and close to Emmaus. Fitzmyer (1985, 1567) dissents and writes: "Lit. 'it is toward evening, and (the day) has declined.' In the Jewish calendaric reckoning this would mean that 'the first day of the week' (24:1) had come to an end; but Luke disregards that, considering the hours after sundown as part of the same day." He also posits that Jesus stayed "in the house that belonged to one of them." Later that evening the two pilgrims returned to Jerusalem and afterward rejoined the eleven disciples where they once again met Jesus. Also, in contradiction to Matthew 28:16-20, Luke 24:42-43 reports that Jesus was the only person who ate a meal in the presence of the eleven disciples and the two travelers. Of course, Christian apologists would argue that this omission is not a contradiction.

Similarly, John 20:19 reports Jesus meeting his disciples Easter Sunday evening in Jerusalem: "Then the same day at evening, being the first day of the week, when the doors were shut where the disciples were assembled for fear of the Jews, came Jesus and stood in the midst, and saith unto them, Peace be unto you." However, in John there is *no* recorded exchange or consumption of food. In brief, the Gospels read like four completely different stories, not like four people recording what they directly eye witnessed at a car accident.

SPECULATION #161 **A Spiritual versus a Physical Bodily Resurrection**

Parts of the Emmaus episode challenge the fundamentalist and evangelical Christian claim of a verified physical, bodily resurrection. Luke 24:16 confirms that initially the two pilgrims did *not* recognize Jesus. After almost a day of travel, Luke 24:31 narrates: "And their eyes were opened, and they knew him" at which time he immediately vanished out of sight. The phrase "eyes were opened" does not support the notion of a physical, bodily resurrection. Stuhlmueller (1968, 163) substantiates this point: "The verb occurs only eight times in the NT; except for Mk 7:35 and Lk 2:23, it is found either in Lk 24 or in Acts, where it always means a deeper understanding of revelation."

Howe (1975, 173-74), writing in the *Journal of the Evangelical Theological Society,* similarly points out: "Luke does not say whether their recognition of Jesus came from viewing his physical form . . . . There is every indication that these disciples knew Jesus during this earthly life, but no indication that they came to believe he was living through visual recognition of his bodily form."

Similarly, Richard C. Carrier (2006)—an atheist, historian, and emeritus editor of the Secular Web—challenges the belief of Jesus's appearance to the two travelers:

> Luke 24.16 records that when Jesus appeared to two men, Kleopas and (presumably) Peter (based on 24.13, 18, and 34), they did not recognize him (*mê epignônai auton*), even after conversing with him, inviting him home, and eating dinner with him. They only conclude that he is Jesus based on his words and behavior (24:31-32). Many translations say that they "recognize" him and then he "vanishes," as if something magical happened. The Greek is more mundane, saying only *autôn de diênoichthêsan hoi ophthalmoi kai epegnôsan auton kai autos aphantos egeneto ap' autôn,* which literally, means, "their eyes were opened and they recognized him and he became hidden from them." In other words, they "see Jesus" in the stranger but then quickly lose sight of this "vision." This could mean the man vanished, or that he merely left, or that they thought he was Jesus for a moment, and this led them to think that he was in fact Jesus. This also suggests that it was not him, but a stranger whom they thought was Jesus. Certainly, there is enough that is odd about this account to place in doubt the belief that Jesus actually appeared to them.

An additional argument refuting the physicality of Jesus's resurrection is Luke's 24:30 narration of a scene when Jesus broke bread with the two pilgrims: "And it came to pass, as he sat at meat with them, he took bread, and blessed it, and brake, and gave it to them." Although Jesus is described as taking bread, braking bread, and giving bread to the two pilgrims, Luke did *not* say that Jesus, in fact, at this point ate any food. (Kilpatrick 1986, 307) In actuality, the first occasion when Jesus consumed any food was later in Luke 24:42. Therefore, the Emmaus episode provides no support for a physical, bodily resurrection.

SPECULATION #162 Problems with Luke's Chronology

Another point of contention of the Emmaus episode deals with the timeline. Luke 24:29 declares that the time of day was "toward evening" and "the day is far spent." Then the two travelers sat down to break bread with Jesus followed by the opening of their eyes and knowing the stranger was Jesus. In verse 33, the two "rose up the same hour and returned to Jerusalem, and found the Eleven gathered together, and them that were with them." Therefore, Luke has these two travelers (one often assumed to be a woman) traveling about eleven kilometers by what is now almost evening time and continuing in the evening when it was dark (even though there was a near full moon it could have been cloudy and dark) to reach the Eleven in Jerusalem. It is unknown exactly how long it would take them to travel in the night under the most favorable weather conditions. However, by one estimate, walking at a comfortable speed of about two miles per hour, it would have taken approximately three and one-half hours to return to Jerusalem. This is assuming that the distance they needed to travel was only eleven kilometers.

This speculated chronology raises another issue. Assuming that the pilgrims set out for Jerusalem prior to the end of Easter Sunday, that is, while it was still light, would they be carrying a torch with them for when it would later become evening time and dark? If the pilgrims did not carry a torch with them, what did they use for lighting while traveling back to Jerusalem when it was dark?

Christian apologists could possibly offer that the two travelers actually left Jerusalem Sunday morning, traveled with Jesus during a good part of the day, and had a meal with him during the late afternoon, perhaps 4:00 p.m. Therefore, it could possibly be argued that there was, in fact, sufficient time to return to Jerusalem and inform the eleven disciples of their meeting with Jesus. Wolfe (1989, 40) refutes this notion.

In Christian apologetics, there is a concept of *The Criteria for Authenticity* to establish the authenticity of the gospel material. Robert Stein (1980, 225-63) wrote a paper on this topic. One such tool is the criterion of Palestinian environmental phenomena. According to this criterion, if a tradition betrays Palestinian social, domestic, agricultural, religious, etc. customs, it is likely that the tradition is not authentic. On the other hand, "the argument here is that the closer we can trace a tradition to the time and environment of Jesus, the more likely it is that that tradition is authentic" (p. 236). Bart Ehrman (1999, 94-95) refers to this concept as the criterion of contextual credibility. This criterion states that "the sayings, deeds, and experiences of Jesus must be plausibly situated in the historical context of first-century Palestine to be trusted as reliable."

Returning to Wolfe (1989, 40), he writes:

> It is usually has been taken for granted that Jesus sat down to eat at a table with these men as soon as they entered the house. However, this assumption is subject to question. Since a Palestinian host usually takes considerable time to prepare food worthy of a guest, Jesus likely was in that Emmaus house for several hours or more before the evening meal was served. At that time, from when the day was 'far gone' until presumably after dark when the food became ready, was undoubtedly spent in conversation.
>
> Luke then went on to describe what transpired when the evening meal finally was served...

Therefore, by the time the two travelers returned to Jerusalem, it had to have been dark. Furthermore, it was probably dark when they set off to return to Jerusalem.

Another peculiar oddity in Luke 24:33 relates to the time frame of Jesus's appearance in Jerusalem to his eleven disciples. Luke states that this meeting occurred on Easter Sunday evening and in Jerusalem. Yet according to Matthew 26:56, all the disciples previously forsook Jesus and fled upon his arrest: "But all this was done, that the scriptures of the prophets might be fulfilled. Then all the disciples forsook him, and fled." Later, Matthew 28:16 reports that the eleven disciples went to the Galilee where they met Jesus at a mountain: "Then the eleven disciples went away into Galilee, into a mountain where Jesus had appointed them." The problem with Matthew's scenario is there was an *insufficient* amount time for the eleven disciples to go to Galilee, a three to four days' walk, and travel back to Jerusalem where Luke's narrative details a meeting with Jesus on Easter Sunday evening.

Finally, Ehrhardt (1964, 182), writing in the *New Testament Studies*, raises yet another possible objection to Luke's chronology. Given that the travelers ate their meal late in the day as clearly implied in verse 29, it must have been dark by the time they returned to the disciples who were residing within Jerusalem's city walls. The problem is that by nightfall the gates of Jerusalem would have been shut, thus preventing entry to the returning travelers.

> Neh 7:1 Now it came to pass, when the wall was built, and I had set up the doors, and the porters and the singers and the Levites were appointed,

> Neh 7:2 That I gave my brother Hanani, and Hananiah the ruler of the palace, charge over Jerusalem: for he *was* a faithful man, and feared God above many.

> Neh 7:3 And I said unto them, Let not the gates of Jerusalem be opened until the sun be hot; and while they stand by, let them shut the doors, and bar *them:* and appoint watches of the inhabitants of Jerusalem, every one in his watch, and every one to be over against his That I gave my brother Hanani, and Hananiah the ruler of the palace, charge over Jerusalem: for he *was* a faithful man, and feared God above many.

> Joshua 2:5 And it came to pass about the time of shutting of the gate, when it was dark, that the men went out: whitter the men went I wot not: pursue after them quickly; for ye shall overtake them."

What then can explain this chronological conflict? One option is that the meeting with the Eleven occurs outside the city center. However, there is no incontrovertible evidence to support such a hypothesis. On the other hand, a practical explanation is that the story is Luke's invention to serve his theological agenda.

SPECULATION #163 The Bread

Another subject that challenges the historicity and reliability of the Christian scriptures relates to the Emmaus narrative and the Passover. Luke 24:30 records that Jesus (1) took bread, (2) blessed it, (3) broke it, and (4) gave it to the two travelers. Later, Luke 24:35 details how the travelers told the

Eleven gathered in Jerusalem about their experience "and how he was known of them in breaking of bread." The issue raised in this speculation is, what was meant by the term *bread* and *to brake (break) bread*?

Many evangelical Christian fundamentalists maintain that their scriptures should be interpreted literally. In contrast, others take the position that at times the Christian scriptures should be rendered in a nonliteral or figurative manner. Therefore, the author could be employing a common idiom of his day or a metaphor or he could be incorporating symbolic speech.

The problem with the Emmaus episode should be very apparent. Assuming that Friday is the first day of Passover, how are these travelers eating bread on the third day of Passover? Only unleavened bread could be eaten during the Passover, and that lasted seven days! However, Luke specifically states that *artos* [i.e., bread (as raised) or a loaf: -(shew-) bread, loaf"; Strong 1890, 16 #740] was broken.

Leviticus 23:6 requires that all Jews to eat unleavened bread for seven days once a year: "And on the fifteenth day of the same month is the feast of unleavened bread unto the LORD: seven days ye must eat unleavened bread." Jesus is recorded to have taught in Matthew 5:17-18 that he did *not* come to abolish the law: "Think not that I am come to destroy the law, or the prophets: I am not come to destroy, but to fulfill. For verily I say unto you, Till heaven and earth pass, one jot or one title shall in no wise pass from the law, till all be fulfilled." Therefore, Jesus seemingly violates the Leviticus 23 injunction. And by extension so too, did the two travelers if they ate the bread.

In their defense, Christian apologists argue that the normal bread consumed today is white, fluffy, and puffed up; but that was not the case with leavened bread two thousand years ago. Instead, they contend that the leavened bread of that time was flat bread, similar to pita bread but so thin that one had to tear not break it. Therefore, they point out the word used for bread in normal parlance *artos* can refer to either leavened or unleavened bread. The question is, is this argument valid?

In the Christian scriptures the Greek word for unleavened bread is *azumos* (*Strong's Concordance* #106; Strong 1890, 8) and it is used 9 times (Mk 14:1, 12; Mt 26:17; Lk 22:1, 7; Acts 12:3; 20:6; 1 Cor 5:7, 8). In contrast, the Greek word for ordinary leavened bread, that is bread with yeast, is *artos* (Strong's #740) and it appears at least seventy-two times in the Christian scriptures. In the Last Supper accounts in Mark 14:22, Matthew 26:26, and Luke 22:19, Jesus took bread with yeasts (*artos*), blessed it, broke it, and gave it to the disciples. Jesus also compared himself to leavened bread with yeasts (*artos*) in John 6:35, where he called himself the "bread of life." Dr. Randall Radic (n.d., Jude 12-15) writes:

> In the *Gr.*, 'to break bread,' is *klasai arton*, and this phrase comes
> from the Hebrew idiom *paras lechem* mxl srP. Both phrases refer to
> partaking of food; just as, even now, the idiom 'to eat salt,' means
> eating a meal among the Arabs. The Hebrew idiom had its origin
> in a Hebrew loaf of bread that was made in cakes as thick as a finger
> and were broken and not cut. Thus the phrase to break bread."

Another argument relates to the earlier discussion about the Last Supper
as a supposed Passover meal. Mark 14:22, Matthew 26:26, and Luke 22:19
employ the Greek word *artos* (bread) and not *azyma*, unleavened bread.
Several writers (Jeremias 1966, 62-66; Stein 1996, 202) point out that the
term *artos* and its Hebrew equivalent terms employed in the Hebrew Bible,
the LXX, the Mishna, and the Targums described showbread, meaning
unleavened bread. Philo, a first-century Jewish scholar, furthermore explicitly
refers to the unleavened bread of the Passover as *artos* (see *De specialibus
legibus* 2.158). Similarly, Bock (1996, 1953) writes that *artos* is sometimes
used as unleavened bread (Ex 29:23; Lev 7:12; 8:26; Num 6:15; Josephus,
Antiquities 3.6,6 §; 8.3.7 §90; *Jewish Wars* 5.5.5 §217). Nonetheless, Stein
(1996, 202)—a senior professor of New Testament interpretation at the
Southern Baptist Theological Seminary, Louisville, Kentucky—raises
a substantial challenge to this notion: "The main difficulty with this
alternative suggestion is that the writers of the Synoptic Gospels clearly
wanted their statements to be understood as indicating that the Last Supper
was part of a Passover celebration (see Mk 14:12, 14, 16; Lk 22:15)."

Taking Stein's hypothesis one step further, it would seem then that Luke
would want his statement to be understood that this event is still taking place
during the seven day period of Passover and to reinforce the understanding
that the Last Supper is part of a Passover celebration.

There is at least one additional shortfall with this Christian apologetic:
there is no evidentiary proof that Luke did not mean regular bread in reference
to the Emmaus episode.

SPECULATION #164 Legend or Historical Narrative

Next, it must be inquired, is the Emmaus episode a legend or a historical
narrative? I. H. Marshall (1973, 84), writing in the *Tyndale Bulletin*, clarifies
this issue. "A legend looks just the same as a historical narrative, so far as *form*
is concerned. What matters is the content, whether the story contains features
which appear to be unhistorical and/or known from folk-lore. It is here that
the matter must be decided."

What then are the elements that can be identified as potentially legendary? According to Marshall (1973, 84), there are five such elements in the Emmaus episode:

(i)   the appearance of a person after his death,
(ii) the appearance to people out for a walk in the country,
(iii) the sudden disappearance of the supernatural being,
(iv) the opening of the eyes of the two men to recognize the stranger, and
(v) the way in which the stranger arrives at the right time to answer their questions.

Marshall (pp. 84-5) continues: "It is not possible to subtract these features from the story and be left with an original, possibly historical nucleus, for there would in fact be nothing left. The features are certainly miraculous."

ISSUE 85: The Disciples' Response to the Two Travelers Who Were on the Road to Emmaus

Mk 16:12 After that he appeared in another form unto two of them, as they walked, and went into the country. 13 And they went and told it unto the residue: *neither believed they them.*	Mt	Lk 24:33 And they rose up the same hour, and returned to Jerusalem, and found the eleven gathered together, and them that were with them, 34 Saying, The Lord is risen indeed, and hath appeared to Simon. 35 And they told what things were done in the way, and how he was known of them in breaking of bread. 36 *And as they thus spake, Jesus himself stood in the midst* of them, and saith unto them.	Jn

Mark 16:12-13 tersely reports an unnamed incident where Jesus appeared to two travelers. Afterwards the two travelers informed the other disciples about Jesus's appearance. However, after giving their report, they were not believed: "neither believed they them." In contrast, Matthew omits any narrative about the two travelers making a report to the disciples in Jerusalem since he had them fleeing earlier (Mt 26:56), presumably to the Galilee.

Luke's narrative has two pilgrims returning to Jerusalem and spending most of the day with the risen Jesus. After finally recognizing Jesus, the two travelers returned to Jerusalem to inform the disciples what they had seen and heard. On Easter Sunday evening they found the eleven disciples. However, before the pilgrims could speak, they were informed that Jesus had appeared to Simon.

Any reference to the Emmaus episode is totally omitted by John.

CHAPTER 12

Easter Sunday Evening to Peter's Recommissioning

PREFACE: INCREASING DIFFERENCES IN THE GOSPEL ACCOUNTS

THE CHRISTIAN SCRIPTURES are not a biography, and they are not written to record history in a modern sense. The purpose of the authors is to evangelize and convince their audiences to accept their belief in Jesus. The primary means of these writers is to provide proofs in the forms of deeds, miracles, signs, and wonders assigned to Jesus. The foremost sign is Jesus's resurrection.

From here on, the Christian scriptures continue their previous trend of "contradiction." Several examples of contradictions include: (1) who first saw Jesus after his resurrection, (2) when was Jesus first and later seen, (3) where was Jesus first and later seen, (4) if Jesus ascended to heaven on Easter Sunday evening or forty days later, and (5) where he ascended. In light of the agenda of these authors, the trustworthiness of these works must be carefully considered and examined. For example, none other than Paul admitted publically, and in writing, that he was willing to lie to convince other people. (Phil 1:18) The means and objectives of the gospel narrators are also occasionally discussed, although not as explicitly and overtly as Paul's.

ISSUE 86: The First to See Jesus on Easter Sunday

1 Cor 15:5 *And that he was seen of Cephas,* then of the twelve.	Mk 16:9. Now when Jesus was risen early the first day of the week, *he appeared first to Mary Magdalene,* out of whom he had cast seven devils.	Mt 28:1 In the end of the sabbath, as it began to dawn toward the first day of the week, *came Mary Magdalene, and the other Mary* to see the sepulchre. Mt 28:9 And as they went to tell his disciples, behold, *Jesus met them* saying, All hail. And they came and held him by the feet, and worshipped him.	Lk 24:33 And they rose up the same hour, and returned to Jerusalem, and found the eleven gathered together, and them that were with them, 34 *Saying, The Lord is risen indeed, and hath appeared to Simon.*	Jn 20:1 *The first day of the week cometh Mary Magdalene* early, when it was yet dark, unto the sepulchre, and seeth the stone taken away from the sepulchre. Jn 20:14 And when she had thus said, *she turned herself back, and saw Jesus standing, and knew not that it was Jesus.*

Paul records that Jesus was first seen by Cephas. In contradiction, Mark claims that Jesus appeared first to Mary Magdalene. In Matthew, the first appearance of Jesus occurs after Mary Magdalene and the other Mary left the tomb on Easter Sunday morning. However, Luke reports that Jesus was seen previously by Simon. Finally, in John, the first appearance of a risen Jesus occurs in the presence of Mary Magdalene.

CONTRADICTION #91 Paul and Luke Contradict Mark, Matthew, and John

Paul, writing in 1 Corinthians 15, one of the oldest sources in the Christian scriptures, reports in verse 5 that the first appearance of Jesus in his list of six who saw the risen Jesus was Peter, also known as Cephas: "And that he was seen of Cephas, then of the twelve." This literal reading of 1 Corinthians 15 assumes that Paul's writing was meant to be interpreted chronologically and not factually. However, Wenham (1992, 104) points out that "Paul's list does not say that it was the first time that Jesus was seen by anyone." Paul provides no indication of the precise time or location of this appearance.

Significantly, Paul does *not* acknowledge the reported appearances to Mary Magdalene (Mk 16:9; Jn 20:14) or any other women (Mt 28:9)!

Mk 16:9 Now when Jesus was risen early the first day of the week, he appeared first to Mary Magdalene, out of whom he had cast seven devils.

Mt 28:9 And as they went to tell his disciples, behold, Jesus met them, saying, All hail. And they came and held him by the feet, and worshipped him.

Jn 20:14 And when she had thus said, she turned herself back, and saw Jesus standing, and knew not that it was Jesus.

Why Paul fails to mention or chose deliberately to omit the names of these women is unknown and subject to considerable speculation. Nonetheless, numerous writers (Jones 1891, 771; O'Collins and Kendall 1987, 635; Setzer 1997, 263; Walvoord 1963, 101; Wink 1983, 177-82; Yarnold 1959, 123) openly acknowledge that the gospel writers seem to plainly state that it was a woman (or women) who first saw the post-resurrected Jesus.

Mark does not report an appearance of Jesus until 16:9. Here, Mark unequivocally states that Jesus appeared first to Mary Magdalene, but he did not clearly indicate the location. Instead, the text openly stated that the appearance occurred sometime after Mary Magdalene fled the tomb. Consequently, Mark directly contradicts Paul.

Matthew omits any reference to a first meeting with Cephas (Simon). Instead, Matthew 28:9 has Jesus making an appearance with Mary Magdalene and the other Mary while on their way back to Jerusalem after leaving the tomb: "And as they went to tell his disciples, behold, Jesus met them saying, All hail. And they came and held him by the feet, and worshipped him." Consequently, on a literal, plain, and with a single reading (excluding all other sources), Matthew reports a first appearance with at least two women.

Luke reports Jesus meeting two travelers on the way to Emmaus, Cleopas and another unnamed person. Later, Luke 24:22-24 narrates that during their dialogue with Jesus (who was unbeknown to them), the two travelers mentioned that several women saw visions of angels [plural; thereby excluding Mark 16:5] and were informed that Jesus was alive, although none saw him [contradicting Mt 28:9-11]. This meeting presumably refers to Jesus's appearance with the two women named Mary, detailed in Matthew 28:1-8 but excludes verses 9-11. Later, during the late afternoon or early evening, they returned to Jerusalem to see the disciples:

Lk 24:33 And they rose up the same hour, and returned to Jerusalem, and found the eleven gathered together, and them that were with them,

Lk 24:34 Saying, The Lord is risen indeed, and hath appeared to Simon.

Several commentators point out that the King James translation is misleading in that it could be thought to mean that Simon, one of the two pilgrims on the way to Emmaus, was the first to see the risen Jesus. The specific problem is who was doing the "saying" in Luke 24:34? For example, McDonald and Porter (2000, 204) have the two travelers telling the eleven disciples that Jesus had risen and appeared to Simon. In contrast, Gilmour, writing in *The Interpreter's Bible* (1951, 7:428-29), states: "Some interpreters needlessly complicate the exegesis of vs. 34 by accepting the reading in Codex Bezae that makes the Emmaus disciples the subject of saying (KJV)." In contrast to the King James, the NRSV (1989, 88) reads: "They were saying" (i.e., adds the words "They were") and referring to the Eleven and their companions gathered in Jerusalem. Therefore, Luke confirms Paul's report in 1 Corinthians 15:3 that Cephas (Simon) was the first to witness an appearance of Jesus.

However, here, too, Luke fails to provide crucial details; he omits precisely when and where the appearance occurred. There have been different attempts to identify the time and place of this apparition.

Plummer (1922, 558) posits that "this manifestation apparently took place after the two had started for Emmaus and before the disciples assembled in Jerusalem." Similarly, Creed (1930b, 298) offers that "we must suppose that the appearance to Peter took place sometime between the journey of the disciples to the tomb (referred to in *vv.* 22 f.) and the return of the two disciples to Emmaus." Wenham (1992, 104) suggests that "being an appearance to Peter alone, it would not have been in a crowded city house; it could hardly have been in Joseph's garden, which had become a centre of interest to both Jewish and Roman authorities and which lay near a busy thoroughfare. Perhaps he had slipped out by the city gate near John's house and had returned to the solitude of Gethsemane?" Here, there is only speculation. Nonetheless, Paul definitely declared and Luke implied that Peter—that is, Peter Simon—first saw Jesus.

Finally, John 20:14-17 is a text completely different from the synoptic Gospels. John narrates that after her second visit Mary Magdalene met Jesus at the tomb where he was buried: "And when she had thus said, she turned herself back, and saw Jesus standing, and knew not that it was Jesus."

Table 62. To Whom, When, and Where Jesus Made His First Appearance?

SCRIPTURE	TO WHOM JESUS WAS FIRST SEEN?	WHEN WAS JESUS FIRST SEEN?	WHERE DID JESUS MAKE HIS FIRST APPEARANCE?
1 Cor 15:5	Peter [Cephas].	Jesus met Peter between Friday evening at sunset and prior to the women arriving at the tomb Easter Sunday morning.	No specific location is detailed. The timeline in the Gospels implies that the visit occurred in the city of Jerusalem or its vicinity.
Mk 16:9	Mary Magdalene.	Sunday morning, early the first day of the week.	The narrative implies that the appearance occurred in the vicinity of the tomb.
Mt 28:9	Mary Magdalene and the other Mary.	Easter Sunday morning.	Jesus meets the women somewhere between the tomb and where the disciples were hiding.
Lk 24:34	Simon.	No specific mention of time. However, Luke's timeline implied that the meeting occurred between Jesus's burial and Easter morning.	No specific location is mentioned.
Jn 20:14-17	Mary Magdalene.	Jesus met Mary Magdalene Easter Sunday morning after her second visit to the tomb.	Jesus meets Mary Magdalene in the garden and outside the tomb.

CONTRADICTION #92 Peter's Investigation of the Tomb Challenges 1 Corinthians 15:5

The apostle Paul declares in 1 Corinthians 15:5 that Peter was the first in his list of six appearances to witness the resurrected Jesus: "And that he was seen of Cephas, then of the twelve." This listing assumes that Paul is writing historicity and not theology. Therefore, Peter had to have seen Jesus sometime between Friday evening after sunset and Sunday morning at about sunrise when the sentinels saw Matthew's angel and the arrival of Mary Magdalene (or possibly in the company of other women).

If Peter did, in fact, previously see Jesus, then Luke's narrative in 24:12, with him running to the tomb after being informed by the women about the two men in the tomb and their message that "he is not here, but is risen" (Lk 24:6), makes no sense. Why would Peter be running to the tomb to verify the women's account if he already had an encounter with Jesus and knew that he was not only alive but also outside of the tomb? Similarly, it is illogical that Peter, in John 20:3, would also run to verify Mary Magdalene's declaration that some people had taken away Jesus: "Peter therefore went forth, and that other disciple, and came to the sepulchre."

SPECULATION #165 Paul's Pious Fraud

John 20:31 declares that the primary purpose of his writing was to convince his audience that Jesus is the Christ, the Son of God, and thus they could obtain life in his name. Luke 1:3-4 reports on the agenda of its author: "It seemed good to me also, having had perfect understanding of all things from the very first, to write unto thee in order, most excellent Theophilus, That thou mightest know the certainty of those things, wherein thou hast been instructed." Finally, the author of Mark 1:1 declares that he was writing the good news. And his good news was that Jesus was the Christos, the Messiah and the Son of God: "The beginning of the gospel of Jesus Christ, the Son of God." This agenda of Mark is repeated at least four times when he used the word *Christos*; four are followed by the title in apposition: Son of God/Blessed (1:1; 14:61), son of David (12:35), and King of Israel (15:32).

The pertinent question is whether or not the Christian scriptures permit pious fraud to achieve this goal. Writing approximately twenty to thirty years prior to the synoptic Gospels, none other than the apostle Paul unequivocally declares that it was permissible to employ virtually any method to win converts and gain souls:

- Rom 3:7-8 *For if the truth of God hath more abounded though my lie unto his glory*; why yet am I also judged as a sinner? And not rather, (as we be slanderously reported, and as some affirm that we say,) Let us do evil, that good may come? *whose damnation is just.*
- 1 Cor 9:20-23 And unto the Jews I become as a Jew, that I might gain the Jews; to them that are under the law, as under the law, that I might gain them that are under the law; To them that are without law, as without law, (being not without law to God, but under the

law to Christ,) that I might gain them that are without law. To the weak become I as weak, that I might gain the weak: I am made all things to all men, *that I might by all means save some.* And this I do for the gospel's sake, that I might partaker thereof with you. (Refuted by Brown 2000, 14-15)

- Phil 1:18 What then? notwithstanding, every way, *whether in pretence, or in truth, Christ is preached; and I therein do rejoice, yea, and will rejoice.*

This last reading is awkward and somewhat arcane. However, this verse is much easier to understand in the NIV rendering: "But what does it matter? The important thing is that in every way, whether from false motives or true, Christ is preached. And because of this I rejoice."

Unequivocally, the Christian scriptures advocate and promote pious fraud. Given that the gospel narrators had access to Paul's epistles, it is speculated that they followed the advice of Paul and employed pious fraud, that is, they incorporated ahistorical portions in their gospels to fulfill their theological agendas.

SPECULATION #166 Peter, Simon, Simon Peter, or Cephas

The gospel narratives of Mark, Matthew, and John contradict Paul's account of the first to witnesses a risen Jesus. Paul's first attestation to the risen Jesus in 1 Corinthians 15:5 is given to Cephas (i.e., Peter): "And that he was seen of Cephas, then of the twelve." Again, this attestation is assuming that Paul's account is to be understood chronologically. Paul's account is later reaffirmed by Luke 24:34: "Saying, The Lord is risen indeed, and hath appeared to Simon."

Despite the attestations in 1 Corinthians 15:5 and Luke 23:34, Lake (1921, 95) points out that there is a major problem attempting to identify who, in fact, was the first person to witness the resurrected Jesus. Ehrman (1991, 463-74; cf. Michaels 1993, 701; Riddle 1940, 169-80) also extensively analyzed this topic and confirmed the concern raised by Lake. However, Allison (1992, 489-95) refutes this thesis. Lake writes that "it is generally held that three names apply to one person, who was the chief of the Twelve Apostles and the first witness to the Resurrection." These three names are Simon, Peter, and Simon Peter.

Mark 3:16 and Matthew 10:2 provide information that Simon was also called Peter. In addition, Luke 5:8 and John 6:8 refer to a "Simon Peter." However, John 1:42 further adds to the confusion by reporting that Jesus changed Simon's name to Cephas.

Table 63. The Names Simon, Peter, Simon Peter, and Cephas Appearing in the Gospels

CATEGORIES	VERSES	Example
The single name "Simon" or "Simon's."	Mk 1:16, 29, 30, 36; Mt 4:18; Lk 4:38; 5:3, 4, 5, 10; 22:31; 24:34	Mk 1:16 Now as he walked by the sea of Galilee, he saw Simon and Andrew his brother casting a net into the sea: for they were fishers.
The name "Simon" carries a patronymic.	Mt 16:17 "Simon bar Jona"	Mt 16:17 And Jesus answered and said unto him, Blessed art thou, Simon Barjona: for flesh and blood hath not revealed it unto thee, but my Father which is in heaven.
	Jn 1:42 "Simon, son of John"	Jn 1:42 And he brought him to Jesus. And when Jesus beheld him, he said, Thou art Simon the son of Jona: thou shalt be called Cephas, which is by interpretation, A stone.
	Jn 21:15, 16, 17 "Simon, (son) of John (but note that in Jn 21:15, 16, 17 "Peter is the name used.)	Jn 21:15 So when they had dined, Jesus saith to Simon Peter, Simon, son of Jonas, lovest thou me more than these? He saith unto him, Yea, Lord; thou knowest that I love thee. He saith unto him, Feed my lambs.
In certain periscopes further specificity is provided.	Mk 3:16	Mk 3:16 And Simon he *surnamed* Peter;
	Mt 4:18	Mt 4:18 And Jesus, walking by the sea of Galilee, saw two brethren, *Simon called Peter,* and Andrew his brother, casting a net into the sea: for they were fishers.
	Mt 10:2	Mt 10:2 Now the names of the twelve apostles are these; The first, *Simon, who is called Peter,* and Andrew his brother; James the son of Zebedee, and John his brother.
	Lk 6:14	Lk 6:14 *Simon, (whom he also named Peter,)* and Andrew his brother, James and John, Philip and Bartholomew.
The combined names "Simon Peter."	Mt 16:16; Lk 5:8; Jn 1:40, 6:8, 68, 13:4, 9; 24, 35; 18:10, 15, 25; 20:2, 6; 21:2, 7, 11, 15	Mt 16:16 And Simon Peter answered and said, Thou art the Christ, the Son of the living God.

| The single name "Peter." | Mt 8:14 (Mk 1:29; Lk 4:38 as "Simon"); Mk 5:37; Lk 8:51; Mt 14:28, 29; Mk 8:29; Lk 9:20 (Mt 16:16 is "Simon Peter"); Mt. 16:22, 23; Mk 8:32, 33; Mt 17:1, 4; Mk 9:2, 5; Lk 9:28, 33; Mt 17:24; Mt 18:21; Lk 12:41; Mt 19:27, Mk 10:28; Mt 26:37, 40; Mk 14:33, 37; Mt 26:58, 69, 73, 75; Mk 14:54, 66, 70, 72; Lk 22:54, 55, 58, 60, 61; Mk 16:7; Jn 13:36; 18:11, 15, 16, 17, 18, 26; 30:3, 4; 21:7 Lk 18:28; Mk 11:21; Mk 13:3; Mt 26:33, 35; Mk 14:29; Lk 22:8, 34 | Mt 8:14 And when Jesus was come into Peter's house, he saw his wife's mother laid, and sick of a fever. |
| Oddity. | Jn 1:42 | Jn 1:42 And he brought him to Jesus. And when Jesus beheld him, he said, Thou art Simon the son of Jona: thou shalt be called Cephas, which is by interpretation, A stone. |

What then is the problem? Lake (1921, 96) identifies several difficulties:

1. "According to Luke 24, 34 the first person to see the risen Lord was Simon, but it is not clear whether this means Simon Peter or some other Simon."

2. "The apostle Peter is only mentioned once in the Pauline Epistles [NB. Ehrman (1991, 467) corrects this fact to twice (Galatians 2:7, 8)]; Cephas is mentioned eight times. Does Paul mean that they are the same person? Is it Paul's intention to identify Peter as Cephas? To call the same man by two names in the same sentence is, to say the least, a curious device."

3. In 1 Corinthians 15:5 "it is of course, possible Cephas is included in the Twelve, but if one had no other information, it would probably be natural to conclude that he was not, in which case he was certainly not identical with Peter."
4. Paul nowhere says Peter is Cephas.

Therefore, it must be asked, who first saw the resurrected Jesus: Simon, Peter, Simon Peter, or Cephas?

Adding to the confusion and expanding on Lake, Ehrman (1991, 463-74), and Annand (1958, 180-87) clearly illustrate that many ancient authors and many ancient texts explicitly and persistently identified two different or separate people: Cephas and Peter. That is Cephas is not Peter. Further elaborating this point, Ehrman (p. 474) stated: "When Paul mentions Cephas, he apparently does *not* mean Simon Peter, the disciple of Jesus."

For example, Origen of Alexandria (186-253) wrote a text *Against Celsus*. In this work he named Simon as Cleopas's companion.

Against Celsus, 262

And in Luke's Gospel, when *Simon and Cleopas* were talking to one another about all that had happened to them, Jesus drew near to them and went with them; and their eyes were holden that they should not know him.

Against Celsus, 268

It is not impossible for the divine nature that Jesus should disappear whenever he wished . . . For it is written in Luke's Gospel that after the Resurrection Jesus took bread and broke it and gave it to Simon and Cleopas, And when they took the bread, their eyes were opened and they knew him; and he vanished out of their sight.

Consequently, Origen has Simon *and* Cleopas, two separate people, traveling on the road to Emmaus.

The problem is that later, Luke 24:34 reports that these two men return to Jerusalem and find the eleven disciples: "And they rose up the same hour, and returned to Jerusalem, and found the eleven gathered together, and them that were with them." In the next verse, the King James Version, reads that before they can give their report they were informed: "Saying, The Lord is risen indeed, and hath appeared to Simon." The questions is who made the statement in verse 35 and what Simon is being talked about?

According to the majority of commentators in Luke 24:34, it is the eleven disciples who declare: "Saying, The Lord is risen indeed, and hath appeared to Simon." However, McDonald and Porter (2000, 204) write: "It was *they* who told 'the eleven' that Jesus had risen and 'appeared to Simon'" (Lk 24:34) (italics in the original). I. H. Marshall (1978, 871) explains that:

> [N]evertheless, some scholars (e.g. K. Lake, 102) have been inclined to accept the reading λέγοντας [["who said," *legantas*, Strong's 3004]] (D Or; the Latin and Syriac are ambiguous) which would make the two disciples the speakers. But the reading of D is no more than a transcriptional error (Metzger, 186), and the meaning of the variant is difficult. Since the two do not know that Jesus has appeared to Simon Peter, they can hardly be referring to him. Another Simon may be meant (cf. the identification of one of the two as Cleopas and the other as his son), but this is a strange kind of self-identification. Dietrich, 158-163, thinks it odd that Peter is referred to in the third person when he is present, and suggests that an independent tradition has been incorporated here. But the premise is weak.

Similarly, others (Ellis 1981, 278; Gilmour 1952, 428-29) criticize making the Emmaus disciples the recipients of the message in Luke 24:34. First, there is no way the Eleven could have known that Jesus had an appearance with that Simon (i.e., one of the two travelers) if they had not spoken to him prior to his journey to Emmaus. Second, the conversation reported by Luke between the two pilgrims and Jesus conveys no hint that either of the two travelers was remotely aware that Jesus had been seen by anyone human, least of all by Simon himself. Instead, Luke 24:22-24 narrates a conversation between the two pilgrims and Jesus.

> Lk 24:22 Yea, and certain women also of our company made us astonished, which were early at the sepulchre;

> Lk 24:23 And when they found not his body, they came, saying, that they had also seen a vision of angels, which said that he was alive.

> Lk 24:24 And certain of them which were with us went to the sepulchre, and found it even so as the women had said: but him they saw not.

Thus, according to the two pilgrims, only an angel reportedly told some women that Jesus was alive.

Third, Lake (1921, 96) points out: "But in this case Simon cannot be Simon Peter, for the text states that the two who returned to Jerusalem found the eleven, which must include Peter, gathered together in that city." Plainly we have an irreconcilable conflict if the Simon reported in Origen's treatise is the same Cephas cited in Paul's 1 Corinthians 15:5 or the same Simon narrated in Luke's Luke 24:34. At the absolute least, the Simon in Origen's treatise should have known that earlier he had seen Jesus as he was later informed by the Eleven gathered in Jerusalem.

Therefore, church tradition presents conflicting if not unclear information as to whether Simon or Cephas are two separate people or Simon and Cephas are referring to the same person to first witness the resurrected Jesus.

SPECULATION #167 Paul's Source That Jesus Was First Seen by Peter

To the critical and observant reader, the omission of certain vital facts is paramount. Paul does not describe the *when*, *where*, or the *character* of these most significant occurrences, the women witnessing the risen Jesus. Appropriately, Byrne (2001, 23) asks: "Why no narrative? . . . Why no narrative, especially, in view of the notice about Peter's visit to tomb, which left him amazed?" (v. 12).

Kaufman (1968, 420n18), writing in his *Systematic Theology*, also raises a similar concern:

> Not only is this explicitly stated in 1 Cor 15:5; it is also suggested by the repeated primacy given to Peter both in many of the other traditions which fail to report directly that he was the first witness (e.g., Lk 24:34; John 20:6; 21:15ff.; and also Lk 22:32; the confession at Caesara Philippi [Mk 8:29]), and in the early church itself, as seen, for example, in the first twelve chapters of Acts.

However, Craig (1984b, 194) argues that since Paul spent fifteen days with Peter (Gal 1:18), he would have known if Peter had such an experience or not: "Then after three years I went up to Jerusalem to see Peter, and abode with him fifteen days." Craig's argument is based on two assumptions taken for granted:

1. Paul actually spent fifteen days with Peter.
2. Peter would have told Paul if he had an experience or not.

To the contrary, research by Ehrman (1990, 474) suggests that "Paul would *not* have gone to Jerusalem, three years after his 'conversion' (Gal 2:18-20), in order to learn more about the life of Jesus from one of his closest disciples, Peter. Instead, he would have gone to confer with Cephas, a leader of the Jerusalem church, perhaps concerning missionary strategy."

Another point that bears consideration relates to the accounts of Paul and Mark. Mark 16:1-8 explicitly omits any discussion about Jesus's encounter with the two travelers to Emmaus. More striking, Mark omits any mention about Peter being the first witness to an appearance of the risen Jesus. For two reasons this omission is highly significant. First, Paul and Mark represent the oldest accounts of church history. Second, church tradition ascribes to Mark the role of Peter's interpreter and secretary.

Toward the end of his life, Papias (ca. 60-130 CE) records that Mark wrote what the apostle Peter had told him. This information was in turn provided to Papias by John the Presbyter: "Mark became Peter's interpreter and wrote accurately all that he remembered of the things said or done by the Lord."

> And the presbyter said this: Mark having become the interpreter of Peter, wrote down accurately, whatsoever he remembered. It was not, however, not in exact order that he related the sayings or deeds of Christ. For he neither heard the Lord nor accompanied Him. But afterwards, as I said, he accompanied Peter, who accommodated his instructions to the necessities [of his hearers], but with no intention of giving a regular narrative of the Lord's sayings. Wherefore Mark made no mistake in thus writing some things as he remembered them. For of one thing he took especial care, not to omit anything he heard, and not to put anything fictitious into the statements. [Eusebius. *History of the Church* 3:39:15. In the Ante-Nicene Fathers: *The Apostolic Fathers with Justin Martyr and Irenaeus* VI. Edited by Philip Schaff]

Therefore, the authority of Mark's gospel is based on Papias, and Papias's authority is based on a certain John the Presbyter.

Later, around the year 180, Irenaeus gave the first historically documented list of the four gospels and their authors:

> Matthew also issued a written Gospel among the Hebrews in their own dialect, while Peter and Paul were preaching at Rome, and laying the foundations of the Church. After their departure, Mark, the disciple and interpreter of Peter, did also hand down to us in writing

what had been preached by Peter. [Irenaeus. *Adversus Haereses* (*Against Heresies* 3.1.1) In the *Ante-Nicene Fathers: The Apostolic Fathers with Justin Martyr and Irenaeus.* Edited by Philip Schaff.]

The key point to recognize is that the two earliest traditions regarding the composition of Mark records that Mark received his information directly from Peter himself.

One additional point also bears consideration. Peter also makes reference to John Mark in 1 Peter 5:13: "The church that is at Babylon, elected together with you, saluteth you; and so doth Marcus my son." In this verse, Peter calls him "my son Mark." This phrase is probably an expression of Peter's close relationship with Mark. If these two early Christian traditions are true, Peter would be the elder apostle and John Mark his dear young friend who wrote down what Peter told him about Jesus.

Now, given that Mark was Peter's secretary and close friend, it seems extremely odd that Mark left out any reference to Peter witnessing the risen Jesus or the appearance of Jesus to the two travelers on the road to Emmaus. Plainly, Mark should have known about this encounter.

Finally, Lindars (1986, 93) makes the following statement: "It should be noted that there is in 1 Corinthians 15:3-5 no suggestion that the appearance to Peter took place on the third day. The reference to the third day is part of the theological statement of the resurrection, deduced from Scripture (verse 4) and perhaps partly from sayings of Jesus himself (cf. Jn 2:22)."

As alleged by Paul and Luke (1 Cor 15:5; Lk 24:34), it seems extraordinary that no account of the appearance of Jesus, first to Peter, has survived. One possible rationale is that Paul was not familiar with this account because it was created approximately a decade later. Wenham (1992, 104) suggests that the meeting with Jesus was "perhaps too personal and sacred to be made a matter of public knowledge." How then does Wenham know that this meeting was too personal or sacred to be a matter of public knowledge? This apologetic is nothing more than speculation.

Conzelmann (1975, 256-57) offers another potential and simplistic explanation for Peter being credited with the first appearance: "Historically speaking, it was the reason for the status of Peter in the primitive church and probably for the founding of the circle of the Twelve." Another explanation posit by Page (1969, 30) is that Peter "would need no introduction to the Corinthian Christians" and his "testimony would carry much weight with the Corinthians."

Regardless of the rationale, it must be reiterated that all explanations, hypotheses, rationales, and theories are nothing more than arguments based on silence, whether they are affirmative or negative. The bottom line is that there is no proof for Paul's claim that Cephas was the first person to see the risen Jesus. This idea is a belief based on an oral tradition.

ISSUE 87: When Jesus Manifested Himself before His Disciples

1 Cor	Mk 16:12 After that he	Mt 28:16	Lk 24:35 And they	Jn 20:19 *Then*
15:5 And that he was seen of Cephas *then of the twelve*	appeared in another form unto two of them, as they walked, and went into the country. 13 And they went and told it unto the residue: neither believed they them. 14 *Afterward he appeared unto the eleven as they sat at meat*, and upbraided them with their unbelief and hardness of heart, because they believed not them which had seen him after he was risen.	Then the eleven disciples went away into Galilee, into a mountain where Jesus had appointed them. 17 And when they saw him, they worshipped him: but some doubted.	told what things were done in the way, and how he was known of them in breaking of bread. 36 And as they thus spake, *Jesus himself stood in the midst of them, and saith unto them, Peace be unto you*. 37 But they were terrified and affrighted, and supposed that they had seen a spirit.	the same day at evening, being the first day of the week*, when the doors were shut where the disciples were assembled for fear of the Jews, came Jesus and stood in the midst, and saith unto them, Peace be unto you.

Mark narrates that Jesus appeared to the eleven disciples after receiving a report from the two travelers. On the other hand, Matthew reports that the eleven disciples eventually saw Jesus while in the Galilee. No specific time reference is provided. In contrast, Luke has the disciples witnessing the risen Jesus on Easter Sunday after they had received a report from the two travelers. John clarifies Luke's report, stating that the time Jesus manifested himself was during the evening.

CONTRADICTION #93 The Number of Disciples Who Saw Jesus

Church tradition contradicts itself as to whether or not Jesus appeared before eleven disciples or twelve disciples. Paul, writing in 1 Corinthians 15:5, states unequivocally that after Cephas, Jesus was witnessed by the Twelve: "And that he was seen of Cephas, then of the twelve." Similarly, Mark 16:14 reported: "And that he was seen of Cephas, then of the twelve:"

In direct contradiction, Luke 24:33 states that following Jesus's post-resurrection he appeared to "the eleven" in Jerusalem: "And they rose up the same hour, and returned to Jerusalem, and found the eleven gathered together, and them that were with them." Therefore, this appearance occurs on Easter Sunday evening.

Luke's narrative provides information that someone was missing, but who? Based on Matthew 27 and Acts 1, one would naturally think that it is Judas because he had already supposedly hanged himself after repenting his treason against Jesus or he died as a consequence of a fall. This topic is discussed later.

> Mt 27:1 When the morning was come, all the chief priests and elders of the people took counsel against Jesus to put him to death:

> Mt 27:2 And when they had bound him, they led him away, and delivered him to Pontius Pilate the governor.

> Mt 27:3 Then Judas, which had betrayed him, when he saw that he was condemned, repented himself, and brought again the thirty pieces of silver to the chief priests and elders,

> Mt 27:4 Saying, I have sinned in that I have betrayed the innocent blood. And they said, What is that to us? see thou to that.

> Mt 27:5 And he cast down the pieces of silver in the temple, and departed, and went and hanged himself.

> Acts 1:18: Now this man purchased a field with the reward of iniquity; and falling headlong, he burst asunder in the midst, and all his bowels gushed out.

John 20:24 states that the missing disciple is Thomas: "But Thomas, one of the twelve, called Didymus, was not with them when Jesus came." Therefore, the question remains, was Jesus appearance witnessed by eleven disciples or twelve disciples?

One rationale challenging the view of Christian apologists is that this "group of Twelve" had to have included Judas because Acts 1:26 records that it was not until *after* the Ascension, some forty-plus days after Jesus's crucifixion, that another person, Mathias, was voted in to replace Judas. (This topic is also discussed later.) "And they gave forth their lots; and the lot fell upon Mathias; and he was numbered with the eleven apostles." However, this

Christian apologetic is meaningless because Judas could *not* have been one of "the eleven" if he was already supposedly dead, according to Matthew 27:5.

Significantly, a few later manuscript copyists edited Paul's 1 Corinthians 15:5 by changing the number "twelve" to "eleven." Perhaps, even more noteworthy, none other than the Vulgate Bible, the Latin translation of the Christian Bible, which is in common use in the Catholic Church, translated Paul's Greek "twelve" with a Latin "eleven."

TABLE 64. Chapter 15 The Douay-Rheims Bible: First Epistle of Saint Paul to the Corinthians

Christ's resurrection and ours. The manner of our resurrection.	*Christ's resurrection and ours. The manner of our resurrection.*
1 Now I make known unto you, brethren, the gospel which I preached to you, which also you have received, and wherein you stand; 2 By which also you are saved, if you hold fast after what manner I preached unto you, unless you have believed in vain. 3 For I delivered unto you first of all, which I also received: how that Christ died for our sins, according to the scriptures: 4 And that he was buried, and that he rose again the third day, according to the scriptures: 5 And that he was seen by Cephas; *and after that by the eleven.*	1 notum autem vobis facio fratres evangelium quod praedicavi vobis quod et accepistis in quo et statis 2 per quod et salvamini qua ratione praedicaverim vobis si tenetis nisi si frustra credidistis 3 tradidi enim vobis in primis quod et accepi quoniam Christus mortuus est pro peccatis nostris secundum scripturas 4 et quia sepultus est et quia resurrexit tertia die secundum scripturas 5 et quia visus est Cephae *et post haec undecim.*

It makes no sense that Saint Jerome, the editor and translator of the Vulgate Bible, changed the number "twelve" to "eleven" unless he recognized that there was an error in the Greek text and sought to correct it. This brings us full circle to the previously raised question, was Jesus witnessed by eleven disciples or twelve disciples? Evidently, the church record is contradictory.

In addition, it is significant that Saint Jerome changed the actual text of Saint Paul in 1 Corinthians 15:5 given that the Catholic Church adopted the Vulgate Bible as the accepted version of the Bible for almost one thousand years. This deliberate editing by Saint Jerome proves that the church did *not* consider the Greek New Testament infallible, inviolable, or sacrosanct, since it was edited.

CONTRADICTION #94 Matthew Contradicts Mark, Luke, and John

Mark 16:14 states that the eleven disciples saw Jesus after they received a report from the two travelers who journeyed to Emmaus and back to Jerusalem. Therefore, the meeting occurred sometime on Easter Sunday. Mark elaborates that this appearance occurred as the disciples sat down to eat. In first century Judean society, eating supper occurred before sunset from approximately 4:00 to 6:00 p.m. As discussed earlier, Jeremias (1966, 44-46) points out that "it was customary to have two meals a day: a very simple breakfast between 10 and 11 a.m. and *the main meal in the late afternoon*." Later, Jeremias (45n1) clarified that the phrase by *late afternoon* meant "in the hours before evening," "in the later hours of the afternoon," "toward evening," or "before evening."

Luke's account is similar to Mark. He too has Jesus appearing before his disciples after the report of the two travelers. To confirm that it was he, Jesus requested some meat to eat. Luke 24:42-43 stated: "And they gave him a piece of a broiled fish, and of an honeycomb. And he took it, and did eat before them." However, this information provided by Luke only meant that there was food in the room at the time. Consequently, it is impossible to determine if Jesus ate this food before, during, or after the disciples' supper.

John 20:19 distinctly clarifies that the time of the appearance was in the evening of Easter Sunday: "Then the same day at evening, being the first day of the week, when the doors were shut where the disciples were assembled for fear of the Jews, came Jesus and stood in the midst, and saith unto them, Peace be unto you." Consequently, John contradicts Mark. Once again, this chronology assumes that Mark's "as the disciples sat down to eat" referred to a time prior to sunset on Easter Sunday.

Finally, Matthew directly contradicts Mark, Luke, and John. In a literal reading of Mark, Luke, and John, the disciples remain in Jerusalem and see the risen Jesus late on Easter Sunday. In contradiction, Matthew must have had the meeting many days later because Matthew's meeting is in the Galilee. Traveling this distance would require approximately three days. It would have been impossible to transverse that distance in a round trip in the time concerned. The only recourse for Christian apologists was to assume that Matthew's appearance was not a first for the disciples but rather a second. However, three rebuttals are evinced: (1) Matthew is thought to be dependent on Mark, (2) Luke omits any direct discussion of the disciples' meeting in a mountain in the Galilee, and (3) why would Matthew omit from his account the meetings in Jerusalem?

CONTRADICTION #95 Why Jesus Manifested Himself to His Disciples

Pagels (1979, 9) offers a rational explanation as to why Paul and the gospel narratives discuss Jesus manifesting himself to his disciples. She suggests that perhaps the purpose was mainly to secure the authority of the original disciples, with, of course, Paul being a unique exception. Therefore, only those who traveled and learned with Jesus between the Resurrection and the Ascension could claim apostolic authority.

Similarly, O'Collins (1988a, 74) adds that "the fish-eating motif also plays its part in depicting the credentials of the apostolic community as authentic witnesses to the resurrection."

Elaborating on this point, Viney (1989, 134) writes:

> By stressing the physical presence of Christ to the disciples—an experience that is closed to future generations—the New Testament writers insured that authority was vested only in those who could claim a line of inheritance from the disciples. *If Pagels is correct, then not only do we know that the Gospel writers increasingly emphasized the bodily reality of the risen Christ, we have some understanding of why they did. The motives had more to do with building church structure than with historical accuracy.* [italics for emphasis]

SPECULATION #168 The Twelve Disciples

A *mathestes* or disciple means a follower or student and can imply a personal relationship with a teacher (i.e., rabbi). "The Twelve" witnesses were a group chosen and ordained by Jesus to accompany him and share his ministry (Mk 3:13-19; Mt 10:1-4; Lk 6:12-16; cf. Jn 1:37-51; 6:70; Acts 1:13). Jesus also named the Twelve as "Apostles" (Lk 6:13). Significantly, the lists of names of "the Twelve" in the synoptic Gospels are different in each account. According to Mark 3:13-19, they were in order: (1) Simon (surnamed Peter), (2) James the son of Zebedee (surnamed Boanergeres), (3) John the brother of James (surnamed Boanerges), (4) Andrew, (5) Philip, (6) Bartholomew, (7) Matthew, (8) Thomas, (9) James the son of Alphaeus, (10) Thaddaeus, (11) Simon the Canaanite, and (12) Judas Iscariot.

A pertinent question is, why were there twelve disciples? Proponents of the Christian scriptures could respond: (1) there were twelve disciples because God, in His wisdom, decided there would be twelve disciples, (2) there were twelve disciples because Jesus decided to appoint twelve disciples (Mk 3:13), (3) the number referred to the twelve tribes of Israel (Mt 19:28; cf. Rev 21:12-14) to be judged, or (4) it symbolized the restoration of Israel.

Below, several rationales offered by Christian apologists and commentators are surveyed. Of course, it must be recognized that their opinion are not the final word. Rather, their opinions are just that—opinions based on silence.

1. That "the Twelve" to which Paul refers was not a literal number but the designation of an office. According to the *Adam Clarke Commentary* (1996), this term is used merely "to point out the society of the apostles, who, though at this time they were only eleven, were still called the twelve, because this was their original number, and a number which was afterward filled up."

2. Did Paul's reference to "the Twelve" contradict Jesus's appearances to ten of the apostles on one occasion (Jn 20:19-23) and eleven on another (Jn 20:26-29)? Not at all. Gordon Fee (1987, 729; cf. G. Hanson 1911, 121-22) suggests that the texts simply used a figure of speech common to all languages, where a body of persons (or groups) who act as colleagues are called by a number rather than a name.

3. J. P. Holding (n.d. One Down, Twelve to Go) posits that "'the Twelve' was a traditional colloquialism that referred to the apostles, originally used by Jesus, that continued to be used (even with, when appropriate, 'the eleven') even when there weren't 12 of them - just as we still refer to a particular college football conference as 'The Big Ten,' even though it has more than 10 teams now!"

4. Summers (1965, 477n11) suggests that "the Twelve" could be just "a 'round number' reference to the apostles. This could be either of several to the 10, to the Eleven, to the group on the mountain, etc.

5. Borchert (1983, 405) suggests that the term "the Twelve" did not necessarily refer to twelve persons. It could simply mean those of the original band which the church saw as representing the new Israel.

6. Bammel (1955, 401-19) posits that the appearance to "the Twelve" and to all the apostles was the same occurrence.

7. Perkins (2012, 181) states that the phrase "then by the Twelve" as incorporated in 1 Corinthians 15:5 "may also be an expansion of the original formula."

The number "twelve" is very auspicious in the Hebrew Bible and noncanonical works. This number is also important because of its literal appearance in scripture and its possible symbolic interpretations. Additional speculated rationales alone or in combination for the twelve apostles include the following:

1. Paralleling the twelve sons of Jacob and the twelve tribes (Gen 35:22).
2. Paralleling the twelve spies who went into the Holy Land (Num 13:1-15).
3. Paralleling the twelve stones in the breastplate of the high priest (Gen 28:13).
4. Paralleling the twelve male descendants of Adam listed in Genesis 4:1-26.
5. Paralleling the twelve loaves of showbread used in the Tabernacle (Lev 24:5).
6. Paralleling the twelve princes of Israel (Num 1:44).
7. Paralleling the select twelve men Joshua commanded representing each tribe (Joshua 4:2).
8. Paralleling the number of hours in a day (Jn 11:9) and the twelve months of the year.
9. Paralleling the twelve constellations (zodiac).
10. Paralleling the number celebrated in the early Jewish document called the Testaments of the Twelve Patriarchs.

Although Christian apologists (e.g., Meier 1997, 672) and fundamentalists may accept the number "twelve" as a literal truth, others, including some believers in Jesus, may recognize that this term is meant nonliterally. What then is the principal argument against the literal number "twelve"? The most probable rationale is that the number twelve served a theological agenda that parallels the twelve tribes. Here, Raymond Collins (1999, 535) maintains that "Jesus' choice of twelve from among his disciples then has eschatological significance, symbolizing a new/renewed people of God."

ISSUE 88: Where Jesus Manifested Himself before His Disciples

1 Cor 15:5	Mk 16:14	Mt 28:16	Lk 24:36 And	Jn 20:19 Then
And that he	Afterward he	Then the	as they thus	the same day at
was seen of	appeared unto	eleven	spake, *Jesus*	evening, being
Cephas, then	the eleven	disciples went	*himself stood*	the first day of
of the twelve:	as they sat	away *into*	*in the midst*	the week, *when*
6 After that,	at meat, and	*Galilee, into*	*of them,* and	*the doors were shut*
he was seen	upbraided	*a mountain*	saith unto	*where the disciples*
of above five	them with	where Jesus	them, Peace be	*were assembled*
hundred	their unbelief	had appointed	unto you. 37	for fear of the
brethren at	and hardness	them. 17 And	But they were	Jews, came Jesus
once; of whom	of heart,	when they	terrified and	and stood in the
the greater part	because they	saw him, they	affrighted, and	midst, and saith
remain unto	believed not	worshipped	supposed that	unto them, Peace
this present,	them which	him: but some	they had seen a	be unto you.
but some are	had seen him	doubted.	spirit.	
fallen asleep.	after he was			
	risen.			

Paul provided no information about where the first disciples saw the risen Jesus. Mark reported that Jesus appeared to the eleven disciples after they received a report from the two travelers. When you read Mark 16:14 alone, it is impossible to determine the location of Jesus's meeting with his disciples. Matthew reported that Jesus met with his disciples in the Galilee. In context, Luke has him meeting his disciples in Jerusalem. So, too, John had Jesus manifesting himself first in Jerusalem.

CONTRADICTION #96 Where Jesus First Manifested Himself before His Disciples

Paul provided no information as to where Jesus first saw his disciples. Instead, 1 Corinthians 15:5 stated: "And that he was seen of Cephas, then of the twelve."

Mark 16:12-14 stated that eleven disciples saw Jesus after they presumably received a report from the two travelers who journeyed to Emmaus. Therefore, the meeting occurred in Jerusalem.

Luke's account was similar to Mark's. He too had Jesus appearing before his disciples after the report of the two travelers from Emmaus. Consequently, Jesus's first manifestation occurred in Jerusalem.

John 20:19 clarified that the time of the first appearance to his disciples was in the evening of Easter Sunday: "Then the same day at evening, being the first day of the week, when the doors were shut where the disciples were assembled for fear of the Jews, came Jesus and stood in the midst, and saith unto them, Peace be unto you." Consequently, John too has Jesus meeting his disciples in Jerusalem.

Matthew directly contradicts the reports found in Mark, Luke, and John. A literal reading of Mark, Luke, and John has the disciples remaining in Jerusalem; and this was where they saw Jesus. In contrast, Matthew 28:16 reported that the meeting was held in the Galilee: "Then the eleven disciples went away into Galilee, into a mountain where Jesus had appointed them."

CONTRADICTION #97 Contradictory Messages and Meeting Places

Mark 16 reported that on Easter Sunday morning several women encountered a young man at the tomb. Mark 16:7 narrated that the young man instructed them: "But go your way, tell his disciples and Peter that he goeth before you into Galilee: there shall ye see him, as he said unto you." Therefore, the disciples were to meet Jesus in the Galilee. This command had a clear echo of Mark 14:28: "But after that I am risen, I will go before you into Galilee."

Matthew 28 related a modified incident when Mary Magdalene and the other Mary found an angel at the tomb. In Matthew 28:2, the narrator specifically stated: "And, behold, there was a great earthquake: for the angel of the Lord descended from heaven, and came and rolled back the stone from the door, and sat upon it." Therefore, the person about to address the two women was not just a mere mortal; he was "an angel of the Lord." In verses 5 and 6, he informed the women not to be afraid and that Jesus was not present since he had already risen. In Matthew 28:7 this angel of the Lord issued a direct and incontrovertible command to these women: "And go quickly, and tell his disciples that he is risen from the dead; and, behold, he goeth before you into Galilee; there shall ye see him: lo, I have told you." As in Mark, the disciples would see a manifested Jesus in the Galilee.

However, after leaving the tomb the women encountered the risen Jesus. In Matthew 28:10 Jesus commanded the women: "Then said Jesus unto them, Be not afraid: go tell my brethren that they go into Galilee, and there shall they see me." For a third time, there was a direct reference to a future meeting in the Galilee with Jesus's disciples.

Naland (1988, 14) raises the following issue: "But why would a divine angel be sent by an omniscient God to relay a message that would then be immediately contradicted?" Not only was the command of the angel of the Lord contradicted, but it was contradicted by Jesus himself, the one for whom the angel was supposedly speaking. The contradiction was that Jesus met the disciples perhaps eight to ten hours later in Jerusalem, not in the Galilee:

> Lk 24:36 And as they thus spake, Jesus himself stood in the midst of them, and saith unto them, Peace be unto you.

> Jn 20:19 Then the same day at evening, being the first day of the week, when the doors were shut where the disciples were assembled for fear of the Jews, came Jesus and stood in the midst, and saith unto them, Peace be unto you.

Recapping, the command of the angel of the Lord and Jesus's own words were contradicted on Easter Sunday evening. Later, these two sets of commands were also contradicted eight days afterward when Jesus made another appearance with his disciples in Jerusalem.

> Jn 20:26 And after eight days again his disciples were within, and Thomas with them: then came Jesus, the doors being shut, and stood in the midst, and said, Peace be unto you.

Incontrovertibly, Luke 24:36, John 20:19, and John 20:26 reported that Jesus met his disciples in Jerusalem, yet his message and those of his angels declared that the disciples would meet Jesus in the Galilee.

SPECULATION #169 Jesus's Means of Transport

Christian apologists and theologians do not agree as to how Jesus entered the locked room. From a literal reading of Luke and John, Jesus seemed to materialize out of the thin air in what can only be categorized as a miraculous and supernatural manner. Unequivocally, neither Luke nor John described Jesus as passing through a locked door in their respective narratives. Therefore, this description served to increase the wonder of Jesus's supernatural appearance in their midst.

Craig (1993, 29) and Gundry (2004, 367) pointed out that Jesus was never said to pass through locked doors in the appearance narratives. He simply appeared miraculously in the closed room, even as he miraculously vanished during the bread breaking in Emmaus. Geisler (1999, 661; 1989a, 160-61; cf. Blair 1973, 259-70) offered several alternative Christian apologetics: (1) Jesus could have used his power to unlock the door, as was done to release Peter from prison (Acts 12:10), (2) he previously performed miracles in his pre-resurrection body, (3) though physical, Jesus's resurrected body by its very nature was supernatural and should be expected to do supernatural things, and (4) according to modern physics, it is only statistically improbable to pass through a door. That is, "physical objects are mostly empty space. All that is necessary for one object to pass through another object is the right alignment of the particles in the two physical objects." Another Christian apologetic cited by Gundry (2004, 370) was that "[T]he glory of Christ's risen body does not exclude physicality, but adorns it."

Craig's response is deficient and inadequate. Does he or anyone else truly believe if any person living in the first century either heard this story or read the narrative that he would *not* interpret the passage that Jesus literally passed through the door or wall to enter the room? Second, the "materialization" apologetic raises several questions regarding Jesus's resurrected body and, more specifically, his clothes or lack of them. For example, Eddy (1990, 328), writing in the *Expository Times*, inquired: "And what about his clothes? Did the risen Lord appear naked (that would be a considerable shock to the Jewish disciples)? If not, what was he wearing? Obviously not the garments of his earthly life, nor the graveclothes: what then? And did their material share the power to appear and disappear, and pass through closed doors?"

SPECULATION #170 John's Negative Motif on the Jews

John was the only author of a gospel to inform his readership that the disciples were assembled behind closed doors or, as the NIV and NRSV rendered, "locked." His sole explanation was "for fear of the Jews." Curiously, John omitted to inform his readership of perhaps the most important fact: why were the disciples in fear of the Jews? Here there can only be speculation. Plainly, the disciples were no threat to the Jewish or Roman leadership.

One rational explanation is that the agenda of John was theological: to continue to cast the Jewish leadership in a negative light. This motif is found numerous times in John:

> Jn 8:44-47 Ye are of your father the devil, and the lusts of your father ye will do. He was a murderer from the beginning, and abode not in the truth, because there is no truth in him. When he speaketh a lie, he speaketh of his own: for he is a liar, and the father of it. And because I tell you the truth, ye believe me not. Which of you convinceth me of sin? And if I say the truth, why do ye not believe me? He that is of God heareth God's words: ye therefore hear them not, because ye are not of God.

> Jn 10:31 Then the Jews took up stones again to stone him.

> Jn 11:53 Then from that day forth they took counsel together for to put him to death.

> Jn 18:39-40 But ye have a custom, that I should release unto you one at the passover: will ye therefore that I release unto you the King of the Jews? Then cried they all again, saying, Not this man, but Barabbas. Now Barabbas was a robber.

> Jn 19:12 And from thenceforth Pilate sought to release him: but the Jews cried out, saying, If thou let this man go, thou art not Caesar's friend: whosoever maketh himself a king speaketh against Caesar.

> Jn 19:15 But they cried out, Away with him, away with him, crucify him. Pilate saith unto them, Shall I crucify your King? The chief priests answered, We have no king but Caesar.

ISSUE 89: What Was the Disciples' Initial Response When the Disciples Saw and Heard Jesus?

Mk 16:14	Mt 28:16 Then	Lk 24:36 And as	Jn 20:19 Then the same
Afterward he appeared unto the eleven as they sat at meat, *and upbraided them with their unbelief and hardness of heart, because they believed not them which had seen him after he was risen.*	the eleven disciples went away into Galilee, into a mountain where Jesus had appointed them. 17 And when they saw him, *they worshipped him: but some doubted.*	they thus spake, Jesus himself stood in the midst of them, and saith unto them, *Peace be unto you.* 37 *But they were terrified and affrighted, and supposed that they had seen a spirit.* 38 *And he said unto them, Why are ye troubled? And why do thoughts arise in your hearts?*	day at evening, being the first day of the week, when the doors were shut where the disciples were assembled for fear of the Jews, came Jesus and stood in the midst, and saith unto them, *Peace be unto you.* 20 And when he had so said, he shewed unto them his hands and his side. *Then were the disciples glad, when they saw the Lord.*

Mark 16:14 reported: "Afterward he appeared unto the eleven as they sat at meat, and upbraided them with their unbelief and hardness of heart, because they believed not them which had seen him after he was risen." Therefore, the disciples did *not* understand and did *not* believe in Jesus's physical bodily resurrection.

In contrast, Matthew detailed only one appearance in Galilee. In Matthew 28:17 the disciples' reaction was reported: "And when they saw him, they worshipped him: but some doubted."

Luke 24:36 reported that Jesus suddenly appeared during the presentation of the report given by the two travelers who were traveling on the road. Upon appearing before the disciples, Jesus said: "Peace be unto you." Next, Luke 24:37 narrated that the disciples were "terrified and affrighted, and supposed that they had seen a spirit." Therefore, the text unequivocally supported the position that they did *not* initially believe in Jesus's physical, bodily resurrection.

Luke 24:41 also verified the fact that the disciples did not believe in Jesus's physical bodily resurrection: "And while they yet believed not for joy, and wondered, he said unto them, Have ye here any meat?" A smoother reading is from the NRSV (1989, 89): "While in their joy they were disbelieving and still wondering, he said to them." Stuhlmueller (1968, 163) clarified this point and stated: "Lk here shows himself possessed of keen psychological insight;

as the Gk text indicates, joy was so great as to leap beyond belief; lit., 'they disbelieved for joy.'"

Finally, John 20:19-20 reported that Jesus "stood in the midst" of the disciples and said, "Peace be unto you." Next, he showed them his hands and his side. "Then were the disciples glad, when they saw the Lord." The unknown is whether or not this narrative meant that the disciples believed in a physical, bodily resurrection or a spiritual resurrection.

CONTRADICTION #98 Contradictory Responses from the Disciples

Mark reported that the disciples did not believe Mary Magdalene's report that she saw Jesus. In Mark 16:12-13, two travelers reported that they too encountered the risen Jesus. Yet the disciples did not believe their report. When Jesus eventually appeared, he criticized them for their lack of belief and stubbornness. However, Mark omitted any description of the disciples' response to seeing the risen Jesus.

In contrast, Matthew 28:17 reported that some disciples doubted when they saw Jesus: "And when they saw him, they worshipped him: but some doubted." The number and identity of those who doubted is unknown.

In total disagreement to Matthew, Luke 24:37 declared that the disciples were terrified and supposed that they had seen a ghost: "But they were terrified and affrighted, and supposed that they had seen a spirit." In the following verse Luke further characterized the disciples as being troubled.

Day (2007; cf. D. Smith 2010, 757-59) offered the following speculation why the disciples were afraid. He wrote:

> The disciples were afraid because they thought they had seen a spirit, the word 'spirit' is being used as a phantom—a manifestation, a resemblance, produced by a wicked spirit, usually pretending to be the spirit of a dead person. (Luke 24:37) The disciples were aware of God's law forbidding communicating with such spirits (Leviticus 19:31; 20:6; Deuteronomy 18:10, 11), and that it was forbidden for a spirit medium to be in the land of Israel (Leviticus 20:27; Deuteronomy 18:10,11; 1 Samuel 28:7-9); thus they had reason for concern that such a spirit might appear to them. They certainly would not want to be used as a medium by such spirits.*

John's gospel stated that in a seemingly miraculous way, Jesus "stood in the midst" of the disciples and then said, "Peace be unto you." This appearance occurred despite the doors being shut. Next, "he showed them his hands and his side. Then were the disciples glad, when they saw the Lord." Consequently, the "glad" response was a secondary response. Jesus's actions following his unexpected arrival seemingly indicate that the disciples' initial response was one of shock or belief that they had seen a ghost or spirit.

SPECULATION #171 The Authenticity of Luke 24:36c

Luke reported that Jesus's first statement to his disciples was "Peace be unto you." In most modern editions of the Christian Bible, the whole of verse 36 from Luke is either omitted from the text or bracketed as doubtful. For example, the NRSV (1989, 89nd) wrote: "Other ancient authorities lack *and said to them, "Peace be with you."* Therefore, the authenticity of this verse is a matter of dispute and remains unresolved by scholars and theologians.

Carson (1991, 647) seems to favor the authenticity of this verse and pointed out that the greeting "is conventional, representing Hebrew šâlōm'alêkem, still in use today." Then Carson added: "But the repetition of the greeting (vv. 21, 26) would eventually prompt the reflective amongst them to recall that Jesus before the cross had promised to bequeath to them his peace (14:27; 16:33)."

ISSUE 90: Jesus's Response to His Disciples' Lack of Belief

| Mk 16:14 Afterward he appeared unto the eleven as they sat at meat, and *upbraided them with their unbelief and hardness of heart*, because they believed not them which had seen him after he was risen. | Mt | Lk 24:38 And he said unto them, Why are ye troubled? And why do thoughts arise in your hearts? 39 *Behold my hands and my feet, that it is I myself: handle me, and see; for a spirit hath not flesh and bones, as ye se me have.* 40 And when he had thus spoken, *he shewed them his hands and his feet.* 41 And while they believed not for joy, and wondered, he said unto them, Have ye here any meat? 42 And they gave him a piece of a broiled fish, and of an honeycomb. 43 *And he took it, and did eat before them.* | Jn 20:19 Then the same day at evening, being the first day of the week, when the doors were shut where the disciples were assembled for fear of the Jews, came Jesus and stood in the midst, and saith unto them, Peace be unto you. 20 *And when he had so said, he shewed unto them his hands and his side.* Then were the disciples glad, when they saw the Lord.

Jn 20:24 But Thomas, one of the twelve, called Didymus, was not with them when Jesus came. 25 The other disciples therefore said unto him, We have seen the Lord. But he said unto them, *Except I shall see in his hands the print of the nails, and put my finger into the print of the nails, and thrust my hand into his side, I will not believe.* 26 *And after eight days again his disciples were within, and Thomas with them: then came Jesus, the doors being shut,* and stood in the midst, and said, Peace be unto you. 27 Then saith he to Thomas, reach hither thy finger, and behold my hands; and further hither thy hand, and thrust it into my side: and be not faithless, but believing. |

Mark reported that Jesus verbally rebuked his disciples for their lack of belief and hardness of heart. However, since Matthew described only an appearance much later in Galilee, his gospel is not relevant to the issue being analyzed. In contrast, Luke and John reported that Jesus attempted to demonstrate to his disciples that he was not a ghost or a spirit by showing parts of his physical body.

Luke 24:39-43 reported that Jesus showed the disciples his hands and feet, permitted touching of his body, and later ate food (fish and honeycomb) in their presence. However, Luke did not explicitly mention if the disciples took Jesus up on his the first two offers, looking at his hands and feet and touching his body.

John 20:19-20 provided no comment about the disciples' initial reaction to seeing Jesus since he appeared suddenly in their midst and started talking. Instead, verse 20 recorded that after Jesus showed them his body, they were glad. During this meeting, Thomas was absent.

CONTRADICTION #99 Initial Contradictory Responses of Jesus to His Disciples

Mark 16:14 reported that Jesus verbally rebuked his disciples for their disbelief and hardness of heart: "Afterward he appeared unto the eleven as they sat at meat and upbraided them with their unbelief and hardness of heart, because they believed not them which had seen him after he was risen."

Matthew did not describe an initial response in Jerusalem. Neither did Matthew record Jesus's initial response to the disciples' lack of faith when it was reported that some doubted while meeting him in the Galilee.

In direct contradiction to Mark, Luke has Jesus attempting to reassure his disciples by demonstrating that he was really a physical and fully materialized person. This he tried to accomplish by showing his hands and feet and by eating.

Similar to Luke, in John, Jesus seemingly tried to allay and dispel any thought that he was not physically risen from the dead. Here, too, he showed the disciples his hands. However, Jesus did not offer to show his feet. Instead, he offered to show his side.

CONTRADICTION #100 John 20:20, 27—Jesus Showing His Hands, Feet, and Side

Luke 24:40 narrates that Jesus showed only his hands and feet to his disciples: "And when he had thus spoken, he shewed them his hands and his feet." Significantly, Luke omitted mention of any wounds borne by Jesus despite the explicit statement: "He shewed them his hands and his feet." Instead, these eight words from the King James translation create the assumption that Jesus had open wounds.

To the contrary, John 20:20 reported: "And when he had so said, he shewed unto them his hands and his side. Then were the disciples glad, when they saw the Lord." Therefore, John omitted any mention of Jesus's feet and added the detail about showing his "side." The issue that requires further consideration is John's addition to Jesus's statement (Jn 20:27), implying that he had a side wound.

The side wound was mentioned only here in John 20 because only John earlier described a Roman soldier piercing Jesus with a spear. This piercing episode was detailed in John 19:34: "But one of the soldiers with a spear pierced his side, and forthwith came there out blood and water." Without the piercing incident in John 19:34 there would not be a need for Jesus to show his side to his disciples as narrated in John 20:20. Eight days later, John 20:27 reported that Jesus again appeared to his disciples but this time with the addition of Thomas: "Then saith he to Thomas, Reach hither thy finger, and behold my hands; and reach hither thy hand, and thrust it into my side: and be not faithless, but believing." N. T. Wright (2003, 658n3) summarized the logical argument by saying that if Jesus had no wounds, he would not have invited Thomas to probe them. An alternative response to Wright is that the author of John was merely referring to what he had already written earlier.

Therefore, one purpose of John's narratives in 20:20 and 20:27 was to corroborate itself with details which seemingly created an illusion that the side-piercing episode was historical. That is, John was attempting to demonstrate that the risen Jesus and the Jesus who was crucified days earlier were one and the same. Obviously, no person living in the first-century would be able to endure a combination of wounds from a lance piercing their side along with having survived a crucifixion.

Last, it was the author of John who corroborated his own written text to fulfill a theological agenda that the events associated with Jesus's crucifixion were prophesied in the Hebrew Bible. That is, John 19:37 stated: "And again another scripture saith, They shall look on him whom they pierced." Yet no other gospel narrator reported or was seemingly aware of the wound to Jesus's side or the soldier's piercing of Jesus's side to fulfill what it said in scripture. Here, history was being replaced with theology.

SPECULATION #172 Seeing and Touching Jesus in Jerusalem

The historicity of Jesus's response to his disciples on Easter Sunday evening in Jerusalem is questioned on three grounds. First, from Luke 24:40: "And when he had thus spoken, he shewed them his hands and his feet" is missing in other ancient manuscripts (NRSV 1989, 89n*e*).

As a side issue, Hilhorst (1983, 165-66), writing in *Estudios Bíblicos*, speculated why: "Only in the Thomas narrative (discussed later), and indirectly in Jn 20:20 and Lk 24:39-40, do the wounds occur?" His research suggested that "there is a widespread conception that the deceased remained in the state in which they died: if someone died a violent death, he retained the wounds through which he died" (e.g., Homer *Od.* 11:40-41, Aeschylus *Eum.* 103, *Aeneas* 6:450, and Lucian *Nec.* 18). Consequently, Hilhorst states, "Possibly this belief that the dead retain their mortal wounds also lies behind the Thomas narratives." However, his thesis fails to address the additional wounds that Jesus must have suffered while being flogged prior to his crucifixion.

Second, this portion of the narrative was not substantiated in Mark or Matthew. Third, by increasing the number of witnesses, the argument (polemic) was stronger against potential skeptics of Jesus's resurrection. Consequently, this entire episode reads like a Christian apologetic invented to convince those who later doubted Jesus's physical, bodily resurrection.

SPECULATION #173 Jesus Eating as a Proof of a Physical Bodily Resurrection

Luke's narrative accounts of Jesus eating food provided no proof of a physical bodily resurrection to the contrary of its advocates. Geisler (1989b,14; 1987, 19) pointed out that this dining episode was the second of at least four occasions during which Jesus was described as eating (the Emmaus episode in Luke 24:30 being the first) after his resurrection. He ate later that evening with ten apostles (Lk 24:42-43; cf. Acts 10:40-41); then he had breakfast with seven apostles (Jn 21:12-13); and finally Jesus ate with the apostles just before his ascension (Acts 1:4). O'Collins (1988a, 171; 1988c, 47; cf. Fitzmyer 1985, 1575) posited that the eating of fish was another example of Luke's attempting to demonstrate the resurrection of a physical body.

Elaborating on the importance of this eating episode, Craig (1989b, 270n28; cf. Anderson 1968, 11) wrote: "Eating would be a failsafe demonstration of corporeality, for after a vision had passed, the food would remain uneaten; but after a real appearance, the food would be gone, having been consumed." Corroborating this point, Talbert (1992, 25; cf. Hannah 1999, 174), wrote: "The significance of this act for Jewish sensitivities is clear: "Angels do not eat (e.g., Tobit 12:19; Josephus *Antiquities* 1.9.2.197; Philo *On Abraham* 118); human beings do eat. For Luke, the risen Lord, no less than the pre-Easter Jesus, is flesh and bones, corporeal, truly human."

However, it is erroneous to maintain that angels do *not* eat. O'Collins (1988a, 69; Goodman 1986, 160-75) refuted the absolute notion stated above:

One should add, however, that in the Jewish tradition eating would not necessarily indicate human bodiliness, whether risen or otherwise (see, for example, Gen 19:1-4; and the mission of Raphael in Tob 3:16-12:22). In the book of Tobit the angel explains that he has not really been eating: "All these days I merely appeared to you and, did not eat or drink, but you were seeing a vision" (Tob 12:9). Nevertheless, Luke's Gentile readers would presumably hold that spirits and angels do not eat and hence be satisfied that eating the fish establishes the risen Jesus' real bodiliness.

Prince (2007, 287; cf. 2005), writing in the *Journal for the Study of the New Testament*, also dispels any notion that eating food or even being palpated were not absolute proof of one's living status. She writes:

> Another ghostly phenomenon found in literature is the reanimated corpse. Modern discussions of these stories often call them revenants, but as one scholar has noted, there is no separate word for this phenomenon in Greek literature. Not surprisingly, these apparitions also appear as they did in life. Revenants are fully palpable, and can engage in the same activities as the living. One of the most extended narratives of this type, although the extant text is not complete, is that of Philinnion, found in Phlegon's *Book of Marvels* 1 . . . . During this period of reanimation, she eats and drinks and has intercourse with the man.

Furthermore, in Genesis 18 there is the account of Abraham entertaining three visitors (angels). After greeting them, Abraham personally had food prepared for his guests. Then, Genesis 18:8 stated: "And he took butter, and milk, and the calf which he had dressed, and set it before them; and he stood by them under the tree, and they did eat." Plainly, the food disappeared. So contrary to Christian apologists, angels come in the form of men and do eat. Therefore, the eating episode provided no support for the physical, bodily resurrection of Jesus.

Finally, in the opinion of Sawicki (1994, 90; cf. 1988, 447-48), the eating motif incorporated the concept of hunger and would serve as a sure proof that it was Jesus.

> Why would hunger be a sure indication that this must be Jesus? Why should we expect the Risen Lord to be hungry? Because at the last supper, Jesus had sworn not to eat again until the reign of God. In Luke 22:15-18, Jesus said (translating literally): "With

desire I desired to eat this Seder with you before my suffer, for I'm telling you that not no more never will I eat it until it is fulfilled in the kingdom of God." Neither will he drink wine again (v. 22:18). Jesus has promised to fast until the kingdom come; so if the Risen Lord is really Jesus, he is going to be pretty hungry.

SPECULATION #174 Questions Raised about Jesus Eating

Jesus's collective eating and drinking episodes are doubtful if not outright rejected by skeptics of the Resurrection. For example, Davis (1985a, 150) wrote in the *Christian Scholar's Review*:

> Surely there are some difficult questions we are entitled to ask here. For example, was the resurrected Jesus genuinely hungry, or was he just accommodating himself to the disciples' level of understanding; i.e., was this the only way for him to prove he was not an apparition? Can "spiritual bodies" get hungry and eat? Isn't eating an aspect of earthly decay? Can ordinary food be digested by glorified bodies? For that matter, how were the atoms and molecules of Jesus' earthly body related to the atoms and molecules of his glorified body?

Similarly, Eddy (1990, 328) inquired:

> *Did* Jesus eat and drink after his resurrection? If so, what became of the food? Was it metabolized, with the obvious sequel of evacuation? And if the body, though "the same body as was crucified," was yet transformed as to be able to appear and disappear, and enter and leave a locked room, did the fish and the honeycomb undergo instant transformation along the same lines as soon as they entered his mouth?

O'Collins (1988a, 68) also raised a theological question about Jesus's new state: "Can a risen body digest food and grow?"

Geisler (1989a, 161; cf. 1989b, 14) addressed this specific issue with two possible Christian apologetics:

> Paul wrote: "Food is for the stomach and the stomach is for food; but will do away with both of them" (1 Cor. 6:13). Because of this verse it is argued that "the resurrection body will not have the anatomy or physiology of the earthly body." However, this inference

is unjustified. First, when Paul wrote that God will destroy both food and the stomach, he was referring to the *process* of death, not to the *nature* of the resurrection body. Second, while the resurrection body does not *need* to eat, it does have the *ability* to eat (Luke 24:30, 42-43; John 21:12-13; Acts 10:41; cf. Acts 1:4, NIV).

Neither of Geisler's answers sufficiently addressed Eddy's argument. Every commentary and explanation regarding Jesus eating after his reported resurrection is nothing more than mere speculation. The eating episodes appear to be legendary embellishments that served a theological agenda.

ISSUE 91: The Powers and Gift Jesus Gave to His Disciples

Mk	Mt 28:18	Lk 24:45 Then	Acts 1:5 For John	Jn 20:21 Then
16:15	And	opened he their	truly baptized with	said Jesus to them
And	Jesus	understanding, that	water; *but ye shall*	again, Peace be
he said	came and	they might understand	*be baptized with the*	unto you: as my
unto	spake	the scriptures, 46 And	*Holy Ghost not many*	Father hath sent
them,	unto	said unto them, Thus	*days hence.*	me, even so send
Go ye	them,	it is written, and thus		I you. 22 *And*
into	saying,	it behooved Christ to	Acts 2:1 *And when*	*when he had said*
all the	All power	suffer, and to rise from	*the day of Pentecost*	*this, he breathed*
world,	is given	the dead the third day:	*was fully come,* they	*on them, and saith*
and	unto me	47 *And that repentance*	were all with one	*unto them, Receive*
preach	in heaven	*and remission of sins*	accord in one place.	*ye the Holy Ghost:*
the	and in	*should be preached in his*	2 And suddenly	23 *Whose soever*
gospel	earth.	*name among all nations,*	there came a sound	*sins ye remit,*
to every	19 *Go ye*	*beginning at Jerusalem.*	from heaven as of	*they are remitted*
creature.	*therefore,*	48 And ye are witnesses	a rushing mighty	*unto them; and*
16 *He*	*and*	of these things. 49 *And,*	wind, and it filled	*whose soever sins*
that	*teach all*	*behold, I send the promise*	all the house where	*ye retain, they are*
believeth	*nations,*	*of my Father upon you:*	they were sitting. 3	*retained.*
and is	*baptizing*	*but tarry ye in the city*	And there appeared	
baptized	*them in*	*of Jerusalem, until ye*	unto them cloven	
shall be	*the name*	*be endued with power*	tongues like as of	
saved;	*of the*	*from on high.* 50 And	fire, and it sat upon	
but he	*Father,*	he led them out as far	each of them. 4 *And*	
that	*and of*	as to Bethany, and he	*they were all filled*	
believeth	*the Son,*	lifted up his hands, and	*with the Holy Ghost,*	
not	*and of*	blessed them. 51 And	and began to speak	
shall be	*the Holy*	it came to pass, while	with other tongues,	
damned.	*Ghost:*	he blessed them, he was	as the Spirit gave	
		parted from them, and	them utterance.	
		carried up into heaven.		

John 20:23 reported that immediately prior to the Doubting Thomas episode, Jesus bequeathed unto his disciples two powers: the power to forgive sins as well as the power to withhold forgiveness. In addition, he granted his disciples the blessing to receive the Holy Ghost.

CONTRADICTION #101 John versus the Three Synoptics and Acts

Perhaps one of the most important ideas taught in John is that the apostles had the power to remit the sins of "whose soever sins."

> John 20:23 If you forgive the sins of any, they are forgiven them;
> if you retain the sins of any, they are retained (NRSV 1989, 113).

> John 20:23 If you forgive anyone his sins, they are forgiven; if
> you do not forgive them, they are not forgiven (NIV 1978, 1225).

Mark 16:16 instructed: "He that believeth and is baptized shall be saved; but he that believeth not shall be damned." Therefore, no power delegating the apostles to forgive sins was mentioned or implied. Instead the power was in the hands of the sinner to be saved by believing and being baptized.

Matthew 28:18 reported that Jesus claimed: "And Jesus came and spake unto them, saying, All power is given unto me in heaven and in earth." Here, too, no power to remit sins was given to the apostles. Instead Jesus instructed that his apostles: "Go ye therefore, and teach all nations, baptizing them in the name of the Father, and of the Son, and of the Holy Ghost."

Luke reads similar to Matthew. Luke 24:47 declared: "And that repentance and remission of sins should be preached in his name among all nations, beginning at Jerusalem." Consequently, here, too, *no* power to remit sins was given to the apostles. Rather, they were commanded to *teach* all the nations.

In Acts 1:5, Jesus informed his disciples prior to his ascension: "For John truly baptized with water; but ye shall be baptized with the Holy Ghost not many days hence." However, being baptized with the Holy Ghost has nothing to do with having the power to forgive sins.

Occasionally there are those instances where it seems inconceivable that some event or concept is omitted from the synoptic narrations and is present in John. This is one of those instances. Not even one of the synoptic writers or the author of Acts discussed the notion that the apostles had the unique power to forgive sins.

CONTRADICTION #102 When the Disciples Received the Holy Ghost

Léon-Dufour (1971, 213), a Catholic apologist, pointed out that "there is a further conflict between John 20:22, where the Spirit is given on Easter day, and Acts 1:4 or Luke 24:49, which promise it on the day of Pentecost." Acts 1 reads:

> Acts 1:3 To whom also he shewed himself alive after his passion by many infallible proofs, being seen of them *forty days*, and speaking of the things pertaining to the kingdom of God:

> Acts 1:4 And, being assembled together with them, commanded them that *they should not depart from Jerusalem, but* wait for the promise of the Father, which, saith he, ye have heard of me.

> Acts 1:5 For John truly baptized with water; *but ye shall be baptized with the Holy Ghost not many days hen*ce.

Therefore, Acts 1:3 reported that this message given by Jesus to his disciples occurred forty days *after* his resurrection. However, the "many days hence" in Acts 1:5 occurred on Pentecost, an additional ten days later (i.e., fifty days after Easter Sunday, see Acts 2:1-4).

> Acts 2:1 And when the day of Pentecost was fully come, they were all with one accord in one place.

> Acts 2:2 And suddenly there came a sound from heaven as of a rushing mighty wind, and it filled all the house where they were sitting.

> Acts 2:3 And there appeared unto them cloven tongues like as of fire, and it sat upon each of them.

> Acts 2:4 And they were all filled with the Holy Ghost, and began to speak with other tongues, as the Spirit gave them utterance.

Furthermore, the author of Acts said that the Father would give the apostles the Holy Ghost *after* Jesus departed. The same author in Luke 24:49 reported that Jesus told them: "And, behold, I send the promise of my Father upon you: but tarry ye in the city of Jerusalem, until ye be endued with power from on high."

In contradiction, John's narrative stated:

> Jn 20:21 Then said Jesus to them again, Peace be unto you: as my Father hath sent me, even so send I you.

> Jn 20:22 And when he had said this, he *breathed on them, and saith unto them, Receive ye the Holy Ghost*:

Therefore, according to John this receiving of the Holy Ghost occurred on "then the same day at evening, being the first day of the week" (v. 19) (i.e., Easter Sunday).

Kaiser, Davids, Bruce, and Brauch (1996, 508-10), writing in *Hard Sayings of the Bible*, offer three Christian apologetic approaches to these verses:

1. "We have a symbolic presentation [[For example in John 14:18]] of what Acts speaks of as a later event. Symbolism is the way of John." That is, "one is historical and the other symbolic." Therefore, "The events may symbolize something (as the raising of Lazarus symbolizes the final resurrection), but they are viewed in themselves as historical."
2. "John presents one type of giving of the Spirit and Acts as another." For example, "John is the impersonal breath of God and Acts is the personal Holy Spirit. John is a sprinkling with the grace of the Spirit and Acts is full empowerment, saturation with the Spirit. John is the Spirit as new life and Acts is the Spirit as empowerment for ministry."
3. John 20:22 looks "as Jesus' symbolic giving or promising the Spirit, which was experientially received on Pentecost . . . For Luke there is no need to mention any previous symbolic giving, for Jesus refers to the promise of the Spirit before his ascension (Acts 1:4-5). Luke is concerned with the reality of the power and how it directs the mission of the church."

What can one say after reading these responses? Obviously these apologists have no concrete or tangible means to explain these unequivocal contradictions other than guesses, hunches, and wishful speculations. What they offer are excuses for an inconvenient truth that these contradictory texts are not reconcilable. Furthermore, Kaiser et al. candidly refuted several of their own apologetics:

1. The first apologetic is rejected because "the disciples do not go out and witness after receiving the Spirit. In fact, they cannot even convince Thomas (Jn 20:24-25). What is more, Thomas would then appear never to receive the Spirit."

2. The second apologetic is rejected because "neither John nor Acts seems to know about two receptions of the Spirit . . . . Thus this approach seems to be an explanation imposed on the texts by the people who read both Acts and John rather than something that either Luke or John thought of."

These Christian apologists concluded their attempt to harmonize these conflicting texts with the following advice: "It will remain for the reader to decide which of these approaches is the most satisfying in that it best fits the data of the texts in question. What is more important than harmonizing the texts is recognizing that both John and Acts do indeed insist that the Holy Spirit is needed for the mission of the church."

Deconstructing this synopsis, these Christian apologists first recommend to go with the most satisfying approach. In other words, the fact that the texts are contradictory is irrelevant. Strangely, they are recommending that one just go with what makes one feel best and avoid the fundamental truth that these texts are contradictory. Second, they subtly and cleverly advise their readers that harmonization of these texts is not the important thing. Instead, they divert the reader to recognize the need of the Holy Spirit for the mission of the church. In other words, *the truth is less important and the word is not as important as the mission of the church.* The fact that these Christian apologists candidly do *not* even recognize the supreme importance of "the truth" and "the word" speaks volumes. Without truth, the church mission can only stand on falsehood.

Perhaps the comment of J. Martin C. Scott (2003, 1209), writing in *John: Eerdmans Commentary on the Bible,* bears consideration: "Despite all the tortuous efforts of scholars to harmonize Acts 2 and John 20:22 (cf. Witherington 1995, 340-41) this is the FE's [Fourth Evangelist's] representation of what Luke describes in terms equally dependent on the imagery of the Jewish scriptures. Even a scholar as conservative as Carson [[1991, 655]] thinks that John's description is 'best understood as a kind of acted parable.'"

In summary John had the disciples receive the Holy Ghost on Easter Sunday evening and Acts 1:4 records that the disciples become recipients of the Holy Ghost on Pentecost. Here there is an incontrovertible contradiction.

CONTRADICTION #103 John Contradicts John—Who Will Send the Holy Ghost?

There is an internal conflict in John regarding who would send the Holy Ghost to the disciples. John 20:22 reported that Jesus breathed on his disciples Easter Sunday evening and said: "Receive ye the Holy Ghost." Therefore, it is Jesus who sent the Holy Ghost. This action of Jesus directly sending the Holy Ghost was also promised earlier by Jesus in John 16:7: "Nevertheless I tell you the truth; It is expedient for you that I go away: for if I go not away, the Comforter will not come unto you; *but if I depart, I will send him unto you.*"

However, even earlier John 14:26 quoted Jesus as saying that it was none other than God the Father who would send the Holy Ghost to the disciples: "But the Comforter, *which is the Holy Ghost, whom the Father will send in my name*, he shall teach you all things, and bring all things to your remembrance, whatsoever I have said unto you."

Thus, in John 14:26, "the Father" sends the Comforter whereas in John 16:7 (later substantiated by John 20:22), "Jesus himself" would send the Comforter. Christian apologists could, of course, point out that Jesus himself would send the Holy Ghost, acting as a mediator between God the Father and the disciples. However, either Jesus was sending the Comforter or the Father was sending the Comforter.

Another Christian apologetic based on John 17:23 is that the Holy Ghost was sent by the Father in the name of Jesus the Son: This verse reads: "I in them, and thou in me, that they may be made perfect in one; and that the world may know that thou hast sent me, and hast loved them, as thou hast loved me." This passage means that "they" both sent it as they are both intimately connected to the Spirit in the triune Godhead.

This Christian apologetic is built on the premise that the essence of God exists as a Trinity: the Son, the Father, and the Holy Ghost. The problem for Christian apologists is that Jesus and the Father are not the same thing. Christian apologists may wish to respond that the Son, the Father, and the Holy Ghost (the Holy Spirit) are one essence, but an essence is not the same thing as a thing.

ISSUE 92: The Doubting Thomas Affair

1 Cor 15:5 And	Mk	Mt	Lk	Jn 20:24 But Thomas, one of the twelve, called
that he was				Didymus, was not with them when Jesus came. 25
seen of Cephas,				The other disciples therefore said unto him, We
then of the				have seen the Lord. But he said unto them, *Except I*
twelve: 6 After				*shall see in his hands the print of the nails, and put my*
that, he was				*finger into the print of the nails, and thrust my hand*
seen of above				*into his side, I will not believe.* 26 And after eight
five hundred				*days again his disciples were within, and Thomas*
brethren at				*with them: then came Jesus, the doors being shut,* and
once; of whom				stood in the midst, and said, Peace be unto you. 27
the greater part				Then saith he to Thomas, reach hither thy finger,
remain unto				and behold my hands; and further hither thy hand,
this present, but				and thrust it into my side: and be not faithless,
some are fallen				but believing. *28 And Thomas answered and said*
asleep. 7 After				*unto him, My Lord and my God. 29 Jesus saith unto*
that, he was seen				*him, Thomas, because thou hast seen me, thou hast*
of James; *then of*				*believed; blessed are they that have not seen, and yet*
all the apostles.				*have believed.*

John 20:19 reported that eight days after Jesus's first post-resurrection appearance to his eleven disciples he once again appeared at the same locale in Jerusalem and the doors were shut. Therefore, by inclusive reckoning, this narrative placed the new meeting, like the first, on a Sunday evening. It also indicated that the disciples stayed in Jerusalem for the entire Passover. During this visit Thomas was now present.

After Thomas arrived the other disciples informed him that they had actually seen Jesus. Thomas declared that he did not believe his fellow disciples and would not believe them except if he could (1) see the nail marks on Jesus's hand, (2) put his finger where the nails were, and (3) put his hand in Jesus's side. Hence the development of the phrase: "the Doubting Thomas." Bonney (1997, 259) posited that "Thomas's words in 20:25 are more likely a sarcastic expression of disbelief than a request for proof . . . He does not demand to see it."

One verse later, John 20:20 reported that Jesus suddenly appeared in their midst. Here Jesus's command to Thomas corresponded almost verbatim to Thomas's prescribed requisites. Also, verse 26 exactly repeated verse 19 in four details: (1) the disciples are again assembled, (2) the doors are shut, (3) Jesus seems to appear almost mysteriously in their mists, and (4) Jesus responds "Peace be unto you." However, this time Thomas was present.

Skinner (2008, 92) pointed out that in verse 27, Jesus's words to Thomas included five imperatives in rapid succession. The first four were affirmative: (1) extend or reach your finger, (2) behold my hands, (3) extend your hand, and (4) thrust it into my side. The final imperative was a negative: "Be not faithless but believing."

John did not report whether or not Thomas actually responded to the invitation to either examine or touch (physically probe) Jesus's wounds (Brown 1990b, 205). Instead John 20:28 reported that Thomas responded, "My Lord and my God." Jesus then replied by declaring: "blessed are they who have not seen and yet believed" (v. 29).

Perhaps, commentators have unfairly dubbed this disciple the Doubting Thomas. After all, Thomas requested virtually no more than his fellow disciples received from Jesus eight days earlier. Furthermore, unlike the disciples who merely described as "glad, when they saw the Lord," Thomas declared, "My Lord and my God."

Finally, Goodman (2009, 11) points out in defense of Thomas that he was "the only one of the disciples not locked away in fear, the only one of the disciples on that third evening after the crucifixion not hiding out in the upper room. And what he was doing we don't know, but it may well have been that he was getting food and water to sustain the disciples during their indefinite stay behind those bolted doors."

SPECULATION #175 Thomas Putting His Hand Inside of God

According to many Christian apologists and evangelicals, Thomas declared that Jesus was Almighty God in the absolute sense. In other words, Jesus's essence is the same as God the Father, and therefore Jesus is the Creator of all space and time. On Easter Sunday evening, ten disciples (except Judas and Thomas) plus the two travelers on the road to Emmaus were present when Jesus suddenly appeared in their midst and conversed with them. Eventually Jesus departed. Later, after an unspecified length of time, the disciples reported to Thomas that Jesus had appeared to them. However, Thomas refused to accept their testimony unless he saw and experienced verifiable proof: (1) saw nail marks on Jesus's hand, (2) placed his fingers in the marks, and (3) placed his hand inside of Jesus's side.

Presumably, Thomas also heard the women's report either directly from them or his fellow male compatriots. However, it is significant to note that even the addition of the empty tomb reported by Peter, the other disciple whom Jesus loved, and the women was insufficient evidentiary proof to convince

Thomas that Jesus had risen from the dead. It would seem that during the next week Thomas had sufficient time to reflect, probe, and question his fellow disciples, the two travelers on the road, and the women that Jesus had, in fact, risen from the dead. Thomas also had time to contemplate the numerous miracles he had heard or actually witnessed that Jesus performed during the past three years and even investigate the empty tomb.

One week later, on Sunday evening, Jesus reappeared and offered Thomas the opportunity to probe his wounds. The text is unclear as to whether or not Thomas took up the challenge to "reach hither thy hand, and thrust it into my side" (Jn 20:27). In the opinion of Dunn (2003, 851), it is a significant fact "that John does not actually describe Thomas as putting finger or hand in Jesus' wound."

Does it seem credible for a first-century Jew (presumably Thomas) to believe that Almighty God, the Creator of the entire universe, and the Creator of all space and time would permit Himself to be brutally humiliated and eventually crucified by Roman soldiers? Or does it seem remotely credible for a first-century Jew (also presumably Thomas) to believe that Almighty God, the Creator of the entire universe, and the Creator of all space and time would permit Thomas, to place a human finger or hand inside of Himself (i.e., Almighty God)? At this time it is assumed that the concept of a Trinity did not exist and, more specifically, that Jesus was God incarnate in human flesh. Nonetheless, this is what Christian apologists and evangelists proclaim. That is, that Almighty God permitted Thomas to place his finger or hand literally inside of God incarnate, in human flesh, and immediately following Thomas declared that Jesus was God. This presumption is rejected by this text.

SPECULATION #176 Refutation of D. A. Carson's Doubting Thomas Hypothesis

In 2010, D. A. Carson published his *Scandalous: the Cross and Resurrection of Jesus*. Chapter 5, "Doubting the Resurrection of Jesus: John 20:24-31," dealt extensively with the apostle Thomas. According to Carson (2010a, 149), Thomas was (1) a devout first-century Jew, (2) a believer in the God of the Bible what Christians call the Old Testament, and (3) an advocate that the God of the Old Testament performed miracles from time to time. These assumptions are presumptuous and pure speculation. Thomas's name occurs only twelve times in the Christian scriptures, of which five were used in the Doubting Thomas episode. (See table 65.)

TABLE 65. Twelve References of Thomas

SOURCE	VERSE	ANALYSIS	
Mk 3:18	And Andrew, and Philip, and Bartholomew, and Matthew, and Thomas, and James the son of Alphaeus, and Thaddaeus, and Simon the Canaanite,	Fact 1: Thomas is identified as one of the apostles.	
		Fact 2: Earlier in verse14 Mark reported that "he [[Jesus]] ordained twelve, that they should be with him and might send them forth to preach."	
Mt 10:3	Philip, and Bartholomew; Thomas, and Matthew the publican; James the son of Alphaeus, and Lebbaeus, whose surname was Thaddaeus;	Fact 1: Thomas is identified as one of the apostles.	
		Fact 2: In verse 1, Matthew reported that, "And when he [[Jesus]] had called upon him his twelve disciples, he gave them power against unclean spirits, to cast them out, and to heal all matter of sickness and all manner of disease."	
Lk 6:15	Matthew and Thomas, James the son of Alphaeus, and Simon called Zelotes	Fact 1: Thomas is identified as one of the apostles.	
		Fact 2: Earlier in verse 13 Luke implied that Thomas was an apostle.	
Jn 11:16	Then said Thomas, which is called Didymus, unto his fellow disciples, Let us also go, that we may die with him	Fact 1: Thomas is a twin.	
		Fact 2: Thomas is a disciple.	
Jn 14:5	Thomas saith unto him, Lord, we know not whither thou goest; and how can we know the way?	Fact 1: Thomas employed the Greek word κυριε or kurios which means lord or master. In this instance, there is no reference to divinity.	
		Fact 2: Thomas asked Jesus a question.	
Jn 20:24	But Thomas, one of the twelve, called Didymus, was not with them when Jesus came.	Fact 1: Thomas was one of the disciples not present when Jesus appeared on Easter Sunday evening.	
		Fact 2: Thomas was called Didymus.	

Jn 20:25 [Note: The word "he" is used instead of the name Thomas.]	The other disciples therefore said unto him, We have seen the Lord. But he said unto them, Except I shall see in his hands the print of the nails, and put my finger into the print of the nails, and thrust my hand into his side, I will not believe.	Fact 1: Thomas did *not* believe the report offered by the disciples. Fact 2: Thomas demanded physical proof before he would believe the report of the other disciples.
Jn 20:26	And after eight days again his disciples were within, and Thomas with them: then came Jesus, the doors being shut, and stood in the midst, and said, Peace be unto you.	Fact 1: It was eight days later. Fact 2: Jesus appears and said, "Peace be unto you."
Jn 20:27	Then saith he to Thomas, Reach hither thy finger, and behold my hands; and reach hither thy hand, and thrust it into my side: and be not faithless, but believing.	Fact 1: Jesus talked to Thomas. Fact 2: Thomas was either commanded or offered the opportunity to put his finger where the nails were and to thrust his hand into Jesus's side.
Jn 20:28	And Thomas answered and said unto him, My Lord and my God.	Fact 1: Thomas answered Jesus. Fact 2: Thomas declared, "My Lord and my God." Fact 3: Thomas did *not* declare that Jesus was Almighty God.
Jn 20:29	Jesus saith unto him, Thomas, because thou hast seen me, thou hast believed: blessed are they that have not seen, and yet have believed.	Fact 1: Jesus is *not* complimenting Thomas. Fact 2: Scholars differ in their interpretation about what Thomas believed. Fact 3: Jesus declared, "blessed are they that have not seen, and yet have believed." This statement excluded Thomas being blessed.
Jn 21:2	There were together Simon Peter, and Thomas called Didymus, and Nathanael of Cana in Galilee, and the sons of Zebedee, and two other of his disciples.	Fact 1: Thomas is fishing with six other disciples. Fact 2: There is no comment about Thomas's beliefs or character prior to this meeting.

| Acts 1:13 | And when they were come in, they went up into an upper room, where abode both Peter, and James, and John, and Andrew, Philip, and Thomas, Bartholomew, and Matthew, James the son of Alphaeus, and Simon Zelotes, and Judas the brother of James. | Fact 1: Thomas and the other disciples [presumably missing Judas] are in a room. |
| | | Fact 2: There is no comment about Thomas's beliefs or character prior to this meeting. |

Not once in the Christian scriptures is there an unequivocal description of Thomas's beliefs or character as stated and embellished by Carson. The importance of these omissions is elaborated below.

Next, Carson went on to argue that Thomas's declaration was an affirmation that Jesus was Almighty God. In support of this position he rejected any notion that Thomas's statement was "an ejaculation of sheer surprise" (p. 154). Carson's argument is that Thomas's first response "My God! my Lord!" was blasphemy. He elaborated:

> Every culture, of course, develops its own forms of vulgarity, profanity, and blasphemy. But it is just about unthinkable to imagine that a devout Jew like Thomas would take on his lips the word "God" as a profane exclamation. But worse, even if we could somehow imagine that Thomas would blaspheme in this way, it would then seem that Jesus approves the blasphemy, since he approves Thomas' words in the next verse.

> No, the text must be taken at face value. Thomas, a first-century monotheistic Jew, addresses Jesus, the resurrected Jesus, with the stunning confession, "My Lord and my God."

Carson's apologetic has several deficiencies. First, Carson did not define or describe what a "devout Jew" is. Second, there is no evidence that in any of the twelve times that Thomas was referred to in the Christian scriptures that he was a "devout" Jew. All we know is that Thomas was a Jewish disciple of Jesus. Thus, Carson cannot claim that it would have been unthinkable to imagine that a devout Jew like Thomas would take on his lips the word "God" as a profane exclamation. This statement is pure speculation.

Second, there is no support for Carson's claim that Thomas was "a first-century monotheistic Jew." For the sake of argument, perhaps Thomas was a proponent of monolatry or henotheism. Monolatry is the recognition of the existence of many gods but with the consistent worship of only one deity.

In contrast, henotheism is not the same thing as monolatry, which is the belief in and worship of one god without at the same time denying that other people can with equal truth worship different gods. Then again, perhaps Thomas had not even worked out in his mind a theological position of what is monotheism. Significantly, it must be remembered that first-century Judaism was *not* monolithic in its beliefs.

Finally, Carson (pp. 155, 161) offered an interesting thought. He wrote:

> We must place Thomas within the framework of the larger narrative of John's Gospel. An entire week passes between verse 25 and verse 26. Verse 26 carefully notes that Jesus appeared to Thomas a week after Thomas had expressed his doubt. One can easily imagine the nature of the probing reflections that occupied his mind and imagination throughout that week: "Jesus alive? It can't be! But the other ten are so very sure. They simply have to be mistaken. But suppose they're not? Is it possible that Jesus really is alive? What would that mean? No, it can't be. I need some evidence. He can't possibly be alive. But suppose that he is."

> How does one put all such pieces together? Thomas had an entire week to mull the matter over. Doubtless he still could not put together what would later be called the doctrine of the Trinity. But he had progressed far enough in his understanding to grasp that if Jesus was truly alive, this was more, even, than a spectacular resurrection: it was the visitation of God Almighty.

Thomas had one week to reflect, probe, and meditate on the claim of his fellow disciples that Jesus had risen. He also had time to contemplate the numerous miracles he had heard about or actually witnessed. And yes, Thomas also had one week to examine God's words recorded in the Hebrew Bible. When Thomas eventually saw Jesus, he exclaimed, "My Lord, my God." Christian evangelists claim that Thomas unequivocally declared that Jesus was Almighty God in the absolute sense.

Does it seem comprehensible for a first-century, monotheistic, and devout Jew to believe that Almighty God, the Creator of the entire universe and the Creator of all space and time, would contract His total essence into a frail human body, the body of Jesus the son of Mary?

Does it seem credible for a first-century, monotheistic, and devout Jew to believe that Almighty God, the Creator of the entire universe and the Creator of all space and time, would permit Himself to be brutally humiliated and eventually crucified by Roman soldiers? For Christian apologists and evangelists to claim that Thomas's declaration affirmed that Jesus was Almighty God in the absolute sense is a matter of belief and faith. However, it is *not* a fact.

Nowhere in the Hebrew Bible is there the slightest hint or suggestion that God, as an act of grace, would permit Himself as God incarnate in human flesh to be brutally humiliated and eventually crucified by Roman soldiers.

Finally, Casey (2010, 487) rejects the claim by conservative Christians that the Doubting Thomas affair was credible. He wrote: "It presupposes that the deity of Jesus, totally absent from the synoptic writers and in conflict with Jesus' Jewish identity, was confessed at a Resurrection appearance, and somehow never passed on by any of the disciples to any of the synoptic writers. This is not historically plausible." [Readers are encouraged to examine Uriel ben-Mordechai's text" *If? The End of the Messianic Lie* (Jerusalem: Above and Beyond, 2011), 402-414. Perhaps, this text offers the most intelligent presentation that refutes the idea that Thomas was declaring that Jesus was divine.]

SPECULATION #177 Thomas and the Gift of the Holy Ghost

C. H. Dodd (1963, 148n2) raised the issue that the author of John 20:22 informed his readers that eight days earlier Jesus breathed on the other disciples and said unto them: "Receive ye the Holy Ghost." Then Dodd continued: "The literal-minded interpreter might ask himself, Did Thomas, then, alone of the apostles, have no share in the gift of the Spirit, and was he alone not given authority in the Church, since he was absent on the crucial occasion?"

SPECULATION #178 Why Is It on the Eighth Day?

John 20:26 reported that Jesus reappeared eight days after his previous appearance: "And after eight days again his disciples were within, and Thomas with them: then came Jesus, the doors being shut, and stood in the midst, and said, Peace be unto you." N. T. Wright (2003, 669) posited: "Now on the eighth day, comes the eighth sign; the sequence was always about the new creation bursting in on the old." These eight signs include the following:

1. Water into wine (2.1-11)
2. The official's son (4.46-54)
3. The paralyzed man at the pool (5.2-9)
4. Multiplication of loaves (6.1-14)

5. The man born blind (9.1-7)
6. The raising of Lazarus (11.1-44)
7. The crucifixion (19.1-37)
8. The resurrection (20.1-29)

In many cultures and religions, numbers convey symbolic meanings. For example, Saint Augustine (cited in Just 2003, 306) espoused that the significance of the number eight was related to Jesus's resurrection: "The Lord's day is called the first of the Sabbath (Mk 16:2; Mt 28:1). But the first day itself falls away when the second follows it. That day, both the eighth and the first, represents eternity."

In the Jewish tradition the number eight indicates something "transcendental," a plane above nature, and beyond the "world of physicality." Examples include the following:

- Eight people went in and out of Noah's ark (Gen 7:7; 10:1).
- A Jewish boy is circumcised on the eighth day (Gen 17:12).
- Eight people escaped Sodom and Gomorrah (Gen 19).
- Abraham had eight sons (Gen 25:1-4, 12, 19).
- The tabernacle was first inaugurated on the eighth day (after seven days of preparation) (Ex 40; Num 7).
- The high priest wore eight holy vestments (Ex 28).
- On the eighth day of dedication the Tabernacle was finally erected, and Moses officiated and offered the communal sacrifices (Ex 40:29)
- On the eighth day a leper made an atonement for his ritual/spiritual uncleanness (Lev 15:10).
- On the eighth day a man made an atonement for his ritual uncleanness due to a discharge (Lev 15:14).
- On the eighth day a woman made an atonement for her ritual uncleanness due to a discharge of blood (Lev 15:30).
- From the eighth day after their birth onward, animals could be offered as sacrifices in the Temple (Lev 27:27).
- The holy convocation of Shemini Atzeret occurred the day after the seventh day of Sukkoth (Lev 23:36). Shemini Atzeret literally means "the assembly of the eighth (day)."
- Eight musical instruments accompanied the psalms of the Levites during the service (i.e., seven instruments and the choir).
- The eight steps of the staircase lead to the external square of the Ezekiel's temple (Ez 40:26).
- David was the eighth son of Jesse (1 Sam 16:6-11; 1 Sam 17:12).

Coincidentally it should be noted that the numerology of Jesus's name in Greek is 888.

> Using the Greek Ionic Ciphered Numeral System scientifically proves this. In this system, each letter of the Greek alphabet is assigned a numerical value. The name of Jesus in Greek is spelled *I H S O U S* (*iota, eta, sigma, omicron, upsilon, sigma*). Substituting in the Greek numeral system the equivalent numerical values to each letter in the name of Jesus and adding them up, the total is 888. The values of each letter are: *iota*, 10; *eta*, 8; *sigma*, 200; *omicron*, 70; *upsilon*, 400; *sigma*, 200. The sum of 10 + 8 + 200 + 70 + 400 + 200 is 888.

Ferguson (1996, 237; cf. Hendricksen 1953, 465), writing in his *The Church of Christ: A Biblical Ecclesiology for Today*, also discusses another possible interpretation of the number eight. He writes:

> Another designation reflecting the custom of numbering the days of the week was "eighth day." The terminology probably originated in a Hellenized Jewish-Christian context where there was a desire to "trump" the Jewish usage that made the Sabbath the climax of the week. It lent itself also to a typological interpretation of "eighth day" in the Old Testament. It is doubtful that the reference to "eight days" in John 20:26 influenced the usage, but it is possible that the passage reflects the same background that led to the adoption of this description. More likely, the passage simply reflects the ancient practice of inclusive numbering according to which the second "first day of the week" would be the "eighth day." The special reason for the adoption of the terminology of "eighth day," however, seems to have been a Hellenistic context where the number eight was a symbol for the heavenly world and the age to come, a symbolism adopted in Jewish apocalyptic writings. Eschatological symbolism made "eighth day" particularly appropriate for the day of the resurrection. As a somewhat more learned, if not esoteric, term this name had a limited currency.

The unknown is whether or not the author of John or his intended readership were aware of the significance of the number eight or if the author employed this number based on the number eight motif in the Hebrew Bible or other traditions.

SPECULATION #179 Jesus Criticized Thomas

Christian apologists contend that Jesus's words in John 20:29 should not be taken as a rebuke. Campbell's (2000, 180-82) review of the literature identified at least three arguments: A negative view of signs-based faith does not exist in the gospel. Since all of Jesus's followers miss the meaning of the crucifixion and empty tomb, it seems strange that Jesus would reprimand only Thomas without reprimanding the other disciples as well. The blessing itself does not convey a sense of rebuke.

Contrary to Christian apologists, it should be recognized that Jesus's statement to Thomas was not a compliment; it was, in fact, a criticism. Jesus was criticizing Thomas for his disbelief and requirement to have a physical verification to support the certainty in the "Risen Lord." Therefore, Jesus declared that those who wanted to only trust their own sight were limited to their own disadvantage whereas "blessed are they that have not seen, and yet have believed." Elaborating this point, Campbell (2000, 181) cites Hendriksen (1953-54, 2:464-65) and Johns and Miller (1994, 532-33) that Thomas is reprimanded because he not only *demands* to see a sign; but unlike the other disciples, "Thomas vocalizes his need for a sign while the other disciples do not." Here there was *no* accolade, honor, or praise of Thomas!

SPECULATION #180 John's Agenda in the Doubting Thomas Episode

What then was the purpose of the famous "Doubting Thomas" story? The purpose of this episode was purely apologetic and theological. Jesus promised that he would return soon. It has now been almost sixty to seventy years after the Crucifixion. By this time many people have started to seriously doubt the Second Coming.

Plainly the story was intended to promote faith in John's readers who did not see Jesus but were perhaps waiting *less* patiently for his return. For that reason, Bater (1969, 60), writing in the journal *Interpretation*, stated that "it is likely that the account is directed squarely at the problem of doubt in the church of John's day." Another possible explanation is that the story of the appearance to Thomas was authored to prove that to believe because one has seen is to be blessed, but that one is far more blessed to believe when one has *not* seen.

The topic of belief is perhaps one of the most important themes found in John and especially here in the Doubting Thomas episode. Elaborating on this topic, N. T. Wright (2003, 669) succinctly wrote: "The cognate verb 'believe' (*pisteuein*) occurs more in this gospel than in Matthew, Mark and

Luke put together; and, perhaps even more surprising, more than in all of Paul's letters put together. The concordance lists ninety-nine occurrences, spread over every chapter in the book except 15, 18, and (oddly) 21."

Three additional apologetic purposes possibly included the following:

1. "It is highly probable (though not certain) that the story grew, that many of the early Christians believed the resurrection to be a spiritual process, and that the story of Thomas was, among others, an imaginative presentation of a supposed fact which could be used to silence an opinion that was dangerous to the Church" [[i.e., Docetism]] (Gorham 1908, 179).

2. "To many minds nothing is more impressive than the conversion of an honest doubter" (Gorham 1908, 179).

3. Wolfe (1989, 128-29) posited that "the nailing and spearing evidently were derived by John from Psalm 22:16 (17 in Hebrew) and Zechariah 12:10 under the erroneous supposition that those passages were prophetically describing the crucifixion of Jesus, and under the further assumption that the crucifixion procedures followed those prophecies meticulously. Since this process of reasoning is now seen to be wholly fallacious, and there is no support for nailing or side stabbing in the Synoptic Gospels, it is fairly certain that these can be dismissed as latter fictions."

In conclusion, John's agenda was promoting *blind* faith in a risen Jesus, as well as the fact that he was the embodiment of God. Furthermore, the Doubting Thomas episode was written to fulfill a theological agenda. In this episode of the Christian scriptures, there is no historicity.

ISSUE 93: Jesus Showing Signs

Mk 8:11 And the Pharisees came forth, and began to question with him, seeking of him a sign from heaven, tempting him.	Mt	Lk	Acts 2:22 Ye men of Israel, hear these words; *Jesus of Nazareth, a man approved of God among you by miracles and wonders and signs, which God did by him in the midst of you, as ye yourselves also know*:	Jn 20:30 *And in many other signs truly did Jesus in the presence of the disciples, which are not written in this book.* But these are written, that ye might believe that Jesus is the Christ, the Son of God; and that believing ye might have life through his name.
Mk 8:12 And he sighed deeply in his spirit, and saith, Why doth this generation seek after a sign? verily *I say unto you, There shall no sign be given unto this generation.*				Jn 21:25 *And there are also many other things which Jesus did, the which, if they should be written every one, I suppose that even the world itself could not contain the books that should be written.* Amen.

John 20:30 reported that Jesus performed many additional signs (miracles) in the presence of his disciples that were not written in his book. The purpose of these signs was to help people to believe in Jesus. In John 21 it was also reported that Jesus performed many other things that were not recorded. Yet in Acts 2:22, Peter addressed a crowd declaring that Jesus proved himself by deeds of power, wonders, and signs that God did through him that they knew.

CONTRADICTION #104 The Number of Signs and Who Witnessed the Signs

John 20:30 stated that Jesus performed many signs in the presence of his disciples that were not recorded. John 21:25 repeated this concept that Jesus did many other things that were not recorded: "And there are also many other things which Jesus did, the which, if they should be written every one, I suppose that even the world itself could not contain the books that should be written. Amen."

The word "signs" (Gr. *Semeion*) appears in the AV seventy-seven times: sign, fifty; miracle, twenty-three; wonder, three, and token, one. Strong's number G4592 (Strong 1890, 65) matches the Greek: "an *indication*, espec. cer. or supernat.: —miracle, sign, token, wonder." Similarly, Thayer's *Greek-English Lexicon* (1886, 573) states: *a sign, mark, token*; 1. univ. that by which a person or a thing is distinguished from others and is known... 2. *a sign, prodigy, portent*, i.e. an unusual occurrence, transcending the common course of nature; a. of signs portending remarkable events soon to happen...b. of miracles and wonders by which God authenticates the men sent by him, or by which men prove that the cause they are pleading is God's..."

Earlier, Mark 8:11-12 reported that Jesus was confronted verbally by several Pharisees. They challenged Jesus to prove himself. Jesus responded that *no* sign would be given to that generation:

> Mk 8:11 And the Pharisees came forth, and began to question with him, seeking of him a sign from heaven, tempting him.

> Mk 8:12 And he sighed deeply in his spirit, and saith, Why doth this generation seek after a sign? verily I say unto you, There shall no sign be given unto this generation.

The unknown is the type of sign that the Pharisees were requesting to see and the type of sign that Jesus was referring to such as: (1) Messianic, (2) pre-resurrection, or (3) post-resurrection. Some posit that an additional unknown is whether or not the generation alluded to by Jesus include his disciples.

Lee (1991, 203 11³) stated that "a sign is a miracle that has some spiritual significance." The significant point is that Jesus unequivocally declared that he would not provide a sign to prove anything. Furthermore, Jesus was not limiting this declaration to one group, the Pharisees. However, his statement was plain and simple; that is, all who live in this generation would not be given a sign. Consequently, this statement by Jesus would seemingly include his disciples. If Lee is correct, then John contradicted Mark.

Yet the author of Acts directly contradicts Mark.

> Acts 2:22 Ye men of Israel, hear these words; Jesus of Nazareth, a man approved of God among you by miracles and wonders and signs, which God did by him in the midst of you, as ye yourselves also know.

However, many of these signs, wonders, and miracles performed by Jesus occurred: (1) between the time that he debated with the Pharisees and (2) after his death.

Below are several examples of signs spanning from approximately the time of Jesus's confrontation with the Pharisees until prior to his arrest in Jerusalem.

Found in Mark only or Mark and the Other Gospels

Mk 8:22 Healing of the blind man at Bethsaida

Mk 9:17 Deliverance of a lunatic boy

Mk 10:46 Healing of two blind men near Jericho

Mk 11:12 Withering of the fig tree

Found Only in Matthew

Mt 14:15-21 Feeding of the five thousand

Mt 14:25-33 Walking upon water

Mt 15:21-28 Deliverance of the Syrophoenician's daughter

Mt 15:32-38 Feeding of the four thousand

Mt 20:29-34 Healing of the blind man near Jericho

Unequivocally, Acts contradicts Mark.

ISSUE 94: Why Jesus Showed His Disciples Many Signs

Mk	Mt	Lk	
			Jn 20:30 And in many other signs truly did Jesus in the presence of the disciples, which are not written in this book. 31 *But these are written, that ye might believe that Jesus is the Christ, the Son of God; and that believing ye might have life through his name.* Jn 21:24 This is the disciple which testifieth of these things, and wrote these things: and we know that his testimony is true.

John states that there were two purposes for detailing the signs performed by Jesus: (1) that the reader might believe Jesus is the Christ, the Son of God, and (2) that by believing the reader might have life through his name.

SPECULATION #181 John's Agenda

John's agenda was to write a missionary and theological text, not one that was historical. This agenda is clearly delineated in John 20:31: "But these are written, that ye might believe that Jesus is the Christ, the Son of God; and that believing ye might have life through his name." Of course, Christian apologists would maintain that it is possible to do both, that is, to write a text that was both historical and missionary/theological. However, astutely, Guthrie (1970, 93) pointed out that "where an author specifically states his own intention, that must always be given more weight than any scholarly conjectures."

To recap, the deliberate agenda of John was both missionary and theological. One such agenda was promoting *blind* faith in a risen Jesus. Although there may be "grains of truth" (historicity) within his gospel, many of the signs were nonhistorical and definitely unconfirmed.

ISSUE 95: Seven Disciples Fishing in the Sea of Tiberias

Mk	Mt	Lk	
			Jn 21:1 After these things Jesus shewed himself again to the disciples *at the sea of Tiberias*; and on the wise shewed he himself. 2 There were together Simon Peter, and Thomas called Didymus, and Nathanael of Cana in Galilee, and the sons of Zebedee, and two other of his disciples. 3 Simon Peter saith unto them, I go a fishing. They say unto him, We also go with thee. They went forth, and entered into a ship immediately; and that night they caught nothing.

John 21 reported that after the events previously detailed (John 20) Jesus showed himself again to seven disciples while fishing in the Sea of Tiberias (the Sea of Galilee). After a night of fishing, the disciples had not caught a single fish. John 21 also informed his reader that this episode represented the third time Jesus had appeared to the disciples as a group. As a result, this event had to have occurred *before* the pre-arranged visit on the mountain in Galilee (see Mt 28:16-20).

SPECULATION #182 The Call to the Lake Metaphor

It is speculated that the historicity of the call to the lake is doubtful. Instead of being a real historical event it is posited that this episode, recorded only in John 21, was really a larger call. Specifically, the author was employing a literary device (metaphor); the disciples were now to become fishermen of the people. Several commentators (Hull 1970, 372; Strachan 1941, 335) discussed the point that the phrase "fishers of men" (cf. Luke 5:10) occurred as early as in Mark 1:17 and had now come full circle: "And Jesus said unto them, Come ye after me, and I will make you to become fishers of men." In other words, the disciples had now been transformed from mortals attempting the physical conquest of nature by fishing for mere fish to followers attempting the conquest of the spiritual world. Therefore, John's call to the lake served as a theological metaphor.

SPECULATION #183 The Symbolism of the Number Seven

The event of the seven disciples fishing at the Sea of Tiberias is recorded *only* in John. Biblical scholars and theologians, both liberal and evangelical, acknowledge that the number seven is a golden thread found throughout the Bible. Carson (1991, 669; cf. Bovon 2001, 267-88) raised the issue regarding the symbolism of the number seven: "It might be tempting to suppose that these *seven* disciples represent, through the symbolism of the number, all of Jesus' followers. But since John does not habitually utilize this number, nor even in this instance mention the number—the reader must do the addition—we cannot be certain."

Articles on the significance of numbers can be found in many standard reference sources and texts. For example, *The International Standard Bible Encyclopedia Online* version (1939) extensively detailed the significance of this number in its entry Number. Two of four sections devoted to the number seven are provided below:

> (1) *Ritual use of seven*—the number 7 plays a conspicuous part in a multitude of passages giving rules for worship or purification, or recording ritual actions. The 7th day of the week was holy (see SABBATH). There were 7 days of unleavened bread (Ex 34:18. etc.), and 7 days of the Feast of Tabernacles (Le 23:34). The 7th year was the sabbatical year (Ex 21:2, etc). The Moabite Balak built Balaam on three occasions 7 altars and provided in each case 7 bullocks and 7 rams (Nu 23:1, 14,29). The Mosaic law

prescribed 7 he-lambs for several festal offerings (Nu 28:11:19, 27, etc.). The 7-fold sprinkling of blood is enjoined in the ritual of the Day of Atonement (Le 16:14, 19), and elsewhere. Seven-fold sprinkling is also repeatedly mentioned in the rules for the purification of the leper and the leprous house (Le 14:7, 16, 27, 51). The leprous Naaman was ordered to bathe 7 times in the Jordan (2 Ki 5:10). In cases of real or suspected uncleanness through leprosy, or the presence of a corpse, or for other reasons, 7 days' seclusion was necessary (Le 12:2, etc.). Circumcision took place after 7 days (Le 12:3). An animal must be 7 days old before it could be offered in sacrifice (Ex 22:30). Three periods of 7 days each are mentioned in the rules for the consecration of priests (Ex 29:30, 35, 37). An oath seems to have been in the first instance by 7 holy things (Ge 21:29 ff and the Hebrew word for "swear"). The number 7 also entered into the structure of sacred objects, for instance the candlestick or lamp-stand in the tabernacle and the second temple each of which had 7 lights (Nu 8:2; Zec 4:2). Many other instances of the ritual use of 7 in the OT and many instructive parallels from Babylonian texts could be given.

(2) *Historical use of seven*—the number 7 also figures prominently in a large number of passages which occur in historical narrative, in a way which reminds us of its symbolic significance. The following are some of the most remarkable: Jacob's 7 years' service for Rachel (Ge 29:20; cf vs 27 f), and his bowing down 7 times to Esau (Ge 33:3); the 7 years of plenty, and the 7 years of famine (Gen 41:53f); Samson's 7 days' marriage feast (Jgs 14:12 ff; cf. Ge 29:27), 7 locks of hair (Jg 16:19), and the 7 withes with which he was bound (vs 7 f): the 7 daughters of Jethro (Ex 2:16), the 7 sons of Jesse (1 Sa 16:10), the 7 sons of Saul (2 Sa 21:6), and the 7 sons of Job (Job 1:2; cf 42:13); the 7 days' march of the 7 priests blowing 7 trumpets round the walls of Jericho, and the 7-fold march on the 7th day (Jos 6:8 ff); the 7 ascents of Elijah's servant to the top of Carmel (1 Ki 18:43 f); the 7 sneezes of the Shunammitish woman's son (2 Ki 4:35); the heating of Nebuchadnezzar's furnace 7 times more than it was wont to be heated (Da 3:19), and the king's madness for 7 times or years (Da 4:16, 23, 25, 32); Anna's 7 years of wedded life (Lu 2:36); the 7 loaves of the 4,000 (Mt 15:34-36 parallel) and the 7 baskets full of fragments (Mt 15:37 parallel); the 7 brothers in the conundrum of the Sadducees (Mt 22:25 parallel); the 7 demons cast out of

Mary Magdalene (Mr 16:9 parallel Lu 8:2); the 7 ministers in the church at Jerus (Ac 6:3 ff), and the 7 sons of Sceva (Ac 19:14, but the Western text represents them as only 2). The number must no doubt be understood literally in many of these passages, but even then its symbolic meaning is probably hinted at by the historian. When a man was said to have had 7 sons or daughters, or an action was reported as done or to be done 7 times, whether by design or accident, the number was noted, and its symbolic force remembered. It cannot indeed be regarded in all these cases as a sacred number, but its association with sacred matters which was kept alive among the Jews by the institution of the Sabbath, was seldom, if ever, entirely overlooked.

Of course, the number seven is also important in the Christian scriptures. However, it is significant to note that John, the author of the last book in the Christian scriptures, Revelation, is filled fifty-nine times with the number seven:

For example, in Revelation, there are

- seven churches (Rev 1:4),
- seven spirits (Rev 1:4),
- seven candlesticks (Rev 1:12),
- seven stars (Rev 1:16),
- seven lamps of fire (Rev 4:5),
- seven spirits of God (Rev 4:5),
- seven seals (Rev 5:1),
- seven horns (Rev 5:6),
- seven eyes (Rev 5:6),
- seven angels (Rev 8:2),
- seven trumpets (Rev 8:2),
- seven thunders (Rev 10:3),
- seven thousand men slain (Rev 11:13),
- seven heads (Rev 12:3),
- seven crowns (Rev 12:3),
- seven plagues (Rev 15:1),
- seven golden vials (Rev 15:7),
- seven mountains (Rev 17:9), and
- seven kings (Rev 17:10).

Here in John 21:1-2 it has been suggested by scholars and theologians that the seven disciples symbolically represented the future church as well as the seven churches in Revelation 2-3. Okure (1998, 1500) also suggested that the "number seven represents fullness." Consequently, the seven disciples could be nothing more than an artificial construction that fulfilled a theological agenda.

ISSUE 96: The Large Catch of Fish

Mk	Mt	Lk	Jn 21:4 But when the morning was now come, Jesus stood on the shore: but *the disciples knew not that it was Jesus.* 5 Then Jesus saith unto them, Children, have ye any meat? They answered him, No. 6 And he said unto them, Cast the net on the right side of the ship, and ye shall find. *They cast therefore, and now they were not able to draw it for the multitude of fishes.* 7 Therefore that *disciple whom Jesus loved saith unto Peter, It is the Lord.* Now when Simon Peter heard that it was the Lord, he girt his fisher's coat unto him, (for he was naked,) and did cast himself into the sea. 8 And the other disciples came in a little ship; (for they were not far from land, but as it were two hundred cubits,) dragging the net with fishes. 9 As soon then as they were come to land, they saw a fire of coals there, and fish laid thereon, and bread. 10 Jesus saith unto them, Bring of the fish which ye have now caught. 11 Simon Peter *went up, and drew the net to land full of great fishes, an hundred and fifty and three*: and for all there were so many, yet was not the net broken.

After a night of fishing, not a single fish was caught. The following morning an unrecognizable Jesus stood on the shore and had a conversation with the disciples, and yet they did not recognize his voice. Jesus informed them where they could catch some fish with their net. Following his instruction they caught a multitude of fish and were unable to pull them in. Almost three hundred feet away (two hundred cubits), the disciple who Jesus loved recognized Jesus and declared that it was Jesus. Immediately Simon Peter clothed himself, since he was apparently naked, jumped overboard, and swam to the shore.

Eventually (v. 9) the other disciples made it to shore and saw some fish cooking on a fire of coals. Upon their arrival, Jesus requested that they bring him some fish that had just been caught. Then Simon Peter promptly and single handedly pulled the catch ashore, a catch containing exactly one hundred and fifty-three large fish, and did so without breaking the net. This was a feat that the other six disciples could *not* accomplish even working *together.*

SPECULATION #184 Speculative Questions Regarding the Fish Catch

There are several questions that must be considered. First, did the disciples literally catch exactly 153 "great fishes"? According to John, exactly 153 great fish were caught. This text, if rendered historically true, implied that the disciples literally counted every fish in the net and remembered the exact number. An alternative discussed below is that the number 153 was ahistorical and employed for its symbolic meaning. In addition, all the fish were large. However, the author of John failed to provide the criterion that was employed to determine if a fish was large, medium sized, or small.

Second, did Simon Peter literally drag the net ashore by himself this tremendous catch, which six other disciples could not pull in together? Christian fundamentalists would argue that the episode recorded in John was factual. However, a speculated alternative is that this episode was a legendary account written to promote Peter over the other apostles.

Third, were 153 large fish usually sufficient number to break a net? An alternative explanation is that the nonbreaking of the net served as a symbolic metaphor. To illustrate this point, Hull (1970, 373) wrote:

> Second, the fact that although there were so many fish, the net was not torn, many suggest that the unity of the church, like that of a seamless robe (19:23), would not be rent by the inclusion of the gentiles. Addressing a situation in which the church was being threatened by schism (cf. John 10; 17; 1 John 2:19), John 21 offered an assurance that the nets may bulge with all sorts of men but they need not break under the strain of such diversity.

Fourth, it is possible that this entire episode was a literary invention with a hidden symbolic or theological agenda. Of course, some proponents could counter that all of the above are correct. On the other hand, it is interesting to note that even C. H. Dodd (1963, 139n1) cautiously pointed out in his *Historical Tradition in the Fourth Gospel* that the evangelist was perhaps "somewhat addicted to numbers, especially large numbers."

SPECULATION #185 The Symbolism of the Number 153

Christian apologists and Christian fundamentalists can point to the incredible catch of 153 fish detailed in John 21 as an example of a sign. To the contrary, there are, in fact, numerous natural or practical explanations other than that of an alleged miracle for this event: The record (1) is hyperbolic (an embellishment), (2) is legendary, or (3) was written to serve a symbolic or theological agenda.

Numerous explanations are based on the symbolism of the number 153. For purposes of clarity, this section will be subdivided into four parts:

TRADITIONAL EXPLANATIONS

Saint Augustine explained about numbers: ten represents the Ten Commandments of the law; seven is the number of the sevenfold spirit (Rev 1:4, 3:1; 1 Cor 12:9-11). Now 7 + 10 = 17, and 153 is the sum of all figures up to 17. Therefore, 1 + 2 + 3 + 4 . . . +17 equal 153 (Parsons 2008b, 38-39). Colson (1914, 67, 72) referred to the resultant of this addition of numbers as a triangular number. Coincidentally, one method of *gematria* (i.e., numerology) for the Hebrew word for "good" (טוב "*Tov*" = 9 + 6 + 2) is 17. A different explanation is that the seven disciples in John 21:2 were present when the 153 fish were caught while John 20:24 reported that ten disciples received the Holy Spirit. Therefore, seven plus ten equals 17. Moreover, Philo also emphasized the importance of seven and ten together (*De opificio mundi* 99). Grant (1949, 274) wrote: "It seems probable, then, that the significance of seventeen is due to its being the sum of the two most scared numbers, and that this significance is multiplied when the number is triangulated." Finally, Gregory the Great (ca. 540-604) simply *multiplied* 17 by 3 and again by 3 (i.e., 17×3^2), and thus arrived at 153.

NINETEENTH-THROUGH TWENTY-FIRST-CENTURY COMMENTARIES AND EXPLANATIONS

Several writers (Brooke 2005, 287-88; Colson 1914-15, 67-76; Grant 1949, 273; Keim 1883, 6:316n1; Neyrey 2006, 337) cited an explanation by Jerome based on his commentary on Ezekiel 15:47. "Writers on the nature and properties of animals who have learned 'fishing' in either Latin or Greek (one of whom is the most learned poet Oppianus Cilix) say there are 153 species of fish." However, Beasley-Murray (2009, 109) and Grant (1949, 273) pointed out that Oppian's writings apparently listed 157 fish! In contrast, Bullinger (1894, 273) stated: "Jerome also sees there is some deeper meaning in the number, and says that there are 153 *sorts* of fish, i.e., all kinds of men enclosed in the Gospel net."

Keim (1883, 6:316n1) cited Volkmar (*Himmelf. Mose.* p. 62), saying that the number (numerology) of the name Simon Peter is one hundred and fifty-three: Shimeon (71), Johanna (53) and Kepha (29); the number related to the fullness of the Gentiles indicated, according to 2 Chronicles 2:17, where Solomon reckoned the strangers in Israel at 153,600; or the 153 fish "refer to the conversion of the Gentiles (100 heathens, 50 Jews, and 3 the Trinity!)."

Bishop John Wordsworth of Salisbury (1843-1911; cf. Hasitschka 2008, 316n25) arrived at his result in a different manner. He used two numbers and employed both multiplication and addition. First he took the square of 12 (which he held to be the church number), and then he *added* the square of 3 (the number of the Godhead), and pointed out that $12^2 + 3^2 = 153$, or $(12 \times 12) + (3 \times 3)$.

Emerton (1958, 86) suggested that Ezekiel 47:10 was a possible source of the number 153, produced by adding the values of the letters of עגלים and noting that גדי produces the related number 17. However, Ackroyd (1959, 94) criticized this hypothesis, pointing out that there are different spellings of various words in different manuscripts. In addition, even Emerton pointed out that this "hypothesis presupposes that readers of a Greek book could be expected to refer to an O.T. passage in Hebrew, which is not explicitly cited, and to recognize in it an example in Hebrew which is not explicitly cited, and to recognize it in an example of *Gematria*." Another possibility suggested by this text is that the number 153 is the numerical value of the name Bezaleel (Ex 35:30), the chief artisan of the Tabernacle and the person in charge of building the Ark of the Covenant. His name means "in the shadow of God." Additional interpretations on the number 153 can be found in the works of other writers (Cardwell 1990, 12-14; Labahn 2006, 125-45; McEleney 1977, 411-17; Owens 1988, 52-54; Parsons 2008b, 38-43; and Trudinger 1990, 11-12).

SELECTED EXPLANATIONS AND INTERPRETATIONS REVIEWED BY BULLINGER (1894, 274-78)

- The expression בני האלהים (*Beni Ha-Elohim*), "Sons of God," occurs in *seven* connections!* Now the *gematria* of this expression is exactly 153. Thus:

ב	=	2
נ	=	50
י	=	10
ה	=	5
א	=	1
ל	=	30
ה	=	5
י	=	10
ם	=	<u>40</u>
		153

- It is very remarkable, in connection with this, that in Job ii:1 we have "*Beni-ha Elohim* with Satan among them." The gematria of this phrase is 1989, and the two factors of this number are 153 and 13 (13 x 153 = 1989).
- The word συνκληρονομοι (*sunkleeronomoi*), "joint-heirs" (Rom viii.17), amounts to 1,071, the factors of which are 153 and 7 (153 x 7=1,071).
- The expression συκληρονομοι δε Χριστου (*sunkleeronomoi de Christou*), "joint heirs with Christ" (viii 8:17), amounts to 2,751. Now the factors of 153, as we have seen, are 9 and 17, and the number 2,751 is three times the *nine* hundred, plus *seventeen*, viz., 3 x (900 + 17) = 2,751.
- The expression κτισις θεου (*ktisis Theou*), "the creation of God," is 1,224, or 8 x 153.
- In the record of the miracle itself there are some remarkable phenomena: -
- The word for "fishes" ιχθυες (*ichthues*), is by gematria 1,224, or 8 x 153.
- The words for "the net" are το δικτυον, and by gematria this also amounts to 1,224, or 8 x 153, for it is unbroken, and carries the

precious freight from "the right side" of the ship safely to the shore, and "not one is lost."

CONTEMPORARY EXPLANATIONS

In more recent times, several writers have offered dubious and wild explanations that John's text was an invention based on another tradition, spiritual allegories. Wahlde's (2010, 883) review of the literature also discussed several theories that make use of gematria: "One proposal was that 153 is gematria for the Hebrew of 'Church of Love,' a phrase that unfortunately echoes nothing in Johannine theology. Another suggests that 17 is the numerical sum of the letters in En-gedi and 153 the sum of for En-eglaim, both of which have eschatological association in Ezek 47."

John Mitchell (1988, 174-76) has suggested that the 153 fishes in the unbroken net were based on a geometrical diagram and *gematria*. The Greek words for *fishes* and *the net*, which appear in the Christian scriptures both amount to 1,224, and that 153 is exactly one-eighth of this amount. Consequently, Mitchell was of the opinion that 153 was not just an arbitrary number.

A further explanation is based on the works of Pythagoras (570-496 BCE). Pythagoreans regarded 153 as a sacred number. According to Mitchell, "it is a traditional practice among teachers of esoteric philosophy to set forth their doctrines in the guise of simple parables which amuse children, enrich popular mythology, and, for those who understand the science of interpreting them, illustrate various cosmological processes." Fideler (1993, 308) discussed two early examples of tales telling how Pythagoras predicted the exact number of "fish in the net." Although no number of fish was given in the stories as they have come down to us, "it is likely that the story was based on the Pythagorean, cosmological geometry, which underlies the later Christian version":

From Porphyry, *The Life of Pythagoras* 27:

> Meeting with some fisherman who were drawing in their nets heavily laden with fishes from the deep, he predicted the exact number of fish they had caught. The fisherman said that if his estimate was accurate they would do whatever he commanded. They counted them accurately, and found the number correct. He then bade them to return the fish alive into the sea; and what is more wonderful, not one of them died, although they had been out of the water a considerable time.

From *Lamblichus, The Life of Pythagoras,* chapter 8:

> One day, during a trip from Sybaris to Croton, by the sea-shore, he happened to meet some fisherman engaged in drawing up from the deep their heavily laden fish-nets. He told them he knew the exact number of fish they had caught. The surprised fisherman declared that if he was right they would do anything he said. He then ordered them, after counting the fish accurately, to return them alive to the sea, and what is more wonderful, while he stood on the shore, not one of them died, though they had remained out of their natural environment quite a little while. Pythagoras then paid the fisherman the price of their fish, and departed for Croton. The fisherman divulged the occurrence, and on discovering his name from some children, spread it abroad publicly. Everybody wanted to see the stranger, which was easy enough to do. They were deeply impressed on beholding his countenance, which indeed betrayed his real nature. (Fideler 1993, 308)

Another explanation of the number 153 is based on the "Measure of the Fish" in Archimedes's treatise *On the Measurement of the Circle.* This text incorporated the whole number ratio 153:265 to accurately approximate the irrational ratio √3, "the measure of the fish" or the *vesica piscis.* Freke and Gandy (1999, 40), both mythicists wrote:

> The sign of the fish is widely used today as a symbol of Christianity, but originally in Pagan sacred geometry. Two circles, symbolic of spirit and matter, are brought together in a sacred marriage. When the circumference of one touches the center of the outer they combine to produce the fish shape known as the *vesica piscis.* The ratio of the height to length of this shape is 153:265, a formula known to Archimedes in the third century BCE as the "measure of the fish." It is a powerful mathematical tool, being the nearest whole number approximation of the square root of three and the controlling ratio of the equilateral triangle.

They based this thesis on the work of Fideler. Fideler (1993, 307) was of the opinion that "those skilled in mathematics would have immediately recognized the story of the153 fish in the net as a geometrical 'story problem.'"

Therefore, "the fact that this mystical fish symbol can be produced from the number of fish that were caught in the account of Jesus' miracle strongly suggests it has been adapted from the original miracle of Pythagoras and that this miracle story encoded sacred geometrical formulae" (Freke and Gandy, 1999, 39).

A simpler speculation is that the Greek word for "net" is *diktuon* [δικτυον], and for "fishes" is *ixthus* (or *ichthues*) [ἰχθύων]. Numerically, both add up to 1,224, which is 8 x 153, the number of the fishes brought ashore in the net.

These explanations contain four cardinal characteristics justifying the hypothesis that the number 153 carried symbolic meanings. First, the original authors of the story probably had access or availability to this well-known ritual via an oral tradition. Second, the density or the parallels between the two texts are self-evident. Third, the distinctive characteristics of (1) fishermen, (2) fishing, (3) the fish, (4) the net, (5) drawing the fish ashore, and (6) the unusual number 153 seems hardly incidental. Fourth, the hypothesis is intelligible. It helps the reader make sense of the text and provides a solution to an otherwise peculiar text. While not all the facts in John parallel the tale of Pythagoras (Jesus did not predict the number of fish, and the fish are eaten), it does become apparent that the account of the "fish in the net" was possibly to some degree modeled after the fish net story. Those seeking a detailed commentary accompanied by numerous illustrations on this topic are referred to Fideler (1999, 291-306) and Mitchell (1972, 174-76). Another option is to type *fish* and the number *153* into any Internet search engine. There one will find a multitude of interpretations.

SPECULATION #186 The Source of the Fishing Story

Another arena of speculation is the source of John's fish story. Numerous writers (Carson 1991, 670; Fortna 1992, 387-99; Howard 1951, 7:803; Labahn 2006, 128; Lüdemann 2004, 125, 157; Neirynck 1990, 321-29; Smith 1988, 1075) discussed or suggested that John's account was perhaps a variation from Luke 5. However, this variant created a paradox: John 21 had the fishing story in the Easter narrative (during the post-resurrection) whereas Luke had the incident occurring prior to Jesus's resurrection.

TABLE 66. Comparison of Luke 5 and John 21

LUKE 5	JOHN 21	ANALYSIS
Lk 5:1 *And it came to pass,* that, as the people pressed upon him to hear the word of God, he stood by *the lake of Gennesaret,*	Jn 21:1 *After these things* Jesus shewed himself again to the disciples at *the sea of Tiberias*; and on this wise shewed he himself.	1. An introductory *time component.* 2. The lake of Gennesart was also called the "Sea of Galilee" and the "lake or sea of Tiberias."
Lk 5:2 And saw *two ships* standing by the lake: but the fishermen were gone out of them, and were washing their nets.	Jn 21:8 And *the other disciples came in a little ship*; (for they were not far from land, but as it were two hundred cubits,) dragging the net with fishes.	3. *There were two ships* involved in these episodes.
Lk 5:3 And he entered into one of the ships, which was Simon's, and prayed him that he would thrust out a little from the land. And he sat down, and taught the people out of the ship.		
Lk 5:4 Now when he had left speaking, *he said unto Simon, Launch out into the deep, and let down your nets for a draught.*	Jn 21:6 *And he said unto them, Cast the net on the right side of the ship, and ye shall find.* They cast therefore, and now they were not able to draw it for the multitude of fishes.	4. Jesus instructed Simon Peter where he would catch some fish.
Lk 5:5 And Simon answering said unto him, Master, *we have toiled all the night, and have taken nothing*: nevertheless at thy word I will let down the net.	Jn 21:3 Simon Peter saith unto them, I go a fishing. They say unto him, We also go with thee. They went forth, and entered into a ship immediately; *and that night they caught nothing.*	5. The disciples *fished all night.* 6. The disciples *caught nothing.*

Lk 5:5 And Simon answering said unto him, Master, we have toiled all the night, and have taken nothing: *nevertheless at thy word I will let down the net.*	Jn 21:6 And he said unto them, Cast the net on the right side of the ship, and ye shall find. *They cast therefore*, and now they were not able to draw it for the multitude of fishes.	7. Simon Peter *followed Jesus's instructions.*
Lk 5:6 And when they had this done, they inclosed *a great multitude of fishes*: and their *net brake.*	Jn 21:11 Simon Peter went up, and drew the net to land *full of great fishes*, an hundred and fifty and three: and for all there were so many, yet *was not the net broken.*	8. There was *a great catch of fish.*
		9. *There was mention of a net*: however, in Luke it is breaking whereas in John it does not break.
Lk 5:7 And they beckoned unto *their partners*, which were in the other ship, that they should come and help them. And *they* came, and filled both the ships, so that they began to sink.	Jn 21:8 And *the other disciples* came in a little ship; (for *they* were not far from land, but as it were two hundred cubits,) dragging the net with fishes.	10. *A group of men* attempted to pull in the catch.
Lk 5:8 When Simon Peter saw it, he fell down at Jesus' knees, saying, *Depart from me; for I am a sinful man*, O Lord.	Jn 21:17 He saith unto him the third time, Simon, son of Jonas, lovest thou me? *Peter was grieved* because he said unto him the third time, Lovest thou me? And he said unto him, Lord, thou knowest all things; thou knowest that I love thee. Jesus saith unto him, Feed my sheep.	11. Peter expressed grief.
Lk 5:9 For he was *astonished*, and all that were with him, *at the draught of the fishes which they had taken*:	Jn 21:11 Simon Peter went up, and drew the net to land *full of great fishes, an hundred and fifty and three*: and for all there were so many, yet was not the net broken.	12. There was again mention of *an amazing catch.*

Lk 5:10 And so was also James, and John, *the sons of Zebedee*, which were partners with *Simon*. And Jesus said unto *Simon*, Fear not; from henceforth thou shalt catch men.	Jn 21:2 There were together *Simon Peter*, and Thomas called Didymus, and Nathanael of Cana in Galilee, and the *sons of Zebedee*, and two other of his disciples.	13. There was mention of *Simon Peter*.
		14. There was mention of *the sons of Zebedee*.
Lk 5:11 And when they had brought their ships to land, they forsook all, and *followed him*.	Jn 21:12 Jesus saith unto them, Come and dine. And none of the disciples durst ask him, Who art thou? *knowing that it was the Lord*.	15. The disciples *recognized Jesus and followed him*.

ISSUE 97: The Disciples Recognizing Jesus at the Sea of Tiberias

Mk	Mt	Lk	
			Jn 21:4 But when the morning was now come, Jesus stood on the shore: *but the disciples knew not that it was Jesus*. 5 Then Jesus saith unto them, Children, have ye any meat? They answered him, No. 6 And he said unto them, Cast the net on the right side of the ship, and ye shall find. They cast therefore, and now they were not able to draw it for the multitude of fishes. 7 *Therefore that disciple whom Jesus loved saith unto Peter, It is the Lord. Now when Simon Peter heard that it was the Lord, he girt his fisher's coat unto him, (for he was naked,) and did cast himself into the sea. 8 And the other disciples came in a little ship*; (for they were not far from land, but as it were two hundred cubits,) dragging the net with fishes. 9 As soon then as they were come to land, they saw a fire of coals there, and fish laid thereon, and bread. 10 Jesus saith unto them, Bring of the fish which ye have now caught. 11 Simon Peter went up, and drew the net to land full of great fishes, an hundred and fifty and three: and for all there were so many, yet was not the net broken. 12 Jesus saith unto them, Come and dine. *And none of the disciples durst ask him, Who art thou? knowing that it was the Lord. 13 Jesus then cometh*, and taketh bread, and giveth them, and fish likewise. 14 This is now the third time that Jesus shewed himself to his disciples, after that he was risen from the dead.

John 21:1-8 reports that seven disciples were fishing about two hundred cubits from the shoreline (i.e., about ninety meters or one hundred yards).

The disciple whom Jesus loved was the first to recognize Jesus: "Therefore that disciple whom Jesus loved saith unto Peter, It is the Lord." Similarly, in John 20:8 it was this disciple who was the first one at the empty tomb to realize what had happened. Peter then jumped overboard to swim to Jesus. However, the text did not incontrovertibly state that Peter recognized Jesus, only that he had been informed of the possibility. At this point, the other disciples seemingly did not recognize Jesus. The reason for this non-recognition was not discussed, although the disciples had seen and conversed with Jesus on two previous occasions.

When the disciples finally made it ashore, they found that Jesus had prepared a meal of fish on a fire of coals and bread. Immediately following, Jesus told them to have breakfast. Then he distributed bread and fish, without eating any himself. Then the narrator in verse 12 stated: "And none of the disciples durst ask him, Who art thou? Knowing that it was the Lord."

ISSUE 98: The Commissioning of Peter

Mk	Mt	Lk	Jn
	Mt 16:18 And I say also unto thee, *That thou art Peter, and upon this rock I will build my church; and the gates of hell shall not prevail against it.* 19 *And I will give unto thee the keys of the kingdom of heaven:* and whatsoever thou shalt bind on earth shall be bound in heaven: and whatsoever thou shalt loose on earth shall be loosed in heaven.		Jn 21:15 So when they had dined, Jesus saith to Simon Peter, Simon, son of Jonas, lovest thou me more than these? He saith unto him, *Yea, Lord; thou knowest that I love thee.* He saith unto him, Feed my lambs. 16 He saith to him again the second time, Simon, son of Jonas, lovest thou me? He saith unto him, *Yea, Lord; thou knowest that I love thee.* He saith unto him, Feed my sheep. 17 He saith unto him the third time, Simon, son of Jonas, lovest thou me? Peter was grieved because he said unto him the third time, Lovest thou me? And he said unto him, Lord, thou knowest all things; *thou knowest that I love thee. Jesus saith unto him, Feed my sheep.* 18 Verily, verily, I say unto thee, When thou wast young, thou girdest thyself, and walkedst whither thou wouldest: but when thou shalt be old, thou shalt stretch forth thy hands, and another shall gird thee, and carry thee whither thou wouldest not. 19 This spake he, signifying by what death he should glorify God. And when he had spoken this, he saith unto him, Follow me. 20 Then Peter, turning about, seeth the disciple whom Jesus loved following; which also leaned on his breast at supper, and said, Lord, which is he that betrayeth thee? 21 Peter seeing him saith to Jesus, Lord, and what shall this man do? 22 Jesus saith unto him, If I will that he tarry till I come, what is that to thee? follow thou me. 23 Then went this saying abroad among the brethren, that that disciple should not die: yet Jesus said not unto him, He shall not die; but, If I will that he tarry till I come, what is that to thee?

Three times (Jn 18:15, 16, 17) during the meal Peter was questioned as to whether he truly loved Jesus. Three times Peter responded affirmatively. After each affirmative reply Jesus responded with a command: "Feed my sheep." Thereby, Peter was rehabilitated and recommissioned, having three times previously denied Jesus. However, the commissioning of Peter was hinted at earlier in Matthew 16:18-19. Matthew reported that Jesus informed Peter that (1) he would build his church on Peter (the rock), (2) the gates of hell would not prevail against the church that Peter would help to build, and (3) Peter would receive "the keys of the kingdom of heaven."

In addition, Jesus informed Peter that he would die. Finally, Jesus instructed Peter: "Follow me."

SPECULATION #187 Peter's Exaltation

The new commissioning of Peter is metaphorically seen in the shepherd image throughout the Hebrew Bible. Implicit in Jesus's statement "Feed my sheep," Peter was exalted *above* the other disciples and placed in charge of both the general community (lambs) and leadership group (sheep). Peter's exalted status was reinforced later by himself in 1 Peter 5:4: "And when the chief Shepherd shall appear, ye shall receive a crown of glory that fadeth not away." N. T. Wright (2003, 676) wrote: "This leads to a new commissioning, seen in terms of the shepherd image which dominated chapter 10."

Peter's triple affirmation in response to his triple denial has the echo of a literary device. Dunn (2003, 845; cf. Wiarda 2004, 181) wrote, "The thrice repeated 'Do you love me?' is obviously framed to echo Peter's threefold denial of Jesus" (18.17-18, 25-27). The three denials narrated in John include the following:

> Jn 18:16-17 But Peter stood at the door without. Then went out that other disciple, which was known unto the high priest, and spake unto her that kept the door, and brought in Peter. Then saith the damsel that kept the door unto Peter, Art not thou also one of this man's disciples? *He saith, I am not.*

> Jn 18:25 And Simon Peter stood and warmed himself. They said therefore unto him, Art not thou also one of his disciples? He denied it, *and said, I am not.*

> Jn 18:26-27 One of the servants of the high priest, being his kinsman whose ear Peter cut off, saith, Did not I see thee in the garden with him? *Peter then denied again*: and immediately the cock crew.

It is postulated that the goal of this section was to demonstrate Peter's primacy in the church and hence it served a theological agenda. N. T. Wright (2003, 677) rejected this thesis because "they [[arguments like this]] remain in my judgment unconvincing." Of course, this is just his scholarly opinion.

Finally, Wiarda (2004, 182) offers an alternative explanation to the Jesus-Peter exchange with its three fold question and response:

As the earlier scene opens, seven of Jesus' disciples decide to go fishing. The narrative tells us that the idea of going out to fish was specifically Peter's. It emphasizes the point by portraying the other six disciples as following his lead (21.3). Since earlier parts of the Gospel have raised certain expectations concerning the role Jesus intends for his disciples, Peter's action will perhaps provoke a question in the reader's mind: what does his decision to go fishing indicate about Peter's commitments and allegiance? This hint of uncertainty with respect to Peter's commitment to the responsibilities of discipleship would adequately account for Jesus' questions and commands in the dialogue to follow.

SPECULATION #188 The Number Three—Fact or a Literary Device (Symbolism)

The number three plays an in ordinate role in the John's gospel narrative. This number also plays an important symbolic role in Matthew. However, especially in the last four chapters of John, the importance of the number three is significantly amplified. It is speculated that the number three has been deliberately embedded into John's text to serve as a literary device.

TABLE 67. The Number Three in Matthew and John

MATTHEW	JOHN
	John 1:1—The Greek term logos ("word") appeared three times.
Mt 1:1-17—The names of Abraham's descendants were manipulated into three sets of fourteen individual male descendants.	
Mt 1:20-24—Three "people" were identified prior to Mary's conception: (1) Joseph, (2) Mary, (3) and the angel.	
Mt 2:11—The Wise Men from the East presented three gifts to the infant Jesus: (1) gold, (2) frankincense, and (3) myrrh.	
Mt 2:12, 13 and 19—Three dreams were reported in the infancy stories.	
	Jn 2:1—A wedding at Cana was held on the third day.

	Jn 2:19-22—Jesus prophesied that he would be resurrected after three days.
Mt 4:4, 6 and 7—The statement "for it was written" was repeated three times.	
Mt 12:40—The sign of Jonah stated that "Jonas was three days and three nights in the whale's belly; so shall the Son of man be three days and three nights in the heart of the earth."	
Mt 16:21—Jesus predicted that he must be killed and on the third day he would be raised to life.	
Mt 17:1—Three disciples went with Jesus up a mountain and witnessed the Transfiguration: Peter, James, and John.	
Mt 17:23—Jesus predicted that he would be killed and on the third day he would be raised to life.	
Mt 20:19—Jesus predicted that on the third day he will be raised to life.	
Mt 26:34—Jesus prophesied that Peter would deny Jesus three times.	Jn 18:17—Jesus prophesied that Peter would deny him three times.
Mt 26:37—It was reported that three disciples went with Jesus into the garden of Gethsemane: Peter and the two sons of Zebedee.	
Mt 26:39-44—Jesus prayed three times at Gethsemane prior to his arrest.	Jn 17:1-5, 6-19, and 20-26—Jesus prayed for three people or groups: (1) for himself, (2) for his disciples, and (3) for all brethren.
Mt 26:40-45—Three times Jesus found his disciples asleep.	
	Jn 18:3—The arresting party consisted of: (1) a detachment of soldiers, (2) some officials from the chief priests, and (3) Pharisees.
	Jn 18:3—The arresting party carried: (1) torches, (2) lanterns, and (3) weapons.

	Jn 18:5, 6, and 8—Three times Jesus said, "I am he."
Mt 26:61—Two witnesses declared that they heard Jesus say he was able to destroy and rebuild the Temple of God and rebuild it in three days.	
Mt 27:40—While on the cross, mockers taunted Jesus, saying, "Thou that destroyest the temple, and buildest it in three days, save thyself."	
Mt 26:70, 72, and 74-75—Peter denied Jesus three times.	Jn 18; 17, 25, and 27—Peter denied Jesus three times.
	Jn 18:13, 24, and 28—Jesus was sent to three people after his arrest: (1) Annas, (2) Caiaphas, and (3) Pilate.
	Jn 18:18—Three groups or people warmed themselves by a fire: (1) the servants, (2) the officers, and (3) Peter.
	Jn 18:29; 19:4, and 13—Three times Pilate came out of his palace and met the Jewish leadership during Jesus's trial.
	Jn 18:38; 19:4, 6—Pilate declared three times that he found Jesus innocent.
	Jn 18:22; 19:1 and 3—Jesus was (1) struck, (2) scourged, and (3) smote.
Mt 27:38—Three people were crucified.	Jn 19:18—Three people were crucified.
	Jn 19:20—A notice fastened to the cross was written in three languages: (1) Aramaic, (2) Latin, and (3) Greek.
Mt 27:45-6—Darkness was over the land for three hours during Jesus's crucifixion: from the sixth hour to the ninth hour.	
	Jn 19:26; 21:7, 20—Three times the phrase "the disciple whom he/Jesus loved" was repeated.
	Jn 19:29-30—Three things were employed to provide Jesus with a drink: (1) vinegar, (2) a sponge, and (3) a stalk of hyssop.

	Jn 19:39-40—Jesus's body was prepared with: (1) myrrh, (2) aloes, and (3) linen.
Mt 27:62—Three groups met on the Sabbath: (1) the chief priests, (2) the Pharisees, and (3) Pilate.	
Mt 27:62-66; 28:4, and 11-15—There were three appearances of the guard.	
Mt 27:63-4—The Jewish leadership recalled Jesus's three-day prophecy.	
Mt 27:64-66—Three times the word "secure" is employed.	
	Jn 20:2, 13 and 15—Three times Mary Magdalene reported words to the effect: "They have taken the Lord" or "she does not know where Jesus's body is to be found [i.e., Mary Magdalene's threefold inquiry where Jesus's body was taken]."
	Jn 20:3—Three people were reported running: (1) Mary Magdalene, (2) Peter, and (3) the disciple whom Jesus loved.
	Jn 20:11, 13, and 15—Three times there was reference to Mary Magdalene crying or weeping.
	Jn 20:12—Mary Magdalene has a dialogue with two angels. Collective, there were three people carrying on a conversation.
	Jn 20:19, 21, and 26—Three times Jesus said, "Peace be with you."
	Jn 21:2—Three disciples at the Sea of Tiberias were specifically named: (1) Simon Peter, (2) Thomas, and (3) Nathanael from Cana.
	Jn 21:11—Exactly 153 fish were caught, and this number is divisible by three.
	21:14, 17, 17—The phrase "the third time" was repeated three times.
	Jn 21:15, 16, and 17—Three times Jesus asked Peter, "Do you love me?"

	Jn 21:15, 16 and 17—Three times Peter affirmed that he loved Jesus.
	Jn 21:15, 16, and 17—Three times Jesus recommissioned Peter by stating, "Feed my lambs" or "Take care of my sheep."
Mt 28:19—The Great Commission required baptizing in the name of the three: (1) the Father, (2) the Son, and (3) of the Holy Ghost.	

ISSUE 99: Peter's Claim about Jesus

Mk	Mt	Lk	Jn 21:17 He saith unto him the third time, Simon, son of Jonas, lovest thou me? Peter was grieved because he said unto him the third time, Lovest thou me? And he said unto him, *Lord, thou knowest all things; thou knowest that I love thee.* Jesus saith unto him, Feed my sheep.

John 21:17 reported that for a third time Peter affirmed his love for Jesus. Twice earlier in verse 16 Peter replied to Jesus's questioning of his fidelity by declaring: "Yea, Lord; thou knowest that I love thee" (v. 15) and "Yea, Lord; thou knowest that I love thee." However, this time Peter added "Lord, thou knowest all things" before he continued "thou knowest that I love thee." In other words, Peter claimed that Jesus possessed the quality of total omniscience.

CONTRADICTION #105 Peter Contradicts Peter

John 21:17 reported that Peter told Jesus that his master knew everything: "He saith unto him the third time, Simon, son of Jonas, lovest thou me? Peter was grieved because he said unto him the third time, Lovest thou me? And he said unto him, Lord, thou knowest all things; thou knowest that I love thee. Jesus saith unto him, Feed my sheep." Therefore, Peter claimed that Jesus possessed the quality of omniscience.

However, previously Peter was instructed by none other than Jesus that his master did *not* know all things. Matthew 24:3 reported that when Jesus was with his disciples at the Mount of Olives they raised a question: "And as he sat upon the Mount of Olives, the disciples came unto him privately, saying, Tell us, when shall these things be? and what shall be the sign of thy coming, and of the end of the world?" After a long oration, Matthew 24:35

reported that Jesus taught them: "But of that day and hour knoweth no man, no, not the angels of heaven, but my Father only."

Mark 13 repeated almost verbatim Matthew 24. However, Mark 13:3-4 specifically identified Peter as one of the disciples who was present: "And as he sat upon the Mount of Olives over against the temple, Peter and James and John and Andrew asked him privately. Tell us, when shall these things be? and what shall be the sign when all these things shall be fulfilled?" In answer to their question, Jesus responded (Mk 13:32): "But of that day and that hour knoweth no man, no, not the angels which are in heaven, neither the Son, but the Father." In no uncertain words, Jesus declared that he was *not* omniscient.

If Jesus was all-knowing as Peter claimed in John 21:17, that would mean Jesus was either wrong (not all-knowing) when he informed Peter (in Mk 13:32 and Mt 24:35) that he did not know all things and, therefore, was, in fact, not all-knowing, or Jesus was lying when he made his statement to his disciples in the Galilee. The only alternative is that Peter did not understand Jesus's concise, direct, and easily understood words.

ISSUE 100: John's Declaration about His Witness

Mk	Mt	Lk	Jn 20:31 And many other signs truly did Jesus in the presence of his disciples, which are not written in this book: *But these are written, that ye might believe that Jesus is the Christ, the Son of God; and that believing ye might have life through his name.*
			Jn 21:24 This is the disciple which testifieth of these things, and wrote these things: and we know *that his testimony is true.* 25 And there are also many other things which Jesus did, the which, if they should be written every one, I suppose that even the world itself could not contain the books that should be written. Amen.

The author of John makes two declarations about his witness, recorded in chapters 20 and 21. At the end of chapter 20, he declared that his purpose in writing the signs (miracles) recorded in his gospel was "that ye might believe that Jesus is the Christ, the Son of God; and that believing ye might have life through his name." Later, at the end of chapter 21, he testified that the things recorded in his gospel were true.

SPECULATION #189 Irrelevancy of John's Trustworthiness

It is meaningless that the author of John declared that his testimony was true. Sarcastically, it must be asked, do advocates and defenders of John suggest that it would be expected or prudent for its author to have written words to the effect: "This is the disciple who testifies concerning these things and the one who has written these things and we know that his testimony *is only partially true?* Therefore, this is to inform you that *many of the details recorded herein are exaggerations and others were written to serve as literary devices* so that you may believe that Jesus is the Christ, the son of God, and that believing, you may have life in his name." Such an action would be absurd, ludicrous, and preposterous.

The problem with any oath or testimony is self-evident: it is only one person's word. A person's sincerity provides *no* credibility to a testimony. Common sense and everyday experience demonstrate that a person taking an oath does not guarantee that everything one will testify to is necessarily true. Errors can be deliberate or accidental. And, "even if people are telling what they sincerely believe to be the truth, it is always possible that they can be mistaken." (Lett 1990) Furthermore, as earlier discussed, it must be remembered that the Christian scriptures approve of *pious fraud* when they support the spread of Christianity. For example, Paul wrote in Philippians 1:18: "What then? notwithstanding, every way, whether in pretence, or in truth, Christ is preached; and I therein do rejoice, yea, and will rejoice."

Dodd (1953, 212-13) identified another problem with John 21:4. He wrote: "This has usually been understood as an editorial note claiming the 'beloved disciple' as the author of the Fourth Gospel. It is, however, not entirely clear that this is the meaning intended."

More forcefully, Grayston (1990, 175) declared: "To claim the beloved disciple's authority for v. 23 is scarcely supported by *He it is who wrote it.* To claim his authority for formal Petrine leadership which overthrows the main teaching of the Gospel is implausible."

Further complicating the issue of the writer's testimony, a review of the literature by Charlesworth (1995) identified almost twenty candidates in identifying the beloved disciple, the possible author of John. In contrast, Hays (2006, 132) pointed out that "the witness-motif is one of the subthemes of the Fourth Gospel, surfacing at three key points in the narrative: the prologue (1:14), death of Christ (19:35), and epilogue (21:24). 21:24 [sic] forms an inclusio to 1:14." Readers seeking arguments in support of the authenticity of John 21 are referred to Chapman (1930, 379-87), Jackson (1999, 1-34), and Köstenberger (2004b, 72-88).

The bottom line is that the identity of John 21 is unknown. To assume that the Christian community at the time John was written knew its author is an argument based on silence. Consequently, the witness reported in John 21:24 is useless given that the identity of the person bearing the witness is unknown.

In conclusion, the testimony of John's trustworthiness is untrustworthy.

SPECULATION #190 The Doubtful Authenticity of John 21:25

There is yet a problem with John; the authenticity of John 21:25 is doubtful. Codex Sinaiticus, also known as Aleph (ℵ) or 01, is the oldest complete fourth-century uncial manuscript of the New Testament. However, the last verse of John 21:25 is a later addition to this manuscript. Research by Milne and Skeat (1938) documented that the manuscript was the work of several scribes and included numerous corrections *including the last verse*. As mentioned above, even Dodd (1953, 212-13) posited that this excerpt from John was "an editorial note."

Skeat and Elliott (2004, 111; cf. Bentley 1986, 122; Metzger 1981, 77) elaborated about the final verse in more detail:

> Now Tischendorf has noted that in the Sinaiticus there is something peculiar about this final verse; the ink, the shapes of the letters, and the whole appearance of the writing of this verse looks slightly different compared with the rest of the page. And he inferred that it had been omitted by the original scribe, and supplied at a later stage by one of the other scribes working on the manuscript.

> Responsible scholars have since questioned or even contradicted Tischendorf's conclusions. Now, however, the question has at last been settled; for ultra-violet light brings up traces of half-effaced writing which show that the scribe actually did stop at the last verse but one, and finished off the book in the usual way by adding a *coronis* or tail-piece, and the title, "Gospel according to John" (which, as in all early manuscripts, is regularly placed at the end, not at the beginning). Subsequently, however, he changed his mind, washed the vellum clean and inserted the final verse, rewriting the tail-piece and title lower down the page.

Interested readers can see the corrected version at the Codex Sinaiticus website. The online version has a fully transcribed set of digital pages, including amendments to the text and two images of each page, with both standard lighting and raking light to highlight the texture of the parchment.

CHAPTER 13

Appearance at the Mountain to the Great Commission

ISSUE 101: Jesus's Appearance at the Mountain

Mk	Mt 28:16 Then the eleven disciples went away to Galilee, into a mountain where Jesus had appointed them. 17 And when they saw him, *they worshipped him: but some doubted.*	Lk	Jn

PERHAPS THE NEXT appearance of Jesus was in a mountain at Galilee. N. T. Wright (2003, 642) wrote: "Neither he [[Matthew]] nor Jesus mention meeting on a mountain, so the comment in verse 16 about Jesus having directed them to go to one remains another unexplained Matthaean puzzle." This detailed event is recorded *only* in Matthew. Matthew narrates that when the people saw Jesus they *proskuneo* (worshipped him), however some doubted.

CONTRADICTION #106 Why the Synoptic Authors Failed to Detail the Other Appearances in John

Why the synoptic authors did not detail the three additional appearances narrated in John is unknown. Unmistakably, these appearances of the risen Jesus were significant.

First, John 20:14-18 indicated that Mary Magdalene met Jesus at the tomb. Jesus gave Mary Magdalene a statement that has been the subject of numerous interpretations: "Jesus saith unto her, Touch me not; for I am not yet ascended to my Father: but go to my brethren, and say unto them, I ascend unto my Father, and your Father; and to my God, and your God." Second, a few verses later, John 20:25-29 reported Jesus's encounter with his apostle Thomas. The Doubting Thomas incident was significant because Jesus asserted the superiority of those who have faith without physical evidence. Finally, the synoptic Gospels omitted any reference to John 21:1-22 detailing the fishing incident at the Sea of Tiberias with seven of Jesus's disciples and Peter's recommission. It was at this time Jesus made Peter the head of the church.

A rational speculation for the absence of these accounts in the synoptic Gospels is that perhaps their authors were unaware of any tradition because they were not yet developed. However, another natural explanation is that John, being the last of the Gospels, embellished and aggrandized the post-resurrection appearances. Once again, his agenda was stated clearly and unambiguously:

> Jn 20:31 But these are written, *that ye might believe* that Jesus is the Christ, the Son of God; and that believing ye might have life through his name.

Unmistakably and overtly, John's agenda was evangelizing, missionizing, and proselytizing (cf. Carson 1991, 661).

SPECULATION #191 Worshipping Jesus Does Not Equate with God

Matthew 28:17 reported that when the eleven disciples saw Jesus in the Galilee they *proskuneo* (worshipped him, however some doubted). Gundry (1994, 595) maintained that the disciples' worshipping Jesus was their acknowledgment of his divinity. To the contrary, the worshipping of Jesus in no way substantiated that he was God in the absolute sense.

The Greek verb *proskuneo* (#4352 in *Strong's Concordance;* Strong 1890, 61) is used in reference to worshipping God *and human persons. However, it also means* showing homage, obeisance, reverence, or supplication to human persons (e.g., kissing the hand, kneeling, or prostrating oneself). Many Christian Bibles (i.e., the AV, ASV, NASB, NIV, NKJV, NLT, NSRV, and RSV) obscure the meaning of this term by rendering *proskuneo* as worshipping. Yet, there are several Christian Bibles that present a different reading:

TABLE 68. Bible Translations of Matthew 28:17

BIBLE	TRANSLATION
J. N. Darby Translation 1890	And when they saw him, they did *homage* to him: but some doubted.
Douay-Rheims Bible	And seeing them they *adored*: but some doubted.
Hebrew Names Version 2000	When they saw him, they *bowed* down to him, but some doubted.
Weymouth New Testament	There they saw Him and *prostrated* themselves before Him. Yet some doubted.
World English Bible	When they saw him, they *bowed* down to him, but some doubted.
Robert Young Literal Translation 1862, 1887, 1898	and having seen him, they *bowed* to him, but some did waver.

The Greek word *proskune* means to adore, bow to the ground, kneel, and pay homage or prostrate oneself. Consequently, the term does *not* refer to praying to Jesus as if he were God in the absolute sense. Instead the Greek word *latreuo* (Strong's Number: 3,000; Strong 1890, 44) is used in of religious service only, and it is applied exclusively to the Father in the Christian scriptures. If Jesus were assumed to be God in the absolute sense by his disciples, it is curious and noteworthy that the term *latreuno* was not ever used in this reference. Furthermore, the NRSV (1989, 89ni) pointed out: "Other ancient authorities lack *worshiped him, and*." (Italics are in the original.)

BeDuhn (2003, 48), in reference to Matthew 28:17, challenged the notion that Jesus was worshipped as if he were thought of as Almighty God. He wrote:

> Here all translations except the NW [[*New World Translation of the Holy Scriptures*]] have recourse to "worship"—a rendering which makes no sense in this context. How can someone worship and doubt at the same time? Notice how all eleven disciples prostrate themselves, but not all believe what they are experiencing. The word can't possibly mean "worship" as we use that word today, as a mental state of reverence, since 'they doubted.' It only refers to the outward physical act of bowing down, which may or may not reflect how the one making the gesture really feels about the person to whom they make it.

In conclusion, the eleven disciples who worshipped Jesus provide *no* support for the belief that he is God. Furthermore, the Greek word employed in Matthew 28:17 for worship does *not* provide incontrovertible evidentiary proof that the disciples thought Jesus was God in an absolute sense.

SPECULATION #192 The Significance of the Mountain

For an unknown reason, great prominence is given to the rendezvous at the mountain in the Galilee. Commentators and scholars have offered speculative reasons as to why Jesus chose to meet his disciples at this mountain. Several of these rationales included the following:

1. The site was chosen because it was convenient to many of Jesus's loyal followers who lived in the Galilee.
2. The mountain probably furnished a location that would be free from distractions and outside disturbances.
3. Matthew attempted to replicate a new Mount Sinai experience.
4. The author adapted the verse from Isaiah 52:7: "How beautiful on the mountains are the feet of those who bring good news, who proclaim peace, who bring good tidings, who proclaim salvation, who say to Zion, 'Your God reigns!'"
5. Moses and Elijah met God at mountains (Horeb/Sinai). Consequently, Matthew similarly indicated that Jesus met these specific prophets on a mountain [However, Matthew did *not* explain how Peter instantly recognized Moses and Elijah; cf. Allison 2005a, 227].
6. It is possible that this was a Hellenistic influence on the description of a lofty meeting place because Ancient Near East traditions taught that the gods resided in such high places.

Elaborating on the Mount Sinai experience, N. T. Wright (2003, 642n33; cf. Allison 1993, 262-65; Aus 2008, 162-64; Baxter 1999, 75; Blomberg 2007, 100; Loewe 1996, 111; O'Toole 1990, 28; Sparks 2006, 660) wrote: "There may be a hint of a 'new Moses' theme, with Jesus on the mountain looking out into the promised land, which is now of course the entire world." If this is so, once again the Christian scriptures are displaying a mania for biblical parallelism and one-upmanship of Moses. However, it must be acknowledged that although many great acts of God were executed on a mountain, it must also be acknowledged that at other times the same acts are done on level ground (e.g., the ten plagues).

SPECULATION #193 The Some Who Doubted and What They Doubted

It should be noted that Matthew added the comment: "But some doubted." Commentators, scholars, and writers have offered a variety of reasons as to why some of the disciples doubted that it was Jesus who they saw at the mountain in the Galilee.

1. Ellis (1968, 577) rendered the phrase *doubted* as "the person concerned is divided in his conviction" and pointed out that the Jerusalem Bible interpreted the passage as "but some hesitated."
2. Réville (1894, 504) offered a different explanation for the phrase "but some doubted." He posited that the text was mutilated and should read: "Some believed, but others doubted."
3. Grayston (1984, 108) translated the verse: "When they saw him, they threw themselves down in submission, though they doubted its effect."
4. Another suggested Christian apologetic is that for some witnesses this encounter might have been their first time seeing Jesus. Consequently they were unaware of his other appearances or there was a lack of a miraculous appearance.
5. Another Christian apologetic is that the phrase "but some doubted" proved the historicity of Jesus's resurrection. The argument runs along the lines that the honesty of the gospel's author is reflected in this admission of the doubts of the apostles. Consequently, this action strengthened the case for Jesus's resurrection.
6. This phrase was incorporated into the text in order to maintain tension in the form of a literary cliffhanger. On the other hand, it has been suggested that the motif of "doubt" reflected the problem of second and third generation Christians who had no direct tie to the original Easter experience. Hence, this phrase is *not* necessarily an example of the criterion of dissimilarity (i.e., an embarrassment).
7. Ceroke (2004, 154), writing for the *New Catholic Encyclopedia*, suggested that the author of Matthew made "use of the tradition of doubt among Jesus' disciples concerning his resurrection to criticize the doubts of the Christian community of his own time, a point that may also be made in Mk 16.14."
8. Ellis (1968, 575) suggested: "The simplest explanation is that the evangelist is quoting facts."

The constructive point to be constantly aware of is that all these interpretations are mere speculations.

Bruner (1990, 810) laid out five main interpretations of worshiped/doubted, including their proponents:

1. *All* worshiped/*All* doubted (thus, among recent scholars, Boring; Hagner, 2: 880, 884).
2. *All* worshiped/*All* had *earlier* (but not now!) doubted (see above).
3. *All* worshiped/*Some of them* doubted (see above; Luz, 4:439; Davies and Allison 3:681 n.23, say that this is the view of "most commentators").
4. *Some* worshiped/*Some* doubted (Gnilka, 2:506; Harrington, 414).
5. *All* worshiped/*Others* (not the Eleven) doubted (Boring, 520, assigns a number of versions here).

Dovetailing on the above, even the apologist N. T. Wright (2003, 643; cf. Horst 1986, 27-30) inquired: "Matthew only has the Eleven there; how many is 'some'? Two or three? Which ones? Were their doubts resolved? What form did their doubts take?"

What then did Matthew mean by "doubt"? Numerous suggestions have been offered. Reeves (1998, 348) identified five possibilities: "1) The eleven worshipped, but some were perplexed by what they saw, 2) The disciples doubted that it was really Jesus, 3) They doubted whether they should worship him, 4) They doubted if submission would have any effect, and 5) They were doubtful about the reception they would get from Jesus, and others."

SPECULATION #194 **Why Some Doubted**

Why should the disciples have doubted Jesus's physical, bodily resurrection as recorded in Matthew? By now, it was at least approximately two weeks after Jesus's crucifixion. The disciples had received and heard numerous reports about the risen Jesus. Furthermore, in Luke 24:36-40 and John 20:19-28 they had, in fact, already seen him and even watched him eat food in their presence (Lk 24:43) (Peterson 2002, 15).

1. The disciples were all informed that he had risen by: (1) Mary Magdalene (Jn 20:18), (2) Mary Magdalene and the other Mary (Mt 28:8), (3) the two on the road including Cleopas (Lk 24:35), (4) Cephas [Simon] had seen Jesus earlier (1 Cor 15:5; Lk 24:34),

and (5) when more than five hundred brethren saw Jesus at one time (1 Cor 15:6).

2. The disciples were informed earlier by Jesus himself that they would find him alive in Galilee (Mk 14:28). Later, the angel(s) at the tomb gave this information to the women who forwarded it to the eleven disciples (Mt 28:8-10; Lk 24:6-11).

3. The disciples made the journey to the Galilee with this expectation.

4. Jesus had previously appeared before them: (1) the ten disciples on Easter Sunday evening saw and ate with him (Jn 20:20), (2) the disciples, including Thomas (but presumably minus Judas), eight days later encountered Jesus (20:26-29), and (3) the seven at the Sea of Tiberias ate with Jesus (Jn 21:12-13).

5. Jesus now appeared alive, in fact, and before them.

TABLE 69. Doubting Jesus's Physical Bodily Resurrection Timeline

TIME	MARK	MATTHEW	LUKE	JOHN
EARLY EASTER SUNDAY MORNING	Mk 16:1 The women came to anoint Jesus's body. This action implied that they did not believe in a physical bodily resurrection.			Jn 20:2 Mary Magdalene believed and reported to Simon Peter and the other disciple that Jesus's body was taken away.
	Mk 16:11 Mary Magdalene was doubted when she described her encounter ("believed not").		Lk 24:11 Mary Magdalene's words seemed like idle tales, and the disciples did not believe them.	

LATER EASTER MORNING				Jn 20:13 Mary Magdalene doubted Jesus's resurrection when she stated to the two angels that "they have taken away my Lord."
A FEW MINUTES LATER EASTER MORNING				Jn 20:15 Mary Magdalene doubted the Resurrection when she stated to Jesus that they had taken away his body.
EASTER SUNDAY AFTERNOON			Lk 24:25 Jesus rebuked the two travelers on the road to Emmaus: "O fools, and slow of heart to believe."	
SOMETIME PERHAPS EASTER SUNDAY AFTERNOON			Lk 24:34 The disciples in Jerusalem knew that Jesus had appeared earlier to Simon.	
			Lk 24:37 But they were terrified and affrighted, and supposed that they had seen a spirit.	

LATE EASTER AFTERNOON or EARLY EASTER SUNDAY EVENING	Mk 16:12-13 The two travelers reported to the rest, but they did not believe them either. [Yet they were told that Jesus appeared earlier to Simon. (It is disputed who was talking in Luke 24:34).].			
EASTER SUNDAY EVENING			Lk 24:40-41 The disciples in Jerusalem "yet believed not" when Jesus appeared before them.	Jn 20:20 This episode implied that the disciples doubted Jesus's physical bodily resurrection since they needed Jesus to show them his body.
LATER EASTER SUNDAY EVENING				Jn 20:25 Thomas doubted the report of the disciples.
SUNDAY EVENING EIGHT DAYS LATER				Jn 20:27 Thomas was invited to touch Jesus's hand and side. This invitation implied his lack of faith.
UNKNOWN DATE: BETWEEN NINE and FORTY DAYS LATER		Mt 28:17 Some doubted Jesus's physical bodily resurrection when they encountered him at a mountain in Galilee.		

Plainly, if some of Jesus's disciples were still doubtful at this point, what more would need to be done to convince them?

ISSUE 102: What Jesus Said to the Eleven Disciples in the Galilee

Mk 16:15	Mt 28:18 And Jesus	Lk 24:44 And he said unto them,	Jn
And he said unto them, *Go ye into all the world, and preach the gospel to every creature. 16 He that believeth and is baptized shall be saved; but he that believeth not shall be damned.*	came and spake unto them, saying, *All power is given unto me in heaven and in earth. 19 Go ye therefore, and teach all nations, baptizing them in the name of the Father, and of the Son, and of the Holy Ghost: 20 Teaching them to observe all things whatsoever I have commanded you: and, lo, I am with you always, even unto the end of the world. Amen.*	These are the words which I spake unto you, while I was yet with you, that all things must be fulfilled, which were written in the law of Moses, and in the prophets, and in the psalms, concerning me. 45 Then opened he their understanding, that they might understand the scriptures, 46 And said unto them, Thus it is written, and thus it behoved Christ to suffer, and to rise from the dead the third day: 47 *And that repentance and remission of sins should be preached in his name among all nations, beginning at Jerusalem.*	

Matthew 28 alone recorded Jesus's meeting with his eleven disciples in the Galilee. However, there is some commonality with Mark 16:15 that the disciples were to preach or teach the gospel. Therefore, following the parallel rendering of several commentators (Aland 1982, 334; Lee 1991, 240; Scroggie 1948, 81), this text will also assume that Mark 16:15-18 took place in the Galilee. In addition, Luke 24:44 echoes or shares to some degree commonality with Mark 16:15-16 and Matthew 28:18-20 with its mention of preaching among all the nations: "And that repentance and remission of sins should be preached in his name among all nations, beginning at Jerusalem." However, a literal reading of Luke in its context has this meeting taking place in Jerusalem and on Easter Sunday evening. An obvious problem with this verse is that nowhere in the Hebrew Bible does it state or even imply that repentance and the remission of sins should be preached in the name of the Messiah, a king of Israel, or a prophet.

CONTRADICTION #107 Jesus's Command to Take the Gospel to All the Nations

Matthew directly contradicted himself in reference to the command to take the gospel to all nations. Matthew 28:19 reads: "Go ye therefore, and teach all nations, baptizing them in the name of the Father, and of the Son, and of the Holy Ghost." Therefore, the command issued by Jesus was to (1) go into the world (all nations) and (2) preach the gospel to all people. This directive is commonly referred to as "the Great Commission."

THE GREAT COMMISSION CONTRADICTS JESUS'S PREVIOUS INSTRUCTIONS

The Great Commission contradicted Jesus's earlier teaching that his message was *only* for the Jews.

> Mt 10:5-6 These twelve Jesus sent forth, and commanded them, saying, Go not into the way of the Gentiles, and into any city of the Samaritans enter ye not: *But go rather to the lost sheep of the house of Israel.*

> Mt 15:24 But he answered and said, *I am not sent but unto the lost sheep of the house of Israel.*

Mark's message is directly contradictory to Jesus's actions. Jesus *only* went to the House of Israel. Of course, some Christian apologists and evangelicals (Carson 1984, 596; Hare 147-48; Hare and Harrington 359-69; Walker 11-13) might possibly argue that the command to go to all the nations of the world was because the Jewish people rejected Jesus. However, this is merely their opinion. An alternative interpretation is that they refer to all people, *including* Israel (Trilling 26-8; Hill; Hubbard 84-7; Keener 1997, 401; 2009b, 720; Meier 1977, 94-102; O'Brien 262-63). [Note: The references in this paragraph are found in D. A. Carson 1984. *Matthew.* p. 596.]

However, it must be recognized that it was the apostle Paul who, against the expressed wishes of Jesus, extended the gospel (Paul's version) to the Gentiles. Paul's rationale was that God wanted to provoke the Jews of his day to emulate the Gentiles, who had obeyed the gospel.

- Rom 10:19 But I say, Did not Israel know? First Moses saith, I will provoke you to jealousy by them that are no people, and by a foolish nation I will anger you [see Deut 32:21].
- Rom 11:11 I say then, Have they stumbled that they should fall? God forbid: but rather through their fall salvation is come unto the Gentiles, for to provoke them to jealousy.
- Rom 11:14 If by any means I may provoke to emulation them which are my flesh, and might save some of them.

THE GREAT COMMISSION CONTRADICTS THE ACTS OF THE APOSTLES

Matthew's Great Commission is completely irreconcilable and contradicted by the accounts recorded twice in the Acts of the Apostles 11:1-3 and 15:1-18. Matthew 28:19-20 recorded that Jesus instructed his eleven disciples at the mountain in the Galilee: "Go ye therefore, and *teach all nations*, baptizing them in the name of the Father, and of the Son, and of the Holy Ghost: Teaching them to observe all things whatsoever I have commanded you: and, lo, I am with you always, even unto the end of the world. Amen." These commands of Jesus are plain and simple. The disciples were to teach all the nations. Nowhere in this commission was there any mention that the teaching to all nations was contingent that these people (1) be circumcised, (2) observe the laws of kashrut (dealing with permissible foods), (3) observe the Jewish Sabbath, or (4) observe other Jewish holy days.

Given that there was an omission of any restrictions to the disciples to teach to all the nations, it makes no sense why the disciples would have opposed Peter's or Paul's outreach in spreading the gospel to the gentiles. The Acts of the Apostles extensively recorded these two conflicts in Acts 11 and Acts 15.

First, approximately eight years after the Jesus's ascension, Peter was condemned for his preaching to the Gentiles. Acts 11:1-2 introduced the controversy: "And the apostles and brethren that were in Judea heard that the Gentiles had also received the word of God. And when Peter was come to Jerusalem, they that were of the circumcision contended with him." Curiously, the disciples knew *nothing* of any such teaching from their Master. How then did Peter deal with the accusation and justify his conduct? He stated that it was the express will of their Master. Specifically, Peter claimed that while in a trance at Joppa he had a vision (11:5) that instructed him to carry the gospel to the Gentiles. Not once did Peter refer to Jesus's Great Commission. Toward the end of this episode the author of Acts 11:18 stated: "When they heard these things, they held their peace, and glorified God, saying, Then hath God also to the Gentiles granted repentance unto life."

TABLE 70. Acts 11 Contradicting Matthew 28:19-20

VERSE	ELABORATION	CONTRADICTION
Acts 11:1 And the apostles and brethren that were in Judaea heard that the Gentiles had also received the word of God.	1. An unknown number of apostles and brothers were located in Judea. 2. They heard that the Gentiles were receiving the word of God.	
Acts 11:2 And when Peter was come up to Jerusalem, they that were of the circumcision contended with him,	1. Peter returned to Jerusalem. 2. Peter was confronted by some who were circumcised.	It made no sense that Peter should have been confronted for carrying out Jesus's command in the Great Commission to "teach all nations."
Acts 11:3 Saying, Thou wentest in to men uncircumcised, and didst eat with them.	1. He was charged with being present with those who were not circumcised. 2. He was charged with eating with those who were not circumcised.	This accusation made no sense in line with Jesus's Great Commission. In order for Peter to "teach all nations," it would be necessary to commune with them.
Acts 11:4 But Peter rehearsed the matter from the beginning, and expounded it by order unto them, saying,	1. First, Peter explained the situation. 2. Then he expounded on it step by step.	
Acts 11:5 I was in the city of Joppa praying: and in a trance I saw a vision, A certain vessel descended, as it had been a great sheet, let down from heaven by four corners; and it came even to me:	1. Peter was in the city of Joppa. 2. Peter fell into a trance. 3. Peter had a vision.	

Acts 11:18 When they heard these things, they held their peace, and glorified God, saying, Then hath God also to the Gentiles granted repentance unto life.	1. Those in Jerusalem listened to Peter's account and had no further objections. 2. They agreed that God granted the Gentiles repentance unto life.	

Four chapters later, Acts reported a second controversy. This time it was Paul who was the apparent violator, performing outreach to the Gentiles. Once again the dispute was resolved in Jerusalem.

TABLE 71. Acts 15 Contradicting Matthew 28:19-20

VERSE	ELABORATION	CONTRADICTION
Acts 15:1 And certain men which came down from Judaea taught the brethren, and said, Except ye be circumcised after the manner of Moses, ye cannot be saved.	1. Some men from Jerusalem (Judea) came to an assembly of Gentile converts (believers) in Antioch, Syria. 2. They started teaching that circumcision "according to the custom of Moses" was a necessary part to be saved.	
Acts 15:2 When therefore Paul and Barnabas had no small dissension and disputation with them, they determined that Paul and Barnabas, and certain other of them, should go up to Jerusalem unto the apostles and elders about this question.	1. Paul and Barnabas, who were in Antioch at the time, did not agree with the teaching brought by these men. 2. They vigorously argued and debated this view with the men from Judea. 3. Finally, the members of the congregation decided to send Paul, Barnabas, and others to Jerusalem to request the opinions of the apostles and elders on this matter of doubt.	It was now almost twenty years after the Crucifixion and Jesus had issued his Great Commission. It made no sense that these men would be challenging Paul's actions if they knew Jesus's Great Commission. Seemingly, these men from Judea were totally unaware of Jesus's Great Commission to teach all nations.

Acts 15:3 And being brought on their way by the church, they passed through Phenice and Samaria, declaring the conversion of the Gentiles: and they caused great joy unto all the brethren.	1. A special escort of church members attended Paul, Barnabas, and the others from Antioch as they made their way to Jerusalem. 2. They recounted to the groups of believers with whom they met in Phoenicia and Samaria how God was calling and converting Gentiles. 3. These successful conversions were a source of great encouragement to these brethren.	
Acts 15:4 And when they were come to Jerusalem, they were received of the church, and of the apostles and elders, and they declared all things that God had done with them.	1. Upon reaching Jerusalem, Paul and Barnabas were welcomed by the church, the apostles, and elders. 2. Paul and Barnabas reported all that God had done through them among the Gentiles. 3. They also apparently provided an explanation of the problem that had arisen in Antioch, which had necessitated their appearance in Jerusalem. [Note: This event marked Paul's third visit to Jerusalem after his conversion.]	
Acts 15:5 But there rose up certain of the sect of the Pharisees which believed, saying, That it was needful to circumcise them, and to command them to keep the law of Moses.	1. Afterward, some of the Pharisees challenged Paul. [Note: Paul was once a Pharisee and thus a "former" member of that group.] 2. They supported the teaching about circumcision and also the keeping of the entire law of Moses.	It made no sense that these Pharisees would have challenged Paul's actions if they knew of Jesus's Great Commission.

Acts 15:6 And the apostles and elders came together for to consider of this matter.	1. Both sides of the issue presented their case to the apostles and church elders assembled together to discuss the matter. 2. They did not give their judgment separately.	It made no sense that there needed to be any discussion if they knew of Jesus's Great Commission.
Acts 15:7 And when there had been much disputing, Peter rose up, and said unto them, Men and brethren, ye know how that a good while ago God made choice among us, that the Gentiles by my mouth should hear the word of the gospel, and believe.	1. There was much arguing. One side insisted that the Gentiles must keep the law of Moses, the other that they were not under the Mosaic covenant at all. 2. After a heated discussion, the apostle Peter stood up and began to relate how Gentiles had originally been brought into the church. He argued: Why should the Gentiles, who had heard the word of the gospel by Paul's mouth, be compelled to submit to circumcision, any more than those that heard it by my mouth? Or why should the terms of their admission now be made harder than they were then?	Again it made no sense that there should have been a heated *dispute if the disciples had been fulfilling Jesus's command to teach all the nations during the past twenty years.*
Acts 15:8 And God, which knoweth the hearts, bare them witness, giving them the Holy Ghost, even as he did unto us;	1. Peter's point was that God gave Cornelius and his house the Holy Spirit without requiring the uncircumcised to first be circumcised. 2. Therefore, accept them just as God accepted us and gave the Holy Spirit as a proof to us that He had accepted them.	It must be kept in mind that Peter's point here is directly related to the issue at hand: circumcision.

Acts 15:9 And put no difference between us and them, purifying their hearts by faith.	1. Peter declared that there was no distinction between the circumcised and the uncircumcised. 2. Those that had their hearts purified by faith were therein made so nearly to resemble one another purified. 3. God purified their hearts by faith. Thus the true circumcision is of the heart, not of the body.	
Acts 15:10 Now therefore why tempt ye God, to put a yoke upon the neck of the disciples, which neither our fathers nor we were able to bear?		
Acts 15:11 But we believe that through the grace of the Lord Jesus Christ we shall be saved, even as they.		
Acts 15:12 Then all the multitude kept silence, and gave audience to Barnabas and Paul, declaring what miracles and wonders God had wrought among the Gentiles by them.	1. Then the entire multitude kept silent and listened to Barnabas and Paul. 2. Paul and Barnabas followed up Peter's speech by listing the things God had done among the Gentiles through their ministry.	The point of mentioning these miracles and wonders was to show that God had accepted the Gentiles without requiring them to first be physically circumcised.
Acts 15:13 And after they had held their peace, James answered, saying, Men and brethren, hearken unto me:	After Paul and Barnabas finished speaking, James the brother of Jesus, the leading elder in the Jerusalem congregation, spoke to the group.	

Acts 15:14 Simeon hath declared how God at first did visit the Gentiles to, take out of them a people for his name.		
Acts 15:15 And to this agree the words of the prophets; as it is written,	James confirmed the words of Peter and then supported them with a quotation from the prophet Amos.	
Acts 15:16 After this I will return, and will build again the tabernacle of David, which is fallen down; and I will build again the ruins thereof, and I will set it up:	In verses 16 and 17, James quoted Amos 9:11-12 from the Greek *Septuagint* translation of the Hebrew scriptures.	
Acts 15:17 That the residue of men might seek after the Lord, and all the Gentiles, upon whom my name is called, saith the Lord, who doeth all these things.		
Acts 15:18 Known unto God are all his works from the beginning of the world.	The meaning of this statement is that this calling of the Gentiles was a part of the divine plan known to God from the beginning of the ages.	

The bottom line is that the disciples seemingly had no knowledge that they were also to spread the gospel to non-Jews.

BIBLICAL COMMENTATORS POINT OUT THE ACTS OF THE APOSTLES CONTRADICTED MATTHEW 28:19-20

Alan Hugh M'Neile (1961, 437), writing in *The Gospel According to St. Matthew*, stated:

The evangelizing of all nations was spoken of in xxxiv. 14. But the difficulty there caused by the words is greater, if possible, in the present passage. If the risen Lord commanded it in one of His latest utterances, the action of the apostles with reference to the Gentiles (see e.g., Gal ii.; Ac. X; xi. 1-18) is inexplicable. . . . Nor is there a hint in Acts or Epistles that when the first apostles confined themselves to Jews, while recognizing S. Paul as the apostle of the Gentiles, it was because of their "reluctance to undertake spiritual responsibilities.". . . . The universality of the Christian message was soon learnt, largely by spiritual experiences of S. Paul, which were authoritative for the Church. And once learnt, they were early assigned to a direct command of Christ. It is impossible to maintain that everything which goes to constitute even the essence of Christianity must necessarily be traceable to explicit words of Jesus.

The same view was maintained in David Hill's (1972, 362) *The Gospel of Matthew* concerning the command to make disciples of all nations:

> The *Sitz im Leben* of the verse probably lies in the life and work of the Church about fifty years after the death of Jesus. Had Christ given the command to "make disciples of all nations," the opposition in Paul's time to the admission of Gentiles to the Church would be inexplicable. It must be presumed that the Church, having learned and experienced the universality of the Christian message, assigned that knowledge to a direct command of the living Lord.

Thus, in plain language, Jesus did not make any such demand.

Beare (1981, 544-45), writing in the *Gospel According to Matthew*, also questioned the command found in Matthew to "make disciples of all nations":

> Obviously enough, if any such command had been known to the apostles, and to the early church, they would not have debated about the legitimacy of such a mission, and the "pillars" of the mother church in Jerusalem could hardly have agreed to restrict themselves to 'the circumcision' while it was left to Paul and Barnabas—two men who had not been among the eleven who received the command—to go to the Gentiles. This alone would be enough to demonstrate that this charge of the risen Jesus is a relatively late formation. The controversy over the admission of the Gentiles is long over, and indeed forgotten.

CONTRADICTION #108 Mark versus Matthew—Jesus's Command to Baptize

Mark contradicts Matthew. Matthew 28:19 instructed the disciples "*to teach all nations* baptizing them in the name of the Father, and of the Son, and of the Holy Ghost." However, in Matthew there is no mention of sins or the remission of sins. Of course, Christian apologists would counter that the omission is not contradiction.

In contradiction, Mark 16:15-16 reported: "And he said unto them, Go ye into all the world, and preach the gospel to every creature. He that believeth and is baptized shall be saved; but he that believeth not shall be damned." Therefore, in Mark, people are saved whereas Matthew omitted any mention of salvation.

The reason Matthew omitted any comment or discussion of forgiveness of sins is remarkable since Matthew is known to be dependent on Mark. N. T. Wright (2003, 643) offered a Christian apologetic: "unless it is seen by implication in the command to baptize. Rather, the Eleven are to be teachers, disciplemakers." However, this Christian apologetic is nothing more than Wright's personal opinion. There is no incontrovertible evidentiary proof to support Wright's hypothesis.

The differences between Mark and Matthew can be seen in the tables below:

TABLE 72. Mark 16:5-6 versus Matthew 28

MARK 16	MATTHEW 28
Mk 16:15 Jesus instructed the disciples to preach the gospel to *every creature* [minor difference in wording].	Jesus instructed the disciples to teach the gospel to *all nations* [minor difference in wording].
Mk 16:16 Jesus claimed that he who believed and was baptized will be saved.	Jesus made *no* claim about being saved through belief or baptism.
Mk 16:16 Jesus claimed that those who did not believe were damned.	Jesus made *no* statement about non-believers being damned.

TABLE 73. Matthew 28:18-20 versus Mark 16

MATTHEW 28	MARK 16
Mt 28:18 Jesus claimed that all power is given to him in heaven and earth.	*No* such claim was made.
Mt 28:19 Jesus specifically instructed his disciples to baptize in the name of the Father, of the Son, and of the Holy Ghost.	*No* such claim was made.
Mt 28:20 Jesus specifically ordered his disciples to teach all the nations to observe all things whatsoever he had commanded them.	*No* such claim was made.
Mt 28:20 Jesus declared that he would always be with his disciples even to the end of the world.	*No* such claim was made.

SPECULATION #195 Did Matthew Write the Trinitarian Formula in the Great Commission?

Biblical scholars generally fall into three categories when they evaluate the authorship of the Trinitarian formula reported in Matthew's Great Commission. First, there are those writers on the extreme left who outright declare that Matthew did not directly quote Jesus. Second, in the middle of the road there are those writers who tactfully state that Matthew modified what Jesus taught. Others who are perhaps in the middle avoid the controversy altogether by reviewing the literature without taking a position. Finally, on the extreme right are writers who argue that the words were preserved accurately (Farmer 1974; Thomas 2002; 2000). For example, Thomas (2000, 52) bluntly states:

> To say that the words represent Jesus' intent even if He did not utter these specific instructions is a presumptuous copout, possibly a concession to gain respectability with the academic intelligentsia, an effort to find a middle ground between the absolute accuracy of the Gospel account and the extreme view that Jesus never said any such thing.

Thomas (2002, 307-08), a conservative evangelical, openly criticized a number of well-known New Testament writers including those he characterized as Evangelical. Below are several writers he identified who missed the mark. The comments of these prominent and renowned commentators speak volumes, refuting the notion that Matthew wrote the Trinitarian formula in the Great Commission.

> Obviously enough, if any such command had been known to the apostles, and to the early church, they would not have debated about the legitimacy of such a mission, and the "pillars" of the mother church in Jerusalem could hardly have agreed to restrict themselves to 'the circumcision' while it was left to Paul and Barnabas—two men who had not been among the eleven who received the command—to go to the Gentiles. This alone would be enough to demonstrate that this charge of the risen Jesus is a relatively late formulation. The controversy over the admission of Gentiles is long over, and indeed forgotten. [Beare, Francis W. *The Gospel According to Matthew* (Peabody, Mass.: Hendrickson, 1981), 149]

> Matthew tells us nothing concerning his view of Christian baptism. Only Matthew records this command of Jesus, but the practice of the early church suggests its historicity (cf. Acts 2:38, 41; 8:12, 38; 9:18 etc.). The threefold name (at most only an incipient trinitarianism) in which the baptism was to be performed, on the other hand, seems clearly to be a liturgical expansion of the evangelist consonant with the practice of his day (thus Hubbard; cf. *Did.* 7.1). There is a good possibility that in its original form, as witnessed by the ante-Nicene Eusebian form, the text read 'make disciples *in my name*' (see Conybeare). This shorter reading preserves the symmetrical rhythm of the passage, where the triadic formula fits awkwardly into the structure as one might expect if it were an interpolation (see H. B. Green; cf. Howard; Hill [*IBS* 8 (1986) 54-63], on the other hand, argues for a concentric design with the triadic formula at its center) . . . [Hagner, Donald A. *Matthew 14-28*, vol. 33B of WBC (Dallas, Tex.: Word Book, 1995), 887-88]

> εἰς τὸ ὄνομα is a favorite phrase of his [Matthew's] (3,2) and occurs nowhere else in the synoptics . . . Matthew edited the story

of Jesus' baptism so as to emphasize the Trinity (see the comments on 3:16-17; cf. 12:28); yet only Jesus' name is associated with baptism in Acts 2:38; 8:16; 10:48; 19:5; 1 Cor 1:13, 15 (cf. Rom 6:3; 1 Cor 6:11; 10:1-4). Therefore Matthew seems to be responsible for the present formula. [Gundry, R. H. 1994. *Matthew: A Commentary on His Handbook for a Mixed Church Under Persecution*, 2nd ed. (Grand Rapids, Mich.: Eerdmans, 1994), 596]

On the other hand, it is not inconceivable that Matthew distilled the essence of Jesus' more detailed parting instructions for the Eleven into concise language using the terminology developed later in the early church's baptismal services. As R. E. O. White reflects: "If Jesus commanded the making of disciples and the baptizing of them 'in my name,' and Matt. expressed Christ's fullest meaning (for disciples 'of all nations') by using the fuller descriptions current in his own day, who shall say that he seriously misrepresented our Lord's intention?" [Blomberg, Craig L. *Matthew*. (Nashville: Broadman, 1992), 432-33]

The term "formula" is tripping us up. There is no evidence we have Jesus' *ipsissima verba* here and still less that the church regarded Jesus' command as a baptismal *formula*, a liturgical form the ignoring of which was a breach of canon law. The problem has too often been cast in anachronistic terms. E. Riggenbach points out that as late as the Didache, baptism in the name of Jesus and baptism in the name of the Trinity coexist side by side: the church was not bound by precise 'formulas' and felt no embarrassment at a multiplicity of them, precisely because Jesus' instruction, which may not have been in these precise words, was not regarded as a binding formula. [Carson, David A. *Matthew*, vol 8 of EBC, edited by F. E. Gaebelein. (Grand Rapids: Zondervan, 1984), 598. Emphasis Carson's]

A table detailing these conflicting points of view has been modified from Thomas (2002, 307):

TABLE 74. Summary of "Genre Override in the Gospels"
Source: Robert L. Thomas in *Evangelical Hermeneutics: The New Versus The Old*. (Grand Rapids: Kregel, 2002), 309. Modified.

Category or Passage	Genre-Override Principles	Grammatical-Historical Principles
historical data	embellished because of writer's theology	factually accurate
harmonization	possible through historical-critical tools	possible through factual reconciliations
allegorization	plentiful to explain alleged discrepancies	unnecessary because no discrepancies exist
authorial skills	authors committed literary blunders	authors were highly skilled
perspicuity	subtle literary clues to hidden meanings	meaning completely obvious
speakers	words misrepresented	words preserved accurately
historical setting	settings falsified	setting represented accurately
eyewitness input	misrepresented	perfectly preserved
meaning	passages with multiple meanings	passages limited to single meaning
Jesus' utterances	single occurrences multiplied	similar sayings on separate occasions
subjectivism	exercised beyond control	reduced to absolute minimum
commissioning of Twelve	scattered sayings compiled by Matthew	given by Jesus on one occasion
exception clause	added by writer of Matthew	spoken by Jesus

One additional point regarding the Great Commission deserves mention. Rabbi Ariel Bar Tzadok (2014) points out that in Matthew 28:19-20, Jesus instructs his disciples to teach all nations "to observe all things whatsoever I have commanded you." So what did Jesus command his disciples? The answer is to be righteous Jews and follow God's instructions that are found in the Torah. Expounding on Rabbi Tzadok's answer it must also be pointed out that Jesus never clearly and unequivocally taught (1) that God existed as a trinity, (2) that he was God incarnate in human flesh, (3) that God became man in human flesh and died on the cross to atone for the sins of mankind, (4) the commandments were to be abrogated, or (5) the Sabbath was to be changed to Sunday.

SPECULATION #196 Misunderstanding Over the Phrase "the Whole Land"

Wolfe (1989b, 134-35; also see earlier 49-50) suggested that the common understanding of Jesus's instruction in Mark to spread the gospel is based on a faulty understanding.

> Verse 15 [[Mk 16:15]], recording what commonly is termed "the Great Commission," is a compacted summary of Luke 24:47, Matthew 28:18-19, and John 20:21. The author of this verse followed faithfully his three sources, not knowing that they had not rendered the underlying Aramaic words of Jesus properly into Greek at this point. The key word here, with consonants **a-r-ts**, carries the triple meaning of earth, world, or land. Since it is pretty certain that Jesus did not have any concept of initiating a world mission, his words, as recorded in this Marcan annex might more properly be rendered into English as, "And he said to them, 'Go throughout the whole land (of Palestine) and preach the Gospel to every ethnic group.'" Luke retained this meaning in his full use of the Greek word *ethne*. Jesus was requesting that his disciples extend their ministry to the whole land of Palestine, including virtually untouched Judaea, and preach to every ethnic group such as Samaritans, Syrians, Lebanese, and any other foreigners who might be sojourning in Palestine, and every social and economic class. This was his Great Commission."

Fitzmyer (1985, 2:1517) also supported the position that "the whole land" referred to Palestine. Assuming that Wolfe's understanding is correct; the ramification challenges a fundamental doctrine of church theology of proclaiming the gospel throughout the entire earth. Instead, believers should only go throughout the whole land of what the Romans later called Palestine and preach the gospel to every ethnic group such as Samaritans, Syrians, Lebanese, and any other foreigners who might be sojourning there.

ISSUE 103: The Signs Jesus Gave to Them That Believed in His Name

Mk 16:17 And these signs shall follow them that believe; In my name shall they *cast out devils; they shall speak with new tongues; 18 They shall take up serpents; and if they drink any deadly thing, it shall not hurt them; they shall lay hands on the sick, and they shall recover.*	Mt	Lk	Jn

Mark records five promises or signs of power that Jesus gave to those who believed in him. These five claims include (1) the power to cast out the devil, (2) the power to speak in new tongues, (3) the power to take up serpents, (4) the power to drink anything deadly and not be hurt, and (5) the power to heal the sick by laying on hands.

SPECULATION #197 Why Some Signs Are Accepted and Others Are Not

Mark 16:17-18 declared: "And these signs shall follow them that believe; In my name shall they cast out devils; they shall speak with new tongues; They shall take up serpents; and if they drink any deadly thing, it shall not hurt them; they shall lay hands on the sick, and they shall recover." Therefore, on a literal, natural, and plain reading, *all* who believe in Jesus's name will possess five signs. These signs are the ability to (1) cast out the devil, (2) speak in tongues, (3) handle serpents, (4) drink any deadly thing with impunity, and (5) lay on hands and heal the sick. However, many churches and theological seminaries accept some of these signs with open hands whereas others seemingly frown on some of these signs. How can this be? Why are some signs accepted when others are not?

In order to explain this contradiction with the facts of history, Christian apologists and New Testament commentators necessitated reinterpreting the words of Mark by adding caveats not presented in the text. For example, Lee (1991, 241) offered a standard Christian apologetic that "what the Lord said here does not mean that every saved believer should have all five signs. It means that each saved believer may have some of these signs but will not necessarily have all."

Unfortunately for Lee and other Christian apologists, Mark 16:17-18 says no such thing. Lee's argument is refuted by a plain faced meaning and natural reading of the text. At the least, this Christian apologetic is nothing more than the opinion of its proponents.

Another rationale that in effect overrides the literal reading of Mark 16:17-18 by Christian apologists is that God has the free will and ability to pass on this power to believers if He (God) so chooses. Plainly, God can choose whomever He wishes, regardless of his or her belief. For example, various religions and cultures have traditions that indicate that certain people have the power to excise or purge foreign entities. However, this Christian apologetic is an argument based on silence. Furthermore, it sounds more like an excuse than a viable answer.

Consequently, Charles Calwell Ryrie (1976, 101), the former chairperson of systematic theology at the Dallas Theological Seminary, wrote: "Mk 16:9-20 These verses do not appear in two of the most trustworthy manuscripts of the N.T., though they are part of many other manuscripts and versions . . . The doubtful genuineness of verses 9-20 makes it unwise to build a doctrine or base an experience on them."

SPECULATION #198 Speaking in New Tongues

Mark 16:17 directly claimed that those who believe in Jesus will be blessed with the gift of new tongues. *Glossolalia* most commonly means "speaking in tongues." This term is derived from two Greek words: *glōssai*, which means tongues or languages, and *lalien*, which means to speak. Jansen (1993, 255), writing for *The Oxford Companion to the Bible,* defined *glossolalia* as "a phenomenon of intense religious experience expressing itself in ecstatic speech." Similarly, Baird (1971, 729), in the *Interpreter's One-Volume Commentary on the Bible,* defined *glossolalia* as "the ecstatic utterance of emotionally agitated religious persons, consisting of a jumble of disjointed and largely unintelligible sounds. Those who speak in this way believe that they are moved directly by a divine spirit and their utterance is therefore quite spontaneous and unpremeditated."

Speaking in tongues appears several times in the Christian scriptures:

> Acts 2:4 And they were all filled with the Holy Ghost, and began to speak with other tongues, as the Spirit gave them utterance [Also see 6, 8, 11].

> Acts 10:46 For they heard them speak with tongues, and magnify God. Then answered Peter,

> Acts 19:6 And when Paul had laid his hands upon them, the Holy Ghost came on them; and they spake with tongues, and prophesied.

1 Cor 12:10 To another the working of miracles; to another prophecy; to another discerning of spirits; to another divers kinds of tongues; to another the interpretation of tongues:

1 Cor 12:28 And God hath set some in the church, first apostles, secondarily prophets, thirdly teachers, after that miracles, then gifts of healings, helps, governments, diversities of tongues.

1 Cor 12:30 Have all the gifts of healing? do all speak with tongues? do all interpret?

1 Cor 13:1 Though I speak with the tongues of men and of angels, and have not charity, I am become as sounding brass, or a tinkling cymbal.

1 Cor 13:8 Charity never faileth: but whether there be prophecies, they shall fail; whether there be tongues, they shall cease; whether there be knowledge, it shall vanish away.

1 Cor 14:26-27 How is it then, brethren? when ye come together, every one of you hath a psalm, hath a doctrine, hath a tongue, hath a revelation, hath an interpretation. Let all things be done unto edifying. If any man speak in an unknown tongue, let it be by two, or at the most by three, and that by course; and let one interpret.

As a side issue, it should be noted that no Hebrew prophet ever mentioned speaking in tongues. Moreover, neither Jesus nor his disciples during Jesus's lifetime ever indulged in such a religious expression.

Perhaps another useful insight can be read in an earlier *Moody Bible Institute Undergraduate Catalog 1999-2000*. The Moody Bible Institute is perhaps one of the foremost conservative evangelical Christian schools of higher learning. Their former position on the Modern Tongues-Speaking movement was issued in their doctrinal statement:

Moody Bible Institute does not endorse the modern tongues-speaking movement for the following reasons:

1. It usually gives an undue prominence to a gift that had only limited value even in New Testament times (1 Corinthians 12-14).

2. It often suggests that tongues-speaking is the necessary evidence of the special work of the Spirit when in fact the New Testament does not say this.
3. It tends to place more emphasis on tongues-speaking as an external manifestation of the Spirit than on the work of the Spirit within to produce character and behavior.
4. It claims that "ecstatic utterance" is also tongues-speaking when there seems to be good reason for believing that the gift in New Testament times was that of speaking in previously unlearned foreign languages.
5. It often fails to see that God sovereignly gives His gifts, not on demand, and that no one gift is for everyone.

We do not deny that God sovereignly gives His gifts, including tongues; we do doubt that most of the emphases of the modern tongues-speaking movement are biblically sound. In stating our position on the modern tongues-speaking movement, we do not mean to detract from the sincerity or Christian character of many within the movement.

In accordance with our long-standing policy against propagating within our fellowship any doctrines not in agreement with our position, we must ask that neither students nor employees propagate the teaching and emphases of the modern tongues-speaking movement within our fellowship. We should rather seek the more excellent way of love and be zealous about more useful and edifying gifts (1 Corinthians 12:13-14:1). (p. 17)

In recent years, the above doctrinal statement has not been incorporated in the Moody's catalog. Instead (2013-2014, 18) they wrote:

SIGN GIFTS OF THE HOLY SPIRIT

The Institute maintains that there is one baptism of the Holy Spirit that occurs at the time a person is born again, placing that one into the body of Christ. MBI also distinguishes between spiritual gifts distributed to believers to equip them for ministry and the "sign gifts," which are understood to have been manifestations of the Holy Spirit to authenticate the messenger and the gospel message during the foundational period of the church. Therefore, the

Institute holds that "sign gifts" are not normative for the church today. While this institutional position is not and must not be a test of fellowship with those whose traditions differ, members of this community will neither practice nor propagate practices at variance with the Institute's position.

The reason that Moody Bible Institute modified its earlier doctrinal statement from their catalog was not explained.

SPECULATION #199 The Purpose of Speaking in Tongues

The Christian scriptures are very clear about the purpose of speaking tongues. Mark 16:17 claimed that it was a promise to believers in Jesus's name. In contrast, Paul declared in 1 Corinthians 14:22 that the purpose of tongues was to be a sign for unbelievers: "Wherefore tongues are for a sign, not to them that believe, but to them that believe not: but prophesying serveth not for them that believe not, but for them which believe."

Donahue (1988, 1009) suggested that the sign of speaking in tongues "may stem from groups within early Christianity who prized such enthusiastic phenomenon." An alternative explanation for tongues was presented by Wolfe (1989, 90). He posited that one obvious rationale for the gift of tongues was: "It is basically a means of religious expression for illiterates who thereby can excel the educated and the theologians."

SPECULATION #200 Sources Regarding Snakes and Drinking Any Deadly Thing

There are several likely sources for the origin of Mark's statements about handling snakes and drinking any deadly thing with impunity. Commentators have suggested several options:

1. In Acts 28:3-5 it is written: "And when Paul had gathered a bundle of sticks, and laid them on the fire, there came a viper out of the heat, and fastened on his hand. And when the barbarians saw the venomous beast hang on his hand, they said among themselves, No doubt this man is a murderer, whom, though he hath escaped the sea, yet vengeance suffereth not to live. And he shook off the beast into the fire, and felt no harm."

2. In *History of the Church*, 3, 39, Eusebius wrote: "He [Papias, around 120 CE] also mentions another miracle relating to Justus, surnamed Barsabas, how he *swallowed a deadly poison*, and received *no harm*, on account of the grace of the Lord."

3. Another version from Philippus Sidetes, *Hist. Eccl.* fragm. in Cod. Barocc. 142, (5ᵗʰ century) states: "Papias reported as he received from the daughters of Philip that Barsabas who is also Justus, [a member of the church of Jerusalem (Acts 1:23)] *challenged by unbelievers, drank the venom of a viper in the name of Christ* and was *protected unharmed.*"

ISSUE 104: Jesus's Claim about the Messiah

Mk	Mt	Lk 24:44 And he said unto them, These are the words which I spake unto you, while I was yet with you, that all things must be fulfilled, which were written in the law of Moses, and in the prophets, and in the psalms, concerning me. 45 Then opened he their understanding, that they might understand the scriptures, 46 And said unto them, *Thus it is written, and thus it behoved Christ to suffer, and to rise from the dead the third day:*	Jn

After a brief prologue, the author of Luke reports that Jesus stated that there were words written in the law of Moses, in the prophets, and in the psalms concerning him. First, Jesus claimed that words were written in the scriptures that Christ (referring to him) would suffer. Second, Jesus stated that it was also written in the scriptures that he would rise from the dead on the third day, meaning three days after his crucifixion.

CONTRADICTION #109 The Messiah's Suffering and Rising

Nowhere in the Hebrew Bible is there a clear and unequivocal instruction that the Messiah would suffer and rise from the dead on the third day. The very notion that a suffering and rising Messiah was not in the expectations of Judaism was demonstrated by the conduct of both the friends and opponents of Jesus when confronted with his teaching on the subject (Mt 16:22; Lk 18:34; Jn 12:34).

Mt 16:21 From that time forth began Jesus to shew unto his disciples, how that he must go unto Jerusalem, and suffer many things of the elders and chief priests and scribes, and be killed, and be raised again the third day.

Mt 16:22 Then Peter took him, and began to rebuke him, saying, Be it far from thee, Lord: this shall not be unto thee.

Mt 16:23 But he turned, and said unto Peter, Get thee behind me, Satan: thou art an offence unto me: for thou savourest not the things that be of God, but those that be of men."

Lk 18:31 Then he took *unto him* the twelve, and said unto them, Behold, we go up to Jerusalem, and all things that are written by the prophets concerning the Son of man shall be accomplished.

Lk 18:32 For he shall be delivered unto the Gentiles, and shall be mocked, and spitefully entreated, and spitted on:

Lk 18:33 And they shall scourge *him*, and put him to death: and the third day he shall rise again. 34 And they understood none of these things: and this saying was hid from them, neither knew they the things which were spoken."

Jn 12:31 Now is the judgment of this world: now shall the prince of this world be cast out.

Jn 12:32 And I, if I be lifted up from the earth, will draw all *men* unto me.

Jn 12:33 This he said, signifying what death he should die.

Jn 12:34 The people answered him, We have heard out of the law that Christ abideth for ever: and how sayest thou, The Son of man must be lifted up? who is this Son of man?

Jn 12:35 Then Jesus said unto them, Yet a little while is the light with you. Walk while ye have the light, lest darkness come upon you: for he that walketh in darkness knoweth not whither he goeth."

Yet Paul, writing approximately 50 CE, recorded the belief that the Messiah was to suffer and rise from the dead on the third day. This formula can be found in the form of a creed recorded in Paul's epistle to the Corinthians:

> 1 Cor 15:3 For I delivered unto you first of all that which I also received, how that Christ died for our sins according to the scriptures;

> 1 Cor 15:4 And that he was buried, and that he rose again the third day according to the scriptures:

A second reference by Paul was perhaps implied four chapters earlier:

> 1 Cor 11:22 What? have ye not houses to eat and to drink in? or despise ye the church of God, and shame them that have not? What shall I say to you? shall I praise you in this? I praise you not.

> 1 Cor 11:23 For I have received of the Lord that which also I delivered unto you, That the Lord Jesus the same night in which he was betrayed took bread:

> 1 Cor 11:24 And when he had given thanks, he brake it, and said, Take, eat: this is my body, which is broken for you: this do in remembrance of me.

> 1 Cor 11:25 After the same manner also he took the cup, when he had supped, saying, This cup is the new testament in my blood: this do ye, as oft as ye drink it, in remembrance of me.

Later, Luke twice reiterates Paul's teaching. First, Luke 24:7 reported a message that two angels gave to several women at the tomb: "Saying, The Son of man must be delivered into the hands of sinful men, and be crucified, and the third day rise again." Later that evening Luke 24:46 reported that Jesus taught this same message to his disciples while they were still in Jerusalem: "And said unto them, Thus it is written, and thus it behoved Christ to suffer, and to rise from the dead the third day."

Contradicting Paul and Luke, the Hebrew Bible expected that the "King Messiah" was to sit physically on the throne of David and rule during his lifetime:

Jer 23:5 Behold, the days come, saith the LORD, that I will raise unto David a righteous Branch, and a King shall reign and prosper, and shall execute judgment and justice in the earth.

Jer 23:6 In his days Judah shall be saved, and Israel shall dwell safely: and this is his name whereby he shall be called, THE LORD OUR RIGHTEOUSNESS.

Jesus never at any time sat on the throne of David, reigned, prospered, or executed judgments and justice in the earth. In addition, neither during Jesus's lifetime was Judea saved nor did Israel dwell safely. Furthermore—and to repeat for emphasis—unequivocally, nowhere in the Hebrew Bible does it explicitly state that an expected "King Messiah" would (1) die and resurrect or (2) require two visits to earth, separated by a period of approximately two thousand years in order to accomplish what he was supposed to do the first time.

Christian apologists have long recognized that Jews living in the first century had no concept of a dying Messiah. Strickland (1959, 223) wrote a doctoral thesis (Southwestern Baptist Theological Seminary), *A Study of the Jew's Rejection of Jesus in the Light of Inter-Biblical Messianic Expectation.* Chapter 6 analyzed the subject of "The Suffering Messiah."

Since the Jewish Messiah was largely a political, this-world figure, it was sometimes thought that he would be mortal like other men. The Apocalypse of Ezra specifically mentions his death, but he was to die in peace at the end of a triumphant and glorious reign. At the end of this age, the Messiah, and all other men will die and something still more glorious have place. To that glorious estate, the Messiah, along with other righteous men, will ascend after resurrection. In this area of thought, itself infrequently expressed, the death of the Messiah has no connection with a vicarious atonement. In most of the writings, the Messiah is not said to die. His departure from the earth is apparently similar to that of Elijah. It is not easy for a Jew to conceive of the Messiah's death; it is not possible for him to conceive of the kind of suffering and death which the New Testament relates.

The concept that Judaism rejected the idea of a suffering and rising Messiah has also been expressly declared multiple times by none other than William Lane Craig:

* 1984b, 201: They had no conception of a dying, much less a rising Messiah. According to Jewish belief, when the Messiah came he

would establish his throne in Jerusalem and reign forever. The idea that the Messiah would die was utterly foreign to them. We find this attitude expressed in John 12:34: "The multitude therefore answered Him, 'We have heard out of the Law that the Christ is to remain forever; and how can You say, 'The Son of man must be lifted up?' Who is this Son of man?'" Here Jesus predicts His crucifixion, and the people are utterly mystified. The Messiah would live forever—so how could He be "lifted up"? It is difficult to overemphasize what a disaster the crucifixion was, therefore, for the disciples' faith. Jesus' death on the cross spelled the humiliating end for any hopes they had entertained that He was the Messiah.

* 1989a, 68: They had no conception of a dying, much less a rising Messiah, for Messiah should reign forever (cf. Jn. 12:34).

* 1989b, 406: They had no conception of a dying, much less a rising Messiah, for Messiah should reign forever (cf. Jn. 12:34).

* 1995, 159: They had no conception of a dying, much less a rising, Messiah, for Messiah should reign forever (cf. Jn. 12:34).

* 2000, 182 Fact 4: *The original disciples believed that Jesus was risen from the dead despite their having every reason not to.* I list three aspects of the disciples' situation following Jesus' crucifixion that put a question mark behind the faith and hope they had placed in Jesus.

☐ Their leader was dead, and Jews had no belief in a dying, much less rising Messiah.

☐ According to Jewish law, Jesus' execution as a criminal showed him out to be a heretic, a man literally under the curse of God.

☐ Jewish beliefs about the afterlife precluded anyone's rising from the dead before the general resurrection at the end of the world.

Finally, in Craig's (2000, 182; cf. Dunn 2003, 619; Novakovic 2012, 216; Wright 1992, 307-08) closing response during a debate, he said:

> It is important to understand with respect to the first aspect of their situation, that in Jewish expectation the Messiah would conquer Israel's enemies and restore the throne of David, not be shamefully executed by them. Jesus' ignominious execution at the hands of Rome was as decisive a disproof as anything could be to a first-century Jew that Jesus was not Israel's awaited Messiah but another failed pretender.

CHAPTER 14

Paul's Marshalling of Arguments in Support of the Resurrection

ISSUE 105: Jesus's Appearance to the More Than Five Hundred Brethren at One Time

1 Cor 15: 6 *After that, he was seen of above five hundred brethren at once; of whom the greater part remain unto this present, but some are fallen asleep.* 7 After that, he was seen of James; then of all the apostles.	Mk	Mt 28:16 Then the eleven disciples *went away into Galilee, into a mountain* where Jesus had anointed them. 17 And when they saw him, they worshipped him: but some doubted.	Lk	Jn

T HE NEXT APPEARANCE of Jesus is recorded in Paul's first letter to the Corinthians. In this account more than five hundred brethren saw Jesus at one time. Paul's rationale here is that John 21:14 declared that there were three previous appearances to the disciples: Easter Sunday, eight days later, on the successive Sunday, and later to the seven at the Sea of Tiberias in the Galilee. Paul omitted any information regarding the exact time or locale of this meeting. Some commentators have speculated that this appearance before the more than five hundred brethren referred to Matthew 28:16.

CONTRADICTION #110 **Lack of Confirmation**

Paul was the only author of the Christian scriptures who mentioned that Jesus met more than five hundred brethren at one time and in one place. This meeting presumably occurred in Galilee on an unspecified date. Taken for granted that Paul's information is correct and that many witnesses were still alive in Judea approximately twenty-five years after Jesus's death, it is noteworthy that neither Mark, Matthew, Luke, or John did not know about the meeting with more than five hundred brethren at one time; or they deliberately omitted this episode from their respective works.

Why did the gospel authors write their respective gospels attempting to report who witnessed the death, the burial, and the post-resurrection appearances as evidentiary proof for these events while only Paul seemingly knew of this event? It would seem logical and sensible for the gospel authors to have included into their narratives the account of this remarkable evidentiary proof that more than five hundred people at one place and time witnessed the resurrected Jesus. Prospective answers here can only be guesses, hunches, and speculations.

Finally, Luke's omission is highly noteworthy and significant. It must be remembered that Luke declared in his preface that he investigated everything carefully from the very first. Assuming at face value that this statement is true, it is seemingly improbable that Luke would have deliberately deleted the names of some of these more than five hundred brethren from a potential list of witnesses.

SPECULATION #201 **Paul's Bogus Challenge**

Paul's implied challenge, questioning the surviving brethren, was bogus surviving brethren was bogus. Paul alone reported in 1 Corinthians 15:6: "After that, he was seen of above five hundred brethren at once; of whom the greater part remain unto this present, but some are fallen asleep." Yamauchi (1974, 14 [730]) clarified this reading by stating that more than five hundred brethren to whom Jesus appeared at the same time, most (*hoi pleiones*, not just "the greater part" as in the King James Version) were still alive at the time Paul wrote. This claim of Christian apologists is a more serious assertion than that Jesus appeared to several individuals or "the Twelve." At first appearance this evidentiary information seems strong. Paul sent a letter to the Corinthians, informing them that there were several hundred eyewitnesses whom he claimed were still alive and could be cross-examined as to the veracity of Jesus's resurrection.

In the opinion of Trail (2001, 282), the significance of the number five hundred is "to substantiate the truth of an event, Jewish law required only two or three witnesses. When Jesus appeared to over 500 witnesses, he provided overwhelming proof of His resurrection." Similarly, Kistemaker (1993, 532) wrote: "In a Jewish court of law, the presence of two or three witnesses was mandatory to prove the veracity of an event. By appearing to five hundred believers at one time, Jesus provided overwhelming proof of being alive."

According to Craig (2010, 232; cf. 2008, 379; 1984b, 194), "he could not have challenged people to ask the witnesses, if the event had never taken place and there were no witnesses." Similarly, C. H. Dodd (1968, 128; cf. Baker 2003, 19; Borchert 1983, 405; Kistemaker 1993, 532; Orr and Walther 1976, 322) replied: "There can hardly be any purpose in mentioning the fact that the most of the 500 are still alive, unless Paul is saying, in effect, 'The witnesses are there to be questioned.'" Therefore, it is claimed that the five-hundred-plus witnesses is one of the strongest arguments in support of Jesus's resurrection. However, Paul's presumed challenge is an illusion.

Contrary to the above, Martin Hengel (quoted by Allison 2005a, 236) challenged the effectiveness of Paul's 1 Corinthians 15:3-8. He posited: "A Jew or Gentile God-fearer, hearing this formal, extremely abbreviated report for the first time, would have difficulty understanding it; at the least a number of questions would certainly occur to him, which Paul could only answer through the narration and explanation of events. Without clarifying delineation, the whole thing would sound enigmatic to ancient ears, even absurd."

Before accepting at face value the argument of these and other Christian apologists, one should inquire about and investigate the evidence. Specifically, one should carefully examine the evidence cited as in the testimony of Paul in order to determine whether or not his remarkable statement has the ability to withstand a critical and objective analysis.

One obvious weakness of Paul's report is that all that exists are other people's accounts of what these eyewitnesses purportedly saw (second-handed information); the accounts are typically sketchy, and they were written many years later. Additional problems, issues, and speculations dealing with Paul's claim include the following:

1. This report lacks verification by any additional sources in the Gospels or other parts of the Christian scriptures. It must be inquired, what happened to this tradition? Given that Paul's statement lacks the criterion of multiple attestations, it is a claim, not a fact. Furthermore, the reality that Paul's report is *not* an eyewitness account of anything must be considered before accepting his statement as factual.

2. According to church tradition, the author of Luke was a friend to Paul. If the story of the five-hundred-plus witnesses were true, it is speculated that *most probably* it would have been inserted into his gospel or the Acts of the Apostles, for it was one of the main proofs of Jesus's resurrection. To the contrary, its absence is a strong argument from silence that this event does not provide support of Jesus's purported physical, bodily resurrection.

3. The identity of the five-hundred-plus brethren is unknown. It is significant to note that Paul did not provide a single clue as to the names of any of these supposed witnesses. Consequently, the absence of this vital information would have made it extremely difficult to identify any of the surviving brethren for questioning. Compounding matters, here, too, it is noteworthy that Paul did not provide a single clue as to the locations of these witnesses. Obviously it would have been virtually impossible to talk to any of these witnesses if it was unknown who they were or where they were located.

4. Paul did not provide any information as to when or where these witnesses saw Jesus. Nor did he record in his letter what the brethren actually witnessed. In addition, Paul did not state whether or not the crowd drew close enough to Jesus to establish a reliable identification. If the crowd got close to Jesus, it remains to be explained how they were able to identify him when his disciples and followers could not while they were in his close proximity (Mt 28:17; Lk 24:31; Jn 20:15). Furthermore, Paul did not provide any information as to how the witnesses were able to verify that their "experience" or "vision" was, in fact, Jesus. In addition, no information was provided as to whether or not the brethren had previously seen Jesus. Even if they had previously seen him, it is unknown whether or not he would have had the same appearance as before his crucifixion as after it.

5. Paul did not provide any information about the nature of the testimony of the five-hundred-plus brethren. Specifically, there was no evidentiary proof that Paul verified the report of *all* the five-hundred-plus brethren (literally interviewed the witnesses). This omission of information raises numerous issues: If Paul literally interviewed these witnesses, when and under what circumstances did it occur? For example, were the eyewitnesses isolated and allowed to give their testimony without collaborating with other witnesses? If not all were examined, then how many? If not all the witnesses were examined, then why were some excluded? Another issue is, why was there no corroboration that Paul actually met any of five-hundred-plus witnesses? In addition, it must be explained how Paul knew that

most of the witnesses were still alive if he was writing from outside of Judea almost twenty years after the event.

6. In another part of the Gospels, Matthew 28:16-17 admitted that some disciples actually saw the resurrected Jesus but doubted: "Then the eleven disciples went away into Galilee, into a mountain where Jesus had appointed them. And when they saw him, they worshipped him: but some doubted." What remains unclear is whether or not the disciples doubted the vision was, in fact, Jesus, had Jesus died, or if what they saw was a vision. Now, going back to the five-hundred-plus witnesses, it must be asked, what did these witnesses believe they had seen? Paul did not provide an answer. Instead, is it possible that some or many of these five-hundred-plus witnesses also had doubts about what they saw.

Virtually none of Paul's readers would have been able to confirm this story. Christian apologists may offer explanations for the issues poised above; however, assumptions, guesses, and suppositions of advocates should not be accepted until they provide positive proof and unassailable evidence that their opinions are actually true. In brief, proponents of Jesus's resurrection must provide incontrovertible evidentiary proofs that substantiate their assumption that Paul's declaration of the five-hundred-plus brethren was one of the strongest arguments in support of Jesus's physical, bodily resurrection.

SPECULATION #202 There Were No Contemporary Objections to Paul's Claim

It is a deceptive assertion by Christian apologists that no contemporaries questioned Paul's claim. Christian apologists poignantly argue that none of the living witnesses who could have exposed Paul's error or none of the secular historians from that era (the first century) raised objection to the belief that five-hundred-plus brethren witnessed the resurrected Jesus. Therefore, they claim that *no* such challenges were initiated by opponents of Jesus's resurrection.

Christian apologists have *no* way of knowing whether or not objections to Jesus's purported physical bodily resurrection were raised. Plainly, since no writings contradicting Paul's words have come down to us, there is *no* proof that there never were any. Perhaps the opposition just did not survive. History has often demonstrated that the victors write the history books and have the last word. Even one of Paul's previous letters cited in an extant epistle, 1 Corinthians 5:9 is known *not* to have survived: "I wrote unto you in an epistle not to company with fornicators." Consequently, the absence of such contemporary opposition by secular historians or anyone else for that matter does not constitute absolute proof that such opposition never actually occurred.

Furthermore, it is presumptuous to think that historians of that era or anyone else would have had any care or concern to write an account rejecting a letter written by Paul to a church (a group of people) in Corinth. That is, there is no reason that they should have cared to respond, even if they knew of Paul's letter. During the mid or late fifties, Christianity was a minor sect. In addition, the writings of Paul were not considered by any stretch of the imagination to be thought of as "scripture" or for that matter anything "special." Again, the epistle of Paul was a letter that he wrote to a congregation in Corinth. Last, there is no evidentiary proof that Paul's epistle to the Corinthians was *widely* recognized outside Christian circles and thus known to contemporary historians. Given that Paul's letter was not widely circulated, it would have been impractical to expect historians of that era to have had contact with it.

Another related yet questionable claim by Christian apologists is that Paul's reference to the five-hundred-plus brethren who saw Jesus at one time had to be true because it was made during the lifetime of some of those brethren. That is, if Paul's claim were untrue, these witnesses could have come forth and denied that it had happened. Of course, this argument makes three assumptions: (1) the brethren had access to Paul's letter although they were almost one thousand miles away, (2) the surviving Jewish-Palestinian brethren could read the letters (presumably written in Greek), and (3) the appearances actually occurred. If the event did not occur, there would have been no eyewitnesses to the fact that it had not happened. Obviously then there could not be any eyewitnesses to such a claim if it did not happen. In other words, how does one disprove an event if it never occurred? After all, the nonexistent is nothing.

In conclusion, the claim that there were no contemporary objections to Paul's epistle is bogus and a sham.

SPECULATION #203 The Impracticality of Sending an Investigator or Letter to Verify Paul's Claim

The Christian apologetic that Paul's indirect challenge for someone to go to Roman, occupy Judea and verify Paul's account, is a pure deception. That is, in 1 Corinthians 15, Paul challenged his readership to go and interrogate the survivors of the five-hundred-plus brethren about their resurrection sightings, knowing full well that the Corinthians would never have the leisure to do so. The fact of the matter is that most people would *not* have had the time, resources, or inclination to personally travel almost a thousand miles to verify Paul's claim. Thus, some may be impressed by the claim and the alluded challenge; in reality, Paul was taking absolutely *no* risks. For example, Price (2004) aptly stated that in the eyes of believers in Jesus: "The mere challenge in such a case functions as sufficient 'proof.'" From the vantage point of skeptics, this challenge is a smoke screen. Finally it must be reiterated that Paul's epistle was a letter to the Corinthians, not a book.

SPECULATION #204 The Logistical Factors and Practicality of Sending an Investigator or Letter to Verify Paul's Claim

Another argument against the evidence of Paul's testimony in 1 Corinthians 15 relates to the reasonableness of sending an investigator to validate the report or a courier (mail carrier) to transmit a letter to verify Paul's claim. Here, too, numerous impediments and obstacles would substantially eliminate any real risk to Paul. Specifically, it was *not* practical for an investigator to examine the witnesses or a courier to deliver a letter to the witnesses.

1. Corinth was approximately 830 miles from Jerusalem by water and 1,500 miles by land. Sending an investigator or courier to Jerusalem would take time since travel was slow. For example, research by Casson (1971, 287, table 3) found that travel between Crete and Alexandria, Egypt was approximately 310 miles. This excursion required three to four days, with average circumstances by sea, traveling at an overall speed of 4.3 or 3.2 knots. Wallace and Williams (1998, 21) added that if traveling was by "coastal ships" (hugging the coast), it took even longer because of the added distance; also ships stayed at ports for undisclosed lengths of time, unloading and reloading cargo.
2. Research (Casson 1974; 1971; Wallace and Williams 1993) confirmed that traveling was potentially a dangerous proposition and fraught with difficulties as reported in the Acts of the Apostles (chapter 27). The Acts of the Apostles reported that Paul alone experienced three shipwrecks during his voyages.
3. Sending an investigator or courier to Jerusalem would have been expensive; it would include the cost of the voyage, food, board, incidental expenses, and compensation for the employee's time and efforts. Who would have assumed the cost to challenge or substantiate Paul's claims?

4. Upon arrival in Roman occupied Judea an investigator or courier would have faced numerous challenges and difficulties to complete the given task. For example, how would the investigator or carrier know who the surviving witnesses were? How would he verify who was a living witness? Furthermore, the investigator/courier would have presumably confronted potential witnesses who refused to answer questions from a stranger out of fear. Many would perhaps seek to remain anonymous and hide because the times were dangerous for Christians and there were numerous spies. Consequently, the potential witnesses would not give interviews. Compounding the investigator's/courier's difficulties, he would have been confronted by having to locate potential witnesses who had moved or scattered (Acts 8:1-5), and he would have to have dealt with local authorities who might have arrested the stranger as a potential nuisance.

5. Either the investigator/courier or Paul could have died before the investigator/courier returned.

6. Paul could have moved before the investigator/courier returned. Paul's First Epistle to the Corinthians is assumed to have been written approximately 54 CE during his "third journey." Dockx (1989, 209-21), in a review of Paul's first journey, revealed that visit durations were no more than three weeks and often several days, although in later journeys he had visitations of longer stays.

7. *If* Paul, in fact, lied and the lie was in fact discovered, he still would have gotten away with his *deceit* by claiming that it must have had something to do with a conspiracy against him. Such a potential argument is found in 2 Corinthians 11:2: "Lest Satan should get an advantage of us: for we are not ignorant of his devices" and in Thessalonians 2:2: "That ye be not soon shaken in mind, or be troubled, neither by spirit, nor by word, nor by letter as from us, as that the day of Christ is at hand." Similarly, those who denied Paul's claims could simply have been accused of being false teachers.

Rom 16:17-18 Now I beseech you, brethren, mark them [[false teachers]] which cause divisions and offences contrary to the doctrine which ye have learned; and avoid them. For they that are such serve not our Lord Jesus Christ, but their own belly; and by good words and fair speeches deceive the hearts of the simple.

Therefore, it would have become a case of his word against theirs or Paul's *divinely revealed* word against theirs. Obviously, too, Paul could have vilified anyone who told a different story that competed with his account. Threats directed at competitors are found in Paul's writings:

Gal 1:9 As we said before, so say I now again, if *any man preach any other gospel* unto you than that ye have received, *let him be accursed.*

8. Finally, it must be inquired, what would a first-century Corinthian skeptic have to gain by disproving Paul's claim? In brief, there would have been no incentive or motive to investigate Paul's assertion. Given that there would be no incentive, no investigation would have been carried out.

Fales (2001, 34) offered the following scenario to ponder: "If I claimed that 500 Tungus [someone living in north eastern Ghana], some of them still alive, had witnessed an aerial flight 20 years ago by one of their shamans, how many would care to make the trip to Siberia—though this would only take perhaps 3 days-to test my claim?"

Paul knew with perfect confidence that there would be *no* opponents to come forth and testify against his claim that a resurrected Jesus appeared and was witnessed before five-hundred-plus brethren at one time. Plainly, if the event did not occur, there would have been no eyewitnesses to the fact that it had not happened. Again it must be asked, how could there have been eyewitnesses that Paul's claim did not happen? Therefore, Paul knew that he was standing on safe ground when he made his claim. The acceptance or rejection of Paul's claim had little to do with it being the type of claim that gullible, superstitious people at that time would have believed. Instead, it dealt with the reality of the first century Mediterranean region, logistics and variables of traveling and communicating over great distances.

In conclusion, there is no evidentiary proof that over five hundred people at one time witnessed the raised Jesus. Furthermore, there is ample reason to believe that Paul's claim was nothing more than a facade, knowing full well that his assertion could *not* have been successfully disproved. Paul's claim of five-hundred-plus witnesses provides no support for Jesus's physical, bodily resurrection.

SPECULATION #205 Numerological Speculations

Kearney, writing in *Novum Testamentum*, offered an interesting hypothesis on the "more than five hundred," i.e., the "holy ones" was based on numerology. He (1980, 267-68) wrote: "Might it not be rather a symbolic number expressing the eschatological fullness signified by the two adverbs just discussed?" He then pointed out that Plutarch's writings indicated that Greek culture at the end of the first century "saw the number five as symbolic of fullness." Second, Philo wrote (*De vita contemplativa*, par. 65; *De vita Mosis*, bk. 2, par. 80; *De specialibus legibus*, bk. 2, par. 176; *De mutatione nominum*, par. 228) that the numeral fifty was symbolic of perfect holiness. Third, Kearney (267-68) offered his own hypothesis:

> I offer the hypothesis that the numeral 500 incorporates this symbolism of holiness in a unique way, as a gematrical equivalent for the Hebrew word מקודשים [[i.e., "holy ones"]] . . . its letters, when given their numerical equivalent, add up to 500 (מ = 40; ק = 100; ו = 6; ד = 4; ש = 300; י = 10; and ם = 40). Thus the holiness of the number fifty has been preserved even while being transformed into the holiness of the number 500, a numeral which points out the relatively large number of the "brothers" who saw the risen Jesus, but even more, indicates symbolically that their sanctification as מקודשים involved a sharing in his glorified condition as the Exalted One.

SPECULATION #206 The Doublet Theory

Another hypothesis raised by some commentators is that the Christophany (vision of Jesus) to the five-hundred-plus witnesses was a "doublet (i.e., repetition or variant) of the Pentecost story in Acts 2:1-4.

> Acts 2:1 And when the day of Pentecost was fully come, they were all with one accord in one place.
>
> Acts 2:2 And suddenly there came a sound from heaven as of a rushing mighty wind, and it filled all the house where they were sitting.
>
> Acts 2:3 And there appeared unto them cloven tongues like as of fire, and it sat upon each of them.
>
> Acts 2:4 And they were all filled with the Holy Ghost, and began to speak with other tongues, as the Spirit gave them utterance.

A review of the literature by Gilmour (1961, 248) suggested that this idea was first proposed by Weisse (1838) and later accepted in part or looked more favourably on the possibility by other scholars (Barrett 1955, Craig 1953, Holl 1921, Pfleiderer 1887, and Dobschütz 1903).

SPECULATION #207 The Issue of Pontius Pilate's Failure to Order an Investigation

A further speculated point about the five-hundred-plus witnesses based on silence relates to Governor Pontius Pilate. Pilate had spies throughout the land. It is assumed that Pilate would have "heard" reports that people, more than five hundred in number, were saying that they had either seen, talked with, or eaten with the man who he had personally ordered to be crucified in front of a large crowd.

> Mt 27:17 Therefore when they were gathered together, Pilate said unto them, Whom will ye that I release unto you? Barabbas, or Jesus which is called Christ?

> Mt 27:20 But the chief priests and elders persuaded the multitude that they should ask Barabbas, and destroy Jesus.

> Mt 27:24 When Pilate saw that he could prevail nothing, but that rather a tumult was made, he took water, and washed his hands before the multitude, saying, I am innocent of the blood of this just person: see ye to it.

This text speculates that it is *not* plausible that Pilate would not have "taken special notice" of five-hundred-plus people claiming that they had seen, spoken to, or eaten with a man who was executed by the state (and buried by Joseph of Arimathea). Given that Pilate would have heard such reports, it must be speculated as to what he would have done.

Perry (1959, 98n3) stated unequivocally: "Herod had no compunction in executing incompetent guards—Acts xii, 19." In this episode, Peter had been previously arrested and imprisoned with four squads of four soldiers (vv. 3-4). With the assistance of an angel he escaped. The next morning Herod made a thorough search for Peter, but he could not be found. Acts 12:19 then reported: "And when Herod had sought for him, and found him not, he examined the keepers, and commanded that they should be put to death. And he went down from Judaea to Caesarea, and there abode." Yet with regard to Jesus's many appearances after his ordered execution, there is not a single written account of any counter measures taken by Pilate! Why?

Caine (1938, 1020) raised four hypothetical points that bear consideration with this issue:

> He would have remembered that Joseph of Arimathea had asked permission to bury Jesus, and he would have sent for Joseph and said, "Did not you tell me that you wished to bury that man? *Did* you bury him? What happened then?"

> And would not Pilate have sent for his centurion and said, "When I asked you if the man had been any while dead, did you not tell me that it was so? What about this report by 500 that he is alive and walking about? Was he not dead? Had he only fainted? Was he resuscitated? If so, by whom? By Joseph of Arimathea? Then both you and Joseph must account to me for what you have done."

> Or if Pilate had been glad of an excuse to ignore and forget the whole miserable matter, would not the Jews, who had set on the tomb a watch which had failed, because (by their own invented account) the disciples of Jesus had come by night and stolen the body away while they slept, have called on Pilate to re-arrest Jesus as one who had not died at all, and therefore had never suffered the penalty of his condemnation, but had, by trickery, escaped it, and was now walking in Galilee free?

> Furthermore, and as a final point, with such a cloud of testimony, what further witness to the truth of the claims of Jesus could the world want? Why should there have been any doubt? Why did not the gospel of Jesus take complete possession of the whole Galilee world—instantly?

SPECULATION #208 The Reliability Factor

Christian apologists often tout the reliability of the witnesses who saw the postmortem resurrection appearances as a proof of Jesus's resurrection. Specifically, they point out (1) there were over five hundred witnesses, (2) the witnesses included men and women, (3) the occurrences took place both during the evening and morning, (4) the locales were in Jerusalem and the Galilee, and (5) they spanned over a period of forty days. However, the reliability of the recorded accounts in the Christian scriptures is not as strong as its proponents suggest.

Many crimes have witnesses who may have observed important details. However, often the credibility of a witness is difficult to determine. In the criminal justice system, research has proven that erroneous or mistaken eyewitness evidence is often responsible for the conviction of innocent people. For example, the first Innocence Project, in 1992, was established by Barry Scheck and Peter Neufeld at the Benjamin N Cardozo School of Law in New York. As of 2011, this project alone has overturned 305 criminal convictions, 18 of which were of prisoners on death row (see http://www.innocentproject.org/understand). The Innocence Project and numerous media investigations have consistently demonstrated that the frequency and importance of eyewitnesses emphasizes the need for reliable interpretation of their evidence.

Since long ago it has been known that the testimony of witnesses should not always be taken at face value and that numerous factors determine the credibility of eyewitness testimony. Consequently, there have been numerous attempts to investigate the correct evaluation, presentation of forensic evidence, and the introduction and implementation of *best practice* procedures within legal offices and police departments. One such effort is ADVOKATE.

ADVOKATE (Bromby and Hall 2002, 143) is an expert advisory software system designed to aid the assessment and credibility of eyewitnesses in forensic and legal investigations. The ADVOKATE acronym refers to eight witness reliability factors to be examined in a case. Below in table 75, the witness reliability factors have been modified to fit the scenario presented by Paul.

TABLE 75. The ADVOKATE System and the Five-hundred-plus Brethren

ACRONYM	RELIABILITY FACTORS (MODIFIED)	MODIFIED BY WALTON (2008)	ANALYSIS of 1 COR 15:6
A:	**Amount** of time the witnesses observed Jesus.	What was the length of time since the witnesses observed the event?	Unknown.
D:	**Distance** from the witnesses.	How close were the witnesses to the event?	Unknown.
V:	**Visibility** conditions at the time.	How favorable were the visibility conditions at the time?	Unknown.
O:	Whether the line of **Observation** was impeded.	Was the line of observation impeded?	Unknown.
K:	Whether Jesus (the person being seen) was **Known** to the witnesses.	Was the person observed known to the witnesses?	Possibly. However, not necessarily all five-hundred-plus brethren had previously seen Jesus.
A:	**Any reasons** for remembering the event or the person Jesus.	Were there reasons (other than the above) for remembering what was observed?	Yes.
T:	**Time** elapsed since the event.	How much time had elapsed since the witnesses observed the event?	Unknown. Presumably about twenty-five years.
E:	**Errors** in description of Jesus.	Were there errors in the description of Jesus?	No descriptions.

Based on the ADVOKATE software system, Paul's testimony of the five-hundred-plus brethren provides virtually no credibility of the witnesses (see table 75).

During the past thirty years, there have been considerable advances in understanding the cognitive processes (cognitive neuroscience, cognitive neuropsychiatry, neuropsychology) and particularly the psychology of evidence and of eyewitness accuracy employed in the courtroom (Brewer and Williams 2005; Kassin et al. 2001, 405-16; Lindsay, Ross, Read and Toglia 2012; Loftus 2003, 207-12; 2002, 41-50; Penrod, Loftus and Winkler 1982, 119-61; Semmler and Brewer 2010, 49-57; Slovenko 2010, 49-57; 2002; Toglia et al. 2007; Wells 1985, 43-66; Wells and Olson 2003, 277-94; Wells, Memon and Penrod 2006, 45-75; Yarmey 2003, 181-89). In the arena of religion, numerous scholars (Allison 2010; DeConick 2008; Le Donne 2011; 2009; McIver 2012, 529-46; Redman 2010, 177-97) have raised hard questions that challenge the credibility of the eyewitness accounts behind the gospel traditions. Yet Christian apologists almost universally ignore the bodies of research that relate to Paul's claim that over five hundred people at one time witnessed the raised Jesus. Beside these avenues, Christian apologists routinely ignore even basic rules of evidence. Iannuzzi (2001, 158) writing in *Handbook of Trial Strategies*, second edition, writes:

> The Rules of Evidence, the rules that govern the submission and admission of physical or documentary evidence, have been designed to protect the integrity of the Trial, to ensure that not a wit of evidence is admitted before it has been fully and well scrutinized for reliability by Advocates for all parties. That scrutiny is accomplished by each Advocate having the opportunity to probe and question the witness who is the conduit for the particular exhibit before it is admitted in evidence.

In no manner would Paul's testimony be acceptable in a modern court of law since opponents of the Resurrection did not have the opportunity to probe and question the witnesses. Neither would his testimony have been acceptable two thousand years ago.

Based on an analysis of psychological research carried on during the past thirty years, Redman (2010, 197) concluded: "The continued presence in Christian communities of eyewitnesses to Jesus' ministry until the time when these events were recorded is a guarantee only of the community's agreed version, not of the exact details of the event itself."

Significantly, the gospel narrations and other parts of the Christian scriptures also provide virtually no credibility for eyewitness accounts of the risen Jesus. Descriptions of a postmortem resurrected Jesus are provided by only two authors (who were not eyewitnesses). Luke 24:37 reported that the witnesses first thought they had seen a ghost and afterward Jesus displayed his hands and feet. John 20:20 and 20:27 reported that Jesus showed his hands and, in contrast, presented his side for examination. The latter implied that Jesus had a side wound from being pierced, while on the cross, by a Roman soldier. On the other hand, John 20:14-16 reported that Mary Magdalene did not recognize Jesus until he spoke to her. Yet Matthew 28:18 reported that some doubted when they saw him. In contrast, Paul stated in Acts 9:3, 22:6, and 26:13 that all he personally saw was a light. Finally, Mark 16:1-8 omitted any description of the risen Jesus.

ISSUE 106: The Appearance to James, Jesus's Step Brother

1 Cor 15: 6-7 After that, he was seen of above five hundred brethren at once; of whom the greater part remain unto this present, but some are fallen asleep. *After that, he was seen of James*; then of all the apostles.	Mk	Mt	Lk	Jn

The next appearance of Jesus cited by Paul was with James. This claim assumes that Paul's account was historical and literally chronological and not necessarily theological. Paul omitted any information detailing precisely when and where this meeting occurred or the interaction that took place during the encounter. Furthermore, Paul was the only writer to mention that Jesus appeared before James.

SPECULATION #209 James, Jesus's Stepbrother, as a Witness

Paul's claim that James, Jesus's stepbrother, saw Jesus is refuted. In a review of the literature, Thiselton (2000, 1207) reported: "Most writers consider it virtually certain that the James in question is the James the brother of Jesus." [So too does this book.] In the eyes of Christian apologists, it is highly significant that Paul recorded that James saw Jesus. Christian apologists (Craig 1984b, 195; De Haan n.d., 12; Habermas 2012, 356-57; 2004, 187; 2003, 21-22; 1980, 37; Habermas and Licona 2004, 67-68) forcefully point out that James was originally an opponent of Jesus and later became the head of the church. Neyrey (1988, 16; cf. Orr and Walther 1976, 318) posited that this "James" was probably the James referred to in Acts and Galatians.

> Acts 12:17 But he, beckoning unto them with the hand to hold their peace, declared unto them how the Lord had brought him out of the prison. And he said, Go shew these things unto James, and to the brethren. And he departed, and went into another place.

> Gal 2:9 And when James, Cephas, and John, who seemed to be pillars, perceived the grace that was given unto me, they gave to

me and Barnabas the right hands of fellowship; that we should go
unto the heathen, and they unto the circumcision.

Rhetorically, Christian apologists inquire, what could account for this
change other than that James saw the resurrected Jesus and believed in him?

RATIONALE FOR JAMES'S APPOINTMENT TO HEAD THE JERUSALEM CHURCH

Price (1995, 87), writing in the *Institute for Higher Critical Studies*,
offered several speculative answers regarding the previously stated rhetorical
questions. He wrote:

> If James were not "turned around" by an appearance of the Risen
> Jesus, how else can we account for his assumption of an early
> leadership role in the Church? The answer is not far to seek. He
> was the eldest brother of King Messiah. Once honored for this
> accident of birth, he did not see fit to decline it. One might well
> remain aloof to a movement in which one's brother was the leader
> yet soon warm to it once the leadership role were offered to oneself.

> The sheer fact of James' blood relation to Jesus is by itself so
> powerful, so sufficient a credential that when we find another, a
> resurrection appearance, placed alongside it in the tradition, we
> must immediately suspect a secondary layer of tradition. And
> fortunately we have a striking historical analogy that will help us
> understand the Tendenz at work in such embellishment. James'
> claim was precisely parallel to that of Ali, the son-in-law and
> nephew of the Prophet Muhammad. Ali's "partisans" (Arabic:
> Shi'ites) advanced his claim to the Caliphate upon the death of
> Muhammad on the theory that the prophetic succession should
> follow the line of physical descent.[68] Later legend claims that
> Ali was entitled to the position on the strength of his piety and

---

[68] Abdulaziz Abdulhussein Sachedina, *Islamic Messianism, The Idea of the Mahdi in
Twelver Shi'ism* (Albany: State University of New York Press, 1981), 6-7; Farhad
Daftary, *The Isma'ilis: Their History and Doctrines* (New York: Cambridge
University Press, 1990), 39.

charisma,[69] a tacit concession that blood relation was no longer deemed adequate for spiritual leadership (cf Mark 3:31-35). Finally he is made, in retrospect, the recipient of new angelic revelations like those of the Prophet himself, taking down the dictation of the *Mushaf Fatima*, one of the Shi'ite holy books.[70]

WHY JAMES'S NAME APPEARS ONLY IN PAUL'S ACCOUNTS

The claim that Jesus was seen by James only appears in the work attributed to Paul. Dunn (2003, 862) unequivocally points out the significance and oddity of this record:

> But we have still to take account of what in many ways is the most striking and astonishing feature of all—that is, the absence of the accounts of the appearances to Peter and to James (brother of Jesus), On almost any reckoning, these must have been regarded as the most significant of the appearances for the initial band of disciples.

What then can explain the absences of these two meetings? Commentators and theologians can only offer their best guess or speculation.

Bammel (1992, 622) posited: "The complete silence of the Gospels about the appearance to James could perhaps result from a rejection of exaggerated leadership claims by James and his followers." Borchert (1983, 405) was of the opinion that "although the appearance to James is not mentioned in the Gospels, through bitter experience Paul learned not to overlook the authority of James (Gal 1:19; 2:9-12; Acts 15:13; 21:18)."

In contrast, Kearney (1980, 281n60) was of the opinion that verses 6-7 were rooted in a Jerusalem tradition.

> Thus the introduction of James into the list was made quite easily, granted his importance in that city. Paul's placing Peter in a parallel phrase likely enough reflects Paul's awareness of James' eventual prominence in Jerusalem at a somewhat more

---

[69] Ignaz Goldziher, *Introduction to Islamic Theology and Law* (Princeton: Princeton University Press, 1981), 175; Sachedina, *Messianism*, 6; but see W.M. Watt, *Islamic Philosophy and Theology* (Edinburgh: The University Press, 1979), 23.

[70] Sachedina, *Messianism*, 22.

developed stage in the primitive community's structure. Citing the appearance to James thus reaffirmed Paul's continued accord with the Jerusalem church, a concern which had earlier motivated his second visit to Jerusalem. (Gal 2:1-10)

Fuller (1960, 14), citing Bammel (1955, 401-19), wrote more forcefully:

The tradition of a primary appearance to James, Bammel suggests, represents a substitution for that to Peter, originating at the time when James took over the leadership of the Jerusalem community from Peter on the latter's departure ca. 42 A.D. That James was in fact the recipient of an appearance is a necessary postulate, since during the earthly life of Jesus he was not a disciple, but apparently a sceptical critic (Mark 3:21, 32-35), yet in Acts 1:14 he is included among the body of disciples.

WHICH JAMES WITNESSED THE RISEN JESUS?

Although most commentators consider it virtually certain that the James in question is James, the brother of Jesus, this is nothing more than a scholarly consensus. However, it is possible that this James was not Jesus's brother. Paul did not specify which James he referred to. Furthermore, James was a common name and appears more than forty times in the Christian scriptures. In the Gospels, three men are recorded with this name in the church: (1) Jesus's brother, (2) the brother of John (whom King Herod ordered put to death), and (3) the son of Alphæus.

JAMES'S OMISSION TO DISCUSS JESUS'S APPEARANCE

If the James referred to by Paul in Acts 15 was the person who presided over the Jerusalem Conference, and if this James wrote the Epistle of James, his omission of Jesus's appearance is quite incomprehensible. Of course, this is an opinion and an argument based on silence. Nonetheless, assuming that an appearance of the risen Jesus took place with James, it was the most important affirmation he could make. Yet James said not a single word about it. Christian apologists could, of course, suggest that this fact was so well-known that it was not necessary for him to declare it. That a person may be assumed to possess certain vital knowledge, which he never claimed, is a novel method of proving a supernatural occurrence to future ages. It is the position of this text that James's negative testimony has greater weight than that of another person (i.e., Paul) given on his behalf and without a word of confirmation.

POTPOURRI

James is irrelevant as a witness to the risen Jesus since, according to the Gospels, Jesus is supposed to have had no relations with his brother; they do not speak of any such appearance to him (cf. Perkins 2012, 181). In addition, it bears repeating that Paul was merely reporting second hand information. Furthermore, for Christian apologists (e.g., Habermas 2004, 183) to argue that Paul had the opportunity to interview the witnesses during his stays in Jerusalem, *interviews which he never included*, is an unacceptable presumption.

Significantly, Luke 1:1-4 claimed to have "carefully investigated everything from the beginning." The unknown is why he would have deliberately omitted such a significant fact. Perhaps his omission was, in fact, a deletion and Luke was, in fact, challenging the historicity of Paul's claim.

Although James is purported to have seen the resurrected Jesus, there is no indication of what he believed he saw. That is, the appearance could have been a spirit, phantom, or ghost. Furthermore, Borchert (1983, 405) added: "It is not insignificant, then, that Paul sets himself in this text at least on a par with these personalities."

In conclusion, there is no irrefutable evidentiary proof as to which James was being cited, or when or where Jesus's appearance to him occurred. Furthermore, there is no incontrovertible evidentiary proof as to why James became a believer in Jesus or more significantly what he supposedly professed. Here there is no support for Jesus's physical, bodily resurrection.

ISSUE 107: The Appearance to All the Apostles

1 Cor 15:7 After that, he was seen of James; *then of all the apostles.*	Mk	Mt	Lk	Jn

The fifth listing of appearances reported by Paul was to "all the apostles." Here too Paul omitted any information regarding the exact time or locale of this meeting.

SPECULATION #210 Who Were the Apostles?

C. G. Kruse (1992, 27), writing in *The Dictionary of Jesus and the Gospels*, defined the term "apostle" (*apostolos*) as "used in the Gospels to designate the twelve disciples called and sent out by Jesus to preach the Gospel of the kingdom and demonstrate its presence by performing signs and wonders." However, Matthew 27:5 and perhaps Acts 1:18 reported that Judas had previously committed suicide. This would then have left only eleven disciples.

On the other hand, the word "apostle" also has, in the Christian scriptures, a larger meaning and denotes some inferior disciples. Examples can be seen in table 76:

TABLE 76. Inferior Examples of the Word "Apostle"

CITATION	APOSTLES	TEXT
Acts 14:14	Barnabas	Which when the apostles, Barnabas and Paul, heard of, they rent their clothes, and ran in among the people, crying out,
Rom 16:7	Andronicus and Junia (Probably)	Salute Andronicus and Junia, my kinsmen, and my fellowprisoners, who are of note among the apostles, who also were in Christ before me.
Phil 2:25	Epaphroditus	Yet I supposed it necessary to send to you Epaphroditus, my brother, and companion in labour, and fellowsoldier, but your messenger, and he that ministered to my wants.

Neyrey (1988, 16; cf. Murphy-O'Connor 1981, 582-89; Orr and Walther 1976, 322) is of the opinion that this group is "surely not 'the Twelve' just mentioned, but other commissioned preachers (see Rom 16:7)." In a similar manner, Craig (1984b, 196) believes that this group was probably a "limited circle somewhat wider than the twelve" and "the facticity of this appearance is guaranteed by Paul's personal contact with the apostles themselves."

Fuller (1980, 39) provided an important overview of four positions regarding the identity of "all the apostles." He wrote: "There has been much discussion as to the identity of "all the apostles." Four positions have been held: (1) that the apostles and the Twelve were identical; (2) that "all the apostles" included the Twelve and others as well; (3) that it included some of the Twelve and others as well' and (4) that it included none of the Twelve and was an entirely different group."

Obviously, one cannot attempt to reject or even defend Paul's claim of "all the apostles" being witnesses to Jesus's resurrection given that there is no accepted definition of the term. This argument should be especially apparent if the meaning of apostles included "others" than just the Twelve. Clearly, Paul's statement in 1 Corinthians 15:7 is vague, ambiguous, and meaningless. There is no incontrovertible evidentiary proof, just hearsay. Consequently, Paul's claim that "all the apostles" saw Jesus provides no proof for Jesus's physical, bodily resurrection.

SPECULATION #211 The Basis of Paul's Claim of Apostleship

Sleeper (1965, 395) posited that according to 1 Corinthians 15:1-11, Paul defined his apostleship in terms of two essential criteria: a commission and a resurrection appearance. Since Paul unequivocally claims that he saw Jesus (1 Cor 15:8), by definition he fulfills the classification of an apostle. Paul's claim that he saw Jesus had profound political implications. Significantly, Paul was putting his vision of the risen Jesus (whether real or imagined) on an equal footing with those of the other apostles. Therefore, Paul was, in effect, insisting that he was an apostle, that is, one specifically called and designated by God (and later Jesus himself) to take a leadership role in the early church. More importantly, Paul stated unequivocally that he was equal to all the apostles (Pyysiäinen 2007, 61, 67-68). The ramifications here are monumental.

Another aspect of Paul's words was his categorization of three types of recipients of apparitions or revelations. First, there were those in the general community such as the five-hundred-plus brethren. Second there were two different leadership groups: the Twelve and the apostles. Last, Crossan (1995, 204) pointed out that there were three specific leaders: Peter, James, and, of course, Paul himself. Therefore, a natural explanation of the entire affair is nothing more than a fictitious account inserted in the interest of Paul's claim about those who saw Jesus.

Habermas (2001, 83), a Christian apologist, is of the opinion that Paul's assertion about those who saw Jesus was "a claim that does not further his own authority. Paul is clearly asserting the historicity of Jesus' appearances, not positioning himself." This opinion is nothing more than that, a claim, a guess, or an opinion.

In contrast, Neyrey (1988, 16) offered a contrasting "guess" or "opinion." He wrote:

> The list, however, is not without shape and formal content. Scholars indicate that the list of people mentioned in 15:5-6 is really *two* lists, which are carefully cast in parallel form:

List One	List Two
1. Cephas	1. James
2. the Twelve	2. all the apostles
3. more than 500	3. Paul

CHAPTER 15

The Ascension

ISSUE 108: The Time and Location of the Ascension

Mk 16:14	Mt	Lk 24:50	Acts 1:2 Until the day in which	Jn 20:19 *Then the same*
Afterwards he appeared unto the eleven as they sat at meat, and upbraided them with their unbelief and hardness of heart, because they believed not them which had seen him after he was risen.		*And he led them out as far as to Bethany*, and he lifted up his hands, and blessed them. 51 *And it came to pass, while he blessed them, he was parted from them, and carried up into heaven.* 52 And they worshipped him, and returned to Jerusalem with great joy.	he was taken up, after that he through the Holy Ghost had given commandments unto the apostles whom he had chosen: 3 To whom also he shewed himself alive after his passion by many infallible proofs, *being seen of them forty days*, and speaking of the things pertaining to the kingdom of God. Acts 1:9 *And when he had spoken these things, while they beheld, he was taken up; and a cloud received him out of their sight.* 10 And while they looked stedfastly toward heaven as he went up, behold, *two men stood by them in white apparel*; 11 Which also said, Ye men of Galilee, why stand ye gazing up into heaven? this same Jesus, which is taken up from you into heaven, *shall so come in like manner as ye have seen him go into heaven.* 12 Then returned they unto Jerusalem from the mount called Olivet, which is from Jerusalem a sabbath day's journey.	*day at evening, being the first day of the week,* when the doors were shut where the disciples were assembled for fear of the Jews, came Jesus and stood in the midst, and saith unto them, Peace be unto you. Jn 20:26 And *after eight days* again his disciples were within, and Thomas with them: then came Jesus, the doors being shut, and stood in the midst, and said, Peace be unto you. Jn 21:1 *After these things Jesus shewed himself again to the disciples at the sea of Tiberias*; and on this wise shewed he himself.
Mk 16:19 *So then after the Lord had spoken unto them*, he was received up into heaven, and sat on the right hand of God.				

A S MENTIONED IN the preface, the Ascension and the Resurrection differ with respect to the fate of Jesus's body. The Ascension involved the disappearance of the body whereas the Resurrection involved an appearance of the resurrected Jesus (Toon 1983, 198). In Mark 16:1-8, the original end of Mark's account, there was no ascension! In contrast, Mark 16:9-14 seemingly reported that Jesus's ascension occurred in Jerusalem when the eleven disciples were gathered. Since this narrative parallels Luke 24:33-43 and John 20:19, it is assumed that Mark reported that Jesus's ascension occurred on Easter Sunday evening.

Matthew omitted an explicit reference of Jesus ascending to heaven. Instead, he reported that Jesus commissioned his disciples in Galilee during an unspecified date. However, this commissioning in Galilee would have precluded an Easter Sunday evening ascension in Jerusalem since it would have required at least three or four days to travel the required distance.

Luke 24:51 declared that Jesus's ascension took place in Bethany, on the "third day" after the Crucifixion, and thus on the evening of Easter Sunday. However, Acts 1:3, 9-12 provided additional details of the account by claiming that Jesus stayed forty days after his crucifixion before he ascended to heaven.

> Acts 1:2-3 Until the day in which he was taken up, after that he through the Holy Ghost had given commandments unto the apostles whom he had chosen: To whom also he shewed himself alive after his passion by many infallible proofs, being seen of them forty days, and speaking of the things pertaining to the kingdom of God:

> Acts 1:9-11 And when he had spoken these things, while they beheld, he was taken up; and a cloud received him out of their sight. And while they looked stedfastly toward heaven as he went up, behold, two men stood by them in white apparel; Which also said, Ye men of Galilee, why stand ye gazing up into heaven? this same Jesus, which is taken up from you into heaven, shall so come in like manner as ye have seen him go into heaven.

Therefore, Acts had the Ascension occur on a Thursday evening and forty days after Jesus's crucifixion. The scholarly consensus is that the author of Luke also wrote Acts. Consequently, Jansen (1967, 67) raised the following point: "If Luke wrote this, why does he not take it into account in the conclusion of his Gospel? And why does he never refer to the forty days again?"

John omitted any discussion or inference of Jesus's ascension. However, John reported that Jesus visited his disciples, with the exception of Thomas, in Jerusalem on Easter Sunday evening. Eight days later, he once again visited his disciples, with Thomas now being present. This second meeting would have precluded an Easter Sunday ascension unless it is claimed that Jesus ascended on Easter Sunday evening, later returned to earth, and then ascended a second time at a future date.

CONTRADICTION #111 Luke 24:50-53 Contradicts John and Possibly Mark

Luke 24:50-53 directly contradicted John and possibly Mark. Luke 24:50 reported that Jesus led his disciples to Bethany located outside the city of Jerusalem. There he ascended to heaven on Easter Sunday evening: "And it came to pass, while he blessed them, he was parted from them, and carried up into heaven" (Lk 24:51).

In contradiction, John recorded two appearances in Jerusalem and one in the Galilee. First, John 20:19-23 reported that Jesus visited his disciples in Jerusalem on Easter Sunday evening while the doors were locked because they were in fear of the Jews. Verse 24 provided information that Thomas was not with them at the time. Eight days later, Jesus once again visited his disciples with Thomas now being present. Consequently, this meeting also occurred on a Sunday evening. However, a second meeting would have precluded an Easter Sunday ascension unless it is argued that

1. Jesus previously ascended to heaven on Easter Sunday evening, returned to earth one week later, and then ascended a second time at a future unspecified date; and
2. Jesus did not ascend to heaven; rather, he remained on earth in places unknown during this one week period (in contradiction to Luke 24:50-53).

Compounding matters further, John 21 recorded a later meeting Jesus had with seven disciples during an unknown amount of time after the Doubting Thomas episode. This chronology would have placed this meeting at the Sea of Tiberias in Galilee almost two weeks after Jesus's crucifixion. The reason this meeting must have occurred after the Doubting Thomas episode is stated in John 21:14: "This is now the third time that Jesus shewed himself to his disciples, after that he was risen from the dead" (i.e., John 20:19-23, 26-29). Again, this third meeting would have precluded an Easter Sunday ascension, unless it is claimed that Jesus previously ascended to heaven on Easter Sunday evening, returned to earth one week later for the Doubting Thomas affair, ascended a second time to heaven, then returned to the earth again (the Galilee), and finally ascended to heaven a third time.

Mark 16 also contradicts Luke. Mark 16:14 reported that Jesus appeared to his eleven disciples as they were sitting at the table and criticized them for their lack of faith: "*Afterwards* he appeared unto the eleven as they sat at meat, and upbraided them with their unbelief and hardness of heart, because they believed not them which had seen him after he was risen." This descriptive narrative parallels Luke 24:33-43 and John 20:19 when Jesus visited his disciples on Easter Sunday evening.

Mark 16:19 then records Jesus's ascension: "So then after the Lord had spoken unto them, he was received up into heaven, and sat on the right hand of God." The unknown factor is how much time elapsed after Jesus spoke to his disciples. Some texts attempt to harmonize the gospel narratives by positing that this ascension occurred in Galilee. If true, this harmonization would then contradict Luke's account of an Easter Sunday evening resurrection since there would be insufficient time to travel the required distance.

In summary, Léon-Dufour (1971, 212-13), a Catholic apologist, concisely delineated the problem:

> The conflict cannot be resolved by a harmonization in which all these appearances take place one after the other, in Jerusalem on Easter Day (Luke, John) and the eighth day (John), then in Galilee (Matthew, John) and back in Jerusalem for the ascension (Luke). This harmonization is unacceptable, because it is contradicted by definite statements in the texts. *According to Luke 24:49, the disciples are to stay in Jerusalem until the day of Pentecost, which excludes any appearance in Galilee. By contrast, Matthew [[28:7]] and Mark [[16:7]] state that the meeting place is to be Galilee.* These different indications of place cannot be reconciled. Here we have a sign that the purpose behind them is not historical but derives from the writers' theological point of view. A historian cannot base his arguments on data of this kind. [italics mine]

CONTRADICTION #112 Acts Contradicts Luke: How Long Jesus Remained on Earth after His Resurrection

Luke and Acts present contradictory information about the length of time Jesus remained on the earth after his resurrection. Luke indicated that

Jesus ascended to heaven on Easter Sunday evening. In contradiction, Acts reports that Jesus ascended to heaven forty days later. Nonetheless many commentators maintain that the author of Luke and Acts are considered to be the same individual.

TABLE 77. The Ascension: The Differences between Luke and Acts

VARIABLE	LUKE	ACTS
LOCATION	Bethany (Lk 24:50).	The Mount of Olives, between Jerusalem and Bethany (Acts 1:12).
TIME	Easter Sunday evening (Lk 24:13-53).	Forty days after the Passion (Thursday) (Acts 1:3).

[Note: Moule (1957, 206n6) pointed out that "there is no necessary discrepancy between Bethany (Lk 24^{50}) and the Mount of Olives (Ac 1^{12}): there is reason to believe that Bethany was on the Mount of Olives. See *The Beginnings of Christianity*, v. 475 f.]

Zweip (1997, 115; cf. Jonge 2013, 151-71) concisely stated the dilemma:

> The chronology of the departure scene is most puzzling. The continuous narrative sequence leaves the unbiased reader with the impression that the ascension took place on Easter Sunday itself (v. 1; 13, 36). This, however, does not square with Acts 1, where the ascension follows forty days after the resurrection (cf. Acts 13:31 "many days"). And if we press the chronology of Lk 24 a little bit further, the ascension took place at night (cf. v. 29).

Zweip (1997, 90-92) then reviewed several attempts to alleviate the chronology "tensions" between Luke 24 and Acts 1.

1. Luke, although "responsible for both versions and asserts that foreign material (either here or in Acts 1, or in both passages) has been *interpolated* into the text."
2. "[I]n Lk 25:51 and Acts 1:9 we simply have accounts *of two separate events* (supra 6 + n.3)."
3. "[A]fter completing the Gospel, Luke received *new information* (notably about the forty days) (supra 6 + n.3)."
4. "[T]here is a *chronological* break in the story-line of Lk 24."
5. "[P]erhaps, Luke was familiar with *two distinct traditions* which he reworked separately, without passing judgement upon them."

The vital point is recognizing that these ingenious solutions are nothing more than guesswork without evidentiary proof. Furthermore, they are just as valid as assumptions, guesswork, and speculations of doubters and skeptics of Jesus's resurrection and the narrations of those events.

Next it is necessary to examine how Matthew's chronology relates to Luke's and Acts'. Matthew's chronology can be interpreted in two ways. First, 28:16-20 can be construed as one event taking place in Galilee. Second, verses 18-20 can be interpreted as taking place at a future time and at a different place.

According to Mark 16:14, 19 (compare with Jn 20:19), Jesus stayed on earth *one* day.

> Mk 16:14 Afterward he appeared unto the eleven as they sat at meat, and upbraided them with their unbelief and hardness of heart, because they believed not them which had seen him after he was risen.

> Mk 16:19 So then after the Lord had spoken unto them, he was received up into heaven, and sat on the right hand of God.

Similarly Luke 24:50-52 reported that Jesus's ascension also occurred on Easter Sunday at Bethany: "And he led them out as far as to Bethany, and he lifted up his hands, and blessed them. And it came to pass, while he blessed them, he was parted from them, and carried up into heaven. And he led them out as far as to Bethany, and he lifted up his hands, and blessed them."

TABLE 78. Time References in Luke 24

VERSE	TIME-REFERENCES
Lk 24:1	*Now* upon the first day of the week
Lk 24:13	that *same day*
Lk 24:33	And they rose up that *same hour*
Lk 24:36	And as they thus spake, Jesus himself stood in the midst of them, and saith unto them, Peace be unto you.
Lk 24:44	And he said unto them [["*Then*"]]

In contradiction, Acts 1:3 claimed that Jesus was seen for "forty days" after his passion: "To whom also he shewed himself alive after his passion by many infallible proofs, being seen of them forty days, and speaking of the things pertaining to the kingdom of God."

Jeremias (1971, 301) challenged the view that Jesus was seen for forty days after his resurrection on Easter Sunday: "Whereas the passion was an observable happening that took place in Jerusalem over the course of a few days, the Christophanies were a variety of events of different kinds which extended over a long period, probably over a number of years, the tradition limited the period of the Christophanies to forty days only at a relatively late stage (Acts 1:3)." And also Heuschen (1965, 22): "The only chronological data which we find in this narrative are in verses 1, 13, 33 and 36; they all narrate facts which took place on the day of the resurrection."

Less radically, perhaps the "forty days" was used as a round number in order to fill the gap between Passover and Pentecost (Acts 2). J. P. Holding (n.d. The Resurrection Narratives Harmonized Contextually) offered yet another and simpler explanation: "The events of John 20:24-21:23 would chronologically occur in the 40 day period which Luke telescopes and brings to an end at his 24:45." Zweip (1997, 92) referred to this apologetic concept as "Luke's compact story-telling technique." However, an analysis of the relevant texts clearly demonstrates that the date of the Ascension was still Easter Sunday.

In contrast, Thomas and Gundry (1988, 246) are of the opinion that the next post-resurrection appearance to the disciples occurred in Jerusalem. They argued Luke 24:44 must not be surmised as the meeting that occurred when Jesus appeared to the ten assembled disciples (Lk 24:36-43) on the evening of Easter Sunday, the same day as the Resurrection. Instead, they postulated that forty days had transpired (Acts 1:3). Hence, they believe that there would have been ample time for a journey to Galilee and back to Jerusalem. Another Christian apologetic offered by Ankerberg and Weldon (n.d. Part 4, #38) is that Jesus made many "appearances in different places over a 40-day period."

However, Moule (1957b, 206) suggested that "perhaps the strongest evidence against the forty days, however is from outside the New Testament." Specifically he pointed to the early liturgy that "there seems to have been no separate festival of the Ascension until the latter part of the fourth century." He continued that "the Ascension is mentioned as a festival earlier, but as observed on the same day as Pentecost—fifty, not forty, days after Easter."

Finally, Maile (1986, 49), writing in *The Tyndale Bulletin* adds:

> It would seem that exact chronology in respect of the ascension was not considered by Luke to have been a part of early Christian proclamation, nor was it important in his own writing generally. Further, it is not only the rest of the NT which is silent in this respect; the number is absent from church tradition until the third century. Even Justin and Irenaeus, both of whom rely heavily

on the Lukan writings for their accounts of the ascension, make no mention of the forty-days, which would seem to indicate, as Lohfink observes, that "they saw in this expression no tradition which ought to be furthered."

In summary, Luke 24 stated that Jesus's ascension occurred on Easter Sunday evening and Acts 1:3 reported that the Ascension occurred forty days later. Yet both works are attributed to the same author.

CONTRADICTION #113 Luke 24:51 Contradicts Luke 23:43

Luke 24:51 unequivocally contradicts Luke 23:43. Luke 23:43 recorded that while on the cross Jesus promised the thief crucified adjacent to him: "To day shalt thou be with me in paradise." This *transportation* would have thus occurred on the day of the Crucifixion (Friday). In direct contradiction, Luke 24:51 recorded that Jesus's ascension was on Easter Sunday evening, technically Monday by the Jewish mode of counting: "And it came to pass, while he blessed them, he was parted from them, and carried up into heaven." Therefore, Jesus was either going to paradise on the day of his crucifixion or on Easter Sunday evening. Here Luke *contradicts* Luke.

Kaiser, Davids, Bruce, and Brauch (1996, 488-89) offered the Christian apologetic that "what Jesus is talking about is where his spirit and the spirit of the thief were to be." A second apologetic offered by this group is the assumption "that paradise is another name for heaven and Jesus was not in heaven until his ascension." They maintain that the term heaven means something more than the term paradise as found in the New Testament. That is, "In 2 Corinthians 12:2-4 it indicates a place that Paul was 'caught up' to, also identified as the 'third heaven' (which is the abode of God), the first two being the place of the birds and the place of the stars."

This first Christian apologetic is nothing more than a wishful excuse. There is no way for these Christian apologists to know that Jesus was not talking about his physical body or know that the thief would have interpreted Jesus's words in this light. The second apologetic is again an example of a word game. It is presumptuous to assume that these Christian apologists understood that Jesus referred to different heavens or that the thief and future readers of the text would have understood that these words referred to different places.

CONTRADICTION #114 Acts 1:9 Contradicts Luke 23:43

Acts 1:9 directly contradicts Luke 23:42-43. Luke 23:43 recorded that that while on the cross Jesus promised the thief crucified adjacent to him that he would end up in paradise on the very day that he was being crucified: "And he said unto Jesus, Lord, remember me when thou comest into thy kingdom. And Jesus said unto him, Verily I say unto thee, *To day shalt thou be with me in paradise.*" However, the Acts of the Apostles recorded:

> Acts 1:9 And when he had spoken these things, while they beheld, he was taken up; and a cloud received him out of their sight.

> Acts 1:10 And while they looked stedfastly toward heaven as he went up, behold, two men stood by them in white apparel;

> Acts 1:11 Which also said, Ye men of Galilee, why stand ye gazing up into heaven? this same Jesus, which is taken up from you into heaven, shall so come in like manner as ye have seen him go into heaven.

The contradiction in Acts 1:9 stated that this ascension of Jesus occurred forty days *after* the passion: "To whom also he shewed himself alive after his passion by many infallible proofs, being seen of them forty days, and speaking of the things pertaining to the kingdom of God:" On the other hand, to the thief in Luke 23:43 Jesus declared that he and the malefactor would *both* be in paradise the *same* day they were crucified. Consequently, either both Jesus and the thief went to paradise on the day of the Crucifixion, or according to Luke 24:51, Jesus went to paradise on Easter Sunday evening; yet Acts 1:9 recorded that Jesus went to Paradise on a Thursday, forty days later. Given that Luke was also the author of Acts, Luke *contradicts* Luke.

TABLE 79. Ascension: Forty Days after Passover

(For key dates see: Hoehner, H. W. "Chronology." In *Dictionary of Jesus and the Gospels*, edited by Joel B. Green, Scot McKnight, I. Howard Marshall, 122. Downers Grove: InterVarsity Press, 1992.)

SUNDAY	MONDAY	TUESDAY	WEDNESDAY	THURSDAY	FRIDAY	SATURDAY
NISAN 10 PALM SUNDAY March 29, 33	NISAN 11 March 30, 33	NISAN 12 March 31, 33	NISAN 13 April 1, 33	NISAN 14 April 2, 33	NISAN 15 JESUS'S DEATH April 3, 33 First day of the Feast of Unleavened Bread	NISAN 16 THE CHIEF PRIESTS VISIT PILATE April 4, 33 Second day of the Feast of Unleavened Bread
NISAN 17 EASTER SUNDAY April 5, 33 Third day of the Feast of Unleavened Bread DAY 1	NISAN 18 April 6, 33 Fourth day of the Feast of Unleavened Bread DAY 2	NISAN 19 April 7, 33 Fifth day of the Feast of Unleavened Bread DAY 3	NISAN 20 April 8, 33 Sixth day of the Feast of Unleavened Bread DAY 4	NISAN 21 April 9, 33 Seventh day of the Feast of Unleavened Bread DAY 5	NISAN 22 April 10, 33 XXXXXX DAY 6	NISAN 23 April 11, 33 XXXXXX DAY 7
NISAN 24 April 12, 33 DAY 8	NISAN 25 April 13, 33 DAY 9	NISAN 26 April 14, 33 DAY 10	NISAN 27 April 15, 33 DAY 11	NISAN 28 April 16, 33 DAY 12	NISAN 29 April 17, 33 DAY 13	NISAN 30 April 18, 33 DAY 14
IYAR 1 April 19, 33 DAY 15	IYAR 2 April 20, 33 DAY 16	IYAR 3 April 21, 33 DAY 17	IYAR 4 April 22, 33 DAY 18	IYAR 5 April 23, 33 DAY 19	IYAR 6 April 24, 33 DAY 20	IYAR 7 April 25, 33 DAY 21

IYAR 8	IYAR 9	IYAR 10	IYAR 11	IYAR 12	IYAR 13	IYAR 14
April 26, 33	April 27, 33	April 28, 33	April 29, 33	April 30, 33	MAY 1, 33	May 2, 33
DAY 22	DAY 23	DAY 24	DAY 25	DAY 26	DAY 27	DAY 28
IYAR 15	IYAR 16	IYAR 17	IYAR 18	IYAR 19	IYAR 20	IYAR 21
May 3, 33	May 4, 33	May 5, 33	May 6, 33	May 7, 33	May 8, 33	May 9, 33
DAY 29	DAY 30	DAY 31	DAY 32	DAY 33	DAY 34	DAY 35
IYAR 22	IYAR 23	IYAR 24	IYAR 25	IYAR 26	IYAR 27	IYAR 28
May 10, 33	May 11, 33	May 12, 33	May 13, 33	May 14, 33	May 15, 33	May 16, 33
DAY 36	DAY 37	DAY 38	DAY 39	DAY 40: THE ASCENSION (ACTS 1)	DAY 41	DAY 42
IYAR 29	SIVAN 1	SIVAN 2	SIVAN 3	SIVAN 4	SIVAN 4	SIVAN 5
May 17, 33	May 18, 33	May 19, 33	May 20, 33	May 21, 33	May 22, 33	May 23, 33
DAY 43	DAY 44	DAY 45	DAY 46	DAY 47	DAY 48	DAY 49
SIVAN 6	SIVAN 7	SIVAN 8	SIVAN 9	SIVAN 10	SIVAN 11	SIVAN 12
May 24, 33	May 25, 33	MAY 26, 33	MAY 27, 33	May 28, 33	MAY 29, 33	May 30, 33
DAY 50: PENTECOST (ACTS 2)						

[NOTE: Some proponents maintain that Jesus's ascension occurred on the seventh of Sivan.]

As a side issue, Vermes (2008, 147) writes: "The alleged need for Jesus remaining with his disciples to give them further instruction about the kingdom of God (Acts 1:3) is rendered superfluous by the promise in John that the Holy Spirit will come to teach them all things (Jn 14:26; 16:13)."

ISSUE 109: Jesus's Ascension

Mk 16:19 So then after the Lord had spoken unto them, *he was received up into heaven*, and sat on the right hand of God.	Mt	Lk 24:50 And he led them out as far as to Bethany, and he lifted up his hands, and blessed them. 51 And it came to pass, while he blessed them, he was parted from them, *and carried up into heaven.* 52 And they worshipped him, and returned to Jerusalem with great joy: 53 And were continually in the temple, praising and blessing God. Amen.	Acts 1:9 And when he had spoken these things, *while they beheld, he was taken up; and a cloud received him out of their sight.* 10 And while they looked steadfastly toward heaven as he went up, behold, *two men stood by them in white apparel;* 11 *Which also said, Ye men of Galilee, why stand ye gazing up into heaven? this same Jesus, which is taken up from you into heaven, shall so come in like manner as ye have seen him go into heaven.*	Jn

Mark 16:19 reported that Jesus "was received up into heaven." The means of this transportation was not detailed. However, Mark stated that Jesus's final destination was in heaven and seated at the right hand of God. In contrast, Matthew contained no ascension scene.

In the Gospel of Luke, the narrative tersely stated that when Jesus parted from his disciples he was "carried up to heaven." Later, in Acts 1:9-11, the ascension narrative reported: (1) "he went up" and (2) a cloud eventually hid him from their sight. Two additional details were appended to this ascension account: (1) two men in white apparel stood by the disciples as Jesus ascended into heaven, and (2) they prophesied the *parousia,* the Second Coming of Jesus.

Similar to Matthew, the Gospel of John omitted any discussion or description of Jesus's ascension.

Hamm (2003, 218; cf. Garland 2011, 969; Green 1997, 860; Kapic 2005, 250; Stempvoort 1959, 34; Tannehill 1996, 362) offers that Luke 23:50-53 directly parallels Sirach's description of the high priest Simeon blessing the people of Israel (the Wisdom of Ben Sira (50:20-23):

> Luke 24:50-53 echoes at least five features of that passage: (1) the raising of the hands (Sir 50:20a || Luke 24:50); (2) the blessing (Sir 50:20b || Luke 24:50-51a); (3) the worshipful prostration (Sir 50:21 || Luke 50:51b); (4) the blessing or praising of God (Sir 50:22a 11 Luke 24:53); and (5) the note of joy (Sir 50:23: a

prayer for joy of heart || Luke 24:52b: disciples return to Jerusalem with great joy).

CONTRADICTION #115 Omissions Detailing the Ascension

There is no explicit account of the Ascension in the oldest Christian sources: the writings of Paul. Paul unequivocally stated in 1 Corinthians 15:3 that Jesus had risen from the dead: "For I deliver unto you first of all that which I also received, how that Christ died for our sins according to the scriptures; and that he was buried, and that he was rose again the third day according to the scriptures." However, Paul often mentioned that Jesus was situated on the right hand or side of God:

> Rom 8:34 Who is he that condemneth? It is Christ that died, yea rather, that is risen again, who is even at the right hand of God, who also maketh intercession for us.

> 2 Cor 6:7 By the word of truth, by the power of God, by the armour of righteousness on the right hand and on the left,

> Eph 1:20 Which he wrought in Christ, when he raised him from the dead, and set him at his own right hand in the heavenly places,

> Col 3:1 If ye then be risen with Christ, seek those things which are above, where Christ sitteth on the right hand of God.

> Heb 1:3 Who being the brightness of his glory, and the express image of his person, and upholding all things by the word of his power, when he had by himself purged our sins, sat down on the right hand of the Majesty on high:

> Heb 1:13 But to which of the angels said he at any time, Sit on my right hand, until I make thine enemies thy footstool?

> Heb 8:1 Now of the things which we have spoken this is the sum: We have such an high priest, who is set on the right hand of the throne of the Majesty in the heavens;

> Heb 10:12 But this man, after he had offered one sacrifice for sins for ever, sat down on the right hand of God;

> Heb 12:2 Looking unto Jesus the author and finisher of our faith; who for the joy that was set before him endured the cross, despising the shame, and is set down at the right hand of the throne of God.

In part, Mark, the oldest gospel account, agreed with Paul and did not have an explicit ascension. Rather, Jesus's ascension appears only in the last twelve passages, the Markan appendix. Mark 16:19 reads: "So then after the Lord had spoken unto them, *he was received up into heaven*, and sat on the right hand of God."

Matthew (see chapter 28), who church tradition declares to have been an apostle and a witness of Jesus's ascension, failed to report this event. It must be remembered that Luke and Acts reported that Jesus defied the law of gravity, mounted into the clouds, and disappeared in the airless space surrounding the earth. Instead, Matthew's narrative ended on an unidentified mountain somewhere in Galilee where he taught the Great Commission to his eleven disciples.

John, the author of the last gospel, a person who church tradition declared to have been an apostle and a witness of Jesus's ascension, also did not report this event. His account in chapter 21 ended with Jesus communicating with Peter at the Sea of Tiberias.

Compounding matters, Schmiedel (1903, 4061) added that there is *no* mention of an ascension in the writings of the early Church Fathers such as Clemens, Romanus, Hermas, Polycarp, or Ignatius. Only Luke provided an exclusive description of Jesus's ascension, although here there is much to doubt regarding the authenticity of this narrative. This topic is examined below.

SPECULATION #212 Manuscript Difficulties

There are thousands of Greek and Latin manuscripts of the New Testament. However, not all of them are of the same value. Most of these manuscripts are only partial texts. The most significant text is referred to as the Sinaitic version (ℵ). Codex Sinaiticus (London, Brit. Libr., Add. 43725; Gregory-Aland nº ℵ (Alef) or 01) is a fourth-century uncial manuscript of the Greek Bible written between the years 330-350. However, only Luke provides details of Jesus's physical bodily ascension. Significantly, his words in 24:51, "carried up into heaven," do not appear in the Sinaitic version, the oldest version of the complete New Testament extant.

In addition, other ancient manuscripts lacked the words "worshipped him." Furthermore, the phrases "was carried up into heaven" and "worshipped him, and" are not even "printed in Nestle's standard edition of the original

Greek text of the New Testament." A similar warning is found in the NRSV (1989, 89nh). With the elimination of the spurious Markan appendix and this interpolated passage in Luke, the four gospels *do not* contain a single reference of Jesus's ascension.

In an analysis of this issue, Parsons (1987, 31) compared the way eight English Bible translations treated seven verses with regard to omissions (Western non-interpolations) from the original text. But first, it is appropriate to explain the term Western non-interpolation.

The Western text type is one of several text types used in textual criticism to describe and group the textual character of Greek New Testament manuscripts. It is the term given to the predominant form of the New Testament text witnessed in the Old Latin translation from the Greek and also in quotations from certain second- and third-century Christian writers, including Cyprian, Tertullian, and Irenaeus. However, the term "Western" is a bit of a misnomer because members of the Western text type have been found in the Christian East, including Syria.

The Western text has the tendency to paraphrase. Words, clauses, and whole sentences are freely changed, omitted or inserted, sometimes with a tendency toward harmonization. Added material comes from oral tradition and the apocryphal literature. Usually it presents longer variants of text, but in the end of the Gospel of Luke and other NT books, it has shorter variants, named Western "non-interpolations." The Western text type consistently omits a series of eight short phrases from verses in the gospel of Luke, the so-called Western non-interpolations: Lk 22:19b-20, 24:3, 24:6, 24:12 [the entire verse], 24:36, 24:40, 24:51, and 24:52. It is noteworthy that eight of the nine non-interpolations are in Luke (and the remaining one is not a true example of the form). The two relevant verses for this discussion are the following:

- Luke 24:51 -- και ανεφερετο εις τον ουρανον [*he was carried up into heaven*] *omitted by* ℵ* D a b d e ff² l (*hiat* r¹) sin (*hiat* cur) geo¹
- Luke 24:52 -- προσκυνης αντεσ αυτον [*worshipped him*] *omitted by* D a b d e ff² l (*hiat* r¹) sin (*hiat* cur) geo²

> The textual theory of Westcott and Hort recognized four text-types—the Neutral, the Alexandrian (these two really being different phases of the same type, and now generally called "Alexandrian"), the Syrian (what we call the Byzantine), and the Western.

> Of these types, in their view, the Alexandrian is restrained, the "Western" is marked by extensive paraphrase and expansion, and the Byzantine is a smooth combination of the two.

It is a good rule of criticism that, when manuscripts go against their tendencies, the significance of this reading is increased. So, for instance, when the "Western" text preserves a *short* reading, that reading is more likely to be original than when it preserves a longer reading. This is the basis on which Hort isolated the "Western Non-interpolations"....

The force of Hort's argument was so strong that for three-quarters of a century most editions and translations (including the Revised Standard Version and the New English Bible) omitted these nine passages. (Robert B. Waltz. 2007)

TABLE 80. Parsons's Analysis of Eight English Bible Translations Dealing with Western Non-Interpolations.

Source: Data from Mikeal C. Parsons, "Treatment of Non-Interpolations in Modern English Translations," *The Departure of Jesus In Luke-Acts: The Ascension Narratives in Context* (Sheffield: JSOT, 1987): 31.

Verse	ERV	ASV	RSV 1962	RSV 1971	RSV CE	NEB	GNB	NIV
24.3	+'	+'	-*	-*	-*	-	+	-
24.6	+'	+'	-*	-*	+'	-*	+	+
24.12	+'	+'	-*	-*	+'	-*	+'	+
24.36	+'	+'	-*	-*	+'	-*	+'	+
24.40	+'	+'	-*	-*	+'	-*	+'	+
24.51	+'	+'	-*	+'	+'	-*	+'	+
24.52	+'	+'	-*	-*	+'	-*	+	+

-   indicates the passage is omitted from the text with no accompanying note.
+   indicates the passage is included the text with no accompanying note.
-*   indicates the passage is omitted from the text but included in a footnote.
+'   indicates the passage is included in the text but accompanied by a footnote that explains that the passage is omitted by some ancient authorities.

The manner in which these eight English Bible translations handle this and other verses speak volumes, challenging the veracity of Jesus's purported physical, bodily resurrection and ascension.

SPECULATION #213 Jesus Sitting at the Right Hand of God

Mark 16:19 stated that Jesus "was received up into heaven and sat on the right hand of God." This is a noteworthy claim. However, an important detail is missing: How did the author of Mark know his declaration to be a fact? Did he actually see Jesus sitting on the right hand side of God? If he did not directly witness this account, where was his incontrovertible evidentiary proof?

Earlier, Mark 16:17-18 talked about various signs given to the followers who believed in his name. Several of these signs included taking up serpents, drinking deadly things, and the laying on of hands. Assuming that these signs were meant figuratively (not literally), it is possible that Mark 16:19 was also meant to be understood symbolically.

On a literal reading, this verse plainly means that one could see God. However, this concept is categorically rejected multiple times in the Christian scriptures. Even the Christian scriptures incontrovertibly instruct: (1) God has no image and (2) God cannot be seen by the human eye, but creation points to His existence.

> Lk 24:39 Behold my hands and my feet, that it is I myself: handle me, and see; for a spirit hath not flesh and bones, as ye see me have.

> Jn 1:18 No man hath seen God at any time; the only begotten Son, which is in the bosom of the Father, he hath declared him.

> Jn 4:24 God is a Spirit and they that worship Him must worship Him in spirit and in truth.

> Rom 1:20 For the invisible things of him from the creation of the world are clearly seen, being understood by the things that are made, even his eternal power and Godhead; so that they are without excuse:

> Col 1:15 Who is the image of the invisible God, the firstborn of every creature:

> 1 Tim 1:17 Now unto the King eternal, immortal, invisible, the only wise God, be honour and glory for ever and ever. Amen.

> 1 Tim 6:16 Who only hath immortality, dwelling in the light which no man can approach unto; whom no man hath seen, nor can see: to whom be honour and power everlasting. Amen.

Some people might say that the "right hand of God" is an allusion of favoritism and that Mark 16:9 did not literally mean that Jesus was sitting at the right hand of God. However, this apologetic is merely a speculation. Perhaps the author was writing literally. As Galvin (1988, 41) poignantly stated: "To confess that Jesus sits at the right hand of God no more implies that Jesus can be seen sitting at the right hand of God than it implies that God has in fact a right hand." Nonetheless, there are several problems with Mark's report:

1. The writer was expressing his belief that Jesus was sitting at the right hand of God. Therefore, this is a claim, *not* a fact.
2. Luke 24:51 stated that Jesus "was carried up into heaven." However, this statement in Luke does *not* appear in the earliest manuscripts of that gospel.
3. The Markan appendix is recognized as being spurious (e.g., Wallace 2011, 29).
4. Matthew or John, two supposed witnesses, did *not* attest to Jesus's ascension.

Finally, Swete (1913, 10) posited: "All references to the Session of the Ascended Christ rest ultimately on the 110th Psalm, *The Lord saith unto my lord, Sit thou at my right hand, until I make thine enemies thy footstool.*"

Unmistakably, this declaration by Mark provides no incontrovertible evidentiary proof for Jesus's physical, bodily resurrection.

SPECULATION #214 Dubious Marching through the Streets at Nighttime

Luke's report of the events leading up to Jesus's ascension is doubtful. A plain meaning and simple reading of the text has the Ascension occurring on Easter Sunday evening. Luke 24:33 has the two travelers from Emmaus returning to Jerusalem and finding eleven disciples and their companions: "And they rose up the same hour, and returned to Jerusalem, and found the eleven gathered together, and them that were with them." This would place eleven disciples plus two travelers and an additional unknown number of companions in one room. A few verses later, Luke 24:36 has Jesus appearing in their midst followed by a dialogue, the eating of some food, and additional teaching.

Luke 24:50 then reports: "And he led them out as far as to Bethany, and he lifted up his hands, and blessed them." This narration is impossible "IF" they were initially meeting *inside* the city of Jerusalem as implied in Luke 24:33: "And they rose up the same hour, and returned to Jerusalem, and found the eleven gathered together, and them that were with them." As discussed earlier, Ehrhardt (1964, 182), writing in the *New Testament Studies*, raised the issue that by nightfall the gates of Jerusalem would have been closed. Consequently, the closed gates would have prevented anyone from leaving the city.

> Neh 7:1 Now it came to pass, when the wall was built, and I had set up the doors, and the porters and the singers and the Levites were appointed,

> Neh 7:2 That I gave my brother Hanani, and Hananiah the ruler of the palace, charge over Jerusalem: for he was a faithful man, and feared God above many.

> Neh 7:3 And I said unto them, Let not the gates of Jerusalem be opened until the sun be hot; and while they stand by, let them shut the doors, and bar them: and appoint watches of the inhabitants of Jerusalem, every one in his watch, and every one to be over against his That I gave my brother Hanani, and Hananiah the ruler of the palace, charge over Jerusalem: for he was a faithful man, and feared God above many.

> Joshua 2:5 And it came to pass about the time of shutting of the gate, when it was dark, that the men went out: whitter the men went I wot not: pursue after them quickly; for ye shall overtake them.

There is yet another problem. It was now the dead of night, and Luke reported that a group of perhaps fifteen to twenty men and women were marching through the streets of Jerusalem with a man who was supposedly crucified by the Roman government as an enemy of the state. Furthermore, their identity must have been well-known as a result of (1) their previous entry into Jerusalem (Mk 11:7-11; Mt 21:8-11; Lk 19:35-40; Jn 12:12-19), (2) Jesus's arrest and marching him to his interrogation and trial (Mk 14:43-53; Mt 26:47-57; Lk 22:47-54; Jn 18:3-12), (3) Jesus's trial before Pilate (Mk 15:1-14; Mt 27:2-25; Lk 23:1-24; Jn 18:29-19:14), (4) Jesus's march to Golgotha (Mk 15:16-23; Mt 27:26-34; Lk 23:26-33; Jn 19:15-17), (5) Jesus's crucifixion (Mk 15:24-25; Mt 27:35-44; Lk 23:33-43; Jn 19:17-23), and (6) information that Jesus's crucifixion coincided with three hours of darkness from noon to 3:00 p.m. (Mk 15:33; Mt 27:45; Lk 23:44-45). In addition, there had to have been some noise created by having fifteen to twenty people marching through the streets during the dead of night, unless it is assumed that they tiptoed bare foot through the streets and they spoke not a single word. Yet nobody seemed to have noticed them or paid any attention to this event. Furthermore, this non-attention took place while Jerusalem was occupied with at least a cohort of Roman soldiers. At the absolute least there would have been guards at the gates (even if they were open), and yet nothing seemed the least bit odd, even though it was several hours after Jesus's execution. If they were noticed, apparently no report is known to exist.

Next, Jesus and his entourage continued on their way to Bethany, and again there was no indication that anyone heard or saw them. Of course, this was when most people would have been sleeping. Then at Bethany, Jesus ascended to heaven from Mount Olivet (Acts 1:12), an event apparently nobody else witnessed except Jesus's followers.

Finally, Luke 24:52 reported that the entourage returned to Jerusalem: "And they worshipped him, and returned to Jerusalem with great joy." It is assumed that the disciples returned to their housing accommodations *within* the walls of the city. Another unknown is whether or not their returning with great joy included any noise making, or did they return during the morning hours. "IF" these events are correct, it is remarkable that Jesus's disciples and followers were not noticed and reported to the Roman officials. Then, too, the problem of the locked city gates would once again confront the disciples, "IF" they were in fact returning to their housing accommodations *within* the city of Jerusalem.

Collectively, Luke's narrative cannot be reconciled with a Roman occupied Jerusalem in the first century and during the week of Passover.

ISSUE 110: Jesus's Final Words

Mk 16:17 And these signs shall follow them that believe; In my name shall they cast out devils; they shall speak with new tongues; 18 They shall take up serpents; and if they drink any deadly thing, it shall not hurt them; they shall lay hands on the sick, and they shall recover.	Mt 28:19 Go ye therefore, and teach all nations, baptizing them in the name of the Father, and the Son, and of the Holy Ghost. 20 Teaching them to observe all things whatsoever I have commanded you: *and, lo, I am with you always, even unto the end of the world. Amen.*	Lk 24:51 And it came to pass, while *he blessed them,* he was parted from them, and carried up into heaven.	Acts 1:6 When they therefore were come together, they asked of him, saying, Lord, wilt thou at this time restore again the kingdom to Israel? 7 *And he said unto them, It is not for you to know the times or the seasons, which the Father hath put in his own power. 8 But ye shall receive power, after that the Holy Ghost is come upon you: and ye shall be witnesses unto me both in Jerusalem, and in all Judaea, and in Samaria, and unto the uttermost part of the earth.*	Jn 21:21 Peter seeing him saith to Jesus, Lord, and what shall this man do? 22 *Jesus saith unto him, If I will that he tarry till I come, what is that to thee? follow thou me.*

Prior to Jesus's ascension, Mark 16:17-18 narrates Jesus's final words which contained five promises or signs of power that Jesus gave to them who believed in him: (1) the power to cast out the devil, (2) the power to speak in new tongues, (3) the power to take up serpents, (4) the power to drink anything deadly and not be hurt, and (5) the power to heal the sick by laying on hands.

Matthew did not have an ascension scene. Consequently, the author of Matthew 28:19-20 only reported Jesus's final teaching to his disciples. This final teaching was the Great Commission: "Go ye therefore, and teach all nations, baptizing them in the name of the Father, and of the Son, and of the Holy Ghost: Teaching them to observe all things whatsoever I have commanded you: and, lo, I am with you always, even unto the end of the world. Amen."

On the other hand, according Luke 24:51, Jesus blessed his disciples prior to parting at Bethany and then there was his ascension. However, the words of his blessing are omitted: "And it came to pass, while he blessed them, he was parted from them, and carried up into heaven."

In Acts 1, a brief conversation was reported just prior to Jesus's ascension. Acts 1:6 first detailed that while at Mount Olivet the disciples asked a question: was Jesus going to restore the kingdom to Israel at this time? In the next two verses Jesus answered their question with his final words: "And he said unto them, It is not for you to know the times or the seasons, which the Father hath put in his own power." Then Jesus followed up by commanding his disciples: "But ye shall receive power, after that the Holy Ghost is come upon you: and ye shall be witnesses unto me both in Jerusalem, and in all Judea, and in Samaria, and unto the uttermost part of the earth."

John did not report an ascension scene. Consequently, in John 21:22, Jesus's last words go back to his conversation with Peter at the Sea of Tiberias when he was recommissioned. Here Jesus answered a question posed by Peter regarding the disciple whom Jesus loved: "Jesus saith unto him, If I will that he tarry till I come, what is that to thee? Follow thou me." However, many commentators and scholars question whether the author of John 20 also penned John 21.

ISSUE 111: The Message of the "Second Coming"

Mk	Mt	Lk.	Acts 1:10 And while they looked steadfastly toward heaven as he went up, behold, *two men stood by them in white apparel; Which also said, 11 Ye men of Galilee, why stand ye gazing up into heaven? this same Jesus, which is taken up from you into heaven, shall so come in like manner as ye have seen him go into heaven.*	Jn

Only in the Acts of the Apostles were two angels reported to be present during Jesus's ascension. First, after Jesus disappeared, the angels asked a rhetorical question: "Ye men of Galilee, why stand ye gazing up into heaven?" Then they followed up with an answer: "this same Jesus, which is taken up from you into heaven, shall so come in like manner as ye have seen him go into heaven." This Second Coming (Gk. *parousia*) referred to the coming of the Son of man as the judge of the world.

ISSUE 112: The Actions of the Disciples after the Ascension

Mk 16:20	Mt	Lk 24:52	Acts 1:25 That he may take part of this ministry and	Jn
And they went forth, and *preached every where*, the Lord working with them, and confirming the word with signs following. Amen.		And *they worshipped him*, and *returned to Jerusalem with great joy:* 53 And were *continually in the temple, praising and blessing God.* Amen.	apostleship, from which Judas by transgression fell, that he might go to his own place. 26 *And they gave forth their lots; and the lot fell upon Matthias; and he was numbered with the eleven apostles.*	
			Acts 2:1 And when the day of Pentecost was fully come, they were all with one accord in one place. 2 And suddenly there came a sound from heaven as of a rushing mighty wind, and it filled all the house where they were sitting. 3 And there appeared unto them cloven tongues like as of fire, and it sat upon each of them. 4 *And they were all filled with the Holy Ghost, and began to speak with other tongues,* as the Spirit gave them utterance.	

According to Mark's report, the disciples followed Jesus's command and went forth and preached everywhere. Matthew failed to provide any information as to whether or not Jesus's command was carried out. In Luke, the author stated (1) they worshipped Jesus, (2) they returned to Jerusalem with great joy, and (3) they were continually in the Temple, praising and blessing God. In contrast, John left no written account of what followed other than this disciple "wrote these things."

However, in Acts there were, in fact, numerous detailed events tracing the history of the church after Jesus's death. Significantly (1) Mathias was named to replace Judas (1:23-26), (2) during Pentecost the disciples were filled with the Holy Ghost and began to speak in tongues, and (3) the disciples preached in Jesus's name (2:13-47).

TABLE 81. Summary of the Substantial Differences between the Gospels and Acts: From the Ascension to Pentecost

MARK and LUKE	ACTS
1. No presence of presumably heavenly messengers during the Ascension.	1. Accentuated by the presence of two presumably heavenly messengers during the Ascension (Acts 1:10).
2. No announced *parousia*.	2. An announced *parousia* (Acts 1:11).
3. No replacement of Judas.	3. Matthias replaces Judas (Acts 1:18-26).
4. No Pentecost.	4. Pentecost (Acts 2).
5. No speaking in tongues.	5. Speaking in tongues (Acts 2:4).

CHAPTER 16

Jesus Appears to Paul

ISSUE 113: When Jesus Appears to Paul

	Mk	Mt	Lk	Acts 9, Acts 22, and Acts 26 [See below]	Jn
1 Cor 15:5 And that he was seen of Cephas, then of the twelve: 6 After that, he was seen of above five hundred brethren at once; of whom the greater part remain unto this present, but some are fallen asleep. 7 After that, he was seen of James; then of all the apostles. 8 *And last of all he was seen of me also, as of one born out of due time.* 9 For I am the least of the apostles, that am not meet to be called an apostle, because I persecuted the church of God. 10 But by the grace of God I am what I am: and his grace which was bestowed upon me was not in vain; but I laboured more abundantly than they all: yet not I, but the grace of God which was with me.					

PAUL'S FIRST LETTER to the Corinthians declared that the resurrected Jesus was witnessed on six separate occasions. These earlier occasions included: (1) Cephas, (2) the Twelve, (3) more than five hundred brethren at once, (4) James, and (5) all the apostles. Finally, Paul concluded that he was a witness to the risen Jesus.

In the Acts of the Apostles there are three accounts of Paul's dramatic conversion (Acts 9, 22, and 26) as a result of seeing the risen Jesus. These texts were written approximately fifty years *after* Paul's conversion experience on the road to Damascus and almost fifty-three years after Jesus's crucifixion. In general, commentators have estimated that this conversion episode occurred between the years 33 to 36. The fact that Paul saw Jesus, and believed that he saw Jesus, is one of the strongest points argued by Christian apologists in support of Jesus's resurrection.

Before proceeding directly into the contradictions and speculations, the three accounts reported in Acts must be examined. They are presented chronologically and in parallel columns. An empty box means that there is no corresponding text. Acts 9 was written in the third person whereas Acts 22 and 26 were written in first person. The accounts started with an explanation that Paul, who at that time also had the name Saul before his conversion, was traveling to Damascus with the approval and authorization of the high priest. Damascus is about 135 miles NNW of Jerusalem. (Note: Throughout the remainder of this issue, the name Paul will be used except in biblical quotations and parts of tables 82-83.)

TABLE 82. Comparison of Paul's Three Visions

ACTS 9: AN ACCOUNT BY LUKE RELATING PAUL'S EXPERIENCE	ACTS 22: PAUL BEFORE A CROWD IN JERUSALEM	ACTS 26: PAUL BEFORE KING AGRIPPA
Acts 9:1 And Saul, yet breathing out threatenings, and slaughter against the disciples of the Lord, went unto the high priest,		
Acts 9:2 And desired of him letters to Damascus to the synagogues, that if he found any of this way, whether they were men or women, he might bring them bound unto Jerusalem.	Acts 22:5 As also the high priest doth bear me witness, and all the estate of the elders: from whom also I received letters unto the brethren, and went to Damascus, to bring them which were there bound unto Jerusalem, for to be punished.	Acts 26:12 Whereupon as I went to Damascus with authority and commission from the chief priests.
Acts 9:3 And as he journeyed, he came near Damascus: and suddenly there shined round about him a light from heaven.	Acts 22:6 And it came to pass, that, as I made my journey, and was come nigh unto Damascus about noon, suddenly there shone from heaven a great light round about me.	Acts 26:13 At midday, O king, I saw in the way a light from heaven, above the brightness of the sun, shining round about me and them which journeyed with me.
Acts 9:4 And he fell to the earth, and heard a voice saying unto him, Saul, Saul, why persecutest thou me?	Acts 22:7 And I fell unto the ground, and heard a voice saying unto me, Saul, Saul, why persecutest thou me?	Acts 26:14 And when we were all fallen to the earth, I heard a voice speaking unto me, and saying in the Hebrew tongue, Saul, Saul, why persecutest thou me? It is hard for thee to kick against the pricks.

Acts 9:5 And he said, who art thou, Lord? And the Lord said, I am Jesus whom thou persecutest: it is hard for thee to kick against the pricks.	Acts 22:8 And I answered, who art thou, Lord. And he said unto me, I am Jesus of Nazareth, whom thou persecutest.	Acts 26:15 And I said, Who art thou, Lord? And he said, I am Jesus who thou persecutest.
Acts 9:6 And he trembling and astonished said, Lord, what wilt thou have me do? And the Lord said unto him, Arise and go into the city, and it shall be told thee what thou must do.	Acts 22:9 And I said, What shall I do, Lord? And the Lord said unto me, Arise, and go into Damascus; and there it shall be told thee of all things which are appointed for thee to do.	Acts 26:16 But rise and stand upon thy feet: for I have appeared unto thee for this purpose, to make thee a minister and a witness both of these things which thou hast seen, and of those things in the which I will appear unto thee;
	Acts 22:10 And I said, what shall I do, Lord? And the Lord said unto me, arise, and go into Damascus; and there it shall be told thee of all things which are appointed for thee to do.	Acts 26:17 Delivering thee from the people, and from the Gentiles, unto whom now I send thee.
		Acts 26:18 To open their eyes, and to turn them from darkness to light, and from the power of Satan unto God, that they may receive foregiveness of sins, and inheritance among them which are sanctified by faith that is in me.
Acts 9:7 And the men which journeyed with him stood speechless, hearing a voice, but seeing no man.	Acts 22:9 And they that were with me saw indeed the light, and were afraid; but they heard not the voice of him that spake to me.	
Acts 9:8 And Saul arose from the earth; and when his eyes were opened, he saw no man: but they led him by the hand, and brought him into Damascus.	Acts 22:11 And when I could not see for the glory of that light, being led by the hand of them that were with me, I came into Damascus.	
Acts 9:9 And he was three days without sight, and neither did he eat nor drink.		
Acts 9:10 And there was a certain disciple at Damascus, named Ananias; and to him said the Lord in a vision, Ananias. And he said, Behold, I am here, Lord.		

Acts 9:11 And the Lord said unto him, Arise, and go into the street which is called Straight, and enquire in the house of Judas for one called Saul, of Tarsus: for, behold, he prayeth,		
9:12 And hath seen in a vision a man named Ananias coming in, and putting his hand on him, that he might receive his sight.		
Acts 9:13 Then Ananias answered, Lord, I have heard by many of this man, how much evil he hath done to thy saints at Jerusalem:		
Acts 9:14 And here he hath authority from the chief priests to bind all that call on thy name.		
9:15 But the Lord said unto him, Go thy way: for he is a chosen vessel unto me, to bear my name before the Gentiles, and kings, and the children of Israel:		
Acts 9:16 For I will shew him how great things he must suffer for my name's sake.		
	Acts 22:12 And one Ananias, a devout man according to the law, having a good report of all the Jews which dwelt there,	
Acts 9:17 And Ananias went his way, and entered into the house; and putting his hands on him said, Brother Saul, the Lord, even Jesus, that appeared unto thee in the way as thou camest, hath sent me, that thou mightest receive thy sight, and be filled with the Holy Ghost.	Acts 22:13 Came unto me, and stood, and said unto me, Brother Saul, receive thy sight. And the same hour I looked upon him.	

Acts 9:18 And immediately there fell from his eyes as it had been scales: and he received sight forthwith, and arose, and was baptized.	Acts 22:13 Came unto me, and stood, and said unto me, Brother Saul, receive thy sight. And the same hour I looked upon him.	
	Acts 22:14 And he said, The God of our fathers hath chosen thee, that thou shouldest know his will, and see that Just One, and shouldest hear the voice of his mouth.	
	Acts 22:15 For thou shalt be his witness unto all men of what thou hast seen and heard.	
	Acts 22:16 And now why tarriest thou? arise, and be baptized, and wash away thy sins, calling on the name of the Lord.	
Acts 9:19 And when he had received meat, he was strengthened. Then was Saul certain days with the disciples which were at Damascus.		
	Acts 22:17 And it came to pass, that, when I was come again to Jerusalem, even while I prayed in the temple, I was in a trance;	
	Acts 22:18 And saw him saying unto me, Make haste, and get thee quickly out of Jerusalem: for they will not receive thy testimony concerning me.	
	Acts 22:19 And I said, Lord, they know that I imprisoned and beat in every synagogue them that believed on thee:	

CONTRADICTION #116 Who Heard Jesus, and What Did They Hear?

Acts contradicts itself in reporting who heard Jesus. After traveling on the road at about noontime, there was a great light from heaven that suddenly shined around Paul. Simultaneously, Acts 9:7 recorded: "And the men which journeyed with him stood speechless, hearing a voice, but seeing no man." Consequently, *all* the men traveling with Paul *heard* a voice. In contradiction, Acts 22:9 narrates: "And they that were with me saw indeed the light, and were afraid; but they heard not the voice of him that spake to me." Therefore, *none* of the men traveling with Paul heard a voice. Plainly, there is an outright contradiction.

So, how then do Christian apologists explain this discrepancy dealing with what was heard by Paul's fellow travelers? Wayne Jackson (2005; cf. Archer 1982, 382; Witherington 1998, 312-13) wrote:

> A common method of reconciliation has been to note that in 9:7 "hearing" (*akouo*) is used with the genitive case, which merely specifies that a "sound" was heard. On the other hand, *akouo* in 22:9 takes an accusative object, which indicates "extent," i.e., though a sound was heard, the extent (the "meaning") was not to the point of comprehension. A. T. Robertson, the prince of grammarians, declared that this approach is "perfectly proper" (*Historical Grammar of the Greek New Testament,* London: Hodder & Stoughton, 1919, p. 506).

> A contemporary scholar suggests that an appropriate harmony is explained best by Luke's use of different sources to compose his document. Professor Daniel Wallace surmises that Luke preserved the precise phraseology of dual sources (cf. Luke 1:3), and that his record reflects the fact that both *akouo* (hear) and *phone* (voice) are capable of different nuances, e.g., hear/understand and sound/ voice. Thus, no contradiction may be charged legitimately, even without the "case" argument (*Greek Grammar Beyond the Basics,* Grand Rapids: Zondervan, 1996, pp. 133-134).

Similarly, W. F. Arndt (1930, 13-14) wrote in his *Does the Bible Contradict Itself?*

> The construction of the verb "to hear" (*akouo*) is not the same in both accounts. In Acts 9:7 it is used with the genitive, in Acts 22:9 with the accusative. The construction with the genitive simply expresses that something is being heard or that certain sounds reach the ear; nothing is indicated as to whether a person understands what he hears or not. The construction with the accusative, however, describes a hearing which includes mental apprehension of the message spoken. From this it becomes evident that the two passages are not contradictory.

In summary, Christian apologists argue: (1) the word "hear" in Acts 22:9 could be used to indicate that it was a sound—not a voice—that the men heard on the road to Damascus or (2) the word "heard" really meant the people traveling with Paul did not understand what was being said.

The Christian apologetic cited above is misleading and deceptive. First, Robertson is often incompletely quoted since apologists fail to quote his contradictory opinion found in his *Word Pictures in the New Testament*. Robertson (1930b, 117-18) wrote:

> In 22:9 Paul says that the men "beheld the light" (*to men phōs etheasantos*), but evidently did not discern the person. Paul also says there, "but they heard not the voice of him that spake to me" (*tēn de phōnēn ouk ēkousan tou lalountos moi*). Instead of this being a flat contradiction of what Luke says in 9:7 it is natural to take it as being likewise (as with the "light" and "no one") a distinction between the "sound" (original sense of [*phone*] as in Joh 3:8) and the separate words spoken. It so happens that [*akouō*] is used either with the accusative (the extent of the hearing) or the genitive (the specifying). It is possible that such a distinction here coincides with the two senses of [*phone*]. They heard the sound (9:7), but did not understand the words (22:9).

What follows next is the portion of Robertson often deliberately omitted by Christian apologists. Key words are placed in italics [which are not in the original] for emphasis.

> *However*, this distinction in case with [*akouō*], *though possible and even probable here, is by no means a necessary one* for in Joh 3:8

where [*phōnēn*] undoubtedly means "sound" the accusative occurs as Luke uses [*ēkousen phōnēn*] about Saul in Ac 9:5. Besides in 22:7 *Paul uses* [*ēkousa phones*] about himself, but [*ēkousa phōnen*] about himself in 26:14, *interchangeably*.

Second, some may proclaim Robertson is "the prince of grammarians" and declare that this approach is "perfectly proper"—in these specific verses. However, this interpretation is not necessarily accepted by all commentators and grammarians. For example, Witherington (1998, 313) paraphrased R. Bratcher [See ET 71 (1959-60), 243-45 Αχονω in Acts 9:7 and 22:9)]. He had "objected to the idea that Luke may be following classical style here on the basis that elsewhere Luke doesn't observe the distinction between having the object in the genitive as opposed to the accusative with verbs such as αχονω (cf., e.g., the accusative in v. 4)."

I. H. Marshall (2007, 355n1) writing in his *Acts: An Introduction and Commentary*, stated: "This distinction may be reflected in the use of the verb 'to hear' with the accusative here of the sound heard, but with the genitive in 9:7 of the source of the sound; but the fact that both constructions are used with regard to what Paul himself heard (accusative in 9:4; 26:14; genitive in 22:7) suggests that the grammatical difference may not be significant."

Similarly, C. K. Barrett (2002, 342) declared in his *The Acts of the Apostles A Shorter Commentary*:

> It is true that in Greek the verb *to hear* takes *sometimes* the accusative and *sometimes* the genitive, and attempts have often been made to explain the difference by means of this fact. But such attempts have often overlooked the further facts that in 9:4 we have *He . . . heard a voice* (accusative) and in 22:7 *I . . . heard a voice* (genitive). *It is doubtful whether Luke was very interested in the question which case should follow the verb.* [italics mine]

Finally, Newman and Nida (1972, 189), writing for the United Bible Societies, *A Handbook on the Acts of the Apostles*, firmly stated:

> However, this conclusion is judged by most scholars as *invalid*; for upon examination of Luke's usage of the verb "to hear" in Acts, *it is clear that he makes no consistent distinction between 'to hear' with the genitive case and "to hear" with the accusative case (see 22:1). The contradiction must remain*, as must the statement in this chapter that Saul's companions remained standing, whereas in 26:14 it is said that they all fell to the ground. Luke has simply told the

same story three times (a narrative which he doubtless considers to be of great importance in the spread of the Christian message throughout the world), and *we must not deny him the freedom of using differences of detail in narrating the event. It is not the responsibility of the translator to try to resolve such difficulties which he thinks may exist, but to translate faithfully what the writer has given him to translate.* [italics mine]

CONTRADICTION #117 Who Quoted the Words of Jesus, Who Had a Vision of Jesus, and Who Received a Commission from Jesus?

Acts presents contradictory information about who received and who quoted the words of Jesus as well as who received a commission from Jesus. As Paul was traveling to Damascus, around noon there was a great light that enveloped him. Acts 26:13 supplemented Acts 9 and Acts 22 with the fact that the light also surrounded those who traveled with him. In all three accounts, Paul inquired who the person was communicating with him. In each narrative, the voice responded that it was none other than Jesus.

Then each of the three accounts from Acts had Paul asking Jesus a question:

> Acts 9:6 And he trembling and astonished said, Lord, what wilt thou have me do?

> Act 22:10 And I said, what shall I do, Lord?

> Acts 26:15 And I said, Who art thou, Lord?

Acts 26:15-18 reported that Jesus responded with a clear message. Paul was commissioned by Jesus to be a witness to those things that he had seen and would see in the future. In addition, Jesus commanded Paul that he would minister unto the Gentiles. The reasons he was instructed to minister to the Gentiles were multifaceted: (1) to open their eyes, (2) to turn them from darkness to light, (3) to turn them from the power of Satan unto God, (4) to give them the opportunity that they may receive forgiveness for their sins, and (5) to let them inherit from Jesus those who were sanctified by faith in Jesus.

In Acts 22:10, the text perhaps implied that Paul received a vision: "And the Lord said unto me, arise, and go into Damascus; and there it shall be told thee of all things which are appointed for thee to do."

However, Acts 9 explicitly and unequivocally contradicts Acts 26. Acts 9:10 clearly states that it was Ananias who received a vision and communiqué directly from Jesus: "And there was a certain disciple at Damascus, named Ananias; and to him said the Lord in a vision, Ananias. And he said, Behold, I am here, Lord." Complementing the vision, Ananias received his commission: (1) he was to go to the home of Judas to find Paul, and (2) he was to place his hand on Paul that he might again receive his sight. Upon receiving this commission, Ananias initially complained because of all the evil things Paul had previously committed. However, Ananias was informed: (1) Paul was Jesus's chosen vessel, and (2) Paul would be shown great things he must suffer for Jesus's name's sake.

CONTRADICTION #118 Who Was Blinded?

Acts contradicts itself in reporting who was blinded. The three relevant chapters in Acts describe that while traveling on the road at about noon there was a great light that suddenly shone. Acts 9:9 reported that for three days Paul was blind: "And he was three days without sight, and neither did he eat nor drink." Similarly, Acts 22:11 reported that Paul lost his sight: "And when I could not see for the glory of that light, being led by the hand of them that were with me, I came into Damascus."

In direct contrast, Acts 26 omitted any mention that Paul was blinded by the light. Consequently, Acts 26 did not mention: (1) Ananias, (2) Ananias's vision and commission, and (3) Paul being led to Damascus to receive a healing. Paul's baptism reads like a completely different story.

CONTRADICTION #119 Who Was Baptized?

Acts 26 directly contradicts Acts 9 and Acts 22. The first two recordings of Paul's conversion describe how Paul became blind due to a great light. Later, Ananias received a vision and command from Jesus to heal an evil enemy. At first Ananias complained but his concerns were relieved. Following his instructions, Paul was healed by Ananias. Later, Acts 9 and Acts 22 reported that Paul was baptized by Ananias.

> Acts 9:18 And immediately there fell from his eyes as it had been scales: and he received sight forthwith, and arose, and was baptized.

> Acts 22:16 And now why tarriest thou? arise, and be baptized, and wash away thy sins, calling on the name of the Lord.

In contrast, Acts 26 omitted any discussion that (1) Paul was blinded, (2) Ananias received a vision and commission to assist Paul, (3) Ananias healed Paul, or (4) Ananias baptized Paul.

CONTRADICTION #120 Galatians Contradicts Acts

Detractors and skeptics posit that there is a direct and unequivocal contradiction between Galatians 1:17-18 and Acts 9:23-26 (see table 83). These opponents maintain that Luke's account leaves no room for a three-year delay in Paul's return to Jerusalem [Damascus-Arabia-Damascus-Jerusalem]. In contrast, Christian apologists contend that there was a literal three-year delay between Acts 9:25 and Acts 9:26 and this delay corresponded with Galatians 1. Consequently, they posit that there is no contradiction between Acts 9:23-26 and Galatians 1:17. This three-year gap has been defended on various grounds:

1. It is "plausible" to believe that Luke simply omitted the references to Paul's Arabian sojourn and return to Jerusalem. That is, there may be details missing in one account that are not in the other, but this does not constitute a contradiction.
2. If the trip to Arabia was not considered important to Paul (in Galatians), why should it be considered important to Luke (in Acts)?
3. *Barnes' Notes on the Bible* states:

> The two accounts, therefore, are like the two parts of a tally; neither is complete without the other; and yet, being brought together, they so exactly fit as to show that the one is precisely adjusted to the other. And as the two parts were made by different individuals, and without design of adapting them to each other, they show that the writers had formed no collusion or agreement to impose on the world; that they are separate and independent witnesses; that they are honest men; that their narratives are true records of what actually occurred; and the two narratives constitute, therefore, a strong and very valuable proof of the correctness of the sacred narrative.

4. That such a time blank should occur in the Acts, and be filled up in Galatians, is not more remarkable than that the flight of the Holy Family into Egypt, their stay there, and their return, recorded only by Matthew (2:12-21), should be so entirely passed over by Luke, that if we had only his Gospel, we should have supposed that they returned to Nazareth immediately after the presentation in the Temple (Lk 2:21-24). (Indeed in one of his narratives, Acts 22:16, 17, Paul himself takes no notice of this period).

5. Actually, the passage in dispute said, "And when Saul was come" (Acts 9:26). Consequently, the word "when" could have been at any time. Therefore, according to Galatians 1:18, the "when" referred to the three years following Paul's return to Damascus.

6. It should be noted that the word is not *apostles,* but *disciples,* meaning the general body of believers. They were afraid of him; many of them had been whipped and persecuted and scourged by him.

In direct contrast to Christian apologists, detractors and skeptics posit that there is a direct and unequivocal contradiction between Acts 9:23-26 and Galatians 1:17. These opponents maintain that Luke's account leaves no room for a three-year delay in Paul's return to Jerusalem. In the order of the Christian apologists' reasoning, detractors counter:

1. To the contrary, it is "plausible" to believe that Luke simply contradicted the references to Paul's Arabian sojourn.

2. The apologetic that "if that trip to Arabia wasn't considered important to Paul (in Galatians), why should it be considered important to Luke (in Acts)?" is an argument based on silence.

3. Barnes's apologetic is rejected by both the Hebrew Bible and Christian scriptures that require a minimum of two concurring witnesses to an account; *not like the two parts of a tally; neither is complete without the other; and yet, being brought together, they so exactly fit as to show that the one is precisely adjusted to the other.*

4. Barnes's apologetic that the differing accounts confirm that the two writers: (1) had formed no collusion or agreement to impose on the world and (2) that they are honest men is bogus. Galatians and Acts were written: (1) at different locals, (2) at different periods of time (decades apart), and (3) by different authors (hundreds of miles apart). The claim that minor discrepancies are evidence that a story is genuine and truthful is nothing more than a smoke screen. The question that begs an answer is, is it not essential whether what is said is true or false even if the speaker is sincere and believed that his testimony is trustworthy?

5. To claim that contradictory accounts prove that Galatians and Acts are independent and thus reliable defies logic. Reliability and validity of testimony exist when there is corroboration of facts.

6. It is fallacious to claim that "such a time blank occurring in the Acts, and filled up in Galatians, is not more remarkable than that the flight of the Holy Family into Egypt, their stay there, and their return thence, recorded only by Matthew, should be so entirely passed over by Luke, that if we had only his gospel, we should have supposed that they returned to Nazareth immediately after the presentation in the Temple." It is the position of doubters and skeptics that the events recorded in Matthew and Luke were embellishments or legendary texts incorporated to fulfill a theological agenda.

7. The "when" could have been at any time (i.e., three years) is a false apologetic. Significantly Luke had Paul in Damascus in one sentence (verse 25) and in Jerusalem in the next (verse 26). Detractors contend that unmistakably then, Luke believed that Paul left Damascus immediately after his conversion and he went to Jerusalem. Macgregor (1954, 125; cf. Parker 1967, 179-80), writing in *The Interpreter's Bible* also challenges this apologetic: "Whereas Paul says that it was 'after three years' that he went up to Jerusalem, Luke compresses this period and writes *when many days had passed*—ἱκαναί, 'an adequate number'— not suggesting any very long period." More important it must be asked what would a typical first-century listener or reader think these words meant hearing or reading Acts independent of Galatians?

8. The argument that the *disciples*, meaning the general body of believers, were afraid of Paul because many of them had been whipped, persecuted, and scourged by him is a deceptive argument. The text clearly states that "ALL" of the disciples were afraid of him. This description seems like a literary exaggeration. Furthermore, it seems dubious that "ALL" the disciples did not believe that he was a real disciple with three years of reports. Finally, it is up to the Christian apologists to prove that Paul had all these disciples whipped, persecuted, and scourged. Where is the proof?

9. In Paul's defense before King Agrippa, he related the circumstances of his conversion at Damascus, after which he said this of his preaching itinerary:

> *Wherefore, O king Agrippa, I was not disobedient*
> *unto the heavenly vision: but declared at Jerusalem,*
> *and through all the country of Judea, and also to the*

Gentiles, that they should repent and turn to God,
doing works worthy of repentance. (Acts 26:19-20)

In another sermon recorded in Acts 22, Paul, again recounting the circumstances of his conversion, gave himself an early preaching itinerary that agreed with what he said to King Agrippa: Damascus first, then Jerusalem, Judea, and the Gentiles (no reference at all to Arabia). In one verse, he had himself in Damascus and then in Jerusalem in the next (Acts 22:16-21). Furthermore, he recounted virtually the same situation described in Acts 9:25-26. The author of Acts is very consistent in his report: there was no excursion to Arabia.

10. It is not probable to believe that three years had passed and somehow news of the great persecutor's conversion had not yet traveled from Damascus to Jerusalem, a distance of only some two hundred miles. Word of Paul's reputation as a persecutor had preceded him to Damascus because the people there were amazed to see him preaching the faith he had once persecuted: "Is not this he that in Jerusalem made havoc of them that called on this name?" they asked (Acts 9:21).

11. How long Paul was in Arabia before returning to Damascus and what he did there is unknown. Neither is it known specifically where in Arabia he visited.

12. Macgregor (1954, 125) adds, "Luke pictures Paul at Jerusalem preaching *boldly in the name of the Lord* [Acts 9:29]—a course which, as in Damascus, is not only historically and psychologically unlikely, but also obviously contradicts the impression left by the Galatians."

13. The exact distance traveled by Paul is unknown. However, a rough estimate can be calculated for the distance between several cities located in the Arabian Peninsula. For example, if the sojourn took place on the edge of the Syrian Desert to the city of Ar'ar, Paul would have traveled 327 miles or 654 miles round-trip. The round-trip journey could have exceeded 1,000 miles *if* Paul traveled deeper into the Arabian Peninsula. However, Lüdemann (2009, 21) speculates that the "Arabia" cited in verse 17 was "according to the language of that time, to the kingdom of the Nabataeans, east of Palestine." Significantly, Kreitzer (1993, 945) pointed out that the most common means of travel was by foot, "making a good day's journey about twenty miles." In the eye of a detractor, it seems dubious that three times (Acts 9, 22, or 26) the author of Acts would have thoughtfully omitted mention of such an excursion given (1) the cumulative round trip distance, (2) the time required to transverse the required miles, and (3) the harsh traveling conditions.

14. Finally, Robert R. Price offers a minority opinion: "To make things worse, there is the serious question of whether the fortnight's visit of Paul to Jerusalem in Galatians 1:18-24 is original to the text either. It bristles with odd vocabulary, even in so short a text and neither Tertullian's text nor Marcion's seems to have contained it. It looks like a Catholicizing interpolation trying to shorten the span between Paul's conversion and his first encounter with the Jerusalem apostles, fourteen years after (Galatians 2:1)."

TABLE 83: Galatians 1:17-18 Contradicts Acts 9:26

Acts 9	Comment	Galatians 1	Comment
		Gal 1:11 But I certify you, brethren, that the gospel which was preached of me is not after man.	Paul testifies that the gospel he has preached was not from a human being.
		Gal 1:12 For I neither received it of man, neither was I taught it, but by the revelation of Jesus Christ.	Paul reports that he received the gospel by Jesus's direct revelation.
		Gal 1:13 For ye have heard of my conversation in time past in the Jews' religion, how that beyond measure I persecuted the church of God, and wasted it:	Paul admits that formerly, he persecuted the church.
		Gal 1:14 And profited in the Jews' religion above many my equals in mine own nation, being more exceedingly zealous of the traditions of my fathers.	
		Gal 1:15 But when it pleased God, who separated me from my mother's womb, and called me by his grace,	

		Gal 1:16 To reveal his Son in me, that I might preach him among the heathen; immediately I conferred not with flesh and blood:	Paul claims that God revealed the truth to him and that his information did not come from a human being.
Acts 9:8 And Saul arose from the earth; and when his eyes were opened, he saw no man: but they led him by the hand, and brought him into Damascus.	While blind, Paul was led to Damascus.		
Acts 9:9 And he was three days without sight, and neither did eat nor drink.	Paul remained blind for three days while in Damascus.		
Acts 9:10-16	In Damascus.		
Acts 9:17 And Ananias went his way, and entered into the house; and putting his hands on him said, Brother Saul, the Lord, even Jesus, that appeared unto thee in the way as thou camest, hath sent me, that thou mightest receive thy sight, and be filled with the Holy Ghost.	In Damascus he was finally healed.		
Acts 9:18 And immediately there fell from his eyes as it had been scales: and he received sight forthwith, and arose, and was baptized.	Still in Damascus, Paul was healed of his blindness and then baptized.		

Acts 9:19 And when he had received meat, he was strengthened. Then was Saul certain days with the disciples which were at Damascus.	Paul remained in Damascus for several days.	Gal 1:17 Neither went I up to Jerusalem to them which were apostles before me; but I went into Arabia, and returned again unto Damascus.	1. Question: What did Paul do? He made a journey from Damascus to somewhere in Arabia and then back to Damascus. 2. Question: Why did Paul travel to Arabia? The text does not provide an answer.
Acts 9:20 And straightway he preached Christ in the synagogues, that he is the Son of God.	Paul remained in Damascus for several days. Furthermore, the word "straightway" means that "immediately" he preached about Jesus.		
Acts 9:21 But all that heard him were amazed, and said; Is not this he that destroyed them which called on this name in Jerusalem, and came hither for that intent, that he might bring them bound unto the chief priests?	Paul stayed in Damascus for several days and amazed people who heard him.		
Acts 9:22 But Saul increased the more in strength, and confounded the Jews which dwelt at Damascus, proving that this is very Christ.	Paul stayed in Damascus for several days attempting to prove to the Jews that Jesus was the Messiah.		
Acts 9:23 And after that many days were fulfilled, the Jews took counsel to kill him:	Consequently, the Jews in Damascus plotted to kill Paul.		

Acts 9:24 But their laying await was known of Saul. And they watched the gates day and night to kill him.	Paul while still in Damascus learned of their plot.		
Acts 9:25 Then the disciples took him by night, and let him down by the wall in a basket.	During the evening, the disciples helped Paul to escape.		
Acts 9:26 And when Saul was come to Jerusalem, he assayed to join himself to the disciples: but they were all afraid of him, and believed not that he was a disciple.	Paul stayed in Damascus for several days. During this time ALL the disciples were: (1) afraid of him and (2) did not believe that he was a disciple.	Gal 1:18. Then after three years I went up to Jerusalem to see Peter, and abode with him fifteen days.	After three years Paul went to Jerusalem to see Peter. It is unknown why he waited so long to go to Jerusalem.
Acts 9:27 But Barnabas took him, and brought him to the apostles, and declared unto them how he had seen the Lord in the way, and that he had spoken to him, and how he had preached boldly at Damascus in the name of Jesus.	Paul left Damascus and traveled to Jerusalem where he met the apostles. 1. The "apostles" referred to in Acts 9:27 were Peter and James, the Lord's brother. 2. Acts 9 does not say that Paul met with *all* of the apostles.		
Acts 9:28 And he was with them coming in and going out at Jerusalem.			
		Gal 1:19 But other of the apostles saw I none, save James the Lord's brother.	**Paul claims that the only other apostle he met was James, the Lord's brother**

		Gal 1:20 Now the things which I write unto you, behold, before God, I lie not	**Paul swears that he is telling the truth: To recap: 1. The gospel that he preached was not from a human being. 2. The gospel was revealed to him by a direct revelation from Jesus. 3. Paul admitted that he formerly persecuted the church. 4. After his conversion, he traveled to Arabia and later returned to Damascus. 5. After three years, Paul traveled to Jerusalem to see Peter. 6. The only other apostle that he saw was James, the Lord's brother.**
Acts 9:29 And he spake boldly in the name of the Lord Jesus, and disputed against the Grecians: but they went about to slay him.			

SPECULATION #215 Reasons to Doubt the Historicity of Paul's Encounter with Jesus

There are three accounts of Paul's dramatic conversion experience while on the road to Damascus. In the first account, Acts 9 tells the story of Paul's conversion in the third person "he." Acts' second telling (Acts 22) of Paul's conversion is reported in the first person "I." This account occurred in a speech Paul presented to his fellow brethren when he was in Jerusalem to defend his ministry. Finally, Acts' third account (Acts 26) of Paul's conversion is also presented in the first person, as his personal testimony to King Agrippa, while defending himself against the accusation of lawlessness that had been charged against him. On a *prima facie* level the episodes detailed in Acts are historically dubious.

- Acts 9:1-2 And Saul, yet breathing out threatenings, and slaughter against the disciples of the Lord, went unto the high priest, And desired of him letters to Damascus to the synagogues, that if he found any of this way, whether they were men or women, he might bring them bound unto Jerusalem.
- Acts 22:4-5 And I persecuted this way unto the death, binding and delivering into prisons both men and women. As also the high priest doth bear me witness, and all the estate of the elders: from whom also I received letters unto the brethren, and went to Damascus, to bring them which were there bound unto Jerusalem, for to be punished.
- Acts 26:10-12 Which thing I also did in Jerusalem: and many of the saints did I shut up in prison, having received authority from the chief priests; and when they were put to death, I gave my voice against them. And I punished them oft in every synagogue, and compelled them to blaspheme; and being exceedingly mad against them, I persecuted them even unto strange cities. Whereupon as I went to Damascus with authority and commission from the chief priests.

First, in the three accounts Paul claimed that he received authority from the high priests in Jerusalem to arrest followers of Jesus who resided in Damascus and bring them back for punishment. The problem with this supposed fact is that the chief priests in Jerusalem had *no* such authority since their jurisdiction did not extend into Damascus.

Second, there is an unusual "coincidence" that is found in the third account of Paul's conversion on the road to Damascus. In Acts 26 Paul and all his compatriots fell to the ground because of a bright shining light. Then Jesus said to Paul *in the Hebrew tongue* as he laid on the ground: "Saul, Saul, why persecutest thou me? It is hard for thee to kick against the pricks." Christian apologists posit that this quotation was a well-known Greek proverb of its day.

Ranke-Heinemann (1994, 163)—a German theologian, chair of history of religion at the University of Duisburg-Essen in Essen, and a skeptical writer—commented:

> This is a quotation from *The Bacchae* by Euripides (d. 406 B.C.). It's no surprise to find a quotation from ancient literature; *the only peculiar thing is that Jesus should quote a Greek proverb to Paul while speaking Aramaic ("in the Hebrew language"). But the really strange thing is that with both Jesus and Euripides we have the*

same "familiar quotation" and the same situation. In both cases we have a conversation between a persecuted god and his persecutor. In Euripides the persecuted god is Dionysus, and his persecutor is Pentheus, king of Thebes. Just like Jesus, Dionysus calls his persecutor to account: "You disregard my words of warning . . . and kick against necessity [literally 'against the goads'] a man defying god" (*Euripides V*, trans. William Arrowsmith [Chicago: University of Chicago Press, 1959], 188 [italics mine].

Quite obviously the author of Acts has borrowed this Dionysus episode and relocated it near Damascus. Paul even uses the plural form of the noun (*kentra*) that Euripides needs for the meter of his line.

However, there is a stronger argument that can be raised about Jesus employing this Greek proverb, an argument that raises doubt regarding the historicity of the incident. Acts 22:3 reported Paul's biography: "I am verily a man which am a Jew, born in Tarsus, a city in Cilicia, yet brought up in this city at the feet of Gamaliel, and taught according to the perfect manner of the law of the fathers, and was zealous toward God, as ye all are this day." In Galatians 1:14 he stated: "And profited in the Jews' religion above many my equals in mine own nation, being more exceedingly zealous of the traditions of my fathers." And in Philippians 3:5-6 Paul added that he was "Circumcised the eighth day, of the stock of Israel, of the tribe of Benjamin, an Hebrew of the Hebrews; as touching the law, a Pharisee; Concerning zeal, persecuting the church; touching the righteousness which is in the law, blameless." To summarize, Paul was (1) a Jew, (2) from the tribe of Benjamin, (3) born in Tarsus, (4) circumcised on the eighth day, (5) a student who studied with the great rabbi Gamaliel, (6) one whose academic accomplishments exceeded that of many of his peers, (7) a Pharisee, and (8) extremely zealous for the law and zealous for the traditions of our fathers.

Therefore, in Paul's own words he was not a Hellenized Jew. Consequently, it seems highly dubious that Jesus would choose to quote a Greek proverb to Paul while speaking Aramaic even if the proverb was well-known.

Third, numerous commentators and writers doubt the veracity of Paul's encounter with Jesus and Paul seeing a corporeal body. Instead they posit that in reality Paul only experienced a vision. Significantly, Paul never reported seeing a physical and corporeal body; all he saw was a light, and he heard a voice. Consequently, Paul's experience clearly was *not* with a physical appearance; it was a nonphysical appearance of a once corporeal body.

The appearance of the nonphysical body is supported in Luke 24 and John 20. Both gospels narrated incidents during which Jesus seemingly walked through walls and closed doors. Consequently, the appearance of a nonphysical body provides no support for (1) an empty tomb or (2) a resurrected physical body.

Fourth, the three accounts offer varied readings due to either omissions or additions to their respective narrations (for examples, see Hedrick 1981, 415-32). In the eyes of Christian apologist Wayne Jackson (1997-2010), "factual 'supplementation' (the addition of non-contradictory details), of course, presents no problem for the perceptive student who is aware of the nature of a *genuine* discrepancy." Yes, many times omission may not be a contradiction; however, in some situations contrary to Christian apologists, omission can be interpreted as contradiction when it is significant and substantial (see below table 84).

Fifth, Acts 9:6 and Acts 22:10 detailed that Paul asked the Lord (Jesus) what he should do. Yet Acts 26 omitted any question Paul asked of the Lord.

Sixth, significantly Acts 9:9 and Acts 22:11 reported that Paul was blinded. There was no mention of any blindness in Acts 26. Consequently, all the details about (1) how Paul became blind, (2) Ananias receiving a prophecy from Jesus, (3) Paul meeting Ananias, (4) Ananias restoring Paul's sight, and (5) Paul being baptized were omitted.

Seventh, Acts 9:16 and Acts 22:14-15 reported that Jesus spoke the Pauline commission directly to Ananias whereas Acts 26:16-18 has Jesus transmitting the commission directly to Paul. In effect, chapter 26 reads like a completely different story. Collectively, these and other differences in the three readings raise doubt to the historicity of this episode.

TABLE 84. Summary of Significant Different Calling/Conversion Accounts

Paul's compatriots *heard* a voice (Acts 9:7).	Paul's compatriots did *not hear* a voice (Acts 22:9).
Paul did *not report* that Jesus *quoted* Euripides (Acts 9:4; 22:7).	Paul quoted Jesus *quoting* Euripides (Acts 26:14).
Paul *asked* the Lord what he should do (Acts 9:6; 22:10).	Paul *omitted* any question asked of the Lord (Acts 26).
Paul was reported blind (Acts 9:9; 22:11).	No mention of Paul's blindness in Acts 26.
No reason is given why Paul could not see (Acts 9:8).	Paul *explained the reason* that he could not see was because of the brightness of the light (Acts 22:11).

Paul *reported* that Ananias was commanded by the Lord to go to Paul and to lay hands on him so he could regain his sight (Acts 9:10-14).	Paul *omitted* that Ananias was commanded by the Lord to go to Paul and to lay hands on him so he could regain his sight (Acts 22).
The Lord spoke the Pauline commission *to Ananias* (Acts 9:16; 22:14-15).	The Lord spoke the Pauline commission *to Paul* (Acts 26:16-18).
Paul *reported that he was baptized* by Ananias (Acts 9:18; 22:16).	Paul *omitted that he was baptized* (Acts 26).

Finally, C. H. Dodd (1957, 9-35) pointed out that it is impossible to count Jesus's appearance to Paul as belonging to the group of the resurrection appearances:

> Outside the canonical Gospels there is little that we can bring into comparison [with the post-Easter appearances]. We have three accounts of the appearance of Christ to Paul, but none of the three constitutes a narrative unit comparable with those which provide the material of the Gospels. The narrative, in all its forms, resembles those of the Gospels in so far that the word of Christ initiates the transaction, that the recognition is the central feature, and that the scene ends with a command of Christ. But the whole situation is so different that the comparison is of little significance.

In conclusion, Paul's story *cannot* be an eyewitness account since the Christian scriptures do *not* provide any incontrovertible evidentiary proof that he actually saw a physical Jesus. Therefore, the only Jesus Paul ever claimed to see was a vision that he assumed was Jesus.

SPECULATION #216 Does the Word *Ophthe* or "Vision" Support a Physical Bodily Resurrection?

What appeared to Paul? Hiltner (1965, 7) inquired: "Did our New Testament friends after the crucifixion, really see their Lord and ours in the flesh on the reported occasions—Jewish nose, endocrine glands, sandals on feet, and literal body cells and limbs and organs?" Paul's 1 Corinthians 15:8 is a matter of intense debate as to what was seen: (1) an embodied Jesus, (2) a vision, or (3) a light (Acts 22:6-8). Numerous articles (Beckwith 1990, 369-73; Davis 1985, 140-52; Geisler 1989a, 148-70); chapters or portions of books (Geisler 2007, 331-36; 1999, 658-64; Gundry 2004, 360-76); entire books (Geisler 1992; Wiebe 1997); and theses (Alfors 1953, Healey 1973, Jevne 1903) have been written on the controversial topic *ōphthē*. Traditional proponents of Jesus's resurrection claim that it was a literal physical body, which the disciples could see and touch. In contrast, skeptics reject this notion.

The Greek word for "appeared" is *ōphthē* (Strong's #3708). According to Moulton and Milligan (1997, 455): "The verb which is used in the LXX as a *t.t.* for appearances of the Divinity and similarly by Paul (1 Cor 9[1], 15[5 ff.]. *al* is found in connexion with dreams in such passages as P Par 51[8] (account of a dream in the Serapeum—B.C. 160)."

N. T. Wright (2003, 323) writes that *ōphthē* occurs eighty-five times in the LXX. Forty-six times it referred "either to YHWH, or YHWH's glory, or an angel of YHWH, appearing to people. The remaining 39 occurrences refer to people appearing before YHWH in the sense of presenting themselves in the Temple; or to objects being seen by people in a straightforward, non-visionary sense; and to people 'appearing', in a non-visionary and unsurprising way, before someone else."

The Septuagint, the Greek version of the Hebrew Bible, often employed the same verb-form *ōphthē'* to indicate that God revealed something to someone but without specifying any kind of physical or visual seeing. In fact, God appeared—*ōphthē*—to Abraham as a voice, not as a vision (Ex 6:3 with Gen 21:1).

Moving to the Christian scriptures, Wright continued:

> It is in fact impossible to build a theory of what people thought Jesus' resurrection appearances consisted of (i.e., whether they were "objective," "subjective" or whatever—these terms themselves, with their many philosophical overtones, are not particularly helpful) on this word alone. The word is quite consistent with people having non-objective "visions"; it is equally consistent with them seeing someone in the ordinary course of human affairs. Its meaning in the present context—both its meaning for Paul, and its meaning in the tradition he quotes—must be judged on wider criteria than linguistic usage alone.

Reiterating the concept that *ōphthē'* has several possible interpretations, Ceroke (2004, 149) wrote in the *New Catholic Encyclopedia*:

> Even if with the majority of NT scholars one prefers "appeared," one cannot deduce the nature of the appearances from this verb.

The most that can be concluded from it is that the experience of the risen Christ to which the verb makes reference had both objective and subjective elements, i.e., the verb implies more than a mere internal visionary experience, but does not necessarily imply the same kind of objective presence of Christ that was the recipients' experience of the objective presence of the historical Jesus.

Furthermore, the word '*ōphthē*' is employed a variety of times in the Christian scriptures. Therefore, if other times *ōphthē* is used in the Christian scriptures it should be possible to determine what Paul meant by "seen" (AV) or "appeared" (NIV), which he used so many times in 1 Corinthians 15.

- 1 Cor 15:5 And that he was seen [*ōphthē*] of Cephas, then of the twelve:
- 1 Cor 15:6 After that, he was seen [*ōphthē*] of above five hundred brethren at once; of whom the greater part remain unto this present, but some are fallen asleep.
- 1 Cor 15:7 After that, he was seen [*ōphthē*] of James; then of all the apostles.
- 1 Cor 15:8 And last of all he was seen [*ōphthē*] of me also, as of one born out of due time.

Several examples of "appeared" (*ōphthē*) employed in the Christian Bible are quite consistent with people having *non-objective* 'visions":

- Mt 17:1-3 And after six days Jesus taketh Peter, James, and John his brother, and bringeth them up into an high mountain apart, And was transfigured before them: and his face did shine as the sun, and his raiment was white as the light. And, behold, there *appeared* unto them Moses and Elias talking with him.

  o Were Moses and Elijah bodily resurrected when they "appeared" to Peter?
  o If they were, what happened to their bodies?
  o Did they die again?
  o If they were not bodily resurrected when they "appeared" to Peter, why was it beyond all doubt that Jesus was bodily resurrected when he "appeared" to Peter?

- Acts 2:3 And there *appeared* unto them cloven tongues like as of fire, and it sat upon each of them.

  o Did real physical fire or something "like as fire" come down from heaven and rest on Peter when it "appeared" on Peter? If so, what was it?
  o Did real physical fire or something "like as fire" come down from heaven and rest on the apostles' heads? If so, what was it?

- Acts 7:1-2 Then said the high priest, Are these things so? And he said, Men, brethren, and fathers, hearken; The God of glory *appeared* unto our father Abraham, when he was in Mesopotamia, before he dwelt in Charran.

  o Nowhere in Genesis 12 does it state that God appeared to Abraham (previously named Abram).
  o It seems that God was in the habit of making bodily appearances. Either that or the word "appeared" in 1 Corinthians 15 does not mean a bodily appearance (Carr n.d. The Resurrection).

- Acts 16:9 And a vision *appeared* to Paul in the night; there stood a man of Macedonia, and prayed him, saying, Come over into Macedonia, and help us.

  o This verse unequivocally reports that Paul had a vision that appeared = *'ōphthe'* to him.
  o Did the man from Macedonia physically travel to Paul when he 'appeared' to him?

- Rev 12:1 And there *appeared* a great wonder in heaven; a woman clothed with the sun, and the moon under her feet, and upon her head a crown of twelve stars:

  o Was there really a woman clothed with the sun?
  o Was there really a woman with the moon under her feet?
  o Was there really a woman who had upon her head a crown of twelve stars?

- Rev 12:3 And there *appeared* another wonder in heaven; and behold a great red dragon, having seven heads and ten horns, and seven crowns upon his heads.

  - Was there really a physical red dragon in heaven?
  - Was there really a physical dragon in heaven with seven heads and ten horns?
  - Was there really a physical dragon in heaven with seven crowns upon his heads?

In addition, one thing that the Christian scriptures plainly demonstrate is that "Peter and Paul were precisely the sort of people to have dreams and visions and to act upon those dreams and visions as though they were real" (Acts 10 and Acts 16) (Carr n.d. The Resurrection).

However, significantly Carr added:

> In 2 Corinthians 12:1-7, Paul boasts of the revelations he has received. He went up to the third heaven (Where's that?) and heard and saw all manner of things. In fact, nowhere in Paul's letters or in the 3 accounts of his conversion in Acts, does Paul or Luke ever state that Paul saw a bodily Jesus. He saw a bright light and heard a voice. A vision—not a physical body—exactly as the use of *'ophthe'* in 1 Corinthians 15 demands.

> In Acts 26:19, it is clearly stated that what Paul saw when he met the resurrected Jesus on the road to Damascus was a vision.

> In 1 Corinthians 15:50, Paul says outright that "flesh and blood cannot inherit the kingdom of God." How could he state more clearly that he did not consider the resurrected Jesus to have a physical body?

> It is often claimed that Paul could not have been teaching about a vision as Jews could not even have conceived of a non-physical resurrection. This argument is refuted by 1 Samuel 28 where Samuel is brought back up. Paul would have been quite familiar with this story and would have been aware that only the witch and not Saul could see Samuel, impossible if Jews could not even conceive of a non-physical vision.

There is another argument based on these Christian scriptures that Paul could not have witnessed a physical, bodily resurrection of Jesus despite the interpreted claim of its adherents. According to Paul, "flesh and blood" cannot inherit the Kingdom of God. *If* interpreted literally, by these words Paul eliminated himself as a witness to a physically resurrected Jesus since only if Jesus had returned from a state of death to resume a physical life would the term resurrection be appropriate. It must be remembered that according to Christian tradition a resurrection is *not* the same as the "resuscitation" or "reanimation" of a body, or the "reincarnation" or "immortality" of a soul.

However, N. T. Wright (2003, 359) claimed that doubters of the "flesh and blood" clause did not mean "physical humanity" in the normal modern sense, "but 'the present physical humanity (as opposed to the future one), which is subject to decay and death.'" Therefore, Wright continued: "The referent of the phrase is not the presently dead but the presently living, who need not to be raised but to be changed."

This response is merely Wright's interpretation and an apologetic at that. However, there are at least two main arguments against his rationale: (1) many equally illustrious and knowledgeable scholars and theologians have interpreted this reading in a contradictory manner and (2) Wright is assuming that he knows and understands what Paul was thinking and writing almost 2,000 years ago. Therefore, Wright is only offering *his* opinion, nothing more and nothing less.

There are in addition several problems of the physical, bodily resurrection model based on Paul's writings. First, in Acts 8:8-9 it was reported that Paul was blinded for three days upon receiving his revelation. Second, Paul, writing in Galatians 1:12, referred to his experience on the way to Damascus as an apocalyptic "revelation" (*di apokalypseōs*). Several verses later, Paul wrote "But when it pleased God" (v. 15) "to *reveal* his Son *in* me" (v. 16). There is no mention of any visual or physical details. Significantly, Paul said "in me." Therefore, this revelation to the blinded Paul could have been nothing more than a voice, a transcendental experience, or the bestowal of spiritual insight. However, plainly it was not the physical appearance of a visible body since Paul was blind at this point in time.

Writing on the subject of revelation, Glen Nelson (2005, Revelation in the Writings of St. Paul) pointed out:

> Of the nineteen times the words *apokalypsis* and *apokalypto* appear in the seven generally recognized letters of Paul, eight denote a claim by Paul that he had received a revelation directly from God, the Spirit, or Jesus Christ. In the other eleven times, while the word may refer to a revelation, it is something that will happen

in the future (e.g., Rom 8:18), is happening in a metaphorical sense in the present, (Rom 1:17, 18), or is used hypothetically (1 Cor 14:6, 26).

The following are the eight occasions when Paul refers to his own experience of a revelation:

Gal 1:12 For I did not receive (the gospel) from a human source, nor was I taught it, but received it through a *revelation* of Jesus Christ.

Gal 1:16 But when God, who had set me apart before I was born and called me through his grace, was pleased *to reveal* his son to (in) me, so that I might proclaim him to the gentiles, I did not confer with any human being.

Gal 2:2 I went up (to Jerusalem) in response to a *revelation*.

Gal 3:23 Now before faith came, we were imprisoned and guarded under the law until faith would be *revealed* . . . but now that faith has come.

1 Cor 2:10 What no eye has seen, nor ear heard, nor the human heart conceived, what God has prepared for those who love him"—these things God has *revealed* to us through the Spirit.

2 Cor 12:1 I must boast. There is nothing to be gained by it, but I will go on to visions and *revelations* of the Lord.

2 Cor. 12:7 But if I wish to boast, I will not be a fool, for I will be speaking the truth. But I refrain from it, so that no one may think better of me than what is seen in me or heard from me, even considering the exceptional character of the *revelations*.

Rom 16:25 Now to God who is able to strengthen you according to my gospel and the proclamation of Jesus Christ, according to the *revelation* of the mystery that was kept secret for long ages but is now disclosed, and through the prophetic writings is made known to all the Gentiles, according to the command of the eternal God, to bring about the obedience of faith.

Here it is asked, do these verses in any manner imply a physical revelation?

Additional problems associated with Paul's physical, bodily resurrection model include the following:

1. The accounts recorded by Paul are suspect because of his agenda.
2. The accounts recorded by Paul in 1 Corinthians (ca. 52-57 CE) were recollections of a supposed event that occurred almost twenty to twenty-five years earlier (ca. 33-35 CE).
3. The accounts recorded by Paul were reinterpreted by later church writers and incorporated into church theology.

Another often overlooked point is how the Greek word *'ōphthē'* should actually be translated. For example, Marxsen (1990, 69) wrote:

> The Greek word is *'ophthē'*, but how exactly this should be translated is a matter of some uncertainty. It can mean, as my translation has suggested, "he appeared." But it can also mean, "he let himself be seen"; or even, "God let him become visible." I do not wish to argue for any one of these over the others, because a clearcut decision is not possible. In each case, though, the reference is to sight. Thus, to put it quite generally, what is being spoken of is a vision.

Prior to finishing this issue, a comment that appeared in a debate with William Lane Craig seems apropos. Lüdemann (2000, 61) stated:

> Paul claims in 1 Corinthians 15:1-11 that Christ appeared "last of all" to him. And he is using the same verb *'ōphthē'* ("he was seen" by me) as he uses for the other apostles. In other words, he claims to have experienced the same appearance as the others had before. Isn't it reasonable to grant that Paul was right on this point—he had the same experience that the others had—and to conclude from his statement that the others had visionary experiences too?

Furthermore, the verb "appeared" used several times in 1 Corinthians 15 is *ōphthē*. This term is as vague and unclear in Greek as in English. The *New Catholic Encyclopedia* second edition (2003,149) stated: "Even if with the majority of NT scholars one prefers 'appeared,' one cannot deduce the nature of the appearance from this verb." Used in the passive voice, as it is here, it means only "was seen" or "appeared" and frequently means "appeared in a vision" (as in the case of Paul's vision, cf. Acts 9.17). Thus, the passage in 1

Corinthians 15:8 cannot mean anything more than that hundreds have seen Jesus in visions and not the physical Jesus in person.

Finally, recently, Pilch (2005, 371-83; cf. 2004; 2002b, 690-707; 1998, 52-60; Craffert 2011, 1-28; 2009, 126-51; 2008, 140, 149; 151; 1989, 331-48; Czachesz 2007, 47-59; Malina and Rohrbaugh 2003b, 327-29; Winkelman 1997, 397-428) posited a fresh and innovative interpretation of Paul's visionary experience on the road to Damascus. In the journal *Hervormde Teologiese Studies* he offered: "Drawing upon psychological anthropology and cognitive neuroscience, I demonstrated how Luke narrated that Paul's call took place in the three stages typical of altered states of consciousness experiences (ASCs) across cultures. Luke's contemporary readers would immediately understand the event and its significance for Paul." At the conclusion of the article Pilch wrote:

> It is possible, however, to gain deeper insights into Paul's statements 'in his own words' by submitting them to a social scientific analysis drawing especially upon psychological anthropology and cognitive neuroscience. These social sciences demonstrate that Paul's call was definitely received in an altered state of consciousness experience. As with all such experiences, the visionary will draw on the latent discourse of his culture to interpret the vision. Paul certainly does this. It was God's intent and initiative to relate to Paul (Gl) in an ASC. Paul considered his call experience and commission to be on par with experiences of the Risen Jesus by others (1 Cor). Paul also drew upon the full meaning of light imagery in his tradition to interpret his call (2 Cor). Finally, he was fully aware that his experience took place in an altered state of consciousness (Phlp) which was a well-known and familiar experience in his culture. It is thus possible to explain Paul's words in other words—not only Luke's, but also those of contemporary science. (pp. 382-83)

In conclusion, no consensus exists among historians, scholars, or theologians on the meaning of the word '*ōphthē*' when it is used as a proof of Jesus's physical, bodily resurrection. Based upon the previous discussions, this text and others reject the argument that the term '*ōphthē*' supports the notion that Jesus had a physical, bodily resurrection.

SPECULATION #217 How Paul Recognized Jesus Without Knowing Him

Paul wrote in 1 Corinthians 15:8: "And last of all he was seen of me also, as of one born out of due time." The account of Paul's testimony is challenged for several reasons. There is nothing to indicate that Paul knew what Jesus looked like beforehand. Specifically, there is no record in any of Paul's writings that he had ever previously seen or heard the corporeal and physical man, Jesus, prior to the Crucifixion. Given that Paul had never seen Jesus prior to his crucifixion, how could he have recognized Jesus several years after his execution? Plainly it is not possible to identify someone who has never been previously seen or even heard. Elaborating on this point, Craig (1993, 30) wrote: "Since Paul had apparently never known the earthly Jesus, it is not clear that he could be expected to recognize him (as opposed to say, an angel), even if he saw him in the light."

Similarly, James D. G. Dunn (1975, 115) wrote: "Paul's seeing was visionary in character; what he saw was non-physical, non-material—strictly speaking, non-objective in that it could not be examined as an object by an observer." Equally forceful, William Lane Craig (1989b, 75n33 and see 333) in another writing stated: "All Paul saw was a light brighter than the sun, and he heard the Lord's voice reprimanding him and commanding him what to do." Plainly, Paul did not observe the physical body of Jesus himself. Therefore, other than an unrecognizable voice that presumably claimed to be Jesus, it is inexplicable how Paul knew Jesus was communicating with him.

CONCLUSION

A
CCORDING TO CHRISTIAN tradition, the only evidence that Jesus intended to demonstrate as a sign of his claimed Messiahship, as well as claimed divinity, was the numerous discussions he had with his disciples regarding his future suffering, death, and resurrection (see Mk 10:34; 14:24-25; Mt 23:37-39; Lk 13:33-35). However, the pertinent question that must be asked relates to the evidence of Jesus's death and claimed physical, bodily resurrection: is the evidence overwhelmingly conclusive to any honestly objective seeker of the truth? This book reveals certainly that this is not the case.

In the preface to this investigation, the late evangelical fundamentalist, William Bright (1999, xii), was quoted:

> During my fifty-five years of sharing the good news of the Savior with the academic world, I have met very few individuals who have honestly considered the evidence and yet deny that Jesus Christ is the Son of God and the Savior of men. To me, the evidence confirming the deity of the Lord Jesus Christ is overwhelmingly conclusive to any honest, objective seeker after truth. However, not all—not even the majority—of those to whom I have spoken have accepted Him as their Savior and Lord. This is not because they were *unable* to believe—they were simply *unwilling* to believe!

In response to Mr. Bright's significant words, the reason that this text rejects Jesus's physical, bodily resurrection is because there is no unequivocal evidence that this historical event occurred.

A second volume to this text will be published. This second volume will directly respond to many of the foremost arguments raised by Christian apologists in support of Jesus's physical, bodily resurrection. In particular, the second volume will review, analyze, and refute the arguments presented by such leading writers as William Lane Craig, Norman L. Geisler, Gary Habermas, Michael Licona, Gerald O'Collins, and N. T. Wright.

Finally, I would like to thank those who took the time to read this text. You had the option to read other books, be with your family and friends, listen to music, exercise, garden, or to do a host of other activities. To the contrary, you dedicated a substantial portion of your time to reading this text. Your time is valuable, respected, and appreciated.

Again, I thank you.

PART III

BIBLIOGRAPHY

BIBLIOGRAPHY

Aarde, A. G. van. 2011. "Regeneration and Resurrection in Matthew - Peasants *in campo* Hearing Time Signals From Scribes." *HTS Teologiese Studies/Theological Studies* 67(3), Att. #1012, 7 pages. Doi: 10.4102/hts. v6713.1012.

Abogunrin, Samuel Oyinloye. 1981. "The Language and Nature of the Resurrection of Jesus Christ in the New Testament." *Journal of the Evangelical Theological Society* 24(1): 55-65.

Ackroyd, Peter R. 1959. "The 153 Fishes in John XXI.11.—A Further Note." *Journal of Theological Studies* 10(1): 94.

Akin, James. 1997. "Last Supper, Was It a Passover Meal?" *Nazareth Resource Library. http://www.cin.org/users/james/questions/q060.htm.*

Aland, Kurt, ed. 1982. *Synopsis of the Four Gospels* 26th edition New York: United Bible Societies.

Aland, Kurt, and Barbara Aland. 1987. *The Text of the New Testament: An Introduction to the Critical Editions and to the Theory and Practice of Modern Textual Criticism.* Grand Rapids: Eerdmans.

Aldrich, J. K. 1870. "The Crucifixion On Thursday—Not Friday." *Bibliotheca Sacra* 27 (July): 401-29.

Alfors, Quinten Hans-Peter. 1953. "The Evidence of the Physical Resurrection of Christ in the Language of John Twenty." Master's thesis, Wheaton College.

Allen, Don. 1893. *The Resurrection of Jesus: An Agnostic's View.* New York: Truth Seeker.

Allen, O. Wesley 1997. *The Death of Herod. The Narrative and Theological Function of Retribution in Luke-Acts.* Atlanta: Scholars Press.

Allison, Dale C. 1985. *The End of the Ages has Come: An Early Interpretation of the Passion and Resurrection of Jesus.* Philadelphia: Fortress Press.

———. 1992. "Peter and Cephas: One and the Same." *Journal of Biblical Literature* 111(3): 489-95.

———. 1993. *The New Moses: A Matthean Typology.* Philadelphia: Fortress Press.

———. 2001. "Matthew." In *The Oxford Bible Commentary*, edited by John Barton and John Muddiman, 844-86. Oxford: Oxford University Press.

———. 2004. *Matthew: A Shorter Commentary.* London: T&T Clark.

———. 2005a. *Resurrecting Jesus: The Earliest Christian Tradition and Its Interpretation.* New York: T&T Clark.

———. 2005b. "Explaining the Resurrection: Conflicting Convictions." *Journal for the Study of the Historical Jesus* 3(2): 117-33.

———. 2008. "The Resurrection and Rational Apologetics." *Philosophia Christi* 10(2): 319-35.

———. 2010. *Constructing Jesus: Memory, Imagination, and History.* Grand Rapids: Baker Academic.

Alsup, John E. 1975. *The Post-Resurrection Appearance Stories of the Gospel Tradition: A History-of-Tradition Analysis with Text-Synopsis.* London: SPCK.

Alward, Joseph Francis. 2000. "How Did Judas Die?" Skeptical Views of Christianity and the Bible. *http://skepticalviewsofchristianity.com/judasdeath.htm*

Anderson, G. W. 1994. "What Today's Christian Needs to Know About the Greek New Testament." The Trinitarian Bible Society," http://www.tbsbibles.org/articles/what-todays-christian-needs-to-know-about-the-greek-new-testament.

Anderson, Hugh. 1964. *Jesus and Christian Origins: A Commentary on Modern Viewpoints.* New York: Oxford University Press.

———. 1965. "The Easter Witness of the Evangelists." In *The New Testament in Historical and Contemporary Perspective. Essays in Memory of G. H. C. Macgregor*, edited by Hugh Anderson and William Barclay, 35-55. Oxford: Basil Blackwell.

Anderson, J. N. D. March 29, 1968a. "The Resurrection of Jesus Christ." *Christianity Today* 12(13): 4-9.

———. April 29, 1968b. "A Dialogue on Christ's Resurrection; Dr. Anderson's Response." *Christianity Today* 12(14): 11-12.

———. 1969. *Christianity: The Witness of History: A Lawyer's Approach.* London: Tyndale Press.

Anderson, Robert. 1895. *The Coming Prince: The Last Great Monarchy of Christendom.* London: Hodder & Stoughton.

Ankerberg, John and John Weldon. 2005. *An Examination of the Alleged Contradictions in the Resurrection Narratives - Part 1, http://www. jashow.org/wiki/index.php?title=An_Examination_of_the_Alleged_ Contradictions_in_the_Resurrection_Narratives-Part_1.*

Annand, Rupert. 1958. "'He Was Seen of Cephas' A Suggestion About the First Resurrection Appearance to Peter." *Scottish Journal of Theology* 11(2): 180-87.

Archer, Gleason L. 1982. *Encyclopedia of Bible Difficulties.* Grand Rapids: Zondervan.

Armstrong, Herbert W. 1952. *The Resurrection was not on Sunday!"* Pasadena, Ca.: Ambassador College.

Arndt, W. F. 1930. *Does the Bible Contradict Itself?* St. Louis: Concordia.

Augustine. 1888. "Lectures Or Tractates on the Gospel According To St. John." In *The Nicene And Post-Nicene Fathers of the Christian Church. Volume VII. The Homilies on the Gospel of John. Homilies on the First Epistle of John. Soliloquies,* edited by Philip Schaff and translated by John Gibb and James Innes. New York: The Christian Literature Company. Available online.

Aune, David E. 1988. *The New Testament in Its Literary Environment.* Philadelphia: Westminster Press.

Aus, Roger David. 2008. *The Death, Burial, and Resurrection of Jesus, and the Death, Burial, and Translation of Moses in Judaic Tradition.* Lanham: University Press of America.

Bacon, Benj. W. 1909. "Notes On Gospel Chronology." *Journal of Biblical Literature* 28(2): 130-48.

Badham, Paul, and Linda Badham. 1982. *Immortality or Extinction?* Totowa, New Jersey: Barnes & Noble.

Baigent, Michael. 2006. *The Mystery of the Jesus Papers: Exposing the Greatest Cover-up in History.* San Francisco: Harper Collins.

Bailey, James L. 1995. "Genre Analysis." In *Hear the New Testament: Strategies for Interpretation,* edited by Joel B. Green, 197-221. Grand Rapids: Eerdmans.

Bailey, James L., and Lyle D. Vander Broek. 1992. *Literary Forms in the New Testament: A Handbook.* Louisville: Westminster/John Knox.

Baird, William. 1971. "The Acts of the Apostles." In *Interpreter's One-Volume Commentary on the Bible,* edited by Charles M. Laymon, 729-67. Nashville: Abingdon.

Baker, Keith. 2003. "The Resurrection of Jesus In Its Graeco-Roman Setting - Part 1." *The Reformed Theological Review* 62(1): 1-13.

Bammel, Caroline P. 1992. "The First Resurrection Appearance to Peter." In *John and the Synoptic,* edited by Adelbert Denaux, 620-31. Leuven: Leuven University Press.

Bammel, E. 1955. "Herkunft und Funktion der Traditionselemente in 1 Kor. 15, 1-11." *Theologische Zeitschrift* 11: 401-19.

Banks, William L. 2005. *Three Days and Three Nights: The Case For A Wednesday Crucifixion Date.* West Conshohocken, Pa: Infinity.

Barbet, Pierre. 1953. *A Doctor at Calvary: The Passion of Our Lord Jesus Christ as Described by a Surgeon.* Translated by Earl of Wicklow. New York: P.J. Kennedy.

Barclay, William. 1955. *The Acts of the Apostles.* Philadelphia: Westminster Press.

———. 1956. *The Gospel of John.* Volume 2 (Chapters 8-21) 2nd ed. Philadelphia: Westminster Press.

Barkay, Gabriel. 1986. "The Garden Tomb: Was Jesus Buried Here?" *Biblical Archaeology Review* 12(2): 40-53, 56-57.

Barker, Dan. 2003. "Did Jesus Really Rise From the Dead?" In *Abuse Your Illusions: The Disinformation Guide to Media Mirages and Establishment Lies*, edited by Russ Kick, 311-20. New York: The Disinformation Company.

Barr, James. 1990. "Luther and Biblical Chronology." *Bulletin of the John Rylands Library* 72: 51-67.

Barrett, C. K. 1955. *The Gospel According to St. John*. London: SPCK.

———. 1978. *The Gospel According to St. John*. Philadelphia: Westminster Press.

———. 1994. *A Critical and Exegetical Commentary on the Acts of the Apostles*. Volume 1. Acts I-XIV. Edinburgh: T&T Clark.

———. 2002. *The Acts of the Apostles*. London: T&T Clark.

Barrick, W. Boyd. 1977. "The Rich Man from Arimathea (Matt 27:57-60) and 1QISA[a]." *Journal of Biblical Literature* 96(2): 235-39.

Bater, Robert R. 1969. "Towards a More Biblical View of the Resurrection." *Interpretation* 23(1): 47-65.

Baxter, Wayne S. 1999. "Mosaic Imagery in the Gospel of Matthew." *Trinity Journal* 20(1): 69-83.

Bauckham, Richard. 1996. "Nicodemus and the Gurion Family." *Journal of Theological Studies* 47(1): 1-37.

———. 1998. *The Gospels For All Christians: Rethinking the Gospel Audiences*. Grand Rapids: Eerdmans.

Beare, Francis Wright. 1981. *The Gospel According to Matthew*. San Francisco: Harper & Row.

Beasley-Murray, Paul. 2000. *The Message of the Resurrection: Christ Is Risen!* Downers Grove: InterVarsity Press.

Beckwith, Francis J. 1990. "Identity and Resurrection: A Review Article." *Journal of the Evangelical Theological Society* 33(3): 369-73.

Beckwith, Roger T. 1989. "Cautionary Notes on the Use of Calendars and Astronomy to Determine the Chronology of the Passion. In *Chronos, Kairos, Christos: Nativity and Chronological Studies Presented to Jack Finegan*, edited by Jerry Vardaman and Edwin M. Yamauchi, 183-205. Winona Lake: Ind.: Eisenbrauns.

BeDuhn, Jason David. 2003. *Truth in Translation: Accuracy and Bias in English Translations of the New Testament.* Lanham: University Press of America.

Ben-Mordechai, Uriel. 2011. *If? The End of a Messianic Lie.* Jerusalem: Above and Beyond.

Benoit, Pierre. 1970. *The Passion and Resurrection of Jesus Christ.* Translated by B. Weatherhead. New York: Herder & Herder.

Bentley, James. 1986. *Secrets of Mount Sinai: The Story of the World's Oldest Bible - Codex Sinaiticus.* Garden City: Doubleday.

Bernard, John Henry. 1928. *A Critical and Exegetical Commentary on the Gospel According to St. John* Vol. II. Edinburgh: T&T Clark.

Binz, Stephen J. 1989. The *Resurrection & the Life.* New London, CT.: Twenty-Third Publications.

Black, C. Clifton. 2011. *Mark.* Nashville: Abingdon.

Blair, E.P. 1969. "Magdalene." In *The Interpreter's Dictionary of the Bible,* edited by George Arthur Buttrick, 221. Nashville: Abingdon.

Blair, G. W. 1973. "A Physicist's Reflection on the Resurrection and Ascension of Christ." *Faith and Thought* 100(2): 259-70.

Blinzler, Josef. 1959. "Josef." In *The Trial of Jesus: The Jewish and Roman Proceedings Against Jesus Christ Described and Assessed from the Oldest Accounts.* Translated by Isabel and Florence McHugh. Westminster, Md.: Newman Press.

———. 1969. *Der Prozess Jesus* 4th edition. Regensburg: Pustet.

———. 1974. "Die Grablegung Jesu in Historischer Sicht." In *Resurrexit*, edited by Edouard Dhanis. 56-107. Vatican City: Editrice Vaticana.

Blomberg, Craig L. 1992. *Matthew*. Vol. 22 of *The New American Commentary*. Nashville: Broadman.

———. 2001. *The Historical Reliability of John's Gospel: Issues & Commentary*. Downers Grove: InterVarsity Press.

———. 2004. *Making Sense of the New Testament: Three Crucial Questions*. Grand Rapids: Baker.

———. 2006. "Book Review: Misquoting Jesus: The Story Behind Who Changed the Bible and Why." *Denver Journal: An Online Review of Current Biblical and Theological Studies*. Volume 6. *http://www.denverseminary.edu/article/misquoting-jesus-the-story-behind-who-changed-the-bible-and-why*.

———. 2007a. *The Historical Reliability of the Gospels*. Downers Grover: InterVarsity Press.

———. 2007b. "Matthew." In *Commentary on the New Testament Use of the Old Testament*, edited by G. K. Beale and D. A. Carson, 1-109. Grand Rapids: Baker.

Bock, Darrell L. 1994. *Luke*. Downers Grove: InterVarsity Press.

———. 1996. *Luke Volume 2: 9:51-24:53*. Grand Rapids: Baker.

———. 2002. *Jesus According to Scripture: Restoring the Portrait from the Gospels*. Grand Rapids: Baker.

Bockmuel, Markus. 1996. *This Jesus: Martyr, Lord, Messiah*. Downers Grove: InterVarsity Press.

Bode, Edward Lynn. 1970. *The First Easter Morning: The Gospel Accounts of the Women's Visit to the Tomb of Jesus*. Rome: Biblical Institute Press.

Boice, James Montgomery. 1978. *God the Redeemer*. Downers Grove: InterVarsity Press.

Bonney, William L. 1997. "Why Did the Risen Jesus Appear to Thomas? An Analysis of John 20:24-29 in the Context of a Synchronic Reading of the Gospel." PhD diss., Fordham University.

Borchert, Gerald L. 1983. "The Resurrection: 1 Corinthians 15." *Review And Expositor* 80(3): 401-15.

Boring, E. Eugene. 1995. "The Gospel of Matthew: Introduction, Commentary, and Reflections." In *The New Interpreter's Bible* Vol 8, edited by Leander E. Keck et al., 89-505. Nashville: Abingdon.

Boring, M. Eugene, and Fred B. Craddock. 2009. *The People's New Testament Commentary.* Louisville, Ky.: Westminster John Knox.

Bornkamm, Günter. 1960. *Jesus of Nazareth.* Translated by Irene and Fraser McLuskey. New York: Harper & Row.

Bostock, Gerald. 1994. "Do We Need an Empty Tomb?" *Expository Times* 105(7): 201-05.

Bousset, Wilhelm. 1906. *Kyrios Christos* 3rd edition. Göttingen: Vandenhoeck & Reichard.

Bovisio, Santiago n.d. "The Valley of Jesus." *http://translate. google.com/translate?hl=en&sl=pt&u=http://www.eurooscar. com/bovisio/santiago-bovisio-reflexao-20.htm&sa=X&oi= translate&resnum=3&ct=result&prev=/search%3Fq%3D%2522 Santiago%2Bbovisio%2522%2B%2522Judas%2522%26hl% 3Den%26sa%3DN*

Bovon, François (2001). "Names and Numbers in Early Christianity." *New Testament Studies* 47(3): 267-88.

Bowen, Clayton R. 1911. *The Resurrection in the New Testament.* New York: G.P. Putnam's Sons.

Boyarin, Daniel. 2001. "'After the Sabbath' (Matt. 28.1)—Once More Into the Crux*." *Journal of Theological Studies* 52(2): 678-88.

Bramer, Daniel Eric. 2010. "Divine Contradiction: The Logic of Blood in the Hebrew and Christian Scriptures." PhD diss., Drew Theological School.

Brandon, S.G.F. 1967. *Jesus and the Zealots*. New York: Charles Scribner's Sons.

Breed, David K. 1948. *The Trial of Christ: From A Legal and Scriptural Viewpoint. Saint Louis:* Thomas Law Book Company.

Brewer, Neil, and Kipling D. Williams, eds. 2005. *Psychology and Law: An Empirical Perspective*. New York: Guilford Press.

Bright, William R. 1999. Foreword to *Evidence That Demands A Verdict* by Josh McDowell. Nashville: Nelsonword.

Briskin, Lawrence. 2004. "Tanakh Sources of Judas Iscariot." *Journal of Bible Quarterly* 32(3): 189-97.

Bromby, Michael C., and Maria Jean J. Hall. 2002. "The Development and Rapid Evolution of the Knowledge Model of ADVOKATE System to Assess the Credibility of Eyewitness Testimony." In *Legal Knowledge and Information Systems JURIX 2002: The Fifteenth Annual Conference,* edited by T. Bench-Capon, A. Daskalopulu, and R. Winkels, 143-52. Amsterdam, Netherlands: IOS Press.

Brooke, George J. 2005. *The Dead Sea Scrolls and the New Testament*. Philadelphia: Fortress Press.

Brooks, James A. 1991. *The New American Commentary: Mark*. Nashville: Broadman.

Broshi, Magen. 1978. "Estimating the Population of Ancient Jerusalem." *Biblical Archaeology Review* 4(2) 10-15.

Brown, Michael L. 2000. *Answering Jewish Objections to Jesus: General and Historical Objections*. Grand Rapids: Baker.

———. 2003. *Answering Jewish Objections to Jesus: Messianic Prophecy Objections* Volume 3. Grand Rapids: Baker.

Brown, Raymond E. 1970. *The Anchor Bible: The Gospel According to John (xviii-xxi)*. Garden City: Doubleday.

———. 1990a. "The Resurrection in Matthew." *Worship* 64(2): 157-70.

———. 1990b. "The Resurrection in John 20—a Series of Diverse Reactions." *Worship* 64(3): 194-206.

———. 1993. *The Birth of the Messiah.* New York: Doubleday.

———. 1994a. *The Death of the Messiah: From Gethsemane to the Grave.* 2 vols. New York: Doubleday.

———. 1994b. *An Introduction to New Testament Christology.* New York: Paulist Press.

———. 1997. *An Introduction to the New Testament.* New York: Doubleday.

Bruce, F. F. 1971. *The New Testament History.* Garden City: Doubleday.

———. 1974. *Jesus and Christian Origins Outside the New Testam*ent. Grand Rapids: Eerdmans.

———. 1997. *New Testament Documents: Are They Reliable? 5ᵗʰ revised edition.* Leicester: Intervarsity Press.

Buchanan, George Wesley. 1996. *The Gospel of Matthew.* Volume 1 Book 2. Lewiston, N.Y.: Mellon Biblical Press.

Buchler, A. 1930. "L'Enternement des Criminels." *Revue des Études Juives* 46: 74-88.

Bruner, Frederick Dale. 1990. *Matthew: A Commentary* Volume 2: The Churchbook Matthew 13-28. Grand Rapids: Eerdmans.

Bryant, Jo-Ann A. 2011. *John.* Grand Rapids: Baker Academic.

Bullinger, E. W. (1894) 1967. *Number In Scripture. Its Supernatural Design and Spiritual Significance.* London: Eyre and Spottiswoode. Reprint, Grand Rapids: Kregel. Citations refer to Kregel edition.

———. 1898. *Figures of Speech Used in the Bible Explained and Illustrated.* London: Messrs. Eyre & Spottiswoode.

———. (1914) 1964. *The Companion Bible: Being the Authorized Version of 1611 with the Structures and Notes . . . and 198 Appendixes.* London:

Oxford University Press. Reprint, London: Lamp Press. Citations refer to Lamp Press edition.

Bultmann, Rudolph. 1964. "Is Exegesis Without Presuppositions Possible?" English Translation in *Existence and Faith: Shorter Writings,* edited and translated by Schubert M. Ogden. London: Collins.

Burkett, Delbert. 2002. *An Introduction to the New Testament and the Origins of Christianity.* Cambridge: Cambridge University Press.

Burkitt, F.C. 1916. "W and Θ in the Western texts of St Mark (continue)." *Journal of Theological Studies* os-17(1): 139-152.

Burridge, Richard A. 2004. *What Are the Gospels? A Comparison With Graeco-Roman Biography* 2nd edition. Grand Rapids: Eerdmans.

Buss, Septimus. 1906. *The Trial of Jesus: Illustrated From Talmud and Roman Law.* London: Society for Promoting Christian Knowledge.

Buttrick, George A. 1951. "Matthew." In *The Interpreter's Bible* vol. vii. 250-625. New York: Abingdon.

Byrne, Brendan. 2001. "Peter as Resurrection Witness in the Lucan Narrative." In *The Convergence of Theology*, edited by Daniel Kendall and Stephen T. Davis, 19-33. New York: Paulist Press.

Cadoux, C. J. 1937. "A Tentative Synthetic Chronology of the Apostolic Age." *Journal of Biblical Literature* 46(3): 177-92.

Cahill, Michael J. 2002. "Drinking Blood at a Kosher Eucharist? The Sound of Scholarly Silence." *Biblical Theology Bulletin* 32(4): 168-81.

Caine, Hall. 1938. *Life of Christ.* New York: Doubleday, Doran & Company.

Cambron, Mark G. 1954. *Bible Doctrines: Beliefs that Matter.* Grand Rapids: Zondervan.

Campbell, W. Thomas. 2000. "The Relationship of the Thomas Pericope To Signs And Belief In The Fourth Gospel." PhD. diss., Southwestern Baptist Theological Seminary.

Capps, Donald. 2000. *Jesus: A Psychological Biography.* St. Louis: Chalice Press.

Cardwell, Kenneth. 1990. "The Fish on the Fire: Jn 21:9." *Expository Times* 102(1): 12-14.

Carlton, Matthew E. 2001. *The Translator's Reference Translation of the Gospel of Matthew.* Dallas: SIL.

Carmichael, Deborah Bleicher. 1991. "David Daube on the Eucharist and the Passover Seder." *Journal for the Study of the New Testament* 13(42): 45-67.

Carmichael, Joel. 1995. *The Unriddling of Christian origins.* Amherst, N.Y.: Prometheus.

Carmichael, Lawrence Garten. 1980. *An Apologetic for the Death, Burial, and Bodily Resurrection of Jesus Christ.* Master's thesis, Western Evangelical Seminary.

Carr, Steven. 1999. "Opening Statement by Steven Carr: Debate with Dr. Paul Marston." Steven Carr Homepage. *http://www.bowness.demon.co.uk/deb.htm*

———. n.d. "The Resurrection." Steven Carr Homepage. http://www.bowness.demon.co.uk/resr.htm

Carrier, Richard. 2002a. More on Vardaman's Microletters." *Skeptical Inquirer* 26(4): 60-61.

———. 2002b. "Pseudohistory in Jerry Vardaman's Magic Coins: The Nonsense of Micrographic Letters." *Skeptical Inquirer* 26(2): 39-41, 61.

———. 2005. "Craig's Empty Tomb & Habermas on Visions" (1999, 2005) [Part 4E of a larger *Review of In Defense of Miracles.*] *http://www.infidels.org/library/modern/richard_carrier/indef/4e.html*

———. 2006. Why I Don't Buy the Resurrection Story. The Secular Web, http://infidels.org/library/modern/richard_carrier/resurrection/

———. 2011-12. "Thallus and the Darkness at Christ's Death." *Journal of Greco-Roman Christianity and Judaism* 8: 185-91.

Carrington, Philip. 1952. *The Primitive Christian Calendar: A Study in the Making of the Marcan Gospel. Volume I Introduction & Text.* Cambridge; Cambridge University Press.

Carroll, John T. 2012. *Luke: A Commentary.* Louisville: Westminster John Knox Press.

Carson, D. A. 1984. *Matthew.* Vol. 8 of *Expositor's Bible Commentary*, edited by Frank E. Gaebelein. Grand Rapids: Zondervan.

———. 1991. *The Gospel According to St. John.* Grand Rapids: Eerdmans.

———. 1994. "The Three Witnesses And The Eschatology of 1 John." In *To Tell the Mystery: Essays on New Testament Eschatology in Honor of Robert H. Gundry*, edited by T.E. Schmidt and M. Silva. 217-32. JSNTSup 100; Sheffield: Sheffield Academic Press.

———. 1995. *Matthew. Chapters 13 Through 28.* The Expositor's Bible Commentary With the New International Version. Grand Rapids: Zondervan.

———. 2007. *New Testament Commentary Survey* 6th edition. Grand Rapids: Baker.

———. 2010a. *Scandalous: The Cross and Resurrection of Jesus.* Wheaton: Crossway.

———. 2010b. "Matthew." In *The Expositor's Bible Commentary Matthew - Mark*, edited by Temper Longman and David E. Garland. Grand Rapids: Zondervan.

Casey, Maurice. 1996. *Is John's Gospel True?* London: Routledge.

———. 2010. *Jesus of Nazareth: An Independent Historian's Account of His Life and Teaching.* London and New York: T&T Clark (Continuum).

Cassels, Walter. 1902. *Supernatural Religion: An Inquiry Into the Reality of Divine Revelation.* London: Watts.

Casson, Lionel. 1971. *Ships and Seamanship in the Ancient World.* Princeton: Princeton University Press.

———. 1994. *Ships and Seafaring in Ancient Times.* Austin, Tex.: University of Texas.

Catchpole, David. 1977. "The Fearful Silence of the Women at the Tomb: A Study in Markan *Theology." Journal of Theology for Southern Africa* 18: 3-10.

———. 2000. Jesus *People: The Historical Jesus and the Beginnings of Community.* London: Darton Longman & Todd.

Catholic Layman, The. 1853. The Passover and the Eucharist. The Catholic Layman 2(19): 74-75.

Cavin, Robert Greg. 1995. "Is There Sufficient Historical Evidence to Establish the Resurrection of Jesus?" *Faith & Philosophy* 12(3): 361-79.

Ceroke C. P. 2003. "Resurrection of Christ." In *The New Catholic Encyclopedia* 2nd ed. 12:145-55. Detroit: Thomson Gale.

Chafer, Lewis Sperry. 1948. *Systematic Theology* Vol. IV Dallas: Dallas Seminary Press.

Chandler, Walter M. 1956. *The Trial of Jesus: From A Lawyer's Standpoint.* Atlanta: Harrison.

Charlesworth, James H. 1995. *The Beloved Disciple: Whose Witness Validates the Gospel of John?* Valley Forge, Pa: Trinity Press International.

Chilton, Bruce. 2008. "Should Palm Sunday Be Celebrated In The Fall?" *Biblical Archaeology Review* 34(2): 28, 86.

Christensen, Michael J. 1979. *C. S. Lewis On Scripture. His Thoughts On The Nature Of Biblical Inspiration, The Role Of Revelation, And The Question Of Errancy.* Nashville: Abingdon.

Chouinard, Larry. 1997. *Matthew.* Joplin, Mo.: College Press.

Clarke, Adam. 1996. *Adam Clarke's Commentary.* Nashville: Abingdon. Electronic Database: Biblesoft.

Clark, Gordon H. 1957. "The Resurrection." *Christianity Today* 1(14): 17-19.

Cline, Darryl. n.d. "Is the Bible Full of Contradictions? The Last Supper and Judas Iscariot." The Pastor's Study, *http://www.biblical-thinking.org/cgi-bin/article.pl?249.*

Collins, Adela Yarbo. 1993. "The Empty Tomb in the Gospel According to Mark." In *Hermes and Athena: Biblical Exegesis and Philosophical Theology,* edited by Eleonore Stump and Thomas P. Flint, 107-40. Notre Dame, Ind.: Notre Dame Press.

———. 2007. *Mark: A Commentary.* Minneapolis: Fortress Press.

Collins, Raymond F. 1999. *First Corinthians.* Collegeville: Liturgical Press.

Colson, F.H. 1914-15. "Triangular Numbers in the New Testament." *Journal of Theological Studies* 16(#61): 67-76.

Connick, C. Milo. 1974. *Jesus the Man, the Mission, and the Message* 2nd ed. Englewood Cliffs: Prentice-Hall.

Connor, John W. 1984. "Misperception, Folk Belief, and the Occult: A Cognitive Guide to Understanding." *The Skeptical Inquirer* 8(4) Summer. 344-54. [Rpt. in *Science Confronts the Paranormal,* edited by Kendrick Frazier. Amherst, N.Y.: Prometheus, 1986. 65-74.]

Conrad, Audrey. 1991. "The fate of Judas; Matthew 27:3-10." *Toronto Journal of Theology* 7(2): 158-68.

Conzelmann, Hans. 1975. *1 Corinthians: A Commentary on the First Epistle to the Corinthians.* Translated by James W. Leitch. Philadelphia: Fortress Press.

———. 1987. *Acts of the Apostles: A Commentary on the Acts of the Apostles.* Translated by James Limburg, A. Thomas Kraabel, and Donald H. Juel. Philadelphia: Fortress Press.

Conway, Colleen M. 1997. *Men And Women in the Fourth Gospel Gender and Johannine Characterization.* Atlanta: Society of Biblical Literature.

Cook, Michael J. 1999. "Christian Appropriation of Passover: Jewish Responses Then and Now." *Lexington Theological Quarterly* 34(1): 18-25.

———. 2001. "Evolving Jewish Views of Jesus." In *Jesus Through Jewish Eyes: Rabbis and Scholars Engage an Ancient Brother in a New Conversation*, edited by Beatrice Bruteau, 3-24. Maryknoll, N.Y.: Orbis.

———. 2008. *Modern Jews Engage the New Testament: Enhancing Jewish Well-Being in a Christian Environment*. Woodstock, Vt.: Jewish Lights.

———. 2010. "Where Jewish Scholars on Jesus Go Awry: Last Supper, Sanhedrin. Blasphemy, Barabbas." *Shofar* 28(3): 70-77.

———. 2011. "How Credible is Jewish Scholarship on Jesus." In *The Jewish Jesus: Revelation, Reflection, Reclamation*, edited by Zev Garber, 251-70. West Lafayette, Ind.: Purdue University Press.

Corley, Katheen M. 1998. "Women and the Crucifixion and Burial of Jesus." *Forum* New Series 1(1): 181-217.

———. 2004. "Mary and the other Women Characters." In *Jesus and Mel Gibson's The Passion of Christ: The Film, the Gospels and the Claims of History*, edited by Kathleen E. Corley and Robert L. Webb, 79-88. London: Continuum.

Cornfeld, Gaalyah, ed. 1982. *The Historical Jesus: A Scholarly View of the Man and His World*. New York: Macmillan.

Cox, S. L. 1993. *A History and Critique of Scholarship Concerning the Markan Endings*. Lewiston: Queenston; Lampeter: Mellon Biblical Press. [This book is Cox's doctoral dissertation completed at The Southern Baptist Theological Seminary in Louisville, Ky.]

Craffert, Pieter F. 1989. "The Origins of Resurrection Faith: the Challenge of a Social Scientific Approach." *Neotestamentica* 23(2): 331-48.

———. 2002. "'Seeing' a Body into Being: Reflections on Scholarly Interpretations of the Nature and Reality of Jesus' Resurrected Body." *Religion & Theology* 9(1 & 2): 89-107.

———. 2008. "Did Jesus Rise Bodily From the Dead? Yes and No!" *Religion & Theology* 15(1&2):133-53.

————. 2009. "Jesus' Resurrection in a Social-Scientific Perspective: Is There Anything New to be Said?" *Journal for the Study of the Historical Jesus* 7(2): 126-51.

————. 2011. "I 'Witnessed' the Raising of the Dead": Resurrection Accounts in a Neuroanthropological Perspective." *Neotestamentica* 45(1): 1-28.

Craig, C. T. 1953. *The First Epistle to the Corinthians. The Interpreter's Bible.* New York: Abingdon.

Craig, William Lane. 1984a. "The Guard at the Tomb." *New Testament Studies* 30(2): 273-81.

————. 1984b. *Apologetics: An Introduction.* Chicago: Moody.

————. 1988. *Knowing the Truth About the Resurrection.* Ann Arbor, Mich.: Servant.

————. 1989a. "On Doubts About the Resurrection." *Modern Theology* 6(1): 53-75.

————. 1989b. *Assessing the New Testament Evidence for the Historicity of the Resurrection of Jesus.* Lewiston: Edwin Mellen.

————. 1993. "From Easter to Valentinus and the Apostles' Creed Once More: A Critical Examination of James Robinson's Proposed Resurrection Appearance Trajectories." *Journal for the Study of the New Testament* 16(52): 19-39.

————. 1995. "Did Jesus Rise From the Dead?" In *Jesus Under Fire*, edited by Michael F. Wilkins and J. P. Moreland, 143-76. Grand Rapids: Zondervan.

————. 1998. "The Evidence of the Missing Body." In *The Case for Christ: A Journalist's Personal Investigation of the Evidence for Jesus*, edited by Lee Strobel, 205-24. Grand Rapids: Zondervan.

————. 2000. "Closing Response." In Jesus' *Resurrection: Fact or Figment?: A Debate Between William Lane Craig and Gerd Lüdemann*, edited by Paul Copan and Ronald T. Tacelli, 162-206. Downers Grove: InterVarsity Press.

———. 2004. "Was Jesus Buried in Shame? Reflections on B. McCane's Proposal." *Expository Times* 115(2): 404-09.

———. 2008. *Reasonable Faith: Christian Truth and Apologetics.* Wheaton: Crossway.

———. 2010. *On Guard: Defending Your Faith With Reason and Precision.* Colorado Springs, Colo.: David C. Cook.

———. 2012. "The Bodily Resurrection of Jesus." In *Christian Apologetics: An Anthology of Primary Sources*, edited by Khaldoun A. Sweis and Chad V. Meister, 362-77. Grand Rapids: Zondervan.

Craig, William Lane, and Gerd Lüdemann. 2000. *Jesus' Resurrection Fact or Figment? A Debate Between William Lane Craig & Gerd Lüdemann*, edited by Paul Copan and Ronald H. Tacelli. Downers Grove: InterVarsity Press.

Cranfield, C. E. B. 1959. *The Gospel According to Saint Mark.* Cambridge: Cambridge University Press.

———. 1990. "The Resurrection of Jesus Christ." *Expository Times* 101(6): 167-72.

———. 1998. *On Romans and Other New Testament Essays.* 137-50. Edinburgh: T&T Clark.

Creed, John Martin. 1930. *The Gospel According to St. Luke.* London: Macmillan.

Crossan, John Dominic. 1991. *The Historical Jesus: The Life of a Mediterranean Jewish Peasant.* San Francisco: HarperSanFrancisco.

———. 1994. *Jesus: A Revolutionary Bibliography.* San Francisco: HarperSanFrancisco.

———. 1995. *Who Killed Jesus? Exposing the Roots of Anti-Semitism in the Gospel Story of the Death of Jesus.* San Francisco: HarperSanFrancisco.

———. 1998. *The Birth of Christianity: Discovering What Happened in the Years Immediately After the Execution of Jesus.* San Francisco: HarperSanFrancisco.

Crossley, James G. 2005. "Against the Historical Plausibility of the Empty Tomb Story and the Bodily Resurrection of Jesus: A Response to N.T. Wright." *Journal for the Study of the Historical Jesus* 3(2): 171-86.

————. 2011. "Manufacturing Resurrection: Locating Some Contemporary Scholarly Arguments." *Neostamentica* 45(1): 49-75.

Culpepper, R. Alan. 1978. "The Passion and Resurrection in Mark." *Review and Expositor* 75(4): 583-600.

Curtis, K. Peter. 1972. "Three Points of Contact Between Matthew and John in the Burial and Resurrection Narrative." *Journal of Theological Studies* 23(2): 440-44.

Czachesz, István. 2007. "Early Views on Jesus's Resurrection Toward a Cognitive Psychological Interpretation." *Nederlands Theologisch Tijdschrift* 61(1): 47-59.

Dake, Finis Jennings. 1961. *Dake's Annotated Reference Bible: The New Testament.* Lawrenceville, Ga.: Dake Bible Sales.

Danby, Herbert. 1933. *The Mishnah.* Oxford: Oxford University Press.

Danker, Frederick W. 1988. *Jesus and the New Age: A Commentary on St. Luke's Gospel.* Philadelphia: Fortress Press.

Daube, David. 1984. *The New Testament and Rabbinic Judaism.* Salem, N.H.: Ayer.

David, Anthony S. 1999. "On the Impossibility of Defining Delusions." *Philosophy, Psychiatry and Psychology* 6(1): 17-20.

Davids, P. H. 1992. "Rich and Poor." In *Dictionary of Jesus and the Gospels,* edited by Joel B. Green, Scot McKnight, and I. Howard Marshall, 701-10. Downers Grove: InterVarsity Press.

Davies, W. D., and Dale C. Allison. 1997. *A Critical and Exegetical Commentary on the Gospel According to Saint Matthew.* London: T&T Clark.

————. 2004. *Commentary in Matthew XIX-XXVIII.* London: T&T Clark.

Davis, Stephen T. 1984. "It is Possible to Know That Jesus Was Raised From the Dead?" *Faith & Philosophy* 1(2): 147-159.

———. 1985. "Was Jesus Raised Bodily?" *Christian Scholar's Review* 14(2): 140-52.

Day, Ronald R. 2007. "Luke 24:39 - Jesus' Appearances in the Locked Room." Jesus and His God: A Restoration Light Site. http://jesus.rlbible.com/?p=215

De Boer, Esther A. 2004. *The Gospel of Mary: Beyond a Gnostic and a Biblical Mary Magdalene.* London: T&T Clark.

DeConick, April D. 2008. "Human Memory and the Sayings of Jesus: Contemporary Experimental Exercises in the Transmission of Jesus Traditions." In *Jesus, the Voice, and the Text: Beyond the Oral and the Written Gospel,* edited by Tom Thatcher, 137-80. Waco, Tex.: Baylor University.

DeHaan, M. R. n.d. *Many Infallible Proofs of the Resurrection Acts 1-3: Four Radio Sermons.* Grand Rapids: Radio Bible Class.

Denaux, Adelbert. 2002. "Matthew's Story of Jesus' Burial and Resurrection (Mt 27, 57-28,20)." In *Resurrection in the New Testament Festschrift,* edited by J. Lambrecht. B. Bieringer, V. Koperski & B. Lataire, 125-45. Leuven: Leuven University Press.

Depuydt, Leo. 2002. "The Date of Death of Jesus of Nazareth." *Journal of the American Oriental Society* 122(3): 466-80.

Derrett, J. Duncan M. 1981. "Miscellanea: a Pauline Pun and Judas' Punishment." *Zeitschrift für die Neutestamentliche Wissenschaft* 72: 131-33.

———. 1982. *The Anastasis: The Resurrection of Jesus as An Historical Event.* Warwickshire, England: P. Drinkwater.

———. 1991. "Miriam and the Resurrection (John 20, 16)." *Bibbia E Oriente* 33(4): 211-19.

deSilva, David A. 2004. *An Introduction to the New Testament: Contexts, Methods & Ministry Formation.* Downers Grove: IVP Academic.

Dewey, Joanna. 2006. "The Women in the Gospel of Mark." *Word & World* 26(1): 22-29.

Dibelius, Martin. 1965. *Die Apostelgeschichte*, edited by E. Haenchen, 64-81, 99-103. Gottingen: Vandenhoeck & Ruprecht.

Dijkhuizen, Petra. 2011. "Buried Shamefully: Historical reconstruction of Jesus' Burial and Tomb." *Neotestamentica* 45(1): 115-29.

Dillon, Richard J., and Joseph A. Fitzmyer. 1968. "Acts of the Apostles." In *The Jerome Biblical Commentary*, edited by Raymond Brown, Joseph A. Fitzmyer, and Roland E. Murphy, 164-214. Englewood Cliffs, N.J.: Prentice-Hall.

Doane, T. W. 1882. *Bible Myths and Their Parallels in Other Religions* 4th edition. New York: Commonwealth.

Dobschütz, Ernest von. 1903. *Ostern und Pfingsten*. Leipzig: J.C. Hinrichs.

Dobson, C. C. 1934. *The Empty Tomb and the Risen Lord*. London: Martin & Parnhan.

Dockx, S. 1989. "The First Missionary Voyage of Paul: Historical Reality or Literary Creation of Luke?" In *Chronos, Kairos, Christos: Nativity and Chronological Studies Presented to Jack Finegan*, edited by Jerry Vardaman and Edwin M. Yamauchi, 209-21. Translated by Edwin Yamauchi. Winona Lake: Eisenbrauns.

Dodd, C. H. 1953. "Note on John 21, 24." *Journal of Theological Studies* 4(2): 212-13.

———. 1957. "The Appearances of the Risen Christ: An Essay in Form-Criticism of the Gospels." In *Studies in the Gospels: Essays in Memory of R. H. Lightfoot*, edited by D. Nineham, 9-35. Oxford: B. Blackwell.

———. 1963. *Historical Tradition in the Fourth Gospel*. Cambridge: Cambridge University Press.

Drazin, M. 1990. *Their Hollow Inheritance: A Comprehensive Refutation of Christian Missionaries*. Safed, Israel: G.M. Publications.

Driver, G. R. 1965. "Two Problems in the New Testament." *Journal of Theological Studies*, N.S., 16(2): 327-37.

Dudrey, Russ. 2000. "What the Writers Should Have Done Better: A Case For the Resurrection of Jesus Based on Ancient Criticisms of the Resurrection Reports. *Stone-Campbell Journal* 3(2): 55-78.

Dunkerley, Roderic. 1957. *Beyond the Gospels: An Investigation into the Information on the Life of Christ to be Found Outside the Gospels.* London: Pelican.

Dunn, James D. G. 1975. *Jesus and the Spirit: A Study of the Religious and Charismatic Experience of Jesus and the First Christians as Reflected in the New Testament.* London: SCM Press.

———. 2003. *Christianity in the Making vol. 1 Jesus Remembered.* Grand Rapids: Eerdmans.

Eddy, G. T. 1990. "The Resurrection of Jesus Christ: A Consideration of Professor Cranfield's Argument." *Expository Times* 101(11): 327-29.

Eddy, Paul Rhodes, and Gregory A. Boyd. 2007. *The Jesus Legend: A Case for the Historical Reliability of the Synoptic Jesus Tradition.* Grand Rapids: Baker.

Edwards, James R. 2002. *The Gospel According to Mark.* Grand Rapids: Eerdmans.

Edwards, William D., Wesley J. Gabel, and Floyd E. Hosmer. March 21, 1986. "On the Physical Death of Jesus Christ." *The Journal of the American Medical Association* 255(11): 1455-63.

Ehrhardt, A. A. T. 1964. "The Disciples of Emmaus." *New Testament Studies* 10(2): 182-210.

Ehrman, Bart D. 1990. "Cephas and Peter." *Journal of Biblical Literature* 109(3): 463-74.

———. 1993. *Orthodox Corruption of Scripture: The Effect of Early Christological Controversies on the Text of the New Testament.* Oxford: Oxford University Press.

———. 2003. *Lost Christianities: The Battles for Scripture and the Faiths We Never Knew.* Oxford: Oxford University Press.

———. 2006. "Dr. Ehrman's Opening Statement." In *Is There Historical Evidence for the Resurrection of Jesus? A Debate Between William Lane Craig and Bart D. Ehrman*: College of the Holy Cross, Worcester, Mass.: *http://www.reasonablefaith.org/ is-there-historical-evidence-for-the-resurrection-of-jesus-the-craig-ehrman*.

———. 2012. *Did Jesus Exist? The Historical Argument for Jesus of Nazareth.* New York: HarperOne.

Eisler, Robert. 1931. *The Messiah Jesus and John the Baptist According to Flavius Josephus' Recently Discovered 'Capture of Jerusalem' and the Other Jewish and Christian Sources.* London: Methuen.

Elliott, J. K. 1982. *Questioning Christian Origins.* London: SCM Press.

Ellis. E. Earle. 1981. *The Gospel of Luke* (NCB). Grand Rapids: Eerdmans.

———. 1999. *The Making of the New Testament Documents.* Leiden: Brill.

Ellis, I. P. 1968. "'But Some Doubted.'" *New Testament Studies* 14: 574-80.

Ellis, Peter F. 1984. *The Genius of John: A Composition-Critical Commentary on the Fourth Gospel.* Collegeville: Liturgical Press.

Emerton, J. A. 1958. "The Hundred and Fifty-Three Fishes in John XXI, 11." *Journal of Theological Studies* 9(1): 86-89.

Enslin, Morton S. 1972. "How the Story Grew: Judas in Fact and Fiction." In *Festschrift to Honor F. Wilbur Gingrich*, edited by Eugene Howard Barth and Ronald Edwin Cocroft, 123-41. Leiden: E.J. Brill.

Espenak, Fred. 2011. "Total Solar Eclipse of 0029 Nov 24." Last Updated: 2011 Jun 15. eclipse.gsfc.nasa.gov/SEhistory/SEplot/SE0029Nov24T.pdf.

Evans, C. F. 1970. *Resurrection and the New Testament.* London: SCM.

Evans, Craig A. 1995. *Jesus and His Contemporaries: Comparative Studies.* Leiden: E. J. Brill.

————. 2001. *Word Biblical Commentary Mark 8:27-16:20* Volume 34B. Nashville: Thomas Nelson.

————. 2003a. *Jesus and the Ossuaries.* Waco, Tex.: Baylor University Press.

————. 2003b. "Jesus and the Ossuaries." *Bulletin for Biblical Research* 13:1: 21-46.

————. 2005a. *Ancient Texts For New Testament Studies: A Guide to the Background Literature.* Peabody, Mass.: Hendrickson.

————. 2005b. "Jewish Burial Traditions and the Resurrection of Jesus." *Journal for the Study of the Historical Jesus* 3(2): 233-48.

————. 2012. *Matthew* (New Cambridge Bible Commentary). Cambridge: Cambridge University Press.

Evans, Craig A., and Donald A. Hager. 1992. *Faith and Polemic: Studies in Anti-Semitism and Early Christianity.* Minneapolis: Fortress Press.

Eymann, David. 1978. "An Evaluation of the Evidence Bearing Upon the Authenticity of Mark 16:9-20." Master's thesis, Western Conservative Baptist Seminary.

Fales, Evan. 2001. "Successful Defense? A Review of In Defense of Miracles." *Philosophia Christ* 3(1): 7-35.

Falkson, Jock. April 25, 2006. *Did Judas Betray Jesus? Or Did Christianity Betray Judas?* Israel Defender. *http://breasy.com/israeldefender/?p=60.*

Farmer, William R. (1956) 1973. *Maccabees, Zealots, and Josephus: An Inquiry Into Jewish Nationalism in the Greco-Roman Period.* Columbia: Columbia University Press. Reprint, Westport, Conn.: Greenwood Press. Citations refer to the Greenwood edition.

————. 1974. *The Twelve Verses of Mark.* Cambridge: Cambridge University Press.

Fee, Gordon. 1987. *The First Epistle to the Corinthians*, NICNT. Grand Rapids: Eerdmans.

Fellows, Richard. n.d. "Mary Magdalene", accessed January 30, 2014. http://members.shaw.ca/rfellows/Site/Magdalene.html.

Fenton, John C. 1963. *The Gospel According to St. Matthew*. London: Penguin.

―――. 1994. "The Ending of Mark's Gospel." In *Resurrection: Essays in Honour of Leslie Houlden*, edited by Stephen Barton and Graham Stanton. 1-7. London: SPCK.

―――. 2001. *More About Mark*. London: SPCK.

Ferguson, Everett. 1996. *The Church of Christ: A Biblical Ecclesiology for Today*. Grand Rapids: Eerdmans.

Fideler, David. 1993. *Jesus Christ, Sun of God: Ancient Cosmology and Early Christian Symbolism*. Wheaton: Quest Books.

Filson, Floyd V. 1960. *A Commentary on the Gospel According to St. Matthew*. London: A. C. & C. Black.

Fine, Steven. 2000. "A Note on Ossuary Burial and the Resurrection of the Dead in First Century Jerusalem." *Journal of Jewish Studies* 51 (1): 69-76.

Finegan, Jack. 1998. *Handbook of Biblical Chronology*. Peabody, Mass.: Hendrickson.

Fitzmyer, Joseph A. 1985. *The Gospel According to Luke (X-XXIV)*. Garden City, N.Y.: Doubleday.

Fortna, Robert T. 1992. "Diachronic/Synchronic Reading John 21 and Luke 5." In *John and the Synoptic*, edited by Adelbert Denaux, 387-99. Leuven: Leuven University Press.

Fotheringham, J. K. 1910. "Astronomical Evidence for the Date of the Crucifixion." *Journal of Theological Studies* 12(October #45): 120-27.

―――. 1934. "The Evidence of Astronomy and Technical Chronology." *Journal of Theological Studies* 35(138 April): 142-62.

Fosdick, Harry Emerson. 1949. *The Man from Nazareth*. New York: Harper.

Fowler, Harold. 1985. *The Gospel of Matthew*. Volume 4. Joplin, Mo.: College Press Publishing.

Fox, Robin Lane. 1991. *The Unauthorized Version: Truth and Fiction in the Bible*. New York: Knopf.

France, R. T. 1986. "Chronological aspects of 'Gospel Harmony.'" *Vox Evangelica* 16: 33-60.

———. 1994. "Matthew." In *New Bible Commentary: 21ˢᵗ Century Edition*, edited by D.A. Carson, R. T. France, J. A. Motyer, and G. J. Wenham, 904-45. Downers Grove: InterVarsity.

———. 2002. *The Gospel of Mark: A Commentary on the Greek Text*. Grand Rapids: Eerdmans.

———. 2007. *The Gospel of Matthew*. Grand Rapids: Eerdmans.

Franklin, Eric. 2001. "Luke." In *The Oxford Bible Commentary*, edited by John Barton and John Muddiman, 922-59. Oxford: Oxford University Press.

Frederick, William. 1911. "CRITICAL NOTE. Did Jesus Eat the Passover?" *Bibliotheca Sacra* 68 (No. 271): 503-11.

Fredriksen, Paula. 1999. *Jesus of Nazareth, King of the Jews*. New York: Knopf.

Freke, Timothy, and Peter Gandy. 1999. *The Jesus Mysteries: Was the "Original Jesus" A Pagan God?* New York: Harmony.

Fruchtenbaum, Arnold G. 2003. "The Little Apocalypse of Zechariah." In *The End Times Controversy*, edited by Tim LaHaye and Thomas Ice, 251-81. Eugene, Ore.: Harvest House.

Fuljenz, Mike. September 13, 2009. "Rare Coins: The Tyre Shekels' Connection to History. Coin News Today." *http://www.coinnewstoday.com/article2/55-rare-coins-the-tyre-shekels-connection-to-history.html*.

Fuller, Reginald H. 1954. "The Mission And Achievement of Jesus; An Examination of the Presuppositions of New Testament Theology." In *Studies in Biblical Theology* 7. London: SCM Press.

———. 1960. "The Resurrection of Jesus Christ." *Biblical Research* 4: 8-24.

———. 1980. *The Formation of the Resurrection Narratives.* Philadelphia: Fortress Press.

———. 1988. "Matthew." In *Harper's Bible Commentary,* edited by James L. Mays, 951-82. San Francisco: Harper & Row.

Gagne, Armand J. 2007. "An Examination and Possible Explanation of John's Dating of the Crucifixion." In *The Death of Jesus in the Fourth Gospel,* edited by G. Van Belle, 411-20. Leuven: Leuven University Press.

Galvin, John P. 1988. "The Origin of Faith in the Resurrection of Jesus: Two Recent Perspectives." *Theological Studies* 49(1): 25-44.

Gardner-Smith, P. 1938. *The Christ of the Gospels: A Study of the Gospel Records in the Light of Critical Research.* Cambridge: Heffer & Sons

Garland, David E. 2011. *Luke: Zondervan Exegetical Commentary on the New Testament.* Grand Rapids: Zondervan.

Geddert, Timothy J. 1989. *Watchwords: Mark 13 in Markan Eschatology.* Sheffield, England: JOST.

———. 2001. *Mark.* Scottsdale, Pa.: Herald Press.

Geisler, Norman L. 1987. "The Apologetic Significance of the Bodily Resurrection of Christ." *Bulletin of the Evangelical Philosophical Society* 10: 15-37.

———.1989a. "The Significance of Christ's Physical Resurrection." *Bibliotheca Sacra* 146(582): 148-70.

———.1989b. "The Battle for the Resurrection." *Fundamentalist Journal* 8(3): 12-15.

———. 1992. *The Battle for the Resurrection* Updated Edition. Nashville: Thomas Nelson.

———. 1999. *Baker Encyclopedia of Christian Apologetics.* Grand Rapids: Baker.

———. 2007. "The Resurrection of Jesus Christ." In *Harmony of the Gospels*, edited by Steven L. Cox and Kendell H. Easley, 331-36. Nashville: Holman.

———. 2013. *Christian Apologetics* 2nd ed. Grand Rapids: Baker.

Geisler, Norman L., and Thomas Howe. 1992. *When Critics Ask: A Popular Handbook on Bible Difficulties*. Grand Rapids: Baker.

Geisler, Norman L., Frank Turek, and David Limbaugh [Forward]. 2004. *I Don't Have Enough Faith to Be an Atheist*. Wheaton: Crossway.

Geldenhuys, N. 1951. *Commentary on the Gospel of Luke*. Grand Rapids: Eerdmans.

Giblin, Charles Homer.1974-1975. "Structural and Thematic Correlations in the Matthean Burial-Resurrection Narrative (Matt. xxvii. 57 - xxviii. 20)." *New Testament Studies* 21(3): 406-20.

Gilmour, S. MacLean. 1952. "The Gospel According to St. Luke: Exegesis." In *Luke; John, vol. VIII of The Interpreter's Bible*, edited by Nolan B. Harmon, 1-434. Nashville: Abingdon-Cokesbury.

———. 1961. "The Christophany to More Than Five Hundred Brethren." *Journal of Biblical Literature* 80(3): 248-52.

———. 1965. "The Evidence for Easter." *Andover Newton Quarterly* 5(4): 7-23.

Goguel, Maurice. 1933. *The Life of Jesus*. Translated by Olive Wyon. New York: Barnes & Noble.

Goodier, Alban. 1949. *The Risen Jesus: Meditations*. New York: P. J. Kenedy & Sons.

Goodman, David. 1986. "Do Angels Eat?" *Journal of Jewish Studies* 37(2): 160-75.

Goodman, Liz. 2009. "Easter Sermon. Romans 14, 15; John 20:19-31." *Journal for Preachers* 32(3): 9-12.

Gorham, Charles Turner. 1908. *The First Easter Dawn: An inquiry Into the Evidence for the Resurrection of Jesus.* London: Watts.

Gosling, F. A. 1999. "O Judas! What have you done?" *Evangelical Quarterly* 71(2): 117-26.

Goulder, Michael. 1976. "The Empty Tomb." *Theology* 79(670): 206-14.

———. 1996. "The Baseless Fabric of a Vision." In *Resurrection Reconsidered*, edited by Gavin D'Costa, 48-61. Oxford: Oneworld.

———. 2005. "Jesus' Resurrection and Christian Origins: A Response to N.T. Wright." *Journal for the Study of the Historical Jesus* 3(2): 187-95.

Grant, Colleen Conway. 1997. "Men and Women in the Fourth Gospel: Gender and Johannine Characterization." PhD diss., Emory University.

Grant, Robert M. 1949. "One Hundred Fifty-Three Large Fish (John 21:11)." *Harvard Theological Review* 42(4): 273-75.

———. 1977. *Early Christianity and Society* New York: Harper & Row.

Grassmick, John D. 1983. "Mark." In *The Bible Knowledge Commentary: An Exposition of the Scriptures by Dallas Seminary Faculty*, edited by John F. Walvoord and Roy B. Zuck, 95-198. Colorado Springs, Colo.: Victor.

Grayston, Kenneth. 1981. "The Empty Tomb." *The Expository Times* 92(9): 263-67.

———. 1984. "The Translation of Matthew 28.17." *Journal for the Study of the New Testament* 6(No. 21): 105-09.

———. 1990. *The Gospel of John.* Philadelphia: Trinity Press International.

Green, Joel B. 1997. *The Gospel of Luke.* Grand Rapids: Eerdmans.

Green, Joel B., Scot McKnight, and I. Howard Marshall, eds. 1992. *Dictionary of Jesus and the Gospels.* Downers Grove: InterVarsity Press.

Greenberg, Gary. 2007. *The Judas Brief: Who Really Killed Jesus?* London: Bloomsbury/Continuum.

Griffith, Stephen F. 1996. "Could It Have Been Reasonable for the Disciples to have Believed that Jesus had Risen from the Dead?" *Journal of Philosophical Research* 21: 307-19.

Groom, N. 2002. "Trade, Incense and Perfume." In *Queen of Sheba Treasures From Ancient Yemen*, edited by St John Simpson, 88-101. London: The British Museum Press.

Guelich, R. 1991. "The Gospel as Genre." In *The Gospel and the Gospels*, edited by P. Stuhlmacher, 173-208. Grand Rapids: Eerdmans.

Gundry, Robert H. 1974. "Recent Investigations into the Literary Genre 'Gospel.'" In *New Dimensions in New Testament Study*, edited by R. N. Longenecker and M. C. Tenney, 97-114. Grand Rapids: Zondervan.

———. 1975. *The Use of the Old Testament in St. Matthew's Gospel, with Special Reference to the Messianic Hope* (Supplements to Novum Testamentum 18), Leiden: E. J. Brill.

———. 1993. *Mark: A Commentary on His Apology for the Cross*. Grand Rapids: Eerdmans.

———. 1994. *Matthew: A Commentary on His Handbook for a Mixed Church Under Persecution*, 2nd ed. Grand Rapids: Eerdmans.

———. 2004. "The Essential Physicality of Jesus' Resurrection According to the New Testament." In *The Historical Jesus: Critical Concepts in Religious Studies. Volume III Jesus' Mission, Death, and Resurrection*, edited by Craig A. Evans, 360-76. London: Routledge. [Originally in Joel B. Green and M. Turner, eds. 1994. *Jesus of Nazareth: Lord and Christ: Essays on the Historical Jesus and New Testament Christology*. Carlise: Paternoster; Grand Rapids: Eerdmans, 204-19.]

Gurtner, Daniel F. 2006. "The Veil of the Temple in History and Legend." *Journal of the Evangelical Theological Society* 49(1): 97-114.

Guthrie, Donald. 1970. *New Testament Introduction*. Downers Grove: InterVarsity Press.

Gwynne, Paul. 2001. "Why Some Still Doubt that Jesus' Body Was Raised." In *The Convergence of Theology: A Festschrift Honoring Gerald O'Collins*, edited by Daniel Kendall and Stephen T. Davis, 355-65. New York: Paulist Press.

Habermas, Gary R. 1980. *The Resurrection of Jesus*. Grand Rapids: Baker.

———. 1984a. "Jesus' Resurrection and Contemporary Criticism: An Apologetic." *Criswell Theological Review* 4(1): 159-74.

———. 1984b. *Ancient Evidence for the Life of Jesus: Historical Records of His Death and Resurrection. Nashville: Thomas* Nelson.

———. 1996. *The Historical Jesus: Ancient Evidence for the Life of Christ.* Joplin, Mo.: College Press.

———. 2001. "On the Resurrection Appearances of Jesus." *Philosophia Christi* 3(1): 76-87.

———. 2003. *The Risen Jesus & Future Hope.* Lanham: Rowman & Littlefield.

———. 2004. "The Case for Christ's Resurrection." In *To Everyone an Answer: A Case for the Christian Worldview. Essays in Honor of Norman L. Geisler,* edited by Francis J. Beckwith, William Lane Craig, and J. P. Moreland, 180-98. Downers Grover: InterVarsity Press.

———. 2012. "Experiences of the Risen Jesus." In *Christian Apologetics: An Anthology of Primary Sources,* edited by Khaldoun A. Sweis and Chad V. Meister, 354-61. Grand Rapids: Zondervan.

Habermas, Gary R., and Michael R. Licona, 2004. *The Case for the Resurrection of Jesus.* Grand Rapids: Kregel.

Haenchen, Ernst. 1971. *The Acts of the Apostles: A Commentary.* Philadelphia: Westminster.

Haggard, Dean Alfred Martin. 1912. "Problems of the Passion Week." *Bibliotheca Sacra* 69(#275): 664-92.

Hagner, Donald. A. 1995. *Word Biblical Commentary Volume 33b, Matthew 14-28.* Dallas, Texas: Word Book.

———. 2012. *The New Testament: A Historical and Theological Introduction.* Grand Rapids: Baker.

Hailey, O. L. n.d. *The Three Prophetic Days: A Harmony of the Apparent Discrepancies in the Gospel Narratives About the Resurrection of Jesus Christ* Part II. Corsicana, Tex.: Author:

Hakola, Raimo. 2009. "The Burden of Ambiguity: Nicodemus and the Social Identity of the Johannine Christians." *New Testament Studies* 55(4): 438-55.

Hamilton, Neill Q. 1965. "Resurrection Tradition and the Composition of Mark." *Journal of Biblical Literature* 84(4): 415-21.

Hamm, Dennis. 2003. "The Tamid Service in Luke-Acts: The Cultic Background Behind Luke's Theology of Worship (Luke 1:5-25; 18:9-14; 24:50-53; Acts 3:1; 10:3, 30." *Catholic Biblical Quarterly* 65(2): 215-31.

Hanauer, James Edward. 1924. "Model of a Columbarium. An Alleged Model of a Sanctuary from the Garden Tomb Grounds." *Palestinian Exploration Quarterly* 56(3): 143-45.

Hanhart, Karel. 1995. *The Open Tomb. A New Approach, Mark's Passover Haggadah (± 72 C.E.).* Collegeville: Liturgical Press.

Hannah, Darrell D. 1999. "The Ascension of Isaiah and Docetic Christology." *Vigiliae Christianae* 53(2): 165-196.

Hanson, G. 1911. *The Resurrection and the Life.* New York: Fleming H. Revell.

Hanson, K. C., and Douglas E. Oakman. 1998. *Palestine in the Time of Jesus: Social Structures and Social Conflicts.* Minneapolis: Fortress Press.

Hare, Douglas, R. A. 1993. *Matthew.* Louisville: John Knox.

———. 1996. *Mark.* Louisville: Westminster John Knox.

Harrington, Daniel J. 1991. *The Gospel of Matthew.* Collegeville: Liturgical Press.

Hasitschka, Martin. 2008. "The Resurrection of Jesus." In *The Gospel of John,* edited by Craig R. Koester and Reimund Bieringer, 311-28. Tübingen, Ger: Mohr Siebeck.

Hays, Richard B. 2003. "Reading Scripture in Light of Resurrection." In *The Art of Reading Scripture*, edited by Ellen F. Davis and Richard B. Hays, 216-38. Grand Rapids: Eerdmans.

Hays, Steve. 2006. *This Joyful Eastertide: A Critical Review of The Empty Tomb*, http://calvindude.org/ebooks/stevehays/This-Joyful-Eastertide.pdf

Healey, Antonette diPaolo. 1973. "The Vision of St. Paul." PhD diss., University of Toronto.

Hedrick, Charles W. 1981. "Paul's Conversion/Call: A Comparative Analysis of the Three Reports in Acts." *Journal of Biblical Literature* 100(3): 415-32.

Heil, John Paul. 1991. *The Death and Resurrection of Jesus: A Narrative-Critical Reading of Matthew 26-28*. Minneapolis: Fortress Press.

———. 1992a. *The Gospel of Mark as a Model for Action*. New York: Paulist Press.

———. 1992b. "The Progressive Narrative Pattern of Mark 14,53-16,8." *Biblica* 73(3): 331-58.

Hendin, David. 1991. "Theory of Secret Inscriptions on Coins is Disputed." *The Celator: Numismatic Art of Antiquity* 5(3): 28-30.

Hendrickx, Herman. 1984. *The Resurrection Narratives of the Synoptic Gospels*. London: Geoffrey Chapman.

Hendricksen, William. 1953. *Exposition of the Gospel According to John. New Testament Commentary. 2 Volumes Complete in One*. Grand Rapids: Baker.

Hengel, Martin. 2001. Das Begräbnis Jesu bei Paulus und die Leibliche Auferstehung aus dem Grabe. In *Auferstehung - Resurrection*, edited by Friedrich Avemaroe and Hermann Lichtenberger, 119-83. Wunt 135. Tübingen.

Henry, Matthew. 1961. *Matthew Henry's Commentary*. Grand Rapids: Zondervan.

Henten, Jan Will, van. 2001. "Daniel 3 and 6 in Early Christian Literature." In *The Book of Daniel: Composition and Reception*, edited by John Collins and Peter W. Flint, 149-69. Leiden: Brill.

Hester, J. David. 1995. "Dramatic Inconclusion: Irony and the Narrative Rhetoric of the Ending of Mark." *Journal for the Study of the New Testament* 17(57): 61-86.

Heuschen, J. 1965. *The Bible on the Ascension.* Translated by F. Vander Heijden. De Pere. Wisc.: St. Norbert Abbey Press.

Hilhorst, A. 1983. "The Wounds of the Risen Jesus." *Estudios Bíblicos* 41(1-2): 165-67.

Hill, David. 1972. *The Gospel of Matthew* NCB. Grand Rapids: Eerdmans.

———. 1985. "Matthew 27:51-53 in the Theology of the Evangelist." *Irish Biblical Studies* 7(2): 76-87.

Hiltner, Seward. 1965. "Psychology and the Resurrection." *Pastoral Psychology* 16(15): 5-7.

Hinks, Dennis. 1999. "Jesus Appears First To Mary, Then To The Other Women." My Journal (part of the Journal 33 Website), accessed January 27, 2014. *http://www.journal33.org/godworld/html/jc-r2a-4.htm.*

Hoeh, Herman L. 1959. "The Crucifixion Was NOT On FRIDAY! "*The Plain Truth.* 24(3):3-6, 15-18, 30-31.

Hoehner, Harold W. 1974a. "Chronological Aspects of the Life of Christ: Part V: The Year of Christ's Crucifixion." *Bibliotheca Sacra* 131(524): 332-48.

———. 1974b. "Chronological Aspects of the Life of Christ: Part IV: The Day of Christ's Crucifixion." *Bibliotheca Sacra* 131(523): 241-64.

———. 1992. "Chronology." In *Dictionary of Jesus and the Gospels,* edited by Joel B. Green and Scot McKnight, 118-22. Downers Grove: InterVarsity Press.

Holding, J. P. n.d. Response to "1001 Errors in the Bible" #431. Tekton Apologetics Ministries. http://www.tektonics.org/uz/wally01.html#fourhun

———. n.d. "The Resurrection Narratives Harmonized Contextually." Tektonics Apologetics Ministries, accessed January 27, 2014. *http://www.tektonics.org/qt/rezrvw.html.*

————. n.d. "One Down, Twelve to Go: Is Reference to the "Twleve" Anachronistic?" Tektonics Apologetics Ministries, accessed January 27, 2014. http://www.tektonics.org/uz/whotwelve.html.

————. n.d. "The Death of Judas Iscariot." Tektonics Apologetics Ministries. *http://www.tektonics.org/gk/judasdeath.php* accessed January 27, 2014.

Holl, K. 1921. *Der Kirchenbegriff des Paulus in seinem Verhältnis zu dem der Urgemeinde. Sitzungsberichte der Preussischen Akademie der Wissenschaften,* 53 (Berlin).

Holmes, Michael W. 2001. "To Be Continued . . . The Many endings of the Gospel of Mark." *Bible Review* 17(4): 12-23, 48-50.

Hölscher, Gustav 1940. *Die Hohenpriesterliste bei Josephus und die Evangelische Chronologie. Sitzungsberichte der Heidelberger Akademie der Wissenschaften - Philosophisch-historische Klasse,* xxx. Heidelberg, pp. 1-33.

Holtzmann, Oscar. 1904. *The Life of Jesus.* Translated by J. T. Bealby and Maurice A. Canney. London: Adam & Charles Black.

Hook, Peter R. 1978. "A Study of the Problem Passages Relating to the Ascension." Master's thesis, Dallas Theological Seminary.

Hooker, Morna D. 1972. "On Using the Wrong Tool." *Theology,* 75: 570-81.

————. 1991. *The Gospel According to Saint Mark.* Peabody, Mass. Hendrickson.

Hoover, Roy W. 2000. "A Contest Between Orthodoxy & Veracity." In *Jesus' Resurrection Fact or Figment? A Debate Between William Lane Craig & Gerd Lüdemann,* edited by Paul Copan and Ronald K. Tacelli, 124-46. Downers Grove: InterVarsity Press.

Horne, Thomas Hartwell. 1856. *A Summary for Evidence for the Genuineness, Authenticity, Uncorrupted Preservation. And Inspiration of the Holy Scriptures* 10th edition. London: Longman, Brown, Green, Longmans, & Roberts.

Horner, Michael. 1996. *"Did Jesus Really Rise From The Dead?"* Debate Between Michael Horner and Dan Barker. The Secular Web. http://infidels.org/library/modern/dan_barker/barker_horner.html.

Horst, P. W. van der. 1986. "Once More: The Translation of οἱ δὲ in Matthew 28.17." *Journal for the Study of the New Testament* 9(No. 27): 27-30.

House, H. Wayne, and Joseph M. Holden. 2006. *Charts of Apologetics and Christian Evidences*. Grand Rapids: Zondervan.

House, H. Wayne, and Randall Price. 2003. *Charts of Bible Prophecy*. Grand Rapids: Zondervan.

Horvath, Anthony. April 6, 2009. "How Many Guards at Jesus' Tomb?" SntJohnny.com /Athanosatos Christian Ministries. *http://sntjohnny.com/front/how-many-guards-at-the-tomb-of-jesus/485.html*.

Howard, Wilbert F. 1951. "The Gospel According to St. John." In *The Interpreter's Bible. Volume 7*, edited by George Arthur Buttrick, 435-811. New York: Abingdon.

Howe, E. Margaret. 1975. " . . . But Some Doubted" (Matt. 28:17): A Re-Appraisal of Factors Influencing the Easter Faith of the Early Christian Community." *Journal of the Evangelical Theological Society* 18(2): 173-80.

Hull, William E. 1970. "John." In *The Broadman Bible Commentary* Volume 9, edited by Clifton J. Allen, 209-376. Nashville: Broadman.

Humphreys, Colin J. 2011. *The Mystery of the Last Supper: Reconstructing the Final Days of Jesus*. Cambridge: Cambridge University Press.

Humphreys, Colin J., and W. G. Waddington. December 22/29, 1983. "Dating the Crucifixion." *Nature* 306(5945): 743-46.

———.1985. "The Date of the Crucifixion." *Journal of the American Scientific Affiliation* 37(March): 2-10.

———1989. "Astronomy and the Date of the Crucifixion." In *Chronos, Kairos, Christos: Nativity and Chronological Studies Presented to Jack Finegan*, edited by Jerry Vardaman and Edwin M. Yamauchi, 165-81. Winona Lake: Eisenbrauns.

———. 1992. "The Jewish Calendar: A Lunar Eclipse And The Date of Christ's Crucifixion." *Tyndale Bulletin* 43 (2): 331-51.

Hurtado, Larry W. 1989. *Mark*. Peabody, Mass.: Hendrickson.

———. 1992. "Gospel (Genre)." In *Dictionary of Jesus and the Gospels*, edited by Joel B. Green and Scot McKnight, 276-82. Downers Grove: InterVarsity Press.

———. 2006. "The New Testament in the Second Century: Text, Collection and Canon." In *Transmission and Reception: New Testament Text-Critical and Exegetical Studies*, volume 4, edited by J. W. Childers and D. C. Parker, 3-27 Piscataway, N.J.: Gorgias Press.

Hynek, R. W. 1936. *Science and the Holy Shroud*. Chicago: Benedictine Press.

Iannuzzi, John Nicholas. 2001. *Handbook of Trial Strategies* 2ⁿᵈ ed. Parmus, N.J.: Prentice-Hall.

Ice, Thomas. 2010. "Preterism and Zechariah 12-14." *http://www.pre-trib. org/articles/view/preterism-and-zechariah-12-14*.

International Standard Bible Online. 1939. "Number," accessed March 3, 2014. http://www.internationalstandardbible.com/N/number.html

Jack, J. W. 1933. *The Historic Christ: An Examination of Dr. Robert Eisler's Theory According to the Slavonic Version of Josephus and Other Sources*. London: James Clarke.

Jackson, Clyo. 1936. "Joseph of Arimathea." *The Journal of Religion* 16(3): 332-40.

Jackson, Hugh. 1975. "The Resurrection Belief of the Earliest Church: A Response to the Failure of Prophecy?" *The Journal of Religion* 55(4): 415-25.

Jackson, W. 1997-2012. "Are the Narratives of Paul's Conversion Repetitious and Contradictory?" ChristianCourier.Com. *http://www.christiancourier.com/ articles/842-are-the-narratives-of-pauls-conversion-repetitious-and-contradictory*.

Jansen, John Frederick. 1967. *No Idle Talk*. Richmond, Va.: John Knox.

———. 1993. *"Glossolalia."* In *The Oxford Companion to the Bible,* edited by Bruce M Metzger and Michael D. Coogan, 255. Oxford: Oxford University Press.

Jarvis, Cynthia A. 1988. "Matthew 28: 1-10." *Interpretation* 42(1): 63-68.

Jenkins, Allan K. 1983. "Young Man or Angel?" *Expository Times.* 94(8): 237-40.

Jensen, P. F. 1970. "History and the Resurrection of Jesus Christ - III." *Colloquium* 3(4): 343-54.

Jeremiah, David. 2013. *The Jeremiah Study Bible: What It Says. What It Means. What It Means for You.* Brentwood, Tenn.: Worthy.

Jeremias, Joachim. 1958. *Heiligengräber in Jesu Umwelt (Mt. 23,29; Lk. 11,47): Eine Untersuchung zur Volksreligion der Zeit Jesu.* Göttingen: Vandenhoeck & Ruprecht. [English title: *Holy Tombs in the Environment of Jesus (Matthew 23.29, Luke 11.47). A Study of the Folk Religion of Jesus' Time.*]1975. *Jerusalem in the Time of Jesus: An Investigation Into Economic and Social Conditions During the New Testament Period.* Philadelphia: Fortress Press.

———. 1966. *The Eucharistic Words of Jesus.* Philadelphia: Fortress Press.

———. 1967. *Theological Dictionary of the New Testament.* Volume 5. [Theologisches Woerterbuch zum Neuen Testament]. Translated and edited by Geoffrey W. Bromiley. 895-99. Grand Rapids: Eeerdmans.

———. 1971. *New Testament Theology.* New York: Charles Scribner's Sons.

Jevne, Charles Arthur. 1903. *The Physical Aspects of Christ's Resurrection.* B. D. Thesis, Chicago Theological Seminary.

Jocz, J. 1976. "Passover." In *The Zondervan Pictorial Encyclopedia of the Bible.* Volume Four, edited by Merrill C. Tenney, 605-11. Grand Rapids: Zondervan.

Johns, Loren L., and Douglas B. Miller. 1994. "The Signs as Witnesses in the Fourth Gospel: Reexamining the Evidence." *The Catholic Biblical Quarterly* 56 (3): 519-35.

Johnson, Benjamin A. 1965. "Empty Tomb Tradition in the Gospel of Peter." Th.D. diss. Harvard University Divinity School.

Johnson, Carl. 2007. "A Thursday Crucifixion Date? But Still an Interment on Friday as We Know?" *http://mb-soft.com/public/crucif.html*

Johnson, Franklin. 1896. *The Quotations of the New Testament from the Old Considered in the Light of General Literature.* Philadelphia: American Baptist Publication Society.

Johnson, Sherman E. 1960. *A Commentary on the Gospel According to St. Mark.* New York: Harper & Brothers.

Johnson, Timothy Luke. 1992a. *The Acts of the Apostles.* Collegeville: Liturgical Press.

———. 1992b. "Luke 24:1-11: The Not-So-Empty Tomb." *Interpretation* 46(1): 57-61.

———. 1996. *The Real Jesus: The Misguided Quest for the Historical Jesus and the Truth of the Traditional Gospels.* San Francisco: HarperSanFrancisco.

———. 1999. *The Writings of the New Testament: An Interpretation.* Minneapolis: Augsburg Fortress.

Jones, William. 1891. "The Story of the Resurrection of the Christ." *Methodist Review* 73(5): 765-73.

Jonge, Jan Henk de. 2013. "The Chronology of the Ascension Stories in Luke and Acts." *New Testament Studies* 59(2): 151-71.

Jonge, Matthijs J. de. 2008. "Mark 16:8 as a Satisfying Ending to the Gospel." In *Jesus, Paul, and Early Christianity Studies in Honor of Henk Jan de Jonge,* edited by Rieuwerd Buitenwerf, Harm W. Hollander and Johannes Tromp, 123-47. Leiden: Brill.

Josephus. (1867) 1960. *Complete Works of Flavius Josephus.* Edinburgh, Scotland. Reprinted as *Josephus, Complete Works.* Translated by William Whiston. Grand Rapids: Kregel. Citations refer to the Kregel edition.

———. 1926. *Life against Apion.* Translated by H. S. J. Thackeray. Cambridge: Harvard University Press.

Juel, Donald H. 1999. *The Gospel of Mark*. Nashville: Abingdon.

Just, Arthur A., ed. 2003. *Ancient Christian Commentary on Scripture: New Testament III Luke*. Downers Grove: InterVarsity Press.

Kaiser, Walter C., Peter H. Davids, F. F. Bruce, and Manfred T. Brauch. 1996. *Hard Sayings of the Bible*. Downers Grove: InterVarsity Press.

Kane, J. Herbert. 1971. *Who Emptied the Tomb?* Chicago: Moody.

Kapic, Kelly, M. 2005. "Receiving Christ's Priestly Benediction: A Biblical, Historical, and Theological Exploration of Luke 24:50-53." *Westminster Theological Journal* 67(2): 247-60.

Karris, Robert J. 1986. "Luke 23:47 and the Lucan View of Judas' Death." *Journal of Biblical Literature* 86(105): 65-74.

Kassin, Saul M., V. Anne Tubb, Harmon M. Hosch, and Amina Memon. 2001. "On the 'General Acceptance' of Eyewitness Testimony Research: A New Survey of the Experts." *American Psychologist* 56(5): 405-16.

Kaufman, Gordon D. 1968. *Systematic Theology: A Historic Perspective*. New York: Charles Scribner's Sons.

Kearney, Peter J. 1980. "He Appeared to 500 Brothers (I Cor. XV 6)." *Novum Testamentum* 22(3): 264-84.

Keener, Craig S. 2003. *The Gospel of John: A Commentary* Volume II. Peabody, Mass.: Hendrickson.

———. 2009a. *The Historical Jesus of the Gospels*. Grand Rapids: Eerdmans.

———. 2009b. *The Gospel of Matthew: A Socio-Rhetorical Commentary*. Grand Rapids: Eerdmans.

———. 2011. *Miracles: The Credibility of the New Testament Accounts*. Two Volumes. Grand Rapids: Baker.

———. 2012. *Acts: An Exegetical Commentary*. Volume 1. Introduction And 1: 1 - 2: 47. Grand Rapids: Baker.

Keim, Theodor. 1883. *The History of Jesus of Nazara* Vol VI. Translated by Arthur Ransom. London: Williams & Norgate.

Kelhoffer, James A. 2000. *Miracle and Mission: The Authentication of Missionaries and Their Message in the Longer Ending in Mark.* Tübingen: Mohr Siebeck.

Kendall, Daniel, and Gerald O'Collins. 1992. "The Uniqueness of the Easter Appearances." *Catholic Biblical Quarterly* 54(2): 287-307.

Kennard, J. Spencer. 1948. "Hosanna" and the Purpose of Jesus." *Journal of Biblical Literature* 67(2): 171-76.

———. 1955. "The Burial of Jesus." *Journal of Biblical Literature* 74(4): 227-38.

Keresztes, Paul. 1989. *Imperial Rome and the Christians Vol. 1, From Herod the Great to About 200 A.D.* Lanham, Md.: University Press of America.

Kilpatrick, G. D. 1986. "Luke 24:42-43." *Novum Testamentum* 28(4): 306-08.

King, Charles. 1945. "The Outlines of New Testament Chronology." *Catholic Biblical Quarterly* 278(January-March): 145-47, 53.

King, Lauren A. 1995. "The New Testament Account of the Resurrection--Is It Credible?" *Religious Quaker Thought* 47(2): 5-38.

King, Rachel H. 1974. "The Torn Veil: A Sign of Sonship." *Christianity Today* 18(13): 722-23.

Kinman, Brent. 1995. *Jesus' Entry into Jerusalem: In the Context of Lukan Theology and the Politics of His Day.* Leiden: E.J. Brill.

———. 2005. "Jesus' Royal Entry into Jerusalem." *Bulletin for Biblical Research* 15(2): 223-60.

Kirby, Peter. 2005. "The Case Against the Empty Tomb." In *The Empty Tomb: Jesus Beyond the Grave*, edited by Robert M. Price and Jeffrey Jay Lowder, 233-60. Amherst, N.Y.: Prometheus.

Kistemaker, Simon J. 1993. *1 Corinthians: Exposition of the First Epistle to the Corinthians*. Grand Rapids: Baker.

Klassen, William. 1996. *Judas: Betrayer or Friend of Jesus?* Minneapolis: Fortress Press.

———. 1999. "The Authenticity of Judas' Participation in the Arrest of Jesus." In *Authenticating the Activities of Jesus*, edited by Bruce Chilton and Craig A. Evans, 389-410. Leiden: Brill.

Klawans, Jonathan. 2001. "Was Jesus' Last Supper a Seder?" *Bible Review* 17(5): 24-33, 47.

Klein, William W., Craig L. Blomberg, Robert L. Hubbard, and Kermit Allen Ecklebarger. 1993. *Introduction to Biblical Interpretation*. Dallas: Word Book.

Kloner, Amos. 1999. "Did a Rolling Stone Close Jesus' Tomb?" *Biblical Archaeology Review* 25(5): 23-29, 76.

Koester, Craig R. 1989. "Hearing, Seeing and Believing in the Gospel of John." *Biblica* 70(3): 327-48.

———. 2003. *Symbolism in the Fourth Gospel: Meaning, Mystery, Community*. Minneapolis: Fortress Press.

Koester, Helmut. 1980. "Apocryphal and Canonical Gospels." *Harvard Theological Review* 73 (1/2): 105-30.

Kokkinos, Nikos. 1989. "Crucifixion in A.D. 36: The Keystone for Dating the Birth of Jesus." In *Chronos, Kairos, Christos: Nativity and Chronological Studies Presented to Jack Finegan*, edited by Jerry Vardman and Edwin M. Yamauchi, 133-63. Winona Lake, Ind.: Eisenbrauns.

———. 2002. "Herod's Horrid Death." *Biblical Archaeology Review* 28(2): 28-31, 31-35, 62.

Komoszewski, J. Ed, James M. Sawyer, and Daniel B. Wallace. 2006. *Reinventing Jesus: How Contemporary Skeptics Miss the Real Jesus And Mislead Popular Culture*. Grand Rapids: Kregal.

Koskenniemi, Erkki, Kirsi Nisula, and Jorma Toppari. 2005. "Wine Mixed with Myrrh (Mark 15.23) and *Crurifragium* (John 19.31-32): Two Details of the Passion Narratives." *Journal of the Study of the New Testament* 27(4): 379-91.

Köstenberger, Andreas J. 2004a. *John: Baker Exegetical Commentary on the New Testament*. Grand Rapids: Baker.

———. 2004b. "'I Suppose' (*oimai*): The Conclusion of John's Gospel in Its Literary and Historical Context," In *The New Testament in Its First Century Setting. Essays on Context and Background in Honour of B.W. Winter on His 65th Birthday* edited by P.J. Williams, Andrew D. Clarke, Peter M. Head & David Instone-Brewer, 72-88. Grand Rapids / Cambridge: Eerdmans.

Köstenberger, Andreas J. and Justin Taylor. 2014. *The Final Days of Jesus: The Most Important Week of the Most Important Person Who Ever Lived*. Wheaton: Crossway.

Kraus, Hans-Joachim. 1993. *Psalms 60-150: A Continental Commentary*. Translated by Hilton C. Oswald. Minneapolis: Fortress Press.

Krodel, Gerhard A. 1986. *Acts*. Minneapolis: Augsbury.

Kruse, C. G. 1992. "Apostle." In *Dictionary of Jesus and the Gospels*, edited by Joel B. Green and Scot McKnight, 27-33. Downers Grove: InterVarsity Press.

Kuhnen, Frithjof. 1982. *Man and Land: An Introduction into the Problems of Agrarian Structure and Agrarian Reform*. Deutsche Welthungerhilfe. Saarbrücke. *http://www.professor-frithjof-kuhnen.de/publications/man-and-land/1-1-1-1.htm*.

Küng, Hans. 1976. *On Being a Christian*. Translated by Edward Quinn. New York: Pocket Books.

Kysar, Robert. 1993. "John's Anti-Jewish Polemic." *Bible Review* 9(1): 26-27.

Labahn, Michael. 2006. "Fishing for Meaning: The Miraculous Catch of Fish in John 21." In *Wonders Never Cease: The Purpose of Narrating Miracle Stories in the New Testament and its Religious Environment*, edited by

Michael Labahn and Bert Jan Lietaert Peerbolte, 125-45. London: T&T Clark.

Lachs, Samuel Tobias. 1987. *A Rabbinic Commentary on the New Testament: The Gospels of Matthew, Mark, and Luke.* Hoboken, N.J.: KTAV; New York: Anti-Defamation League.

Lake, Kirsopp. 1907. *The Historical Evidence for the Resurrection of Jesus Christ.* New York: G.P. Putnam's Sons.

———. 1912. "The Date of Herod's Marriage With Herodias and the Chronology of the Gospels." *The Expositor.* 4(8): 462-77.

———. 1921. "Simon, Cephas, Peter." *Harvard Theological Review* 14(1): 95-97.

———. 1933. "The Death of Judas." In *The Acts of the Apostles. The Beginnings of Christianity.* Volume V. edited by Kirsopp Lake and Henry J. Cadbury, 22-29. London: Macmillan.

Lampe, G. W. H. 1966. "Easter." In *The Resurrection: A Dialogue by G. W. H. Lampe and D. M. MacKinnon*, edited by William Purcell, 30-60. Philadelphia: Westminster Press.

Lane, William L. 1974. *The Gospel According to Mark.* Grand Rapids: Eerdmans.

Lange, John Peter. (1862) 1954. *Commentary on the Holy Scriptures.* Grand Rapids: Zondervan. (Citation refers to 1954 reprint)

Lasker, Daniel J. 2004. "The Date of the Death of Jesus: Further Reflections." *Journal of the American Oriental Society* 124 (1): 95-99.

Lavoie, Gilbert R. 2000. *Resurrected: Tangible Evidence Jesus Rose from the Dead, Shroud's Message Revealed 2000 Years Later.* Allen, Tex.: ThomasMore.

Law, Stephen. 2011. "Evidence, Miracles, and the Existence of Jesus." *Faith and Philosophy* 28(1): 129-51.

LeBec, A. A. 1925. "The Death of the Cross: A Physiological Study of the Passion of Our Lord Jesus Christ." *The Catholic Medical Guardian* [London] 3:126-32.

Le Donne, Anthony. 2009. *The Historiographical Jesus: Memory, Typology and the Son of David. Waco, Tex.:* Baylor University Press.

———. 2011. *The Historical Jesus: What Can We Know and How Can We Know It?* Grand Rapids: Eerdmans.

Lee, Alfred. 1958. "The Last Twelve Verses of Mark: A Study of Authenticity." Master's thesis, Harding College.

Lee, G. M. 1969. "The Guard at the Tomb." *Theology* 72 (April, No. 586): 169-75.

Lee, Witness. 1991. *The New Testament Recovery Version*. Anaheim, Calif.: Living Stream Ministry.

Lenowitz, Harris. 1998. *The Jewish Messiahs: From Galilee to Crown Heights*. New York: Oxford University Press.

Lenski, R. C. H. 1943. *The Interpretation of St. John's Revelation*. Columbus, Ohio: Wartberg Press.

Léon-Dufour, Xavier. 1971. *Resurrection and the Message of Easter*. Translated by R.N. Wilson. New York: Holt, Rinehart & Winston.

Leske, Adrian. 1998. "Matthew." In *The International Bible Commentary*, edited by William R. Farmer, 1253-330. Collegeville: Liturgical Press.

Lett, James. 1990. "A Field Guide to Critical Thinking." *Skeptical Inquirer Magazine*. Winter 1990. Available online at: http://www.scribd.com/doc/16779053/Critical-Thinking-Field-Guide-by-James-Lett

Levine, Amy-Jill. 1999. "Anti-Judaism and the Gospel of Matthew." In *Anti-Judaism and the Gospels*, edited by William R. Farmer, 9-36. Harrisburg, Pa.: Trinity Press International.

———. 2002. "Matthew, Mark, and Luke: Good News or Bad?" In *Jesus, Judaism, Christian Anti-Judaism,* edited by Paula Fredriksen and Adele Reinhartz, 77-98. Louisville: Westminster John Knox.

———. 2007. "Theory, Apologetic History: Reviewing Jesus' Jewish Context." *Australian Biblical Review* 55: 57-78

Lewis, C. S. 1952. *Mere Christianity.* New York: Macmillian.

Licona, Michael R. 2010. *The Resurrection of Jesus: A New Historiographical Approach.* Downers Grove: IVP Academic.

———. 2011. "Press Release: Michael Licona Response to Norm Geisler." In Parchment & Pen Blog. http://www.reclaimingthemind.org/blog/2011/09/press-release-michael-licona-response-to-norm-geisler.

Lightfoot, R. H. 1950. *The Gospel Message of St. Mark.* Oxford: Clarendon Press.

Lilly, Joseph L. 1940. "Alleged Discrepancies in the Gospel Accounts of the Resurrection" *The Catholic Biblical Quarterly* 2(2): 98-111.

Lindars, Barnabas. 1986. "Jesus Risen: Bodily Resurrection But No Empty Tomb." *Theology* 89(728): 90-96.

Locks, Steve. 2003. "Faith Alone." In: *Conundrums. Leaving Christianity.* http://www.users.globalnet.co.uk/~slocks/conundrums.html.

Lindsay, R.C.L, David F. Ross, J. Don Read, and Michael P. Toglia, eds. 2012. *The Handbook of Eyewitness Psychology Volume II: Memory for People.* New York: Routledge.

Lindsey, Hal. Apr 6, 2012. "The Week that Changed the World." The Hal Lindsey Report. http://www.itbn.org/index/detail/ec/dnYmxlNDpbyAyh67L2hIhFY-0ELmwAb.

Loewe, William P. 1996. *The College Student's Introduction to Christology.* Collegeville: Liturgical Press.

Loftus, Elizabeth. 2002. "Memory Faults and Fixes." *Issues in Science and Technology* 18(Summer): 41-50.

———. 2003. "Memory in Canadian Courts of Law." *Canadian Psychology* 44(3): 207-12.

Loisy, Alfred. 1907. *Les Évangiles Synoptiques*. Volume 1, Paris: Ceffonds (Haute-Marne): Chez l'Auteur.

Long, Thomas G. 1997. *Matthew*. Louisville: Westminster John Knox.

Longenecker, Richard N. 1981. "The Acts of the Apostles." In *The Expositor's Bible Commentary*, Vol. 9, edited by F. E. Gaebelein, Grand Rapids: Zondervan.

Lorenzen, Thorwald. 1995. *Resurrection and Discipleship: Interpretive Models, Biblical Reflections, Theological Consequences*. Maryknoll, New York: Orbis.

Lowder, Jeffrey Jay. 2000. "An Emotional Tirade Against Atheism." The Secular Web, *http://www.infidels.org/library/modern/jeff_lowder/zacharias.html*.

———.2005. "Historical Evidence and the Empty Tomb Story: A Reply to William Lane Craig." In *The Empty Tomb: Jesus Beyond the Grave*, edited by Robert M. Price and Jeffrey Jay Lowder, 261-306. Amherst, N.Y.: Prometheus.

Lowe, W. L. 1892. *The Hebrew Student's Commentary on Zechariah Hebrew and LXX*. London: Macmillan.

Lowery, D. K. 1984. "Lord's Day." In *Evangelical Dictionary of Theology*, edited by Walter A. Elwell, 648-50. Grand Rapids: Baker.

Luccock, Halford E. 1951. "The Gospel According to St. Mark." In *The Interpreter's Bible Volume 7*, edited by George Arthur Buttrick. 629-917. Nashville: Abingdon.

Lüdemann, Gerd. 1999. *The Great Deception and What Jesus Really Said and Did*. Amherst, N.Y.: Prometheus.

———. 2000. "Second Rebuttals." In *Jesus' Resurrection: Fact or Figment?: A Debate Between William Lane Craig & Gerd Lüdemann*, edited by Paul Copan and Ronald H. Tacelli, 60-62. Downers Grove: InterVarsity Press.

————. 2004. *The Resurrection of Christ: A Historical Inquiry.* Amherst, N.Y.: Prometheus.

————. 2005/6. "Will Secularism Survive." *Free Inquiry* 25: 35.

————. 2009. "The First Three Years of Christianity." *Toronto Journal of Theology* 25(1): 19-40.

Lunn, Nicholas. 2009. "Jesus, the Ark, and the Day of Atonement: Intertextual Echoes in John 19:38-20:18." *Journal of the Evangelical Theological Society* 52(4): 731-46.

Lyons, William John. 2004. "On the Life and Death of Joseph of Arimathea." *Journal for the Study of the Historical Jesus* 2(1): 29-53.

Luz, Ulrich. 2005a. *Studies in Matthew.* Translated by Rosemary Selle. Grand Rapids: Eerdmans.

————. 2005b. *Matthew.* 21-28. Translated by Rosemary Selle. Philadelphia: Augsburg Fortress.

Maas, A. J. 1898. *The Gospel According to Saint Matthew.* St. Louis: B. Herder.

MacArthur, John. 1989. *The MacArthur New Testament Commentary Matthew 24-28.* Chicago: Moody.

————. 2005. *The MacArthur Bible Commentary.* Nashville: Thomas Nelson.

Maccoby, Hyam, 1986. *The Mythmaker: Paul and the Invention of Christianity.* New York: Harper & Row.

————. 1992. *Judas Iscariot and the Myth of Jewish Evil. New* York: Free Press.

Macgregor, G. H. C. 1954. "The Acts of the Apostles." In *The Interpreter's Bible,* Volume IX, edited by George Arthur Buttrick. 1-353. Nashville: Abingdon.

Mack, Burton L. 1991. *A Myth of Innocence: Mark and Christian Origins.* Philadelphia: Fortress Press.

Mackay, Cameron. 1963. "The Third Day." *The Church Quarterly Review* 164(July/September): 289-99.

Mackinnon, D. M. 1967. "Sacrament and Communal Meal." In *Studies in the Gospels: Essays in Memory of R. H. Lightfoot,* edited by D. E. Nineham, 201-07. Oxford: Basil Blackwell.

MacQuarrie, John. 1977. *Principles of Christian Theology* 2nd edition. New York: Charles Scribner's.

Madison, Leslie P. 1963. *Problems of Chronology in the Life of Christ.* Unpublished Th.D. diss., Dallas Theological Seminary.

Magness, Jodi. 2005. "Ossuaries and the Burial of Jesus and James." *Journal of Biblical Literature* 124(1): 121-54.

Maier, Paul L. 1989. "The Date of the Nativity and the Chronology of Jesus' life." In *Chronos, Kairos, Christos: Nativity and Chronological Studies Presented to Jack Finegan,* edited by Jerry Vardaman and Edwin M. Yamauchi, 113-30. Winona Lake, Ind.: Eisenbrauns.

Maile, John F. 1986. "The Ascension in Luke-Acts." *Tyndale Bulletin* 37: 29-59.

Malina, Bruce J. 1993. *The New Testament World Insights From Cultural Anthropology.* Rev. ed. Louisville: Westminster John Knox.

———. 2001. *The New Testament World: Insights From Cultural Anthropology* 3rd ed. Louisville: Westminster John Knox.

Malina, Bruce J. and Richard L. Rohrbaugh. 1998. *Social-Science Commentary on the Gospel of John.* Minneapolis: Fortress Press.

———. 2003a. *Social-Science Commentary on the Synoptic Gospels* 2nd ed. Minneapolis: Fortress Press.

———. 2003b. *Social-Science Commentary on the Gospel of John.* Minneapolis: Fortress Press.

Mann, C. S. 1986. *Mark: A New Translation with Introduction and Commentary.* The Anchor Bible, Volume 27. Garden City, N.Y.: Doubleday.

Manson, T. W. 1951. "The Cleansing of the Temple." *Bulletin of the John Rylands Library* 33(2): 271-82.

Maples, Kevin. 2007. "The Function of Paschal Allusions in John's Crucifixion Narrative: An Examination of John's Typological Depiction of the Death of Jesus." Master's thesis, Southeastern Baptist Theological Seminary.

Mariottini, Claude F. 2006. "Republicans v. Democrats = Old Testament v. New Testament." August 7, 2006. Dr. Claude Mariottini - Professor of Old Testament (blog), accessed February 27, 2011. *http://doctor. claudemariottini.com/2006_08_01_archive.html*

Marsh, Gideon W. B. 1908. *Messianic Philosophy: An Historical and Critical Examination of the Evidence for the Existence, Death, Resurrection, Ascension, and Divinity of Jesus Christ.* London: Sands.

Marshall, I. Howard. 1973. "The Resurrection of Jesus in Luke." *Tyndale Bulletin* 24: 55-98.

———. 1978. *The Gospel of Luke: A Commentary on the Greek text.* Grand Rapids: Eerdmans.

———. 1980. *The Acts of the Apostles.* Grand Rapids: Eerdmans.

———. 2007. *The Book Acts.* Downers Grove: InterVarsity Press.

Martin, Don. 2013. "Greek, How Should a Knowledge of it be Viewed?" Bible Truths, *www.bibletruths.net/Archives/BTAR323.htm.*

Martin, James. April 20, 2011. "Why Did Judas Do It?" Huff Post Religion http://www.huffingtonpost.com/rev-james-martin-sj/why-did-judas-betray-jesus_b_851613.html

Martin, Michael. 2011. "Skeptical Perspectives on Jesus' Resurrection." In *The Blackwell Companion to Jesus,* edited by Delbert Burkett, 285-300. Malden, Mass.: Wiley-Blackwell.

Martin, Raymond A. 1995. *Studies in the Life and Ministry of the Historical Jesus.* Lanham: University Press of America.

Marxsen, Willi. 1990. *Jesus and Easter: Did God Raise the Historical Jesus From the Dead?* Translated by Victor Paul Furnish. Nashville: Abingdon.

Mastin, B. A. 1969. "The Date of Triumphal Entry." *New Testament Studies* 16 (1): 76-82.

Matson, Dave. 1997 (November-December). "On the Matter of Proof." *The Skeptical Review Online*, *http://www.theskepticalreview.com/ tsrmag/976proof.html*.

Matson, Mark A. 1992. "The Contribution of the Temple Cleansing by the Fourth Gospel." *Society of Biblical Literature Seminar Papers* 31: 489-506.

McBride, Dennis. 1996. *The Gospel of Mark: A Reflective Commentary.* Dublin: Dominican Publications.

McCane, Byron R. 1999. "'Where No One Had Yet Been Laid': The Shame of Jesus' Burial." In *Authenticating the Activities of Jesus*, edited by Bruce Chilton and Craig A. Evans, 431-52. Leiden: E.J. Brill.

McDonald, Lee Martin, and Stanley E. Porter. 2000. *Early Christianity and Its Sacred Literature.* Peabody, Mass.: Hendrickson.

McDowell, Josh. 1981. *The Resurrection Factor.* Nashville: Thomas Nelson.

McDowell, Josh, and Don Stewart. 1980. *Answers to Tough Questions Skeptics Ask About the Christian Faith.* Nashville: San Bernardino, Calif.: Here's Life Publishers.

McEleney, N. J. 1977. "153 Great Fishes (John 21,11)—Gematriacal Atbash," *Biblica* 58 (3):411-17.

McGehee, Michael. 1986. "A Less Theological Reading of John 20:17." *Journal of Biblical Literature.* 105(2): 299-302.

McGlynn, Moyna. 2012. "Easter Sunday: Luke 24.13-49." *The Expository Times* 123(6): 285-87.

McIver, Robert K. 2012. "Eyewitnesses as Guarantors of the Accuracy of the Gospel Traditions in the Light of Psychological Research." *Journal of Biblical Literature* 131(3): 529-46.

McKenzie, John L. 1968. "The Gospel According to Matthew." In *The Jerome Bible Commentary*, edited by *Raymond E., Joseph A. Fitzmyer and Roland E. Murphy Brown*, 62-114. Englewood-Cliffs, N.J.: Prentice-Hall.

M'clintock, John and James Strong. (1873) 1969. "Jesus Christ." *Cyclopedia of Biblical, Theological, and Ecclesiastical Literature* Vol. IV. 873-901. New York: Harper. Reprint, New York: Arno Press. Citations refer to the Arno edition.

Meacham, William. 2009. "What Did John 'See and Believe' in the Tomb? Countless Easter Sermons and Many Bible Commentators May Have Got It Wrong." *The Expository Times* 120(7): 322-26.

Meeus, Jean. 2003. "The Maximum Possible Duration of a Total Solar Eclipse." *Journal of the British Astronomical Association*, 113(6), 343-48.

Meier, John P. 1977. "Two Disputed Questions in Matt 28:16-20." *Journal of Biblical Literature* 96(3): 407-24.

———. 1991. *Marginal Jew: Rethinking The Historical Jesus Volume One: The Roots of the Problem and the Person*. New York: Doubleday Anchor Bible Reference Library.

———. 1997. "The Circle of Twelve: Did it Exist During Jesus' Public Ministry?" *Journal of Biblical Literature* 116(4): 635-672.

Menken, M. J. J. 1984. "The References to Jeremiah in the Gospel According to Matthew." *Ephemerides Theologicae Lovanienses* 60(1): 5-24.

Mershman, Francis. 1912. "The Last Supper." In *The Catholic Encyclopedia* Vol. 14, 341-42. New York: Encyclopedia Press.

Metzger, Bruce M. 1981. *Manuscripts of the Greek Bible: An Introduction to Greek Palaeography*. New York: Oxford University Press.

Metzger, Bruce M. and Bart D. Ehrman. 2005. *The Text of the New Testament: Its Transmission, Corruption, And Restoration* 4th edition. New York: Oxford University Press.

Meyer, Eduard. 1923. *Ursprung und Anfänge des Christentums* Volume III. Stuttgart and Berlin: J.G. Gott'sche Buchandlung.

Meyer, Heinrich August Wilhelm. 1883. *Critical and Exegetical Handbook to the Acts of the Apostles.* Translated by Paton J. Gloag and William P. Dickson. New York: Funk & Wagnalls.

Michaels, J. Ramsey. 1993. "Peter." In *Dictionary of Paul and His Letters,* edited by Gerald F. Hawthorne and Ralph P. Martins, 701-03. Downers Grove: InterVarsity Press.

Middletown Bible Church. 2014. "Eating and Dressing." Bible Times and Customs. Middletown Bible Church. http://www.middletownbiblechurch.org/biblecus/biblec.htm.

Miller, Glenn. March 5, 1997. "Do the Resurrection Accounts Hopelessly Contradict One Another?" Christian-Thinktank, *http://www.christian-thinktank.com/ordorise.html.*

———. November 15, 2002. "Good Question . . . *is the Tomb Story Flawed Because the Term 'Rolled' is Used?"* Christian ThinkTank. *http://www.christian-thinktank.com/rocknroll.html.*

Miller, Susan. 2004. "'They Said Nothing to Anyone': The Fear and Silence of the Women at the Empty Tomb (Mk 16.1-8)." *Feminist Theology* 13(1): 77-90.

Milne, H. J. M., and T. C. Skeat. 1938. *Scribes and Correctors of the Codex Sinaiticus.* London: British Museum.

Minear Paul S. 1976. "'We Don't Know Where . . .' John 20:2." *Interpretation* 30(2): 125-39.

Mitchell, John. 1972. *City of Revelation: On the Proportion and Symbolic Numbers of the Cosmic Temple.* London: Garnstone Press.

———. 1988. *The Dimensions of Paradise: The Proportions and Symbolic Numbers of Ancient Cosmology.* London: Thames & Hudson.

M'Neile, Alan Hugh. (1915) 1961. *The Gospel According to St. Matthew.* London: Macmillan. Reprint of 1915 edition. Citation refer to the 1961 edition.

Moedder, Hermann. 1948. "Die Todesursache bei der Kreuzigung." *Stimmer der Zeit* 144: 50-9.

Moiser, Jeremy. 1995. "The Resurrection: Recent Official Pronouncements and Recent Exegesis." *Downside Review* 113(393): 235-47.

Montague, George T. 2010. *Companion God: A Cross-Cultural Commentary on the Gospel of Matthew*. New York: Paulist Press.

Montefiore, C. G. 1968. *The Synoptic Gospels In two volumes*. New York: KTAV.

Montefiore, Hugh. 1960. "When Did Jesus Die?" *The Expository Times* 72(2): 53-54.

Moore, George Foot. 1971. *Judaism in the First Centuries of the Christian Era: The Age of the Taanaim*, vol. I. New York: Schocken.

Morison, Frank [pseudonym for Albert Henry Ross]. 1930. *Who Moved the Stone?* London: Faber & Faber.

Morris, Leon. 1971. *The Gospel According to John*. Grand Rapids: Eerdmans.

———. 1995. *Apocryphon of John*. Grand Rapids: Eerdmans.

Moshe, Beth. 1987. *Judaism's Truth Answers the Missionaries*. New York: Bloch.

Mosse, Martin. 2007. *The Three Gospels: New Testament History Introduced by the Synoptic Problem*. Milton Keynes, England: Paternoster.

Motyer, S. 1987. "The Rending of the Veil: A Markan Pentecost?" *New Testament Studies* 33(1): 155-57.

Moule, C. F. D. 1957. "Expository Problems: The Ascension - Acts i. 9." *The Expository Times* 68: 205-09.

———. 1965. *The Gospel According to Mark*. Cambridge: Cambridge University Press.

Moulton, J. H., and G. Milligan. (1930) 1997. *Vocabulary of the Greek Testament*. London: Hodder & Stoughton. Reprint, Peabody, Mass.: Hendrickson. Citations refer to the Hendrickson edition.

Moxnes, Halvor. 1988. *The Economy of the Kingdom.* Philadelphia: Fortress Press.

Muncaster, Ralph O. 2000a. *What is the Proof for the Resurrection?* Eugene, Ore.: Harvest House.

———. 2000b. *How Do We Know Jesus is God?* Eugene, Ore.: Harvest House.

Murphy-O'Connor, Jerome. 1981. "Tradition and Redaction in 1 Cor 15:3-7." *Catholic Biblical Quarterly* 43(4): 582-89.

Myllykoski, Matti. 2002. "What Happened to the Body of Jesus?" In *Fair Play: Diversity and Conflicts in Early Christianity. Essays in Honour of Heikki Räisänen,* edited by Kari Syreeni, 43-82. Leiden: Brill.

———. 2006. "Being There: The Function of the Supernatural in Acts 1-12." In *Wonders Never Cease: The Purpose of Narrating Miracle Stories in the New Testament and Its Religious Environment,* edited by Michael Labahn and Bert Jan Lietaert Peerbolte, 146-79. London: T&T Clark.

Naland, John K. 1988. "The First Easter: The Evidence for the Resurrection Evaluated." *Free Inquiry* 8(2): 10-20.

Naluparayil, Jacob Chacko. 2000. *The Identity of Jesus in Mark: An Essay On Narrative Christology.* Jerusalem: Franciscan Printing Press.

Nathan, Bruce. 1980. "An Isogogical and Exegetical Study of Marx 16:9-20." Master's thesis, Concordia Theological Seminary.

National Oceanic and Atmospheric Administration (NOAA), The. June 9, 2009. "National Weather Service Glossary." http://www.weather.gov/glossary/

Neirynck, Frans. 1972. "The Uncorrected Historic Present in Lk. XXIV.12." *Ephemerides Theologicae Lovanienses* 48(3-4) 548-53.

———. 1990. "John 21." *New Testament Studies* 36(3): 321-36.

Nelson, Glen. 2005. *Revelation* in the Writings of St. Paul: Paul's Idiosyncratic Use of *Apokalyps. Biblical Theology: for Study and Life. http://www3. sympatico.ca/glancy.nelson/nt-paul-and-apocalyptic.htm.*

New International Version (NIV). 1978. Grand Rapids: Zondervan.

Newman, Barclay A., and Eugene A. Nida. 1972. *A Handbook on the Acts of the Apostles.* New York: United Bible Societies.

Newman, Barclay M., and Philip C. Stine. 1988. *A Handbook on the Gospel of Matthew.* New York: United Bible Societies.

Neyrey, Jerome H. 1988. *The Resurrection Stories.* Wilmington, Del.: Michael Glazier.

———. 1993. "Limited Good." In *Handbook of Biblical Social Values,* edited by John J. Pilch and Bruce J. Malina, 122-27. Peabody, Mass.: Hendrickson.

———. 2006. *The Gospel of John.* Cambridge: Cambridge University Press

Nichol, Francis D. ed. *The Seventh-day Adventist Bible Commentary.* Volume 5. Hagerstown, Md.: Review & Herald.

Nicholas, Wyatt. 1990. "Supposing Him to be the Gardener' (John 20, 15): A Study of the Paradise Motif in John." *Zeitschrift fur die Neutestamentliche Wissenschaft*: 81(Issues 1/2): 21-38.

Nodet, Étienne. 2010. "On Jesus' Last Supper." *Biblica* 91(3): 348-69.

Nolland. John. 2005. *The Gospel of Matthew: A Commentary on the Greek Text (New International Greek Testament Commentary).* Grand Rapids: Eerdmans.

Norris, John Pilkington. 1877. *A Key to the Narratives of the Four Gospels.* London: Rivingtons.

Nourse, Edward Everett. 1911. "New Testament Chronology." In *The New International Encyclopædia.* Volume 14, edited by Daniel Coit Gilman, Harry Thurston Peck, and Frank Moore Colby, 484-88. New York: Dodd, Mead & Company.

Novakovic, Lidija. 2012. *Raised From the Dead According to Scripture*. London: Bloomsberry T&T Clark.

O'Collins, Gerald. 1988a. "Did Jesus Eat the Fish (Luke 24:42-43)?" *Gregorianum* 69(1): 65-76.

———. 1988b. "The Fearful Silence of Three Women (Mark 18:8c)." *Gregorianum* 69(3): 489-503.

———. 1993. *The Resurrection of Jesus Christ: Some Contemporary Issues*. Milwaukee, Wisc.: Marquette University Press.

———. 1999. "Resurrection and New Creation." *Dialog* 38(1): 15-19.

O'Collins, Gerald, and Daniel Kendall. 1987. "Mary Magdalene As Major Witness to Jesus' Resurrection." *Theological Studies* 48(4): 631-46.

O'Connell, Jake H. 2010. "The Reliability of the Resurrection Narratives." *European Journal of Theology* 19(2): 141-52.

O'Day, Gail R. 1995. "The Gospel of John." In *The New Interpreter's Bible* Vol 9, edited by Leander E. Keck et al., 493-865. Nashville: Abingdon.

Ogg, George. 1940. *The Chronology of the Public Ministry of Jesus*. Cambridge: Cambridge University Press.

O'Herlihy, Donal J. 1946. "The Year of the Crucifixion." *Catholic Biblical Quarterly* 8(3):298-305.

Okure, Teresa. 1998. "John." In *The International Bible Commentary: A Catholic and Ecumenical Commentary for the Twenty-First Century*, edited by William R. Farmer, 1438-502. Collegeville, Minn.: Liturgical Press.

Olmstead, A. T. 1942. "The Chronology of Jesus' Life." *Anglican Theological Review* 24(1): 1-26.

Opočenská Jana. 1997. "Women at the Cross, at Jesus' Burial, and After the Resurrection Mk 15:40; 16:10." *Reformed World* 47(1): 40-48.

Ordal, Z. J. 1923. *The Resurrection of Jesus, An Historical Fact.* Minneapolis: Augsburg.

O'Rahilly, A. 1941. "The Burial of Christ: Peter and John at the Tomb." *Irish Ecclesiastical Record* 59:150-71.

O'Reilly, Bill, and Martin Dugard. 2013. *Killing Jesus: A History.* New York: Henry Holt.

Oropeza, B. J. 2010. "Judas' Death and Final Destiny in the Gospels and Earliest Christian Writings." *Neotestamentica* 44(2): 342-61.

Orr, James. 1908. *The Resurrection of Jesus.* London: Hodder & Stoughton.

Orr, William F. and James Arthur Walther. 1976. *I Corinthians: The Anchor Bible.* New York: Doubleday.

Osborne, Grant R. 2006. *The Hermeneutical Spiral: A Comprehensive Introduction to Biblical Interpretation.* Downers Grove: IVP Academic.

———. 2010. *Matthew: Exegetical Commentary on the New Testament.* Grand Rapids: Zondervan.

Osborne, Kenan B. 1997. *The Resurrection of Jesus: New Considerations For Its Theological Interpretation.* New York: Paulist Press.

Osiek, Carolyn. 1993. "The Women at the Tomb: What Are They Doing There?" *Ex Auditu* 9: 97-107.

Osler, Mark William. 2009. *Jesus on Death Row: The Trial of Jesus and American Capital Punishment.* Nashville: Abingdon.

O'Toole, Robert F. 1990. "The Parallels Between Jesus and Moses." *Biblical Theology Bulletin* 1990 20(1): 22-29.

———. 1992. "Last Supper." In *Anchor Bible Dictionary.* Volume 4, edited by David Noel Freedman, 234. New York: Doubleday.

Owens, O. T. 1988. "One Hundred and Fifty Three Fishes." *Expository Times* 100(2): 52-4.

Oygen, Gert van. 2003. "Irony as Propaganda in Mark 15:39? In *Persuasion and Dissuasion in Early Christianity, Ancient Judaism, and Hellenism.* edited by Pieter W. van der Horst, Maarten J. J. Menken, Joop F. M. Smit and Gert van Oygen, 125-142. Leuven: Peeters.

Packham, Richard. 1998. "The Man With No Heart: Miracles and Evidence." The Secular Web, *http://www.infidels.org/library/modern/richard_packham/heart.html.*

Page, Donald Eugene. 1969. *ΗΓἐΡΘΗ the Historicity of the Resurrection of Jesus.* New York: The General Theological Seminary. [Paper in partial fulfillment of the requirements for the Degree of Bachelor of Sacred Theology]

Pagels, Elaine. 1979. *The Gnostic Gospels.* New York: Random House.

———. 1995. *The Origin of Satan.* New York: Vintage Books.

Pagels, Elaine, and Karen L. King. 2007. *Reading Judas: The Gospel of Judas and the Shaping of Christianity.* New York: Penguin.

Palmer, Darryl. 1974. "The Resurrection of Jesus and the Mission of the Church." In *Reconciliation and Hope: New Testament Essays On Atonement and Eschatology,* edited by Robert Banks, 205-23. Grand Rapids: Eerdmans.

Parambi, Baby. 2003. *The Discipleship of the Women in the Gospel According to Matthew: an Exegetical Theological Study of Matt 27:51b-56, 57-61 and 28:1-10."* Roma: Editrice Pontificia.

Parker, D. C. 2008. *An Introduction to the New Testament Manuscripts and Their Texts.* Cambridge: Cambridge University Press.

Parker, Pierson. 1967. "Once More, Acts and Galatians." *Journal of Biblical Literature* 86(2): 175-182.

Parsons, Mikeal C. 1987. *The Departure of Jesus in Luke-Acts: the Ascension Narratives in Context.* Sheffield, England: Journal for the Study of the New Testament Supplement Series 21.

———. 2008a. *Acts*. Grand Rapids: Baker.

———. 2008b. "Exegesis "by the Numbers": Numerology and the New Testament." *Perspectives in Religious Studies* 35(1): 25-43.

Patte, Daniel. 1996. *The Gospel According to Matthew: A Structural Commentary on Matthew's Gospel*. Valley Forge, Pa.: Trinity Press International.

Peake, Arthur S. 1920. *A Critical Introduction to the New Testament*. New York: Charles Scribner's Sons.

Pennells, Stephen. 1983. "The Spear Thrust: (Mt. 27.49b, v. I / Jn 19.34)." *Journal for the Study of the New Testament* 6(No. 19): 99-115.

Penrod, Steven, Elizabeth Loftus, and John Winkler. 1982. "The Reliability of Eyewitness Testimony: A Psychological Perspective." In *The Psychology of the Courtroom*, edited by Norbert L. Kerr and Robert M. Bray. 119-61. New York: Academic Press.

Perkins, Pheme. 1992. "I Have Seen the Lord" (John 20:18): Women Witnesses to the Resurrection." *Interpretation* 46(1): 31-41.

———. 2012. *First Corinthians*. Grand Rapids: Baker.

Perrin, Norman. 1977a. *The Resurrection According to Matthew, Mark, and Luke*. Minneapolis: Fortress Press.

———. 1977b. *The Resurrection Narratives: A New Approach*. London: SCM.

Perrin, Norman, and Dennis C. Duhing. 1982. *The New Testament: An Introduction*. 2nd ed. New York: Harcourt Brace Jovanovich.

Perry, John M. 1986. "The Three Days in the Synoptic Passion Predictions." *Catholic Biblical Quarterly* 48(4): 637-54.

Perry, Michael C. 1959. *The Easter Enigma: An Essay on the Resurrection with Special Reference to the Data of Psychical Research*. London: Farber & Farber.

Pervo, Richard I. 2009. *Acts: A Commentary*. Minneapolis: Fortress Press.

Petersen, Norman R. 1980. "When Is the End Not the End? Literary Reflections on the Ending of Mark's Narrative." *Interpretation* 34(2): 151-66.

Peterson, David G. 2009. *The Acts of the Apostles.* Grand Rapids: Eerdmans.

Peterson, Eugene H. 2002. "Resurrection Breakfast: John 20:1-14." *Journal for Preachers* 25(3): 13-17.

Pfleiderer, Otto. 1887. *Das Urchristentum, Seine Schriften and Lehren, in Geschichtlichem Zusammenhang Beschrieben.* Berlin: Georg Reimer.

Phillips, John. 2002. *Exploring 1 Corinthians: An Expository Commentary.* Grand Rapids: Kregel.

Phillips, Wendell. 1975. *An Explorer's Life of Jesus.* New York: Morgan Press.

Pilch, John J. 1998. "Appearances of the Risen Jesus in Cultural Context: Experiences on Alternate Reality." *Biblical Theology Bulletin* 28(2): 52-60.

————. 2002. "Paul's Ecstatic Trance Experience Near Damascus in Acts of the Apostles." *Hervormde Teologiese Studies* 58(2): 690-707.

————. 2004. *Visions and Healing in the Acts of the Apostles: How the Early Believers Experienced God.* Collegeville: Liturgical Press

————. 2005. "Paul's Call to be a Holy Man (Apostle): In His Own Words and In Other Words." *Hervormde Teologiese Studies* 61(1/2): 371-83.

Plevnik, Joseph. 1980. "The Origin of the Easter Faith according to Luke." *Biblica* 61(4): 492-508.

Plummer, Alfred. 1922. *A Critical and Exegetical Commentary on the Gospel According to S. Luke* 4th ed. Edinburgh: T&T Clark.

Plummer, Robert L. 2005. "Something Awry in the Temple? The Rendering of the Temple Veil and Early Jewish Sources that Report Unusual Phenomena in the Temple Around AD 30." *Journal of the Evangelical Theological Society* 48(2): 301-16.

Polhill, John B. 1992. *Acts, New American Commentary*. Nashville: Broadman.

Pokorný, Petr. 1987. *Genesis of Christology: Foundations of the New Testament*. Edinburgh: T&T Clark.

Pope, Marvin H. 1988. "Hosanna—What It Really Means." *Bible Review* 4(2): 16-25.

Powell, Baden. 1859. *Order of Nature: Considered in Reference to the Claims of Revelation*. London: Longman, Brown, Green, Longmans, & Roberts.

Powell, Mark Allan. 1998. *Jesus as a Figure in History*. Louisville: Westminster/ John Knox.

Pratt, John P. 1991. "Newton's Date for the Crucifixion." *Quarterly Journal of Royal Astronomical Society* 32(September): 301-04.

Pregeant, Russell. 2009. *Encounter with the New Testament: An Interdisciplinary Approach*. Minneapolis: Fortress Press.

Price, J. Randall. 2003. "Historical Problems with a First-Century Fulfillment of the Olivet Discourse." In *The End of Times Controversy*, edited by Tim LaHaye and Thomas Ice, 377-98. Eugene, Ore.: Harvest House.

Price, Robert M. 1985. "Ancient Evidence for the Life of Jesus: Historical Records of His Death and Resurrection by Gary R. Habermas. Reviewed by Robert M. Price." *Religious Humanism* 19(3): 147-50.

———. 1989. "Jesus' Burial in a Garden: The Strange Growth of the Tradition." *Religious Traditions* 12:17-30.

———. 1993. *Beyond Born Again: Towards Evangelical Maturity*. Eugene, Ore.: Hypatia Press.

———. 1995. "Apocryphal Apparitions:1 Corinthians 15:3-11 as a Post-Pauline Interpolation." *Journal of Higher Criticism* 2/2 (Fall 1995): 69-99. Reprinted in: *The Empty Tomb: Jesus Beyond the Grave*, edited by Robert M. Price and Jeffrey Jay Lowder, 69-104.

———. 2003. *The Incredible Shrinking Son of Man: How Reliable is the Gospel Tradition?* Amherst, N.Y.: Prometheus.

―――. 2004. "Reviews: James Patrick Holding's *The Impossible Faith or, How Not to Start an Ancient Religion.*" http://www.robertmprice. mindvendor.com/rev_holding.htm

Prince, Deborah Thompson. 2005. *Vision of the Risen Jesus: The Rhetoric of Certainty in Luke 24 and Acts 1.* PhD diss. Notre Dame, Indiana.

―――. 2007. "The 'Ghost' of Jesus: Luke 24 in Light of Ancient Narratives of Post-Mortem Apparitions." *Journal for the Study of the New Testament* 29(3): 287-301.

Pyysiäinen, Ilkka. 2007. "The Mystery of the Stolen Body: Exploring Christian Origins." In *Explaining Christian Origins and Early Judaism: Contributions From Cognitive and Social Science*, edited by Petri Luomanen, Ilkka Pyysiäinen, and Risto Uro, 57-72.Leiden: Brill.

Quast, Kevin. 1989. *Peter and the Beloved Disciple: Figures for a Community in Crisis. Journal for the Study of the New Testament*, Supplement. Series. 32. Sheffield: JSOT Press.

Radic, Randall. n.d. "Jude 12-15. Grace Notes." accessed February 4, 2014. *http://www.realtime.net/~wdoud/jude/jude06.html.*

Ralston, Thomas N. 1924. *Elements of Divinity*, edited by T. O. Summers. New York: Abingdon.

Ramsey, A. Michael. 1946. *The Resurrection of Christ.* London: Longmans, Green.

Ranke-Heinemann, Uta. 1994. *Putting Away Childish Things.* Translated by Peter Heinegg San Francisco: HarperSanFrancisco.

Redman, Judith C. S. 2010. "How Accurate Are Eyewitnesses? Bauckham and the Eyewitnesses in the Light of Psychological Research." *Journal of Biblical Literature* 129(1): 177-97.

Reece, S. 2002. "Seven Stades to Emmaus." *New Testament Studies* 48(2): 266-64.

Reed, David A. 2005. "Saving Judas"—A Social Scientific Approach to Judas' Suicide in Matthew 27:3-10." *Biblical Theology Bulletin* 35(2): 51-59.

Reeves, Keith H. 1998. "They Worshipped Him, And They Doubted: Matthew 28:17." *The Bible Translator* 49(3): 344-49.

Reicke, Bo. 1975. *The New Testament Era: The World of the Bible from 500 B.C. to 100 A.D.* Translated by D.E. Green. Philadelphia: Fortress Press.

Reid, Barbara E. 2005. *The Gospel According to Matthew.* Collegeville: Liturgical Press.

Reimarus, Hermann Samuel. 1971. *Reimarus: Fragments*, edited by Charles H. Talbert and Translated by Ralph S. Fraser. Philadelphia: Fortress Press.

Reiner, Erica. 1968. "Thirty Pieces of Silver." *Journal of the American Oriental Society* 88:186-90.

Reinhold, Roy E. n.d. "Jesus (Yeshua) was Crucified on a Wednesday Afternoon Part 2. Prophecy Truths." http://ad2004.com/prophecytruths/Articles/Prophecy/3dayspt2.html

Renan, Ernst. 1864. *The Life of Jesus.* Paris: Trübner.

———. 1898. *The Apostles: Including the Period from the Death of Jesus Until the Greater Missions of Paul.* Translated by Joseph Henry Allen. Boston: Roberts Brothers.

Rensberger, David. K. 1988. *Johannine Faith and Liberating Community.* Philadelphia: Westminster John Knox.

Réville, Albert. 1894. "The Resurrection of Jesus." *The New World: A Quarterly Review of Religion, Ethics and Theology.* Volume 3(September): 498-527.

———. 1897. *Jésus de Nazareth* vol. 2. Paris: P. Fischbacher.

Richards, John Evan and Aiyar, S. Srinivasa. 1915. *The Illegality of the Trial of Jesus: The Legality of the Trial of Jesus.* N.Y.: Platt & Peck.

Richardson, Peter. 2006. "The Beginnings of Christian Anti-Judaism, 70-c. 235." In *The Cambridge History of Judaism*, edited by Steven T. Katz, 244-58. Cambridge: Cambridge University Press.

Riddle, Donald W. 1940. "The Cephas-Peter Problem, and a Possible Solution." *Journal of Biblical Literature* 59(2): 169-80.

Robertson, Archibald Thomas. 1930a. *Word Pictures in the New Testament Volume I. The Gospel According to Matthew and the Gospel According to Mark*. Nashville: Broadman.

———. 1930b. *Word Pictures in the New Testament Volume III. The Acts of Apostles*. Nashville: Broadman.

Robinson, Edward. 1993. "The Resurrection and Ascension of Our Lord." *Bibliotheca Sacra* 150(Jan-March): 9-34. [Reprint of *Biblica Sacra* 2 No. 5 (1845): 162-90.]

Robinson, J. A. T. 1976. *Redating the New Testament*. London: SCM.

Robinson, James M. 2006. *The Secrets of Judas; The Story of the Misunderstood Disciple and His Lost Gospel*. San Francisco: HarperSanFrancisco.

Robinson, John T. 1985. *The Priority of John*, edited by J. F. Coakley. London: SCM Press.

Ross, J. M. 1987. "The Genuineness of Luke 24:12." *Expository Times* 98(4): 107-08.

Routledge, Robin. 2002. "Passover and the Last Supper." *Tyndale Bulletin* 53(2): 203-21.

Ruckstuhl, Eugen. 1965. *Chronology of the Last Days of Jesus*. Translated by Victor J. Drapela. New York: Desclee.

Rusk, Roger. 1974, March 29. "The Day He Died." *Christianity Today* 18(3): 4-6/720-22

Ryrie, Charles Caldwell. 1976. *The Ryrie Study Bible: New American Standard Translation*. Chicago: Moody.

Saarnivaara, Uuras 1954. "The Date of the Crucifixion in the Synoptics and John." *Lutheran Quarterly* 6(2): 157-60.

Salvoni, Fausto. 1979. "The So-Called Jesus Resurrection Proof (John 20:7)." *Restoration Quarterly* 12 (1/2): 72-76.

Samuelsson, Gunnar. 2011. *Crucifixion In Antiquity: An Inquiry Into the Background of the New Testament Terminology of Crucifixion.* Tübingen: Mohr Siebeck.

Sanders, E. P. 1985. *Jesus and Judaism.* Philadelphia: Fortress Press.

———. 1993. *The Historical Figure of Jesus.* London: Allen Lane.

———. 2000. "How Do We Know What We Know About Jesus." In *Jesus Two Thousand Years Later,* edited by James H. Charlesworth and Walter P. Weaver, 38-61. Harrisburg, Pa: Trinity Press International.

Sawicki, Marianne. 1988. "Recognizing the Risen Lord." *Theology Today* 44(4): 447-48.

———. 1994. *Seeing the Lord: Resurrection and early Christian practices.* Minneapolis: Fortress Press.

Schaeffer, Susan E. 1991. "The Guard at the Tomb (Gos. Pet. 8:28-11:49 and Matt 27:62-66; 28:2-4, 11-16): A Case of Intertextuality?" *Society of Biblical Literature Seminar Papers*, edited by Eugene H. Lovering, 499-507. Atlanta, Ga.: Scholars Press.

Schleiermacher, Friedrich. 1975. *The Life of Jesus,* edited by Jack C. Verheyden, and translated by S. Maclean Gilmour. Philadelphia: Fortress Press.

Schlier, Heinrich. 2008. *On the Resurrection of Jesus Christ.* Translated by Michael Sullivan. Rome: 30Giorni.

Schmiedel, Paul Wilhelm. 1903. "Resurrection-and Ascension-Narratives." In *Encyclopædia Biblica.* Vol. IV, edited by T. K. Cheyne and J. Sutherland Black, 4039-087. New York: Macmillan.

Schnabel, Eckhard J. 2012. *Acts: Zondervan Exegetical Commentary on the New Testament.* Grand Rapids: Zondervan.

Schnackenburg, Rudolf. 1982. *The Gospel According to St. John.* New York: Crossroads.

———. 1990. *The Gospel According to St. John.* Volume Three. Translated by Kevin Smyth. New York: Crossroads.

Schnelle, Udo. 2004. *Das Evangelium Nach Johannes.* Leipzig: Evangelische Verlagsanstalt.

Schneiders, Sandra M. 1983. "The Face Veil: A Johannine Sign (John 20:1-10)." *Biblical Theology Bulletin* 13(3): 94-97.

Schnelle, Udo. 2004. *Das Evangelium Nach Johannes.*Leipzig: Evangelische Verlagsanstalt.

Schonfield, Hugh J. 1974. *The Jesus Party.* New York: Macmillan.

Schreckenberg, H. 1982. "Josephus, Flavius." In *The International Standard Bible Encyclopedia,* edited by Geoffrey W. Bromily, 1132-133. Grand Rapids: Eerdmans.

Schreiber, J. 1981. "Die Bestattung Jesu: Redaktionsgeschichtliche Beobachtungen zu Mark 15:42-47 par." *Zeitschrift für die Neutestamentliche Wissenschaft* 72(3/4): 141-71.

Schweizer, Eduard. 1967. *The Lord's Last Supper According to the New Testament.* Translated by James M. Davis and edited by John Reumann. Philadelphia: Fortress Press.

———. 1977. *The Good News According to Matthew.* Atlanta: John Knox.

Scott, J. Martin C. 2003. "John." In *Eerdmans Commentary on the Bible,* edited by James D. G. Dunn and John W. Rogerson, 1161-212. Grand Rapids: Eerdmans.

Scroggie, W. Graham. 1948. *A Guide to the Gospels.* Old Tappan, New Jersey: Fleming H. Revell.

Seigle, Mario. 2006. "Centuries-Old Documents Show Evidence for a Wednesday Crucifixion." *The Good News: A Magazine*

of Understanding, http://www.ucg.org/doctrinal-beliefs/
centuries-old-documents-show-evidence-wednesday-crucifixion

Semmler, Carolyn, and Brewer, Neil. 2010. "Eyewitness Memory," In *The Cambridge Handbook of Forensic Psychology*, edited by Jennifer M. Brown and Elizabeth A. Campbell, 49-57. Cambridge: Cambridge University Press.

Senior, Donald. 1972. "The Fate of the Betrayer: A Redactional Study of Matthew XXVII, 3-10." *Ephemerides Theologicae Lovanienses* 48: 372-426.

———. 1976. "The Death of Jesus and the Resurrection of the Holy Ones (MT 27:51-53)." *Catholic Biblical Quarterly* 38(3): 312-29.

———. 1992. "Matthew's Account of the Burial of Jesus Mt 27, 57-61." In *The Four Gospels: Festschrift Frans Neirynck*. Volume II, edited by F. Van Segroeck, 1443-448. Leuven: Leuven University Press.

———. 1998. *Abingdon New Testament Commentaries: Matthew*. Nashville: Abingdon.

Shafto, G. R. H. 1930. *The Reality of the Resurrection*. New York: Fleming H. Revell.

Shamoun, Sam. n.d. "Responses to Understanding-Islam: The Resurrection Account." *http://www.answering-*islam.org/Responses/Learner/resurrection.htm.

Shanks, Hershel. 2008. "Emmaus: Where Christ Appeared." *Biblical Archaeology Review* 34(2): 41-50, 80.

Sheehan, Thomas. 1986. *The First Coming: How the Kingdom of God Became Christianity*. New York: Random House. The electronic edition 2000. http://www.infidels.org/library/modern/thomas_sheehan/firstcoming/two.html#e3.

Sheppard, W. J. Limmer. 1929. "The Resurrection Morning." *The Expository Times* 40(4):182-87.

Sigal, Gerald. 1981. *The Jew and the Christian Missionary: A Jewish Response to Missionary Christianity* New York: KTAV.

———. 2012. *The Resurrection Fantasy: Reinventing Jesus.* USA: Xlibris.

Simonetti, Manlio, ed. 2002. *Ancient Christian Commentary on Scripture: New Testament Ib Matthew 14-28.* Downers Grove: InterVarsity Press.

Singer, Tovia. 1998. "Zechariah 12." *Let's Get Biblical Study Guide.* Monsey, N.Y.: Outreach Judaism.

Sire, James W. 2006. *Why Good Arguments Often Fail.* Downers Grove: InterVarsity Press.

Skeat, T. C., and T. C. Elliott, eds. 2004. *The Collected Biblical Writings of T. C. Skeat.* Leiden: Brill.

Skinner, Christopher William. 2008. "John and Thomas: Gospels In Conflict? A Study In Johannine Characterization In Light of the Thomas Question." PhD diss. Catholic University of America.

Sleeper, C. Freeman. 1965. "Pentecost and Resurrection." *Journal of Biblical Literature* 84(4): 389-99.

Slick, Matthew J. 1995-2011a. "Extraordinary Claims Require Extraordinary Evidence." **CHRISTIAN APOLOGETICS & RESEARCH MINISTRY.** *http://carm.org/extraordinary-claims-require-extraordinary-evidence.*

———. 1995-2011b. "Hasn't The Bible Been Rewritten So Many Times That We Can't Trust It Anymore?" **CHRISTIAN APOLOGETICS & RESEARCH MINISTRY.** http://www.carm.org/questions/rewritten. htm

Slovenko, Ralph. 2009. *Psychiatry in Law/Law in Psychiatry* 2nd ed. New York: Routledge.

Smith, Barry D. 1991. "The Chronology of the Last Supper." *Westminster Theological Journal* 53(1): 29-45.

———. 1993. *Jesus' Last Passover Meal.* Lewiston, N.Y.: Edwin Mellen.

Smith, C. W. F. 1960. "No Time for Figs." *Journal of Biblical Literature* 79(4): 315-27.

———. 1962-1963. "Tabernacles in the Fourth Gospel and Mark." *New Testament Studies* 9(2):130-46.

Smith, D. Moody. 1988. "John." In *Harper's Bible Commentary*, edited by James L. Mays, 1044-076. San Francisco: Harper & Row.

Smith, Daniel A. 2010. "Seeing a Pneuma(tic Body): the Apologetic Interests of Luke 24:36-43)." *Catholic Biblical Quarterly* 72(4): 752-72.

Smith, Dennis Edwin. 2003. *From Symposium to Eucharist: The Banquet in the Early Christian World.* Minneapolis: Fortress Press.

Smith, Jay, Alex Chowdhry, Toby Jepson, and James Schaeffer. 2014. "101 Cleared-Up Contradictions in the Bible." Debate.org.uk, http://www. debate.org.uk/debate-topics/apologetic/contrads/.

Smith, Robert. 1983. *Easter Gospels: The Resurrection of Jesus According to the Four Evangelists.* Minneapolis: Augsburg Publishing.

Smith, Wilbur M. 1971. "The Indisputable Fact of the Empty Tomb." *Moody Monthly* 71(9): 38-40.

Solowey, Saul S. 1987. *The Original and the Pretenders.* Ft. Lauderdale, Fla.: Land Publishing.

Sparks, Kenton L. 2006. "Gospel as Conquest: Mosaic Typology in Matthew 28: 16-20." *Catholic Biblical Quarterly* 68(4): 651-63.

Sparrow Simpson, W. J. 1905. *Our Lord's Resurrection.* London: Longmans, Green.

Stagg, Frank. 1969. "Matthew." In *The Broadman Bible Commentary* Volume 8, edited by Clifton J. Allen, 81-253. Nashville: Broadman.

Stanton, G. N. 1977. "Presuppositions in New Testament Criticism." In *New Testament Interpretation: Essays on Principles and Methods*, edited by I. H. Marshall, 60-71. Grand Rapids: Eerdmans.

Stauffer, Ethelbert. 1960. *Jesus and His Story.* Translated by D. M. Barton. London: SCM.

Stecchini, Monica, and Jan Sammer. 1996. "Who was Mary Magdalene?" *http://www.metrum.org/gosen/index.htm.*

Stein, Robert H. 1977. "Was the Tomb Really Empty?" *Journal of the Evangelical Theological Society* 20(1): 23-29.

———. 1980. "The 'Criteria' for Authenticity." In *Gospel Perspectives,* Vol. 1. *Studies of History and Tradition in the Four Gospels,* edited by R. T. France and David Wenham, 225-63. Sheffield, England: JSOT Press.

———. 1996. *Jesus the Messiah: A Survey of the Life of Christ.* Downers Grove: InterVarsity Press.

———. 2008. *Mark.* Grand Rapids: Baker.

Stempvoort, P. A. van. 1958. "The Interpretation of the Ascension in Luke and Acts." *New Testament Studies* 5(1): 30-42.

Stewart, John. 1932. "The Dates of the Nativity and the Crucifixion of our Lord—A New Discovery." *Evangelical Quarterly* 4(3 July): 290-315.

Stone, Perry. 2010. *Secrets beyond the Grave.* Lake Mary, Fla.: Charisma House.

Stott, John R.W. 1971. *Basic Christianity.* Grand Rapids: Eerdmans.

Strachan, R. H. 1941. *The Fourth Gospel: Its Significance and Environment* 3rd ed. London: SCM.

Strickland, Rowena Rue. 1959. "A Study of the Jew's Rejection of Jesus In The Light of Inter-Biblical Messianic Expectation." PhD diss., Southwestern Baptist Theological Seminary.

Strobel, Lee.1998. *The Case for Christ: A Journalist's Personal Investigation of the Evidence for Jesus.* Grand Rapids: Zondervan.

Strong, James. 1890. *The Exhaustive Concordance of the Bible.* New York: Methodist Book Concern.

Stuhlmueller, Carroll. 1968. "The Gospel According to Luke." In *The Jerome Biblical Commentary,* edited by Raymond Brown, Joseph A. Fitzmyer, and Roland E. Murphy. 115-64. Englewood Cliffs, N.J.: Prentice-Hall.

Summers, Ray. 1965. "The Death and Resurrection of Jesus: John 18-21." *Review And Expositor* 62(4): 473-81.

Swain, Lionel. 1993. *Reading the Easter Gospel.* Collegeville: Liturgical Press.

Swanson, Reuben ed. 1995. *New Testament Greek Manuscripts: Variant Readings Arranged in Horizontal Lines Against Codex Vaticanus.* Sheffield, Eng: Sheffield Academic Press. [Note: This multi-volume work is composed of 9 volumes.]

Swete, Henry Barclay. 1913. *The Ascended Christ: A Study in the Earliest Christian Teaching.* London: MacMillan.

―――. 1927. *The Gospel According to St. Mark: The Greek Text with Introduction Notes and Indices.* 3rd ed. London: MacMillan.

Sylva, Dennis D. 1986. "The Temple Curtain and Jesus' Death in the Gospel of Luke. *Journal of Biblical Literature* 105(2): 239-50.

Tabor, James D. 2006. *The Jesus Dynasty: The Hidden History of Jesus, His Royal Family, and the Birth of Christianity.* New York: Simon & Schuster.

Talbert, Charles H. 1977. *What is a Gospel?* Philadelphia: Fortress Press.

―――. 1992. "The Place of the Resurrection in the Theology of Luke." *Interpretation* 46(1): 19-30.

―――. 1997. *Reading Acts: A Literary and Theological Commentary on the Acts of the Apostles.* New York: Crossroads.

Tannehill, Robert C. 1996. *Luke.* Nashville: Abingdon Press.

Tatum, W. Barnes. 1998. "Jesus' So-Called Triumphal Entry: On Making An Ass of the Romans." *Forum* 1(1): 129-43.

Taussig, Hal. 2004. "Book Review: The Resurrection of the Son of God by N. T. Wright." *Union Seminary Quarterly Review* 58(3-4): 244-249.

Taylor, Joan E. 1998. "Golgotha: A Reconsideration of the Evidence for the Sites of Jesus' Crucifixion and Burial." *New Testament Studies* 44(2): 180-203.

Taylor, Vincent. 1953. *The Gospel According to St. Mark*. London: Macmillan.

Tenney, Merrill C. 1976. *John: The Gospel of Belief: An Analytic Study of the Text*. Grand Rapids: Eerdmans.

Thayer, Joseph Henry. 1886. *A Greek-English Lexicon on the New Testament*. New York: American Book Company.

Theissen, Gerd, and Annette Merz. 1998. *The Historical Jesus: A Comprehensive Guide*. Minneapolis: Fortress Press.

Thiselton, Anthony C. 2000. *The First Epistle to the Corinthians: A Commentary on the Greek Text*. Grand Rapids: Eerdmans.

Thomas, Robert L. 2000. "Historical Criticism and the Great Commission." *The Master's Seminary Journal* 11(1): 39-52.

———. 2002. *Evangelical Hermeneutics: The New Versus the Old*. Grand Rapids: Kregel.

Thomas, Robert L., and Stanley N. Gundry, eds. 1988. *The NIV Harmony of the Gospels*. San Francisco: Harper & Row.

Thompson, Donald Argyle. 1980. *The Controversy Concerning the Last Twelve Verses of the Gospel According to Mark*. Walton-on-Thames, Surrey [England]. Bible Christian Unity Fellowship.

Thompson, Mary R. 1995. *Mary Magdala: Apostle and Leader*. New York: Paulist Press.

Tiede, D. L. 1984. "Religious Propaganda and the Gospel Literature of the Early Church." *ANRW* 2. 25/2: 1705-29 [*Aufstieg und Niedergang der romischen Welt*].

Till, Farrell. n.d. "The Mary Magdalene Problem: A Reply to: Tomb Visitor Checklist Do the Gospels Contradict Over Who Went to Jesus' Tomb? by Robert Turkel (aka James Patrick Holding)." Tektonics Apologetics Ministries. *http://www.theskepticalreview.com/jftill/mary/problem.html*

Tilley, Terrence W. 2000. "The Historical Fact of the Resurrection." In *Theology and the Social Sciences*, edited by Michael Horace Barnes, 88-110. Maryknoll, N.Y.: Orbis.

Time. April 7, 1997. "Inside the Web of Death." *Time* 149(14): 28-47.

Tinsley, E. J. 1965. *The Gospel According to Luke*. Cambridge: Cambridge University Press.

Tipler, Frank. J. 1994. *The Physics of Immortality: Modern Cosmology, God and the Resurrection of the Dead*. New York: Doubleday.

Tobin, William J. 1968. "The Petrine Primacy Evidence of the Gospels." *Lumen Vitae* 23(1): 27-70.

Toglia, Michael P., J. Don Read, David F. Ross, R.C.L. Lindslay. eds. 2007. *The Handbook of Eyewitness Psychology: Volume I: Memory for Events*. Mahwah, N.J.: Lawrence Erlbaum.

Tolbert, Malcolm O. 1970. "Luke." In *The Broadman Bible Commentary* Volume 9, edited by Clifton J. Allen, 17-188. Nashville: Broadman.

Toon, Peter. 1983. "Historical Perspectives on the Doctrine of Christ's Ascension Part 1: Resurrected and Ascended: The Exalted Jesus." *Bibliotheca Sacra* 14(559): 195-205.

Topel, John. 2012. "What Were the Women Afraid Of? (Mark 16:8)." *Journal of Theological Interpretation* 6(1): 79-96.

Torah Learning Resources. 2010. "Holidays Do Not Fall Out On Particular Days Of The Week." Torah Learning Resources. http://www.dailyhalacha.com/m/halacha.aspx?id=1143.

Torrey, R. A. September 26, 1969. "Christ's Crucifixion-Friday or Wednesday? Was Jesus Really Three Days and Three Nights in the Heart of the Earth?" *Sword of the Lord* 35(39): 1, 22-23

Trail, Ronald. 2001. *An Exegetical Summary of 1 Corinthians 10-16*. Dallas: SIL International.

Triestman, Mitch. 1997. *To the Jew First: A Textbook on Jewish Evangelism.* Levittown, Pa.: Lifeline.

Troki, Isaac. (1850) 1970. *Faith Strengthened.* Translated by Moses Mocatta. New York: Hermon Press. Citations refer to the Herman Press edition.

Trotter, Andrew H. 2005. "Ascension of Jesus Christ." In *Dictionary for Theological Interpretation of the Bible*, edited by Kevin J. Vanhoozer, 38-40. Grand Rapids: Baker.

Troxel, Ronald L. 2002. "Matt 27.51-4 Reconsidered: Its Role in the Passion Narrative, Meaning and Origin." *New Testament Studies* 48(1): 30-47.

Trudinger, Paul. 1990. "The 153 Fishes: A Response and a Further Suggestion." *Expository Times* 102(1): 11-12.

Turlington, Henry E. 1969. "Mark." In *The Broadman Bible Commentary* Volume 8, edited by Clifton J. Allen, 265-402. Nashville: Broadman.

Turner, Cuthbert Hamilton. 1898. "Chronology of the New Testament" In *A Dictionary of the Bible Dealing With Its Language, Literature and Contents Including the Biblical Theology* Volume I, edited by J. Hastings, 403-15. New York: Charles Scribner's Sons.

Turner, David L. 2005. *Cornerstone Biblical Commentary: The Gospel of Matthew and the Gospel of Mark.* Carol Stream, Ill.: Tyndale House.

Turner, H.E.W. 1965. "The Chronological Framework of the Ministry." In *Historicity and Chronology in the New Testament,* edited by D.E. Nineham, 59-74. London: SPCK

Tzadok, Ariel Bar. August 13, 2014. "An Orthodox Rabbi Reads the Christian Bible, Lesson 23 Matthew, Chapter 27c-28." www.koshertorah.com.

Tzaferis, Vassilios. 1985. "Crucifixion -- The Archaeological Evidence." *Biblical Archaeology Review* 11(1): 44-53.

Ulansey, D. 1991. "The Heavenly Veil Torn: Mark's Cosmic "Inclusio." *Journal of Biblical Literature* 110(1): 123-25.

The United States Geophysical Survey (USGS). January 9, 2013a. "Magnitude / Intensity Comparison." *http://earthquake.usgs.gov/learn/topics/mag_vs_int.php*.

———. January 9, 2013b. "At What Magnitude Does Damage Begin to Occur in an Earthquake?" *http://gallery.usgs.gov/audios/81*

Vardaman, Jerry. 1989. "Jesus' Life: A New Chronology." In *Chronos, Kairos, Christos" Nativity and Chronological Studies Presented to Jack Finegan*, edited by Jerry Vardaman and Edwin M. Yamauchi, 55-82. Winona Lake, Ind.: Eisenbraums.

———. 1998. "A Provisional Chronology of the New Testament: Jesus Through Paul's Early Years." In *Chronos, Kairos, Christos" Nativity and Religious Studies in Memory of Ray Summers*, edited by E. Jerry Vardaman, 313-20. Macon, Ga.: Mercer University.

Vermes, Geza. 2008. *The Resurrection: History & Myth*. New York: Doubleday.

Villers, Pieter G. R. de. 2010. "The Powerful Transformation of the Young Man in Mark 15:51-52 and 16:5." *HTS Teologiese Studies/Theological Studies* 66(1), Art #893, 7 pages. DOI: 10.4102/hts.v66i1.893

Vine, W. E. 1939. *A Comprehensive Dictionary of the Original Greek Words With Their Precise Meanings For English Readers*. McLean, Va.: MacDonald Publishing Company.

Viney, Donald Wayne.1989. "Grave Doubts About The Resurrection." *Encounter* 50(2): 125-40.

Viviano, Benedict T.1990. "The Gospel According to Matthew." In *The New Jerome Biblical Commentary*, edited by Raymond E. Brown, Joseph A. Fitzmyer, and Roland E. Murphy, 630-74. Englewood Cliffs, N.J.: Prentice-Hall.

Waetjen, Herman C. 2005. *The Gospel of the Beloved Disciple*: A Work in Two Editions. London: T&T Clark.

Wahlde, Urban C. von. 2010. *The Gospel and Letters of John*. Volume 2. Grand Rapids: Eerdmans.

Wakefield, Samuel. 1869. *A Complete System of Christian Theology.* Cincinnati: Jennings & Graham.

Walvoord, John F. 1963. "Christ in His Resurrection." *Bibliotheca Sacra* 120(478): 99-108.

Wall, Robert W. 2002. *The Acts of the Apostles.* In NIB 10, edited by L. E. Keck, 1-368. Nashville: Abingdon.

Wallace, Daniel B. 2011. "The Textual Reliability of the New Testament: Opening Remarks." In *The Textual Reliability of the New Testament: Bart D. Ehrman and Daniel B. Wallace: a Dialogue,* edited by Robert B. Stewart, 27-46. Minneapolis: Fortress Press.

Wallace, J. Warner. 2013. *Cold-Case Christianity: A Homicide Detective Investigates the Claims of the Gospels.* Colorado Springs, Colo.: David C. Cook.

Wallace, Richard and Wynne Williams. 1993. *The Acts of the Apostles.* London: Duckworth.

———. 1998. *The Three Worlds of Paul of Tarsus.* London: Routledge.

Walton, Douglas. 2008. *Witness Testimony Evidence: Argumentation, Artificial Intelligence, and Law.* Cambridge: Cambridge University Press.

Waltz, Robert B. 2007. "The Western Non-Interpolations." *http://skypoint. com/members/waltzmn/WestNonInterp.html.*

Waterman, Mark M. W. 2006. *The Empty Tomb Tradition of Mark: Text, History, and Theological Struggles.* Los Angeles: Agathos Press

Waters, Kenneth L. 2005. Matthew 28:1-6 as Temporally Conflated Text: Temporal-Spatial Collapse in the Gospel of Matthew." *The Expository Times* 116(9): 295-301.

Watson, Alan. 1995. *The Trial of Jesus.* Athens: The University of Georgia Press.

———.1998. *The Digest of Justinian* Vol 2. Philadelphia: University of Pennsylvania Press.

Watson, Francis. 1987. "'Historical Evidence' and the Resurrection of Jesus." *Theology* 90(737): 365-72.

Watson, William. 1911. "Review of Baldensperger's Urchristliche Apologie: Die Älteste Auferstehungskontroverse." *Review of Theology and Philosophy* 6(December): 343-46.

Weather Channel Interactive. 2008. *http://www.weather.com/outlook/travel/ businesstraveler/wxclimatology/monthly/graph/ISXX0010?from=searchhttp:// www.weather.com/outlook/travel/businesstraveler/wxclimatology/monthly/ graph/ISXX0010*

Weiss, Johannes. 1917. *Das Urchristentum*: *Göttingen: Vandenhoeck & Ruprecht.* [Cited in C.G. Montefiore, *The Synoptic Gospels In Two Volumes*. New York: KTAV.]

Weiss, L. 1904. *Some Burning Questions: Pertaining to the Messiahship of Jesus and Christology in General. Why Jews Do Not Accept Them.* Third Edition. Columbus, Ohio: Rabbi L. Weiss.

Weisse, C. H. 1838. *Die Evangelische Geschichte* Vol. II. Leipzig: Breitkopf und Härtel.

Wells, Gary L. 1985. "The Eyewitness." In *The Psychology of Evidence and Trial Procedure*, edited by Saul M. Kassin and Lawrence S. Wrightsman. 43-66. Beverly Hills, Calif.: Sage.

Wells, Gary. L., Amina Memon, and Steven D. Penrod. 2006. "Eyewitness Evidence: Improving Its Probative Value." *Psychological Science in the Public Interest* 7(2): 45-75.

Wells, Gary L., and Elizabeth A. Olson. 2003. "Eyewitness Testimony." *Annual Review of Psychology* 54: 277-94.

Wenham, D. 1973. "The Resurrection Narratives in Matthew's Gospel." *Tyndale Bulletin* #24: 19-54.

Wenham, John W. 1981. "When Were the Saints Raised? A Note on the Punctuation of Matthew xxviii. 51-3." *Journal of Theological Studies* 32(1): 150-53.

———. 1992. *Easter Enigma: Are the Resurrection Accounts In Conflict?* 2nd ed., Grand Rapids: Baker.

Wesley, John. 1755. *Explanatory Notes Upon the New Testament.* London: William Bowyer.

Westcott, Brooke Foss. 1881. An *Introduction to the Study of the Gospels* 6th ed. Cambridge: Macmillan.

Whiston, William, translator. (1867) 1960. *The Complete Works of Flavius Josephus.* Grand Rapids: Kregel. [Citations refer to the Kregel edition.]

White, Ellen G. (1888) 1950. *The Great Controversy Between Christ and Satan.* Oakland, Calif.: New York: Pacific Press. Reprint, Mountain View, Calif.: Pacific Press. Citations refer to the 1950 edition.

———. (1898) 1940. *The Desire of the Ages.* Mountain View, Calif.: Pacific Press. Reprint, London: Pacific Press. Citations refer to the 1940 edition.

———. (1917). 1943. *The Story of Prophets and Kings.* Mountain View, Calif.: Pacific Press. Citations refer to the 1943 edition.

Whitlark, Jason A., and Mikeal C. Parsons, 2006. "The 'Seven Last Words: A Numerical Motivation for the Insertion of Luke 23.34a." *New Testament Studies* 52(2): 188-204.

Wiarda, Timothy. 2004. "Scenes and Details in the Gospels: Concrete Reading and Three Alternatives." *New Testament Studies* 50(2): 167-84.

Wiebe, Phillip. 1997. *Visions of Jesus.* Oxford: Oxford University Press.

Williams, Joel F. 1994. *Other Followers of Jesus: Minor Characters as Major Figures in Mark's Gospel.* Sheffield: Sheffield Academic Press.

———. 1999. "Literary Approaches to the End of Mark's Gospel." *The Journal of the Evangelical Theological Society* 42(1): 21-35.

Williams, Joel Stephen. 2000. *The Real Jesus of History. Kērygma.* http://www.afn.org/~afn52344/realjesus.html.

Williams. N. P. 1920. *The First Easter Morning: A Suggested Harmony of the Gospel Narratives.* New York: Macmillan.

Wingo, Earle L. 2011. *The Illegal Trial of Jesus.* Ontario, Ca.: Chick Publications.

Wink, Walter. 1983. ""And the Lord Appeared First to Mary": Sexual Politics in the Resurrection Witness." In *Social Themes of the Christian Year: A Commentary on the Lectionary,* edited by Dieter T. Hessel, 177-82. Philadelphia: Geneva Press.

Winkelman, Michael. 1997. "Altered States of Consciousness and Religious Behavior." In *Anthropology of Religion: A Handbook,* edited by Stephen D. Glazier, 393-428. Westport, Conn.: Greenwood Press.

Winter, Paul. 1958. "I Corinthians XV 3b-7." *Novum Testamentum* 2(2): 142-50.

———. 1961. "On the Trial of Jesus." *Studia Judaica* (Volume 1), Berlin: Walter de Gruyter & Co.

Winter, C. S. 1998. "The Arrest of Jesus." *Forum* 1(1): 145-62.

Witherington, Ben. 1995. *Conflict and Community in Corinth: A Socio-Rhetorical Commentary on 1 and 2 Corinthians.* Grand Rapids: Eerdmans.

———. 1998. *The Acts of the Apostles: A Socio-Rhetorical Commentary.* Grand Rapids: Eerdmans.

———. 2001. *The Gospel of Mark: A Socio-Rhetorical Commentary.* Grand Rapids: Eerdmans

Witherup, Ronald D. 1987. "The Death of Jesus and the Raising of the Saints: Matthew 27:51-54 in Context." In *Society of Biblical Literature Seminar Papers,* edited by Kent Harold Richards, 574-85. Atlanta. Ga.: Scholars Press.

Wolfe, Rolland E. 1989. *How the Easter Story Grew From Gospel to Gospel.* Lewiston: Edwin Mellen.

Wrede, William. 1901. *Das Messiassgeheimnis in den Evangelien.* [*The Messianic Secret.* Translated by J.C.G. Greig. Cambridge: James Clarke. 1987].

Wright, Arthur. 1893. "On the Date of the Crucifixion." *The Biblical World* 2(October): 275-82.

Wright, N.T. 1992. *The New Testament and the People of God.* Minneapolis: Fortress Press.

———. 1996. *Jesus and the Victory of God.* Volume 2. Philadelphia: Fortress Press.

———. 1999. *The Challenge of Jesus: Rediscovering Who Jesus Was and Is.* Downers Grove: InterVarsity Press.

———. 2003. *The Resurrection of the Son of God.* Minneapolis: Fortress Press.

Wylen, Stephen M. 1996. *The Jews in the Time of Jesus.* New York: Paulist Press.

Yadin, Yigael. *The Temple Scroll: The Hidden Law of the Dead Sea Sect.* New York: Random House.

Yamauchi, Edwin M. March 29, 1974. "Easter -Myth, Hallucination, or History? Part two." *Christianity Today* 18(12): 12-16.

Yang, Jayoon. 2003. "Other Endings of Mark as Responses to Mark: an Ideological-Critical Investigation into the Longer and Shorter Ending of Mark's Gospel." PhD diss., University of Sheffield, UK.

Yarmey, A. Daniel. (2003). "Eyewitness Identification: Guidelines and Recommendations for Identification Procedures in the United States and in Canada." *Canadian Psychology,* 44(3): 181-89.

Yarnold, G. D. 1959. *Risen Indeed: Studies in the Lord's Resurrection.* New York: Oxford University Press.

Yeager, Randolph O. 1982. *The Renaissance New Testament. Volume Eight.* Gretna: Pelica.

Yosef, Uri. 2001-2011. "Zechariah 12:10 - A Piercing Look at A False Claim. Lesson notes." MessiahTruth.Com, http://thejewishhome.org/counter/Zech12_10.pdf

Young, Robert. 1970. *Analytical Concordance to the Bible* 22nd American edition. Grand Rapids: Eerdmans.

Zangenberg, Jürgen. 2007. "Buried According to the Customs of the Jews: John 19, 40 in Its Material and Literary Context." In *The Death of Jesus in the Fourth Gospel*, edited by G. Van Belle, 873-92. Leuven: Leuven University Press.

Zimmermann, Ruben. 2008. "Symbolic Communication Between John And His Reader: the Garden Symbolism in John 19-20." In. *Anatomies of Narrative Criticism: The Past, and Futures of the Fourth Gospel as Literature*, edited by Tom Thatcher and Stephen D. Moore, 221-35. Atlanta: Society of Biblical Literature.

Zugibe, Frederick T. 1983. "Death by Crucifixion." *Canadian Society Forensic Science Journal* 17(1): 1-13.

———. 1989. "Questions About Crucifixion: Does the Victim Die of Asphyxiation? Would Nails in the Hand Hold the Weight of the Body?" *Bible Review* 5(2): 35-43.

———. 2005. *Crucifixion of Jesus: A Forensic Inquiry.* 2nd ed. New York: M. Evans.

Zweip, A. W. 1997. *The Ascension of the Messiah in Lukean Christology.* Leiden: Brill.

———. 2004. *Judas and the Choice of Matthias: A Study on Context and Concern of Acts 1:15-26.* Tübingen: Mohr Siebeck.

INDEX OF SUBJECTS

P

INDEX OF NAMES IN REFERENCES

C

M

N

O

Lightning Source UK Ltd.
Milton Keynes UK
UKOW01f2354130616

276264UK00001B/91/P